Microsoft® Office 2010 for Teachers

William J. Gibbs
DUQUESNE UNIVERSITY

Patricia J. Fewell
EASTERN ILLINOIS UNIVERSITY

PEARSON

Boston Columbus Indianapolis New York San Francisco Upper Saddle River
Amsterdam Cape Town Dubai London Madrid Milan Munich Paris Montréal Toronto
Delhi Mexico City São Paulo Sydney Hong Kong Seoul Singapore Taipei Tokyo

Vice President and Editorial Director: Jeffrey W. Johnston
Acquisitions Editor: Kelly Villella Canton
Associate Editor: Anne Whittaker
Editorial Assistant: Annalea Manalili
Director of Marketing: Margaret Waples
Executive Marketing Manager: Krista Clark
Marketing Manager: Darcy Betts
Production Project Manager: Elizabeth Gale Napolitano
Full-Service Project Management: Element LLC
Composition: Element LLC
Manager, Central Design: Jayne Conte
Cover Designer: Suzanne Behnke
Cover Image: © sandozcooper/Fotolia
Printer/Binder: Edwards Brothers Malloy
Cover Printer: Lehigh-Phoenix Color/Hagerstown
Text Font: Times

Library of Congress Cataloging-in-Publication Data

Gibbs, William J.
Microsoft office 2010 for teachers / William J. Gibbs, Patricia J. Fewell.
p. cm.
Rev. ed. of: Microsoft office for teachers. 3rd ed. © 2009.
Includes index.
ISBN-13: 978-0-13-269619-7
ISBN-10: 0-13-269619-3
1. Microsoft Office. 2. Teachers—In-service training. 3. Education—Data processing. 4. Computer-assisted instruction. I. Fewell, Patricia J. II. Gibbs, William J. Microsoft office for teachers. III. Title.

HF5548.4.M525F49 2013
005.5—dc23

2012004651

10 9 8 7 6 5 4 3 2 1

PEARSON

ISBN-10: 0-13-269619-3
ISBN-13: 978-0-13-269619-7

This book is dedicated to our families:
Earl and Joy Longman and the Longman gang; Annette, Lauren, and Liam Gibbs; and James and Helen Gibbs.

About the Authors

William J. Gibbs

Dr. Gibbs is an associate professor at Duquesne University. He holds a Ph.D. and a master's degree in Instructional Systems from The Pennsylvania State University. Dr. Gibbs teaches courses in instructional design, e-learning, human–computer interaction, interface design, and digital multimedia. Dr. Gibbs has given numerous technology training seminars and workshops on Microsoft Office, Web development, and interactive multimedia applications.

Dr. Gibbs has been actively involved in original research projects that have resulted in scholarly publications and conference presentations. He has given presentations at state, national, and international conferences on numerous topics related to the use of technology for teaching and learning. In addition, Dr. Gibbs has published a number of research articles on topics ranging from technology-based learning, developing e-learning applications, online learning, computer-mediated communication, and human–technology interaction.

Patricia J. Fewell

Professor Fewell is a professor emeritus and former chair of the Department of Secondary Education and Foundations at Eastern Illinois University. She received her Ed.D. from Illinois State University. She has been certified as a K–12 media specialist within the state of Illinois. She is involved in teacher certification, serving on numerous accreditation teams in the state and nationally. She gives presentations on technology applications in the classroom at state, national, and international conferences.

Professor Fewell enjoys the dog, two cats, and horses that live with her and help her in her garden and "mini farm" at the end of a dead-end road out of town.

Brief Contents

Contents

Preface

Conceptual Framework

In this book, computers and associated software are presented as tools or means to accomplish educational tasks. From this perspective, we examine various types of computer software, including word processing, presentation, database, and spreadsheet applications. Each category of software is presented as part of the Microsoft Office suite, comprising Word, PowerPoint, Access, Excel, and Publisher, as well as through a combination or integration of the Office products. We offer specific instructions and recommendations for using these products in the classroom and provide teachers, students, and administrators with a starting point to develop their technological knowledge and integrate technology into the educational environment.

Word processing, database, and spreadsheet applications can improve work efficiency, expand the range of tasks performed, improve accuracy and effectiveness, and reduce the amount of time needed to perform routine tasks. However, the initial time needed to learn these applications can be an obstacle. We address this issue in three ways. First, we present a visually illustrated and nontechnical approach to learning the Microsoft Office 2010 suite. The book includes screen captures supplemented with text descriptions, work templates, and projects to help you learn and use these applications without the frustration often experienced when studying intensive technical manuals. Second, because we believe it is useful to build on the suggestions and work of others, we have created work templates and exercises that demonstrate the usefulness of the Microsoft Office suite and the diversity of its applications. You can quickly and easily tailor these templates and exercises to meet your specific needs. Third, the book focuses on various projects—such as creating newsletters and posters or making presentations to parent groups or the school board—as a springboard for learning the Microsoft Office suite. Throughout the chapters, you will find projects for students, teachers, and administrators. For example, students often create multimedia presentations to present class research, many pre-service teachers prepare class newsletters for parents, and administrators frequently spend time analyzing data. Word processing, database, spreadsheet, and presentation development skills are fundamental to these tasks. The projects in this book focus on these types of tasks to cultivate basic computer proficiency. Using nontechnical and graphically illustrated how-to procedures, teachers, students, and administrators complete real-world, computer-based projects and develop skills in word processing, database management, the use of spreadsheets, and presentations.

This book is written for individuals with basic computing skills. The activities described in the book require a computer capable of running Microsoft Office 2010.

What Is New and Improved?

Although we have published previous editions of *Microsoft Office for Teachers,* this version has been designed to support use of new Microsoft Office 2010. Additionally, we have worked on enhancements to improve the format and content of previous versions of the book:

- *Revised chapters for Office 2010*—All chapters have been updated for Microsoft Office 2010. Office 2010 offers a number of new features, many of which are highlighted in the chapters.

- *Windows Live*—Windows Live enables people to use Office 2010 remotely from any location. The Windows Live environment is reviewed, and its features are highlighted in this book.
- *Project activities*—Many of the chapter activities have been completely revised, and new projects have been added. There are now three types of major activities or projects in each chapter: projects for students, projects for teachers, and projects for administrators. The tasks in these projects are tailored to the type of work these individuals might perform with the Office software.
- *Windows 7*—At the time of this writing, Windows 7 is the most current Windows operating system. Appendix A has been revised to reflect the new features of the operating system, and appropriate revisions have been made in the chapters.
- *PDToolkit*—The new PDToolkit site offers additional Web exercises and completed examples of in-text activities for download.
- *Updated National Educational Technology Standards (NETS) for students, teachers, and administrators*—The most recent NETS-S, NETS-T, and NETS-A standards are located on the inside front cover of this text, for easy access and reference.

Organization of the Text

Chapter 1, Technology and the School, introduces the text and offers information on state and national technology standards for teachers and students related to integrating technology in the classroom.

Chapter 2, Getting Started with Office, addresses the Microsoft Office 2010 interface, including taskbars, menu options, and the Ribbon. It also presents information about using the Quick Access Toolbar.

Chapter 3, Word 2010, discusses word processing, including creating a new Microsoft Word document and modifying an existing one. It focuses on writing a newsletter, creating SmartArt diagrams, creating a webpage document, and using Word templates. In the chapter activities, students create word processing documents. They use the copy, cut, paste, and formatting options, as well as WordArt and Clip Art to create documents.

Chapter 4, PowerPoint 2010, introduces Microsoft PowerPoint. It focuses on the fundamentals and how they apply to developing a presentation. The chapter presents information on slide layout, design, graphics and Clip Art, and presentation printing.

Chapter 5, Excel 2010, focuses on Excel fundamentals and their application to education. It presents step-by-step instructions for creating workbooks and editing and manipulating data in worksheets. Activities include creating a workbook, entering data into a worksheet, and editing data, performing calculations, charting data, and creating and using PivotTables.

Chapter 6, Access 2010, presents detailed instructions for creating databases, entering information, and searching a database using Access. It also shows how to save files, prepare mail, merge documents, and print reports.

Chapter 7, Publisher 2010, discusses preparing brochures, postcards, and flyers with Publisher software, using many of the same processes used in Word.

Chapter 8, Integrating Office 2010, builds on the previous chapters and presents readers with ideas on integrating the various Office products to increase work efficiency and enhance the quality of materials created.

Chapter 9, Multimedia and Web Technologies, examines the foundations of multimedia Web services and the Office applications. It explores the Office programs in Windows Live. Teachers, students, and administrators can use the Windows Live environment to create and share multimedia content, organize files, and communicate with others.

Although the chapters are related to each other, they can be used independently and out of sequence. Teachers who want students to create a monthly newsletter will find Chapter 3 useful; teachers who want students to create book report presentations or perform analyses on data will find Chapters 4, 5, and 9 informative.

Features of the Book

Advance Organizers

Each chapter begins with a set of advance organizers to prepare readers for the main topics. They include the following:

- Chapter outline
- Learning objectives: *What you are going to learn.*
- Overview, which provides the rationale for the topics and discusses their use

Project Activities

The chapters present projects for students, teachers, and administrators. The projects involve specific tasks (e.g., creating a newsletter) that relate to the work of students, teachers, and administrators. Step-by-step instructions are given for manipulating the technical aspects of various applications to complete the projects. Using text and graphics, the steps necessary to accomplish the project as well as the rationale for performing specific software functions are illustrated.

New PDToolkit

Accompanying *Microsoft Office 2010 for Teachers* is a new website containing completed examples of the exercises and activities referenced in each chapter, as well as additional Web activities designed to facilitate further learning and practice.

The PDToolkit site is available free for six months after you register with the password that comes with this book. After that, it is available by subscription for a yearly fee. Be sure to explore and download the resources available at the website.

CourseSmart and Other E-Books

CourseSmart is an exciting new choice for teachers looking to save money. As an alternative to purchasing the printed book, teachers can purchase an electronic version of the same content at a reduced price. With a CourseSmart eTextbook, teachers can search the text, make notes online, print out readings that incorporate notes, and bookmark important passages for later review. For more information, or to purchase access to the CourseSmart eTextbook, visit www.coursesmart.com.

Acknowledgments

A number of the ideas in this text were conceived or provided by classroom teachers to whom we are most grateful. We would like to especially thank Richard Rechenberg, a teacher at Holy Sepulcher School, for allowing us to use his science project PowerPoint template as a guide for one of the projects for teachers. We would like to thank the teachers at the Prairieland Elementary School for their ideas. Bridgette Belasli graciously provided work samples that proved most useful and helped guide us in developing practical examples. Terry Hyder spent many hours reviewing drafts of the text. Her suggestions were invaluable, and we greatly appreciate her efforts.

The following reviewers also provided invaluable advice: Rhonda Bonnstetter, Southwest Minnesota State University; Margaret Kostal, Amherst County High School; Elizabeth Pocius, Seminole County Public Schools; David K. Pugalee, The University of North Carolina at Charlotte; Jean Rockwell Warner, Rider University.

Mostly, we thank our families for their understanding and support as we developed this book. Earl Longman, Joy Longman, and Suzanne Schertz; and Annette Gibbs, Lauren Gibbs, Liam Gibbs, and James and Helen Gibbs, your encouragement made this book possible.

1 TECHNOLOGY AND THE SCHOOL

Chapter Outline

- What You Are Going to Learn
- Chapter Overview
- About the Book and Using Technology
- Expectations of Teachers
- Expectations of Students
- Expectations of Administrators
- Projects for Everyone
- Copyright and the Classroom
- Acceptable Use Policies
- Summing It Up
- References and Resources

WHAT YOU ARE GOING TO LEARN

At the completion of this chapter you will be able to:

- Identify the International Society for Technology in Education standards for teachers
- Note technology standards for students
- Note technology standards for administrators
- Be aware of copyright issues
- Be aware of acceptable use policies (AUPs) in school districts
- Identify production activities throughout the text

CHAPTER OVERVIEW

This chapter discusses the contents of this text and provides an overview of its structure and scope. It offers information regarding technology standards for teachers, students, and administrators that can serve to establish a context for integrating technology in the school. In addition, the chapter presents an overview of acceptable use policies and copyright law.

ABOUT THE BOOK AND USING TECHNOLOGY

In order to comply with the International Society for Technology in Education (ISTE) and the National Council for Accreditation of Teacher Education (NCATE) standards, teachers, including pre-service teachers, and administrators must possess computer skills beyond the basics. In today's educational environment, there is constant pressure for school personnel to become competent with technology because of increased access to computing, networking, and communications technology, among other reasons.

The effective use and integration of technology into teaching and learning is a complex process. Teachers and administrators, not technology, should direct this integration. The acquisition and configuration of sophisticated computing and networking systems is essential for technology integration. It is shortsighted, however, to perceive hardware and software as the only requirements for successful integration and utilization. As Earle (2002) points out, it is comparatively straightforward to situate computing hardware in physical locations. However, it is another matter to integrate technology into teaching, learning, and the curriculum. Schools' curricula should be at the heart of all technology integration efforts. Schools must invest in technology training and development for teachers. Teachers must understand the basics of technology for successful implementation of that technology in the classroom. They must have an opportunity to learn about appropriate and effective uses of technology and practice using computers, software, and other communication devices. In addition, schools and teachers must seek innovative ways to foster teachers' willingness to invest the time and energy needed to use technology effectively.

This book serves as a supplement to computer application texts used in colleges of education. It may also be used as a basis for in-service teacher education or with administrators for application examples. This book includes examples and exercises based on the work teachers, students, and administrators routinely perform each day in the school environment. It provides a technological foundation for beginning teachers and administrators to guide them to more advanced skill levels. This introduction to technology should serve as an initial step for teachers and administrators as they begin using and integrating technology in their schools.

EXPECTATIONS OF TEACHERS

Many teachers struggle with how to effectively use computers and software not merely as tools to facilitate the presentation of information but also as tools for students to build their own knowledge. The expectations for teachers to integrate technology into the classroom are high. Teachers are expected to use technology not only for class management but also to facilitate and support the curriculum, which can be challenging.

Each state has specific standards for teachers to follow when implementing technology in the curriculum. Many states have adopted or adapted the standards of the ISTE, which has been a leader in the field of establishing technology standards. As teachers begin to integrate technology into their classes, the ISTE standards provide an invaluable resource to guide their efforts.

Addressing the development of student knowledge and skills to meet the ISTE standards is beyond the scope of this book. However, the text gives specific illustrations for using and integrating Microsoft Office products into the classroom environment, which will provide you with the knowledge and skills to meet many of the standards. The ISTE standards for teachers are divided into the following sections:

1. Facilitate and Inspire Student Learning and Creativity
2. Facilitate and Inspire Student Learning and Creativity
3. Model Digital-Age Work and Learning
4. Promote and Model Digital Citizenship and Responsibility
5. Engage in Professional Growth and Leadership (ISTE, 2008)

The ISTE National Educational Technology Standards (NETS) and Performance Indicators for Teachers are located on the inside front cover of this book.

EXPECTATIONS OF STUDENTS

Because technology is now an integral part of the curriculum, learning standards have been developed throughout the nation to provide a basis of expectations for what students should know and be able to do utilizing technology. For instance, ISTE has developed technology standards for students that are divided into the following sections:

1. Creativity and Innovation
2. Communication and Collaboration
3. Research and Information Fluency
4. Critical Thinking, Problem Solving, and Decision Making

5. Digital Citizenship
6. Technology Operations and Concepts (ISTE, 2007)

The ISTE NETS and Performance Indicators for Students are located on the inside front cover of this book.

EXPECTATIONS OF ADMINISTRATORS

Administrators play a pivotal role in the application of technology not only in the curriculum but throughout the school system—from the classroom to the cafeteria. Administrators must understand the implications and application of technology for the most meaningful operation of the school setting. In many schools, the principal is the curriculum leader and must be able to lead by example in the application of technology throughout the school. ISTE has developed technology standards for administrators that are divided into the following sections:

1. Visionary Leadership
2. Digital Age Learning Culture
3. Excellence in Professional Practice
4. Systemic Improvement
5. Digital Citizenship (ISTE, 2009)

The ISTE NETS and Performance Indicators for Administrators are located on the inside front cover of this book.

PROJECTS FOR EVERYONE

New to this edition are examples of Microsoft Office products that everyone can use for everyday life. These examples show that the use of technology is pervasive inside and outside the classroom and that skills learned inside the school building can be applied to everyday life.

COPYRIGHT AND THE CLASSROOM

As noted in the ISTE standards for teachers, administrators, and students, ethical issues are addressed within the digital citizenship standards. Specifically, Standard 4 for teachers addresses ethical issues:

> Teachers understand local and global societal issues and responsibilities in an evolving digital culture and exhibit legal and ethical behavior in their professional practices. Teachers . . . advocate, model, and teach safe, legal, and ethical use of digital information and technology, including respect for copyright, intellectual property, and the appropriate documentation of sources. (ISTE, 2008)

Central to modeling expectations is appropriate respect for and use of copyright laws. Copyright laws are federal laws pertaining to the legal rights to use original works. These laws set forth rights and conditions regarding how individuals may use or copy materials. The Copyright Act covers eight broad categories:

1. Literary works
2. Musical works
3. Dramatic works, including any accompanying music
4. Pantomimes and choreographed works
5. Pictorial, graphic, and sculptural works
6. Motion pictures and other audiovisual works
7. Sound recordings
8. Architectural works

A copyrighted work may be used or copied under certain conditions:

- *Public domain*—Public domain works belong to the public as a whole, such as government documents and works with an expired copyright or no existing protection.
- *Permission*—Permission may have been given for the proposed use by the copyright owner.

- *Legal exemption*—Use of the work constitutes an exemption, such as a parody.
- *Fair use*—Use of the work for educational purposes according to certain restrictions. (Newsome, 1997)

Public domain work is a creative work that is not protected by copyright and may be freely used by all. For works created after 1978, the copyright is valid for the life of the work's producer plus 70 years (or if the work is a corporate authorship, the shorter of 95 years from publication or 120 years from creation). Works published before 1923 are now in the public domain.

The Copyright Act of 1976, Section 107, established fair use, or guidelines that allow educators to use and copy certain copyrighted materials for nonprofit educational purposes. Copyright issues can be convoluted, particularly in terms of computer-based media and materials available on the Web. School districts provide teachers with specific guidelines for using copyrighted materials in their classes. It is in your best interest to ascertain and adhere to policies advocated by your school.

Copyright law sets out four factors to be considered in determining fair use:

1. The purpose and character of the use, including whether such use is of commercial nature or is for nonprofit educational purposes
2. The nature of the copyrighted works
3. The amount and substantiality of the portion used in relation to the copyright work as a whole
4. The effect of the use on the potential market for or value of the copyrighted works (U.S. Copyright Office, March 2011)

The distinction between fair use and infringement may be unclear. There is no specific number of words, lines, and so on that may be safely taken without permission. Acknowledgement of the source does not substitute for obtaining permission. In addition, ownership of a book, an image, a software program, or other works does not confer copyright ownership. The right to copy, display, or otherwise use material must be specifically granted.

The following are general recommendations to follow when contemplating using copyrighted materials:

- When computer software is intended for one computer, it should be used on only one computer.
- If the picture, video, audio, or text you would like to use does not belong to you (that is, you did not create it), you should ask permission from the individual or entity that produced the materials.
- You should never reprint material from the Internet unless it specifically says "copyright free." You should ask permission for any material that you wish to use. Even if the material is copyright free, you must cite the source when you reuse it.
- For a project that contains any kind of music, the material needs to be evaluated to determine whether the music, the words, or the performance is copyrighted. It is wise to operate under the assumption that all works are protected by either copyright or trademark law unless conclusive information indicates otherwise. A work is not in the public domain simply because it has been posted on the Internet.

ACCEPTABLE USE POLICIES

To further address the issue of ethical use of computers, computer software, the Internet, and the World Wide Web, many schools have acceptable use policies (AUPs). AUPs are agreements among students, parents/guardians, teachers, administrators, and staff that govern the use of school and school district computers, networks, and the Internet. AUPs vary greatly from school district to school district. Some schools have separate AUPs for students, teachers, and staff personnel. AUPs generally address access to and transmission of data and information within the school and any technology-based device in the school or personal device brought into the school. Generally, AUPs include the following key elements:

- *A preamble*—Explains why the policy is needed and that the school's code of conduct applies to online activity.
- *A definition section*—Defines the key words used in the policy.

- *A policy statement*—Describes what technology-based devices are covered under the AUP and under what circumstances students can use those devices.
- *An acceptable use section*—Defines appropriate student use of the technology available in the school. This includes the parameters of student use of network technology.
- *An unacceptable use section*—Gives clear examples of what constitutes unacceptable student use.
- *A violations/sanctions section*—Explains how to report violators and to whom to address questions about the AUP. Some AUPs note that violations will be handled in accordance with the general student disciplinary code for the school.

A typical AUP has a section where students and parents sign the document, acknowledging that they are aware of the information contained in the policy, and their intentions of abiding by the policies outlined in the document. It is a teacher's responsibility to monitor student use of the computers in the classroom and school. A teacher also has a responsibility for abiding by the AUPs set by the school district.

SUMMING IT UP

This chapter provides an overview of the book and presents standards that set expectations for how teachers should integrate technology into their classrooms and how students use technology, and an overview of technology standards for school administrators. As you work through the book, you will likely find many useful opportunities to use Microsoft Office products to enhance your teaching and learning activities and the operation of the school. At the same time, you will identify ways to help your students meet established technology standards.

References and Resources

Bloom, B. (Ed.). (1956). *Taxonomy of educational objectives.* New York: David McKay.

Earle, R.S. (2002). The integration of instructional technology into public education: Promises and challenges. *Educational Technology, 42*(1), 5–13. Retrieved November 12, 2004, from http://isites.harvard.edu/fs/docs/icb.topic87187.files/Earle02.pdf.

International Society for Technology in Education. (2007). *NETS for students.* Retrieved March 4, 2011, from www.iste.org/standards/nets-for-students.aspx.

International Society for Technology in Education. (2008). *NETS for teachers.* Retrieved March 4, 2011, from www.iste.org/standards/nets-for-teachers.aspx.

International Society for Technology in Education. (2009). *NETS for administrators.* Retrieved March 4, 2011, from www.iste.org/standards/nets-for-administrators.aspx.

Newsome, C. (1997). *A teacher's guide to fair use and copyright.* Retrieved September 21, 2007, from http://home.earthlink.net/~cnew/research.htm.

U.S. Copyright Office. (March 2011). *Copyright basics.* Retrieved March 4, 2011, from www.copyright.gov/circs/circ1.pdf.

U.S. Copyright Office. (July 2011). *Reproduction of copyrighted works by educators and librarians.* Retrieved July 8, 2011, from www.copyright.gov/circs/circ21.pdf.

SELECTED WEBSITES

U.S. Copyright Office
www.copyright.gov

Reproduction of Copyrighted Works by Educators and Librarians
www.copyright.gov/circs/circ21.pdf

A Teacher's Guide to Fair Use and Copyright
http://home.earthlink.net/~cnew/research.htm

Copyright Laws for Teachers from Educational CyberPlayGround
www.edu-cyberpg.com/Teachers/copyrightlaw.html

Copyright from Legal Information Institute
http://topics.law.cornell.edu/wex/Copyright

10 Big Myths About Copyright Explained
www.templetons.com/brad/copymyths.html

Model Acceptable Use Policy
www.justice.gov/criminal/cybercrime/rules/acceptableUsePolicy.htm

Acceptable Use Policy from the Indiana Department of Education
www.doe.in.gov/olt/aup/welcome.html

Acceptable Internet Use Policy from the Virginia Department of Education
www.doe.virginia.gov/support/safety_crisis_management/internet_safety/acceptable_use_policy.shtml

Copyright & Fair Use from Stanford University Libraries
http://fairuse.stanford.edu

2 GETTING STARTED WITH OFFICE

Chapter Outline

WHAT YOU ARE GOING TO LEARN

At the completion of this chapter you will be able to:

- Open the Microsoft Office suite
- Use the icons on the Ribbon
- Use the File tab (or Backstage) and understand the actions associated with it
- Modify the Quick Access Toolbar
- Add a hyperlink to a document

CHAPTER OVERVIEW

This chapter provides an introduction to the Ribbon, menus, and functions available in the Microsoft Office suite. Each Office application has additional components in the ribbons and menus that are unique to that program. After studying this chapter, you will be able to customize your Quick Access Toolbar and use basic commands common to all the Office products.

WORKING WITH THE MICROSOFT OFFICE SUITE

The Microsoft Office suite may include any or all of the following products: Word, Excel, PowerPoint, Access, Publisher, Outlook, and OneNote. Most standard Professional Office editions for Windows include these products. All ribbons, menus, and help information function similarly from product to product. The compatibility makes working with the Office applications easier and requires less of a learning curve. To view ribbons, menu items, and help information, an Office program (e.g., Word) must be open.

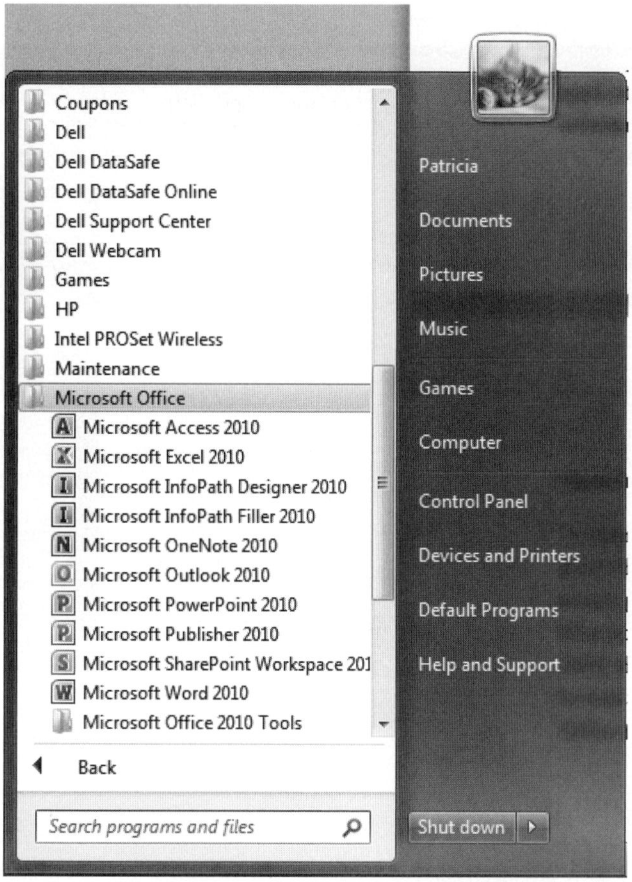

FIGURE 2.1 Opening Microsoft Office

Opening Office Applications

To open any of the Office applications, click Start on the Windows taskbar. On the Start menu, move the mouse pointer to All Programs, and the Programs submenu appears. Move the mouse pointer to Microsoft Office, and the Microsoft Office submenu appears. Click the Microsoft application that you want to open. *Note:* Depending on how you installed Office 2010, the menu items for the application may appear in various locations on the Start menu. In most cases, they can be found under All Programs or under Programs within the Microsoft Office folder (see Figure 2.1).

Opening Microsoft Office

To see examples of some of the similarities between the various Office programs, open Microsoft Office Word 2010 by clicking on the icon in the menu noted in Figure 2.1. You will be able to see the Ribbon and other components that are similar throughout the Microsoft Office suite (see Figure 2.2):

- *Quick Access Toolbar*—Displays quick access buttons such as buttons for the Undo and Save commands
- *Ribbon*—Displays groups of related commands in tabs
- *Title bar*—Displays the name of the open file and the program that is now open
- *Program window controls*—Minimize the program window, restore the window to full size, and close the window
- *Help*—Displays the Help screen to get assistance using Microsoft Office
- *Scrollbars*—Allow different work areas to be displayed within a document
- *Zoom controls*—Allow you to zoom in or out of the view of a document
- *Document window controls*—Control the format of the document being viewed
- *Status bar*—Displays information about the current file

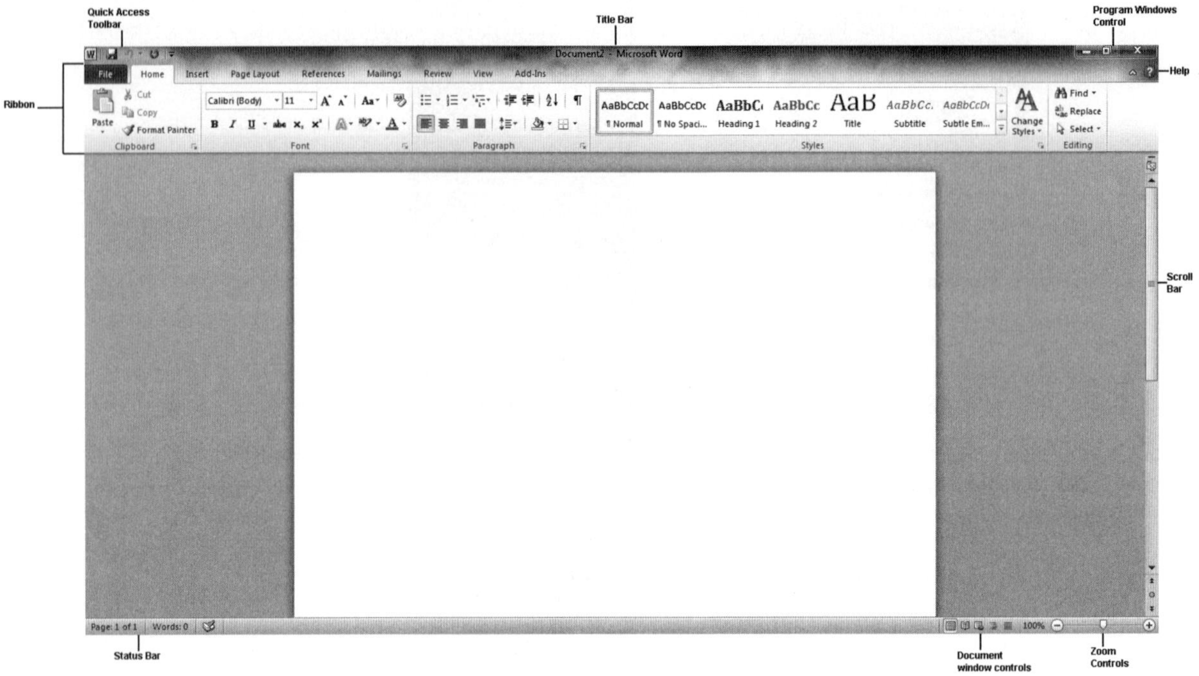

FIGURE 2.2 Screen Components

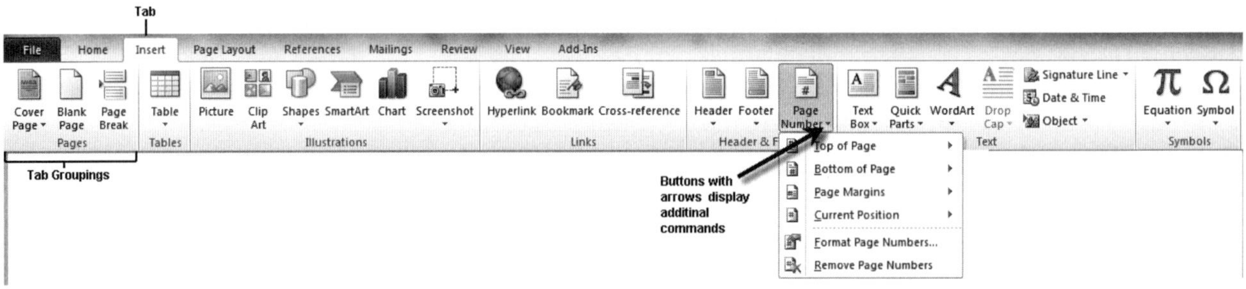

FIGURE 2.3 The Microsoft Word Ribbon

The Ribbon in Microsoft Office

The Ribbon is organized into groups or categories of commands, which relate to a function. The Ribbon is arranged in tabs, and each tab holds related commands (see Figure 2.3).

As you make changes in documents, such as changing the size or style of text if you have the text highlighted, the program will provide a preview of what the type or style will look like if you apply it to the document.

The Quick Access Toolbar

The functions that automatically appear on the toolbar are Program Icon, Save, Undo, and Redo. You can add commands and customize the toolbar by choosing commands from the pull-down menu (see Figure 2.4).

The Help Function in Microsoft Office

The Help function allows you type a word or phrase that you would like to learn about. To utilize the Help function online, you must be connected to the Internet. You can also browse the Help screen. To activate the Help window, click the question mark at the top-right corner of the screen (see Figures 2.5 and 2.6).

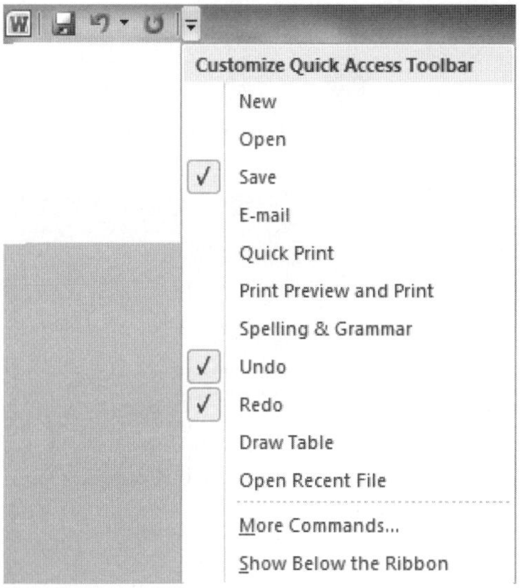

FIGURE 2.4 The Quick Access Toolbar

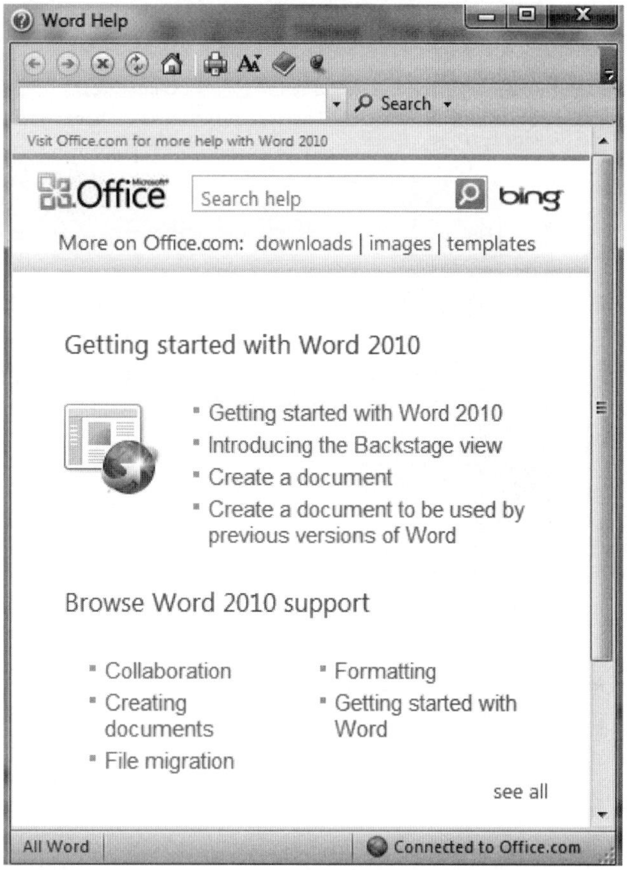

FIGURE 2.5 The Help Screen Connected to the Web

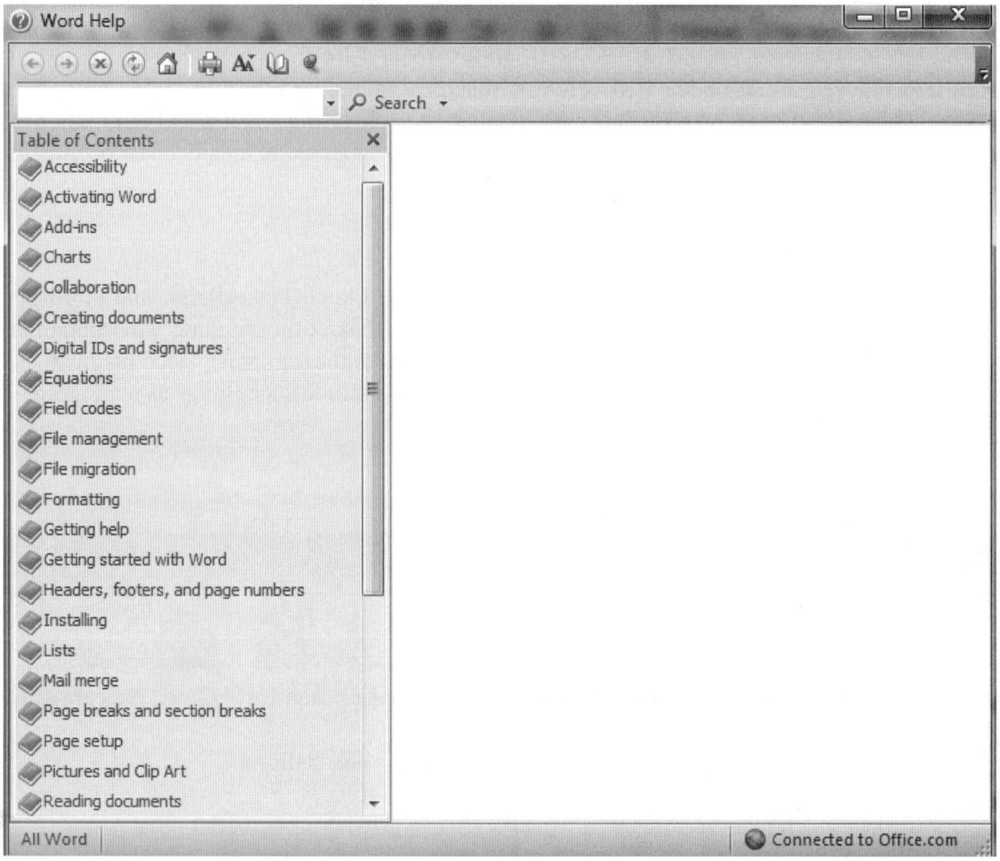

FIGURE 2.6 The Computer Help Screen

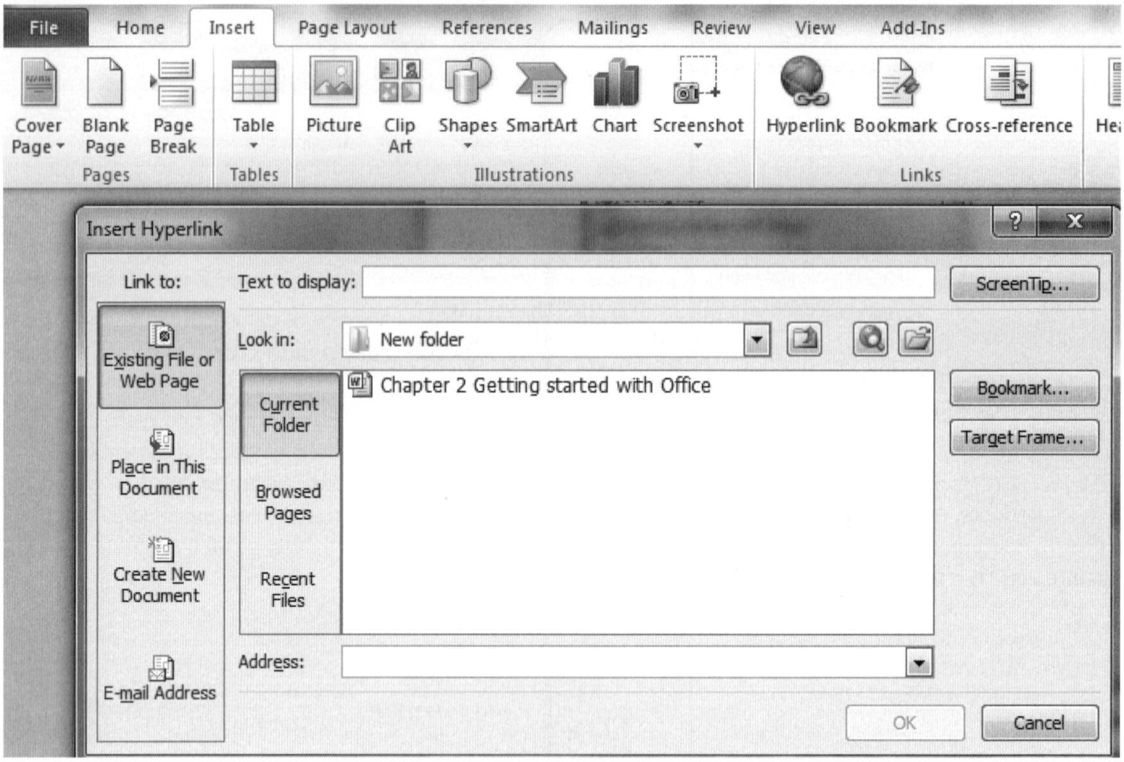

FIGURE 2.7 Inserting a Hyperlink

Inserting a Hyperlink

A hyperlink is a reference or navigational element in a document that allows you to go to another section in the same document, anther document, or (if you're connected to the Internet) a separate webpage. To apply hyperlinks in a document, select the text or image to which you would like to attach a hyperlink. Click the Insert tab on the Ribbon and click on the Hyperlink icon (see Figure 2.7). Type the URL address linked to, including http:// in the address, then click OK. As you can see with the icons listed along the side of the window in Figure 2.7, you can insert a link to an existing webpage or to a page in the document, create a new document, or link to an e-mail address.

Inserting Clip Art

Clip art is predrawn artwork that can be added to Word, Excel, PowerPoint, and Publisher documents. On the Ribbon, click the Insert tab, and the Illustration grouping will contain an icon for clip art (see Figure 2.8). Keep in mind that wherever the cursor is placed on the document is where the clip art will be placed. Clip art can also include such things as photographs, sounds, and movies.

FIGURE 2.8 The Clip Art Icon

Once the Clip Art icon is clicked, a Clip Art pane appears. This pane allows you to search for a particular subject area of clip art, from a variety of media types. If you are connected to the Internet, you can search for clip art on Office Online as well as other clip art sources (see Figure 2.9). To select the particular clip art, use the mouse pointer to move over the image, and a pull-down menu appears, allowing you to insert the clip art into your document.

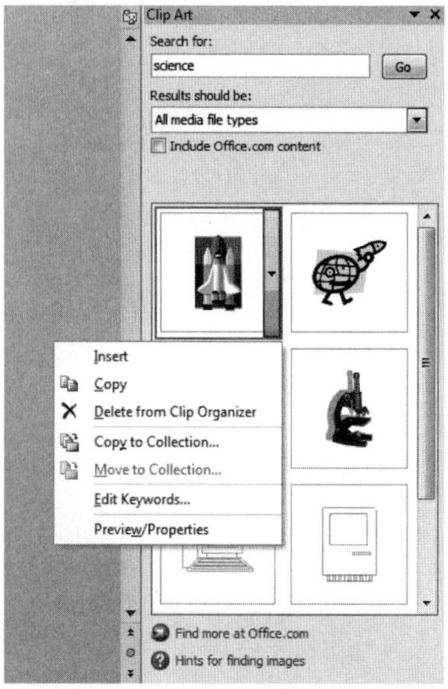

FIGURE 2.9 Selecting Clip Art

The File Tab

The File tab replaces the Microsoft Office Button found in earlier versions of the Office suite. The File tab is where you can see the Microsoft Office Backstage view, where you manage your files and save, create, and find settings options (see Figure 2.10).

SUMMING IT UP

This chapter gives an overview of the toolbars and options that are available in the Microsoft Office products. As you open the Office applications, you will see that these applications have some of the same options no matter what program you are using. This commonality gives you an interface for using Office and makes learning the programs easy.

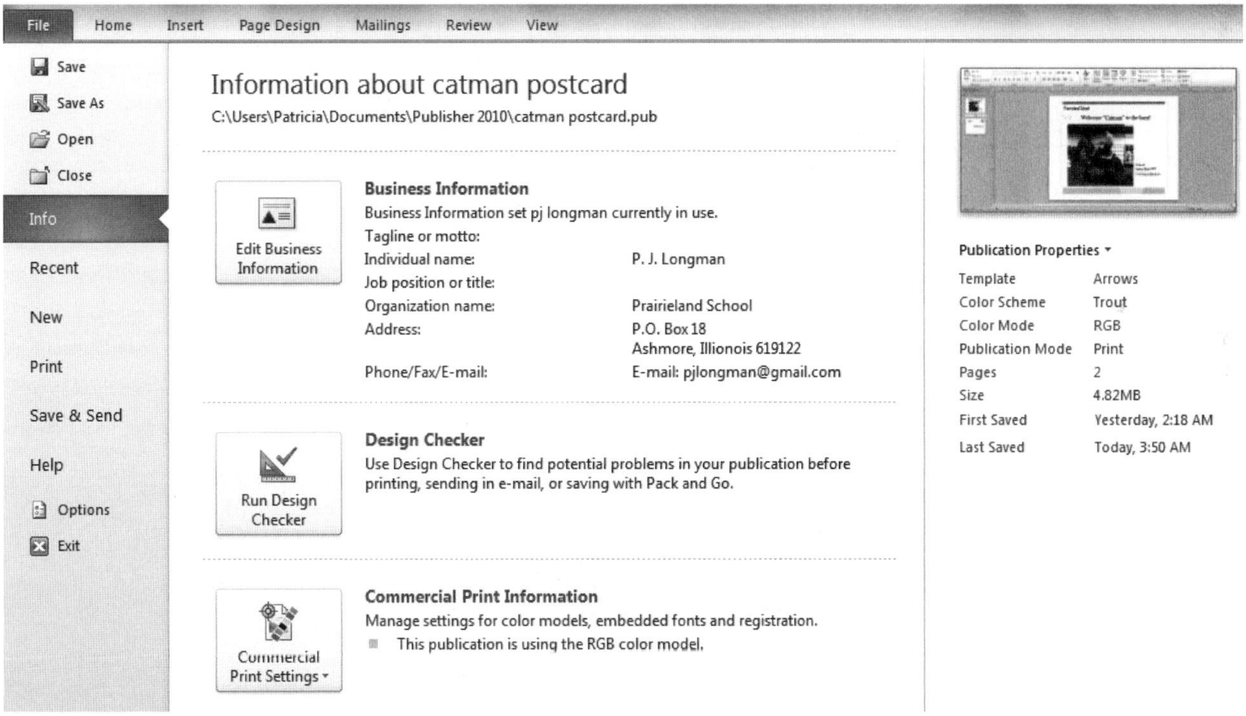

FIGURE 2.10 The File Tab Information Page

3 WORD 2010

Chapter Outline

- What You Are Going to Learn
- Chapter Overview
- How You Can Use Word
- NETS for Teachers
- What's New in Word 2010
- Working with Word
- Project for Teachers: Writing a Newsletter
- Project for Students: Creating a Diagram
- Project for Administrators: Creating a Webpage
- Project for Everyone: Using a Template for Mailings
- Summing It Up
- References and Resources

WHAT YOU ARE GOING TO LEARN

At the completion of this chapter you will be able to:

- Create a new word processing document
- Navigate the Word workspace
- Spell-check a document
- Format a document
- Add clip art and pictures to a document
- Working with text boxes
- Insert a hyperlink into a document
- Create a table in a document
- Create a diagram
- Save a document as a webpage
- Use a template

CHAPTER OVERVIEW

This chapter provides an introduction to Word 2010. It focuses on Word fundamentals and how to apply them to a variety of learning activities. The various activities for educators and students present instructions on how to use many of the tools in Word 2010 for creating, editing, and manipulating information in a word processing document. The exercises provide real-life activities that you do on a daily basis that may make your classroom or school more productive and provide a richer educational experience for students. The following section provides ideas on how you can use Word at a variety of cognitive levels.

HOW YOU CAN USE WORD

As a teacher, you can use Word in a variety of activities for both you and your students. You may want to examine Bloom's taxonomy of cognitive levels in conjunction with the National Educational Technology Standards for Teachers. You can use Word to accomplish instruction and learning at a variety of levels and address multiple standards:

- *Knowledge*—Students can create their own worksheets to practice materials and create flashcards to use in practicing such things as content vocabulary or the periodic table facts.
- *Comprehension*—Students can create book reports on recently read trade books, find more information about a topic such as gene therapy, create a webpage, and use Word to explain a lab experiment and report the results.
- *Application*—After reading *My Side of the Mountain* by Jean Craighead George and further research, students can create a brochure for other students who want to investigate falconry. After reviewing angles in geometry, students can research the works of Dutch artist M. C. Escher and repeating patterns such as triangles used in Islamic art and architecture; they can then write a report identifying the patterns and analyze one of the designs they found in their research.
- *Analysis*—After reading *Hatchet* by Gary Paulsen, students can organizing the skills Brian Robeson acquired during his adventure into a resume to get a job next summer. The students could develop a questionnaire to determine the type of recycling their parents and the community schools do and analyze what else may be done.
- *Synthesis*—After reading *My Side of the Mountain*, students can invent a survival kit for any situation. After investigating the properties of kites (geometry), students can create a script for creating and flying kites.
- *Evaluation*—Students can establish criteria and write a critique of a video presented in class; or students can write a letter to the school board, suggesting how recycling could be improved at the school.

NETS FOR TEACHERS*

Word can be utilized in the classroom to address the following standards:

- *Facilitate and Inspire Student Learning and Creativity*—Teachers use their knowledge of subject matter, teaching and learning, and technology to facilitate experiences that advance student learning, creativity, and innovation in both face-to-face and virtual environments.
- *Design and Develop Digital-Age Learning Experiences and Assessments*—Teachers design, develop, and evaluate authentic learning experiences and assessment, incorporating contemporary tools and resources to maximize content learning in context and to develop the knowledge, skills, and attitudes identified in NETS for Teachers.
- *Model Digital-Age Work and Learning*—Teachers exhibit knowledge, skills, and work processes representative of an innovative professional and digital society.

WHAT'S NEW IN WORD 2010

Microsoft Word is the word processing component of the Microsoft Office suite. It is a productivity tool for you and your students to use. When you open Word, you are basically rolling an "electronic piece of paper" on the screen. With simple clicks of a mouse, you can easily manipulate text materials, add graphics to text, check spelling and grammar, place words in column or table format, and include links to the Web in documents. The finished product may be saved on a memory device, printed on paper, or saved as a webpage for posting to the World Wide Web. As a teacher who knows how to use Word, you can produce all types of interesting materials and facilitate student production of materials.

Word 2010 uses the Ribbon instead of a menu bar, as with Word 2007. The major difference you will find in this version of Word is in formatting effects in text: You can use fills of color or shapes such as reflection. There are new picture editing tools, including cropping tools and artistic effects, such as a color glow around pictures. Office has more themes that you can apply to a document, or you can create your own. SmartArt graphics include new diagrams and chart layouts. When paired with online access, Microsoft Word enables you to co-author features through Windows Live, which allows you to share documents with others via the Web.

WORKING WITH WORD

The primary purpose of this chapter is to introduce you to the fundamental components and features of Word so you can use them in productive ways. To accomplish this objective, you will work through examples throughout the chapter. Although the examples are specific, the steps and procedures they present for developing Word documents, tables, and webpages are generic and apply to a variety of classroom management tasks and learning activities. As you work through the chapter's content, you can substitute your own examples for these to make the finished product unique.

Opening Word 2010

To create a Word document, you need to open Word 2010. Click Start on the Windows taskbar; move the mouse pointer over All Programs, and the Programs submenu appears. Move the mouse pointer over Microsoft Office and click, and the Office submenu appears. Click Microsoft Word 2010, and Word 2010 opens (see Figure 3.1). The Word workspace is delineated by tabs at the top of the Ribbon that are activated when selected, allowing the user to utilize the tools located on each tab. There are certain menus that appear when you need them, such as Table Tools when a table is created or selected within a document. As you go through creating a document, you will use the various tabs.

The Word workspace appears as shown in Figure 3.2. The Ribbon on the Word workspace is delineated by tabs at the top of the Ribbon that are activated when selected, allowing the user to utilize the tools that are located on each tab. The Ribbon is divided into the following tabs: File, Home, Insert, Page Layout, References, Mailings, Review, View, and Add-Ins. When the Home tab is activated, you see the following groupings on the Ribbon: Clipboard, Font, Paragraph, Styles, and Editing. When you click the arrow next to Font, the Font dialog box will appear (see Figure 3.3). You can use this dialog box to make changes in the font used in a document.

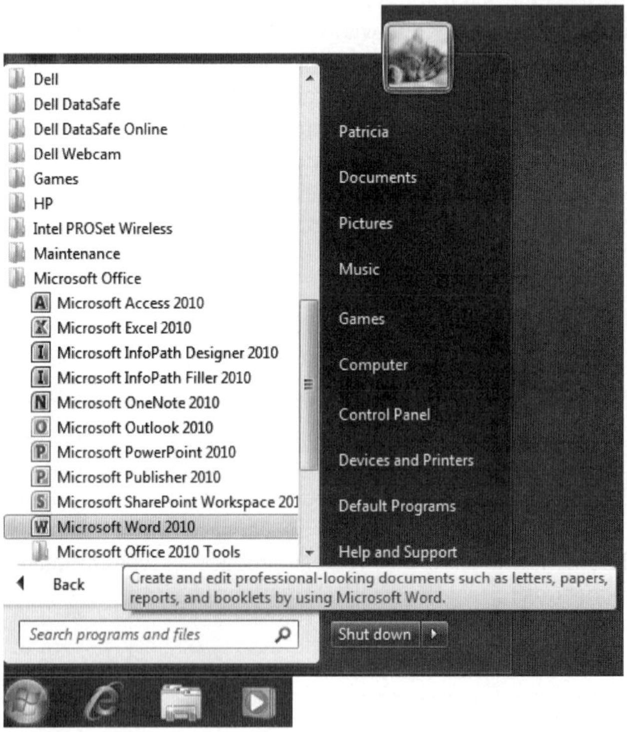

FIGURE 3.1 Starting Word

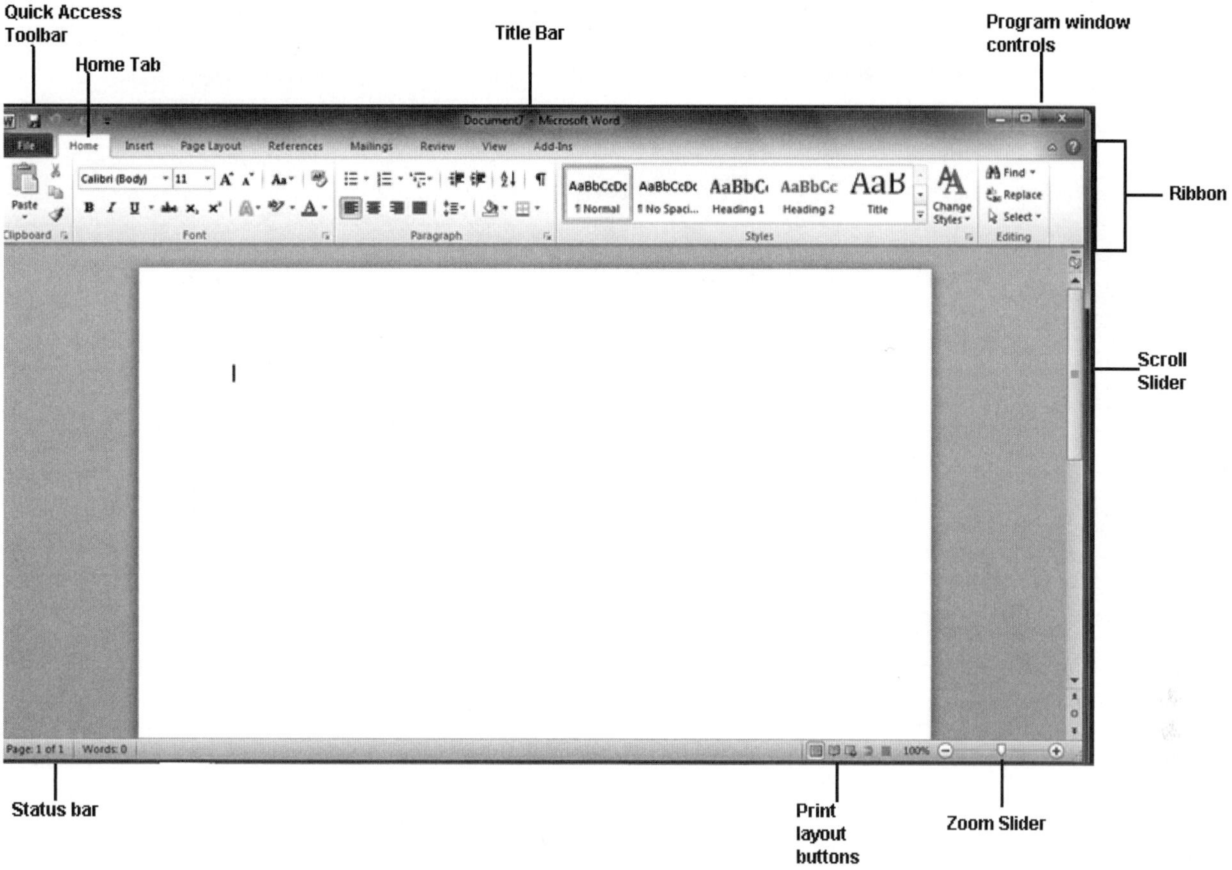

FIGURE 3.2 The Word Workspace

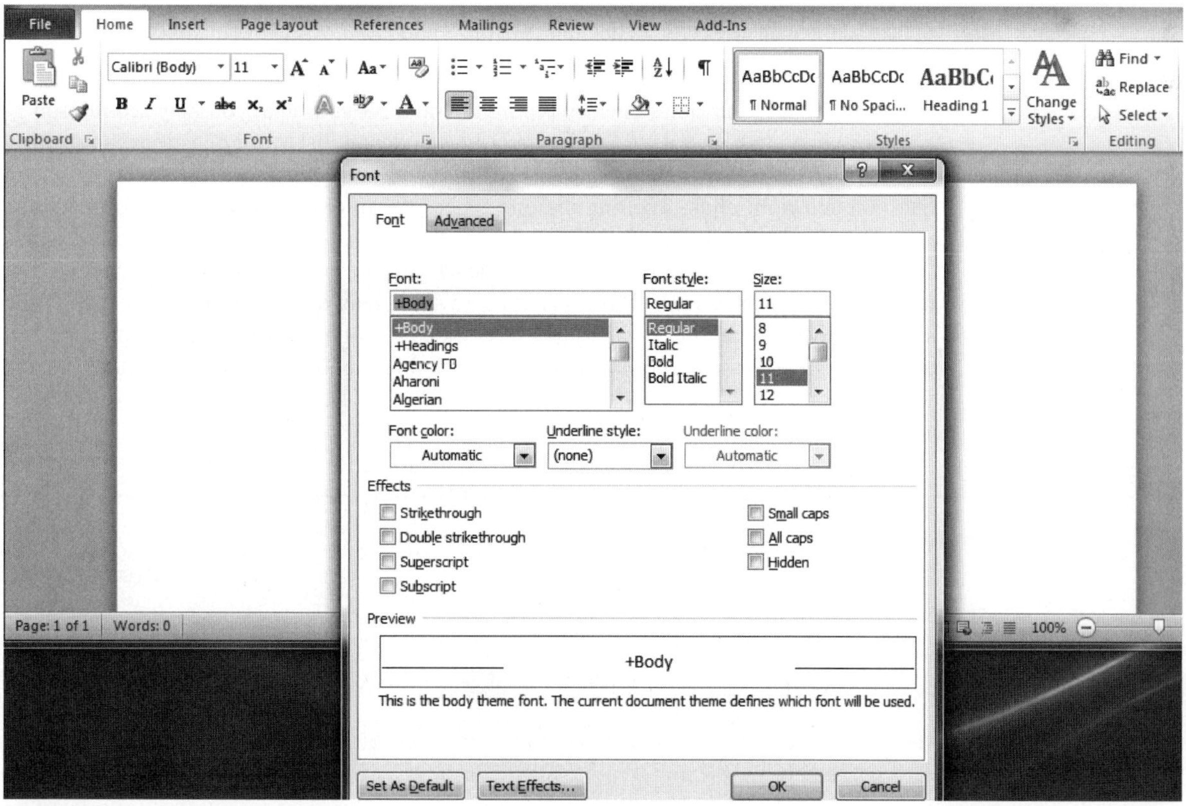

FIGURE 3.3 The Home Tab of the ribbon, with a Dialog Box

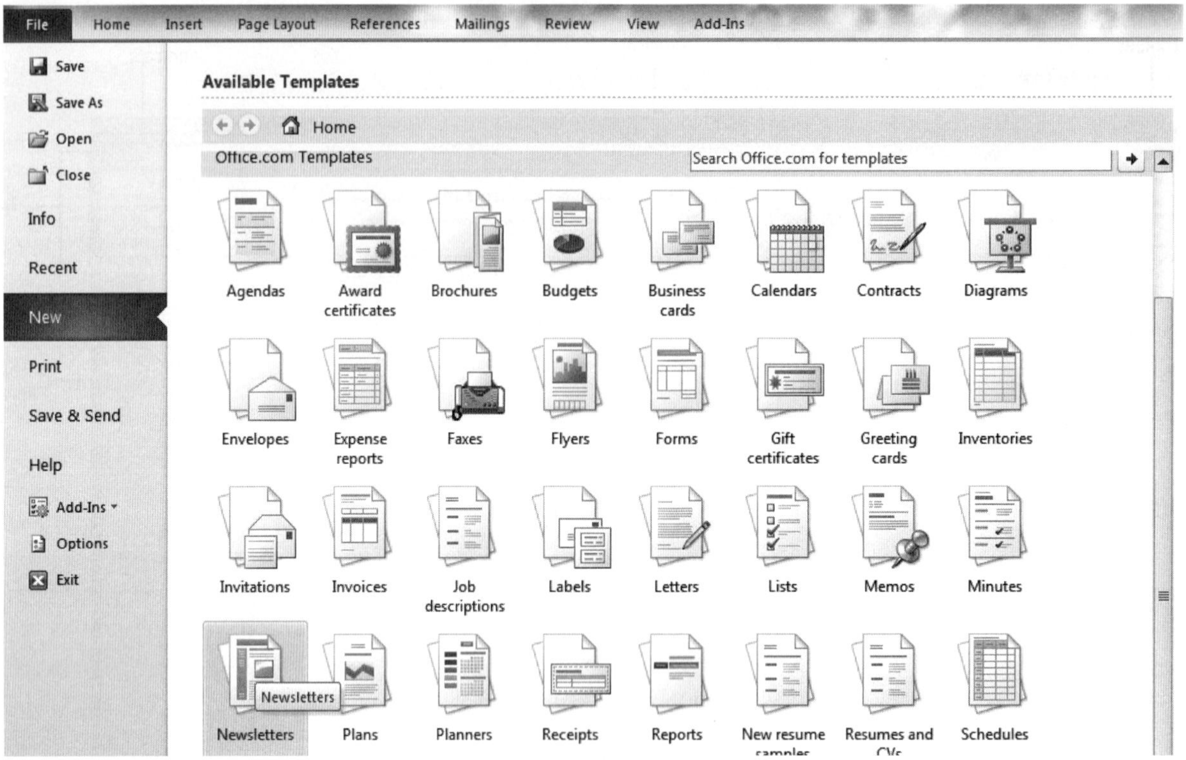

FIGURE 3.4 New Templates Available from www.office.com

PDToolkit for *Microsoft® Office 2010 for Teachers*

Go to PDToolkit for **Microsoft® Office 2010 for Teachers** to locate a completed version of the diagram in the Examples folder (Newsletter Example Finished.docx).

PROJECT FOR TEACHERS: WRITING A NEWSLETTER

This section presents an example of a project that you, as a teacher, could develop a newsletter for your classroom. If you have access to the Web, you can click on File and click on Newsletters on the template page (see Figure 3.4). You are then taken to the Microsoft website, where you can select the template of your choice.

In this example, instead of selecting one of Word's templates, you are going to create your own:

1. Under the File tab, select a new blank document (see Figure 3.5).
2. Create a title for your newsletter by typing the title. As you type, you may see red squiggly lines under some words; these squiggly lines indicate that Word questions the spelling of those particular words (see Figure 3.6). Place your mouse cursor over a word that is in question and right-click. Spelling options appear, as do other options to perform actions related to the word in question.

   As you type, words wrap to the next line. If you press the Enter key, Word creates a new paragraph. By default, Word inserts 1.15 lines between paragraphs. To change the spacing between lines and paragraphs, select the Paragraph section of the ribbon and click the down arrow at the corner of the paragraph dialog box (or you can select the Line and Spacing icon) (see Figure 3.7).

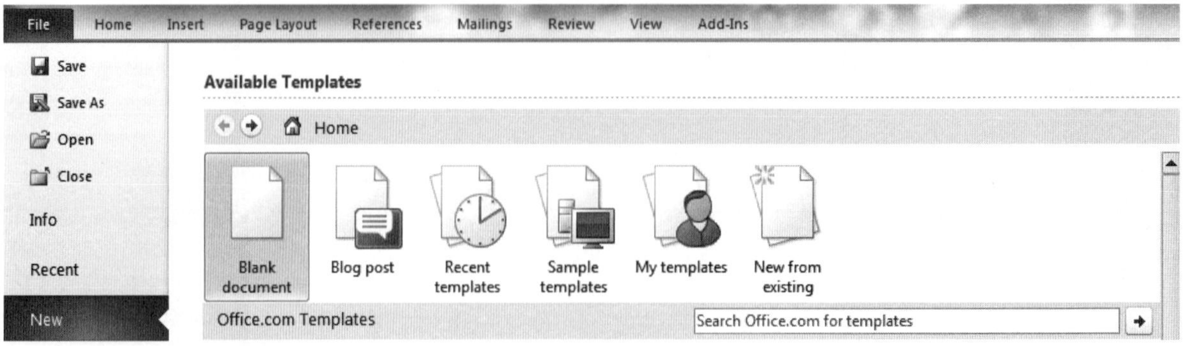

FIGURE 3.5 A New Blank Document

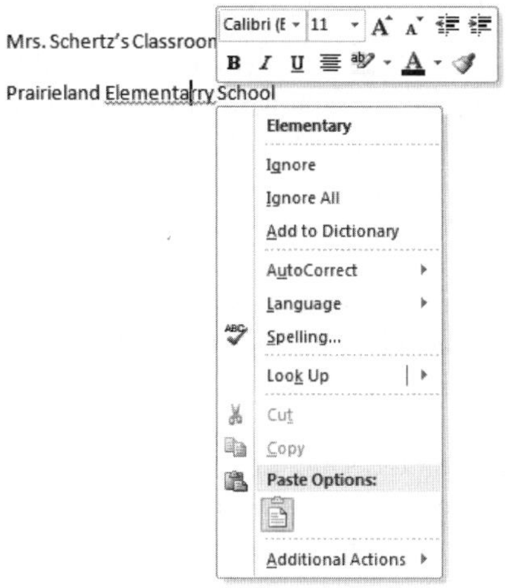

FIGURE 3.6 Spelling Correction

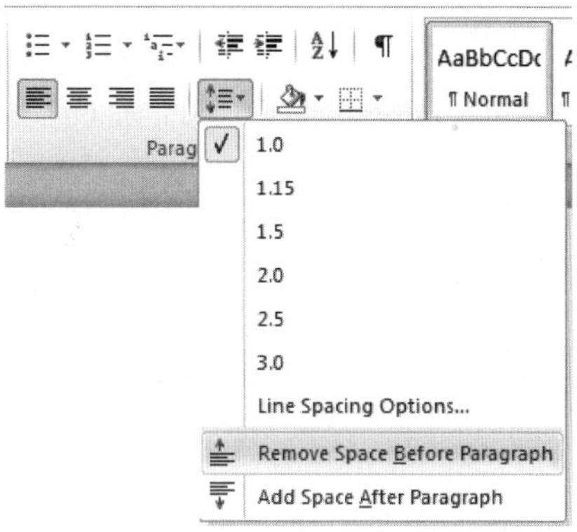

FIGURE 3.7 The Line and Spacing Icon Menu

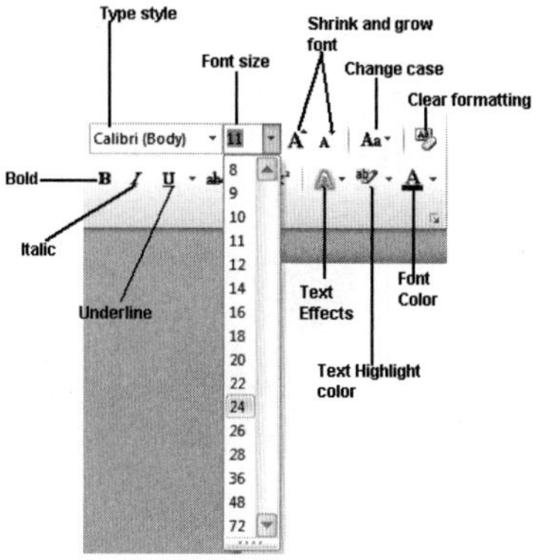

FIGURE 3.8 The Font Section of the Home Tab

3. Once text has been typed in, select words, lines, or paragraphs by doing the following:
   - Drag the cursor over sections of type and hold down the mouse button.
   - Double-click anywhere inside a word you want to select.
   - Click inside the left margin to select the entire line of text.
   - Double-click inside the left margin to select a paragraph.
4. Highlight (or select) the title of the newsletter. Then, to increase the size of the text and utilize the text effects, select the Font section of the Home tab of the Ribbon (see Figure 3.8). Increase the font size to 24 (see Figure 3.9). (Note that there are 36 points to 1 inch.)
5. With the title still selected, click on the arrow next to Text Effects from the Font section of the Home ribbon and select Gradient Fill—Orange (or whatever text effect you choose).
6. Center the title on the page by using the Paragraph section of the Home ribbon and selecting the Center icon (see Figure 3.10). (Alternatively, you can select the down arrow in this section and then select Center under General—Alignment.)
7. To add visual interest to your document, insert some clip art. To do so, place the cursor next to the left side of the title of your newsletter (in this case, Mrs. Schertz's Classroom Newsletter). From the Insert tab select the Clip Art icon. You will be focusing on the Illustrations section of the insert for this action. Select Clip Art by moving your mouse pointer over the icon and clicking on the icon (see Figure 3.11). Once the clip art has been clicked, a Clip Art task pane appears on the right side of the Word workspace.

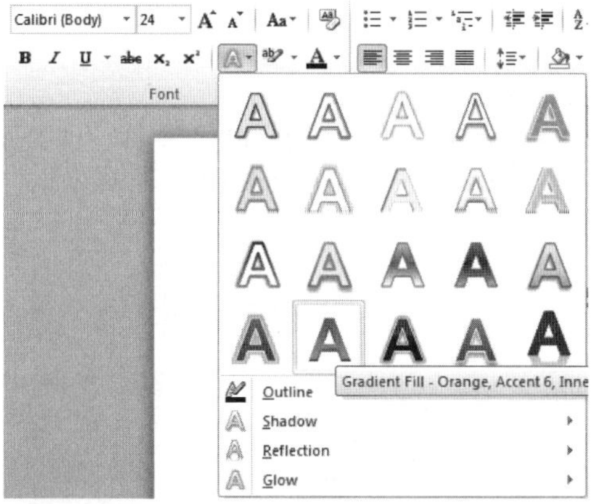

FIGURE 3.9 Text Effects

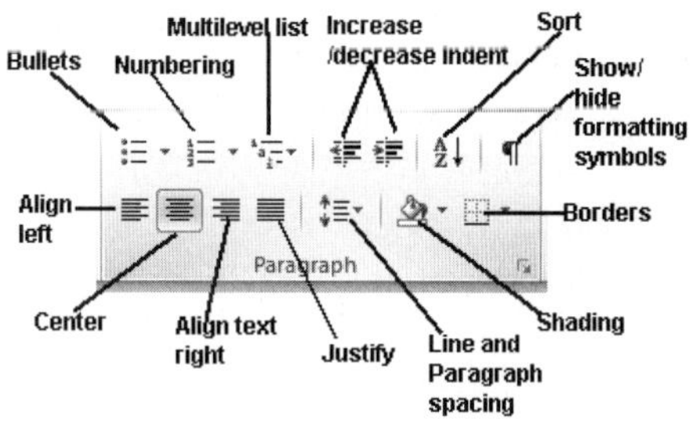

FIGURE 3.10 The Paragraph Section of the Home Tab

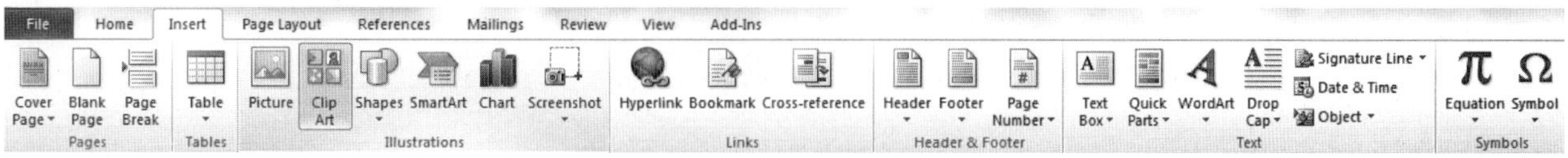

FIGURE 3.11 The Insert Tab

FIGURE 3.12 The Clip Art Pane

8. In the Clip Art task pane, type school in the Search For pane. If your computer is connected the Web, you can access the clip art from Office Online, which adds to the selection possibilities. In this illustration, select the school bus or whatever clip art you wish (see Figure 3.12).
9. Once the clip art has been placed in the document, a new ribbon section appears that deals with the manipulation of clip art. This ribbon section appears only when a picture or clip art has been selected by clicking on the object. Select Drop Shadow Rectangle from the Picture Tools section of the Ribbon (see Figure 3.13).
10. When you place the mouse pointer over the clip art, the pointer turns into a four-arrow icon. Right-click on the clip art, and a clip art action pane appears. Select Wrap Text, and a second pane appears. From this pane, select Tight (see Figure 3.14).
11. While holding down the left mouse button, drag the picture to the top of the page, move the clip art to one side to allow the title and clip art to be on the same line (see Figure 3.15). You can also resize the clip art by placing the mouse cursor over the circles on the edge of the clip art and holding down the left mouse button and then dragging. In addition, the green circle on the clip art allows you to rotate the clip art on the page.
12. Under the title of your school, press Enter two times to add some space between the title of the newsletter and the body of the material you are now going to insert. After doing so, select the Insert ribbon and the Text Box icon on the ribbon. Of the options, select Draw Text Box for this illustration (see Figure 3.16).

FIGURE 3.13 Picture Tools

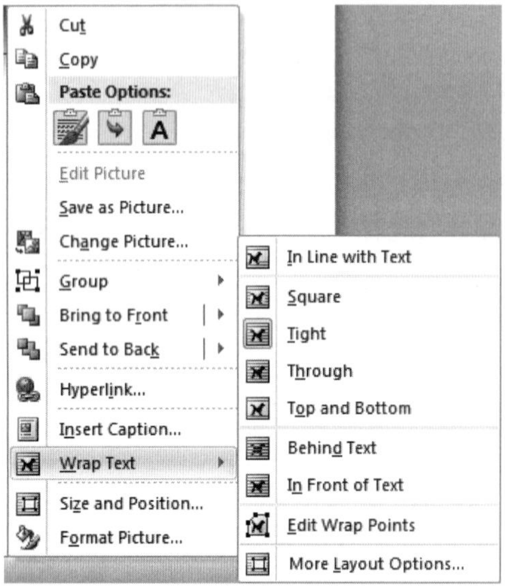

FIGURE 3.14 Wrapping Text

FIGURE 3.15 Clip Art and Title

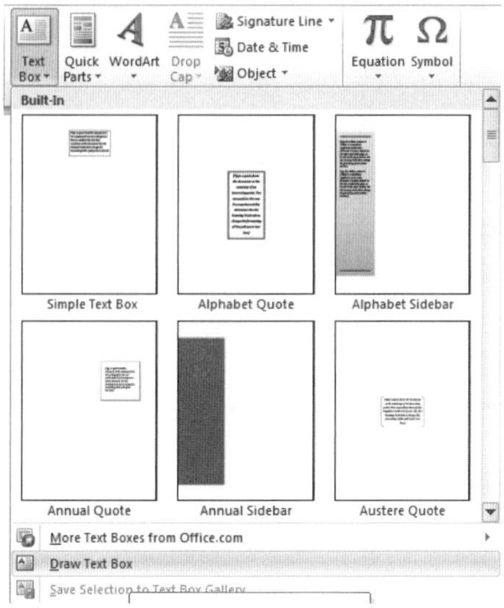

FIGURE 3.16 Text Box Selection

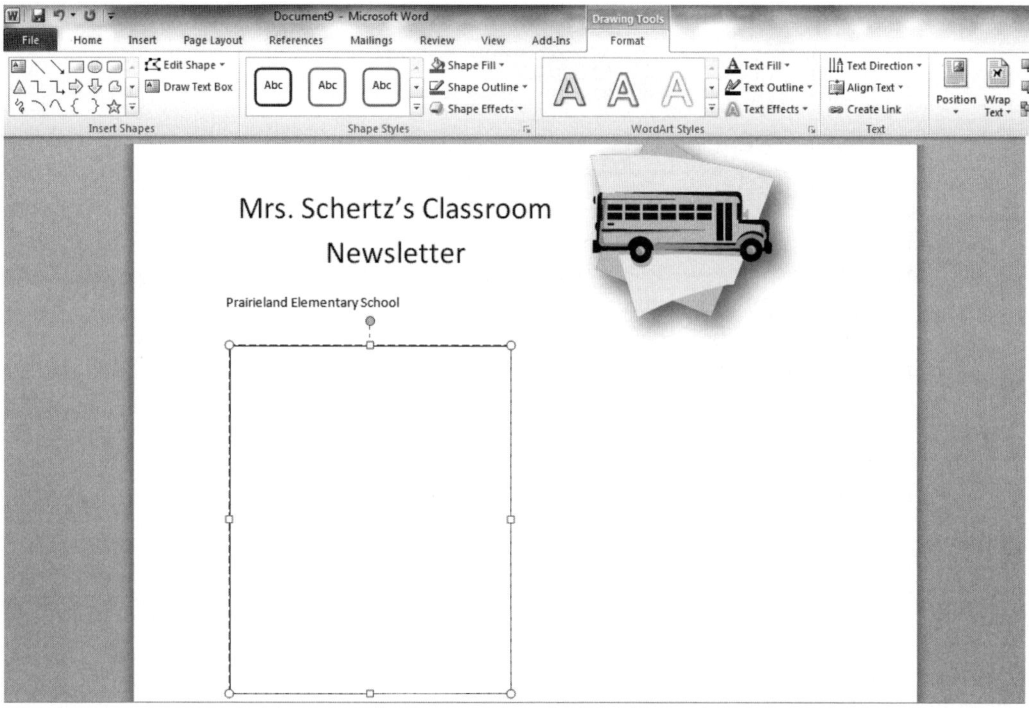

FIGURE 3.17 Drawing Tools

13. The cursor turns into a crosshair icon when the Draw Text Box has been selected from the list. While holding down the left mouse button, drag the crosshair icon down and to the right to about the middle of the page and release. A box appears, where you can start typing. Also, a Text Box Tools Formatting ribbon appears (see Figure 3.17).
14. Once the text box has been created, a cursor appears in the box, and you can start typing information in the box. Create a title for this section on the newsletter, such as This Week's Highlights. Make the title a little larger and make the type boldface by using tools in the Font section of the Ribbon. Type text in your newsletter about the upcoming week.
15. Create a second text box. To do so, highlight the text box you created earlier, hold down the Ctrl key and press C (i.e., Ctrl+C) at the same time. This is a shortcut to copy items and ensures that the new text box is exactly the same size as the first one. Then press Ctrl+V, which is a shortcut for pasting documents that are on the Clipboard that have been copied. You can do the same thing by selecting Copy and Paste from the first section of the Home ribbon. You can remove the text in the second box by highlighting the text and pressing the Delete key. Title the second box Upcoming Events. In this box, add the upcoming events that are happening at your school.
16. Across the bottom of the page draw a third text box. Title this section of the newsletter Spelling Words for This Week. Using the Home ribbon, make the text 18 points in size, use one of the glow effects, and center the text. After doing so, press Enter once. From the Insert tab, select Insert Table and highlight boxes to create a 3-by-6 table (see Figure 3.18).
17. Once the table has been inserted, click in each of the cells of the table and type in spelling words that students will need to know for your class. You can add some clip art to the table if you'd like.
18. You can add a border around the newsletter by selecting the Page Layout tab and then selecting Page Borders. You will see a pane appear once you have clicked on Page Borders. Select a border type by clicking on the options to create a border for the newsletter (see Figure 3.19).
19. Spell-check your newsletter to make sure you haven't missed any spelling errors. To do a spell-check of your document, select the Review tab on the ribbon and select the Spelling and Grammar icon (see Figure 3.20).
20. You will periodically want to save documents so you don't lose your work. To do so, select the File tab of the Ribbon. If you want to save a document for use by others who may have different versions of Office, you may do so by selecting the Save As button from the

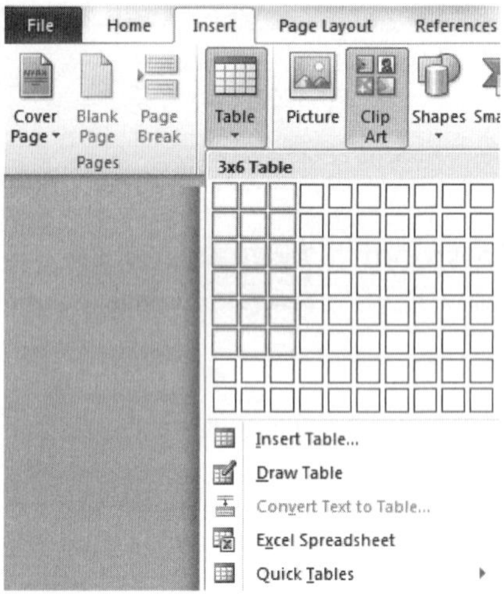

FIGURE 3.18 Inserting a Table

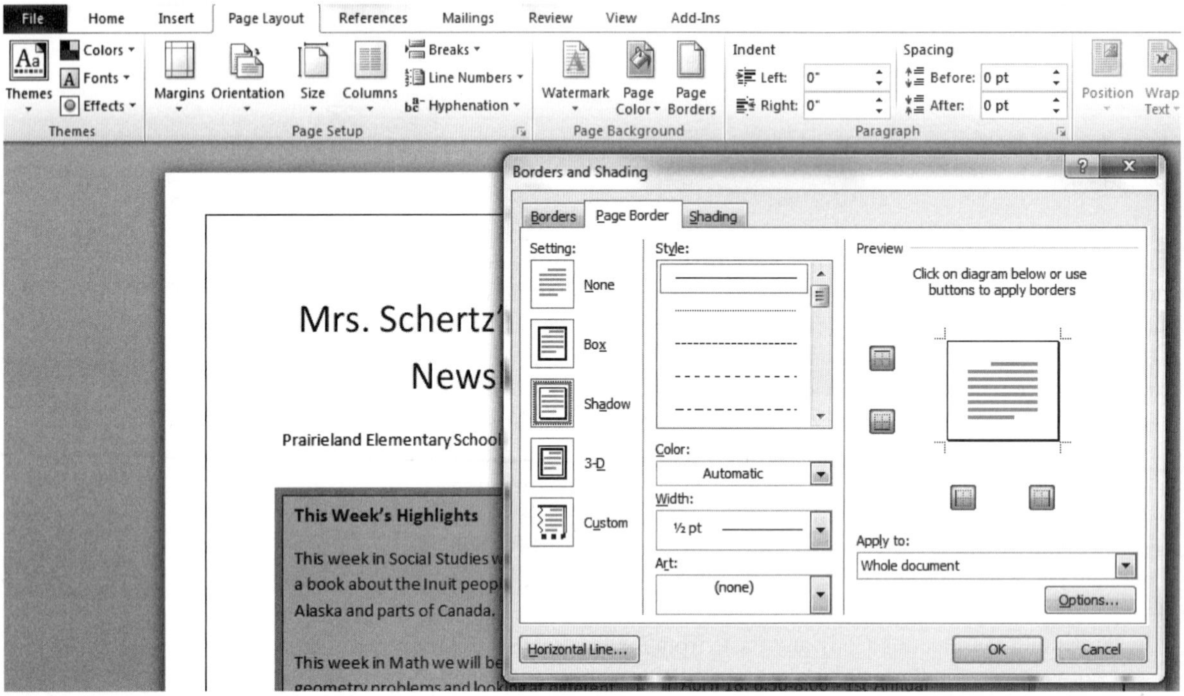

FIGURE 3.19 Adding Borders

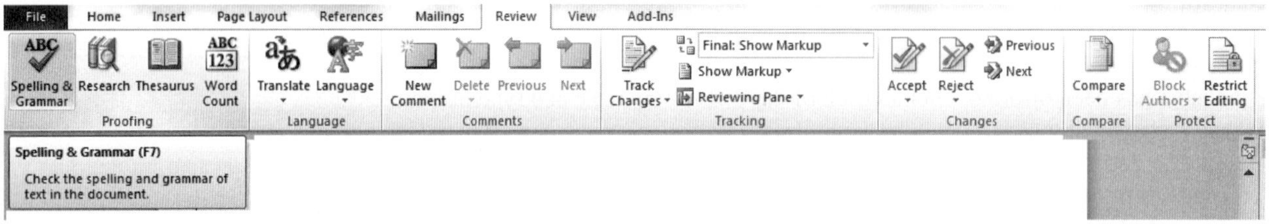

FIGURE 3.20 Spell-Checking a Document

list of options under the File tab. You may also want to use Save As if you want to save a document using a different name. To save the newsletter to an earlier version of Word, select the down arrow on the Save As Type bar and select Word 97-2003 Document. You will notice that you can save the file in a variety of formats, including PDF, Template, and Other Formats, allowing you a variety of finished products (see Figure 3.21). The finished newsletter might look as shown in Figure 3.22.

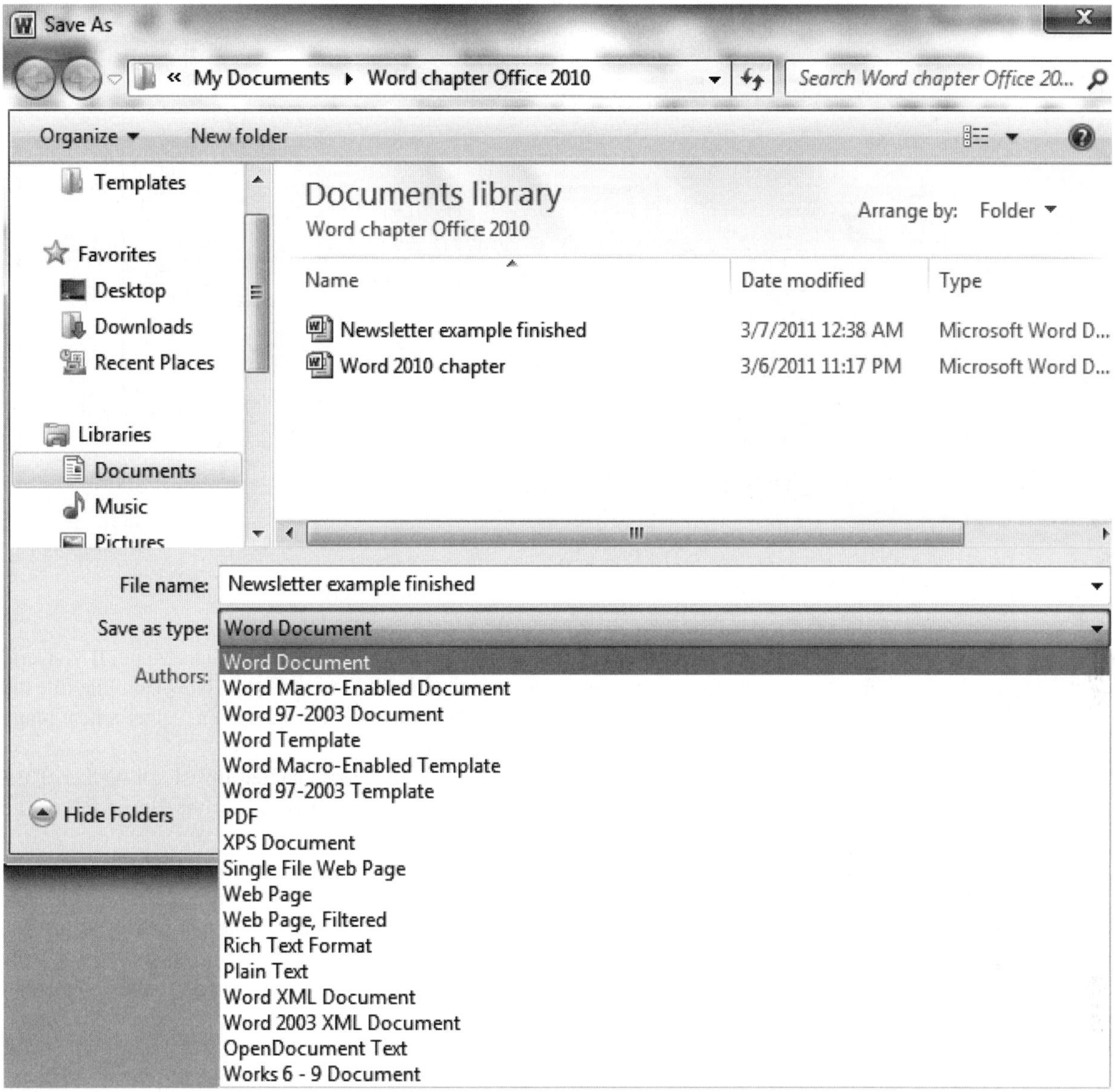

FIGURE 3.21 Saving the Newsletter

21. To print the newsletter, select File from the Ribbon and then select Print. The page where your cursor is located will show as the preview page. Because your newsletter is only one page, a print preview will show on the screen; you can use it to review the document prior to printing. Then you can determine the number of copies of the document to print, the printer to use, and which pages to print if your document is more than one page. Once all selections are made, click on the Print icon, and the document prints to the specified printer (see Figure 3.23).

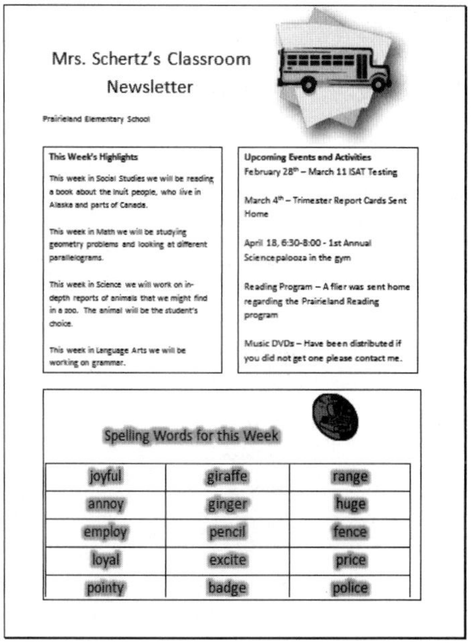

FIGURE 3.22 The Finished Newsletter

PROJECT FOR STUDENTS: CREATING A DIAGRAM

Periodically, students are asked to provide a diagram of an idea or provide visual images of a process or an organization. For example, when a class is talking about inherited traits, the teacher might ask the students to show the heritage of a horse to give an idea what horses might have as their specialty due to their breeding, which is very similar to a family tree for people. This would be part of a report a student may give on selective breeding of animals or general genetics. To create such a diagram, follow these steps:

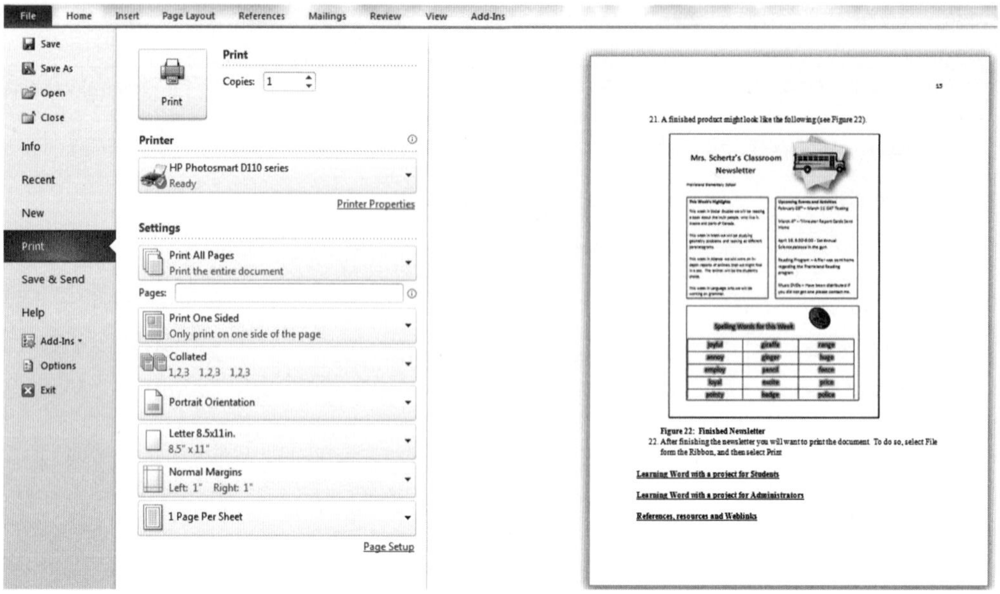

FIGURE 3.23 Printing a Document

PDToolkit for *Microsoft® Office 2010 for Teachers*

Go to PDToolkit for **Microsoft® Office 2010 for Teachers** to locate a completed version of the diagram in the Examples folder (Pedigree of a Quarter Horse named Investor.docx).

1. Open a new document in Word by clicking on the Word icon in the Start Menu. If you kept the Word program open from the previous document, you can select New from the File tab on the Ribbon. When the available templates are listed on the screen, select a new blank document and click on Create (see Figure 3.24).
2. Press Enter once and type in Pedigree of a Quarter Horse named Investor's Walker. Then highlight the new text and select Title from the Styles Listing on the Home tab of the Ribbon (see Figure 3.25).
3. For this particular diagram, you want to use the landscape orientation for the page. To change the orientation of the page, select the Page Layout tab on the Ribbon and click on Orientation. Select the landscape orientation by clicking on the appropriate icon (see Figure 3.26).
4. Press Enter twice to add some space after the title. Select the Insert tab on the Ribbon and then select SmartArt. On the menu, select Hierarchy and then select the horizontal hierarchy (see Figure 3.27).
5. To complete the diagram use the information found shown in Figure 3.28.

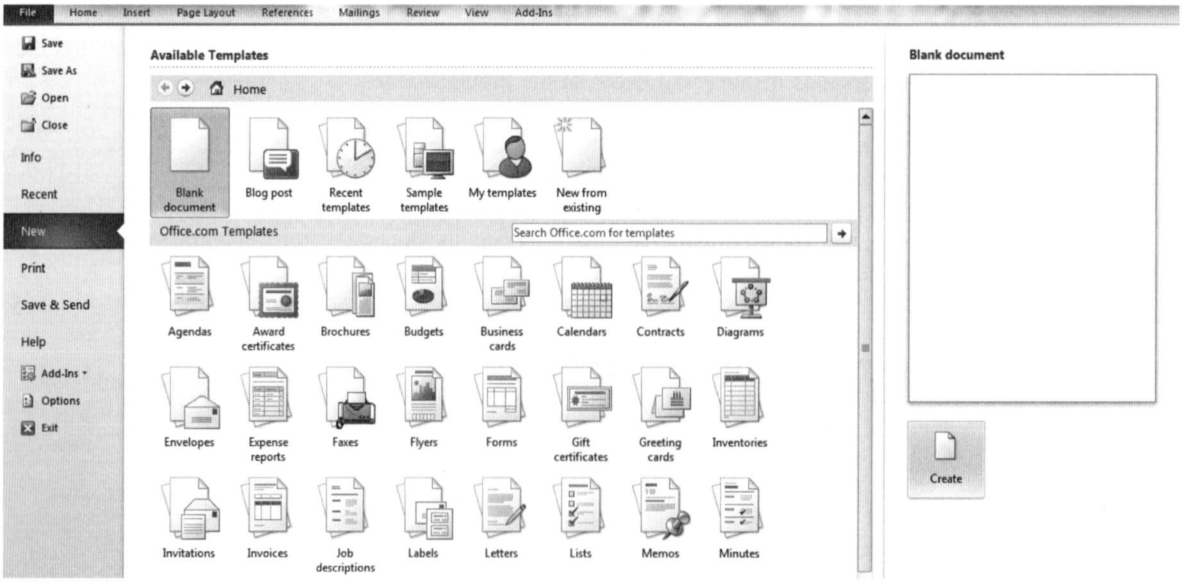

FIGURE 3.24 Creating a New Blank Document

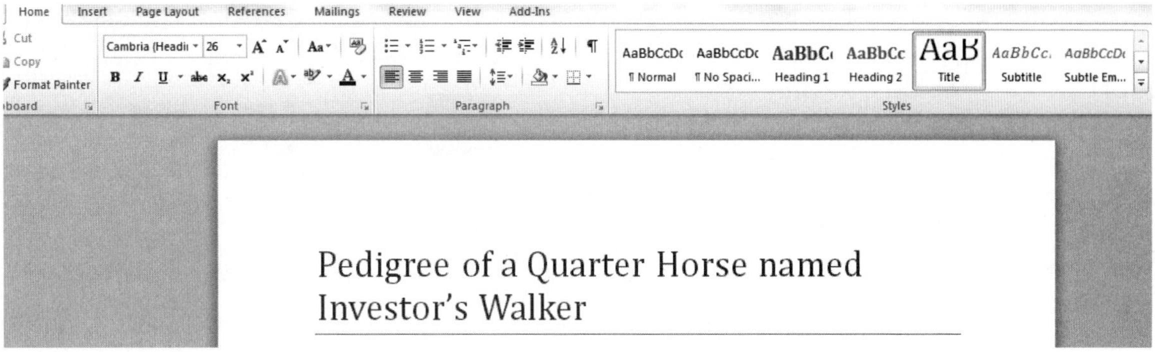

FIGURE 3.25 Using the Title Style

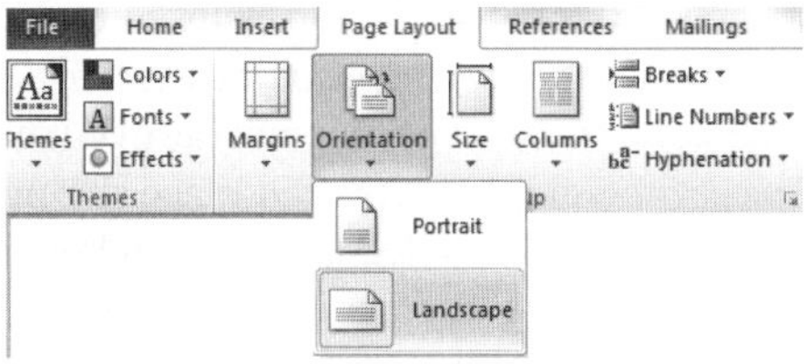

FIGURE 3.26 Page Orientation

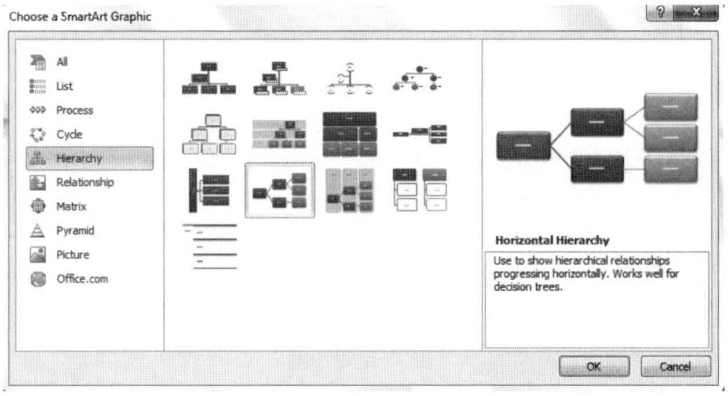

FIGURE 3.27 The Horizontal Hierarchy

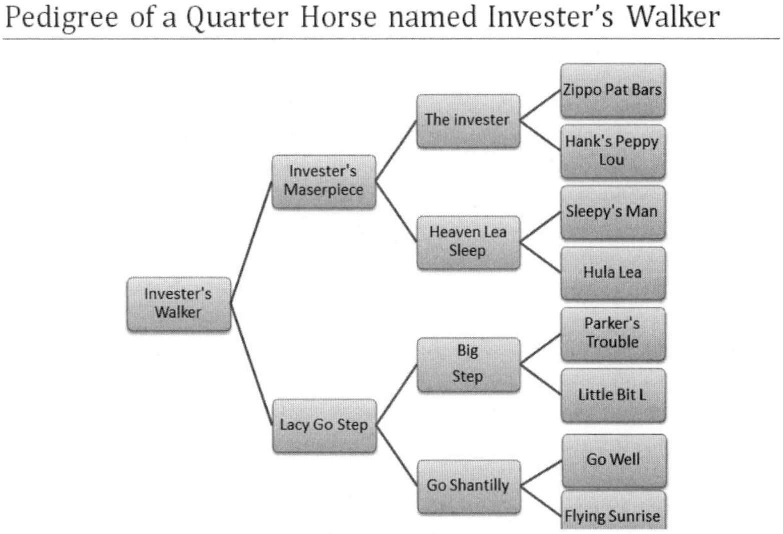

FIGURE 3.28 Finished Pedigree of Investor's Walker

6. In the space for text in the boxes you can type the ancestors of Investor's Walker. The tree shown in Figure 3.28 does not have enough boxes for Investor's Walker's entire heritage. To add boxes to the lineage, place the curser in the last box on the bottom and from the Smart Tools Ribbon click on Add Shape. This will add an additional box for the horse's lineage (see Figure 3.29).

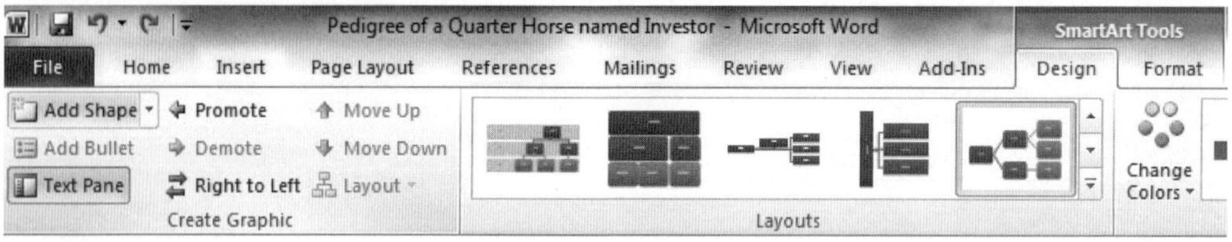

FIGURE 3.29 Adding Shapes

7. To add additional shapes behind the last series, on the SmartArt Tools Ribbon click on the down arrow next to Add Shape and select Add Shape Below. To add a second box, click on the new empty box and then click on Add Shape. You need to add boxes until you have two sets of parents for each of the last set of horses listed in the chart (see Figure 3.30).
8. You can change the style and color scheme of the chart by selecting Design on the SmartArt Tools Ribbon and clicking the style of diagram desired (see Figure 3.31).
9. To increase the size of the graphic, you can place the mouse cursor on a corner of the graphic until it turns into a double-sided arrow. Then hold down the left mouse button and drag the mouse to create the size of graphic you desire.
10. Save the document by selecting File and Save. Indicate where to save the file and in what format (see Figure 3.32).
11. After saving the document, you may choose to print it or copy and paste it into a report that the student is writing about quarter horses.

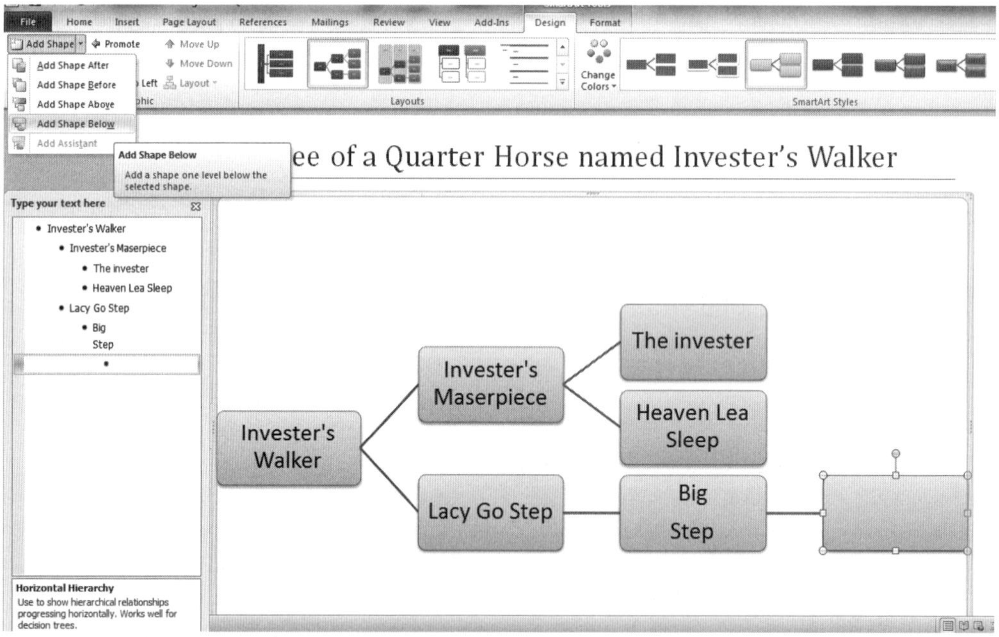

FIGURE 3.30 Adding Shapes Below a Selected Shape

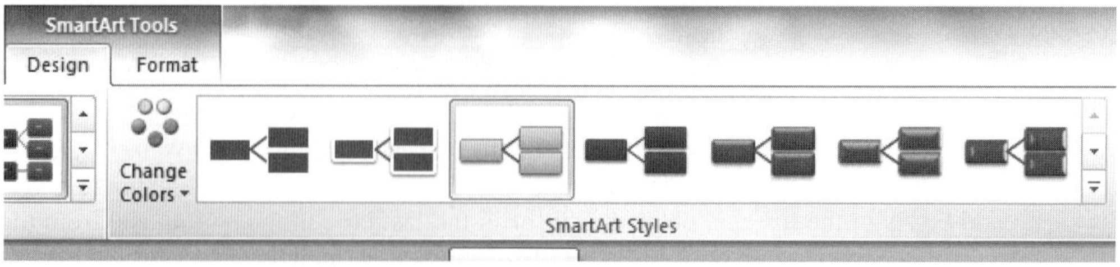

FIGURE 3.31 Changing the SmartArt Style

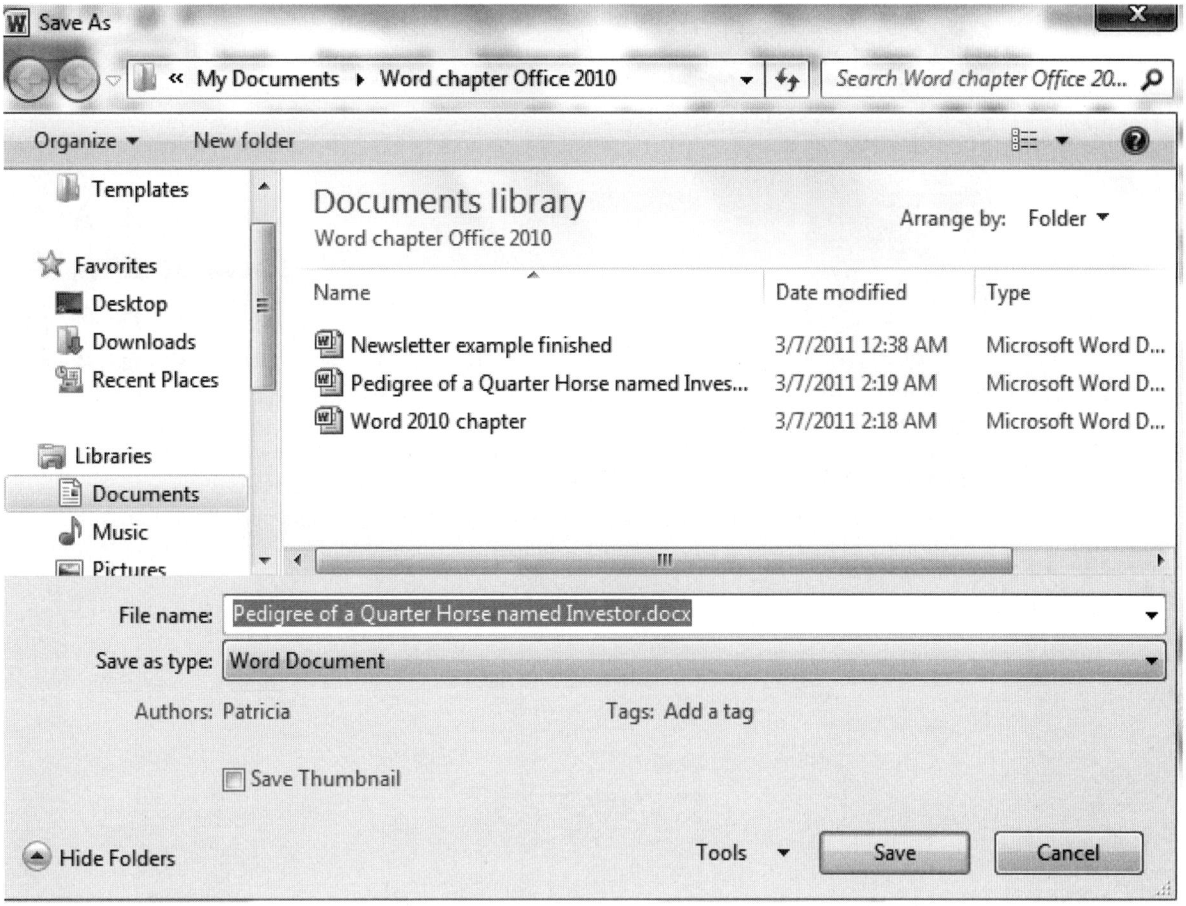

FIGURE 3.32 Saving the Document

PROJECT FOR ADMINISTRATORS: CREATING A WEBPAGE

As an administrator, a teacher, or a student, you may be called upon to create a webpage. Word allows you to save a document as a webpage. You will want to check with the technology coordinator in your school to find out if there are any requirements that must be utilized when creating webpages that will be linked or published on the school website. But keep in mind that a webpage does not necessarily have to be published on the Web for all to see. For teachers and/or administrators who want to allow students to go to specific websites related to a topic, a webpage can be created and shared with students via CD, thumb drive, or central server where students can access the information.

One subject that administrators and teachers must address is copyright in the classroom and in the school. You will now work on creating a copyright webpage with links to other websites that can provide additional information. Follow these steps:

1. Open Word, select File, select Blank Document, and click on Create to start the new document.
2. Once the Word workspace appears, press Enter twice to move the cursor down the page. Select the Insert tab on the Ribbon and select the WordArt icon. The WordArt gallery appears (see Figure 3.33).
3. Select the style of WordArt you want. A text box appears, allowing you to type in the title of the page. Title the document Copyright Basics.
4. In the Drawing toolbar, select Text Effects. A pane appears, allowing you to select transform styles of lettering. Select one that appeals to you. The text on the page will reflect the style as you mouse over the style (see Figure 3.34).
5. Move the text box by moving the mouse cursor over the text box until the cursor turns into a four-arrow cursor. Hold down the left mouse button and drag the text box to the center of the page from left to right at the top of the page. You have just created the title of your webpage (see Figure 3.35).

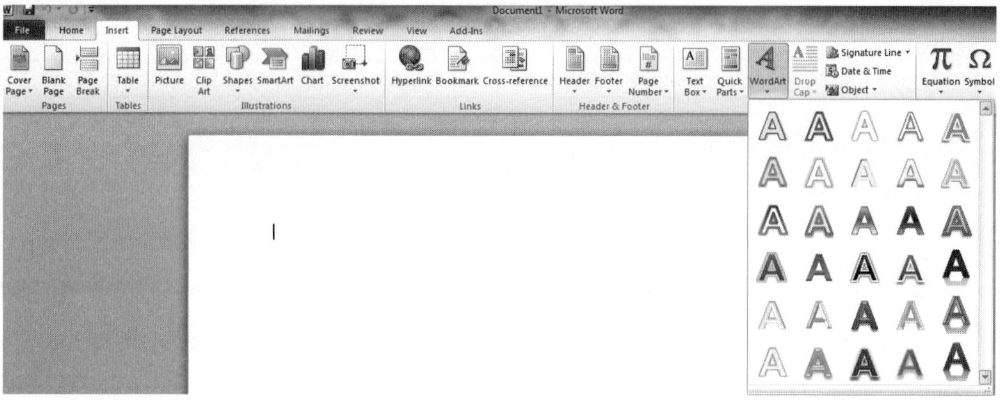

FIGURE 3.33 Inserting WordArt

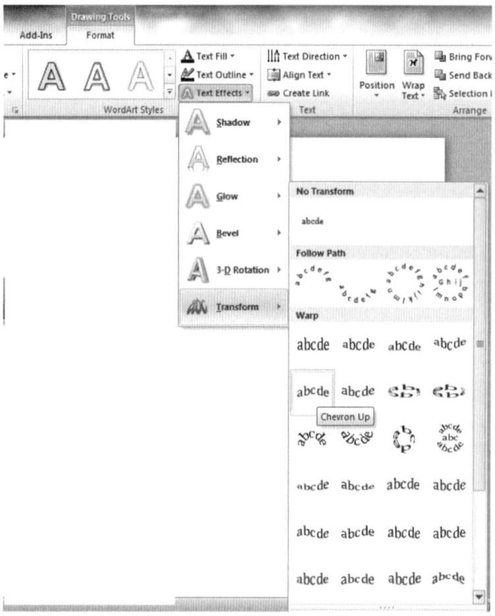

FIGURE 3.34 Transform Text Effects

FIGURE 3.35 Creating the Title of a Webpage

6. After creating the title, type in information related to copyright (see Figure 3.36).
7. Highlight all the text you have typed in and select the Page Layout tab on the Ribbon. Select Columns from the Page Setup section of the Ribbon and select two columns (see Figure 3.37).
8. The document will reflect the two columns. Place the cursor above the "When can copyrighted materials be used?" paragraph and press the Enter key to move some of the paragraph text to the second column (see Figure 3.38).
9. Below the paragraphs add another title: Websites for Additional Information on Copyright (see Figure 3.39).
10. Select the Insert tab from the Ribbon and select Hyperlink. A Hyperlink pane appears (see Figure 3.40).
11. You will want to Link to: Existing File or Webpage. You can look in browsed pages, or you can type in the address to create a hyperlink. You can also type in the text to be displayed or use the title provided when you use browsed pages. Figure 3.41 shows the websites that can be used are in the following figure. As an example you can type in the following webpage address: www.copyright.gov. The addresses in this case were copied and pasted in the table from the address line in the Insert Hyperlink pane.
12. To create a background for the webpage, select the Page Layout tab from the Ribbon and then select Page Color. Select Fill Effects from the pane that appears, using settings similar to what is shown in Figure 3.42. If you use a background color that is too dark, it will be difficult to read the text on the webpage. If you click on Texture or Patterns, you see additional effects that can be used in addition to the gradient.

What is copyright?

Copyright law is a set of federal laws pertaining to the legal right to use original works. These laws set forth rights and conditions regarding how an individual may use or copy materials.

The Copyright Act covers eight broad categories:

1. Literary works
2. Musical works
3. Dramatic works, including any accompanying music
4. Pantomimes and choreographic works
5. Pictorial, graphic and sculptural works
6. Motion pictures and other audio visual works
7. Sound recordings
8. Architectural works

   (Talab, 1986, p.6)

When can copyrighted materials be used?

- Public domain – work belonging to the public as a whole, such as government documents and works with an expired copyright or no existing protection.
- Permission – Permission has been given for the proposed use by the copyright owner.
- Legal exemption – Use constitutes and exemption, such as a parody.
- Fair use – Use for educational purposes according to certain restrictions.

Four Standards for determining fair use exemption:

1. The purpose and character of the use
2. The nature of the copyrighted work
3. The amount and substantiality of the portion used in relation to the copyrighted works as a whole
4. The effect of the use upon the potential market for, or value of, the copyrighted work.

FIGURE 3.36 The Text for the Copyright Page

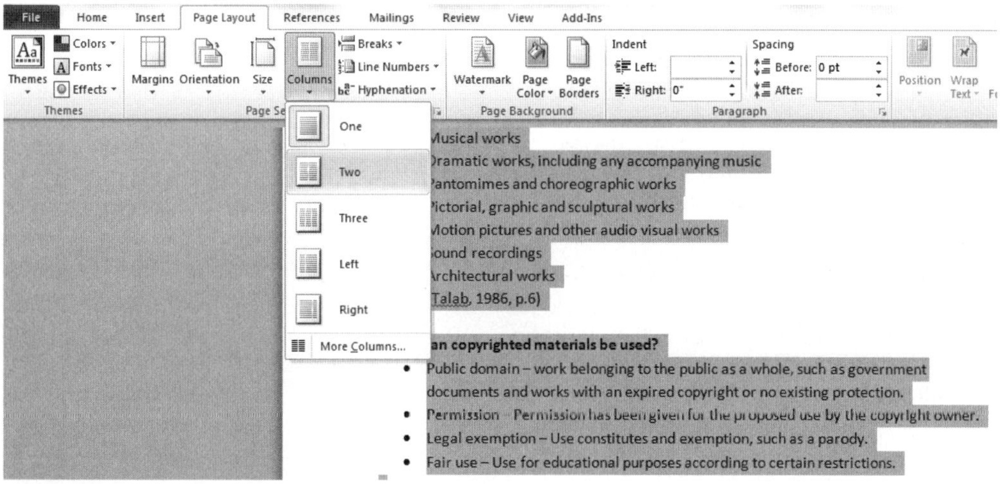

FIGURE 3.37 Creating Columns

13. To save your document as a webpage, select the File tab on the Ribbon, select Save As, use the pull-down menu next to Save as Type, and select webpage (see Figure 3.43). You may want to check with your technology coordinator at your school to see if he or she has a preference as to the type of webpage you create to make sure it is compatible with the protocol used at the school for webpages.

14. To see how the page looks when posted to the Web, close the Webpage document. Then from the Start button go to Documents and select the Copyright webpage. The page will launch in the browser on your computer, and if your computer is has access to the Internet, you will be able to link to the websites on the page. The finished website should look similar to the one shown in Figure 3.44.

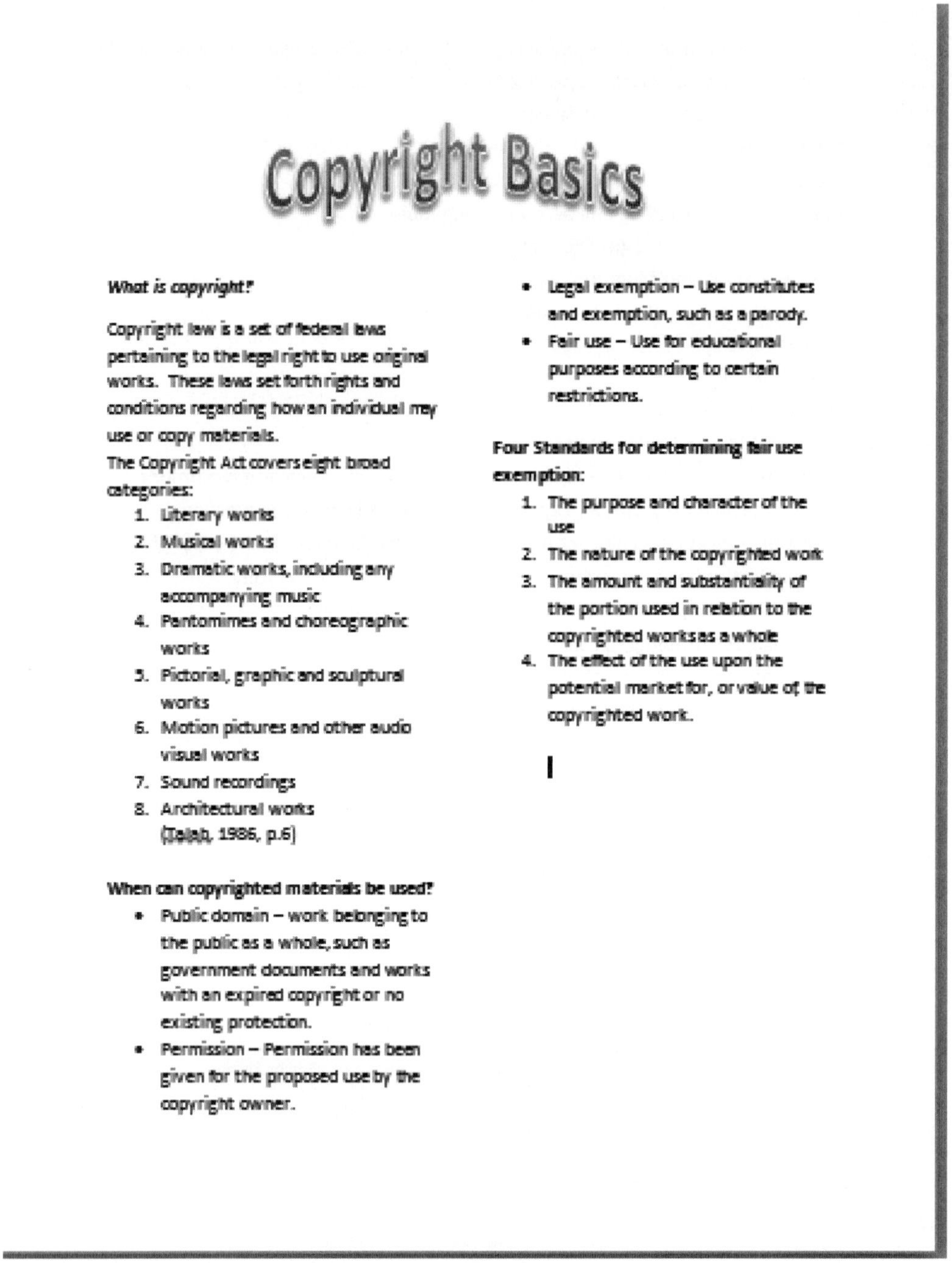

Copyright Basics

What is copyright?

Copyright law is a set of federal laws pertaining to the legal right to use original works. These laws set forth rights and conditions regarding how an individual may use or copy materials.
The Copyright Act covers eight broad categories:

1. Literary works
2. Musical works
3. Dramatic works, including any accompanying music
4. Pantomimes and choreographic works
5. Pictorial, graphic and sculptural works
6. Motion pictures and other audio visual works
7. Sound recordings
8. Architectural works
(Talab, 1986, p.6)

When can copyrighted materials be used?

- Public domain – work belonging to the public as a whole, such as government documents and works with an expired copyright or no existing protection.
- Permission – Permission has been given for the proposed use by the copyright owner.
- Legal exemption – Use constitutes and exemption, such as a parody.
- Fair use – Use for educational purposes according to certain restrictions.

Four Standards for determining fair use exemption:

1. The purpose and character of the use
2. The nature of the copyrighted work
3. The amount and substantiality of the portion used in relation to the copyrighted works as a whole
4. The effect of the use upon the potential market for, or value of, the copyrighted work.

FIGURE 3.38 Moving Text in Columns

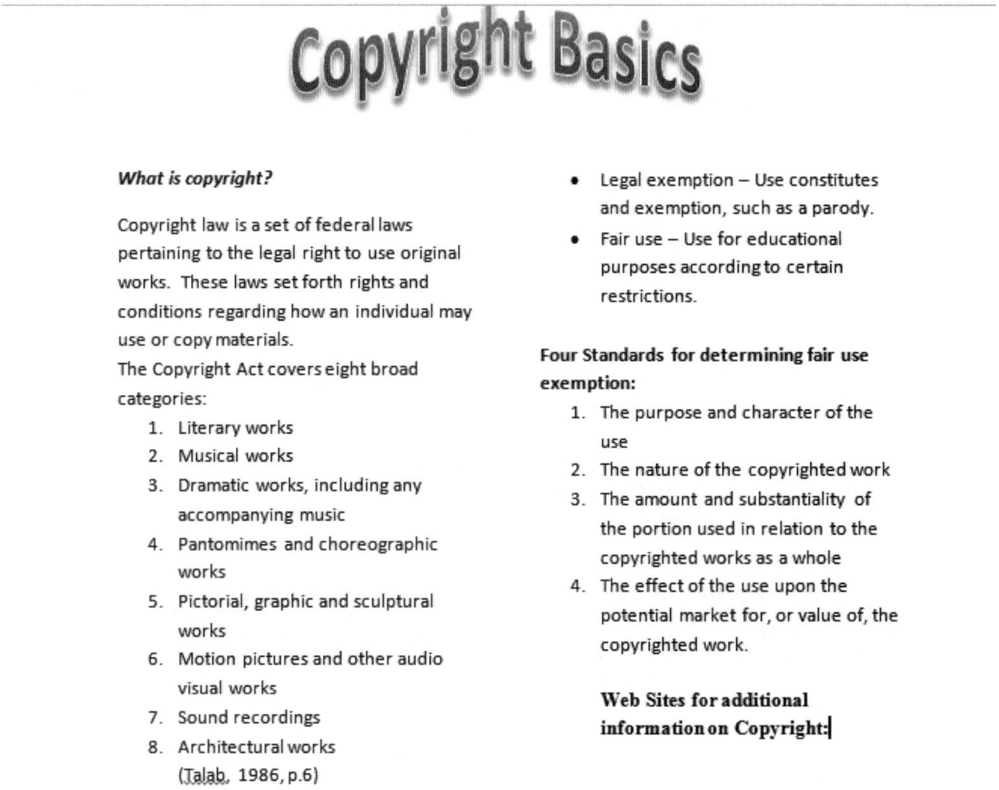

Copyright Basics

What is copyright?

Copyright law is a set of federal laws pertaining to the legal right to use original works. These laws set forth rights and conditions regarding how an individual may use or copy materials.

The Copyright Act covers eight broad categories:

1. Literary works
2. Musical works
3. Dramatic works, including any accompanying music
4. Pantomimes and choreographic works
5. Pictorial, graphic and sculptural works
6. Motion pictures and other audio visual works
7. Sound recordings
8. Architectural works (Talab, 1986, p.6)

- Legal exemption – Use constitutes and exemption, such as a parody.
- Fair use – Use for educational purposes according to certain restrictions.

Four Standards for determining fair use exemption:

1. The purpose and character of the use
2. The nature of the copyrighted work
3. The amount and substantiality of the portion used in relation to the copyrighted works as a whole
4. The effect of the use upon the potential market for, or value of, the copyrighted work.

Web Sites for additional information on Copyright:

FIGURE 3.39 Websites for Additional Information

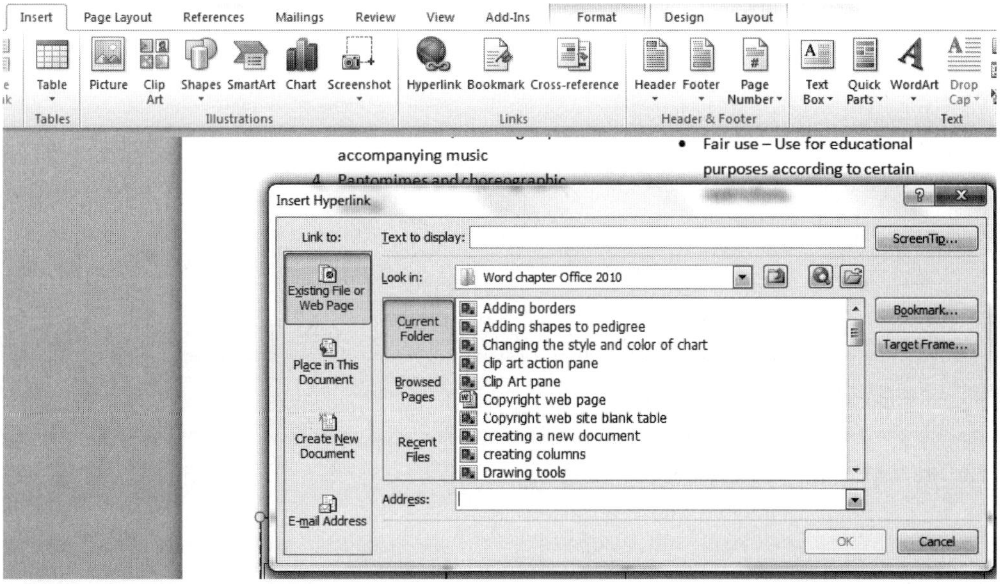

FIGURE 3.40 Inserting a Hyperlink

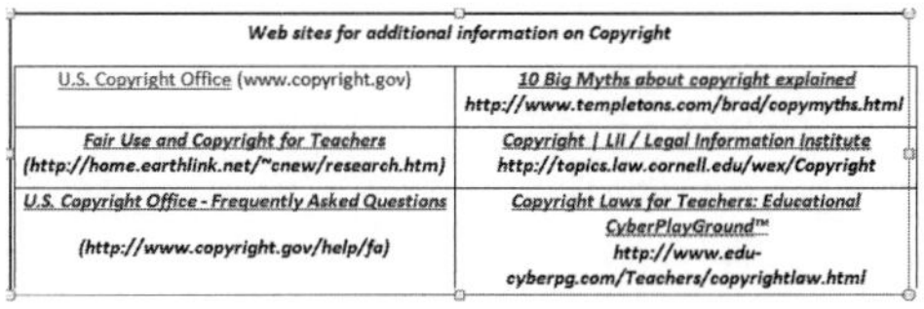

Web sites for additional information on Copyright	
U.S. Copyright Office (www.copyright.gov)	10 Big Myths about copyright explained http://www.templetons.com/brad/copymyths.html
Fair Use and Copyright for Teachers (http://home.earthlink.net/~cnew/research.htm)	Copyright | LII / Legal Information Institute http://topics.law.cornell.edu/wex/Copyright
U.S. Copyright Office - Frequently Asked Questions (http://www.copyright.gov/help/fa)	Copyright Laws for Teachers: Educational CyberPlayGround™ http://www.edu-cyberpg.com/Teachers/copyrightlaw.html

FIGURE 3.41 Websites for Copyright

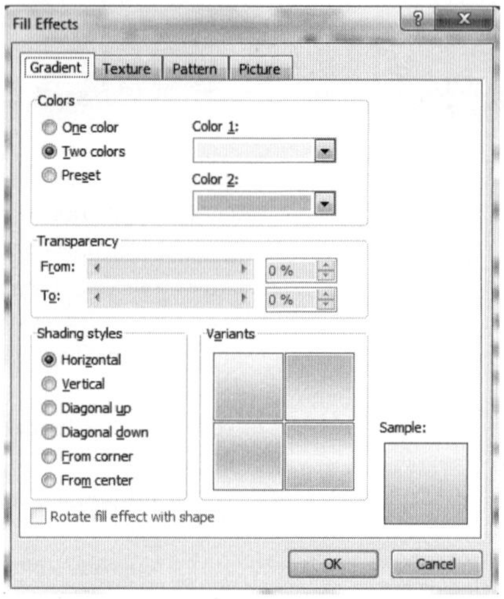

FIGURE 3.42 Fill Effects

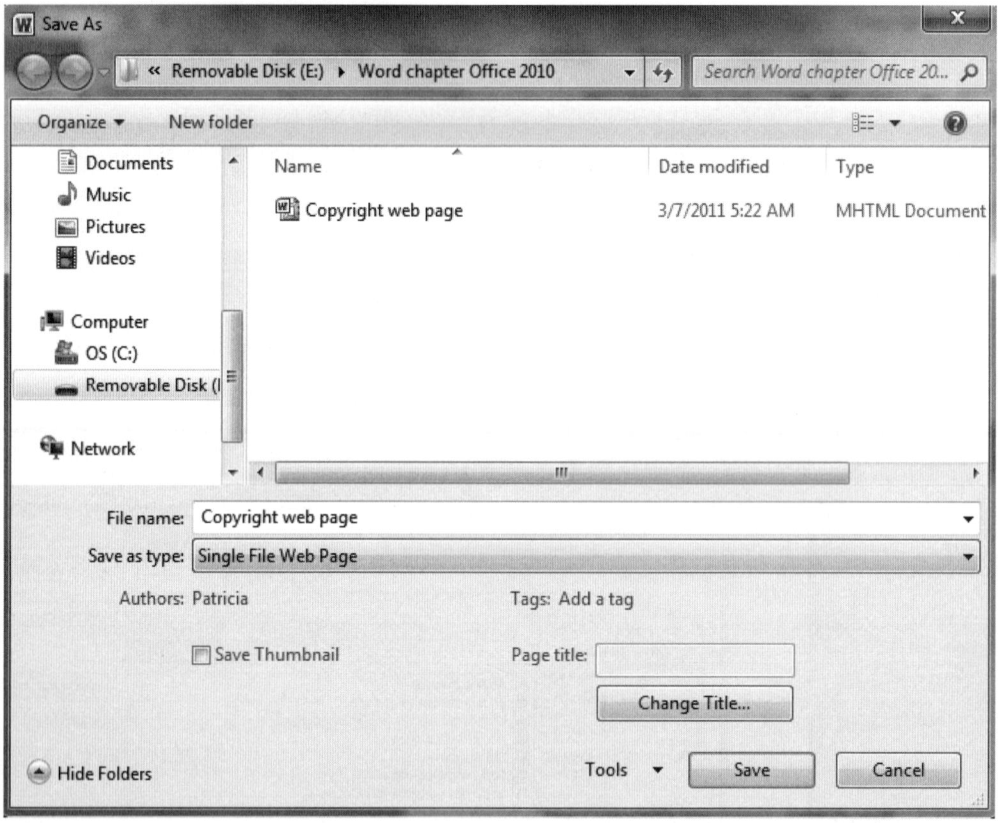

FIGURE 3.43 Saving as a Webpage

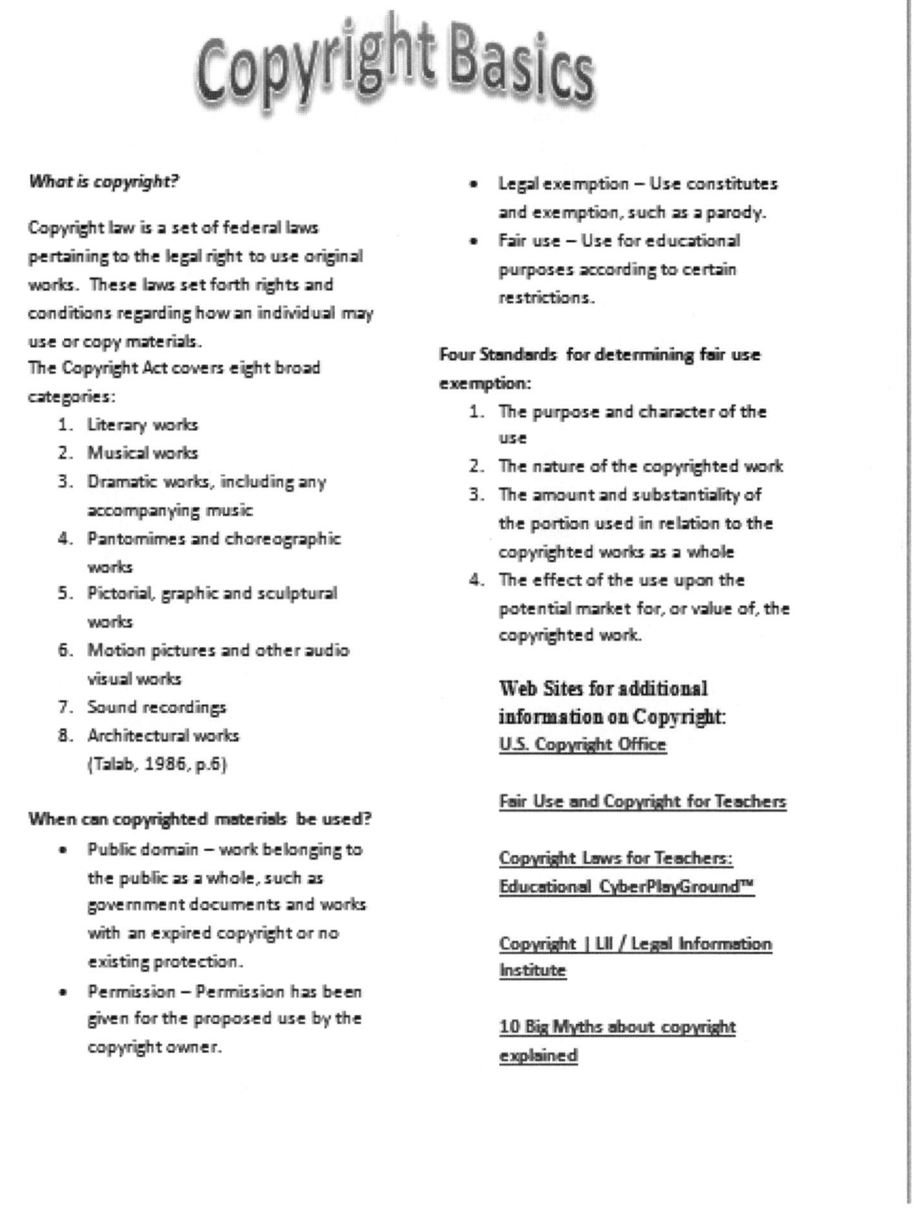

Copyright Basics

What is copyright?

Copyright law is a set of federal laws pertaining to the legal right to use original works. These laws set forth rights and conditions regarding how an individual may use or copy materials.
The Copyright Act covers eight broad categories:

1. Literary works
2. Musical works
3. Dramatic works, including any accompanying music
4. Pantomimes and choreographic works
5. Pictorial, graphic and sculptural works
6. Motion pictures and other audio visual works
7. Sound recordings
8. Architectural works
(Talab, 1986, p.6)

When can copyrighted materials be used?

- Public domain – work belonging to the public as a whole, such as government documents and works with an expired copyright or no existing protection.
- Permission – Permission has been given for the proposed use by the copyright owner.
- Legal exemption – Use constitutes and exemption, such as a parody.
- Fair use – Use for educational purposes according to certain restrictions.

Four Standards for determining fair use exemption:

1. The purpose and character of the use
2. The nature of the copyrighted work
3. The amount and substantiality of the portion used in relation to the copyrighted works as a whole
4. The effect of the use upon the potential market for, or value of, the copyrighted work.

Web Sites for additional information on Copyright:

U.S. Copyright Office

Fair Use and Copyright for Teachers

Copyright Laws for Teachers: Educational CyberPlayGround™

Copyright | LII / Legal Information Institute

10 Big Myths about copyright explained

FIGURE 3.44 The Copyright Webpage

PROJECT FOR EVERYONE: USING A TEMPLATE FOR MAILINGS

Educators are often asked to write letters to all types of individuals and entities. Word has several templates that allow you to create letters on letterhead rather than plane paper. These templates offer a variety of documents for which the "shell" is already created. Templates are also available from Microsoft Online. In the following steps, you will use a template to create a letter to your local senator:

1. Open a new document in Word and select Sample Template. A screen appears, showing the installed templates available on your computer (see Figure 3.45).
2. Select Adjacency Letter, make sure the Document radio button is selected, and click Create.
3. The beginning template will look similar to the one shown in Figure 3.46. You will be basically filling in the blanks to make sure the letter looks professional and the spacing for the letter is correct.

PDToolkit for *Microsoft® Office 2010 for Teachers*

Go to PDToolkit for **Microsoft® Office 2010 for Teachers** to locate a completed version of the letter in the Examples folder (Letter to Senator Durban.docx).

4. Once you have filled in the blanks for the letter, the finished product may look something like Figure 3.47.
5. When the letter is complete, you will want to create an envelope to send the letter in. Keep your letter document open and select the Mailings tab from the Ribbon. Highlight the senator's name and mailing address. By doing this, you will not have to type the name and address again. Select Envelopes from the Create section on the Mailings section of the Ribbon (see Figure 3.48).
6. A pane appears, with the information that will be printed on the envelope and directions on how to place the envelope in the printer. Once the envelope is in place, click on the Print button, and the printer will print your envelope. You can also print labels in the same fashion (see Figure 3.49).

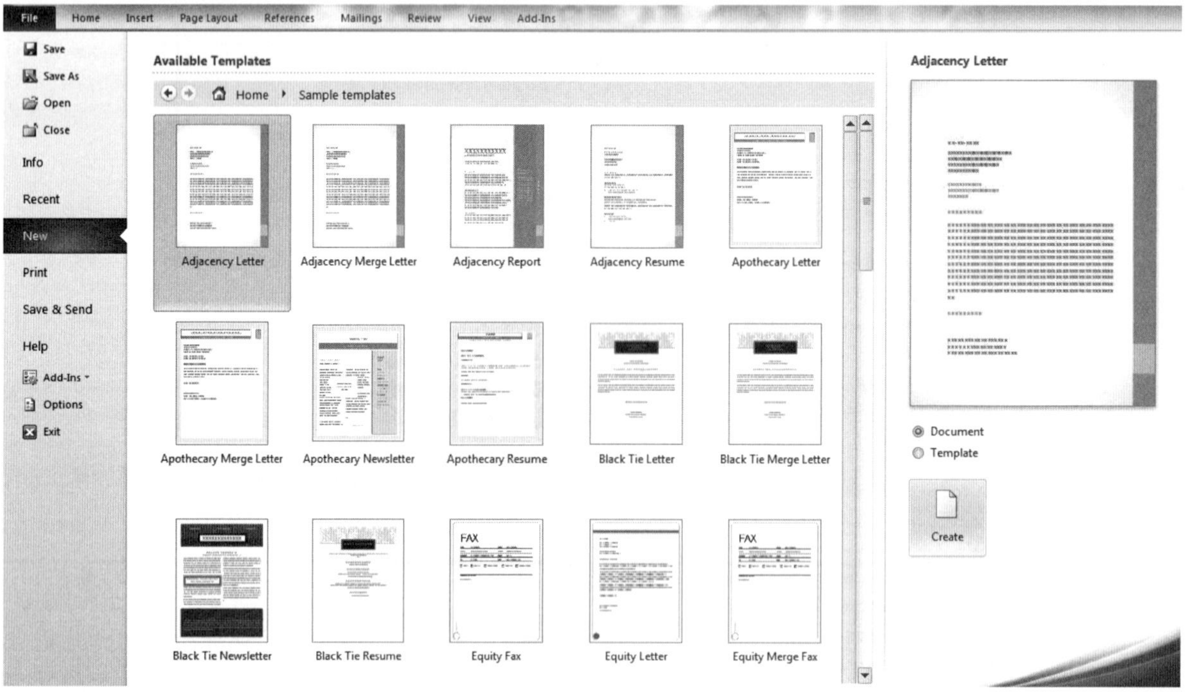

FIGURE 3.45 Template Letter Selection

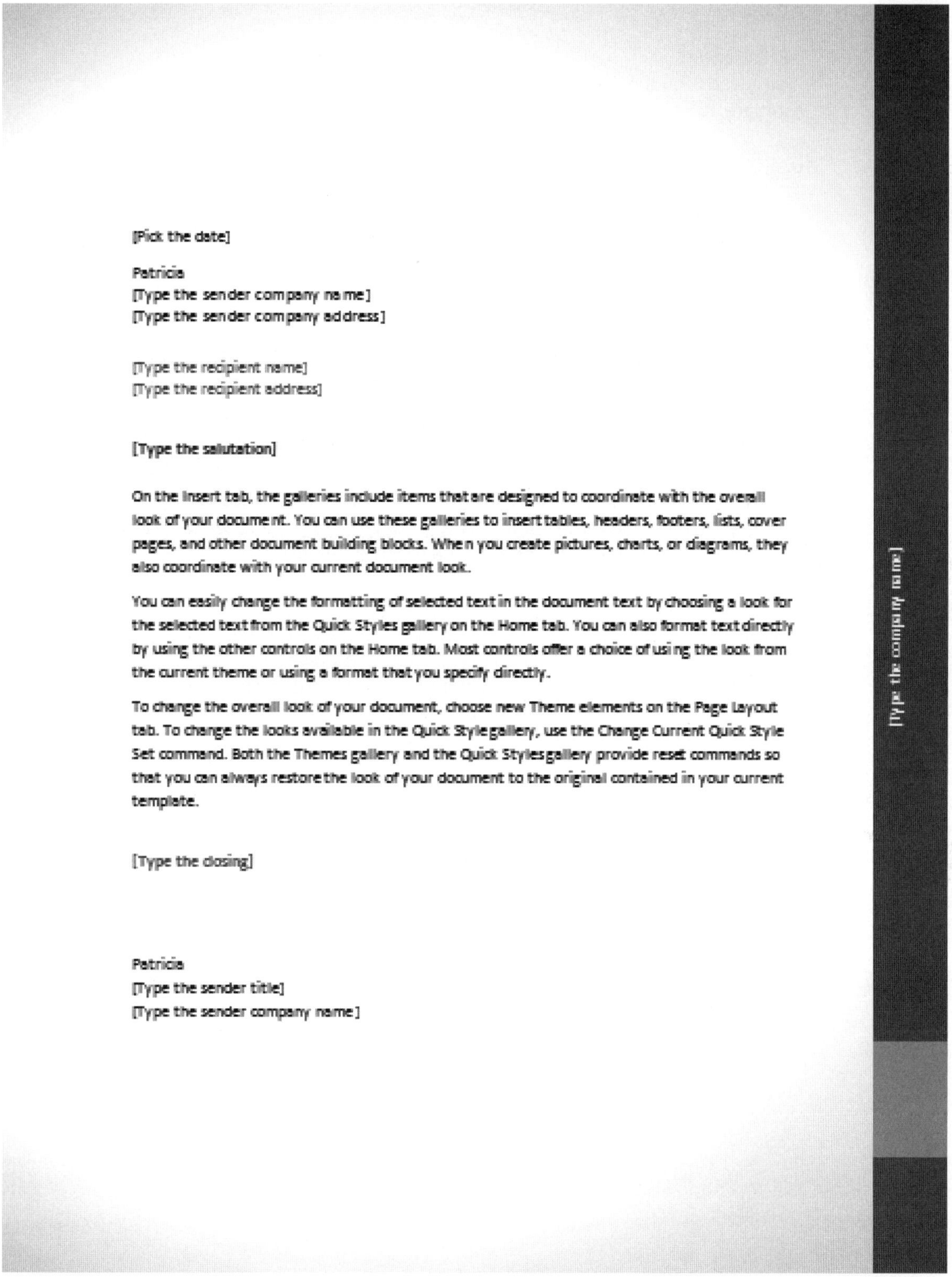

[Pick the date]

Patricia
[Type the sender company name]
[Type the sender company address]

[Type the recipient name]
[Type the recipient address]

[Type the salutation]

On the Insert tab, the galleries include items that are designed to coordinate with the overall look of your document. You can use these galleries to insert tables, headers, footers, lists, cover pages, and other document building blocks. When you create pictures, charts, or diagrams, they also coordinate with your current document look.

You can easily change the formatting of selected text in the document text by choosing a look for the selected text from the Quick Styles gallery on the Home tab. You can also format text directly by using the other controls on the Home tab. Most controls offer a choice of using the look from the current theme or using a format that you specify directly.

To change the overall look of your document, choose new Theme elements on the Page Layout tab. To change the looks available in the Quick Style gallery, use the Change Current Quick Style Set command. Both the Themes gallery and the Quick Styles gallery provide reset commands so that you can always restore the look of your document to the original contained in your current template.

[Type the closing]

Patricia
[Type the sender title]
[Type the sender company name]

[Type the company name]

FIGURE 3.46 A Letter Template

3/11/2011

Patricia Fewell
Prairieland School
Ashmore, IL

Honorable Richard Durban
711 Hart Senate Office Building
Washington, DC 20510

Dear Senator Durban,

The Senor class of Prairieland School will be making a trip to Washington, DC to participate in the convention of young inventors during the week of November 7 - 11, 2011. There are 12 students who will be attending the convention during that time frame, and we were hoping that you or one of your staff members might be able to meet with our group. We are excited about representing Illinois at the convention and even more at the opportunity of meeting with the people who do the important work of governing our country. Please do have someone from your office contact me via mail or email at pjfewell@yahoo.com, so we can make the students' schedule work with yours. We do look forward to this opportunity.

Sincerely,

Patricia Fewell
Principal
Prairieland School

FIGURE 3.47 A Letter to a Senator

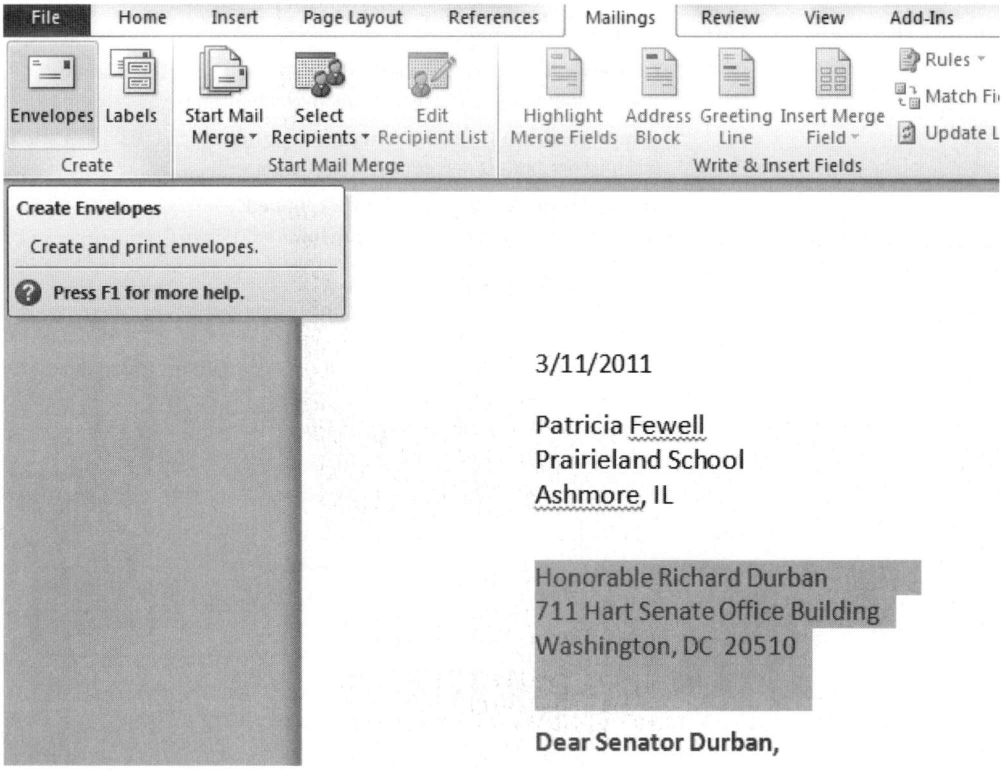

FIGURE 3.48 Selecting Envelopes

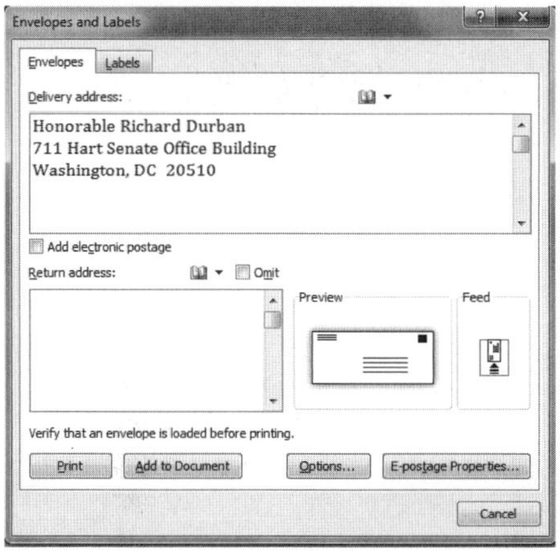

FIGURE 3.49 Printing an Envelope

SUMMING IT UP

In this chapter, you created a newsletter, a diagram, and a webpage with hyperlinks; you also used a template to create a letter and an envelope. You can use these techniques yourself and teach them to your students. These and other activities allow you to fulfill some of the ISTE standards for teachers, making you and your classroom look more professional and providing technology that enhances student learning.

References and Resources

Bloom, B. (Ed.). (1956). *Taxonomy of educational objectives.* New York: David McKay.

George, J.C. (1991). *My side of the mountain.* New York: Puffin Books.

International Society for Technology in Education. (2008). *NETS for teachers.* Retrieved March 4, 2011, from www.iste.org/standards/nets-for-teachers.aspx.

U.S. Copyright Office. (March 2011). *Copyright basics.* Retrieved March 4, 2011, from www.copyright.gov.

SELECTED WEBSITES

Nets for Teachers Website
www.iste.org/standards/nets-for-teachers.aspx

Site to Select Templates
www.office.com

U.S. Copyright Office
www.copyright.gov

Fair Use and Copyright for Teachers
http://home.earthlink.net/~cnew/research.htm

Copyright Laws for Teachers: Educational CyberPlayGround
www.edu-cyberpg.com/Teachers/copyrightlaw.html

Copyright from Legal Information Institute
http://topics.law.cornell.edu/wex/Copyright

10 Big Myths About Copyright Explained
www.templetons.com/brad/copymyths.html

4 POWERPOINT 2010

Chapter Outline

- What You Are Going to Learn
- Chapter Overview
- How You Can Use PowerPoint 2010
- NETS for Teachers
- NETS for Students
- What Is New in PowerPoint 2010
- About PowerPoint
- Working with PowerPoint
- Project for Students: Presenting Weather Data
- Project for Teachers: Using a Template for Scientific Investigation
- Project for Administrators: Making a Presentation to the School Board
- Summing It Up
- References

WHAT YOU ARE GOING TO LEARN

At the completion of this chapter you will be able to:

- Start PowerPoint and create a new presentation
- Navigate the PowerPoint workspace
- Add slides to a presentation in a variety of layouts
- Create charts
- Add clip art to a slide
- Add slide transitions
- Save a presentation
- Print a presentation
- Copy a presentation to a CD
- Share a presentation using Windows Live

CHAPTER OVERVIEW

This chapter provides an introduction to PowerPoint 2010. It focuses on helping you learn PowerPoint fundamentals and applying them in developing a presentation. This chapter provides instructions on how to use many of the tools in PowerPoint 2010 for creating, editing, and manipulating information in slide presentations. The exercises provided throughout the chapter give specific step-by-step instructions for quickly accomplishing real-life activities that you do on a daily basis.

HOW YOU CAN USE POWERPOINT 2010

As a teacher, you can use PowerPoint in innovative ways to support various educational activities for you and your students. This section examines ways in which you can use PowerPoint to support learning in relationship to Bloom's cognitive domain of learning outcomes, a prevalent categorization of learning (Dick, Carey, & Carey, 2008), and the National Educational Technology Standards for Teachers. The following items identify ways PowerPoint can be used to achieve learning outcomes at a variety of cognitive levels:

- ***Knowledge***—(a) Students can create their own electronic flashcards within PowerPoint. The electronic flashcards can include pictures, text, audio, video, or any combination of media. (b) Students can be given several historic time periods (e.g., 1861–1865, 1939–1945) and can use PowerPoint to present quotes and images that characterize those periods. (c) Students can use PowerPoint to create a shape-coloring book. With PowerPoint, they can draw shapes and figures and label them and then print the slides for coloring.
- ***Comprehension***—(a) Students can create visual stories with images, text, and other media that summarize or describe historical events. (b) Using a digital camera and PowerPoint, they can visually (without words) describe the habitat in which they live or the habitats of certain animals. (c) For a physics activity, students, using a digital camera and PowerPoint, can assemble a slide show of images that visually (without words) describes types of motion (forward, backward, upward, and downward).
- ***Application***—(a) Students can use PowerPoint to draw the solar system, labeling each planet and the sun as well as drawing the planets in the appropriate relative positions and sizes. (b) Students can use PowerPoint to visually demonstrate concepts such as justice, legality, happiness, politics, and peace.
- ***Analysis***—(a) Students can use PowerPoint to draw shapes and figures and then classify them as rectangles, circles, ellipses, and so on. (b) Similarly to photo galleries on news websites, students can use PowerPoint and a digital camera to compile a series of photographs that explains important events occurring during the week or month. (c) Often what people see is not what is actually taking place. Some students can be given a digital camera and the task of taking action photographs of class members at work or on break. The photographer then infers what is taking place in a photograph or what the subject is thinking. He or she then compiles the photographs and inferences in PowerPoint. After the teacher reviews the PowerPoint slide show, the photographer presents it to the class and explains his or her inferences. Those in the photographs are then given a chance to describe what was really taking place or what they were thinking.
- ***Synthesis***—Students can be asked to compile an inventory of images that represent concepts such as peace, justice, family, hope, and health. They could then ask their grandparents and parents to identify a visual inventory of objects that represents those same concepts. The students then need to integrate and/or compare the two inventories and draw conclusions about how the inventories are the same and/or different.
- ***Evaluation***—Students could use PowerPoint to make a convincing case for why we should or should not be involved in space travel or other activities.

NETS FOR TEACHERS*

PowerPoint can be utilized in the classroom to address the following standards:

- ***Facilitate and Inspire Student Learning and Creativity***—Teachers use their knowledge of subject matter, teaching and learning, and technology to facilitate experiences that advance student learning, creativity and innovation in both face-to-face and virtual environments:
  - Promote, support, and model creative and innovative thinking and inventiveness
  - Engage students in exploring real-world issues and solving authentic problems using digital tools and resources

  - Promote student reflection, using collaborative tools to reveal and clarify students' conceptual understanding and thinking, planning, and creative processes
  - Model collaborative knowledge construction by engaging in learning with students, colleagues, and others in face-to-face and virtual environments

- ***Design and Develop Digital-Age Learning Experiences and Assessments***—Teachers design, develop, and evaluate authentic learning experiences and assessment, incorporating contemporary tools and resources to maximize content learning in context and to develop the knowledge, skills, and attitudes identified in the NETS•S:
  - Design or adapt relevant learning experiences that incorporate digital tools and resources to promote student learning and creativity
  - Develop technology-enriched learning environments that enable all students to pursue their individual curiosities and become active participants in setting their own educational goals, managing their own learning, and assessing their own progress
  - Customize and personalize learning activities to address students' diverse learning styles, working strategies, and abilities, using digital tools and resources

- ***Model Digital-Age Work and Learning***—Teachers exhibit knowledge, skills, and work processes representative of an innovative professional and digital society:
  - Demonstrate fluency in technology systems and the transfer of current knowledge to new technologies and situations
  - Collaborate with students, peers, parents, and community members using digital tools and resources to support student success and innovation
  - Communicate relevant information and ideas effectively to students, parents, and peers using a variety of digital-age media and formats
  - Model and facilitate effective use of current and emerging digital tools to locate, analyze, evaluate, and use information resources to support research and learning

NETS FOR STUDENTS*

Applications of PowerPoint to educational activities could address the following standards:

- ***Creativity and Innovation***—Students demonstrate creative and innovative thinking, construct knowledge, and develop innovative visual materials using technology.
- ***Communication and Collaboration***—Students use mediated materials to communicate and engage with one another and to support one another's learning.
- ***Research and Information Fluency***—Students apply digital tools to gather, evaluate, and use information.
- ***Critical Thinking, Problem Solving, and Decision Making***—Students use critical thinking skills to plan and conduct research, manage projects, solve problems, and make informed decisions using appropriate digital tools and resources.

WHAT IS NEW IN POWERPOINT 2010

The PowerPoint 2010 interface is characterized by the Ribbon, which includes a number of tabs. The organization of tabs is based on the type of activity you might perform when creating a presentation, such as animation and slide shows. Certain tabs display only when you need them. For instance, when you click an image, the Picture Tools tab displays.

Some new and very useful features of PowerPoint 2010 include the ability to open multiple presentation files at the same time and exchange slides between them. The Backstage view provides an area to access frequently performed tasks related to managing files, such as opening, saving, and sharing files; printing; and document properties. PowerPoint 2010 allows you to create a video of a presentation so you can make the presentation available to a wider audience. In addition, you can link to videos such as those found on YouTube and other websites. For additional information about PowerPoint 2010 features, see the What's New section of Microsoft Office PowerPoint Help.

ABOUT POWERPOINT

PowerPoint 2010 is an application you can use to create presentation materials. With PowerPoint, you can create electronic slide shows to display on a computer, printed handouts, overhead transparencies, 2-inch-by-2-inch slides, and Web documents.

There are many ways to use PowerPoint 2010. Teachers can write and present lecture notes and give students printed handouts of the PowerPoint presentation for review and note taking. Teachers and students can create presentations that include multimedia elements, such as animation, statistical charts and graphs, photographs, video, and audio, to enrich or give emphasis to instructional content. In addition, these presentations can be put on the Web. Media of special school activities may be incorporated into a self-running slide show and displayed at school events. Students can be assigned research projects that require them to collect and analyze data and to present their findings in a multimedia slide show format. Such a task may cause students to think visually and to collect information in various media formats (in addition to text) and employ them to more fully convey complex concepts. For instance, a student who has researched the rotation of planets in our solar system is likely to have greater impact on his or her audience using animation or video of planet orbits than if he or she attempts to explain the information with only text or the spoken word. As you become familiar with PowerPoint, you are likely to find many more innovative ways to incorporate it into your classroom activities.

WORKING WITH POWERPOINT

When opening PowerPoint 2010, you enter the Normal view. It is a workspace composed of several tabs and panes. Figure 4.1 depicts the different areas of the workspace. The top portion of the screen is referred to as the Ribbon, which contains tabs for functions and tools to assist

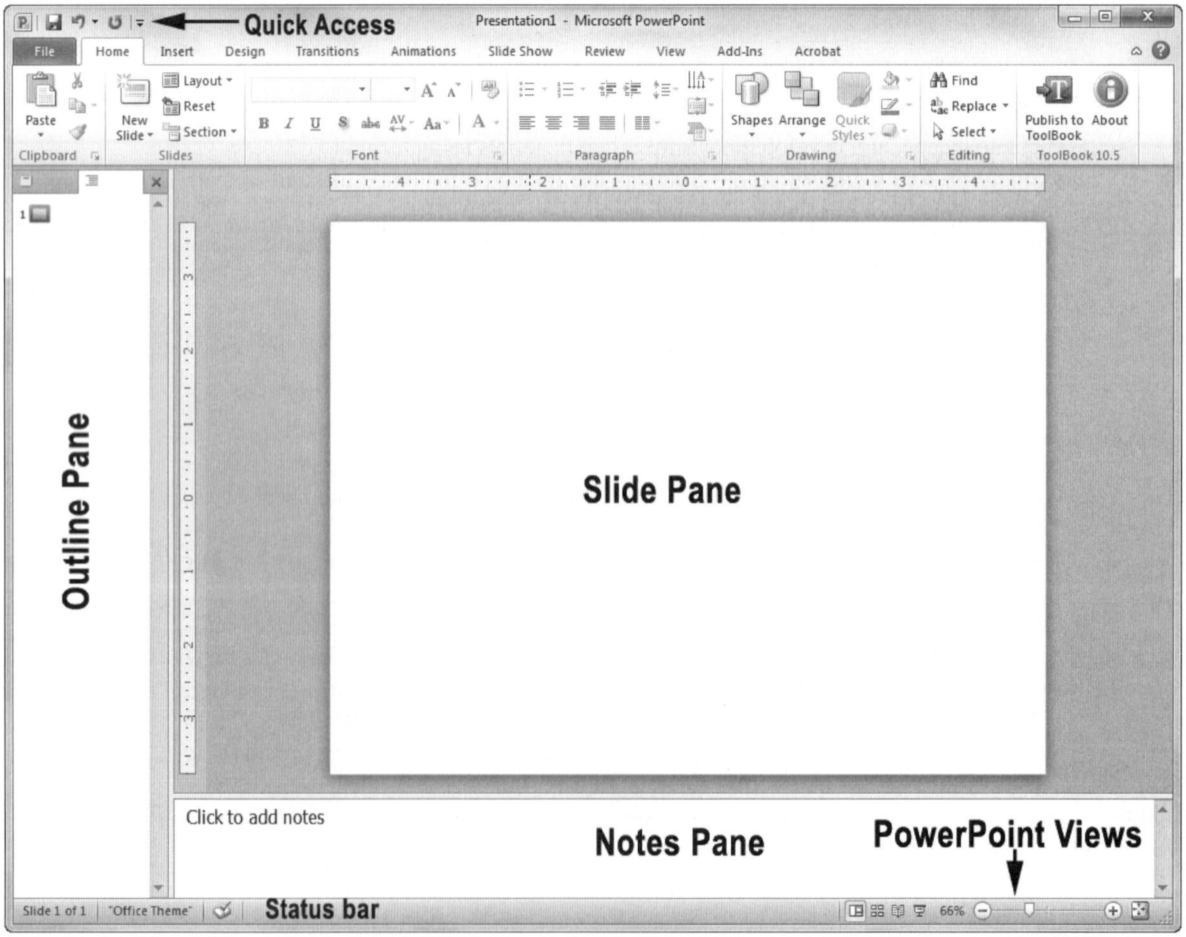

FIGURE 4.1 The PowerPoint Workspace

in creating a presentation. For additional workspace, you can minimize the Ribbon by right-clicking on a Ribbon tab and selecting Minimize the Ribbon.

The middle portion of Figure 4.1 shows three panes—Outline, Slide, and Notes—that divide the PowerPoint workspace. This is the area where most of the slide development work is done. When text, graphics, drawn objects, and so on are added, they appear here and can be arranged and modified to create a professional-looking slide. The size and positioning of the panes vary from view to view. You can adjust the size of each pane by positioning the mouse over the pane border (until the cursor changes to double arrows), clicking the left mouse button, and dragging the pane border to the desired size.

The Outline and Slides tabs display a text outline or miniature slides of your presentation, depending on the tab selected. With the Outline tab selected, you can enter the text for your presentation and organize it in list, paragraph, or slide format. With the Slides tab selected, you see thumbnail images of your slides. When you click on text in the Outline tab or the thumbnails in the Slides tab, the corresponding slide appears in the Slide pane.

In the Notes pane, you type notes about your presentation that remind you of a particular point to be made. You can add clip art and pictures to your notes pages. Click Notes Page in the Presentation Views group on the View tab to open the notes pane. You can then insert objects by clicking the Insert tab and selecting any of the illustration options. The objects and pictures only appear in the notes page or when printing your slides with notes. When viewing your presentation in the Slide show, notes do not display. Exit the notes page by clicking on the View tab and then click Normal in the Presentation Views group.

If your computer is equipped with two monitors (e.g., laptop and projector), you can use the Slide Show view, which allows you display the slide show to an audience while you control the slide as well as read notes for each slide. Turn on the Presenter view by clicking on the Slide Show tab and checking the Use Presenter View option. When you view your slide show, slides appear on one screen (i.e., projector), and the Presenter view appears on the screen the audience does not see.

Located at the bottom of the screen, the status bar gives information about the number of slides in your presentation, the current slide number, and the design theme used by the current slide. In addition, the status bar contains the PowerPoint view buttons. PowerPoint provides three views of your presentation: Normal (with Outline and Slides tabs), Slide Sorter, and Slide Show. You can switch between views by clicking the buttons on the View toolbar located in the lower right of the PowerPoint screen. The Normal view has three panes: Outline, Slide, and Notes. In these panes, you can work on all the components of your presentation. The Slide Show view displays your presentation without menus and toolbars. When you're presenting to an audience, you use the Slide Show view. You can preview your presentation in the Slide Show view at any time by clicking the Slide Show button. The Slide Sorter view displays miniatures of each slide in the presentation. In this view, you can reorder the slide sequence, delete slides, and add transitions. Finally, the Zoom slider allows you to zoom in and out on the slide work area. Right-click on the status bar to change the information and options that it displays.

PDToolkit for *Microsoft® Office 2010 for Teachers*

You can find files that correspond to the chapter activities at http://pdtoolkit.pearson.com.

PROJECT FOR STUDENTS: PRESENTING WEATHER DATA

Suppose you assign students the task of creating a school weather station. Divide the class into several weather research teams. Students record the daily high and low temperatures, measure precipitation, and calculate wind speed and direction. You correspond with other geographically dispersed schools and arrange for your students to share and compare weather data with them. Students track weather trends throughout the year and each month report their collection methods and analysis to the class. Your classroom is equipped with a computer and projector, and you encourage students to use PowerPoint to present their findings. PowerPoint can help them create visual slide shows with images, colors, text, and animation effects. To create the weather station slides, follow these steps:

1. Open PowerPoint. Click Start on the Windows taskbar. On the Start menu, click All Programs, move the mouse pointer over Microsoft Office, and click Microsoft PowerPoint 2010. The PowerPoint workspace appears. You are in PowerPoint's Normal view, and your presentation has one blank slide.

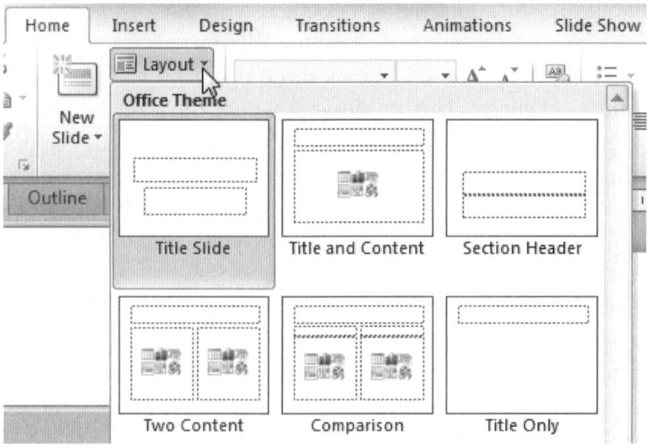

FIGURE 4.2 Slide Layout

Creating a Title Slide and Inserting Text (Slide 1)

Slide layout.

2. PowerPoint offers numerous layouts, such as Title Slide, Title Only, Title and Content, and Blank. To prepare the first slide, click Layout in the Slide group of the Home tab to view slide layouts (see Figure 4.2). Single-click a layout, and the current slide changes to that layout. You can also scroll through layouts by clicking the up and down scroll arrows on the right side of the list.

   The first slide in a presentation is typically a title slide. PowerPoint assigns the slide a title layout when you create the presentation. If your layout is not a Title slide, click Layout on the Home tab and select the Title Slide layout. You may also right-click on the slide and select Layout from the menu. Figure 4.3 illustrates a Title slide layout.

   You are now in the Normal view of PowerPoint's workspace. You can give the slide a title. On a title slide, there are two text boxes: one for a title and the other for a subtitle (see Figure 4.3).

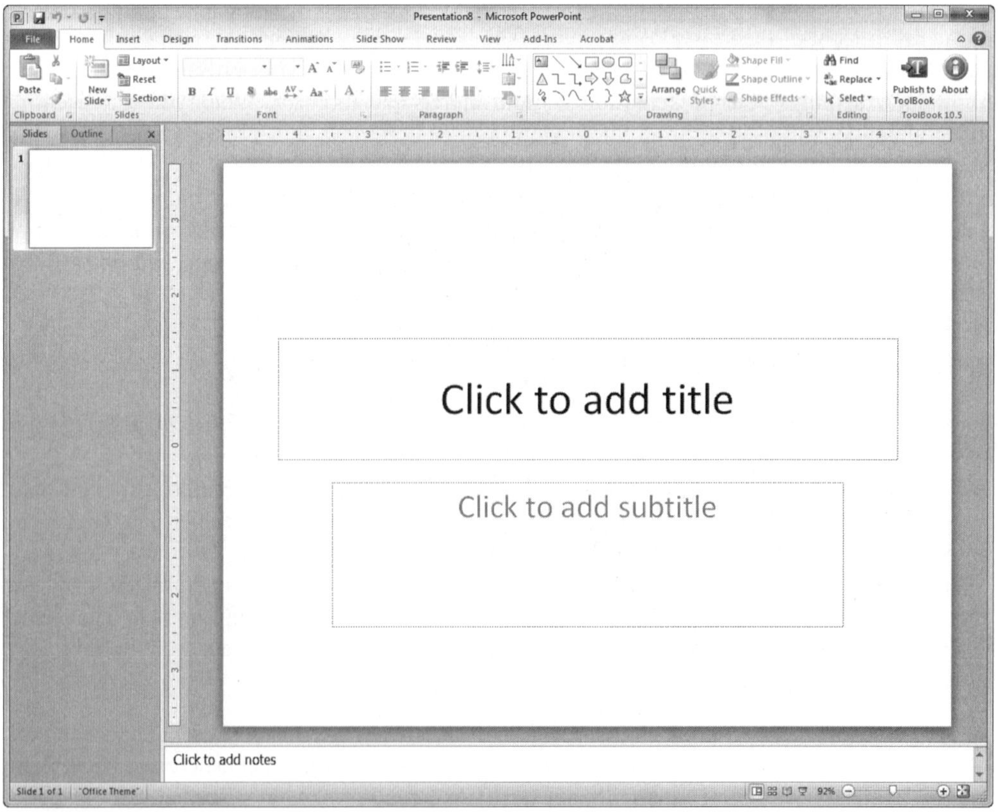

FIGURE 4.3 A Title Slide Layout

3. Click inside the text box labeled Click to Add Title and type the following title for the presentation: Our Weather Station: Precipitation Amounts. Notice that prior to clicking in the Click to Add Title box, the border is a thin dashed line. Clicking inside the box causes the border to change to a thicker dashed line, indicating that it is selected and you can begin typing. Deselect the text box by clicking anywhere outside it.
4. Click inside the Click to Add Subtitle box and type By the Research Weather Team: and the students' names to signify that this presentation will be a report about precipitation by the school's weather team.

ADDING A DESIGN THEME Design themes consist of predefined colors, layout formats, and font styles that give a presentation a specific look. When you apply a design theme, each existing slide receives the same treatment, as do all new slides. PowerPoint provides a number of themes that you can apply to a presentation. It is a good idea to add a theme when starting a presentation. If you add themes after creating numerous slides, you may need to realign objects and reformat text, depending on the themes selected.

To add a design theme, follow these steps:

1. For the weather team's presentation example, select a theme titled Flow. Click on the Design tab, and thumbnail images of the themes appear. Move the mouse cursor over a theme, and the theme attributes display on the slide. As the cursor moves over a theme, its title displays. Click the More option in the Themes group to display a list of all themes (see Figure 4.4). Click on a theme to apply it to your slide.
2. To remove the design, select Office Theme in the Themes group of the Design tab. The slide should now look similar to the one shown in Figure 4.5.

Title Only Slide (Slide 2)

You can now add a second slide to the weather station presentation. For this slide, you will choose a Title Only layout, which provides a text area for the slide title. The Title Only layout refers to the slide's title and not to the title slide of the presentation.

After entering a title, you will create a second text box in which to type the purpose of the presentation. When you are finished, the slide will look similar to the one shown in Figure 4.6.

FIGURE 4.4 The More Arrow

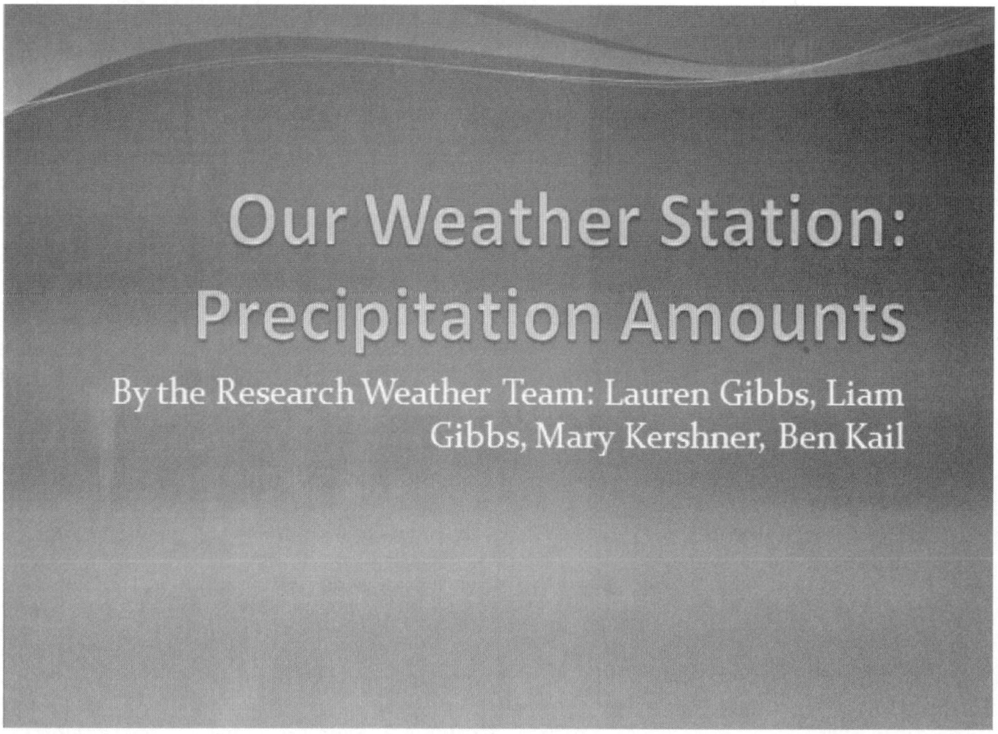

FIGURE 4.5 Slide 1

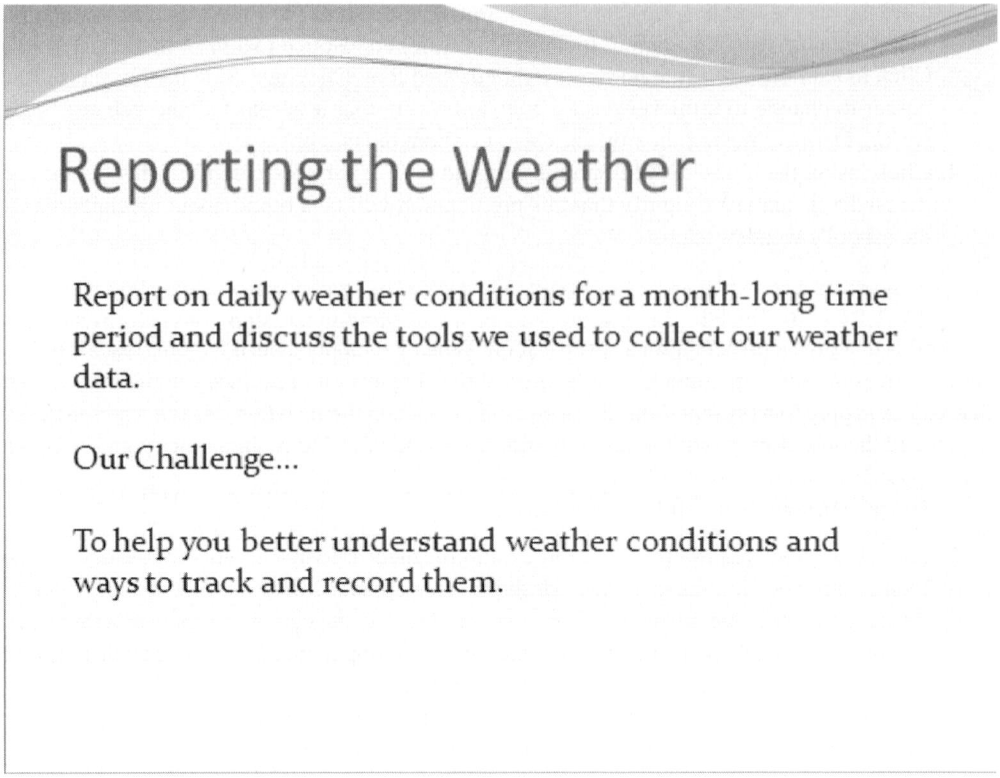

FIGURE 4.6 A Title Only Slide

To add the next slide, follow these steps:

1. Two ways to add a new slide include: Click the New Slide button in the Slides group on the Home tab or use the key combination Ctrl+M.
2. PowerPoint adds a new slide to the presentation and by default assigns it a Title and Content layout. You want the layout to be Title Only, so click Layout in the Slides group on the Home tab and click the Title Only layout option.
3. Add a title to slide 2 by clicking inside the Click to Add Title box and typing the following: Reporting the Weather. Another way to add a title is by making the Outline tab (on the left side of screen) active. Select the small slide icon that corresponds to slide 2 and type the title (see Figure 4.7). The title appears in the slide pane while you're typing.
4. Slide 2 presents the purpose of the presentation. Currently, it has one text box that contains the slide title. Create a second text box for the text describing the presentation's purpose. Create a text box by clicking the Insert tab and then select the Text Box tool in the Text group (see Figure 4.8). When you click on the Text Box tool, the mouse cursor changes to the vertical line (see Figure 4.9).
5. Place (click) the cursor in the slide pane where you want the text box to begin. While holding down the left mouse button, drag the cursor to the right side of the slide pane. Release the mouse, and a blank text box appears (see Figure 4.10). When you drag the text box across the slide, the text wraps to the next line. Alternatively, you could select the text tool

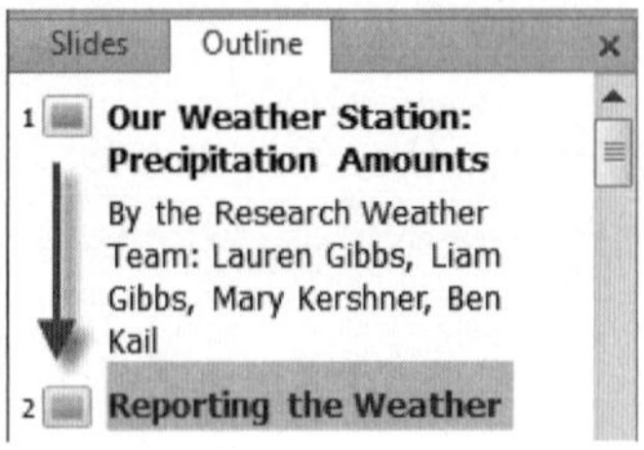

FIGURE 4.7 Slide Title in the Outline Tab

FIGURE 4.8 The Text Box Tool

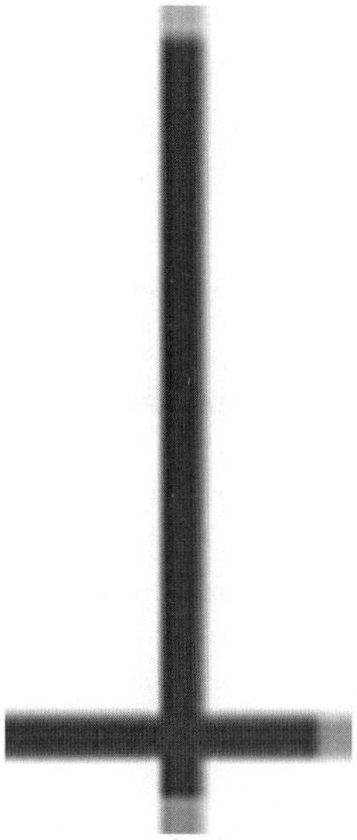

FIGURE 4.9 The Cursor After Selecting a Text Box

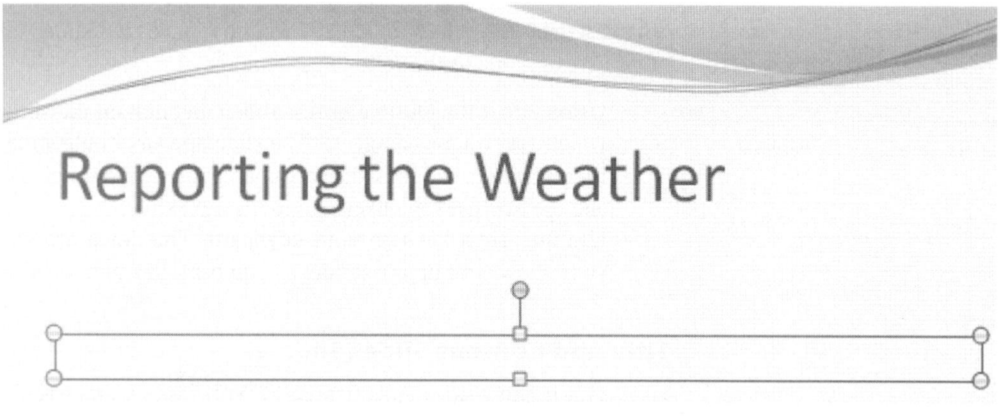

FIGURE 4.10 An Empty Text Box

and simply click in the slide pane and type. However, when you use this method, the text does not wrap and runs off the slide while you're typing.

6. Now, type the purpose of the presentation:

   Report on daily weather conditions for a month-long time period and discuss the tools we used to collect our weather data.
   Our Challenge . . . ?
   To help you better understand weather conditions and ways to track and record them.

7. Change the font style and size by clicking the text box border and then selecting a desired font style and size from the Font group. When you click a text box, a border appears with a dashed line (see Figure 4.11), indicating that you can insert or modify text. Clicking the text box border a second time changes it to a solid line (see Figure 4.12). A solid line indicates that the contents are selected. Any changes (e.g., to font size or style) alter the entire contents of the box.
8. If you chose the Flow theme, PowerPoint assigned the slides a font type of Constantia. To change it, click the text object to select it and then click the border of the object so it changes from a dashed line to a solid line. Make the Home tab active and in Font group click the small downward arrow in the Font box to display a list of available fonts. Select a font by clicking on the font name.

FIGURE 4.11 A Dashed Line Text Box Border

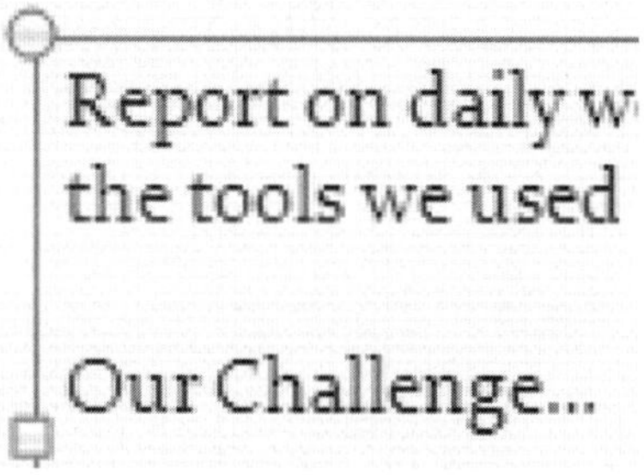

FIGURE 4.12 A Solid Line Text Box Border

9. To change the font size, click the small downward arrow in the font size box, located on the right side of the font type box. Select a size of 18 or 24 by clicking on the number. Currently, the text is set to Times New Roman font and 24 points.
10. The slide should look like the one shown earlier, in Figure 4.6.

NAVIGATING BETWEEN SLIDES You now have two slides and can navigate from one to the other by using one of the following methods:

- Using either the Outline or the Slide tab, click on the slide icon that represents the slide to which you want to navigate. The slide appears in the slide pane.
- In the slide pane, click the scrollbar arrows. The up arrow takes you to the previous slide, and the down arrow takes you to the next slide.
- Use the arrow keys on your keyboard. The down arrow moves you forward through the slide show. The up arrow moves you back through the slide show.

Title and Content Slide (Slide 3)

Next, you'll add a third slide. Choose a Title and Content layout, which provides text areas for the slide title and a text list. When you enter text into a list, PowerPoint separates it with bullets, checkmarks, hyphens, and so on. Using lists is an easy and useful way to format text on a slide. When you are finished, the slide will look similar to the one shown in Figure 4.13.

To add the next slide, follow these steps:

1. Add a new slide by selecting New Slide from the Slides group of the Home tab. Choose a Title and Content layout.
2. Click in the Click to Add Title box and type the following title: Weather Reporting Tools.
3. Click inside the Click to Add Text box and type The tools we used:.
4. Press Enter, and a bullet character (in this case, an ellipse) appears on the next line. In Figure 4.13, notice that the first line uses the bullet character and that the remaining lines indent with an arrow character. After typing the first line in the bulleted list and pressing

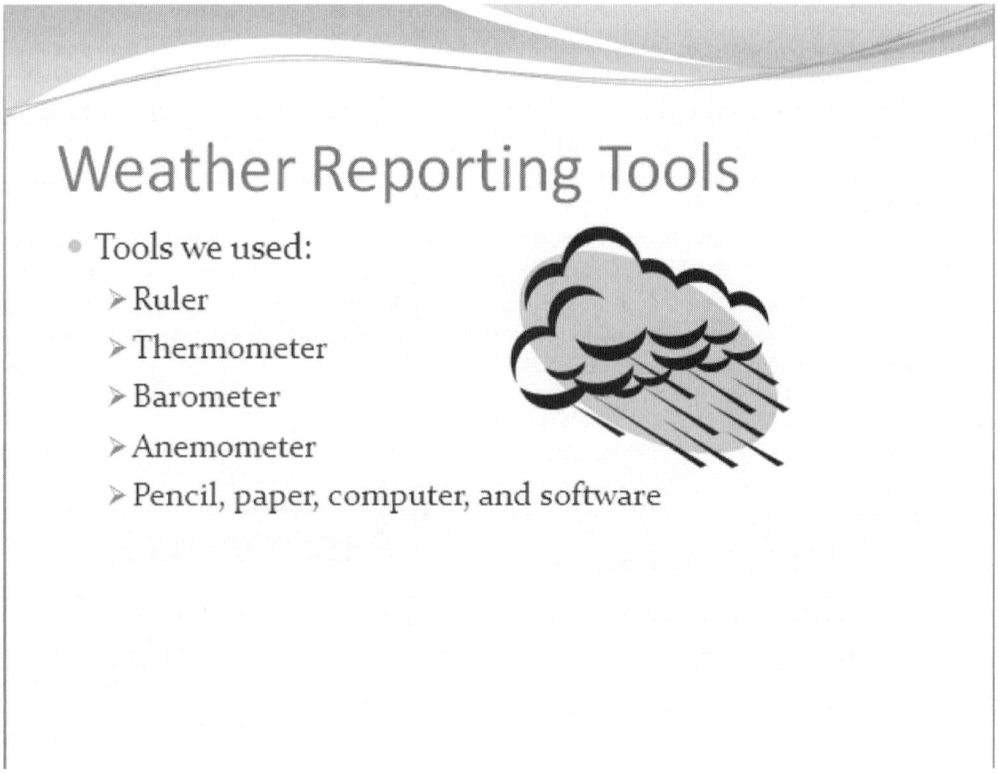

FIGURE 4.13 A Title and Content Slide

Enter, the next text line (Ruler) does not indent. To indent it, position the cursor at the beginning of the line and press the Tab key. Type Ruler and press Enter; subsequent lines indent.

5. Type the remaining items:
   - Thermometer
   - Barometer
   - Anemometer
   - Pencil, paper, computer, and software
6. As you indent these lines, the bullets become ellipses different in color from the first bullet item. To change the ellipses to arrows, select the five indented bullet items. Position the cursor before the word Ruler and, while holding down the left mouse button, drag downward to after the word software and release the mouse. The text should appear highlighted; highlighting text in this manner is referred to as *selecting*. With the text selected, click the right mouse button in the highlighted area, select Bullets, and then choose arrow bullets from the submenu. If you do not see this option, choose Bullets and Numbering. The Bullets and Numbering dialog box appears, which presents various bullet types. Select the arrow bullet type by clicking the Bulleted tab and clicking the appropriate option.
7. To deselect the text, click anywhere outside the text box.

ADDING CLIP ART

1. Insert a clip art image that represents weather. To insert clip art, make the Insert tab active and click the Clip Art button in the Images group (see Figure 4.14). The task pane displays the Clip Art options (see Figure 4.15). Using the Search In and Results Should Be options, you can specify the location that you want to search and the file types that you are seeking (e.g., sounds, movies, photographs, clip art).
2. In the Search For box, type weather and click *Go*. Small images (thumbnails) representing weather clip art are displayed in the task pane (see Figure 4.15). If you do not want any of the images, you may also click the Find More at Office.com link at the bottom of the task pane.
3. Select the rain clouds image. Insert it on the slide by clicking it. You can also insert the image by selecting Insert from the drop-down menu that becomes available by positioning the mouse cursor over the image icon and clicking the downward arrow that appears on the right side of the thumbnail.

MOVING CLIP ART AND RESIZING TEXT OBJECTS

1. There are eight small sizing handles around the image (see Figure 4.16) that you can use to resize it. The handles also indicate that you selected the object. If you do not see the sizing handles around a clip art image, click on the image to select it, and the handles appear.

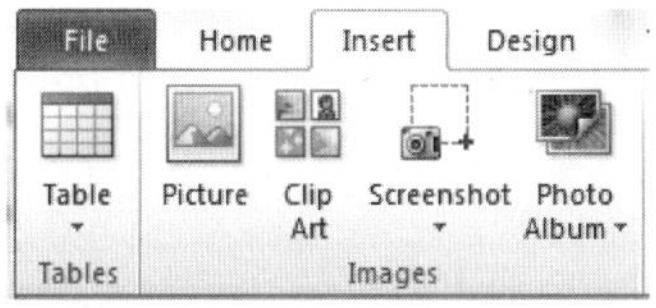

FIGURE 4.14 Clip Art

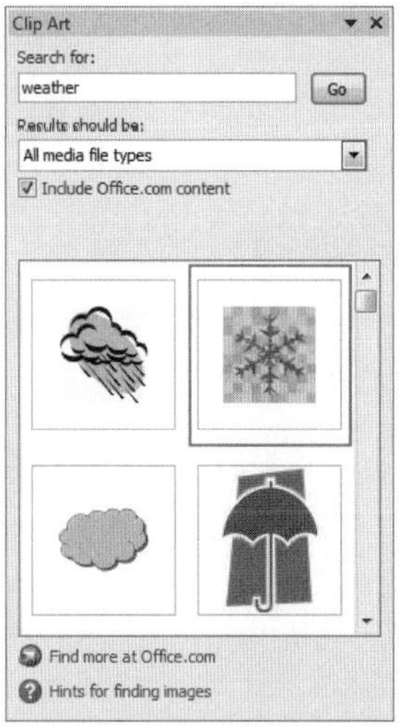

FIGURE 4.15 Inserting Clip Art

FIGURE 4.16 Sizing Handles

2. To make the image larger, move the mouse cursor over one of the sizing handles, and the cursor changes to an arrow. Click the upper-left sizing handle of the image and, while holding down the left mouse button, drag the sizing handle to the upper left. The image resizes. Pressing the Ctrl key while dragging resizes the image proportionally. If you need to reposition the image, click the left mouse button in the center of the image and, while holding down the left mouse button, drag the image to the desired location. You may also notice a green dot attached to the sizing handle. Dragging this dot to the left or right rotates the image.

Adding a Title, Text, and Picture to a Slide (Slide 4)

This slide has a Two Content layout. When you are finished, the slide will look similar to the one shown in Figure 4.17.

1. Add a new slide by selecting New Slide from the Slides group on the Home tab.
2. Select the Two Content layout from the layout options. After clicking the layout, the slide view looks as shown in Figure 4.18.
3. Click inside the Click to Add Title box and type the following title: Making an Anemometer.
4. Click inside the Click to Add Text box on the left side of the screen and type the following text list:
   - *2 cardboard strips*
   - *4 cups*
   - *Pencil*
   - *Ruler & stapler*
   - *Scissors*
   - *Watch with second hand*
5. Add a picture to the slide. Because you are making an anemometer, you could create a paper and pencil drawing of it, scan the drawing, and save it on the computer.
6. Notice that the slide has a placeholder for content (refer to Figure 4.18). The six icons in the placeholder area represent different types of content you can add to a slide, such as tables, graphs, clip art, pictures, diagrams, and media (audio and video).
7. Click the Insert Picture icon, and the Insert Picture dialog box appears. Click the image one time to select it and then click the Insert button.
   You can find files that correspond to the chapter activities at http://pdtoolkit.pearson.com.
8. Position the picture on the slide by clicking in its center and, while holding down the left mouse button, drag it to the desired location (refer to Figure 4.17).

PDToolkit for *Microsoft® Office 2010 for Teachers*

Go to PDToolkit for **Microsoft® Office 2010 for Teachers** to locate the drawing of the anemometer in the WeatherData folder within the Examples folder (anemometer.tif).

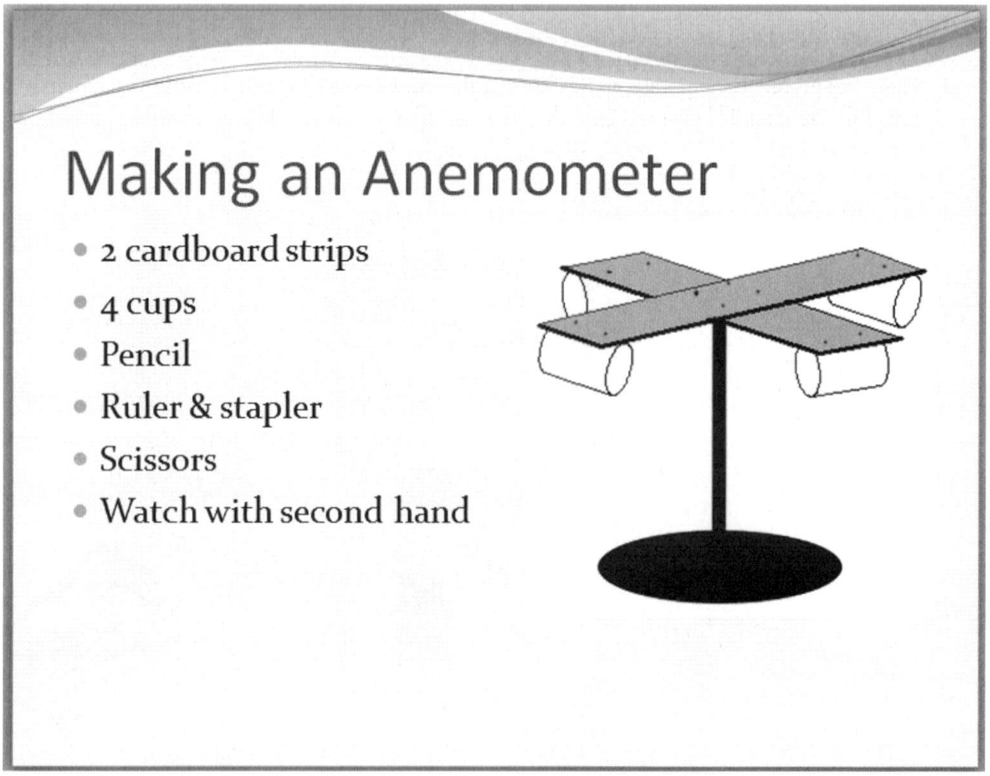

FIGURE 4.17 A Two Content Slide

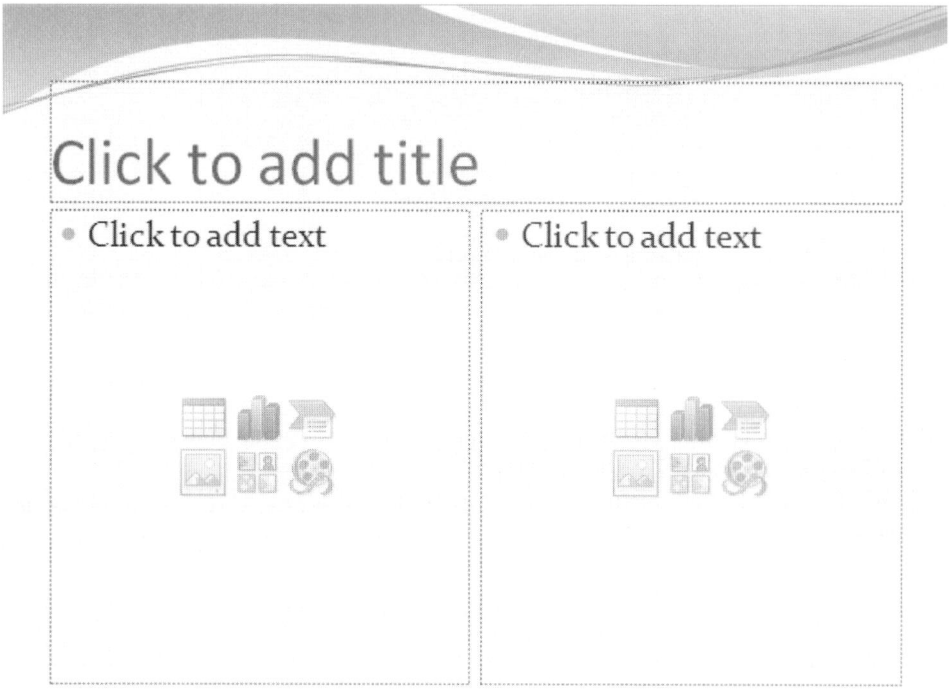

FIGURE 4.18 A Two Content Layout

Title Slide (Slide 5)

The first portion of the presentation covers the goals of the project, weather reporting tools, and directions for making an anemometer. You now will change the presentation topic and discuss weather data collected in October. You need to convey to your audience that you are changing topics, and a way to accomplish this is to insert a title slide. The complete slide will look similar to Figure 4.19.

FIGURE 4.19 Title Slide for a New Topic

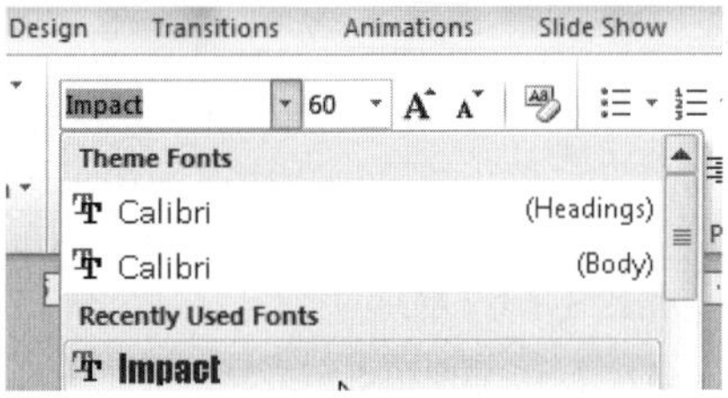

FIGURE 4.20 Font Selection

1. Add a new slide.
2. Select Title Slide layout from the Layout option in the Slides group on the Home tab.
3. Click in the Click to Add Title box and type Our Weather in October.
4. Click in the Click to Add Subtitle box and type Weather data: Recorded October 1 through October 31.

MODIFYING TEXT You can now adjust the font type, style, size, and positioning of the text.

1. To modify the title, click the title text box to select it. A dashed-line border with sizing handles appears. Click the border again to change its appearance from a dashed line to a solid line. As you pass the mouse pointer over the border, the cursor changes to a four-pointed cross. When the border is selected, changes (e.g., font size or style) can be made to the contents of the text box.
2. In the Font group on the Home tab, click the small downward arrow in the font box to display a list of fonts (see Figure 4.20). Select a font by clicking on the font name. For this slide, set the font set to Impact. If you want to choose a different font, scroll through the font list and click a font name.
3. Click the small downward arrow in the font size box to display a list of font sizes. Select a size by clicking on the number. In this case, choose a font size of 60 (see Figure 4.21).
4. In the Font group, set the font style to bold and the text to shadow by clicking the Bold (B) and Shadow (S) icons (see Figure 4.22). In the Paragraph group (Home tab), click the Center icon to center the text (see Figure 4.22). The Center icon centers the contents inside the text box. It does not center the text box relative to the screen.
5. With the title selected, click the Format tab, and in the WordArt Styles group click the down arrow for Text Effects and select Shadow and then Perspective Diagonal Upper Left (see Figure 4.23).
6. Select the title and align it in the top of its own text box. PowerPoint provides options for aligning text in the top, middle, or bottom of the text box. To align the text in the top of the box, go to the Home tab and in the Paragraph group click Align Text and select Top (see Figure 4.24).
7. Click the subtitle text box under the title and set the font style to shadow (S).
8. With the subtitle selected, align it in the bottom of its own text box.

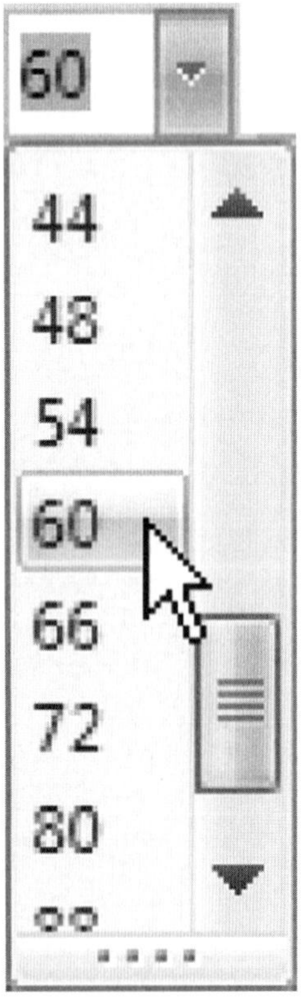

FIGURE 4.21 Font Size

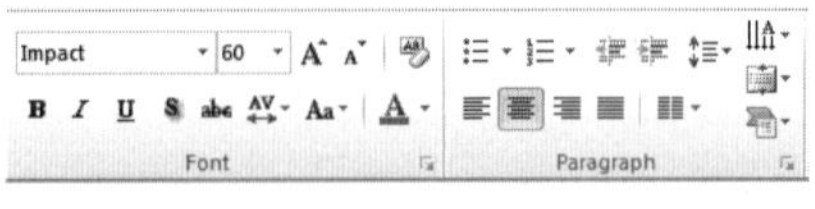

FIGURE 4.22 Font Attributes

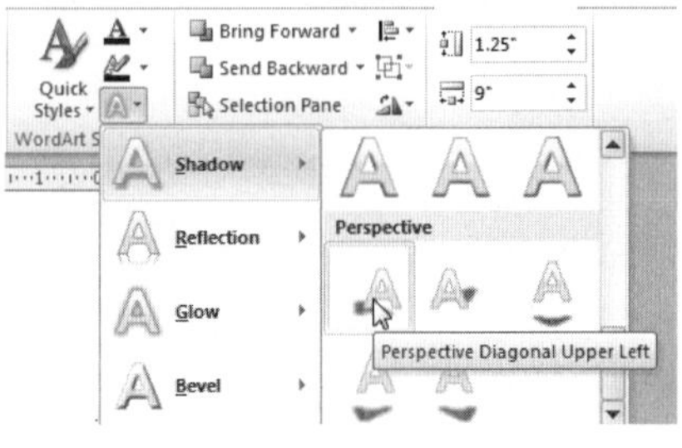

FIGURE 4.23 Font Styles

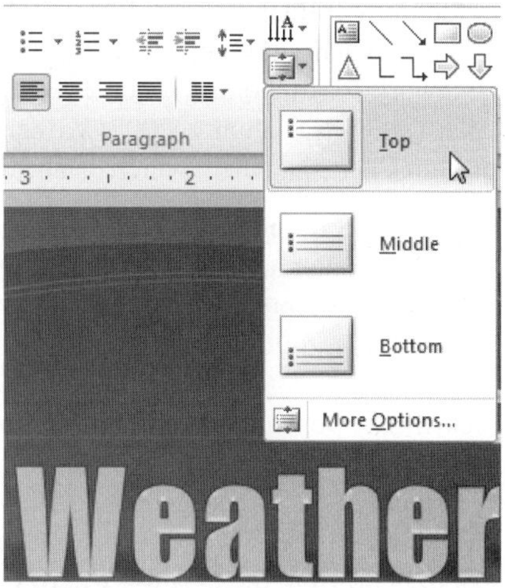

FIGURE 4.24 Alignment

9. Move the subtitle to the lower portion of the slide by selecting it, clicking on its border, and then dragging the box. Alternatively, you can align the entire subtitle text box at the bottom of the screen by doing the following:
   - Select the object (subtitle).
   - Click the Arrange button in the Drawing group (on the Home tab). Pass the mouse pointer over Align and in the drop-down menu click Align to Slide. A check appears next to the Align to Slide menu item. The menu disappears. Click Arrange in the Drawing group. Pass the mouse pointer over Align and in the drop-down menu click Align Bottom. The text box appears toward the bottom of the slide.
   - You can also find the alignment options by selecting the object (subtitle) and then clicking the Align button in the Arrange group on the Format tab.
10. Click the subtitle text box to select it. Click the Format tab and in the WordArt Styles group click the down arrow for Text Effects and select Shadow and then Perspective Diagonal Upper Left.

ADDING A SCREENSHOT FROM VIDEO The weather research team reporters Leah and Katie have been recording daily weather conditions and making weather reports from the field, using their iPods. Leah's says making the videos is as simple as going outside, turning her iPod sideways (horizontally), and pressing Record. For the presentation, they want to take a screenshot of a video frame and put it onto this title slide.

After each recording, they copy the video file from the iPod to a home computer. They plug the iPod's USB cable into the computer and using Windows Explorer view the iPod files (see Figure 4.25). They then drag the video file from the iPod folder to a folder on the home computer and name it LeahKatie_Oct12.mov.

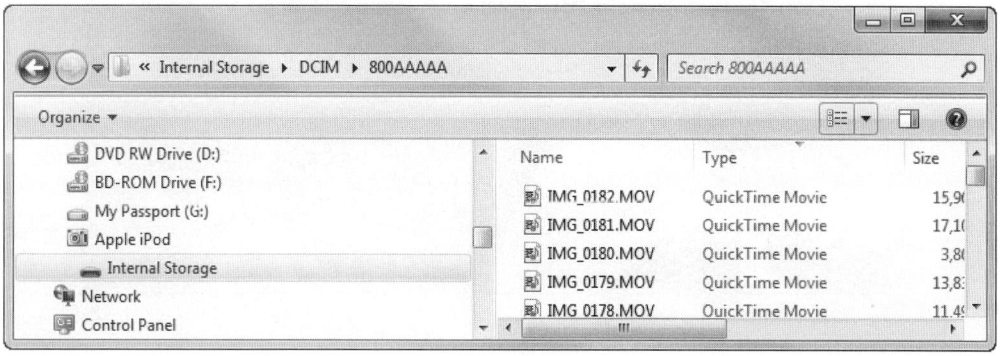

FIGURE 4.25 Windows Explorer: iPod

PDToolkit for *Microsoft® Office 2010 for Teachers*

Go to PDToolkit for **Microsoft® Office 2010 for Teachers** to locate the corresponding file in the WeatherData folder within the Examples folder (LeahKatie_Oct12.mov).

The iPod saves video in the .mov format. A .mov file is a QuickTime container or wrapper movie file format that stores audio and video information. QuickTime, developed by Apple Computer Inc., provides a framework for audio and video encoding/decoding, the QuickTime player, and the movie file format (.mov) (Delahunty, 2007; Wong, 2009). So to view the video (.mov file), the computer needs QuickTime installed, which can be downloaded from Apple.com.

1. To make the screenshot of a video frame, double-click the video file to open it. You can find files that correspond to the chapter activities at http://pdtoolkit.pearson.com. Go to the frame of the video that they want to capture.
2. Open PowerPoint (if it is not already open) and go to the title slide (Our Weather in October).
3. Click the Insert tab. Click the Screenshot button (Images group) and then click Screen Clipping (see Figure 4.26).
4. Once you select Screen Clipping, the screen gets shaded and the cursor changes to the cross (+). Click the location on the screen where you want to begin the capture. With the left mouse button pressed, drag down to the location where you want the screen capture to end (see Figure 4.27).
5. When you release the mouse button, the screenshot appears in the slide (see Figure 4.28).
6. Resize the screenshot so that it fits between the title and subtitle.
7. Right-click on the screenshot and select Format Picture. The Format Picture box displays (Figure 4.29). Click on the Size category and set the Scale Height and Width to 62%. Click OK.
8. Position the image so it is equally spaced between the main title and subtitle. Select all three objects: title, screenshot, and subtitle. On the Home tab, click Arrange in the Drawing group. Select Align and Distribute Vertically.
9. Arrange the three objects so they are left-aligned.
10. Click on the screenshot to select it. Make sure nothing else is selected. The Picture Tools tab becomes active.
11. Click Format under Picture Tools. Click the down arrow under Picture Styles and select the Rotated, White option (see Figure 4.30).
12. With the screenshot still selected, click Picture Effects and choose Reflection, Full Reflection 8 pt offset (see Figure 4.31).

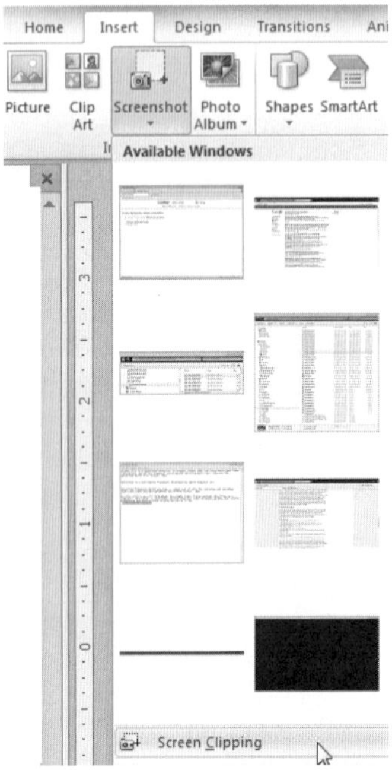

FIGURE 4.26 Screenshot

FIGURE 4.27 Screenshot Capture

FIGURE 4.28 Screenshot in Slide

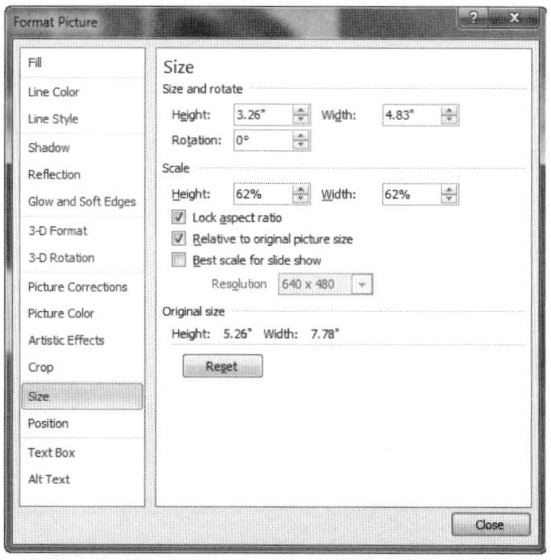

FIGURE 4.29 The Format Picture Box

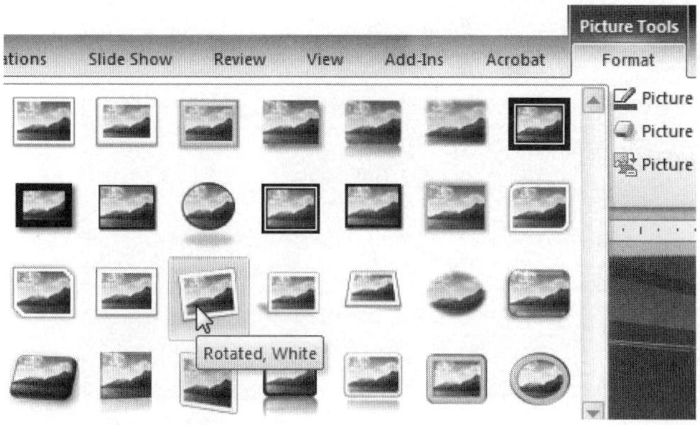

FIGURE 4.30 Picture Styles

FIGURE 4.31 Picture Effects

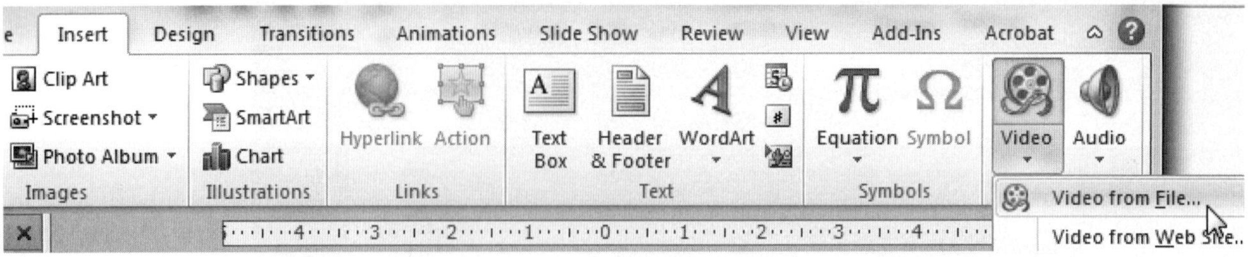

FIGURE 4.32 Insert Video

Adding a Video Report (Slide 6)

To being this section, reporters Leah and Katie want to include a video report that they recorded with an iPod.

1. Create a new Title Only slide.
2. Add the title iPod Weather Report: October 12. Add a text effect such as Shadow, Perspective. Click somewhere away from the title to deselect the title.
3. Click the Insert tab. Click the Video button and select Video from File (see Figure 4.32).
4. Using the Insert Video box, browse to the LeahKatie_Oct12.mov file and then click the Insert button.
5. The video is too large for the slide. Right-click the video and select Format Video from the menu. On the Format Video box, click the Size category and type 65% for the Scale Width and Height. Click Close.
6. Click the Play button on the video to play it (see Figure 4.33). Alternatively, click the Slide Show tab and then click the From Current Slide button (in the Start Slide Show group). The slide will display in the Slide Show view. Click the Play button on the video to play it. To exit the Slide Show view, press the Escape (Esc) key or right-click on the slide and click End Show.

Adding Web Video (Slide 7)

For the next slide, the research team wants to embed a video from the Web.

1. Create a new Title Only slide.
2. Add the title Weather Researchers and add a text effect to it.

FIGURE 4.33 Video Play Control

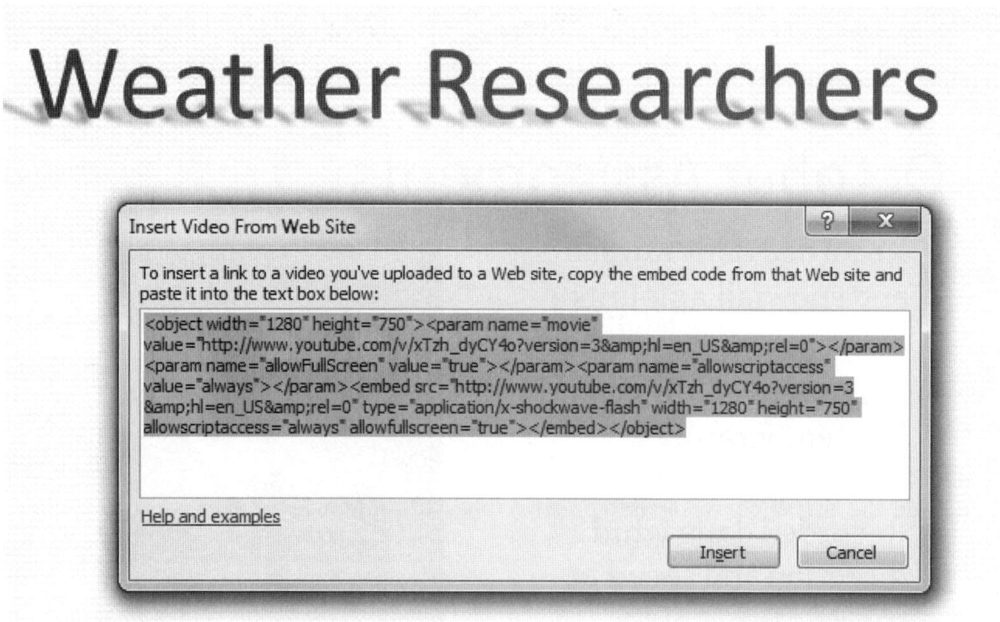

FIGURE 4.34 Inserting a Video Box

3. Click the Insert tab. Click Video and select *Video from Web Site*.
4. Go to www.youtube.com/user/NOAAWP.
5. Click on the Videos link and then click on one of the videos to preview it.
6. Click the Share button under the video controls. Click the Embed button. When the Embed options display, check only the Use Old Embed Code option.
7. A box displays with the embed code. Copy the code and paste in to the Insert Video from Web Site box (see Figure 4.34).
8. With the video selected, click Format on the Video Tools tab (see Figure 4.35). Click Video Effects. Select Shadow, Perspective and then Perspective Diagonal Upper Right.
9. Right-click on the video and select Format video. In the Size category, set the scale width and height to 200%.

FIGURE 4.35 Video Tools

Adding a Title, Text, and Content Slide (Slide 8)

1. For this slide, choose the Two Content layout. The final slide will look similar to the one shown in Figure 4.36.
2. Add a new slide by selecting New Slide from the Slides group on the Home tab.
3. Choose the Two Content layout from the Slides group.
4. Click in the Click to Add Title box and type the following title: October Assignments.
5. Enter the following three items in the bullet list on the left side of the two content areas:
   - Recorded daily rainfall and snowfall amounts
   - Recorded daily high and low temperatures
   - Recorded daily wind direction and speed at specific times of day

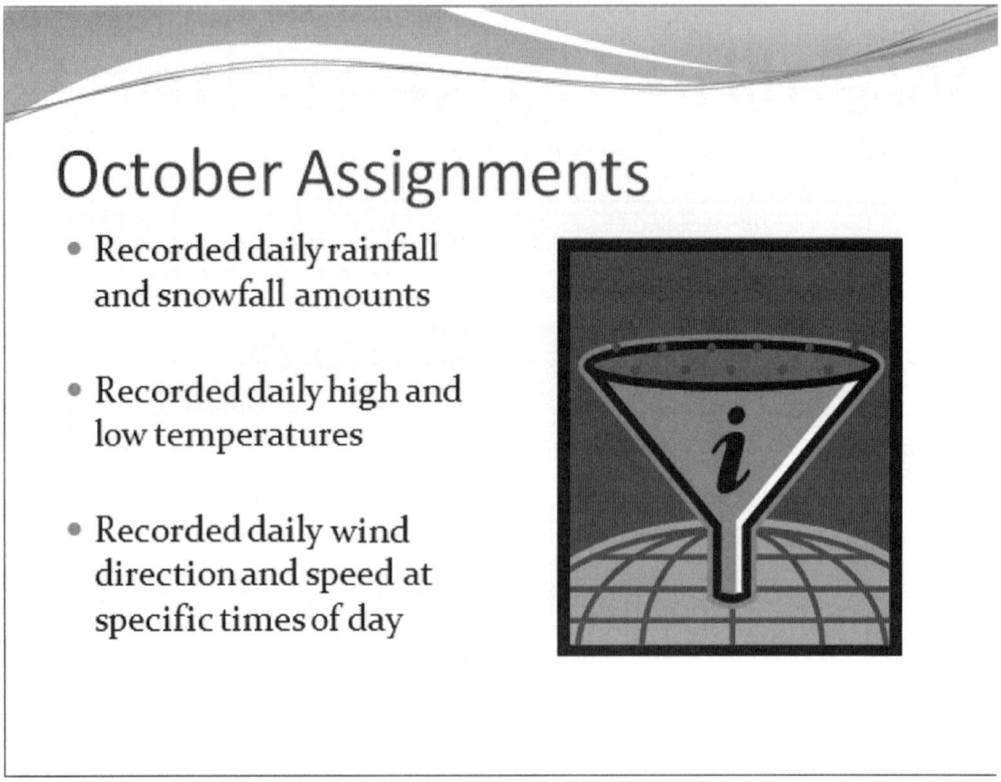

FIGURE 4.36 The Completed Slide

6. Set the line spacing. The list items are close together, and readers may have difficulty discerning one item from another. Select the list text box and click on its border so it becomes a solid line. Click the Line Spacing button in the Paragraph group on the Home tab and select Line Spacing Options. The Paragraph box appears (see Figure 4.37).
7. Type *30* in the After box located in the Spacing area, to add space between list items.
8. Click the Clip Art icon in the content area on the right side of the slide to add a clip art image. Adjust its size and position as needed.

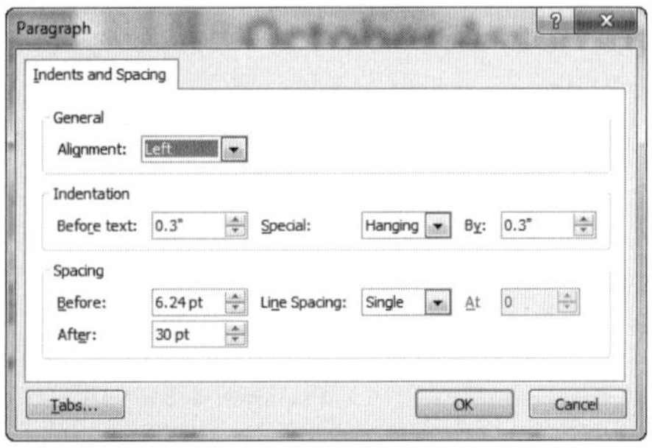

FIGURE 4.37 Line Spacing

Adding a Title Only Slide with an Object (Slide 9)

For this slide, choose a Title Only layout. You will insert an Excel worksheet onto the slide to represent the data recorded for the first 15 days in October. The final slide will look similar to the screen shown in Figure 4.38.

1. Add a new slide by selecting New Slide from the Slides group on the Home tab.
2. Choose the Title Only layout.
3. Click in the Click to Add Title box and type the following title: Storing Weather Data.
4. Place an Excel worksheet on the slide. Click anywhere on the slide to deselect the title. Click the Insert tab and select Object in the Text group. The Insert Object dialog box appears (see Figure 4.39).

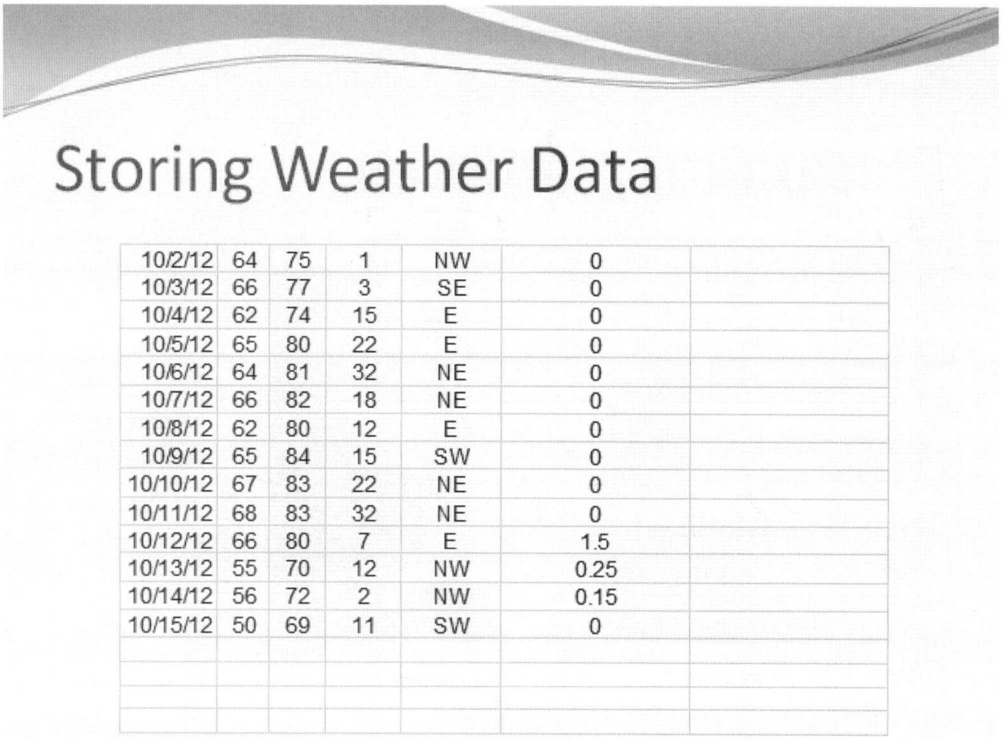

10/2/12	64	75	1	NW	0	
10/3/12	66	77	3	SE	0	
10/4/12	62	74	15	E	0	
10/5/12	65	80	22	E	0	
10/6/12	64	81	32	NE	0	
10/7/12	66	82	18	NE	0	
10/8/12	62	80	12	E	0	
10/9/12	65	84	15	SW	0	
10/10/12	67	83	22	NE	0	
10/11/12	68	83	32	NE	0	
10/12/12	66	80	7	E	1.5	
10/13/12	55	70	12	NW	0.25	
10/14/12	56	72	2	NW	0.15	
10/15/12	50	69	11	SW	0	

FIGURE 4.38 The Completed Slide with a Worksheet

5. Click the Create from File option. Click Browse, and the Browse dialog box appears.
6. Locate the worksheet named OctoberWeatherData.xlsx Click the OctoberWeatherData.xlsx file one time to select it and then click OK, and you return to the Insert dialog box.
7. Click OK, and the worksheet appears on the slide. Adjust the size of the worksheet by clicking and dragging the corner to expand or contract it.

PDToolkit for *Microsoft® Office 2010 for Teachers*

Go to PDToolkit for **Microsoft® Office 2010 for Teachers** to locate the corresponding file in the WeatherData folder within the Examples folder.

Adding a Chart Slide (Slide 10)

You want to add another slide to the presentation, which will include a chart. Suppose a weather research team located in Charleston, Illinois, and another team in Philadelphia, Pennsylvania, want to compare precipitation amounts for the month of October over a three-year period. Figure 4.40 shows one way to present the data.

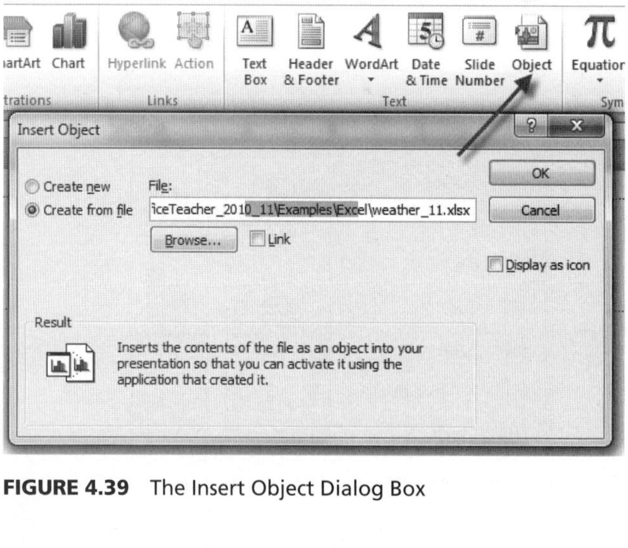

FIGURE 4.39 The Insert Object Dialog Box

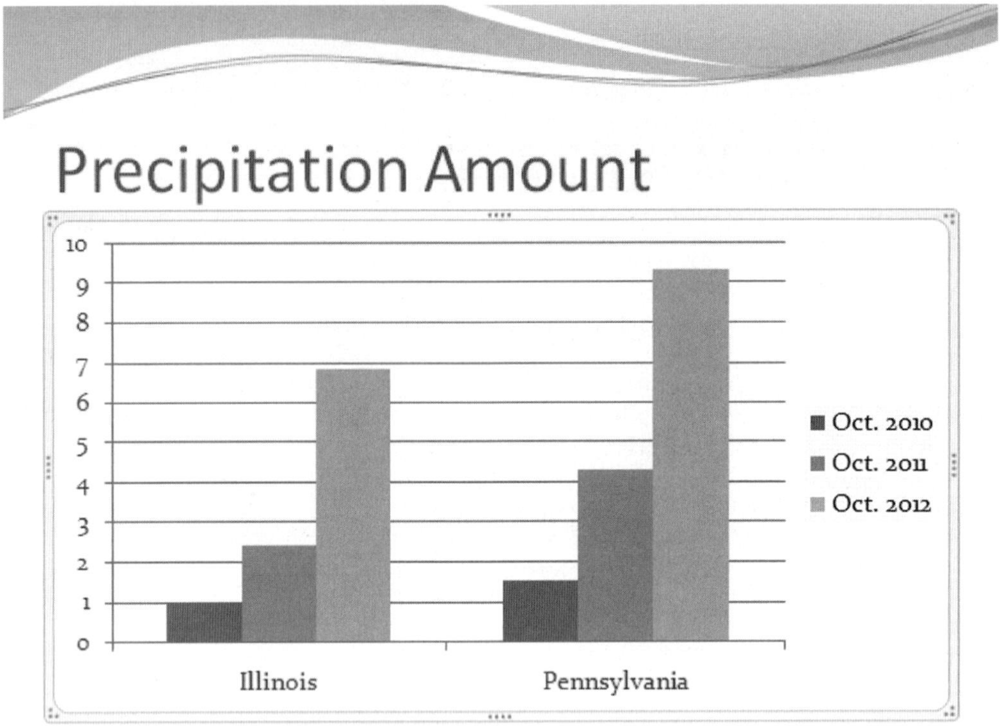

FIGURE 4.40 A Column Chart Emphasizing State

1. Add a new slide by selecting New Slide from the Insert menu.
2. Choose the Title and Content layout.
3. Click in the Click to Add Title box and enter the following title: Precipitation Amount.
4. Click the Insert Chart icon, and the Insert Chart box appears (see Figure 4.41). On the left side of the Insert Chart box, select Column and, under the column subtype area, choose Clustered Column and click OK. An Excel worksheet opens, showing sample data.
5. Enter the data shown in Figure 4.42. Notice that there are Category 3 and Category 4 items with data that do not display in the chart. You can either delete these data items or simply drag the Range rectangle so that it encompasses only the data to be shown in the chart.

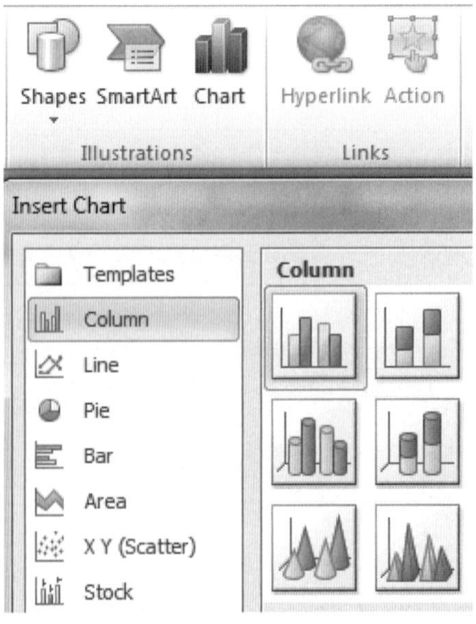

FIGURE 4.41 The Insert Chart Option

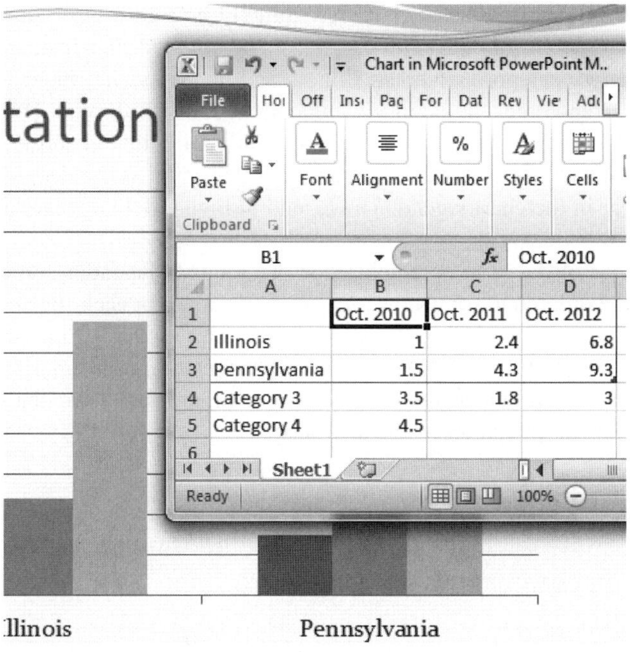

FIGURE 4.42 Data Entry

In this example, the Range rectangle encompasses data in cells A1 down through cell D3. To close the data sheet, click the Close button (X) on the upper-right corner of the data sheet.

6. Close the Excel worksheet and view the chart (see Figure 4.43). If you need to edit the data, click the chart, and the Chart Tools tab becomes active. Under the Chart Tools tab, click the Design tab and in the Data group click Edit Data.

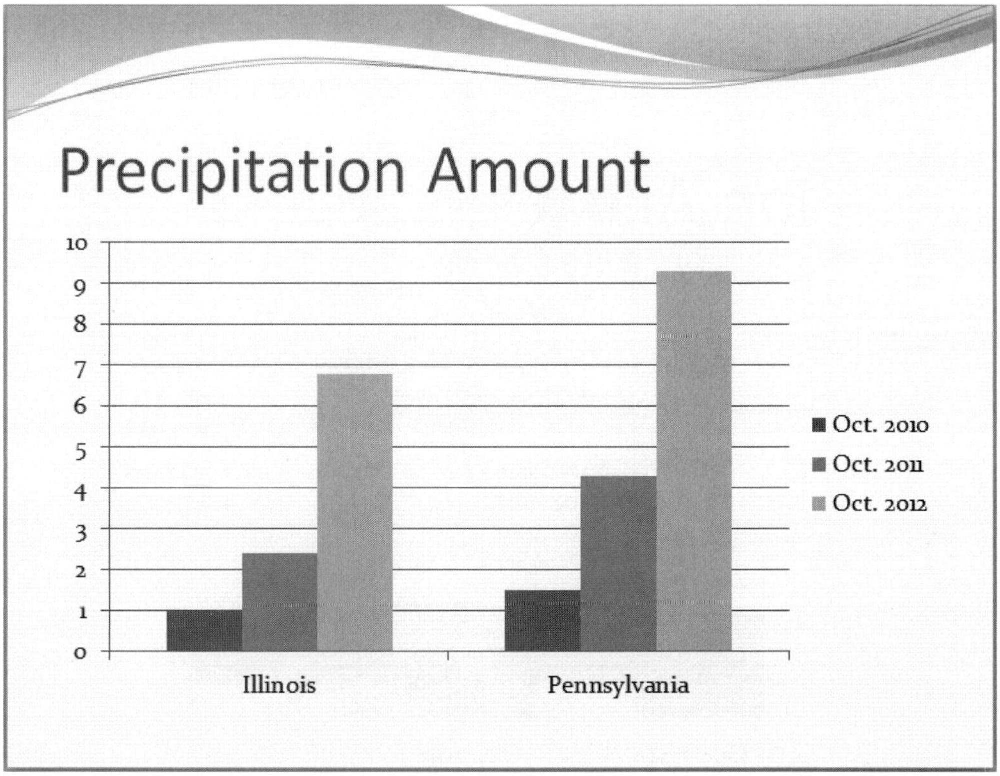

FIGURE 4.43 A Chart Emphasizing Time

ORDERING DATA Before continuing, review quickly how to order data in the data sheet. The ordering of data in Excel determines how data are plotted. For instance, in the previous example, there are two categories labeled Illinois and Pennsylvania. Enter the Illinois data in cells A2 through D2 and enter the Pennsylvania data in cells A3 through D3. PowerPoint plots the Illinois data first on the left side of the chart, with data points in subsequent columns and rows appearing next and so on. Notice in Figure 4.42 that row 1 is the data series column. Data entered there appear in the chart legend. The legend in Figure 4.43 appears on the right side of the chart.

Various aspects of data can be emphasized or grouped, depending on their ordering. For example, data can be ordered to show how precipitation varied for each state over time, as shown in Figure 4.43. Alternatively, placing the states in the data series column and time periods in Categories 1, 2, and 3 (see Figure 4.44) emphasizes precipitation over time. The ordering of data illustrated in Figure 4.44 produces the chart shown in Figure 4.45. The chart emphasizes time period and plots the state categories as the data series.

Inserting a Chart (Slide 11)

In this example, you will create the chart shown in Figure 4.45 by using the Insert Chart command.

1. Add a new slide.
2. Choose the Blank layout.
3. Make the Insert tab active and click the Chart button. The Insert Chart box appears. Click Column and then Clustered Column. Click OK. An Excel worksheet displays.
4. Enter the data as shown in Figure 4.44 and move the Range rectangle so that it encompasses cells A1 through C4. Close the worksheet.

CHANGING THE CHART LAYOUT

5. Click the chart to select it, and the Chart Tools tab becomes active. Click the Design tab and in the Chart Layouts group select Layout 2. Clicking the More arrow in the Chart Layouts group will display the available chart layouts. Move the mouse cursor over each item, and the layout name appears. When you select a layout, the chart appearance changes, and a Chart Title box appears at the top of the chart. Type October Precipitation: Illinois and Pennsylvania in the Title box.

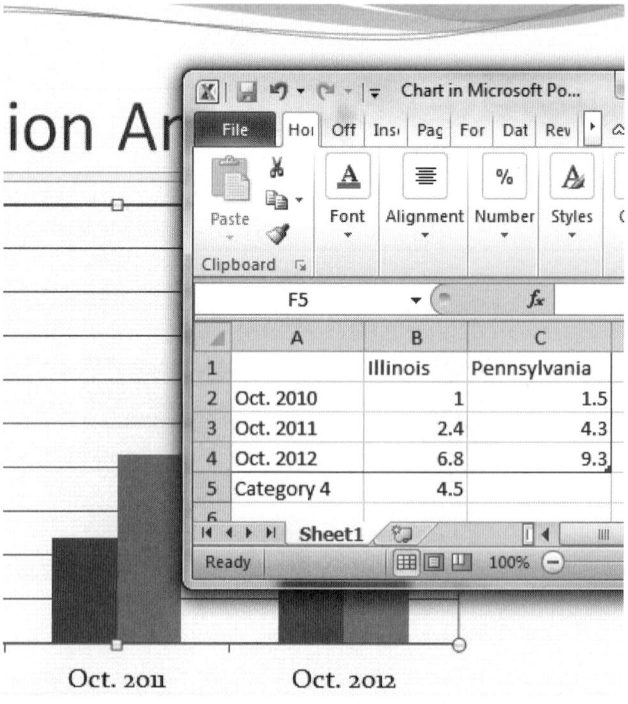

FIGURE 4.44 Editing Data

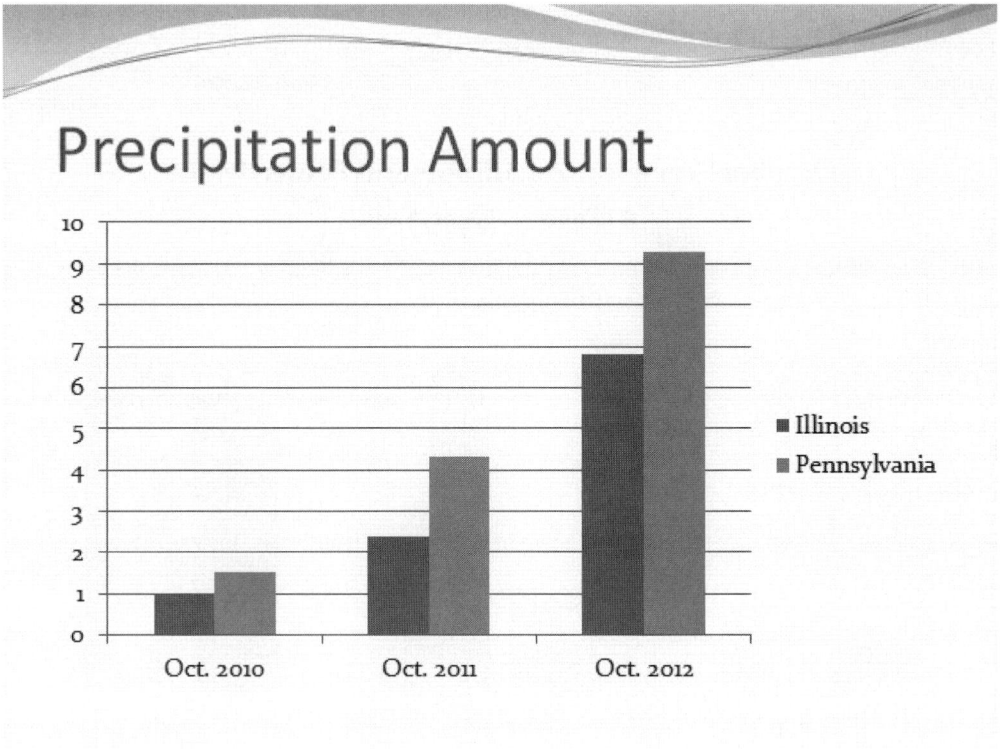

FIGURE 4.45 The Completed Data Slide

6. Enlarge the chart by clicking and dragging one of the sizing handles (three small dots) around its borders.
7. Click the chart to select it, and the Chart Tools tab becomes active. Click the Design tab and in the Chart Styles group choose Style 39 or another style of your choice.
8. With the chart selected, position the cursor over its border, right-click, and select Format Chart Area. The Format Chart Area box displays. On the left portion of the box, click Border Color, and the Border Color options display. Select No Line and then click Close.

CHANGING THE CHART TYPE

1. To change the chart type, click on the chart, and the Chart Tools tab becomes active. Click the Design tab and in the Type group click Change Chart Type. The Change Chart Type box appears, and from it you can choose another type.
2. Edit the chart by double-clicking in the chart area and then selecting the commands on the Chart Tools Design tab or right-clicking in the chart area and selecting Edit Data or Change Chart Type.

Adding a Title and Text Slide Using the Slide Sorter (Slide 12)

Next, you'll add another slide with a Title and Content layout. For this slide, you'll use the Slide Sorter to make a copy of an existing slide, paste it, and alter its text to create the next slide. Copying and pasting slides in the Slide Sorter is one of the many approaches you can use to work efficiently. When you are finished, the slide will look similar to the one shown in Figure 4.46.

1. Click the Slide Sorter View button located in the lower-right portion of the PowerPoint workspace to enter the Slide Sorter (see Figure 4.47). The Slide Sorter presents images of each slide in the slide show (see Figure 4.48). In this view, slides can be easily copied, pasted, reordered, and deleted. To reorder a slide, click on it and drag it to a new location in the slide show sequence. To delete a slide, click on it and press Delete. You can also accomplish many of the previously mentioned tasks in the Slide pane of the Normal view.

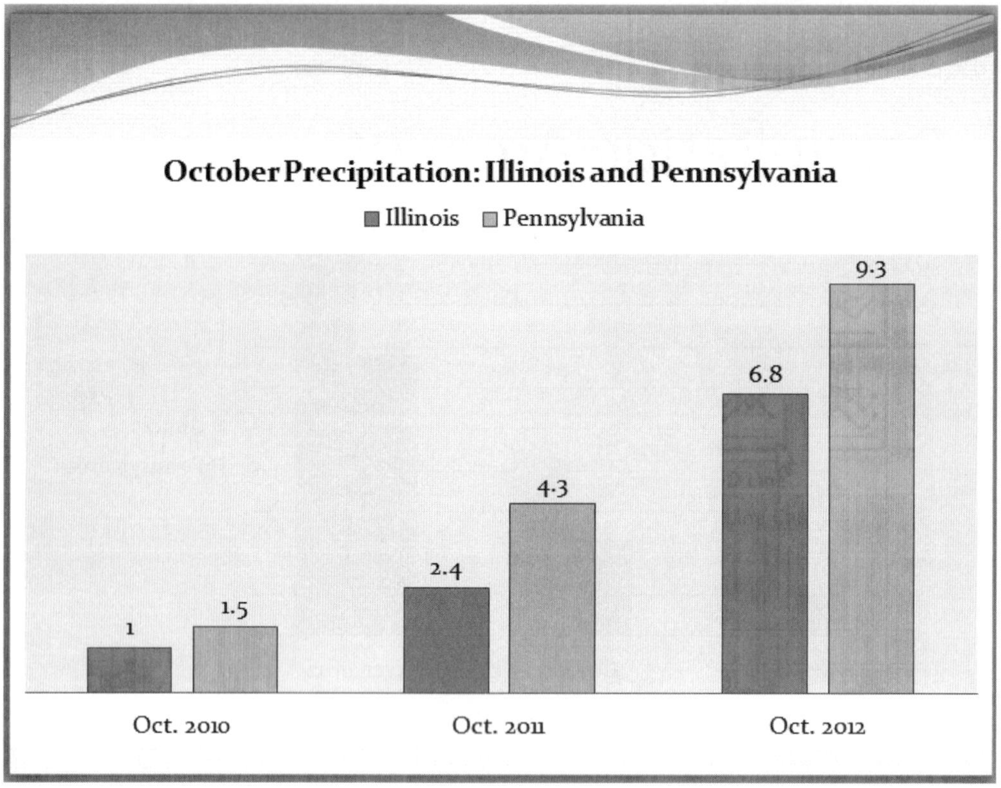

FIGURE 4.46 The Completed Findings Slide

FIGURE 4.47 The Slide Sorter

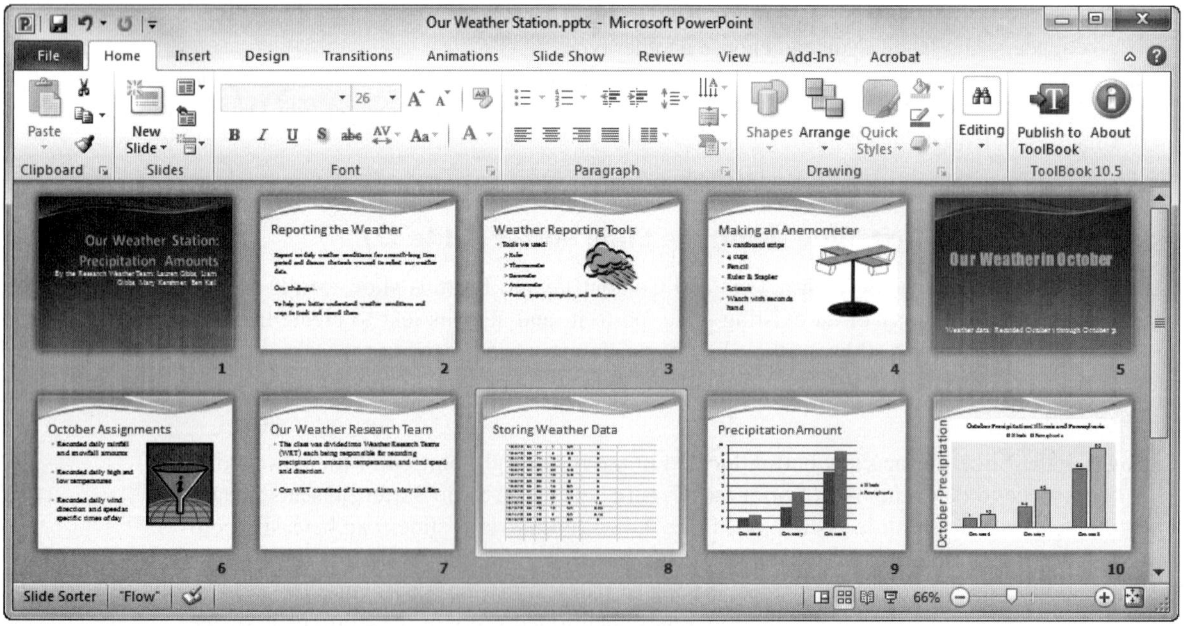

FIGURE 4.48 The Slide Sorter View

2. To copy and paste a slide, click one of the Title and Content layout slides (e.g., slide 3) to select it. A border appears around the slide. With the slide selected, click Copy on the Clipboard group of the Home tab or press Ctrl+C. Click the last slide in the presentation and click Paste in the Clipboard group or press Ctrl+V. A new slide appears. Note that the pasted slide appears after the slide you selected.
3. There are now two duplicates. Change the text on the slide you just pasted. Double-click it to exit the Slide Sorter and return to the Normal view.
4. The title box has text in it that can be replaced with Our findings. To replace the text, click on the Title box to select it. A dashed-line border appears around the box. Click on the border again, and it changes to a solid line. Press Delete, and the text changes to Click to Add Title. Type the new title: Our findings.
5. To enter bullet items, click the bulleted list text box to select it. As in the previous step, press Delete, and the text changes to Click to Add Text. Type a new list by entering the following items:
   - Average low temperature = 58.6
   - Average high temperature = 73.7
   - Total precipitation = 5.9
6. Select the bulleted list text box. Choose Line Spacing from the Paragraph group on the Home tab and select 3.0.

Adding a Title, Text, and Content Slide (Slide 13)

To complete the presentation, you need to add one more slide. Again, you'll use the Slide Sorter to copy and paste a slide.

1. Click the Slide Sorter View button to enter the Slide Sorter.
2. Click a Two Content slide (e.g., the slide with the anemometer image) to select it and then copy it. Right-click the last slide in the presentation and select Paste.
3. To change the text on the slide, double-click slide 12 to exit the Slide Sorter and return to the Normal view. The slide you create will look like the screen shown in Figure 4.49.

FIGURE 4.49 The Completed Team Slide

4. Replace the text in the title text box with Weather Reporting Team.
5. Enter the bullet items. Click the bulleted list text box to select it. A dashed-line border appears around the box. Click on the border again, and it changes to a solid-line pattern. Press Delete, and the text changes to Click to Add Text. Type the new list. Enter the following items:
   - From Lauren, Liam, Mary, and Ben, this has been our monthly weather report. . . .
   - Until next time—Thanks!!!
6. Select the text list and then click Line Spacing in the Paragraph group of the Home tab. Select the Line Spacing options and type 30 in the After box.
7. Delete the existing clip art image. Click it to select it and then press Delete. Add clip art representative of the topic and position it in a desired location.

Previewing a PowerPoint Presentation in the Slide Show View

You can now view the presentation in the Slide Show view. Click the Slide Show button located in the lower-left portion of the PowerPoint workspace to enter the Slide Show view. Advance the slides by clicking the left mouse button. To exit the Slide Show view, press the Escape (Esc) key or click the right mouse button on the slide and select End Show from the menu. Remember that at any point when you are developing the presentation, you can view it in the Slide Show view.

Saving the Presentation

It is a good idea to save your work frequently. Keep in mind that even though you see your presentation onscreen, it may not be saved. The more often you save your work, the less chance there is of losing a presentation or a portion of it. Any portion of your presentation that you do not save disappears when the computer is turned off. There are three save options available by clicking the File tab: Save, Save As, and Save and Send. Under Save As, there are numerous options for saving the workbook, including options for the Web and for earlier Office versions.

SAVE When you create a new presentation and select *Save*, the Save As dialog box appears, prompting you to determine a location in which to save the file, give the file a name, and specify a file format. When saving a new presentation, you will likely do the following:

1. Click in the Save In box to specify the location to save the presentation.
2. Type a name in the File Name field.
3. Assign a file format by clicking in the Save As Type box.
4. If you do not provide a name, PowerPoint gives the presentation the name Presentation1 .pptx. By default, PowerPoint appends the .pptx extension to the file name and saves the file in a presentation (*.pptx) format. Additionally, you can save the file as a PowerPoint show format by selecting the PowerPoint Show .ppsx option in the Save as type box. Click the Office button, File tab select Save as, and then select the PowerPoint Show option.
5. Once you have designated a location, name, and format for your presentation, PowerPoint saves all future changes accordingly.

PDToolkit for *Microsoft® Office 2010 for Teachers*

Go to PDToolkit for **Microsoft® Office 2010 for Teachers** to locate the completed example in the WeatherData folder within the Examples folder (Our Weather Station_2011.pptx).

SAVE AS The Save As option allows you to save an existing presentation in a different location, under a different file name, or in a different file format.

PDToolkit for *Microsoft® Office 2010 for Teachers*

Go to PDToolkit for **Microsoft® Office 2010 for Teachers** to locate the completed example in the WeatherData folder within the Examples folder (Our Weather Station_2011.ppsx).

SAVE TO WEB You can save PowerPoint files for the Web by uploading them to Windows Live. After uploading a file to Windows Live, you can access it from anywhere. You can also edit the file as well as preview it in a Slide Show view. To use Windows Live, you need to create an account by going to https://login.live.com. The account creation process is simple and takes only a few minutes. (See "Sharing the Template" in the "Project for Teachers" section for more details about Windows Live.) After you create an account, click the File tab, select Send & Save, and then select Save to Web.

Adding Slide Transitions

You can add slide transitions, such as wipes, dissolves, and fades, between slides. The effects display when viewing the presentation in the Slide Show view.

1. Make the Animations tab active.
2. Select a transition from the Transition to This Slide group. To add a transition to all slides, click Apply to All after selecting the transition. If you want to add a transition to only a single slide, select the slide and then choose a transition. You can also adjust the speed of the transition using the options on the Transition to This Slide group.
3. For this example, click a transition (e.g., blinds horizontal, blinds vertical wipe, dissolve, and so on) and then click Apply to All Slides.
4. Set the speed of the transition and a sound.
5. Under Advance Slide, check On Mouse Click so the slide advances and the transition takes place when the mouse button is clicked.
6. You can also select Automatically After to advance slides after a designated number of seconds. Checking this option and specifying a number of seconds sets the transition to occur and the slide to advance automatically after the specified time. This option is useful for creating self-running slide shows.
7. Checking both On Mouse Click and After (and specifying a time) sets the transition to occur automatically after the preset number of seconds. To advance the slide before the designated time, click the mouse.
8. Set the transition to apply to all the slides by clicking Apply to All Slides. To preview the transitions, click the Preview button on the Animations tab.

PDToolkit for *Microsoft® Office 2010 for Teachers*

Go to PDToolkit for **Microsoft® Office 2010 for Teachers** to locate the corresponding file in the WeatherData folder within the Examples folder.

Spell-Checking a PowerPoint Presentation

You can check a presentation for spelling errors by selecting Spelling in the Proofing group on the Review tab. When PowerPoint does not recognize a word, it displays it in the Spelling box (see Figure 4.50). In most cases, PowerPoint offers suggestions for correcting misspelled words. When you click Ignore, the spell checker disregards the suggestion. When you click Ignore All, it disregards all future instances of the word in the spell-check session. You can make a suggested change by clicking Change. Change All changes all future instances of the word in the spell-check session.

If the word in the Not in Dictionary box is spelled correctly and PowerPoint does not recognize it, you can add it to PowerPoint's dictionary by clicking Add. Clicking Suggest causes PowerPoint to search the currently selected dictionary for possible suggestions of the correct word. Clicking AutoCorrect adds the spelling mistake to a list of errors and automatically corrects it on subsequent occurrences. The Ignore button changes to Resume when you exit the spell-check session. Clicking Resume resumes the session. Clicking Close closes the Spelling dialog box.

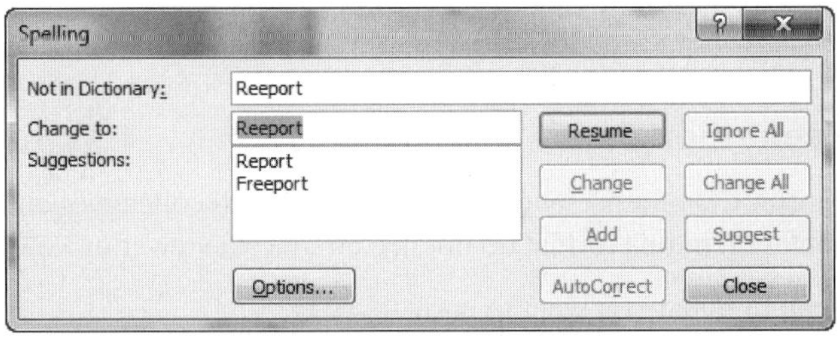

FIGURE 4.50 Spell-Checking

Printing a PowerPoint Presentation

PowerPoint provides several options for printing, including slides, handouts, notes, or an outline. For this example, you want to print handouts of the presentation. This is particularly useful if you want students or audience members to take notes while they listen to the presentation.

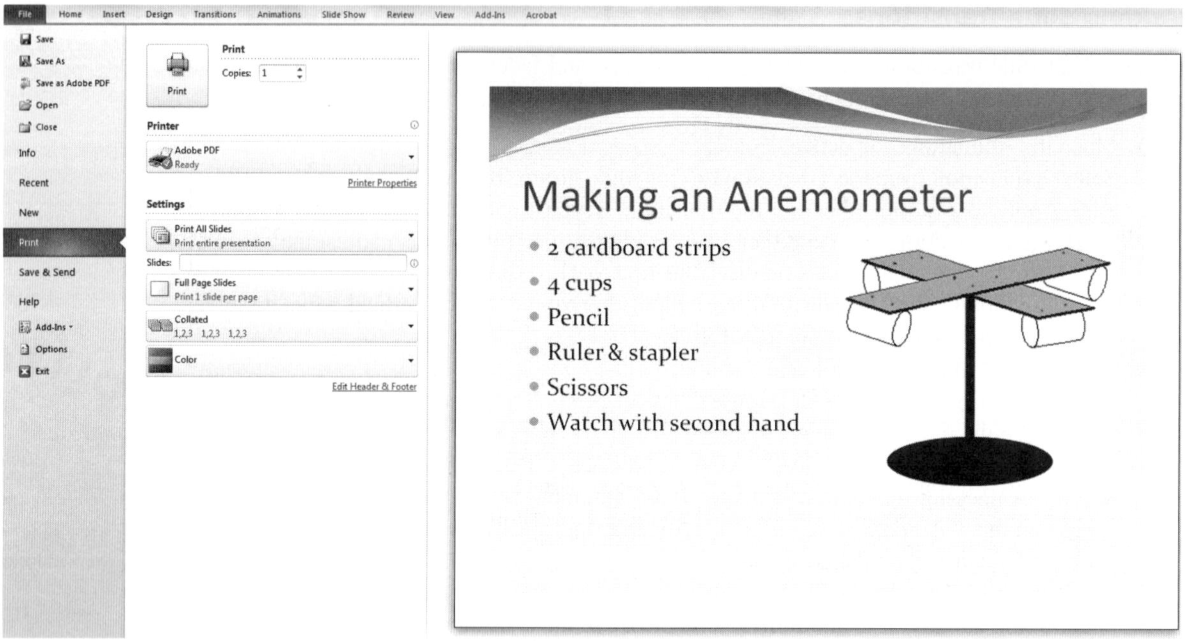

FIGURE 4.51 The Print Box

1. To print, click the File tab and select Print, and the Backstage appears (see Figure 4.51).
   - *Print*—Click the Print button to print the presentation.
   - *Copies*—Specifies the number of copies you want to print.
   - *Printer*—Designates a printer to print the slide. Other options include printer, PDF, XPS, and fax.
   - *Print All Slides*—This option allows you to print the entire presentation or selected slides.
   - *Slides*—Specifies a range of slides to print.
   - *Full Page Slides*—Specifies whether to print slides, handouts, notes, or the outline. For this presentation, select Handouts by clicking the down arrow. Click Handouts from the drop-down list. When the Handouts option is selected, the Handouts area becomes active, and you can specify how many slides to print on each page of the handout. Select six slides per page.
   - *The Preview area on the right*—Allows viewing of the workbook, workbook selection, or chart prior to printing. Often the data you enter into a worksheet extend beyond the viewing area of your computer monitor. Print Preview allows you to see what a printed copy of your worksheet will look like prior to its being printed.

Packaging a Presentation on CD

You can make an autorun CD of a presentation and share it with colleagues and students. Those who view your presentation in this format do not need to have a viewer or PowerPoint installed.

1. Open the presentation that you want to copy to a CD.
2. Click the File tab, select Save & Send, and then select Package Presentation for CD from the File menu. The Package for CD box will be displayed.
3. Type a name for the CD in the Name the CD box (e.g., Weather Research).
4. The Add button allows you to add additional files to the CD. To the left of the Add button is the name of the file that will be copied.
5. Click the Copy to CD button, and recording begins. When recording is complete, several files appear on the CD, and the CD title corresponds to the title you typed in the Name the CD box.

PROJECT FOR TEACHERS: USING A TEMPLATE FOR SCIENTIFIC INVESTIGATION

Rick Rechenberg, a teacher at Holy Sepulcher School in Butler, Pennsylvania, developed a PowerPoint template that he gives to students to help them prepare for the Pennsylvania Junior Academy of Science (PJAS). For PJAS, students conduct a scientific investigation. After completing their experiments, each student makes a 10-minute presentation to a panel of judges at a local university. Students receiving first-place ribbons have an opportunity to go on to a state meeting at The Pennsylvania State University. Holy Sepulcher School students have been very successful at PJAS because of teachers' efforts to prepare them. Additionally, Mr. Rechenberg's template guides students' work. It helps to ensure that their investigations and presentations are consistent and thoroughly prepared. Along with the template, Mr. Rechenberg provides students a detailed instruction sheet that describes, among other things, what goes on each slide, due dates, and how students should save and turn in files.

In this activity, you will develop some of the main slides of Mr. Rechenberg's template of 35 slides. Additionally, you will see how to share these PowerPoint files with students and parents and, if needed, to work on them collaboratively.

The template has a minimalist design. It is prepared so students do not have to worry about formatting issues such as font size, centering, or spacing. This helps students to focus foremost on research methodology and content rather than thinking about PowerPoint design. In addition, it reduces printing problems in situations where overhead transparencies or handouts might be needed. You will add a design template at the end of the activity.

Title Only Slide (Slide 1)

1. Open PowerPoint and create a Title Only slide.
2. Add the following title: Highlight & place your title here (see Figure 4.52).
3. Type the following in the subtitle field: Highlight & write in your name here, School name, and Grade?

FIGURE 4.52 Template for Slide 1

Title and Content Slide (Slide 2)

1. Create a Title and Content slide.
2. Add the title Investigation Question (see Figure 4.53).
3. Add the following content:
   - Highlight & write your "Investigation Question" here
   - Highlight & give a BRIEF overall description of your investigation. What you will be testing and how you will do it. Do not give a detailed procedure here. Do not call the items you are testing independent variables in this paragraph

Title and Content Slide (Slide 3)

4. Create a Title and Content slide.
5. Add the title Interest (see Figure 4.54).
6. Add the following content: Highlight & give the reason for your interest in doing this investigation or explain what led you to want to do this investigation. The more personal and real-life you make it the better.

Title and Content Slide (Slide 4)

7. Create a Title and Content slide.
8. Add the title Research (see Figure 4.55).
9. Add the following content:
   - Highlight & write your Big Question here.
   - Highlight & write your 1st area of research.
   - Highlight & write your 2nd area of research.
   - Highlight & write your 3rd area of research.
   - Highlight & write your 4th area of research.
   - Highlight & write your 5th area of research.

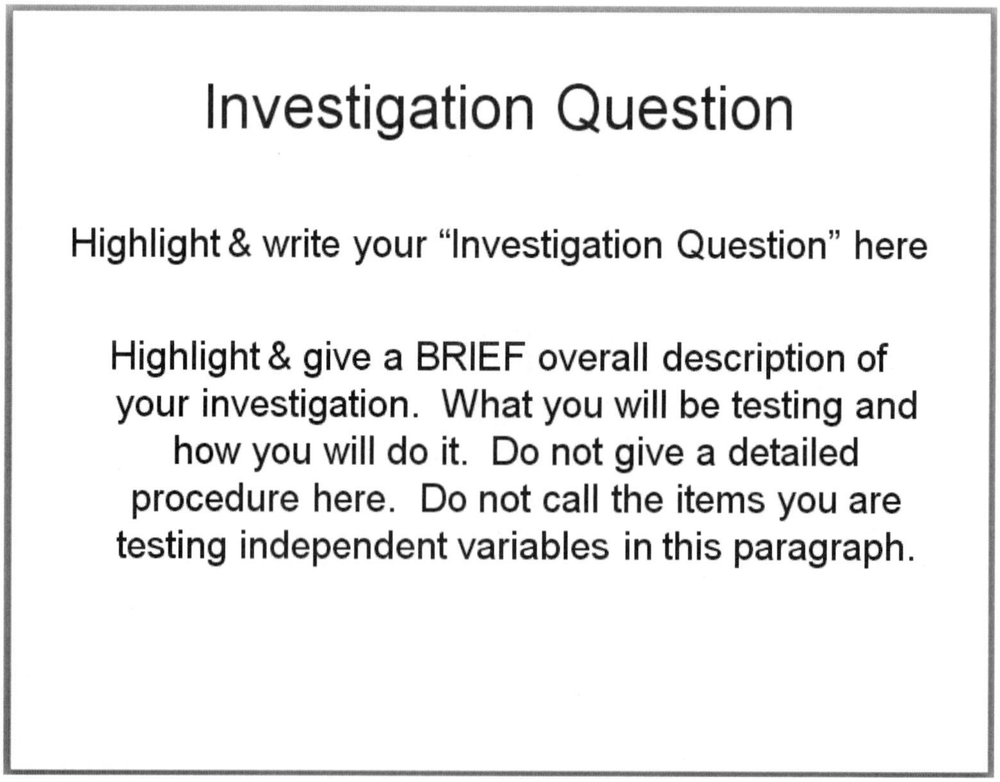

FIGURE 4.53 Template for Slide 2

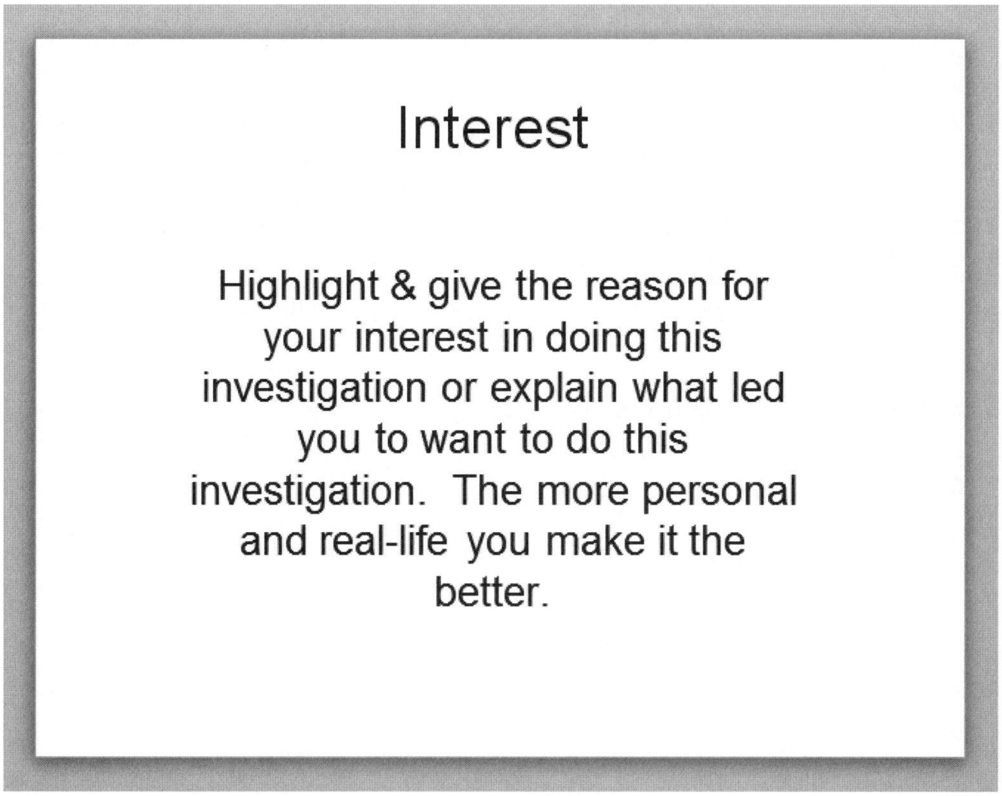

FIGURE 4.54 Template for Slide 3

FIGURE 4.55 Template for Slide 4

Title and Content Slide (Slide 5)

10. Create a Title and Content slide.
11. Add the title Research.
12. Add the following content: Highlight & copy to this page the research information that takes up too much room on page 4. Delete this page if you don't need it.

Title and Content Slide (Slides 6–8)

13. Create a Title and Content slide.
14. Add the title Highlight & replace these two sentences with the title of your first picture/diagram/chart about something from your research (see Figure 4.56).

Title and Content Slide (Slide 9)

15. Create a Title and Content slide.
16. Add the title Hypothesis (see Figure 4.57).
17. Add the following content:
    - Highlight & write your hypothesis in the top of this area.
    - Highlight & replace this section with your reasons for your hypothesis. Be sure to back this hypothesis up with some facts from your research. Give scientific reasons!

Two Content Slide (Slide 10)

18. Create a Two Content slide.
19. Add the title Materials (see Figure 4.58).
20. Add the following two columns of content:
    - Highlight these two sentences to add list of materials. Hit Enter after each item to add the next item. Place ½ of the materials on this left side.
    - Highlight these two sentences to add list of materials. Hit Enter after each item to add the next item. Place ½ of the materials on this right side.

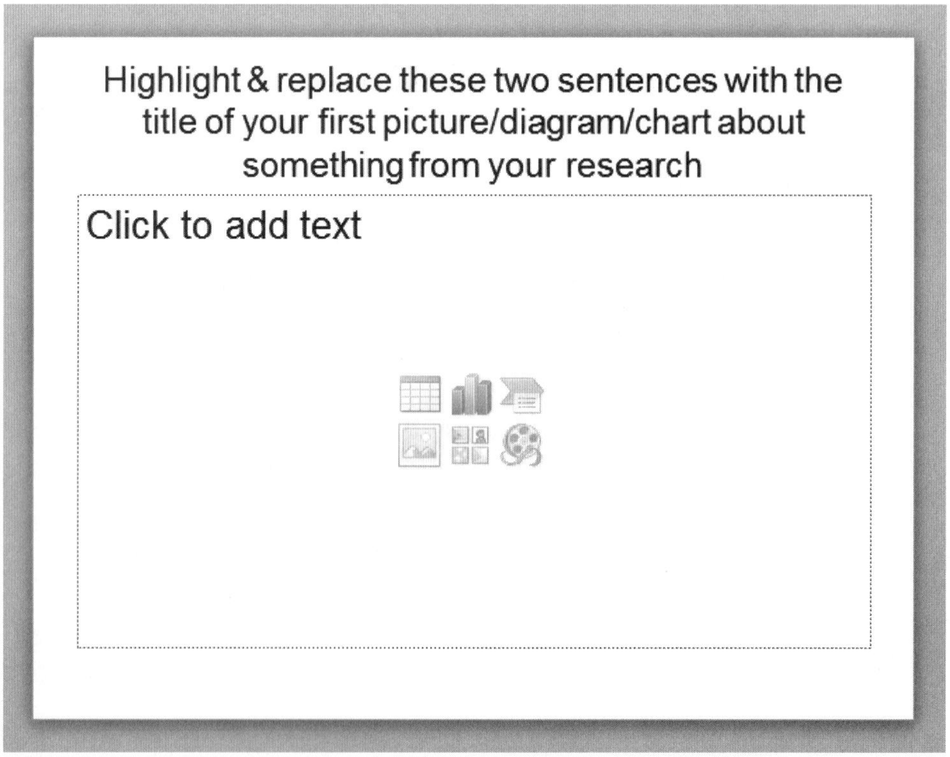

FIGURE 4.56 Template for Slides 6–8

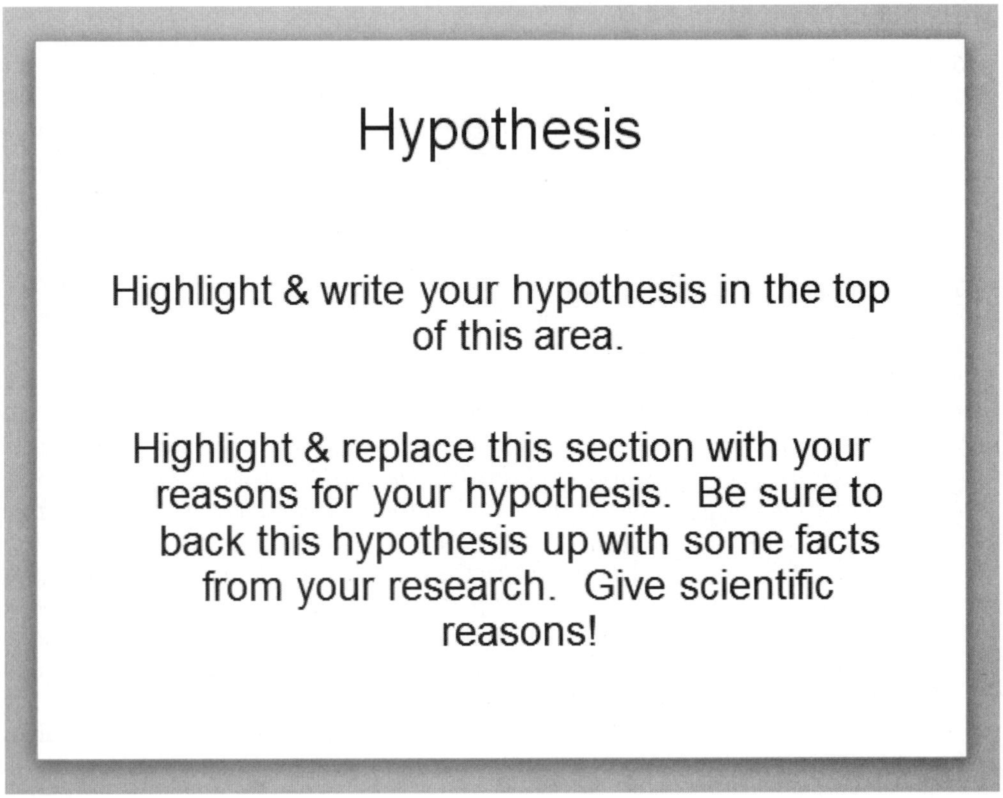

FIGURE 4.57 Template for Slide 9

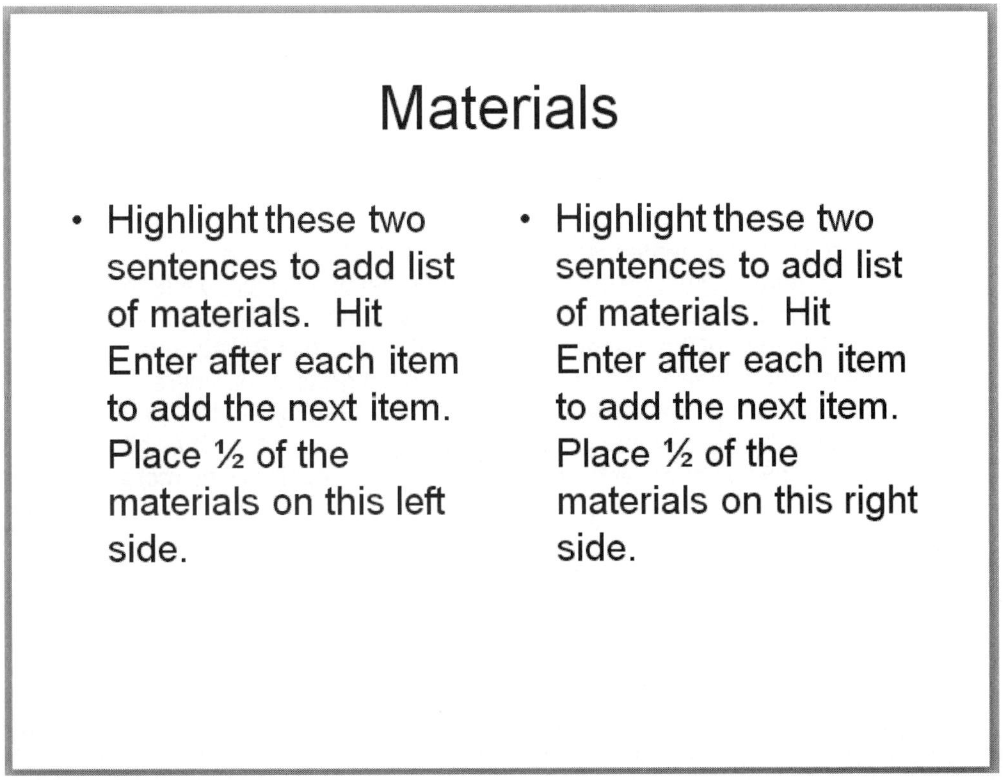

FIGURE 4.58 Template for Slide 10

Title and Content Slide (Slide 11)

21. Create a Title and Content slide.
22. Add the title Procedure.
23. Add the following content (noting that 1 begins the ordered list):
- 1. Highlight these four sentences & write first step in the procedure. Hit Enter after each step to add the next step. Place no more than 12 total lines on this page. Place any additional lines on the next page.

Title and Content Slide (Slide 12)

24. Create a Title and Content slide.
25. Add the title Procedure (see Figure 4.59).
26. Add the following content:
- *15. Highlight these sentences & write additional steps for the procedure. To change the procedure number of this step to match up with what is written on the previous page, do the following. Click in front of the sentence—click on Format, then Bullets and Numbering, then Numbered. Choose the top group of numbers that are followed by a period. Then in the bottom right of the box, choose the number that you want this page to start with. Then hit OK. Hit Enter after each step to add the next step. Place no more than 12 total lines on this page.*

27. Note that the list on this slide begins at 15. By default, PowerPoint sets the list number to 1. The number 15 simply indicates that the list continues from the previous slide. You need to adjust this number to correspond to the correct number of items in your list. Right-click on the list number and select Numbering. Select Bullets and Numbering. On the Bullets and Numbering box, click the Numbered tab and increment or decrement the number in the Start At box.

Title and Content Slide (Slide 13)

28. Create a Title and Content slide.
29. Add the title Variables, Constants, & the Control.

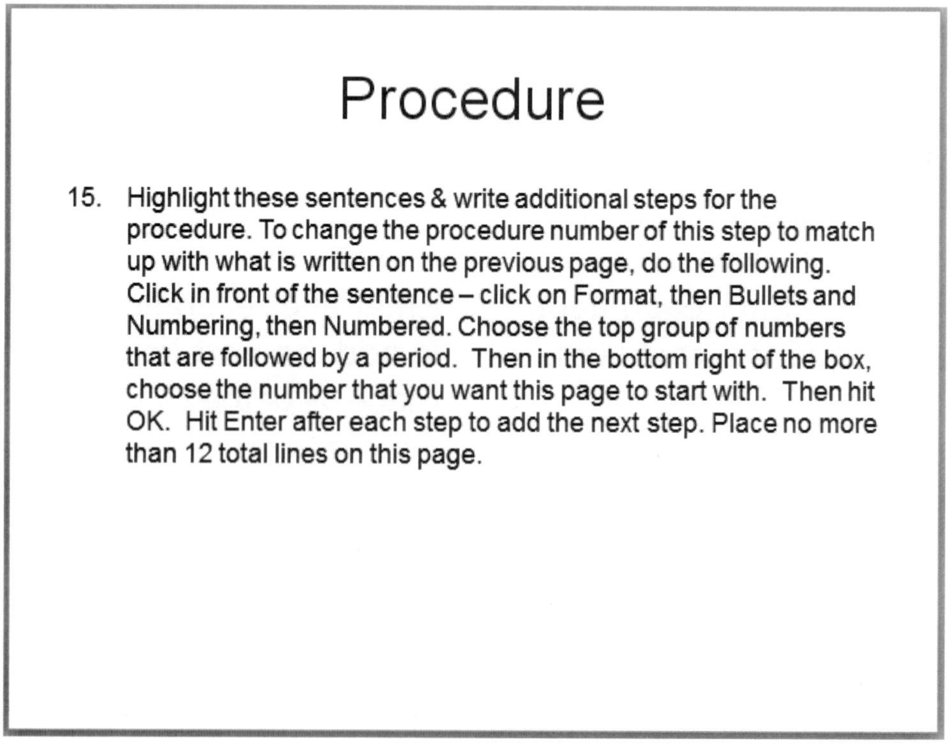

FIGURE 4.59 Template for Slide 12

30. Add the following content:
    - Independent Variable: DO NOT DELETE "Independent Variable." Highlight & replace these three sentences with your independent variables. This is the part of the experiment that you are changing.
    - Dependent Variable: DO NOT DELETE "Dependent Variable." Highlight & replace these three sentences with your dependent variable. This is the part of the experiment that you are measuring.
    - Constants: DO NOT DELETE "Constants." Highlight & replace these three sentences with the constants. This is the part of your experiment that always stays the same.
    - The Control: DO NOT DELETE "The Control." Highlight & replace these three sentences with your control. This is one of the independent variables that you will compare the others to.

Title and Content Slide (Slides 14–31)

Slides 14 through 31 consist of slides for tables and figures/graphs (see Figures 4.60 and 4.61).

31. Create Title and Content slides.
32. For the table slides, add the title Click & write in the title of your 1st table here.
33. For the figure/graph slides, add the following text:
    - Paste Graph #1 above this window, then delete this line.
    - Highlight this bullet point & type an analysis statement of Graph #1. Hit Enter to add more analysis statements.

Title and Content Slide (Slide 32)

34. Create a Title and Content slide.
35. Add the title Possible Errors.
36. Add the following content:
    - Highlight and state any parts of your experiment in which errors could have occurred. Hit Enter to list more possible errors. You should have at least one possible error. Please don't write possible errors that would make you look like you didn't think things through☺!

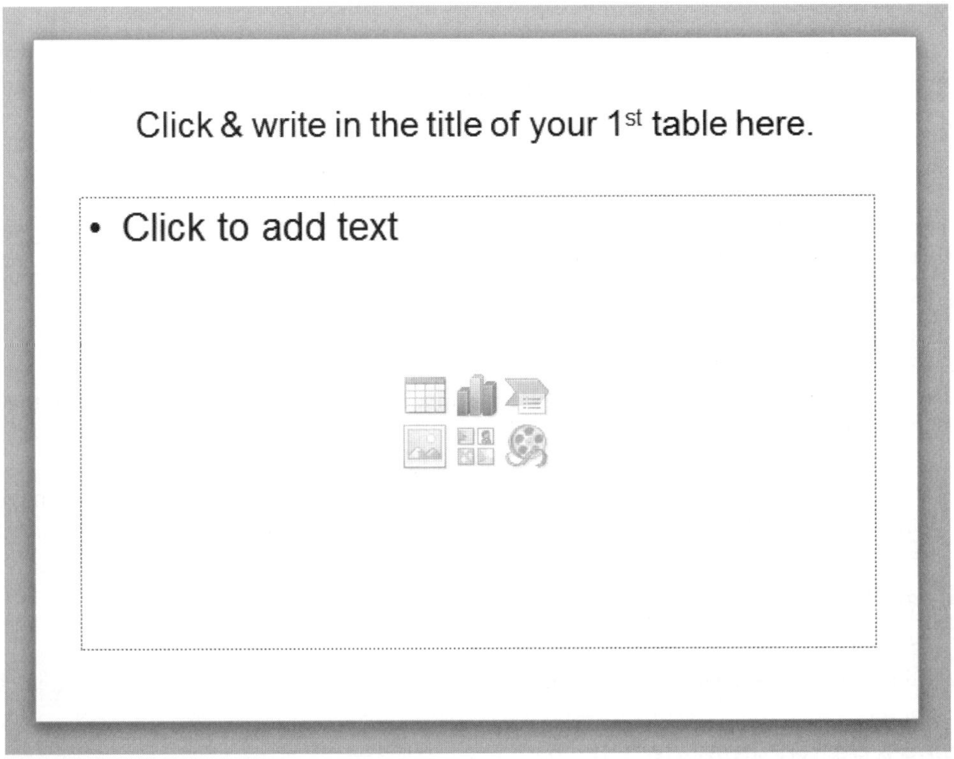

FIGURE 4.60 Template Table for Slides 14–31

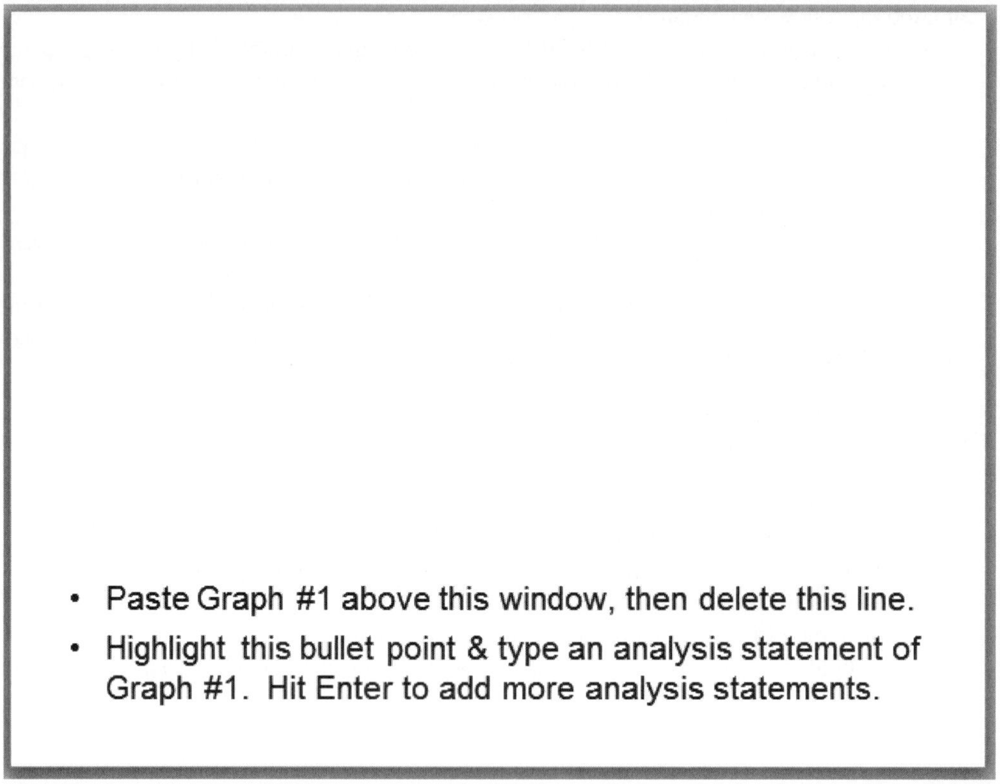

FIGURE 4.61 Template Graph for Slides 14–31

Title and Content Slide (Slide 33)

37. Create a Title and Content slide.
38. Add the title Conclusions (see Figure 4.62).
39. Add the following content:
    - YOU MUST FILL OUT BOTH CONCLUSIONS PAGES!—FILL IN EACH BULLET ASKED FOR ON BOTH PAGES! Delete this line after reading
    - Highlight & restate your hypothesis here.
    - Click & write in your first conclusion. Be sure to reference your research in some of these statements. Hit Enter to add in more conclusions.

Title and Content Slide (Slide 34)

40. Create a Title and Content slide.
41. Add the title Conclusions.
42. Add the following content:
    - My hypothesis was (supported, partially supported, or not supported). Never say that you were "Right" or "wrong."
    - Offer some "real-life" applications of your findings.
    - Tell of any future research that you would like to do that's related to your work. (Then go back and delete any slides you did not use!)

Title and Content Slide (Slide 35)

43. Create a Title and Content slide.
44. Add the following content: Thank You.

Adding a Design Template

Now you'll add a design style theme to a student's presentation created with PJAS template.

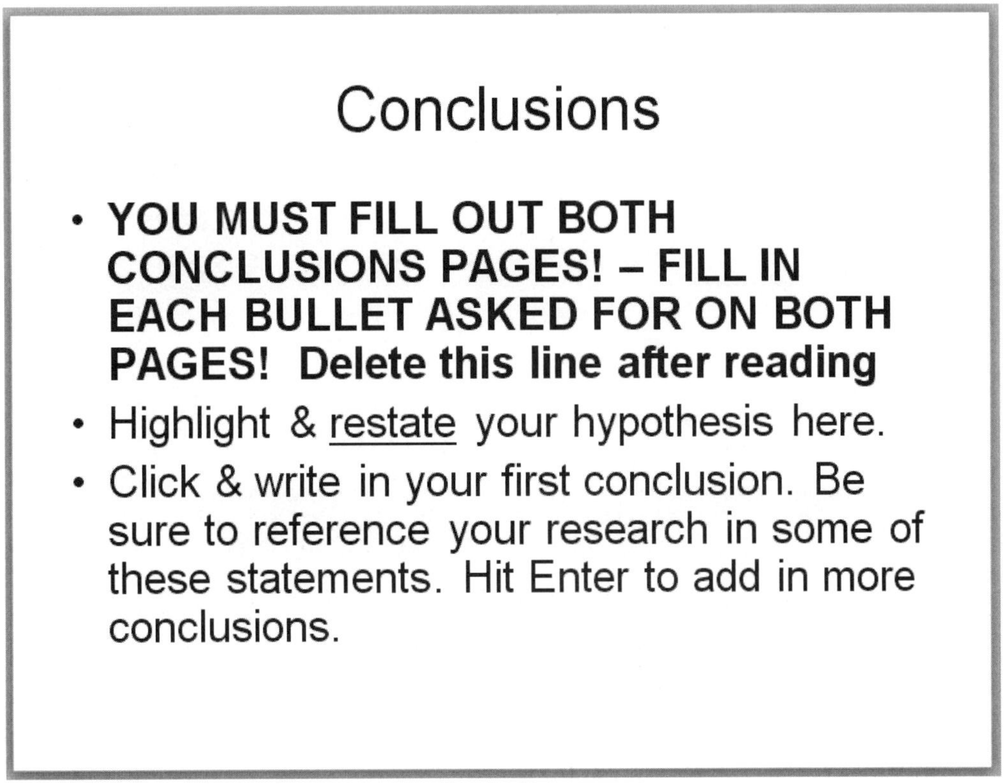

FIGURE 4.62 Template for Slide 33

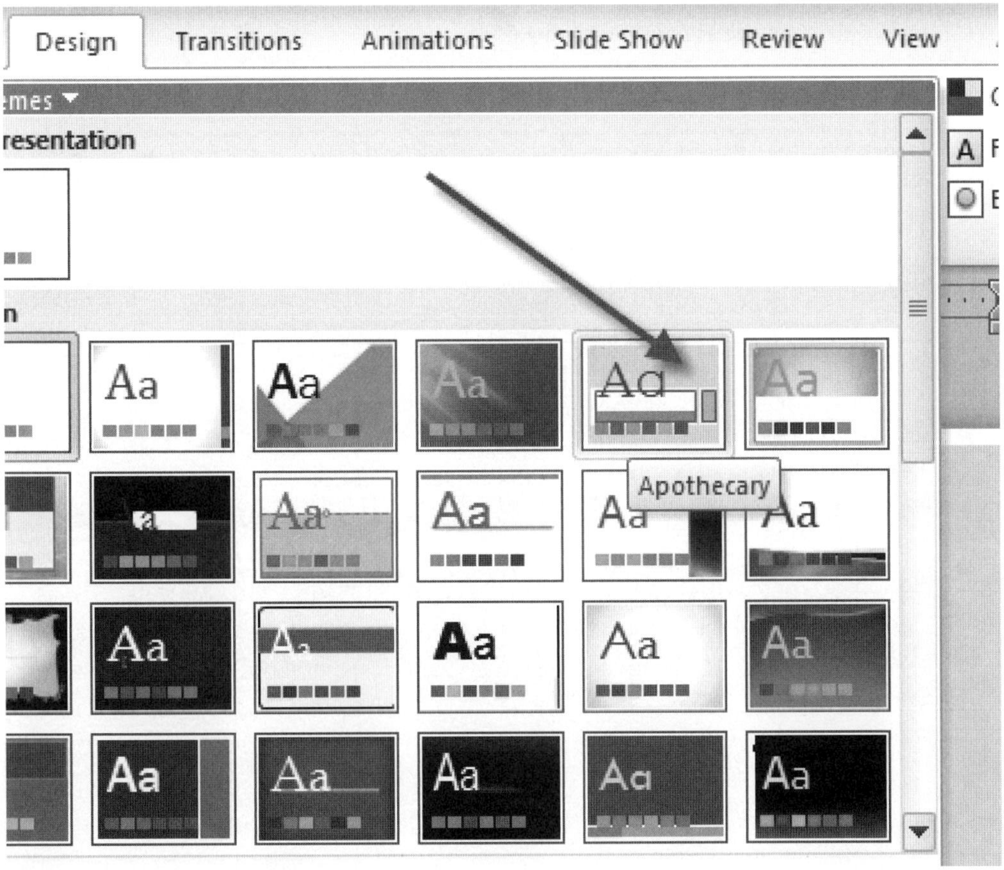

FIGURE 4.63 A Design Theme

FIGURE 4.64 Slides with This Design Theme

PDToolkit for *Microsoft® Office 2010 for Teachers*

Go to PDToolkit for **Microsoft® Office 2010 for Teachers** to locate the corresponding file in the Examples folder.

1. Open the PJAS_StudentExample_NoDesignTemplate.pptx file.
2. Click the Design tab. Click the More arrow in the Themes category and select the Apothecary theme (see Figure 4.63). All the slides should not have the Apothecary theme applied to them (see Figures 4.64 and 4.65).

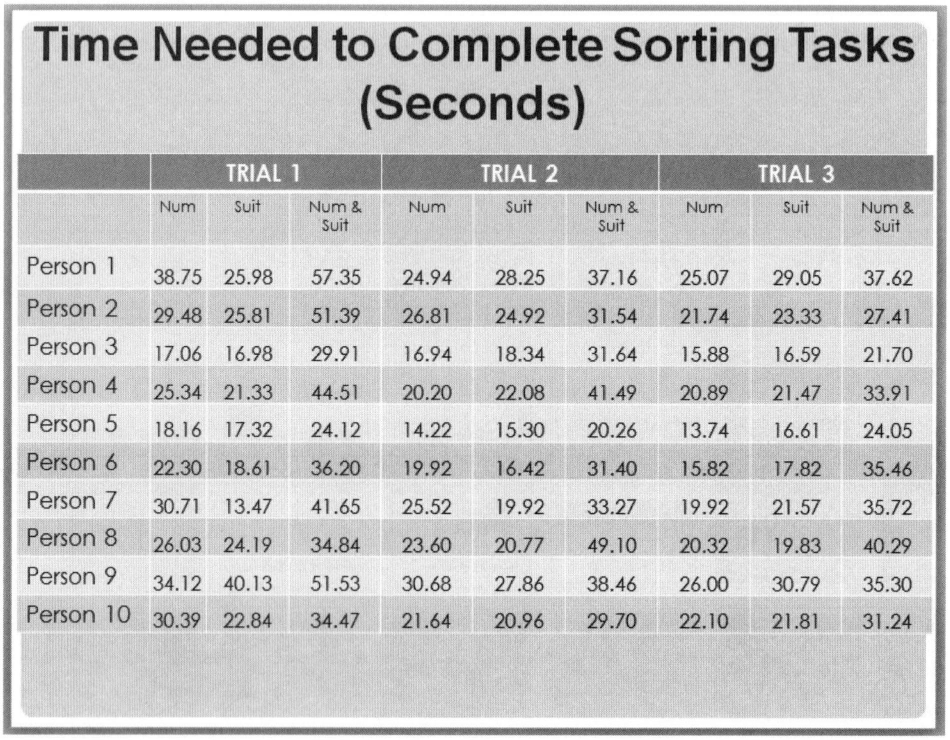

Time Needed to Complete Sorting Tasks (Seconds)

	TRIAL 1			TRIAL 2			TRIAL 3		
	Num	Suit	Num & Suit	Num	Suit	Num & Suit	Num	Suit	Num & Suit
Person 1	38.75	25.98	57.35	24.94	28.25	37.16	25.07	29.05	37.62
Person 2	29.48	25.81	51.39	26.81	24.92	31.54	21.74	23.33	27.41
Person 3	17.06	16.98	29.91	16.94	18.34	31.64	15.88	16.59	21.70
Person 4	25.34	21.33	44.51	20.20	22.08	41.49	20.89	21.47	33.91
Person 5	18.16	17.32	24.12	14.22	15.30	20.26	13.74	16.61	24.05
Person 6	22.30	18.61	36.20	19.92	16.42	31.40	15.82	17.82	35.46
Person 7	30.71	13.47	41.65	25.52	19.92	33.27	19.92	21.57	35.72
Person 8	26.03	24.19	34.84	23.60	20.77	49.10	20.32	19.83	40.29
Person 9	34.12	40.13	51.53	30.68	27.86	38.46	26.00	30.79	35.30
Person 10	30.39	22.84	34.47	21.64	20.96	29.70	22.10	21.81	31.24

FIGURE 4.65 Table Slide with This Design Theme

Sharing a Template

Once a teacher has made a template, there are a number of ways to distribute it to students. For example, the teacher can create an e-mail distribution list through which the template is sent as an attachment.

1. In PowerPoint click the File tab and then Save and Send.
2. Click the Send as Attachment button. The default e-mail program on your computer opens, and from it you can send the file.

A possible drawback to this approach is when you notice editing mistakes in your file after you send it. You must resend a corrected version, which may confuse some recipients. Additionally, recipients' inboxes can become full quickly.

An alternative approach that teachers can employ with PowerPoint 2010 is to use Windows Live services to distribute files.

First, a teacher creates a template (or any other type of file) for students, uploads it to SkyDrive of Windows Live Services (a space to manage files), and makes it available for students to view, download, and edit, if needed. The steps in the following section illustrate this example. Another way Windows Live Services may be used is for a teacher to upload a model template for students to view. Students then use Office Web Apps in Windows Live Services to create their own presentations. When a presentation is ready, they can share it with the teacher and other students. When sharing files, permissions can be set so that others (e.g., the teacher) can edit the file. Editing changes are reflected in the student's file. Once the presentation is complete, it can be downloaded to a computer. Even if a student does not have Office, he or she can use Office Web Apps, the files from which can then be downloaded by the instructor or someone who has the Office software.

In the following example, you'll use SkyDrive to upload a file and make it available for students to view and download.

1. Create a Windows Live login by going to https://login.live.com. The account creation process is simple and takes only a few minutes. After you create the account, Windows Live sends an e-mail to you. Use that e-mail to activate your account. Once the account is activated, you can access Windows Live Services, such as Hotmail, Messenger, and SkyDrive.
2. Log in to your account at https://login.live.com by typing the Windows Live ID (which you can find in the e-mail address you provided during account creation) and password (see Figure 4.66). Click the Sign In button.

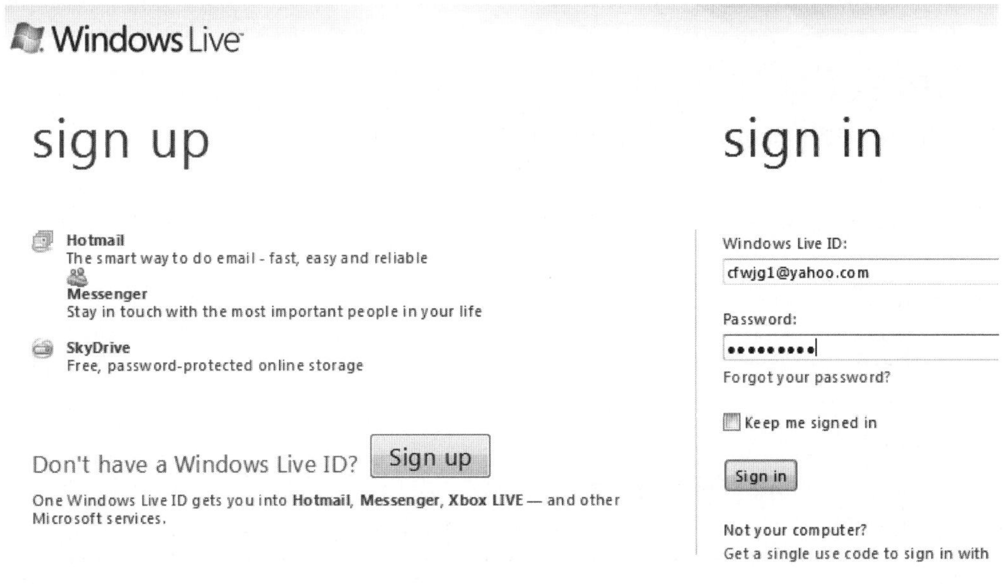

FIGURE 4.66 Windows Live Login

3. Once you are logged in, click the SkyDrive link to upload or download and otherwise manage files (see Figure 4.67).
4. Click Add Files (see Figure 4.68) to upload the PowerPoint template you created earlier.
5. In the Select a Folder area, create a new folder or access the My Documents folder in SkyDrive (see Figure 4.69).
6. Double-click My Documents to open it. You now see the area where you can drop documents (see Figure 4.70) into the My Documents folder. You can drag files from the local computer to this area, drop them, and they will be uploaded to SkyDrive.

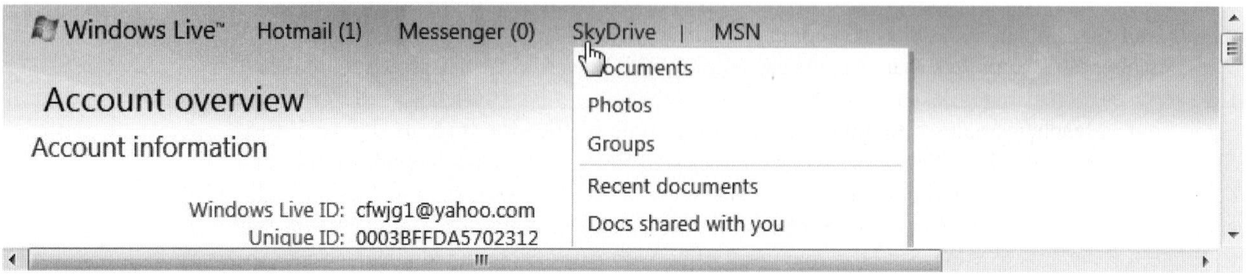

FIGURE 4.67 Accessing SkyDrive

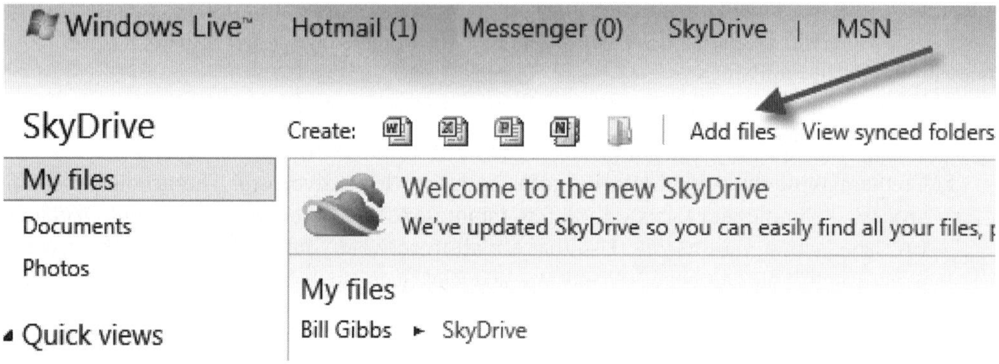

FIGURE 4.68 SkyDrive: Adding Files

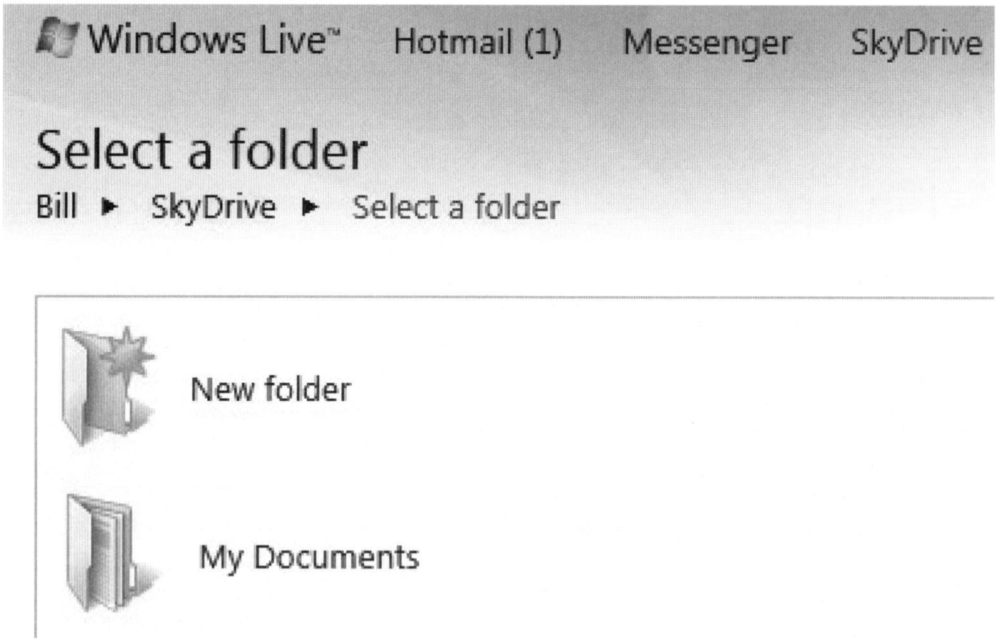

FIGURE 4.69 SkyDrive: Selecting a Folder

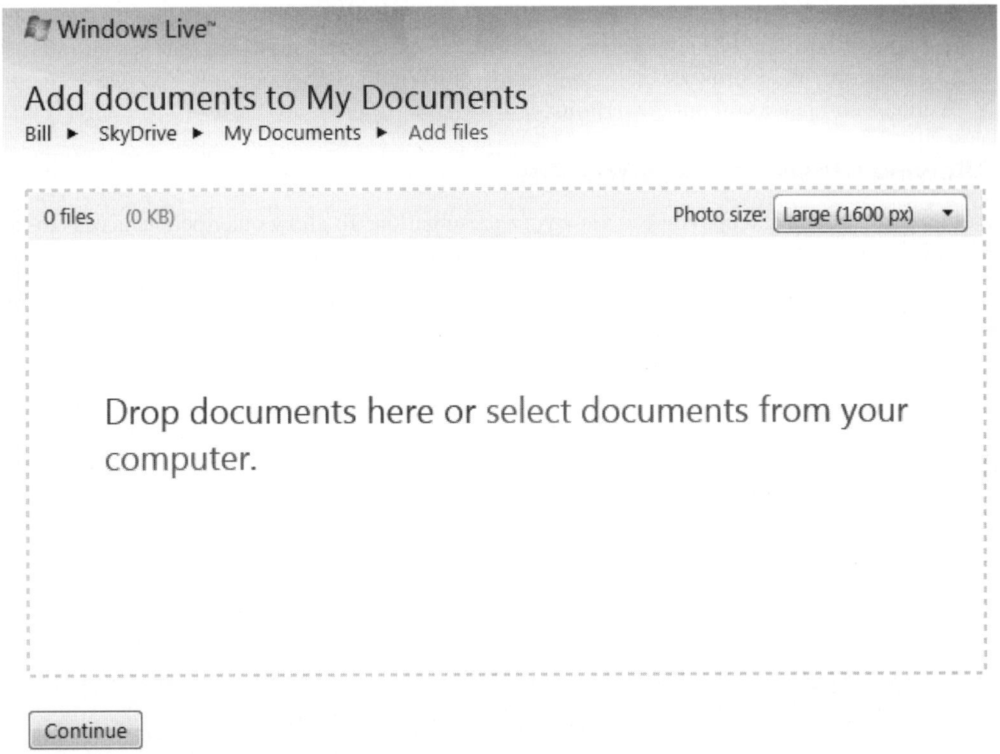

FIGURE 4.70 SkyDrive: Dropping Documents Here

7. In this example, use Windows Explore to locate the PJAS_StudentExample_DesignTemplate.pptx file on the local computer and then drag it from Explorer to the Drop Document Here space in SkyDrive (see Figure 4.71).
8. A copy of the file appears in SkyDrive (see Figure 4.72). Click Continue.

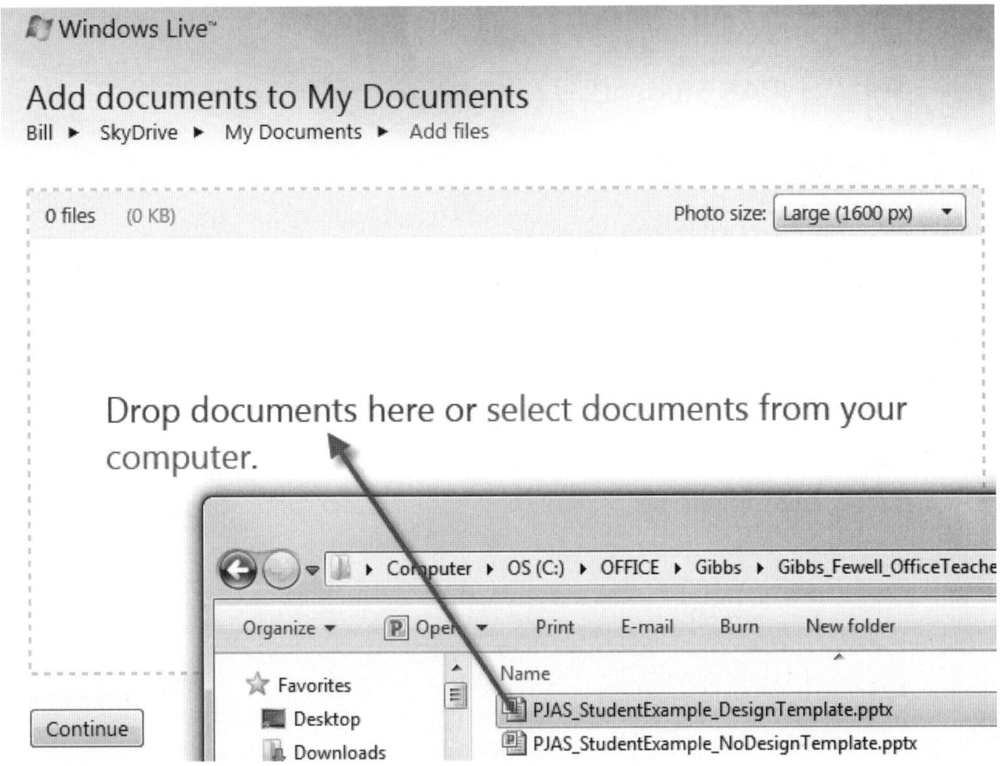

FIGURE 4.71 Dragging a File from Windows Explore to SkyDrive

9. You see a list of the files you uploaded to the SkyDrive My Documents folder (see Figure 4.73). You can now access the PowerPoint file from anywhere that has an Internet connection and a browser by logging in to your Windows Live account. You can even edit it on a computer without PowerPoint.

Allowing Others Access to Your File

At this point, no one except you can view your presentation. To allow other people access to the PJAS PowerPoint file, you need to provide them a link to your file.

10. Click Get a Link on the right side of the screen (see Figure 4.73). If you do not see Get a Link, a file might be selected. Notice in Figure 4.73 that neither presentation files are selected. To see the Get a Link option, click somewhere (e.g., on Name or Date Modified) on the screen to deselected the file.
11. There are two options for Get a Link. The first option makes the presentation available to only those with permission or those who sign in to Windows Live. The second option makes the presentation available to everyone. For this example, copy the Share with Everyone link. People will be able to only view the presentation, not edit it, unless you give them permission to do so.

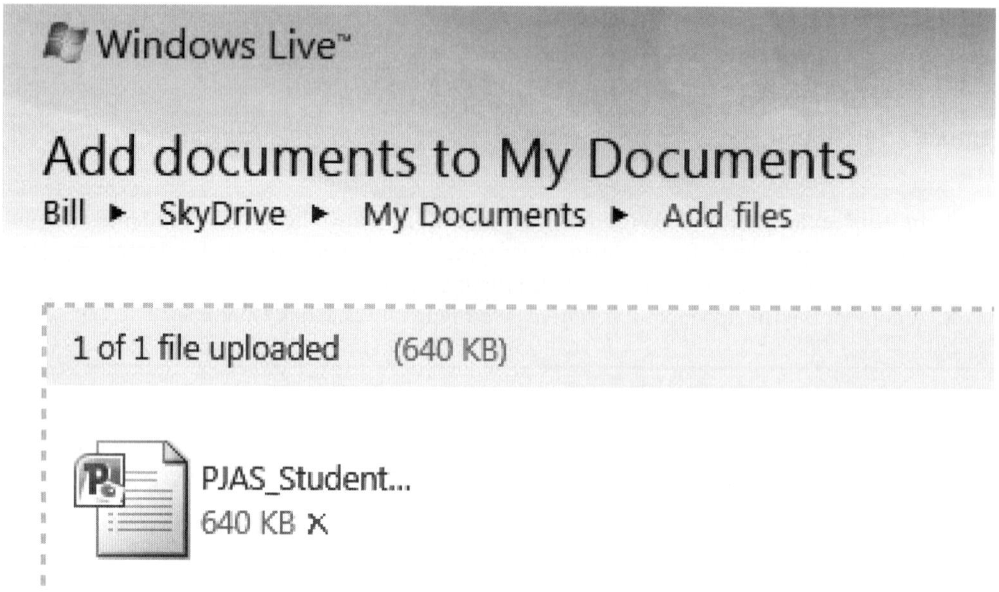

FIGURE 4.72 SkyDrive: An Uploaded Document

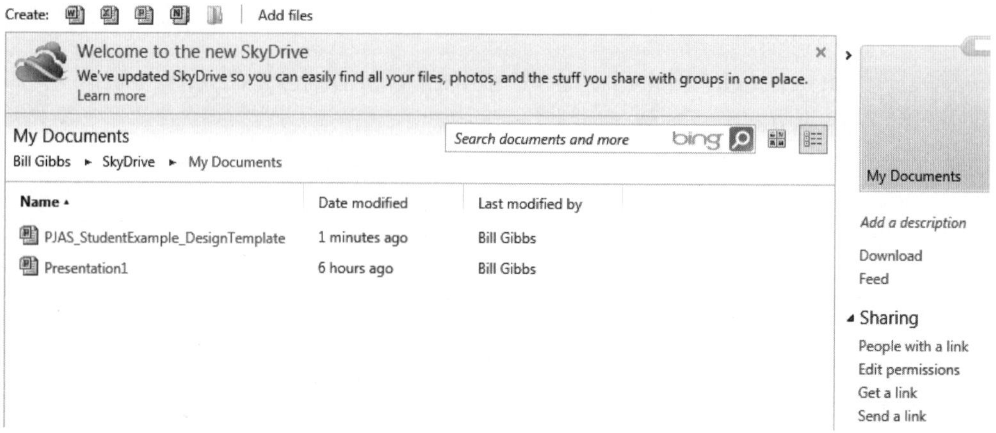

FIGURE 4.73 SkyDrive My Documents: List of Uploaded Documents

12. Click in the Share with Everyone box (see Figure 4.74) and copy the link (using Ctrl+C). E-mail the link to anyone who would like to view the presentation or download it.
13. When someone gets the link, he or she can click it to access the folder (My Documents) in your SkyDrive space (see Figure 4.75). Alternatively, he or she can copy the link and paste it in the address bar of the browser.
14. In your SkyDrive space, a person (the visitor) can click on the file name (PJAS_StudentExample_DesignTemplate.pptx) to open it in View in Browser mode (see Figure 4.76). To close out this mode and go back to SkyDrive, click the File tab and select Close. To download the file, click the File tab and select Download a Copy.

PDToolkit for *Microsoft® Office 2010 for Teachers*

Go to PDToolkit for **Microsoft® Office 2010 for Teachers** to locate the corresponding file in the Examples folder.

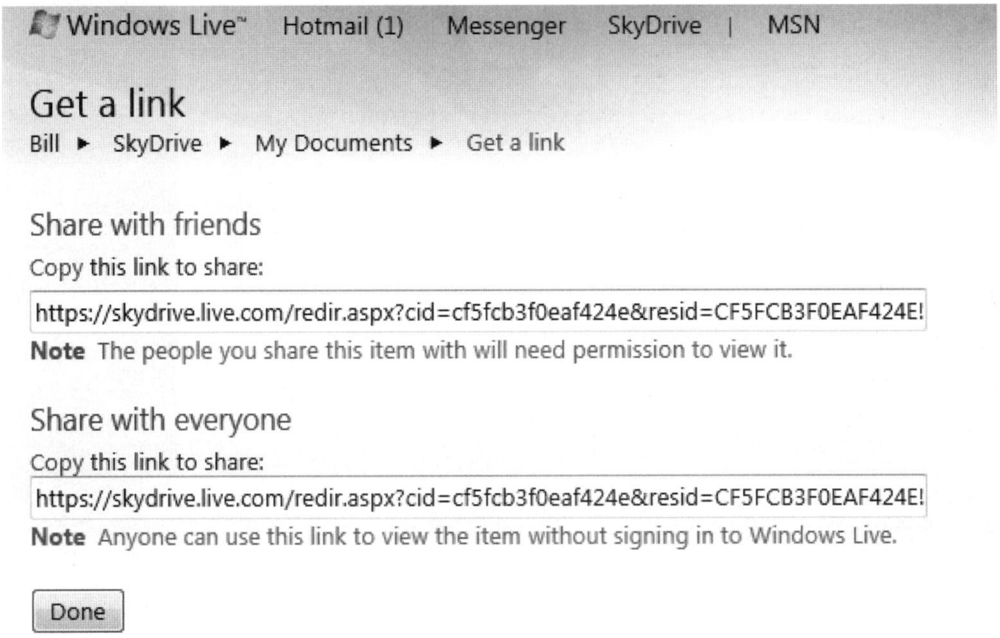

FIGURE 4.74 Sharing a PowerPoint File

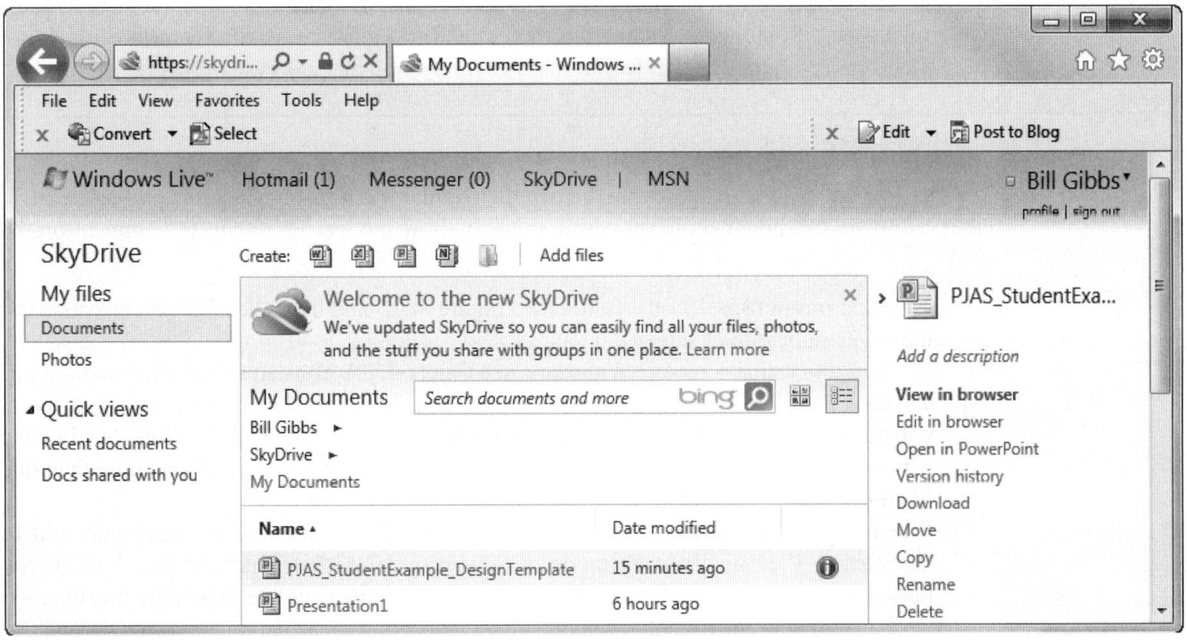

FIGURE 4.75 Sharing a PowerPoint File

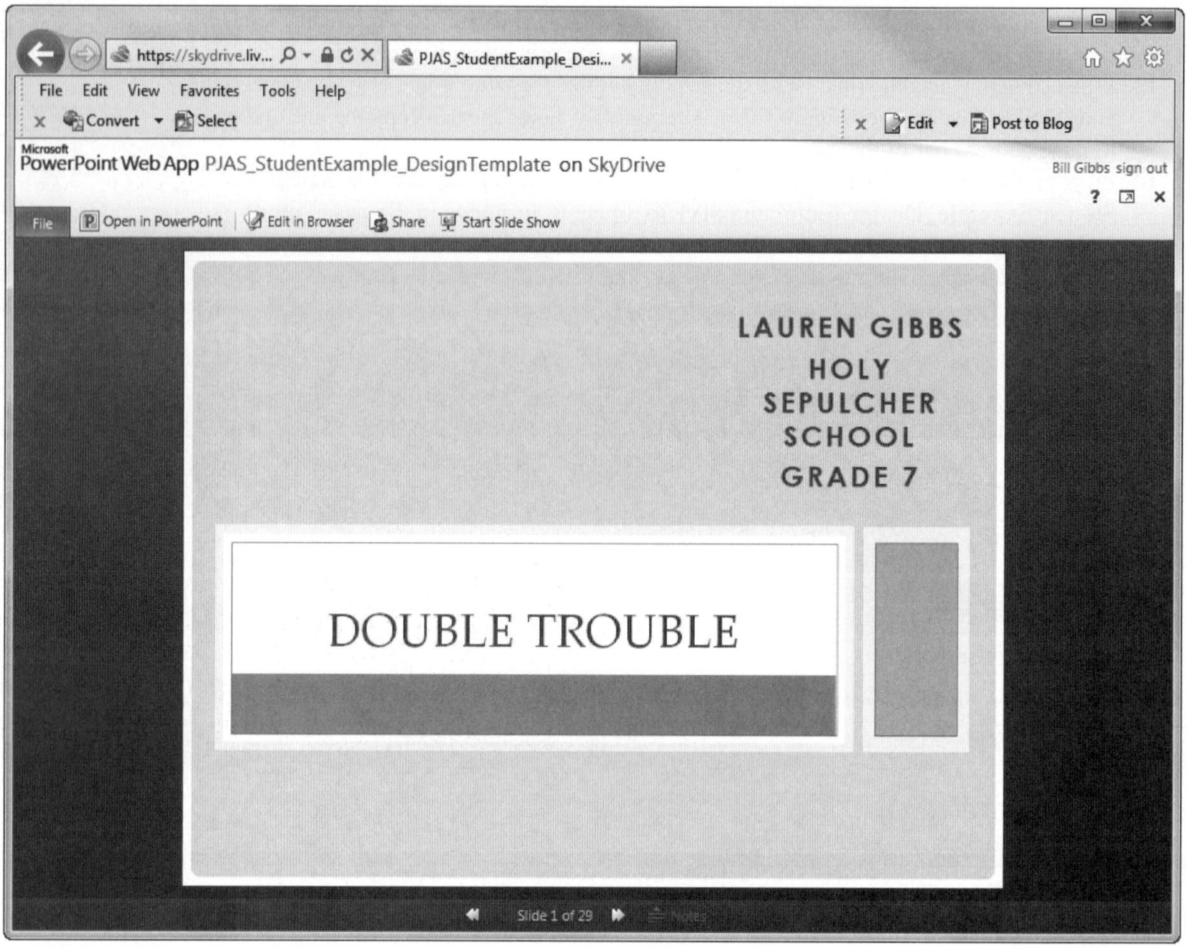

FIGURE 4.76 PowerPoint in a Browser

15. To view the file in the Slide Show mode, click Start Slide Show. The presentation displays in the browser as a slide show (see Figure 4.77). When making presentations at meetings such as PJAS, students could store their files in SkyDrive and run them in Slide Show mode on any computer that has an Internet connection and a browser.

Setting Permissions

You can set permissions to allow specific people to edit a file. This may not be appropriate in all cases. However, a student could set permissions to allow the teacher to edit or comment on the work.

16. To set permissions, select the folder (see Figure 4.78) and then click Edit Permissions (on the lower-right side of screen).

The Edit Permissions screen appears (see Figure 4.79). You can select which individuals can view the file and which ones can edit it. Notice in Figure 4.79 that one person (Lauren Gibbs) has permission to edit. Additionally, people who may be added as friends will have permission to edit. Permissions get applied to folders, not files. If you have more than one file in a folder, then people will be able to view those files as well.

17. When Lauren Gibbs, the person to whom you gave edit permissions, clicks on Edit in Browser in View in Browser mode, a PowerPoint interface displays that Lauren can make changes to the presentation (see Figure 4.80). This could be especially useful when working collaboratively with someone on a PowerPoint presentation.

FIGURE 4.77 Slide Show View in a Browser

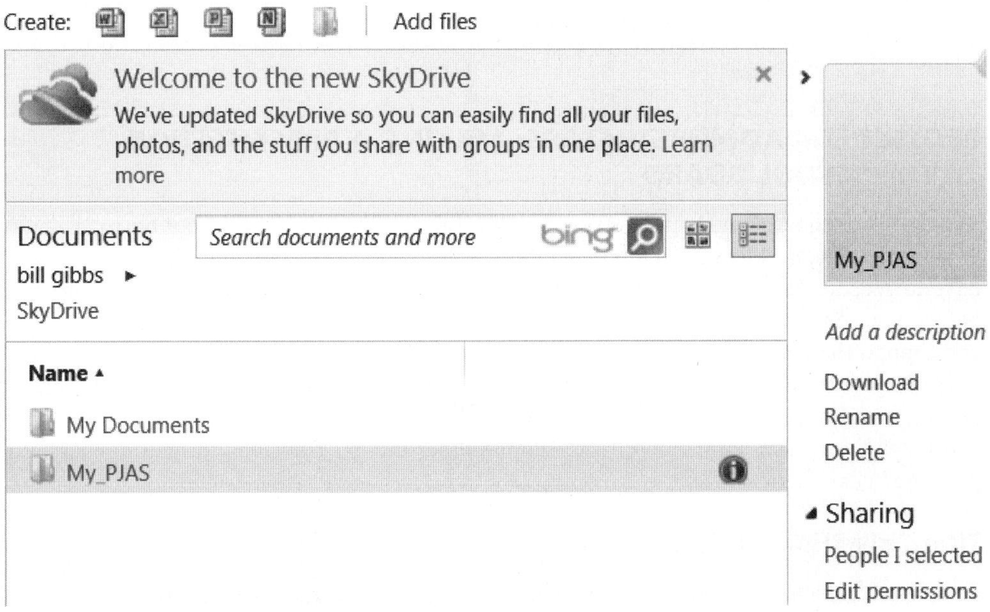

FIGURE 4.78 Folder Permissions

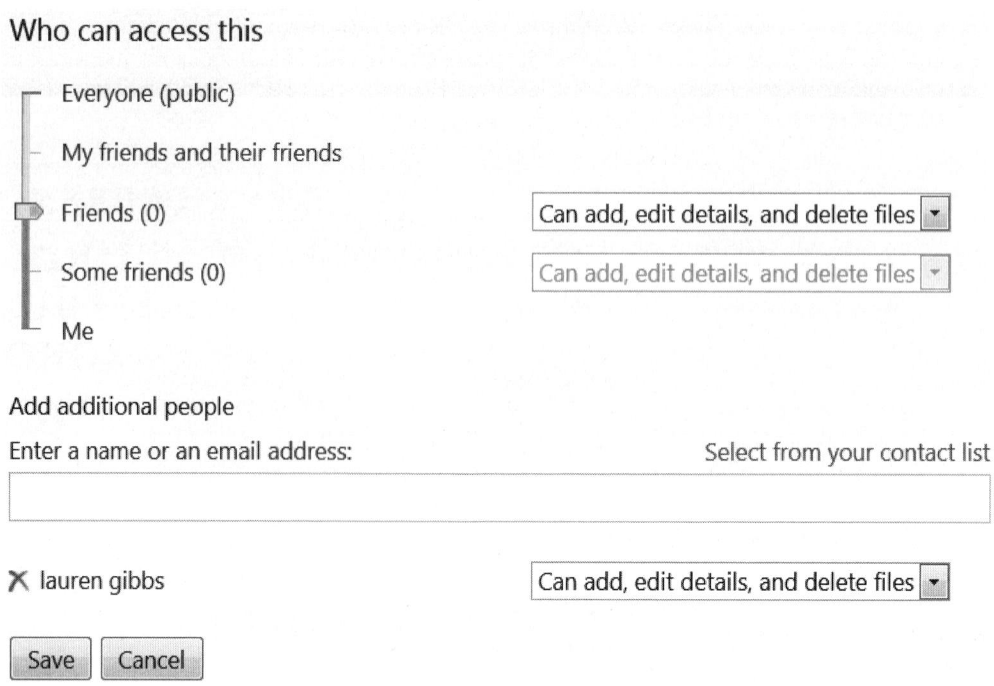

FIGURE 4.79 Editing Permissions

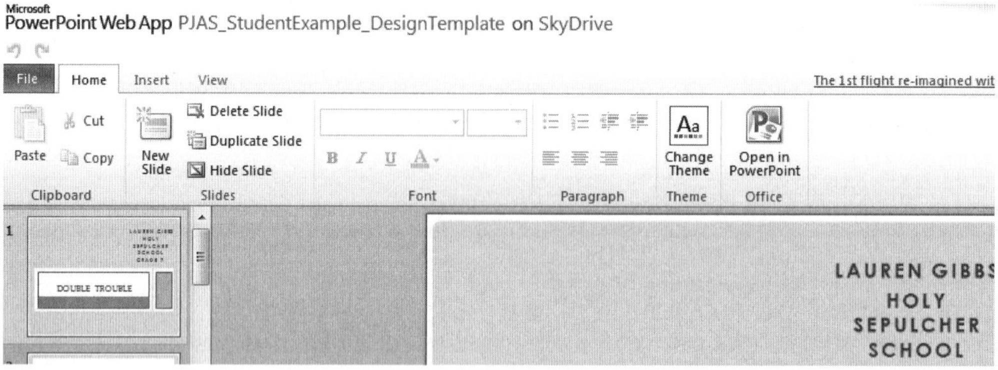

FIGURE 4.80 Editing in a Browser

PROJECT FOR ADMINISTRATORS: MAKING A PRESENTATION TO THE SCHOOL BOARD

Suppose your superintendent asked you to deliver a presentation to the school board. The topic is your plan for establishing new graduation requirements. The superintendent gives you two days to prepare and states emphatically, "Dazzle them!" You begin to consider all the tasks before you, one of which is creating high-quality, easy-to-understand visuals that illustrate and support the points of your talk. Knowing that the room is equipped with a computer and a video projector as well as a smartboard, you decide to develop your visuals using PowerPoint 2010. PowerPoint will enable you to create a visual slide show with images, colored charts and graphs, text, and animation effects, among other things. The steps for getting started are presented next.

Title Only Slide (Slide 1)

To view a completed version of the school board presentation, open SchoolBoard_Complete.pptx.

1. Open PowerPoint. A blank presentation opens, with one title slide. If you do not see a blank title slide, select Layout from the Slides group of the Home tab and click Title Slide.

2. Insert text in the title slide. Click inside the Click to Add Title box and type the title of the presentation: Level Five. With the text box selected and the border as a solid line, click the small down arrow in the Font Size box on the Formatting toolbar. Select a text size of 105.
3. Click anywhere outside the text object to deselect it.
4. Add a subtitle by clicking inside the *Click to Add Subtitle* box and type Board Work Session *By Lauren M. Gibbs.*
5. Select a theme from the Themes group on the Design tab. Apply a theme of your choice by clicking its icon. Figure 4.81 shows an example of a completed slide.

PDToolkit for *Microsoft® Office 2010 for Teachers*

Go to PDToolkit for **Microsoft® Office 2010 for Teachers** to locate the corresponding file in the Examples folder.

Title Only Slide (Slide 2)

6. Add a new slide by clicking New Slide or pressing Ctrl+M.
7. Select Title Only.
8. Click in the Click to Add Title box and enter Our Future Goals.
9. Create a text box where you will place the text describing the presentation's purpose. Select the Text Box tool in the Text group of the Insert tab. The mouse cursor changes to a vertical line when you click on the Text Box tool. Click in the slide pane where the text box begins and, while holding down the left mouse button, drag it to the right side of the slide pane. Release the mouse button, and a blank text box appears.
10. Type the purpose of the presentation in the text box:

    Establish new graduation requirements and standards that ensure high levels of student achievement versus traditional time and attendance requirements.

    Our challenge . . .

    Invent a new system that prepares ALL graduates for society.

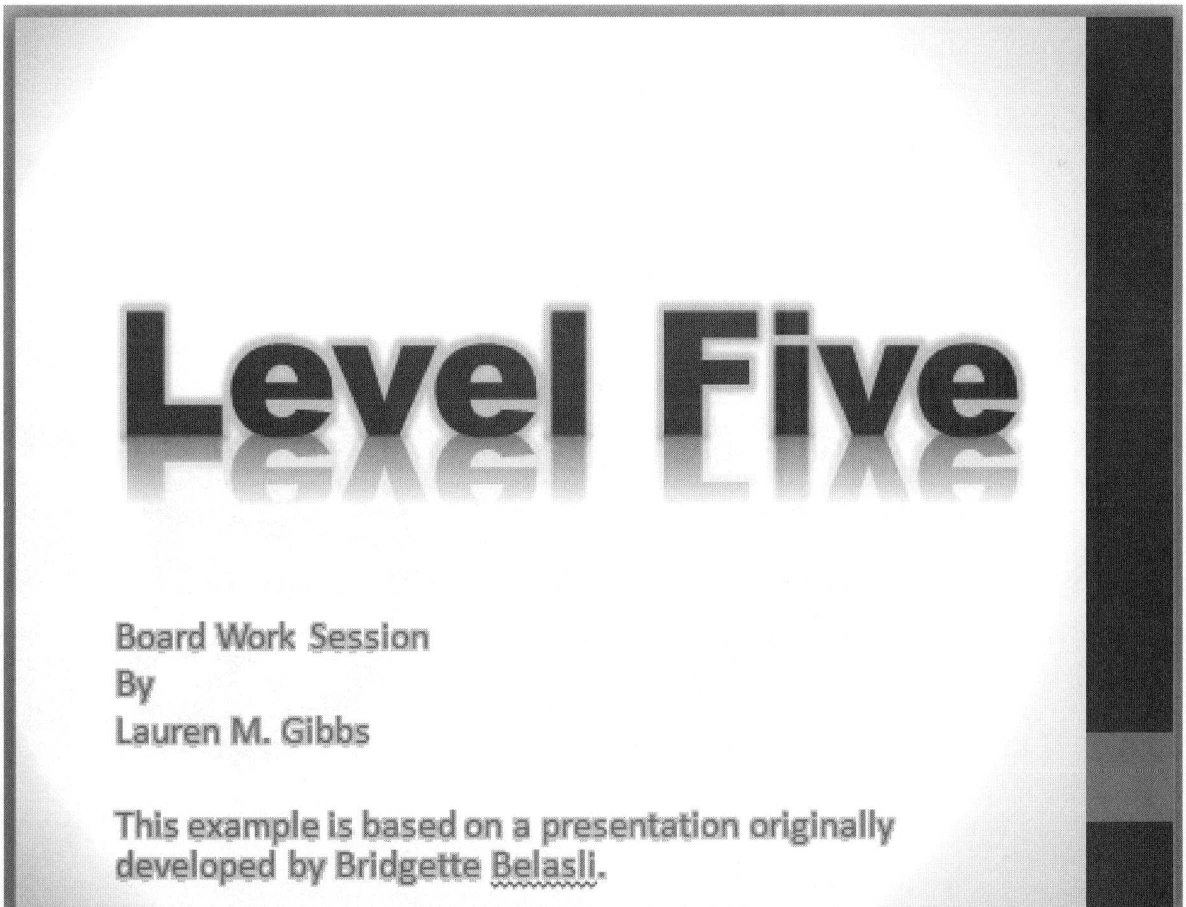

FIGURE 4.81 A Completed Title Slide

11. With the text box selected and the border as a solid line, click the small down arrow in the Font box on the Formatting toolbar. Select Arial font by clicking on the font name.
12. With the text box selected and the border as a solid line, click the small down arrow in the Font Size box on the Formatting toolbar. Select a text size of 24.

Title and Content Slide (Slide 3)

1. Add a new Title and Content slide.
2. Click in the Click to Add Title box and type the title Time-Based System.
3. Click inside the Click to Add Text box, type Credits based on:, and press Enter.
4. Indent subbullets. With the cursor positioned at the beginning of the line, press the Tab key. Type the following bullet items and press Enter after each line:
   - Time spent in class
   - Grade of D or better
   - Lack of consistency or uniform expectations for performance to earn diploma

   Each item will indent under the Credits Based On text.
5. Select the three indented bullet items. Right-click in the selected area and select Bullets and then click the checkmark bullets cell.
6. Click anywhere outside the text box to deselect the text.
7. Select the Insert tab and then click Clip Art. Enter a search term or key word (e.g., education) in the Search For box of the task pane to search for an image.
8. When PowerPoint retrieves the images that relate to your search term, click one of them to insert it onto the slide.
9. Position and resize the image on the slide. Figure 4.82 shows an example of a completed slide.

Two Content Slide (Slide 4)

1. Add a new Two Content slide.
2. Click inside the Click to Add Title box and type the title Performance-Based System.

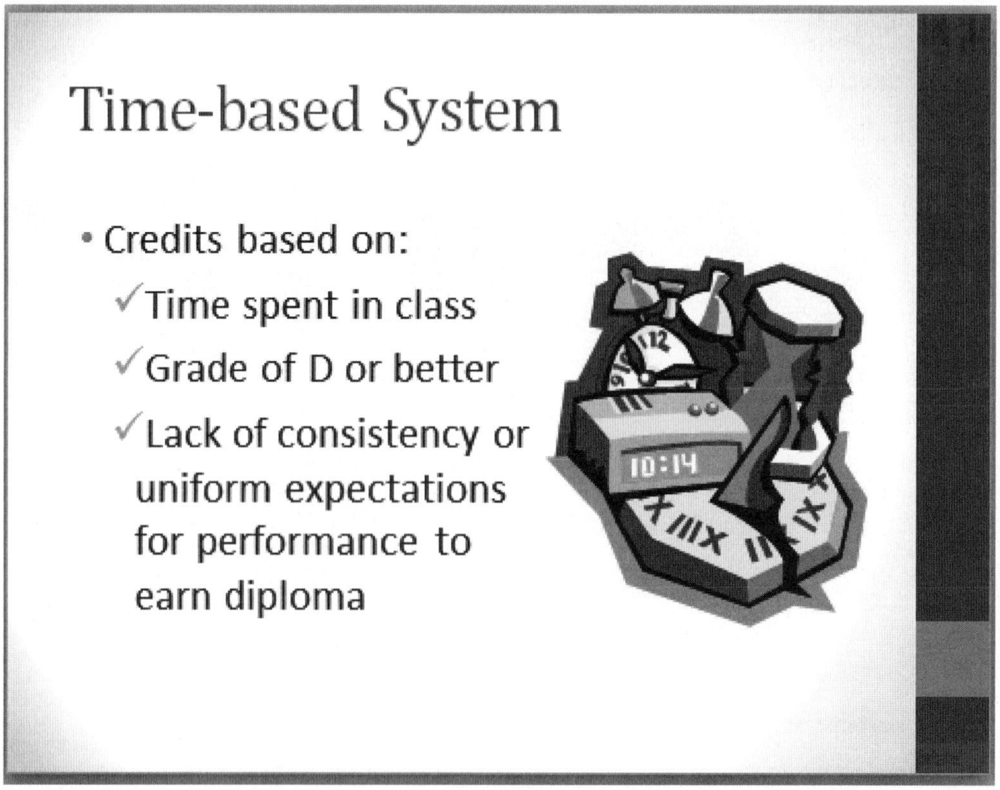

FIGURE 4.82 Completed Title and Content

3. Click inside the Click to Add Text box and type the following text list:
   - Students demonstrate proficiency in all graduation requirements.
   - Seat time and passing grade no longer earns a degree.
4. Add a picture or clip art to the slide. Click the Clip Art icon in the content area on the right side of the slide to add a clip art image.
5. Position the picture or clip art on the slide by clicking in its center and, while holding down the left mouse button, drag it to a desired location. Figure 4.83 shows an example of a completed slide.

Title Slide (Slide 5)

At this point in the school board presentation, the topic focus changes, and you can indicate this shift in focus by using a title slide.

1. Add a new Title slide.
2. Click in the Click to Add Title box and type the title Why Change? In this example, the font size is 80.
3. Set the font style to bold and the text to shadowed by clicking the Bold (B) and Shadow (S) icons.
4. Click in the Click to Add Subtitle box and type Some important reasons. In this example, the font size is 36. Set the font style to bold.

Title and Content Slide (Slide 6)

The next slide states reasons change is needed. This slide will have a Title and Content layout. Because there is an existing slide with a Title and Content layout, you will use the Slide Sorter to copy and paste it.

1. Click the Slide Sorter View button located in the lower-right portion of the PowerPoint workspace to enter the Slide Sorter.
2. Click the Title and Content slide (e.g., slide 3) to select it.

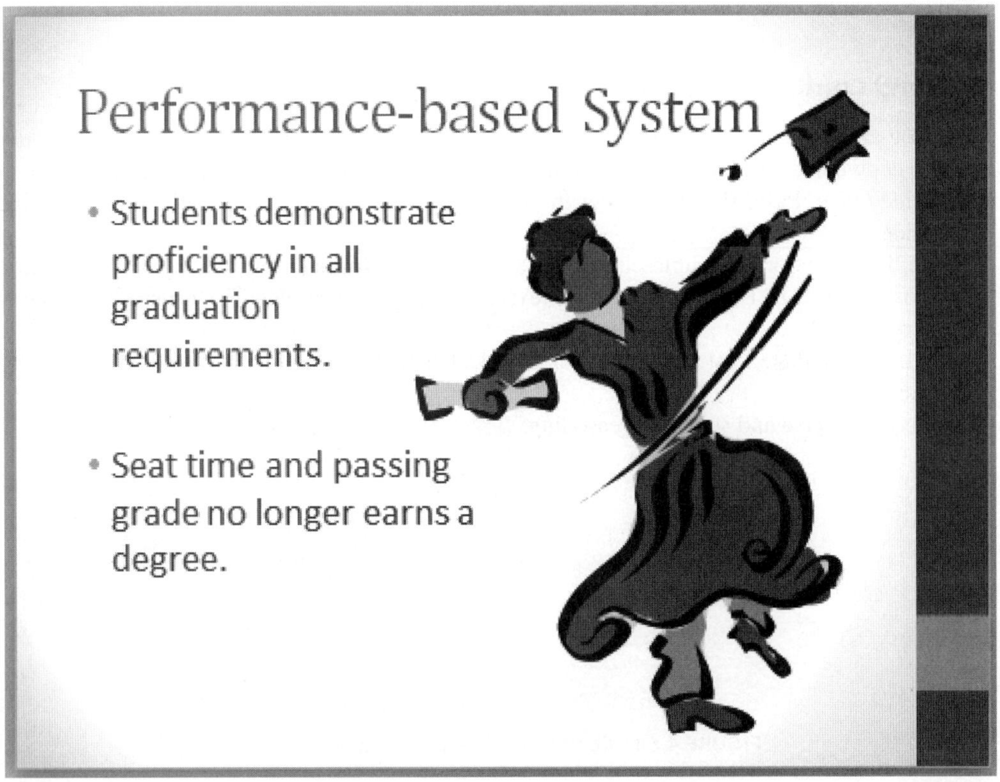

FIGURE 4.83 Completed Title and Content

3. With the slide selected, choose Copy. Click the last slide in the presentation and select Paste. There are now six slides.
4. Double-click the slide to exit the Slide Sorter and return to Normal view.
5. Click on the Title box to select it. Click on its border again, and it changes to a solid line. Press the Delete key, and the text changes to Click to Add Title. Type the new title America Is Unprepared.
6. Click the bulleted list text box to select it. Press the Delete key, and the text changes to Click to Add Text. Type a new list, entering the following items:
   - ". . . wherever the people are well informed they can be trusted with their own government . . ." Thomas Jefferson. (The Jefferson Monticello)
   - Provide students with a proper background in history, economics, government, language, literature, science, technology, philosophy, and the arts.
7. Add clip art.

Title and Content Slide (Slide 7)

1. Add a new Title and Content slide.
2. Click in the Click to Add Title box and enter the following title: Skills Needed: Critical Thinking & Problem Solving.
3. Click the Insert Chart icon, and the Insert Chart box appears.
4. On the left side of the Insert Chart box, select Bar; then under Chart Subtype, select the Cluster Bar format by clicking the appropriate icon.
5. Click OK to set the chart options. An Excel worksheet opens, with sample data.
6. In the data sheet, type (%) of Jobs Requiring Skills in the Category 1 cell of column A and (%) of Today's Workforce with Skills in the Category 2 cell of column A. Adjust the column widths as needed (see Figure 4.84).
7. Enter three time periods for the data series: 1960 in the data series column B, row 1; 1985 in the data series column C, row 1; and 2005 in the data series column D, row 1.
8. Enter the values 10, 30, and 60 in cells B2, C2, and D2, respectively.
9. Enter the values 4, 14, and 20 in cells B3, C3, and D3, respectively.
10. Set the Range rectangle so that it encompasses cell A1 through cell D3 (see Figure 4.84).
11. Close the worksheet by clicking Close on the upper-right corner. Figure 4.85 shows an example of a completed slide.

Title and Content Slides (Slide 8 and 9)

1. You already have a slide (slide 6) with a Title and Content layout, so use the Slide Sorter to copy it and paste it. Because you need two more slides with this layout, paste the copied slide twice. Paste the slides after the last slide (slide 7). The presentation now has nine slides.
2. In the Slide Sorter, double-click slide 8 to return to Normal view. Click on slide 8's title box to select it. Delete the existing text and type The Five New Performance Standards Are.
3. Click the bulleted list text box to select it. Delete the existing text and enter the following items:
   - Quantitative and scientific reasoning
   - Communication (including a culminating project)

	A	B	C	D
1		1960	1985	2005
2	(%) of Jobs Requiring Skills	10	30	60
3	(%) of Today's Workforce with Skills	4	14	20
4	Category 3	3.5	1.8	3
5	Category 4	4.5	2.8	5

Sheet1

FIGURE 4.84 Completed Title and Content

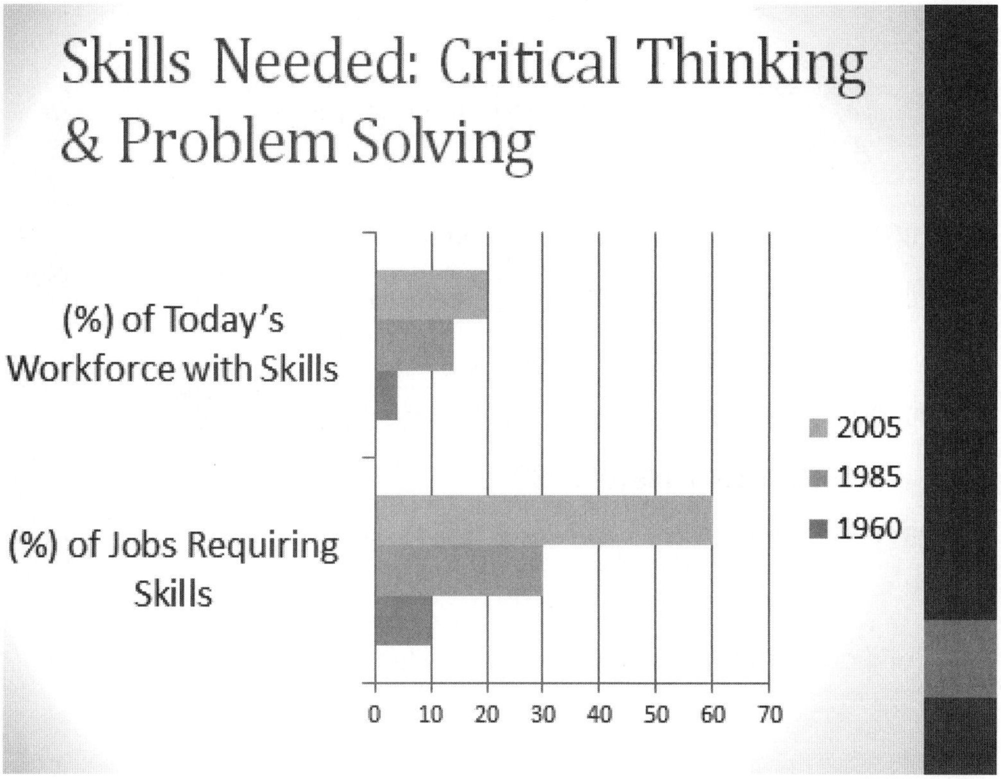

FIGURE 4.85 A Completed Slide

- Citizenship (including a service learning component)
- Culture
- School-to-career (including an education and future plans and a field experience)

4. Add clip art.
5. Repeat steps 2–4 for slide 9. Enter the following title: What Will Be Done to Ensure That All Students Meet These Standards?
6. Enter the following list items:
   - Students who perform poorly on the 4th, 7th, and 10th grade WASL exams will be identified for additional support.
   - Support programs will exist in K–12.
   - Students will be given multiple chances to show they can meet the standards.

Two Content Slide (Slide 10)

To complete the presentation, add one more slide with a Two Content layout. Again, use the Slide Sorter to copy and paste a slide.

1. Click the Slide Sorter View button to enter the Slide Sorter.
2. Click a Two Content slide (e.g., slide 4) to select it. Copy the slide and paste it after the last slide.
3. Replace the text in the title text box with Gradual Phases.
4. Enter the following bulleted items:
   - 2008 Communication Requirements
   - 2009 Quantitative and Scientific Reasoning Requirements + Requirements for 2008
   - 2010 Citizenship and Culture Requirements + Requirements for 2009
   - 2011 School-to-Career and Life Skills Requirements + Requirements for 2010
   - Certificate of Mastery required for Graduation

Figure 4.86 shows an example of a completed slide.

FIGURE 4.86 A Completed Slide

PDToolkit for *Microsoft® Office 2010 for Teachers*

Go to PDToolkit for **Microsoft® Office 2010 for Teachers** to locate additional Web Activities for this chapter in the Web Activities folder.

Additional Activities Using PowerPoint

- Have students create a genealogy presentation that includes various font types and styles, design templates, and clip art that complement the older-style photographs that students scan and include in the presentation. The presentations should depict at least one generation, beginning with the most recent generation.
- Have students present a book report on *Charlotte's Web.* The presentation should include photographs or clip art of all the animals depicted in the book.
- For a science project, have students make an anemometer. While making this device, students should document the process with a camera and notes. Compile the notes and photographs in a PowerPoint presentation and present it to the class. The presentation may also include video of the anemometer rotating.
- Create a class or school presentation portfolio. Have students collect photographs, write stories and poems, and create drawings representative of their positive feelings and attitudes about the class or school. Incorporate the photographs, stories, drawings, and so forth into a self-running presentation displayed in public areas (e.g., school lounge). The presentation may also include audio and video segments of school activities, students, and teachers.
- Create an art exhibit presentation. Scan students' drawings and artwork into a PowerPoint presentation. Save the presentation as a webpage and distribute it on the Web for parents, teachers, and classmates to view.
- Assign a design theme and give a background color to only one slide in a presentation.
- Assign a design theme to a presentation and assign a different template to one slide.
- Create a five-slide presentation that includes linked action buttons.
- Create a slide that imports a chart created in Excel.

SUMMING IT UP

This chapter presents many fundamentals to help you get started with PowerPoint. You created a few presentations consisting of varying slide layouts. The slides contained text, clip art, and a chart. We discussed saving presentations in presentation (.pptx) and how to use Windows Live to upload PowerPoint files to the Web.

References

Delahunty, J. (2007). *How to play MOV files.* Retrieved July 18, 2011, from www.afterdawn.com/guides/archive/how_to_play_mov_files.cfm.

Dick, W., Carey, L., & Carey, J.O. (2008). *The systematic design of instruction.* Boston: Allyn & Bacon.

Thomas Jefferson Monticello and University of Virginia. (N.D.). *Quotations on education.* Retrieved July 22, 2011, from www.monticello.org/site/jefferson/quotations-education.

Wong, Y.-L. (2009). *Digital media primer: Digital audio, video, imaging and multimedia programming.* Upper Saddle River, NJ: Prentice Hall.

5 EXCEL 2010

Chapter Outline

WHAT YOU ARE GOING TO LEARN

At the completion of this chapter you will be able to:

- Start Excel and create a new workbook suitable for use in a variety of student learning activities
- Navigate the Excel workspace
- Add, modify, and manipulate data in a worksheet
- Chart worksheet data
- Add worksheets to a workbook
- Add formulas and functions in a worksheet
- Save a workbook
- Save workbooks as Web documents
- Print a workbook

CHAPTER OVERVIEW

This chapter provides an introduction to Excel 2010. It focuses on Excel fundamentals and how to apply them to a variety of learning activities. The various activities for educators and students present instructions on how to use many of Excel's tools to create workbooks and edit and manipulate data in worksheets. The exercises in this chapter give specific examples and step-by-step instructions for using Excel to accomplish a variety of tasks that you perform regularly. Studying the chapter contents and working through the activities will enable you to create workbooks suitable for many classroom learning activities.

HOW YOU CAN USE EXCEL

Microsoft Excel can be used in innovative ways to support various educational activities that benefit students, teachers, and school administrators. This section examines ways in which Excel can be used to support educational activities in relation to types of learning outcomes and the National Educational Technology Standards for Students. Looking first at types of learning, the ways in which Excel can be used by students include the following:

- *Knowledge*—(a) Students can create their own Excel worksheets of historical facts, vocabulary words, multiplication tables, or science facts. As they read and study, they can enter these facts into the worksheet. (b) Data in the worksheets could then be linked across applications to create electronic flashcards within PowerPoint, or they could be used to create printed flashcards in Word. (c) Students can create worksheets that list all the states in the United States, the date when each state became part of the union, and the population of each state.
- *Comprehension*—(a) Students can create book or laboratory reports that include data tables from Excel that help them interpret results and explain a topic or experiment. (b) Using a worksheet based on state information, students could summarize state data and contrast one state with another.
- *Application*—(a) Students can collect precipitation data for specific regions and, after examining these data, classify regions as low-, moderate-, or heavy-precipitation areas. They could then assess whether there are relationships between the data and regional characteristics, such as population, employment, and recreational activities.
- *Analysis*—(a) Students could use Excel to project costs for a summer vacation traveling from their home town to Yellowstone National Park. (b) Based on the travel data collected, students could make inferences about the fastest route, the least expensive route, and arrival time.
- *Synthesis*—(a) Students could integrate participation data, temperature data, and population density for specific regions of the United States to formulate projections about the most livable areas in the country.
- *Evaluation*—(a) Students could make recommendations about the best cars or bicycles to purchase, based on data (cost, safety features, and so on) entered into a worksheet.

NETS FOR TEACHERS*

Excel can be utilized in the classroom to address the following standards:

1. *Facilitate and Inspire Student Learning and Creativity*—Teachers use their knowledge of subject matter, teaching and learning, and technology to facilitate experiences that advance student learning, creativity, and innovation in both face-to-face and virtual environments.
2. *Design and Develop Digital-Age Learning Experiences and Assessments*—Teachers design, develop, and evaluate authentic learning experiences and assessment incorporating contemporary tools and resources to maximize content learning in context and to develop the knowledge, skills, and attitudes identified in the NETS•S.
3. *Model Digital-Age Work and Learning*—Teachers exhibit knowledge, skills, and work processes representative of an innovative professional in a global and digital society.

NETS FOR STUDENTS*

Applications of Excel to educational activities could address the following:

- *Creativity and Innovation*—Students demonstrate creative and innovative thinking, construct knowledge, and develop innovative materials and processes using technology.
- *Communication and Collaboration*—Students use mediated materials to communicate and work collaboratively and to support the learning of others.
- *Research and Information Fluency*—Students apply digital tools to gather, evaluate, and use information.
- *Critical Thinking, Problem Solving, and Decision Making*—Students use critical thinking skills to plan and conduct research, manage projects, solve problems, and make informed decisions using appropriate digital tools and resources.

WHAT IS NEW IN EXCEL

The Excel Ribbon replaced many of the menus and toolbars of earlier versions. The associated commands and functions have been grouped under tabs intended to help you get your work done more quickly. The organization of tabs is based on the type of activity you might perform when working with data and worksheets.

Some new and useful features of Excel 2010 include the ability to customize the Ribbon. You can now add your own tabs and groups to the Ribbon. The Backstage view provides an area to access frequently performed tasks related to managing files, such as opening, saving, and sharing files; printing; and document properties. Excel has improved charting capabilities. The number of data points that can be created is limited only to computer memory. Additionally, there are more themes and styles to help you present data professionally. For additional information about Excel features, see the What's New section of Microsoft Office Excel Help.

ABOUT EXCEL

Excel is a tool that you and your students can use to record, organize, and analyze information. With Excel, you can perform mathematical calculations, sort data, and produce charts and graphs to visually represent information, among other things.

You can use Excel for many student learning and classroom management activities. Teachers can create Excel workbooks that contain information about student learning progress, and they can create electronic grade books for entering and calculating student performance scores. In addition, they can create worksheets to record and maintain information about classroom equipment and supply costs. School administrators can use Excel for scheduling, budgets, research, and data analysis. Students can use Excel as an electronic data recorder to help collect, record, and analyze information and data sets. They can manage projects with it. When given an assignment that requires a team effort, students can log project details and progress to ensure that the team is on task and on schedule. These are only a few applications of Excel. As you become familiar with it, you are likely to find many more innovative ways to incorporate it into your classroom management and student learning activities.

WORKING WITH EXCEL

The primary purpose of this chapter is to introduce fundamental components and features of Excel so that you can use Excel in productive ways. To accomplish this objective, this chapter presents several activities. Although the examples are specific, the steps and procedures they present for developing workbooks and worksheets are generic and applicable to a variety of classroom management tasks and learning activities. As you work through the chapter's content, you can substitute your own examples for those that appear here.

A WORD ABOUT THE EXCEL WORKSPACE

Before you create a workbook and corresponding worksheets, it is important to examine the Excel workspace, including the screen layout, functions, and tools. When you open Excel, it presents a new blank document, referred to as a *workbook*. Figure 5.1 shows a new workbook. The Ribbon, located in the top portion of the workbook, contains functions and tools to assist you with entering, modifying, and analyzing data. For additional workspace, you can minimize the Ribbon by right-clicking on a Ribbon tab and selecting Minimize the Ribbon. With a few exceptions, the tabs on the Ribbon are the same as those in other Office applications. You may notice, for example, that except for the Formulas and Data tabs, Excel's Ribbon is almost identical to that of Word. The Formulas tab contains four main groups, labeled Function Library, Defined Names, Formula Auditing, and Calculation. With the tools in these tabs, you can write formulas and include in worksheets Excel functions that can assist you with performing calculations and data analysis. The Data tab has five major groups: Get External Data, Connections, Sort & Filter, Data Tools, and Outline. These tabs offer functions for acquiring, organizing, and examining data. For example, you may have data in a text file that you want to import into a worksheet. The Get External Data group provides an option to import the file.

As shown in Figure 5.1, the Home tab contains seven groups, two of which (Number and Cells) are unique to Excel. The Number group provides options for number formatting: Currency Style, Percent Style, Comma Style, Increase Decimal, and Decrease Decimal. Number format allows you to set how Excel displays the cell values in a worksheet. The Currency Style option sets the cell format to a dollar value. Percent Style sets the cell value to a percentage. The Comma Style option sets the cell value to a number with a decimal point. Finally, Increase and Decrease Decimal specify the number of decimal points in a cell value.

The Cells group contains options to insert and delete rows and columns and to set the cell formatting options. The Alignment group is similar to Word's Paragraph group. However, it contains the Wrap Text and Merge and Center options. Wrap Text, when clicked, wraps the text in the cell. The Merge and Center option combines multiple cells into a single cell and aligns the cell's contents to Center.

Below the Ribbon is the worksheet area where you perform most of your data entry, modification, and analysis. This is also referred to as the Normal view. There are several alternative views available in a worksheet, such as Page Layout (worksheets are laid out side to side) and Page Break (allows you to see page breaks in a document). These options are found under the View tab.

PDToolkit for *Microsoft® Office 2010 for Teachers*

You can find files that correspond to the chapter activities at http://pdtoolkit.pearson.com.

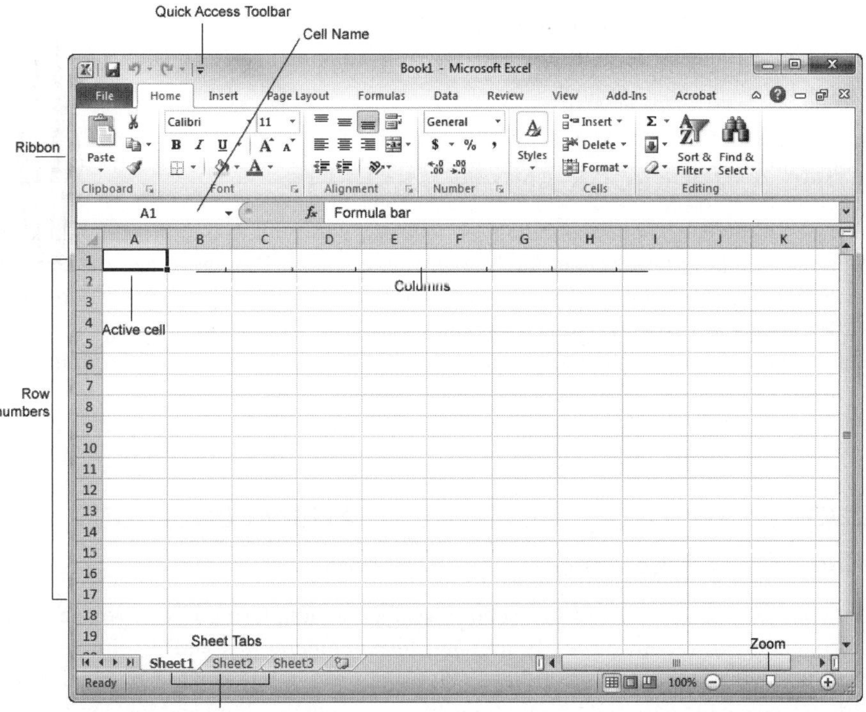

FIGURE 5.1 The Excel Workspace

A new workbook is made up of three blank worksheets, or sheets. When a workbook opens, Sheet 1 appears foremost on the screen, with Sheets 2 and 3 layered behind it. The Sheet tabs can be used to navigate sheets. Each worksheet contains column and row headings, cells, gridlines, worksheet tabs, and scrollbars. Excel labels columns with letters (e.g., A, B, and C) and rows with numbers. Columns extend vertically down the worksheet, and rows extend horizontally. Excel designates cell names by the intersection of the column and row. For example, cell A1 is located in the first row (row 1) in column A. When you click inside a cell, its name or cell reference appears in the cell name box. Gridlines separate cells, columns, and rows.

Worksheet tabs and scrollbars are located at the bottom right of the worksheet. The tabs allow you to easily move between worksheets. Clicking on a tab moves the selected worksheet to the foreground.

As data sets become large, columns and rows extend beyond the viewing areas of a computer monitor. To see them, you scroll using the scrollbars and arrows located to the right of the worksheet. If you click or hold down the mouse button on the scroll arrows, the screen moves in the corresponding direction. You can also drag a scrollbar in the desired direction while holding down the mouse button. The zoom control can be used to zoom in and out of worksheets so that data can be viewed more easily.

MOVING ABOUT IN A WORKSHEET

In an Excel worksheet, there are several ways to move across cells, columns, and rows. When you open a new workbook, cell A1 is active and ready for input. Begin to type, and the information appears in the cell as well as in the formula bar. After typing the information, pressing Enter moves the active cell down one row. Pressing the keyboard arrow keys moves the active cell in the direction corresponding to the arrow key. For instance, if the active cell is A1 and you press the down arrow key, the active cell moves down from A1 to A2.

Pressing the arrow keys does not move the active cell when you are editing a cell's contents. If cell B2 contains a misspelled word, double-click in the cell, and the cursor appears in the cell as a flashing line (insertion point). The arrow keys allow you to move the cursor within the cell so that you can edit the word. To move the active cell when in Edit mode, you press Enter or the Tab key.

Pressing the Tab key moves the active cell one column to the right. Pressing the Tab key while holding down the Shift key moves the active cell one column to the left. Clicking the cursor in any cell on the worksheet makes that cell active. Clicking and typing in a cell that contains information replaces the cell's contents. Double-clicking in a cell that contains information enables you to edit the cell's contents.

CREATING A WORKBOOK AND WORKSHEETS

To create a workbook and corresponding worksheets, you need to open Excel. Click the Start button on the Windows taskbar. On the Start menu, click All Programs, and the Programs list appears. Click Microsoft Office to expand the Microsoft Office list. Click Microsoft Office Excel 2010, and Excel opens. *Note:* Depending on how you installed Excel, it may be in a different location on the Start menu. In most cases, it can be found under All Programs or within the Microsoft Office folder. An Excel workbook opens, containing three blank worksheets (see Figure 5.2). Cell A1 is the active cell. If you begin to type, the information appears in cell A1.

PROJECT FOR TEACHERS: TRACKING WEATHER CONDITIONS

Entering Data in a Worksheet

Suppose you and your students form a school weather station. Using Excel, you set up a worksheet for students to record the daily low and high temperatures and precipitation. You are interested in having students collect these data to observe weather patterns. Each month you ask them to analyze the data and present their findings (monthly high and low temperatures and precipitation) to the class.

PDToolkit for *Microsoft® Office 2010 for Teachers*

Go to PDToolkit for **Microsoft® Office 2010 for Teachers** to locate a completed version of the letter in the Examples folder. To view an example of the final workbook, open the weather.xlsx file. You can also view an expanded version of the file by opening weather_Master.xlsx.

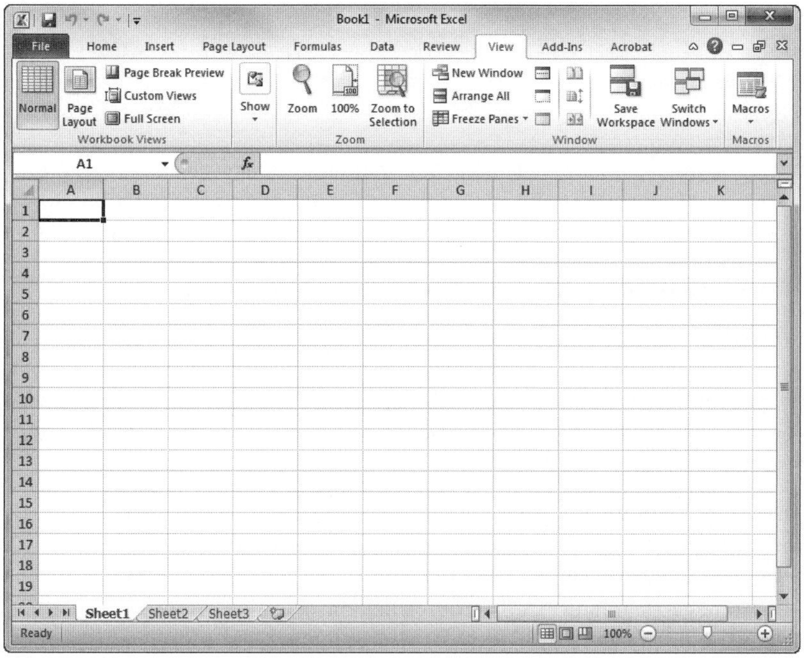

FIGURE 5.2 A Blank Worksheet

In this example, you will create a simple monthly weather reporting sheet:

1. Check that cell A1 is the active cell, indicated by a black frame around its border. Enter Weather Data for Charleston IL: October 2012 into A1 and then press Enter. As you type, the text appears in the formula bar. Weather Data for Charleston, IL: October 2012 appears in cell A1, and cell A2 becomes the active cell after you press Enter. Note that although Weather Data for Charleston IL: October 2012 may appear to extend beyond cell A1 to cells B1, C1, and D1, it is contained only in cell A1.
2. Create titles to describe the weather data. With cell A2 active, type Day and then press the Tab key; cell B2 becomes active. Type Temperature in cell B2 and press the Tab key two times, leaving cell C2 empty. Continue to enter the following data titles, beginning in cell D2 and ending in cell G2: Rain Fall (inches), Avg. Low, Avg. High, and Total Precipitation. When complete, your screen should look like the one shown in Figure 5.3.
3. Format the data titles. Adjust the columns and cells so that all the data titles are readable. The main title for these data is Weather Data for Charleston IL: October 2012, which should extend across columns A through G. To extend it, use the Merge command.
4. Select cells A1 through G1. Click in cell A1 and, while holding down the mouse button, drag across to cell G1. Click the Merge and Center button (see Figure 5.4). The seven cells merge into one, and the text becomes centered.
5. Merge cells B2 and C2 so that the Temperature title appears as a header for the daily low and high temperatures. Select cells B2 and C2. Click in cell B2 and, while holding down the mouse button, drag across to cell C2. Click the Merge and Center button. The two cells merge into one, and the text becomes centered.
6. Create titles to indicate the low and high temperatures for each day of the month. Make cell B3 active by clicking in it. Type Low, and press the Tab key. In cell C3, type High.

FIGURE 5.3 Data Labels

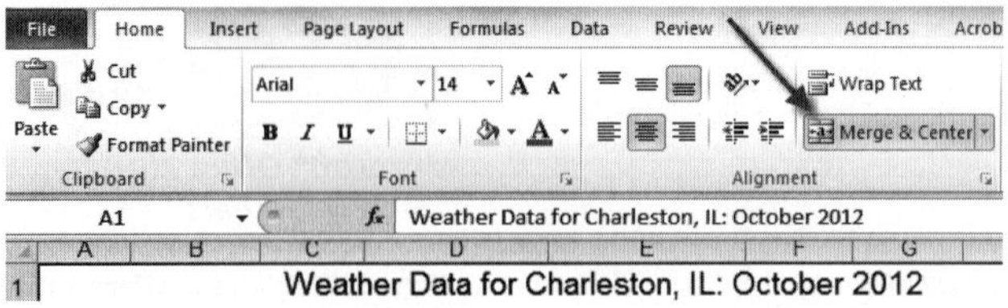

FIGURE 5.4 Merge and Center Sheet Title

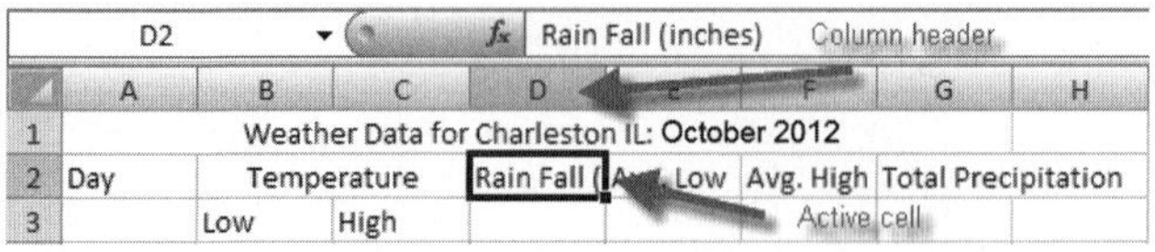

FIGURE 5.5 Adjusting Column Width

Modifying Worksheets: Adjusting Columns and Rows

You have probably noticed that the formatting of the worksheet contents appears incomplete. The cell contents cannot be seen, or they extend beyond the cell borders and into other cells. In this section, you will adjust the column widths and format the data titles. There are several ways to adjust the column width. For your purposes, Excel's AutoFit Column Width is a good option. Follow these steps:

1. Adjust the width of a specific column by clicking on the column header or clicking within a cell (see Figure 5.5). In Figure 5.5, Rain Fall (inches) does not fit in the cell D2 and needs to be adjusted. Click in cell D2.
2. On the Home tab and in the Cells group, click the selection arrow under Format and select AutoFit Column Width (see Figure 5.6). The column width adjusts to fit the cell contents.

Alternatively, you could format all the column titles simultaneously by clicking the cell A2 header and, while holding down the mouse button, dragging across to the G2 header. The columns are highlighted, or selected, as you drag across them. With the column titles selected, click the selection arrow under Format in the Cells group and select AutoFit Column Width. The columns adjust to the data. Deselect the columns by clicking anywhere else on the worksheet.

3. In the Format options, there are several additional items useful for formatting cells:
   - *Column Width*—Displays a box in which you can enter a dimension for the column width.
   - *Hide (columns, rows, or sheets)*—Hides a column, row, or selected set of columns or rows. This option is useful for viewing only specific segments of your data set.
   - *Unhide (columns, rows, or sheets)*—Reveals columns or rows that have been hidden using the Hide option. To reveal a hidden column or row, select the columns to the left and right of the hidden column and choose Unhide.
   - *Default Width*—Defines a standard width for all columns in a worksheet. However, the standard width will not apply to columns that have been adjusted previously. To set a standard width, click the Format option in the Cells group and select the Default Width submenu item. The Standard Width box appears, and in it you can specify a width value and then click OK. All previously unadjusted columns are set to the designated width.

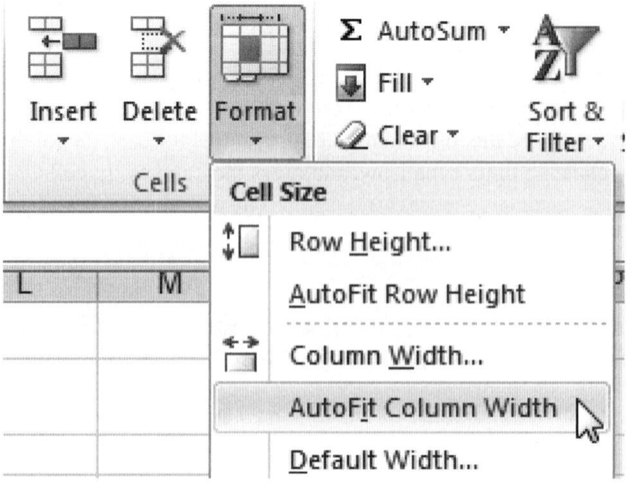

FIGURE 5.6 Using AutoFit Column Width

Adjusting Row Height

To make the data title more pronounced, you can increase the height of the second row to set it apart from the main title and weather data. To do so, follow these steps:

1. Click in any cell of row 2. On the Home tab, click the selection arrow under Format in the Cells group and select Row Height. Enter a row height of 24 and click OK. The row height increases across all columns (see Figure 5.7).
2. Notice that the titles are aligned at the bottom of row 2. To align the text in the center of row 2, click the row number to select row 2. Click the selection arrow under Format in the Cells group and select Format Cells. The Format Cells box appears (see Figure 5.8).
3. You can also right-click in row 2 and select Format Cells from the shortcut menu. Click the Alignment tab. Under Horizontal and Vertical, select Center and click OK. The text appears in the center of row 2 (see Figure 5.9).
4. Continue to enter data. For this example, enter the day of the month, temperatures (low and high), and rain fall, in inches, for each day. The average temperature and total precipitation will be handled later.
5. You want column A to contain dates corresponding to each day of the month, so format the column for this data type. Select column A by clicking on the column header. Click the selection arrow under Format in the Cells group and select Format Cells, and the Format Cells box appears (see Figure 5.10).
6. Click the Number tab, select Date from the Category area, choose a date type or the way you want the date to appear, and then click OK.
7. Click in cell A4 and type the first date, 10/01/12. You may notice an #### error after typing the date; this indicates that the column width is too narrow. If this occurs, select column A by clicking on the column header and then click the selection arrow under Format in the Cells group and select AutoFit Column Width. Your screen should look as shown in Figure 5.11.
8. Press the Tab key to accept the data, and cell B4 becomes active. Type the low temperature for the day and press the Tab key to make cell C4 active. Type the high temperature for the day. Press the Tab key again to make cell D4 active and type the amount of rain fall (in inches) for that day. Press Enter to move down to the next row.
9. Format cells containing temperatures and precipitation amount as General. Select the range of cells or columns to be formatted. From the Format options (the Cells group on

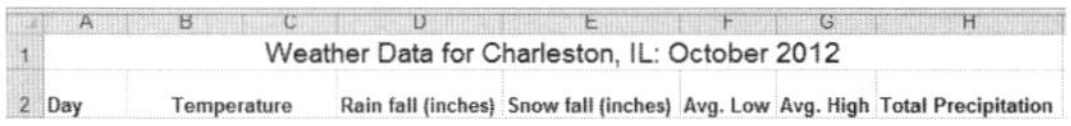

FIGURE 5.7 Increasing Row Height

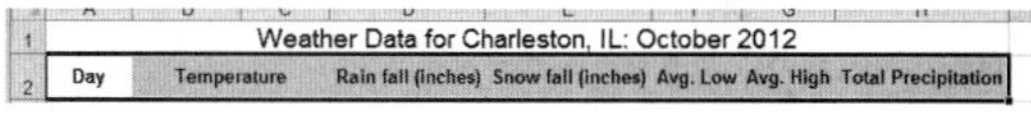

FIGURE 5.9 Center-Aligned Text

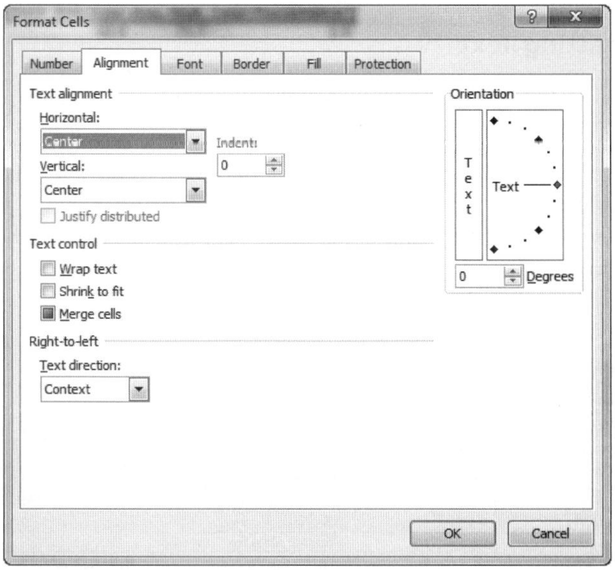

FIGURE 5.8 The Format Cells Box

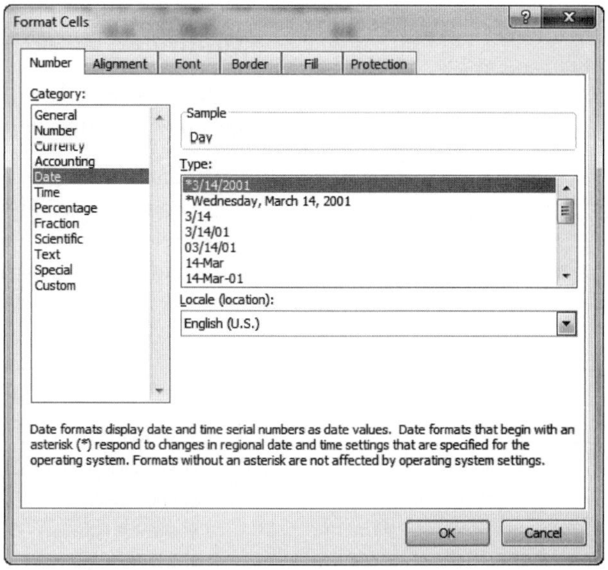

FIGURE 5.10 The Format Cells Box

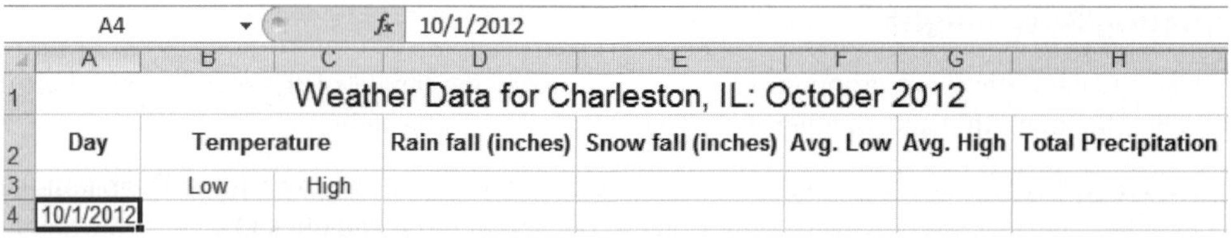

FIGURE 5.11 Entering Data

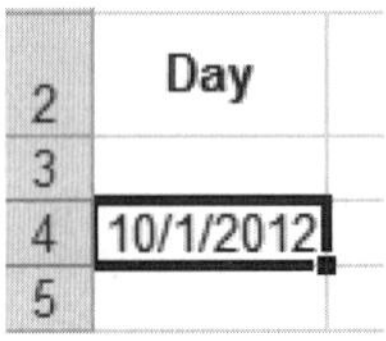

FIGURE 5.12 Auto Filling Cells

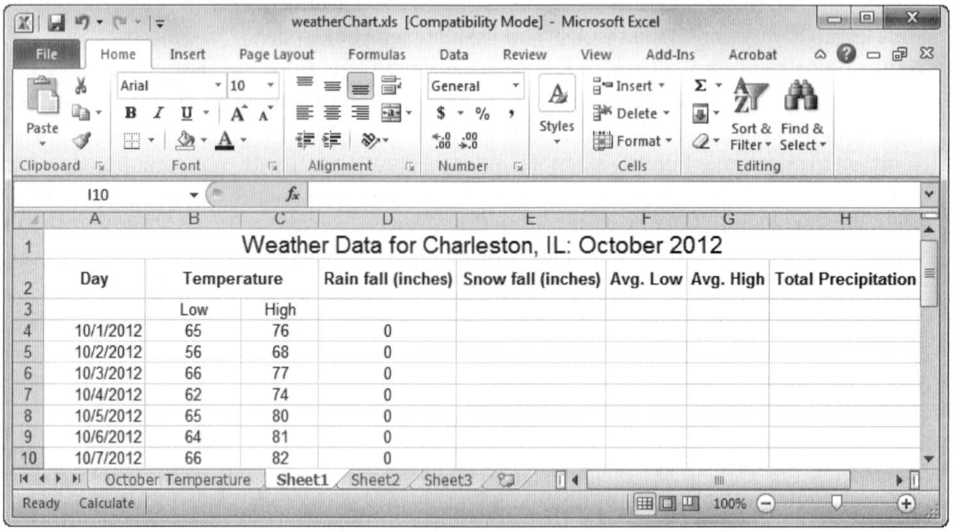

FIGURE 5.13 A Completed Worksheet

Home tab), select Format Cells. In the Format Cells box, click the Number tab and under Category select General.

10. Enter a date, low and high temperatures, and rain fall amounts for each day of the month. Remember to press the Tab key to move to a cell in the adjacent column on the right. If you prefer, you can auto fill the date column by dragging the selection down. After entering the first date, click in the cell to make it active. At the bottom right of the active cell is a small square (see Figure 5.12). Position the cursor over it and, while holding down the mouse button, drag down, and the dates will auto fill. Drag down to cell A34, and the data that appears in the cell should be 10/31/12. When you are finished, the worksheet should look similar to Figure 5.13.

Modifying Worksheets: Formatting Text

In this section, you will adjust the text of the worksheet by modifying the font type, size, style, and color of cell contents. Follow these steps:

1. Click in cell A1. Set the font type to Arial. Click the Home tab. In the Font group, click the Font box (see Figure 5.14) and select Arial.
2. Set the font size to 14 by clicking the Font Size box in the Font group (on the Home tab) and selecting *14*. Figure 5.15 shows the result of the font type and size changes.

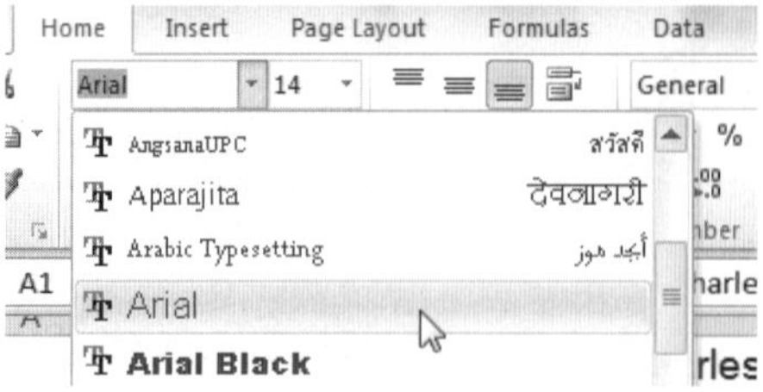

FIGURE 5.14 Font Type

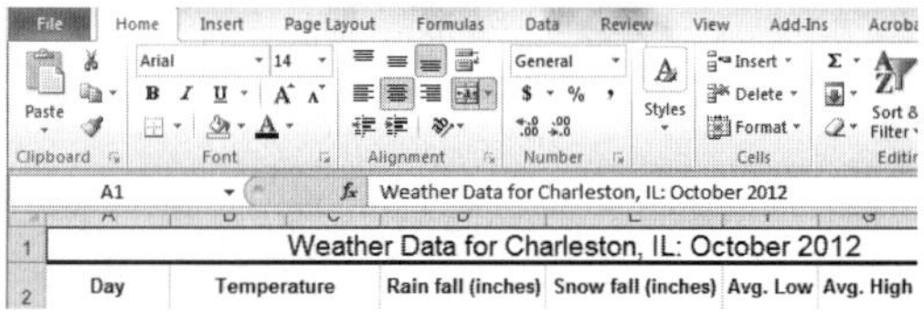

FIGURE 5.15 Adjusted Font Type and Size

3. To adjust the font style of the titles, select cells A2 through G2 by clicking in cell A2 and, while holding down the mouse button, dragging to cell G2. Click the Bold button in the Font group (on the Home tab). The Bold button appears as a **B** on the formatting toolbar (see Figure 5.16).
4. After setting the style to Bold, you may notice that portions of the titles in columns D through G do not display. To adjust this, select cells D2 through G2 and then on the Home tab click the selection arrow under Format (in the Cells group) and select AutoFit Column Width.
5. Set the row color. On the left side of the worksheet, click the row heading number 2, which represents the second row. Clicking *2* selects the entire row. Alternatively, you can select cells A2 through G2 by dragging across them.
6. On the Home tab in the Font group, click the down arrow located on the right side of the Fill Color tool. A palette of color choices appears (see Figure 5.17). Click on the black square, and the row fill color changes to black.
7. Both the fill color and the font color are set to black, so you cannot see the text titles (Day, Temperature, Rain Fall (inches), Avg. Low, Avg. High, and Total Precipitation). With row 2 selected, click the down arrow located on the right side of the Font Color tool. The color choices palette appears (see Figure 5.18). Click on the white square, and the font color changes to white. Row 2 should now have a black background with white text (see Figure 5.19).
8. Set the style of row 2. Select row 2 on the Home tab click Cell Styles in the Styles group, and the cell styles box appears. Move your cursor over the styles to see their effects. Select Accent 1, and the font and background colors of the row change (see Figure 5.20).

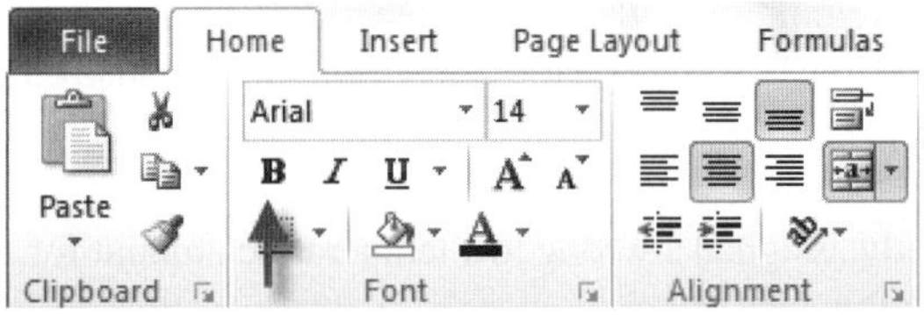

FIGURE 5.16 Setting Font Styles

FIGURE 5.19 Row Text and Background Color

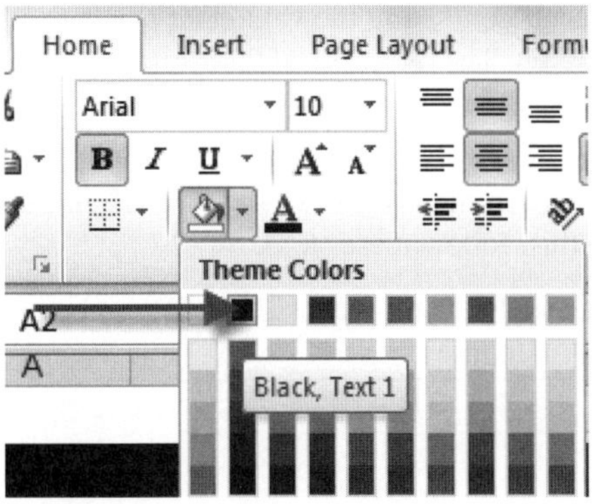

FIGURE 5.17 Setting the Fill Color

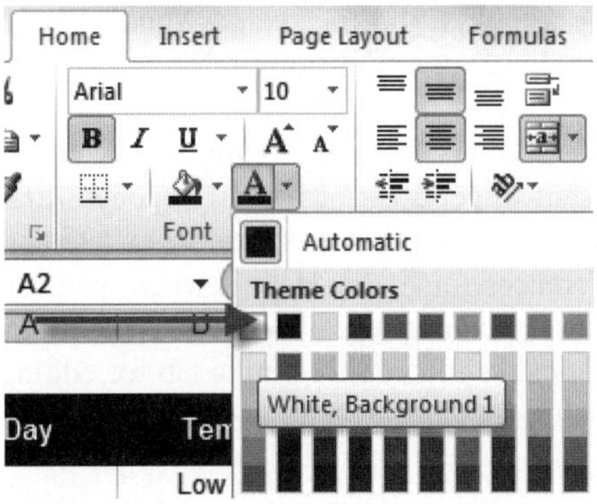

FIGURE 5.18 Setting the Font Color

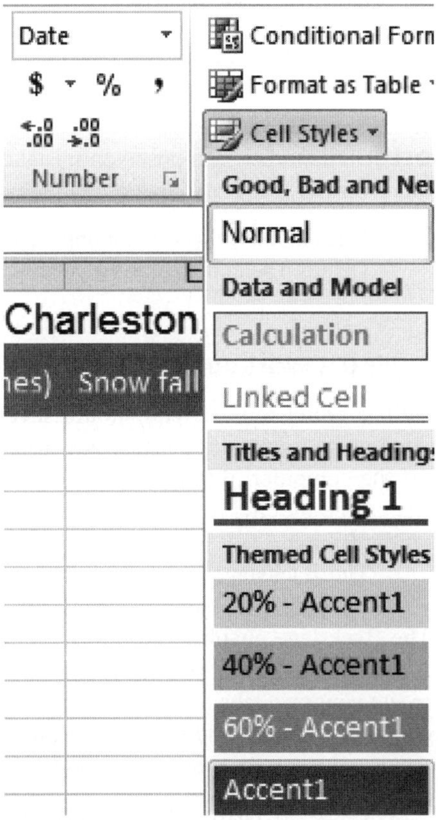

FIGURE 5.20 Cell Styles

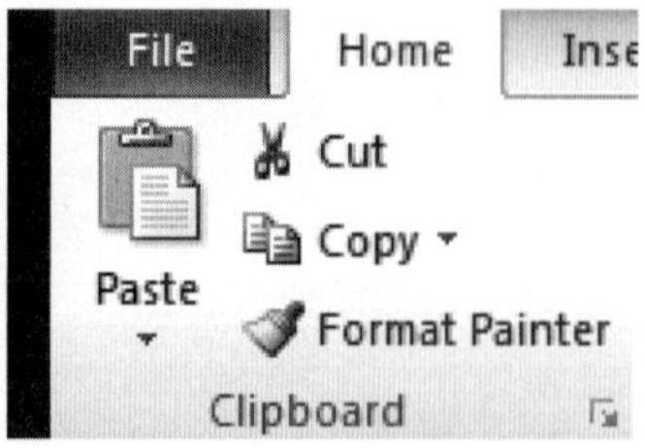

FIGURE 5.21 The Format Painter Icon

9. You can apply the same attributes (font type, color, and so on) to the Low and High titles under Temperature. One way to set these attributes is to select cells B3 and C3 and repeat the steps previously presented. Alternatively, using the Format Painter icon in the Clipboard group (see Figure 5.21), you can apply the attributes of one cell or a group of cells to another cell or range of cells.
10. For example, select cells E2 and F2 and then click the Format Painter icon. Click cell B3, and the attributes of cells E2 and F2 are applied to B3 and C3. Notice that Excel applies the attributes to the same number of cells that you selected prior to clicking the Format Painter icon.

Modifying Worksheets: Editing Data

In this section, you will alter the data entered into the school weather station workbook. Specifically, you will edit the contents of a cell, replace the contents of a cell, and delete data.

EDITING DATA Suppose that one of the titles is misspelled in the school weather station worksheet. Assume that the last column title is spelled Total Percipitation instead of Total Precipitation. To fix this, follow these steps:

1. Double-click cell G2, which contains the misspelled title. After double-clicking in the cell, the cursor appears inside the cell as a flashing line, referred to as the insertion point. You are now able to edit the text (e.g., select, add, delete).
2. Select the second and third letters of Percipitation and, with the letters selected, type re. Press Enter or the Tab key to accept the changes and move the active cell. You can also edit Percipitation on the formula bar.

REPLACING DATA Suppose you inadvertently assigned a wrong low temperature amount for a particular day in the worksheet. To fix this, follow these steps:

3. You may have entered 23 for the low temperature on October 2 when, in fact, it should have been 64. To correct this error, click on the cell containing the value that needs to be changed. Click cell B5. Type the new temperature 64. The old value of 23 is replaced with 64. Press Enter or the Tab key to accept the change and move the active cell.

DELETING DATA Suppose you mistakenly entered data in the Avg. Low and Avg. High columns for October 2 and now need to remove it. To fix this, follow these steps:

4. Click on the cell(s) containing the data you want to delete. Select cells E4 and F4 and press Delete. The contents of the cell are removed.

Saving a Workbook: The Backstage

Before going too far, you should save the workbook. It is important to save your Excel documents frequently because any unsaved portion of a workbook disappears when you turn off the computer. Before you save, you need to take a look at the Backstage. You enter the Backstage by clicking the File tab. You exit it by clicking on any another tab (e.g., Home) on the Ribbon.

The Backstage is an area where you can manage your files (see Figure 5.22). With it you can open, close, and save files. You can use Recent to get a list of recently opened files. The Backstage enables you to get information about a file, to print files, and to exit Excel. Additionally, the Options item allows you to set preferences for Excel. Here is where you can create your own tabs on the Ribbon. For example, let's say you use several commands on different Ribbon groups and want to combine them for efficiency. You could set up a tab for editing that is unique to the work you're doing. Here are the steps.

1. Click File tab to enter the Backstage.
2. Click Options and click Customize Ribbon.

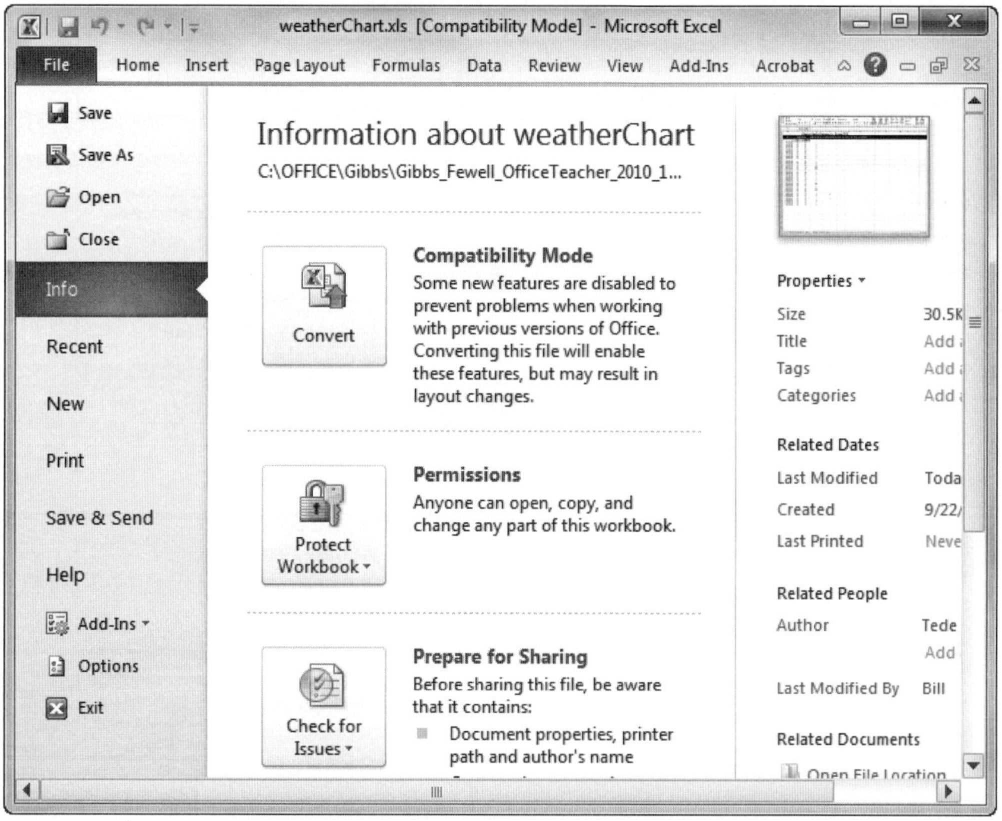

FIGURE 5.22 The Backstage

3. Click the New Tab button (see Figure 5.23). You see New Tab (Custom) listed under Main Tabs. Right-click on it, select Rename, and type the tab name Office for Teachers 2010.
4. There is also New Group (Custom) listed under your new tab. Right-click it, select Rename, and type the group name Editing Office for Teachers.
5. With your new group selected, click on an item/command on the left (under Choose Commands From). Then click the Add button in the middle of the screen. The command is placed in your group. (You can remove items by right-clicking on them and select Remove.) The new tab and group appear on the Ribbon (see Figure 5.24).

Saving and Naming a Workbook

There are three save options available by clicking the File tab: Save, Save As, and Save and Send. Under Save As, there are numerous options for saving a workbook, including options for the Web and for earlier Office versions.

SAVING A WORKBOOK When you create a new workbook and then select Save, the Save As dialog box appears, requesting that you assign the file a location in which to be saved, give the file a name, and specify a file format. When saving a new workbook for the weather station example, you do the following:

1. Click in the Save In box or the address box to specify the location to save the workbook.
2. Type the name weatherStation.xlsx in the File Name field.
3. Assign a file format by clicking in the Save As Type box. The weather station file should be saved as Excel Workbook*.xlsx.
4. If you do not provide a name, Excel gives the workbook the name of Book1.xlsx. By default, Excel appends the .xlsx extension to the file name and saves the file in Microsoft Excel workbook (*.xlsx) format. A number of formats are available for saving documents, including Web Page, Microsoft Excel 97–2003, XML Data, PDF, and CSVtext (.txt).

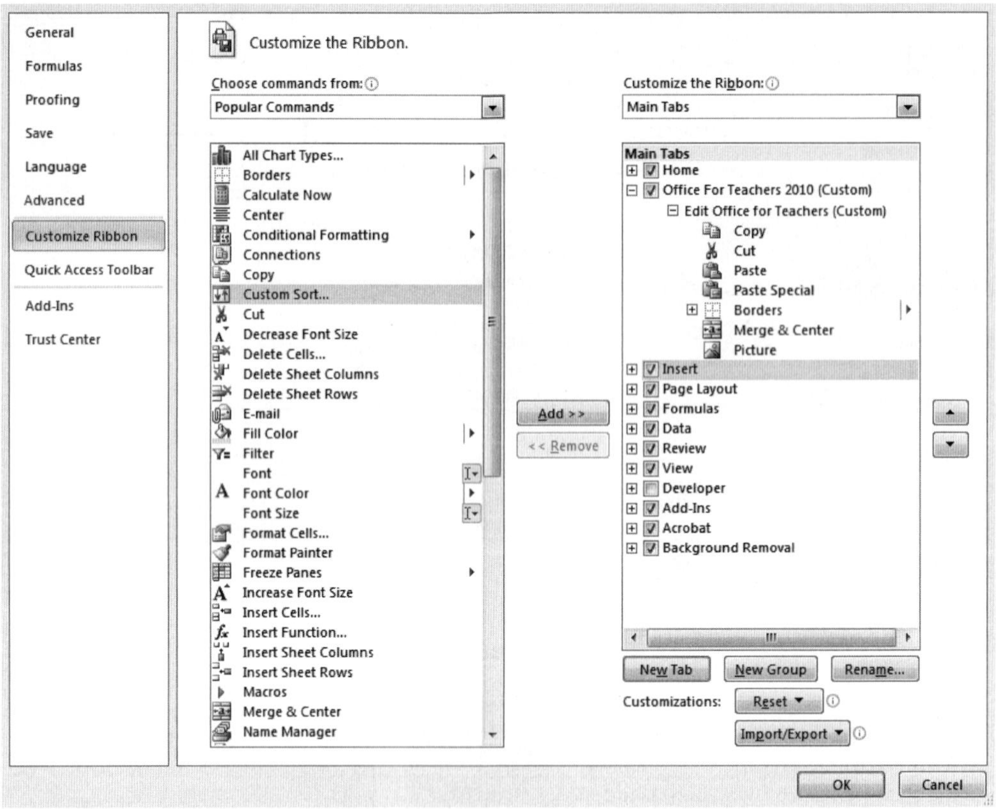

FIGURE 5.23 Custom Ribbon Options

5. Once you have designated a location, name, and format for your workbook, Excel saves all future changes accordingly. When saving a file, you can also click the Save icon on the Quick Access Toolbar.

USING THE SAVE AS OPTION The Save As option allows you to save an existing Excel workbook in a different location, under a different file name, or in a different file format.

USING THE SAVE AND SEND OPTION Excel workbooks can be sent via e-mail or saved in a variety of ways including:

- *Send Using E-mail*—You can save your workbook in a variety of formats (e.g., Excel workbook PDF, XPS) and then send it to e-mail or fax.
- *Save to Web*—You can save your document as a webpage and publish it online. Alternatively, if you want to save a workbook as a webpage, you can select Save As and in the Save As Type box and choose either Web Page (.htm; .html) or Single File Web Page (.mht; .mhtml), both of which can be viewed in a browser.
- *Save to SharePoint*—You can save your workbook and share it with others. With SharePoint, you can set up spaces with which you share information, manage documents, and publish files to work collaboratively (in Microsoft SharePoint 2010 and 2011).

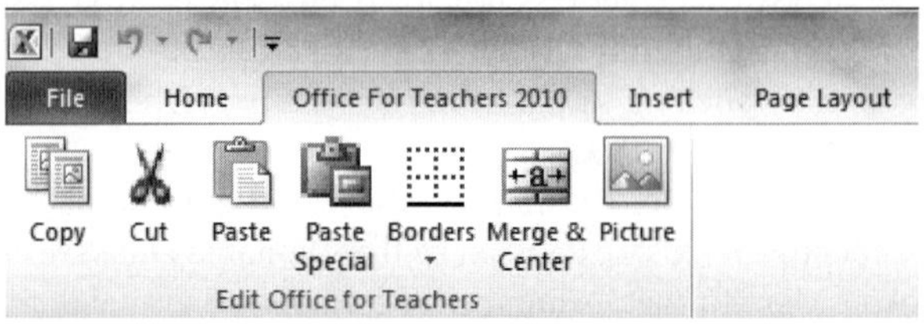

FIGURE 5.24 A Customized Ribbon

- *Change File Types*—You can change the file format. For instance, you can save your workbook as Excel 97-2003 or as a template. In addition, you can save your workbook in Portable Document Format (PDF) or XML Paper Specification (XPS), which is Microsoft's platform-independent and trustworthy format for electronic paper (Microsoft Corporation, 2010).

Modifying Worksheets: Inserting Rows and Columns

In the following sections, you'll continue with the weather station worksheet. You will add data to a worksheet and perform calculations. To modify the worksheet, follow these steps:

1. Suppose that after creating the weather station worksheet, you found that you overlooked a date, October 4, and a column for snowfall. To add the October 4 data and a Snowfall column, first insert a row below rows 6 and 7 and then insert a column after Rain Fall (Inches). These actions provide the space to place the previously unrecorded data.

INSERTING A ROW

2. Excel places the newly inserted row above the cursor position or active cell. For example, if the active cell is row 23, the contents of row 23 are pushed down into row 24, and the inserted row becomes row 23.
3. To insert the October 4 data, position the cursor within row 7. On the Home tab, click the selection arrow under Insert in the Cells group and select Insert Sheet Rows. A new empty row appears.
4. Enter the following data in row 7: 10/4/12, 62, 74, 0. If you auto filled your date column in earlier steps, then you may have more than 31 days because you added the extra row. You can delete the extra row by clicking the row number to select it and then clicking the selection arrow under Delete in the Cells group and choosing Delete Sheet Rows.

INSERTING A COLUMN

5. Insert a column after Rain Fall (Inches) to place the snowfall amounts. Excel places the newly inserted column to the left of the cursor position or active cell. For example, if the active cell is in column E, the contents of column E are pushed to the right, into column F, and the inserted column becomes column E.
6. Click anywhere in column E (Avg. Low). On the Home tab, click the selection arrow under Insert in the Cells group and select Insert Sheet Columns. A new empty column appears, in which you can enter snowfall amounts (see Figure 5.25). Add the title Snowfall (Inches) to cell E2.
7. After inserting a column or row, the Format Painter icon appears and presents cell-formatting options. Clicking the down arrow next to the Format Painter icon displays a list of formatting choices. You can format the inserted row or column like the row or column adjacent to it, or you can clear the formatting. Select the default option: Format Same As Above for a row and Format Same As Left for a column.

Formulas

Excel allows you to write formulas to make calculations. A formula can be a series of numbers, cell references, or names that, when placed in a specific sequence or combination, produce a new value. All formulas start with an equals sign (=). Suppose you want to place the sum of three cells (A1, A2, and A3) of data into a new cell, A4. Double-click in cell A4 to activate the formula bar. On the formula bar, type an equals sign (=) and then type the formula A1+A2+A3 to add the values in the three cells (see Figure 5.26).

This formula adds the contents of cells A1, A2, and A3, and the sum of the cells appears in cell A4. After typing the formula, click the Enter Formula option or press Enter. You can cancel the formula by clicking the Cancel Formula option.

FIGURE 5.25 Inserting a Column

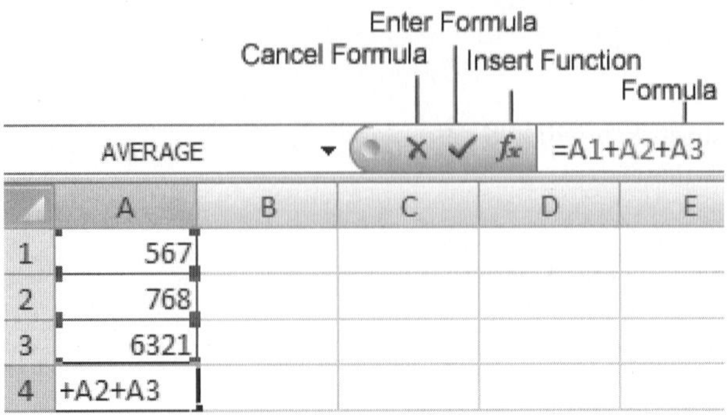

FIGURE 5.26 A Cell Formula

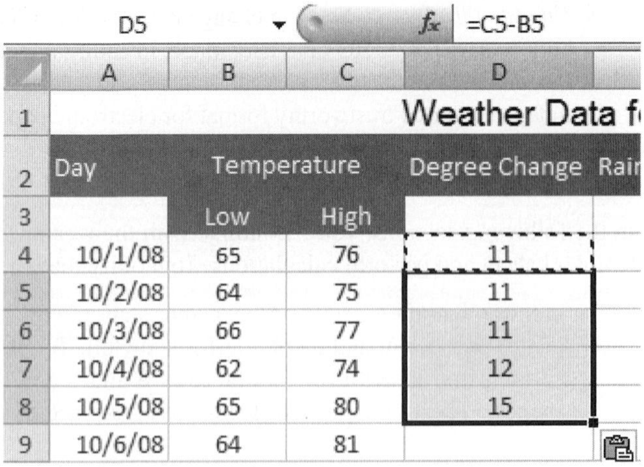

FIGURE 5.27 Copying and Pasting Formulas

For the weather station example, suppose you want to determine the differences between the low and high temperatures for a particular number of days. To get a cursory look at how many degrees the temperature increased, you can calculate the differences between the low and high temperatures for the first five days in October:

1. Insert a column to calculate the temperature difference. In the weather station workbook (weather.xls), click anywhere in column D. Click the selection arrow under Insert in the Cells group and click Insert Sheet Columns. A new empty column appears to calculate the temperature differences. You can also right-click in the cell and select Insert.
2. Click in cell D2 and give the column the title Degree Change. Notice that a portion of the title in D2 does not display. To adjust the title, select cell D2 and then click the selection arrow under Format in the Cells group and then choose AutoFit Column Width.
3. Calculate temperature differences for the first five days of October. Begin by subtracting the low temperature in cell B4 from the high temperature in C4 to get the difference.
4. Click in the cell that corresponds to October 1, which is D4. Type an equals sign (=) followed by C4-B4. Excel displays the Formula Cancel and Enter options. Double-clicking in cell D4 makes the formula options appear automatically. The complete formula should look like this: =C4-B4.
5. Click the Enter Formula option or press Enter to accept the formula. If the temperatures in cells C4 and B4 in your workbook were 76 and 65, respectively, 11 should appear in cell D4.

COPYING AND PASTING FORMULAS You could calculate the temperature differences for October 2 through October 5 by entering a formula for each day. However, a more expedient approach is to copy the formula in cell D4 and paste it for each of the other days. Follow these steps:

6. Click in cell D4 to make it active.
7. Click the Copy button in the Clipboard group on the Home tab or press Ctrl+C. Notice that the cell becomes surrounded with a marquee (blinking dots) border to indicate that the computer copied the cell contents.
8. Click in cell D5 to make it active and, while holding down the mouse button, drag to cell D8, which should correspond to October 5. All cells from D5 to D8 should be selected.
9. Click the Paste button in the Clipboard group (Home tab) or press Ctrl+V. The formula is pasted in each cell, and the calculated values are displayed (see Figure 5.27).
10. Click in each cell of column D and look closely at the formulas. Excel automatically adjusts each cell reference to the appropriate row. For example, cell D5 contains the formula =C5-B5, cell D6 contains the formula =C6-B6, and so on. The automatic referencing of cells is referred to as relative addressing.
11. Use the Auto Fill option. Notice in Figure 5.27 that cells D5 through D8 have a black border around them. A small square appears at the bottom right of the border. Pass the mouse over the square, and the cursor changes to a cross. With the cursor positioned over the square, drag down, and Excel copies the formula of the previous cell, with relative addressing.

12. A review of the data in column D indicates that the greatest temperature change between October 1 and October 5 occurred on October 5, with a difference of 15 degrees between the low and high temperatures.

Functions

In the previous example, you created a formula (=C4-B4) to calculate the differences between daily low and high temperatures. Excel provides built-in formulas called *functions* that perform calculations. For instance, to find the average temperature change for October 1 through October 31, you could use the AVERAGE function. For this example, you will place the average temperature difference in cell D35. Follow these steps:

1. Copy and paste or use Auto Fill to complete the degree change column so that column D (Degree Change) has values for each day of the month up until October 31.
2. Click in cell D35 at the bottom of column D, after the last degree change figure.
3. On the formula bar, click the Insert Function option, and the Insert Function box appears (see Figure 5.28). This box presents a number of functions that you can use. You can also search for function. Click AVERAGE under Select a Function and then click OK.
4. The Function Arguments box appears (see Figure 5.29) and requests a defined range of cells for the average. Enter the cell range D4 through D34.
5. To define the cell range for the function arguments, click in the beginning cell, D4. While holding down the mouse, drag to cell D34. D4:D34 displays in the Number 1 field of the Function Arguments box, indicating that the average of these cells will be calculated. Click OK. These steps average the values in cells D4 through D34 by placing the following function in cell D35:=AVERAGE (D4:D34).

The result is 15.09. The AVERAGE formula is built into Excel, and thus we refer to it as a function. Alternatively, you could write your own formula to average the column D values, but it would be less efficient to do so. Entering the function =AVERAGE (D4:D34) into cell D35 produces the same result as entering the formula =(D4+ D5+ D6+ D7+ D8+ ··· D34)/31.

THE STRUCTURE OF FUNCTIONS In Figure 5.30, notice that the structure of the function begins with an equals sign followed by the function name. The function arguments (I4:I18), or the range of cells on which the SUM function is performed, are enclosed in parentheses.

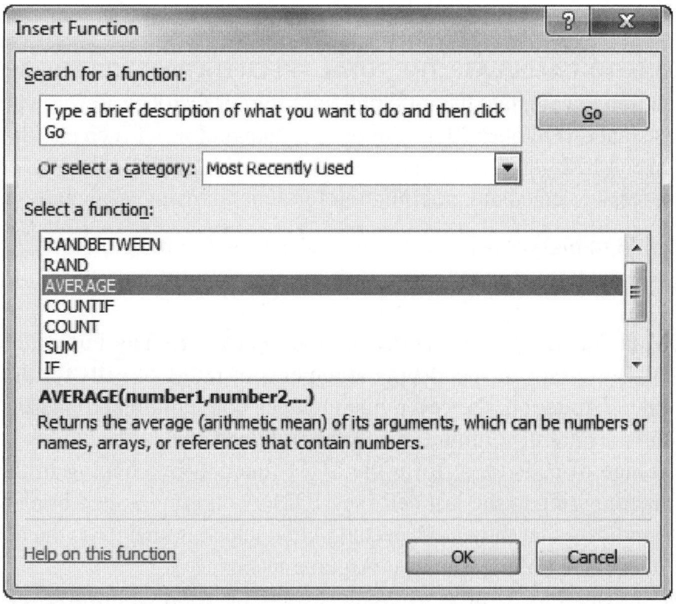

FIGURE 5.28 The Insert Function Box

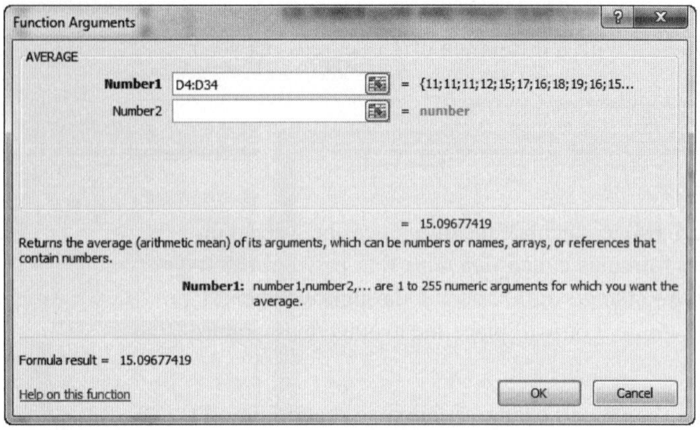

FIGURE 5.29 The Function Arguments Box

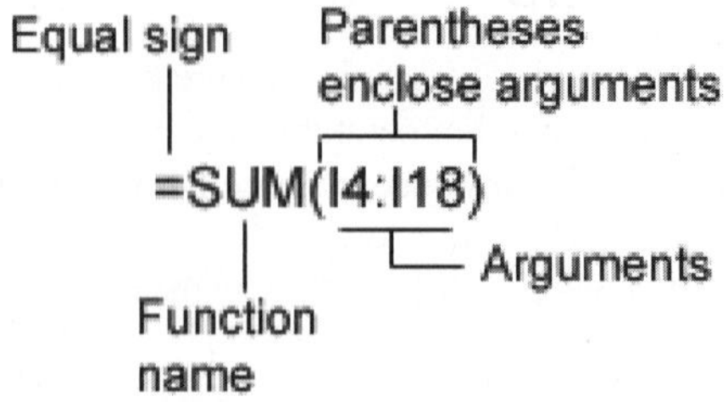

FIGURE 5.30 Function Structure

USING FUNCTIONS TO CALCULATE THE AVERAGE LOW AND HIGH TEMPERATURES Calculate the average low and high temperatures for the month of October:

1. Click in cell G3 to make it active. G3 will record the average low temperature.
2. On the formula bar, click the Insert Formula option. The Insert Function box appears.
3. Click AVERAGE under Select a Function and then click OK. The Function Arguments box appears, and in it you can specify the arguments or range of cells for the AVERAGE function. For the average low temperature, the argument or cell range is B4 through B34 (B4:B34). Select the range of cells by clicking in the beginning cell (i.e., B4) and dragging to the last cell (i.e., B34). A marquee (blinking dots) border appears around the cells to indicate that they are selected. After selecting the cells, the cell range appears in the Number 1 field of the Function Arguments box. Click OK.
4. Noticed that the average low temperature appears in cell G3.
5. To calculate the average high temperature, click in cell H3. Repeat the preceding steps 2 and 3 for the high temperature in cells C4 through C34.
6. Notice that the average low and high temperatures for October are 58.64516 and 73.741935, respectively. These cells can be formatted to display only one decimal point.
7. Select cells G3 and H3. On the Home tab, click the selection arrow under Format (in the Cells group) and choose Format Cells. Click the Number tab and under Category select Number. In the Decimal Places box, type 1 or use the down arrow to decrease the decimal places.

USING FUNCTIONS TO CALCULATE THE TOTAL PRECIPITATION FOR THE MONTH You can use the SUM function to calculate the total precipitation for October. Before performing the calculations, suppose that on October 29, the amount of snowfall was 1 inch and that on October 31, it was 0.5 inch. In cell F32 you would enter the value 1 and in cell F34 you would enter the value 0.5. Follow these steps to calculate precipitation for a month using a function:

1. Click in cell I3 to make it active. I3 will record the total precipitation.
2. On the formula bar, click the Insert Formula option, and the Insert Function box appears.
3. Click SUM under Select a Function and then click OK. The Function Arguments box appears, and in it you can specify the arguments or range of cells for the SUM function. For the total precipitation, the cell range includes both columns E and F. (Remember that snowfall amounts are in column F for October 29 and 31.)
4. Select the range of cells to perform the SUM function by clicking in the beginning cell (i.e., E4) and dragging to the last cell (i.e., F34). A blinking dotted border appears around the cells to indicate that they are selected. After selecting the cells, the cell range appears in the Number 1 field of the Function Arguments box.
5. Click OK on the Function Arguments box. The total precipitation for October is 5.9 inches.

Moving and Copying Data

This section describes how to copy and move data within a worksheet; you will often need to perform these tasks when working with data sets.

MOVING DATA Suppose you entered the October snowfall amounts incorrectly. Instead of snowfall events occurring on October 29 and 31, they actually took place on October 26 and 28, so these values need to be moved to the appropriate cells. To fix this, follow these steps:

1. Select cells F32 and F34. Click cell F32 to make it the active cell and, while holding down the mouse button, drag downward to cell F34.
2. Position the cursor over the border of the selected area, and the cursor changes to a four-point arrow. Click on the border and drag the selection to the appropriate cells, F29 and F31. As you drag the selection, its border becomes shaded, and it snaps to the cell's border.
3. Release the mouse button when the values are over cells F29 and F31, and the values move.
4. Another way to move data is to select the data that you want to move and click the Cut button in the Clipboard group (Home tab) or press Ctrl+X. Click in the location where you want to move the data. Click the Paste button or press Ctrl+V.

PDToolkit for *Microsoft® Office 2010 for Teachers*

Go to PDToolkit for **Microsoft® Office 2010 for Teachers** to locate a completed version of the letter in the Examples folder. To practice using the IF function, open the NumberPatterns.xlsx or the Jellybeans.xlsx files. The NumberPatterns.xlsx worksheet uses the IF function along with the AND logical function. The Jellybeans worksheet uses the IF function along with the OR logical function.

COPYING DATA Data can be copied from one group of cells to another or from one column to another. Suppose you want to make a copy of column A (the days of the month) on the right side of your worksheet to more easily view the precipitation amounts with their corresponding dates. To do so, follow these steps:

1. Select cells A4 through A34.
2. Position the cursor over the border of the selected area, and the cursor changes to a four-point arrow. Press the Ctrl key while clicking on the border and drag the selection to the desired column, J. As you drag the selection, its border becomes shaded, and it snaps to the column's border. Note that pressing Ctrl while moving the selection copies it to the destination. If you do not press Ctrl, Excel moves the selection instead of copying it.
3. Release the mouse when the values are over column J, and the selection is copied.
4. Another method of copying data is to select the data that you want to copy and click the Copy button in the Clipboard group (on the Home tab) or press Ctrl+C. Click in the location where you want to copy the data. Click the Paste button or press Ctrl+V.

Charting Excel Data

When you complete this section, you will have produced the line chart shown in Figure 5.31. Follow these steps:

1. In the weather.xlsx file, select the range of cells from B3 through C34, which are the low and high temperatures for the month of October.
2. Click the Insert tab and then click the selection arrow for Line in the Charts group. Select the Line with Markers chart type (see Figure 5.32). The Charts group offers options for column, line, bar, area, and scatter chart types. There is also an Other Charts option that includes surface, donut, bubble, and radar categories. Notice within each type that the charts are categorized and that icons of the chart types appear. Clicking on an icon selects that particular chart type. Moving the cursor over the icons displays a pop-up description of the charts.
3. The Line chart displays in the worksheet. Click the chart to select it, and the Chart Tools tab becomes active. Under the Chart Tools tab, click the Design tab and then click the More arrow in the Charts Layout groupand select Layout 1 (see Figure 5.33). In the Chart Styles group, select Style 2.
4. Click on the chart title and type October Low and High Temperature. Click on the axis title and type Temperature.
5. Click on the Series line for the high temperature to select it (see Figure 5.34). Under the Chart Tools tab, click the Format tab and then click the selection arrow for Shape Outline in the Shape Styles group (see Figure 5.35).

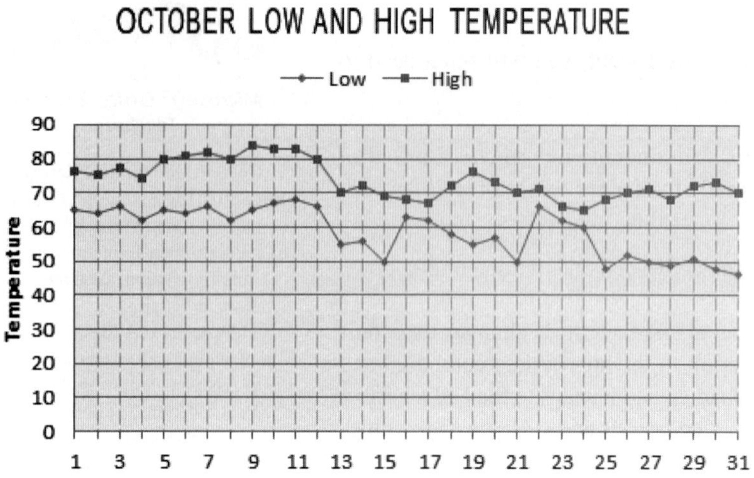

FIGURE 5.31 A Completed Chart

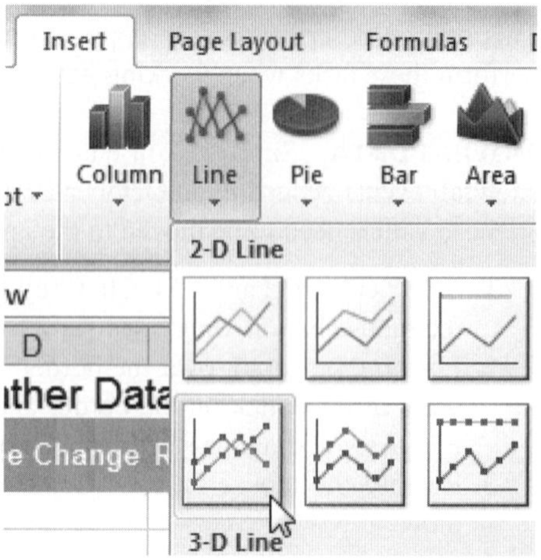

FIGURE 5.32 A Line Chart

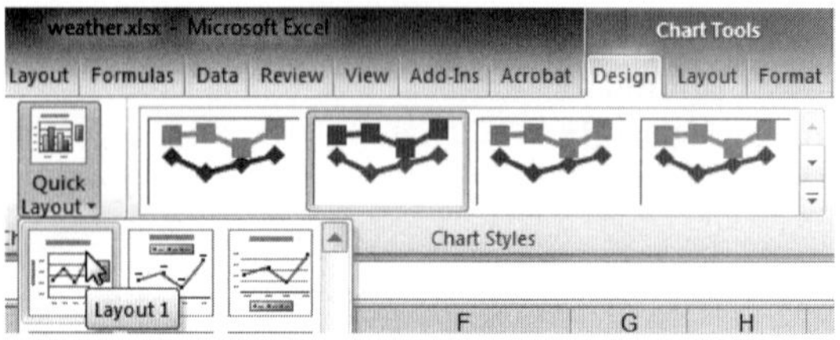

FIGURE 5.33 A Chart Layout

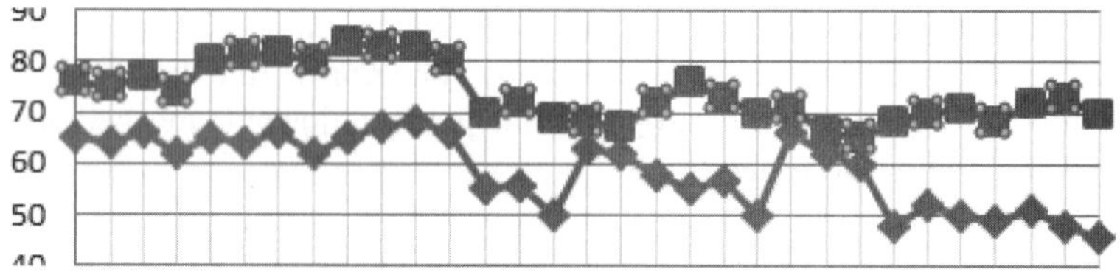

FIGURE 5.34 Chart Series Lines

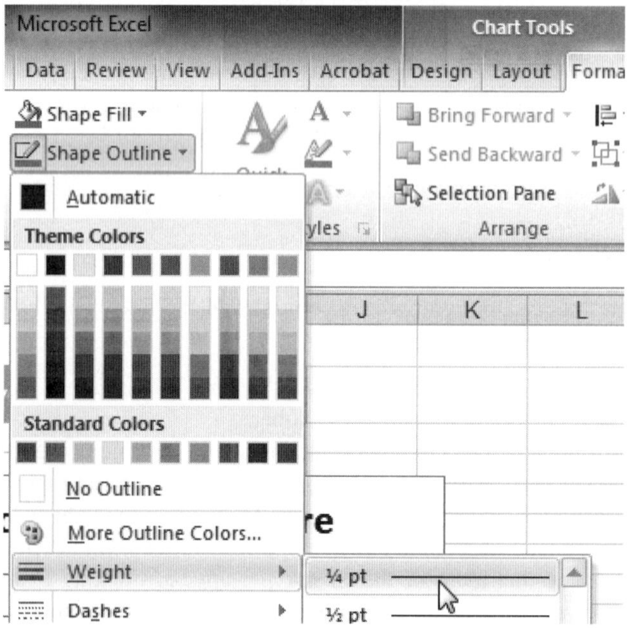

FIGURE 5.35 Selecting Chart Series Lines Weight

6. Select Weight and ¼ pt to set the weight of the high temperature series line. Repeat this step for the low temperature series line.
7. Click the chart if it is not already selected. Right-click on the Horizontal/Category Axis and select Format Axis. The Format Axis box appears.
8. Click on Axis Options on the left side of the box. For intervals between labels, choose Specify Interval Unit and type the number 2. This will show the temperature at two-day intervals.

9. For Major Tick Marks, select Outside, and for Position Axis choose On Tick Marks (see Figure 5.36). These options display every other date on the horizontal axis. They place tick marks on the chart and center the horizontal axis values on them.
10. Click the Number option on the left side of the Format Axis box. If the dates on the horizontal axis take up too much space, change them. With Number on the left side of the Format Axis box selected, choose Custom (under Category). In the Format Code box, type d;@ and click the Add button. Click Close. This changes the horizontal axis so that only the day appears (see Figure 5.37).
11. Click the chart to select it, and the Chart Tools tab becomes active. Click the Layout tab under Chart Tools. In the Labels group, choose Legend and Show Legend at Top.

Modifying the Chart

ADJUSTING THE X-AXIS LABELS: ORIENTATION Notice that as you click on various sections of a chart, they become selected. For example, clicking on the chart title October Low and High Temperature selects it. A border and four small dots appear around it, indicating that it is selected (see Figure 5.38). Once selected, the title can be moved, edited, or deleted.

ADJUSTING THE X-AXIS LABELS: FONT TYPE, STYLE, AND SIZE The steps to adjust the labels on the X-axis labels:

1. To adjust the font on the X-axis, right-click the X-axis labels section (the numbers representing the days of month) located below the columns (see Figure 5.39). A border and four small dots on the X-axis label indicate that it is selected.
2. Choose Font from the shortcut menu, and the Font box appears. Set the font to Arial, size 10, and check the Equalize Character Height option (see Figure 5.40).

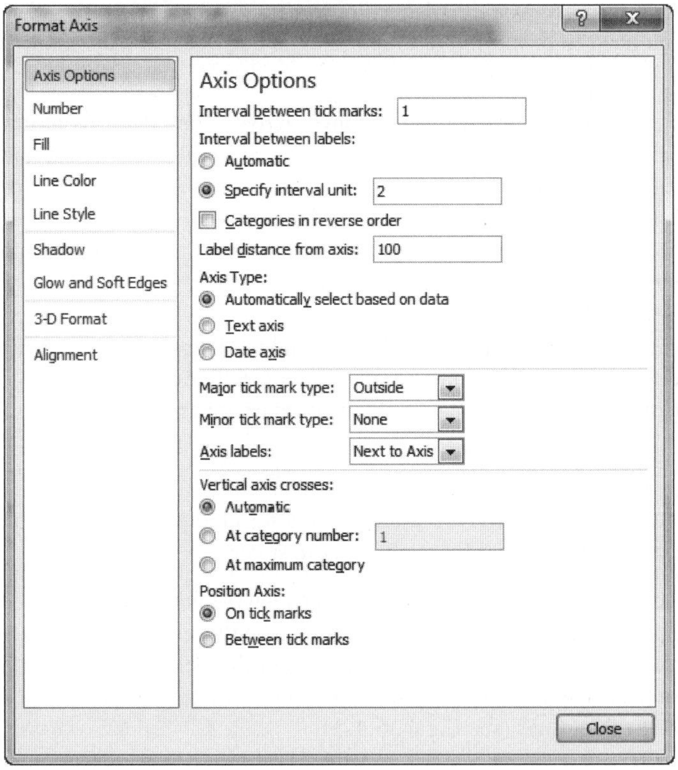

FIGURE 5.36 The Format Axis Box

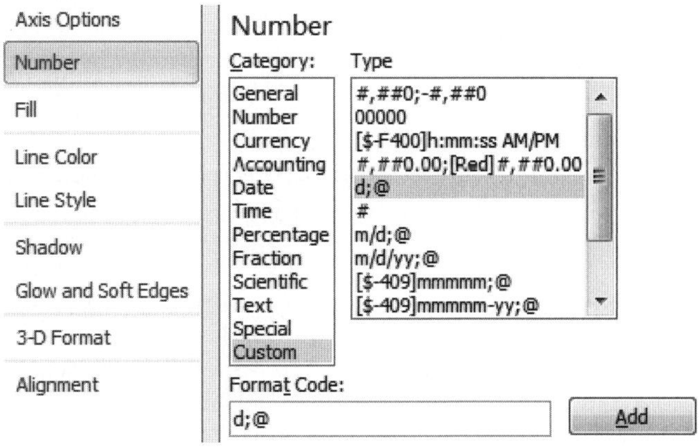

FIGURE 5.37 The Axis–Date Format

FIGURE 5.38 A Chart Title

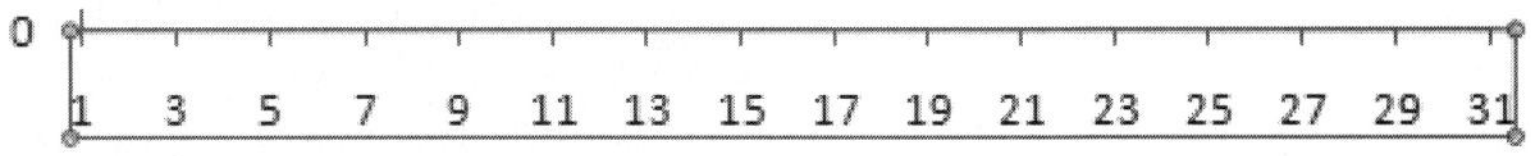

FIGURE 5.39 The Chart X-Axis

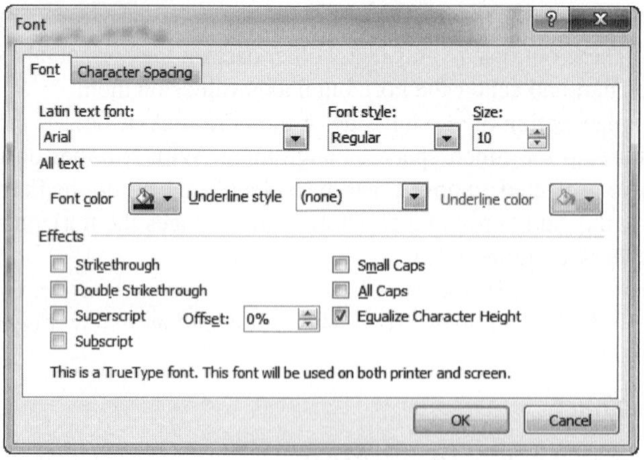

FIGURE 5.40 The Chart X-Axis Font

ADJUSTING DATA LABELS: FONT TYPE, STYLE, AND SIZE

1. Click the Chart title (October Low and High Temperature). Clicking on the title selects it, as indicated by the four small dots that appear around it.
2. Right-click the chart title and select Font from the shortcut menu. Set the font type to Arial and the size to 12 points and select All Caps. Click OK to accept the changes to the chart title.

ADJUSTING CHART GRIDLINES Gridlines are horizontal and vertical lines that run through the chart. They provide a visual referent for the data series lines and the X- and Y-axes. However, the lines in your chart may interfere with the visual clarity of the data points, so they can be adjusted. In this example, you want to see exactly where the data points fall in terms of data and temperature. As a result, you need to turn on both the horizontal and vertical axes. Follow these steps:

1. Click the chart to select it, and the Chart Tools tab becomes active. Click the Layout tab. In the Axes group, click the Gridlines option and select Primary Vertical Gridlines and then Major Gridlines. If the horizontal gridlines are not already present, click the Gridline option again and select Primary Horizontal Gridlines and Major Gridlines.
2. With the chart still selected, click the selection arrow under Gridlines in the Axes group (on the Chart Tools Layout tab). Select Primary Vertical Gridlines and then More Primary Vertical Gridlines. The Format Major Gridlines box appears. Click Line Color on the left side of the Format Major Gridlines box. Choose Solid Line and set Transparency to 55%.
3. Click the Line Style option on the left side of the Format Major Gridlines box. Set the line width to 0.75 point and set the dash type to Long Dash, the third option from the bottom of the list.

ADJUSTING THE CHART BACKGROUND COLOR To direct attention to the plot area, you can change the background color of the chart to light blue. Follow these steps:

1. Click in the plot area. You can accomplish this by clicking between the major gridlines (see Figure 5.41). Be careful not to click on data series lines or mistakenly select the gridlines.
2. The Chart Tools tab becomes active. Click the Format tab and then click the selection arrow below Shape Fill (in the Shape Styles group). On the Shape Fill options panel, click Olive Green, Accent 3, and Lighter 80% (see Figure 5.42).

Spell-Checking an Excel Workbook

1. Open the weather.xlsx workbook.
2. Check the workbook for spelling errors. Click the Review tab and click the Spelling button in the Proofing group. If your workbook contains spelling errors or words Excel does not recognize, the Spelling dialog box appears (see Figure 5.43).

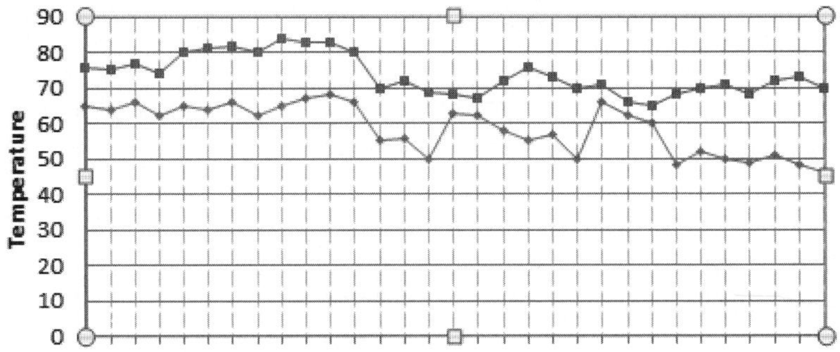

FIGURE 5.41 Selecting Major Gridlines

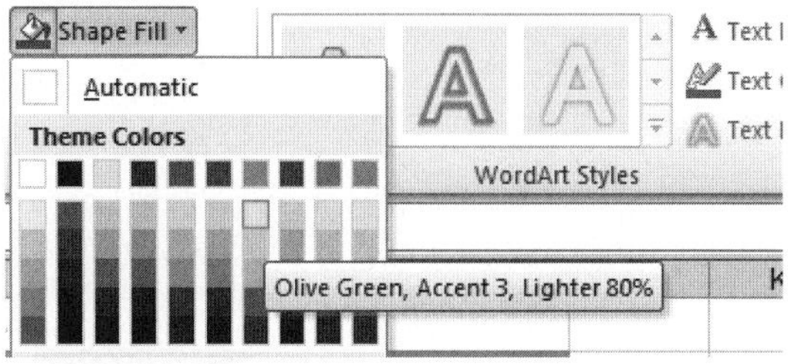

FIGURE 5.42 Shape Fill Options

When Excel does not recognize a word, it shows the word in the Not in Dictionary section of the Spelling dialog box. For example, in Figure 5.43, Excel encountered a misspelling of the word *Precipitation* (*Percipitation*). Excel offers suggestions for changing the word. Clicking Ignore Once ignores the suggestion. Clicking Ignore All ignores all future instances of the word in the spell-check session. You can change the word to Excel's suggestion by clicking Change. Change All changes all future instances of the word in the spell-check session. If a word identified in the Not in Dictionary is spelled correctly and Excel does not recognize it, you can add it to Excel's dictionary by clicking Add to Dictionary. AutoCorrect adds the spelling mistake to a list of errors and automatically corrects it on subsequent occurrences. Close closes the Spelling dialog box.

Printing an Excel Workbook

1. Open the weather.xls workbook.
2. To print the weather.xls workbook, click the File tab and then select Print in the Backstage (see Figure 5.44). There are a number of print options, some of which are described here:
   - *Print button*—You click this button to print.
   - *Copies*—You can specify the number of copies to print.
   - *Printer*—You can designate a printer to print the workbook. Other options include PDF, XPS, and fax.
   - *Settings*—Excel has several printing options. You can print the active sheet, an entire workbook, a worksheet, or selected cells within a worksheet. Printing worksheets or selections from a worksheet is particularly useful, for example, when students and teachers share and discuss their data analysis results.
   - *Pages*—You can specify a range of pages to print.
   - *Print One Sided*—You can specify whether to print on one side of the paper or on both sides.

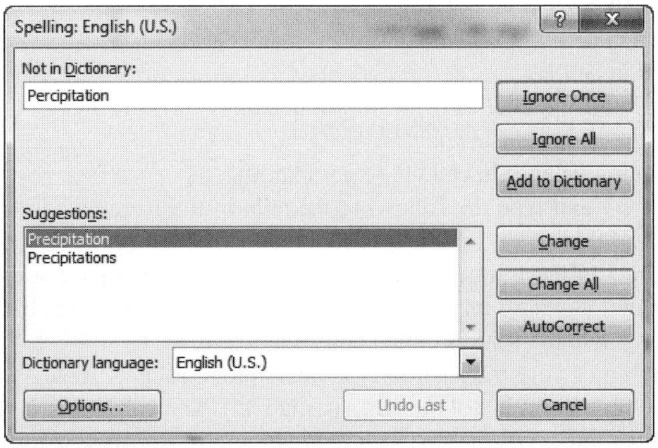

FIGURE 5.43 Checking Spelling

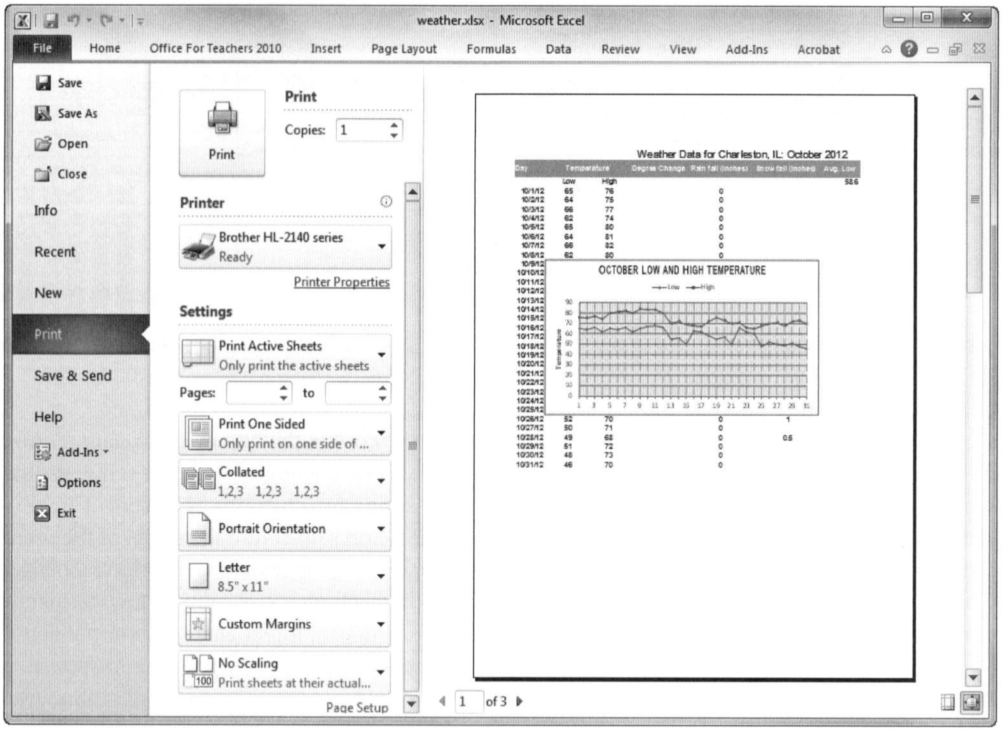

FIGURE 5.44 Backstage: Printing

PDToolkit for *Microsoft® Office 2010 for Teachers*

Go to PDToolkit for **Microsoft® Office 2010 for Teachers** to locate a completed version of the letter in the Examples folder. As an example of an Excel project that a teacher and students could develop is a checkbook minder.

The Preview area on the right allows viewing of the workbook, a workbook selection, or a chart prior to printing. Often the data you enter into a worksheet extend beyond the viewing area of your computer monitor. Print Preview allows you to see what a printed copy of your worksheet will look like prior to its being printed.

PROJECT FOR TEACHERS AND STUDENTS: CREATING A CHECKBOOK MINDER

As an example of an Excel project that a teacher and students could develop is a checkbook minder. To create one, follow these steps:

1. Open a new workbook and save it as checkbook.xlsx.
2. Type Date in cell A1. Click on the column A heading to select all rows in the column. On the Home tab in the Number group select Short Date to format the cells for the transaction date.
3. Type Transaction in cell B1.
4. Type Description in cell C1.
5. Skip a column and type Withdraw in E1.
6. Type Deposit in cell F1.
7. Type Balance in cell G1.
8. Type Cleared in cell H1.
9. Press the Ctrl key and click on the column headings for E, F, and G. On the Home tab in the Number group select Currency.
10. Type a beginning balance in cell G2 (e.g., $2,500).
11. Click in cell G3 and type the following formula in the formula bar: =SUM(G2-E3+F3) (see Figure 5.45).
12. Click in cell G3 to make it active. Notice the small square at the bottom right of the cell. Click and drag it down for as many cells as you think you will need. In this example, copy the formula relative to its surrounding cells down to row 15.
13. You can now enter your transaction type descriptors, such as ATM Withdraw, Check, or Deposit by typing them in column B. Alternatively, you can create a drop-down list that contains these items. Assume that you have three types of transactions: ATM Withdraw, Check, and Deposit.

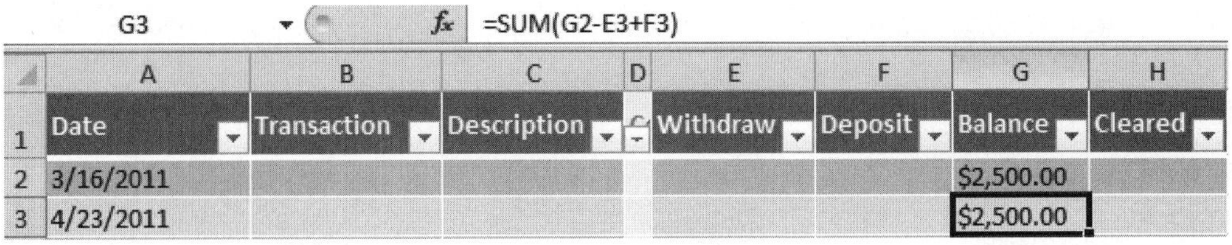

FIGURE 5.45 Formula

14. To create the drop-down list, click in cell B4 to make it active. Click the Data tab. In the Data Tools group click Data Validation (see Figure 5.46).
15. In the Data Validation box under the Settings tab select List Under Allow. In the Source box type ATM Withdraw, Check, and Deposit. Make sure you separate items with commas (see Figure 5.47). Click OK.
16. You should notice that cell B4 has a drop-down list arrow next to it (see Figure 5.48). Click in cell B4 to make it active. Notice the small square at the bottom right of the cell. Click and drag it down for as many cells you think you will need. In this example, you copied the drop-down list down to row15. Now, instead of typing the transaction type, you can select it from the list.

Formatting the Checkbook

1. Click row 1 to make the entire row active. On the Styles tab, click Cell Styles and select Accent 1 (see Figure 5.49).
2. Click the column headings so that all the columns are selected.
3. Click the Format As Table button and select the Table Style Medium 9 (see Figure 5.50).

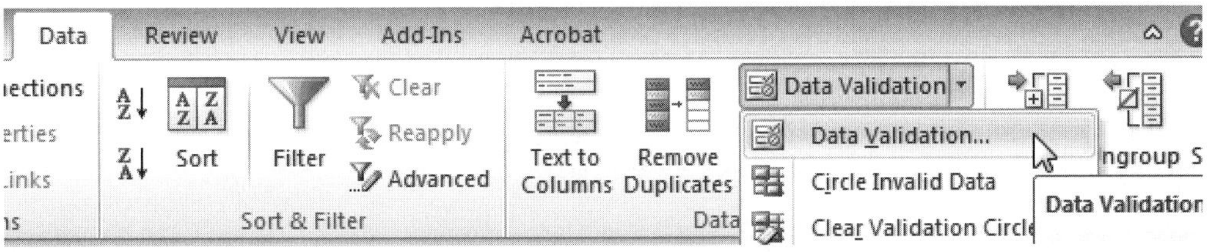

FIGURE 5.46 A Drop-Down List

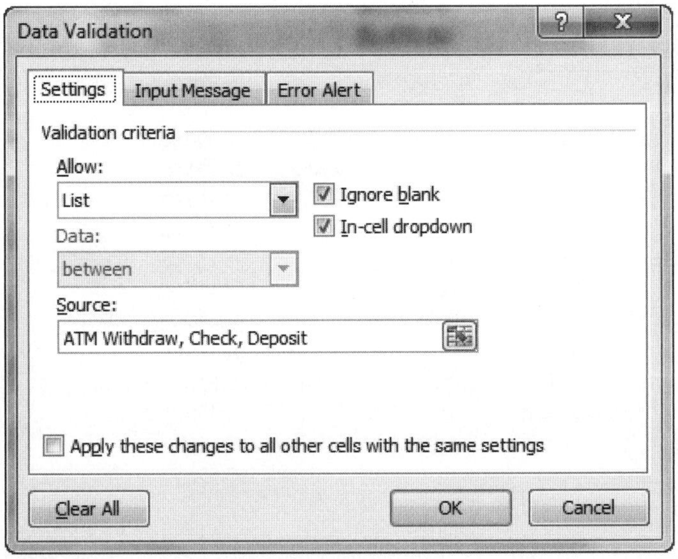

FIGURE 5.47 The Data Validation Box

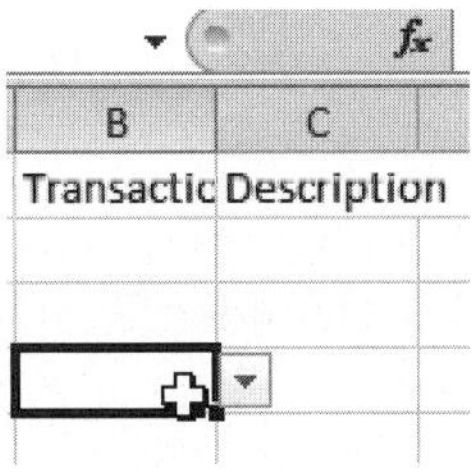

FIGURE 5.48 A Drop-Down List

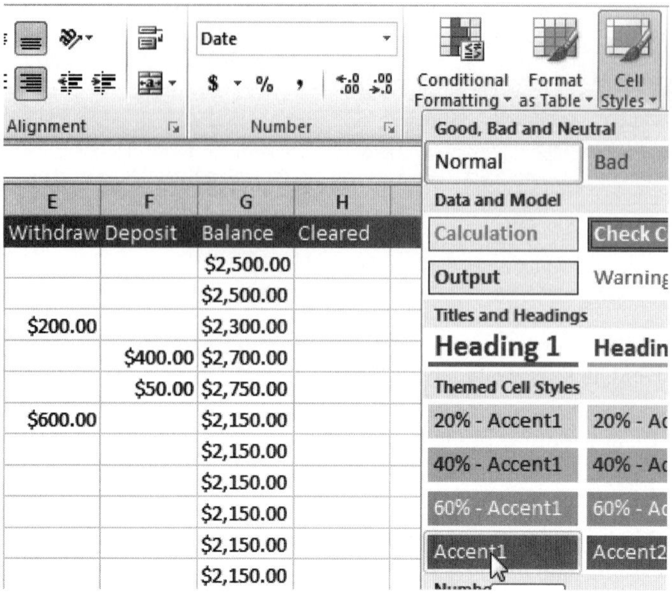

FIGURE 5.49 A Cell Style

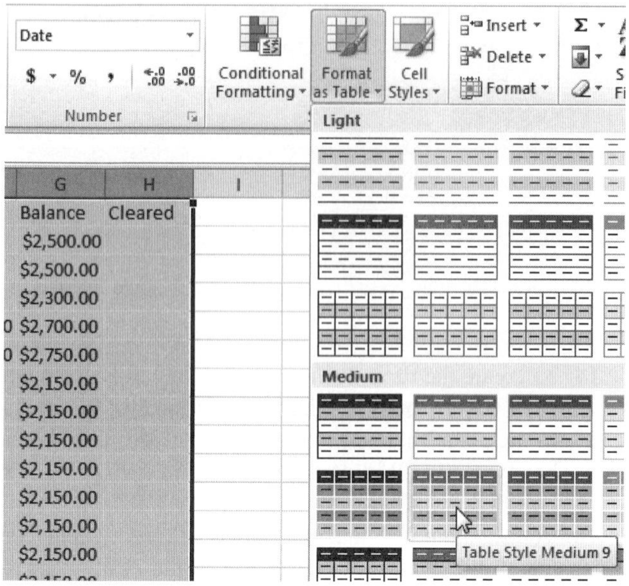

FIGURE 5.50 A Table-Style List

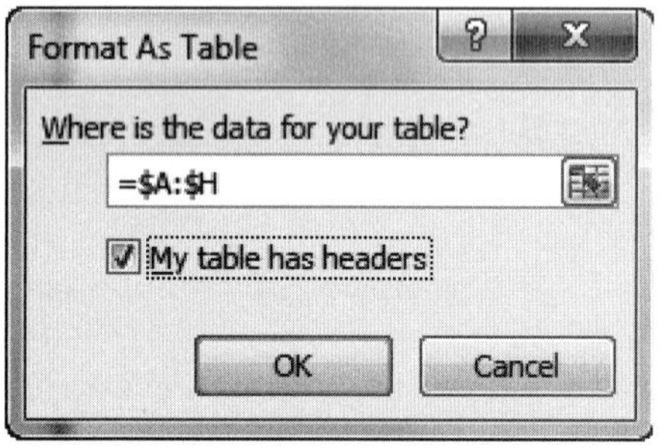

FIGURE 5.51 Format As Table Box

4. On the Format As Table box, note the cell range. In this example, it is =$A:$H, which means that all cells in columns A through H will be formatted.
5. Check the My Table Has Headers option. Click OK (see Figure 5.51).
6. With the columns still selected, go to the Home tab, and in the Cells group, choose Format and then AutoFit Column Width.
7. Select row 1. On the Home tab in the Cells group, click Format Row Height. In the Row Height box type 25.

The finished check book should look similar to Figure 5.52.

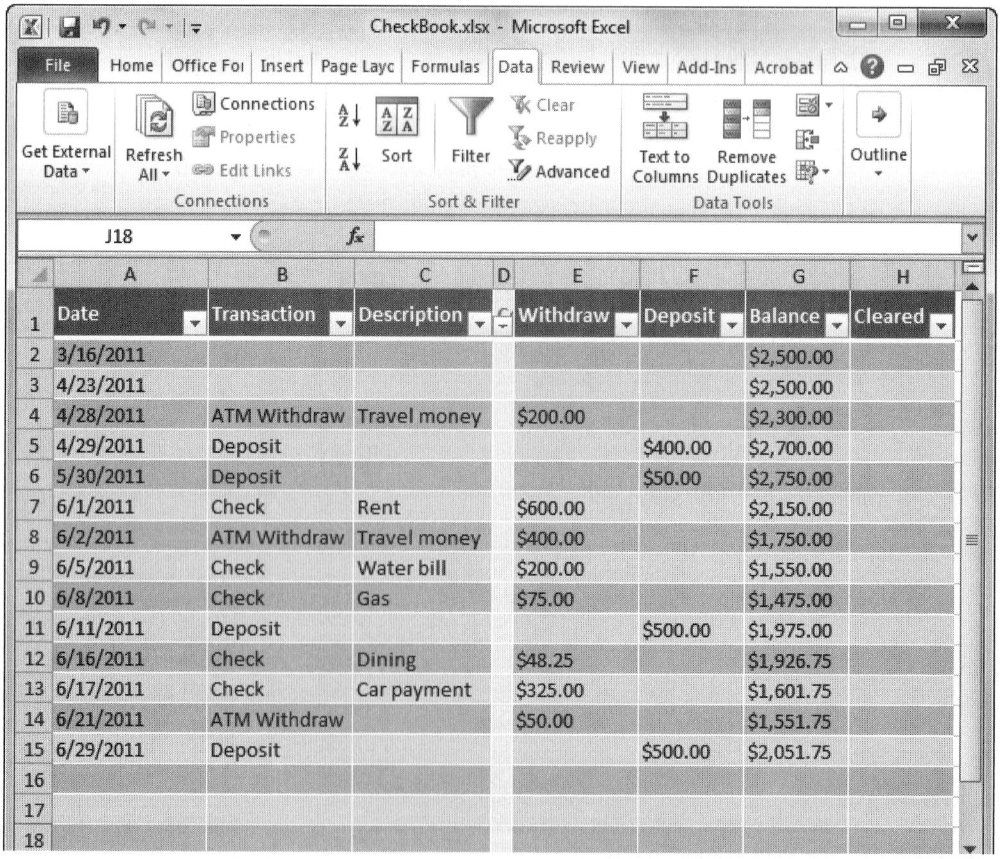

FIGURE 5.52 A Finished Checkbook

PROJECT FOR STUDENTS: CALCULATING FUTURE VALUE (HOW MUCH DO I NEED TO SAVE?)

Suppose you want to have students calculate the future value of their savings or how much they will need to save each month to acquire a specific amount of money over a period of time. Using Excel's PMT function, you can do this easily:

1. Open a new workbook and save it.
2. In cell A1, type Purpose of Savings.
3. In cell B1, type Loan Amount. Select column A and format it as Currency (in the Number group of the Home tab).
4. In cell C1, type Interest Rate. Select column B and format it as Percentage.
5. In cell D1, type Duration in Years.
6. In cell E1, type Amount to Save Each Month. Select column D and format it as Currency.
7. In cell A2, type Saving for College.
8. In cell B2, enter a value for Future Amount. For this example, enter $50,000.
9. In cell C2, enter the annual interest rate of 6%.
10. In cell D2, enter the duration in years. In this example, you will examine savings over an 18-year period so type 18 in cell D2.
11. In cell E2, enter the PMT function =PMT(C2/12,D2*12,0,B2) and press Enter (see Figure 5.53). You should see –$129.08, which is the amount you will need to save each month to eventually save $50,000 in 18 years.

    The PMT function takes the following four arguments:

    - *Rate*—Interest rate
    - *Nper*—Total number of payments
    - *Pv*—Present value
    - *Fv*—Future value

In this example, for the first argument (Rate), you take the interest rate and divide it by 12 for each month (C2/12) to get the monthly interest rate. The second argument (Nper) is the duration, 18 years. You need a monthly amount, so multiply the value in cell D2 by 12 (D2*12). The third argument (Present Value) is zero because you have not saved any money yet. The final argument (Future Value) is the value in cell A2, or the amount you ultimately want to have saved: $50,000.

12. Click the Format As Table button and select Table Style Medium 3. In the Format As Table box, note the cell range. In this example, it is =$A:$E. Check the My Table Has Headers option and click OK.

    The completed calculator should look as shown in Figure 5.54.

PDToolkit for *Microsoft® Office 2010 for Teachers*

Go to PDToolkit for **Microsoft® Office 2010 for Teachers** to locate a completed version of the letter in the Examples folder. Suppose you want to have students calculate the future value of their savings or how much they will need to save each month to acquire a specific amount of money over a period of time.

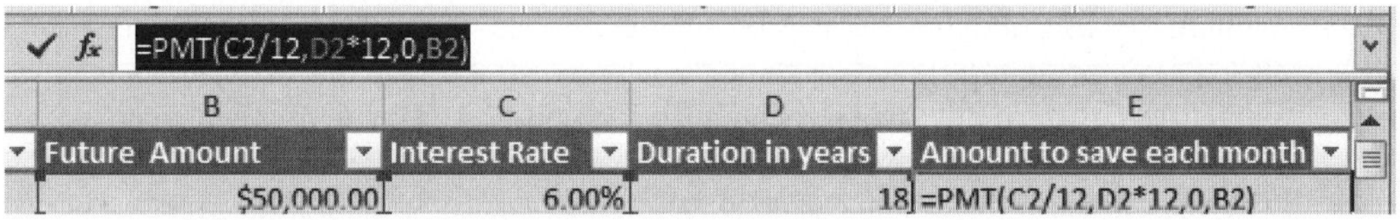

FIGURE 5.53 The PMT Function

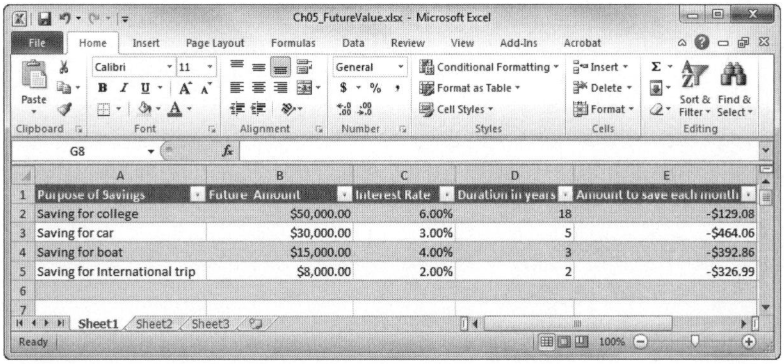

FIGURE 5.54 A Completed Future Value Calculator

PROJECT FOR TEACHERS: CREATING A MORTGAGE PAYMENT CALCULATOR

It is sometimes difficult to get a sense of how much interest rates affect the amount we pay toward a loan. A perfect illustration of this is when an individual takes on a home mortgage. The cost of the home may be $120,900, but the borrower pays more than that amount due to the interest involved. To encourage financial literacy, the mortgage payment calculator activity can help give students (and you) a sense of how much you actually pay when taking out a loan. When you complete the activity, you and your students can change the loan amounts, interest rates, and payment periods to see how much borrowers pay. Follow these steps:

1. Open a new workbook and save it.
2. In cell A1, type Mortgage Information.
3. In cell A2, type Loan Amount.
4. In cell A3, type Interest Rate.
5. In cell A4, type Duration in Years.
6. In cell A5, type Monthly Payment.
7. In cell B1, type A 15 Year Mortgage Example.
8. In cell B2, type the loan amount. In this example, assume the loan amount is $192,735.40. Format cell B2 for Currency.
9. In cell B3, type the interest rate—in this case, 3.81%. Format cell B3 for Percentage.
10. In cell B4, type the duration, 15 Years.
11. In cell B5, type, the PMT formula =PMT(B3/12,B4*12,B2). Format cell B5 for Currency (see Figure 5.55).

Here the PMT function takes three arguments: Rate, interest rate; Nper, total number of payments; and Pv, present value. In this example, for the first argument (Rate), you take the interest rate of 3.81% and divide it by 12 for each month (B3/12). For the second argument (Nper), the duration is 15 years. You need a monthly amount, so multiply the value in cell B4 by 12 (B4*12). The third argument (Present Value) is the loan amount of $192,735.40, the value in cell B2. This gives us the monthly payment, which should appear in cell B5 (refer to Figure 5.55).

Calculating Principal and Interest

Now suppose that you want to figure out how much of a monthly payment goes to the principal and how much goes to interest. Follow these steps:

12. Type Month, Principal Paid, Interest Paid, and Balance in cells A9, B9, C9, and D9, respectively (see Figure 5.56).
13. Under the Month heading, you need a number to represent each month, starting from 0 and continuing to 180 (the total number of months for a 15-year mortgage). Beginning with cell A10, you could type 0 and continue through to cell A190 so that your numbers range from 0 to180. Instead of typing 0 is cell A10, 1 in cell A11, 2 is cell A12 and so on, type 0 in cell A10 and then in cell A11 type the formula =A10+1 and press Enter.
14. Next, click in cell A11 to make it active. Note the square in the bottom-right corner of the cell. Position the mouse pointer over the square until it changes to a solid cross

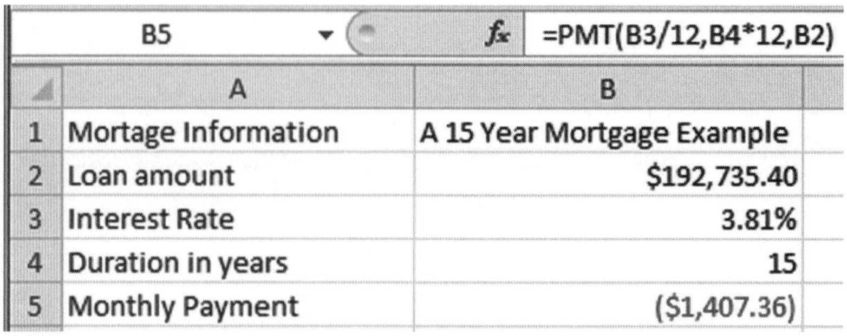

B5 | fx =PMT(B3/12,B4*12,B2)

	A	B
1	Mortage Information	A 15 Year Mortgage Example
2	Loan amount	$192,735.40
3	Interest Rate	3.81%
4	Duration in years	15
5	Monthly Payment	($1,407.36)

FIGURE 5.55 The PMT Function for a Mortgage Calculator

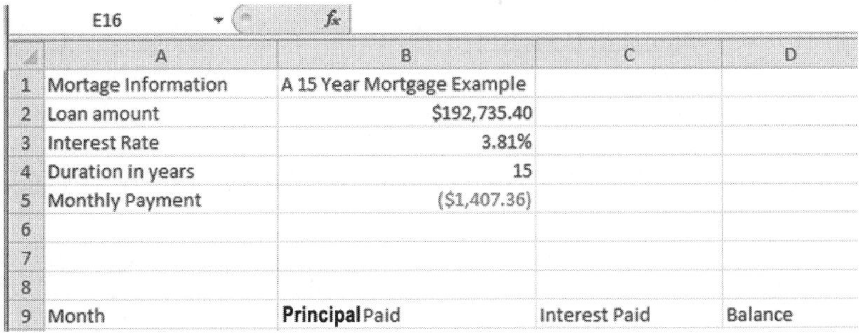

FIGURE 5.56 Principal and Interest

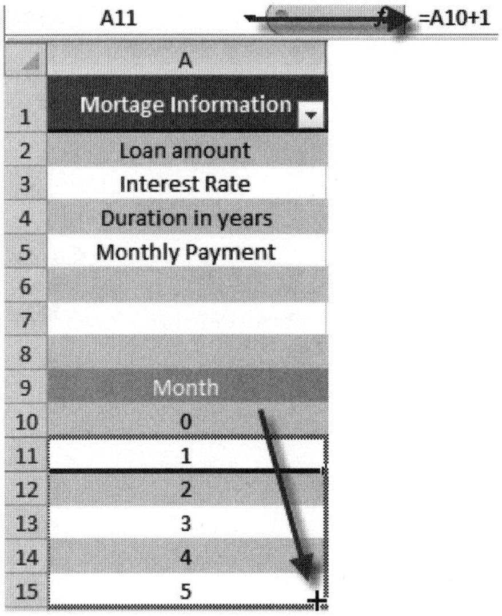

FIGURE 5.57 Representing 180 Months

(see Figure 5.57). With the cursor as a cross, click the left mouse button and drag down until you have 180 months. If you being at cell A11, you must drag down to cell A190 so that cell A10 begins with 0 and cell A190 ends with 180, representing the 180 months in the 15-year period.

15. Click in cell B11 and type the PPMT formula =PPMT($B$3/12,A11,$B$4*12,$D$10), which tells how much of the principal you pay each month. Press Enter (see Figure 5.58).
16. The PPMT function takes four arguments: Rate, the interest rate; Per, the period for which the payment on principal is calculated, which must be a number between 1 and the total number of payments (Nper); Nper, the total number of payments; and Pv, the present value. In this example, for the first argument (Rate), you use the interest rate 3.81% and divide it by 12 for each month (B3/12). Because you want to use the absolute value for the interest rate, column and row references are preceded by a $, as in $B$3/12. The second argument (Per), the period for which the payment on principal is calculated, is represented by the numbers (0 through 180) that you entered in column A. Each pay period is represented in column A, rows 11 through 190. To get the third argument (Nper), number of payments, you take the value is cell B4 (15 years) and multiply it by 12 (B4*12). The fourth argument (Present value) is the loan amount of $192,735.40, the value in cell B2. This gives you the amount you pay on the principal in each payment.

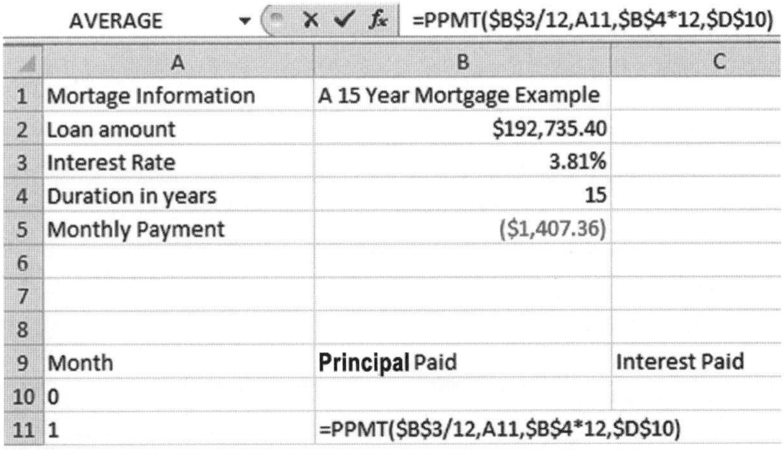

FIGURE 5.58 The PPMT Formula

Calculating Interest

17. Click in cell C11. Type the formula =$B$5-B11. To calculate the amount of interest paid each month, subtract the amount of principal (cell B11) from the monthly payment in cell B5. You need to use the absolute value for the monthly payment, so begin column and row references with $, as in $B$5 (see Figure 5.59).

Calculating the Loan Balance

18. Click in cell D11. Type the formula =D10+B11. To calculate the monthly balance on the loan, subtract that current month's principal from the previous month's balance. For example, in cell D10 is the opening balance for pay period 0. In cell B11 is the amount paid this month (pay period 1) toward the principal, represented as –$795.42. Thus, D10 plus –$795.42 gives the current balance for pay period 1. At this point, your worksheet should look similar to Figure 5.60.
19. Copy the formula in cells B11, C11, and D11 for each of the 180 months. To do this, click in cell B11 and with the left mouse button pressed, drag to cell D11 (see Figure 5.61).

Note the square in the bottom-right corner of cell D11. Position the mouse pointer over the square until it changes to a solid cross. With the cursor as a cross, click the left mouse button and drag down to row 190, or until you have a total of 180 months. A relative reference to the

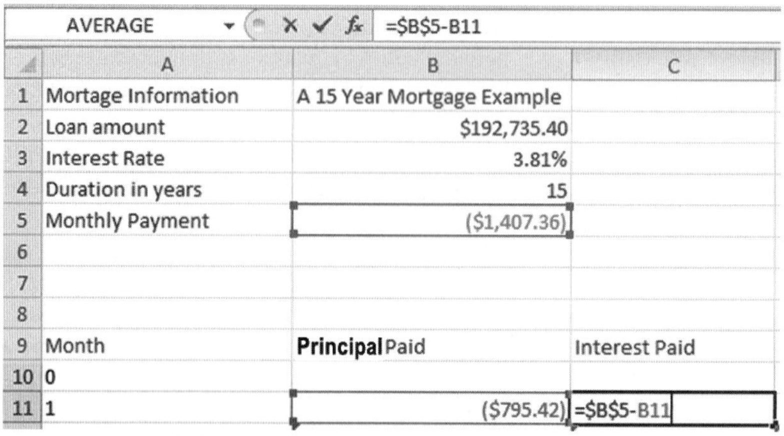

AVERAGE =$B$5-B11

	A	B	C
1	Mortage Information	A 15 Year Mortgage Example	
2	Loan amount	$192,735.40	
3	Interest Rate	3.81%	
4	Duration in years	15	
5	Monthly Payment	($1,407.36)	
6			
7			
8			
9	Month	Principal Paid	Interest Paid
10	0		
11	1	($795.42)	=$B$5-B11

FIGURE 5.59 Calculating Interest

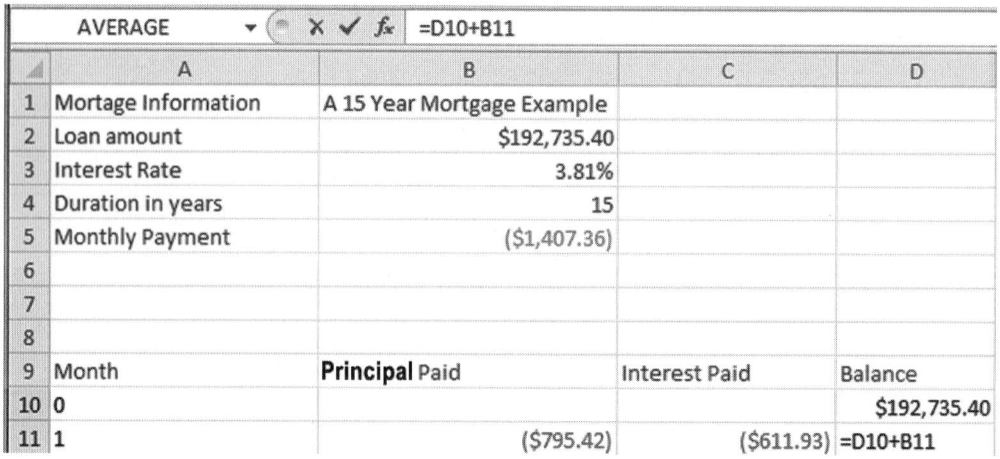

AVERAGE =D10+B11

	A	B	C	D
1	Mortage Information	A 15 Year Mortgage Example		
2	Loan amount	$192,735.40		
3	Interest Rate	3.81%		
4	Duration in years	15		
5	Monthly Payment	($1,407.36)		
6				
7				
8				
9	Month	Principal Paid	Interest Paid	Balance
10	0			$192,735.40
11	1	($795.42)	($611.93)	=D10+B11

FIGURE 5.60 Calculating the Loan Balance

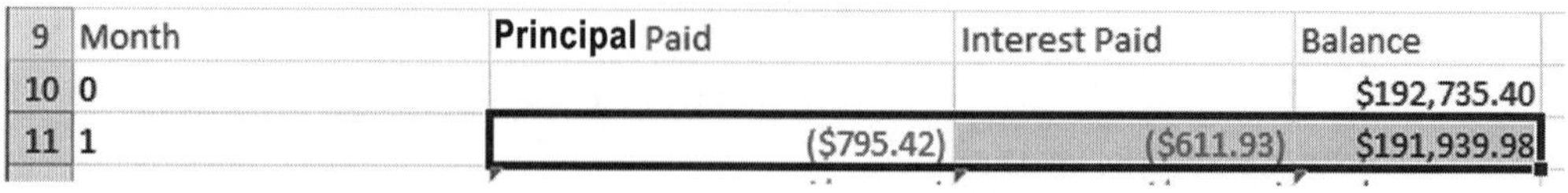

9	Month	Principal Paid	Interest Paid	Balance
10	0			$192,735.40
11	1	($795.42)	($611.93)	$191,939.98

FIGURE 5.61 Copying Cell Formulas

177	167	($1,346.27)	($61.09)	$17,895.42
178	168	($1,350.54)	($56.82)	$16,544.88
179	169	($1,354.83)	($52.53)	$15,190.05
180	170	($1,359.13)	($48.23)	$13,830.92
181	171	($1,363.45)	($43.91)	$12,467.47
182	172	($1,367.77)	($39.58)	$11,099.70
183	173	($1,372.12)	($35.24)	$9,727.58
184	174	($1,376.47)	($30.89)	$8,351.11
185	175	($1,380.84)	($26.51)	$6,970.26
186	176	($1,385.23)	($22.13)	$5,585.04
187	177	($1,389.63)	($17.73)	$4,195.41
188	178	($1,394.04)	($13.32)	$2,801.37
189	179	($1,398.46)	($8.89)	$1,402.90
190	180	($1,402.90)	($4.45)	$0.00

FIGURE 5.62 Cell Formulas for 180 Months

formulas in cells B11, C11, and D11gets copied for all rows. You should see that at 180 months, the balance is zero (see Figure 5.62).

Formatting the Mortgage Payment Calculator

20. Click the column headings so that all the columns are selected.
21. Click the Format As Table button and select Table Style Medium 17.
22. In the Format As Table box, note the cell range. In this example, it is =$A:$H, which means that all cells in columns A through H will be formatted.
23. Check My Table Has Headers and click OK.
24. With the columns still selected, go to the Home tab, and in the Cells group, choose Format and then AutoFit Column Width.
25. Select row 1. On the Home tab in the Cells group, click Format Row Height. In the Row Height box type 25.
26. Select row 9. On the Home tab in the Styles group, click Cell Styles and choose Accent 3. The formatted mortgage payment table should look similar to the one shown in Figure 5.63.

	A	B	C	D
1	Mortage Information	A 15 Year Mortgage Example	Column1	Column2
2	Loan amount	$192,735.40		
3	Interest Rate	3.81%		
4	Duration in years	15		
5	Monthly Payment	($1,407.36)		
6				
7				
8				
9	Month	Principal Paid	Interest Paid	Balance
10	0			$192,735.40
11	1	($795.42)	($611.93)	$191,939.98
12	2	($797.95)	($609.41)	$191,142.03
13	3	($800.48)	($606.88)	$190,341.54
14	4	($803.02)	($604.33)	$189,538.52
15	5	($805.57)	($601.78)	$188,732.94
16	6	($808.13)	($599.23)	$187,924.81
17	7	($810.70)	($596.66)	$187,114.11
18	8	($813.27)	($594.09)	$186,300.84
19	9	($815.85)	($591.51)	$185,484.99

Sheet1 Sheet2 Sheet3

FIGURE 5.63 A Formatted Mortgage Payment Table

PROJECT FOR ADMINISTRATORS: CREATING PIVOTTABLE AND PIVOTCHART REPORTS

A PivotTable report allows you to quickly summarize large amounts of data dynamically and to generate easily adjustable summary tables. Without writing complex formulas, you can shift, or "pivot," columns and rows to perform in-depth and diverse analyses.

With a PivotChart report, you can generate graphical representations of data in a PivotTable report. The arrangement of data presented in a PivotChart report can be easily modified. Each PivotChart report has a corresponding PivotTable.

There are many levels at which schools can assess their effectiveness. Ideally, four types of data should be collected as indicators of a school's accomplishments and improvement: (a) data on student learning and achievement, (b) demographic data, (c) data on school programs and processes, and (d) perception data (Learning Points Associates & NCREL, 2004). This example focuses on perception data, which can help school administrators address the attitudes and ideas of the school community. You will use a sample of data collected from a perception survey sent to members of the school community. A selection of the survey questions is presented below. Respondents rated their opinions on a 10-point scale from 0 to 9, with 0 indicating strongly disagree (SD) and 9 indicating strong agree (SA). In addition, the survey collected data about the respondents' education level, school/grade level affiliation, and position, such as teacher or community business owner who might hire graduates.

The following are examples of the survey items:

1. I am satisfied with the school.
2. I am satisfied with our educational programs.
3. Science and math programs are our strength.
4. Art and music programs are our strength.
5. Reading and writing programs are our strength.
6. Athletics programs are our strength.
7. The skills of our graduates are adequate.
8. Students spend an adequate amount of time on homework.
9. Student transportation needs are adequately accommodated.
10. Technical facilities are sufficient.
11. Technology is used effectively to enhance learning.
12. Facilities are accessible to students with disabilities.
13. Communications with school staff are useful.
14. Written communications about students (e.g., report cards, newsletters) are available in a language I understand.
15. School administrators listen and take my opinions into consideration in terms of school policy decisions.
16. My level of education:
    - *HSD*—High school diploma
    - *COL*—College degree
    - *MAD*—Master's degree
    - *MA+*—Beyond a master's degree
17. The school or grade level with which I am affiliated:
    - *PRE*—Preschool
    - *KD8*—Kindergarten through eighth grade
    - *MID*—Grades 9 through 10
    - *HHS*—High school (grades 11 through 12)
    - *ALL*—Not affiliated with a specific school or grade level but a member of the community
18. Respondent type:
    - Alumnus (of the high school)
    - Parent
    - Teacher
    - Community citizen
    - Community businesses (owner or manager)
    - School administrator

PivotTable Report: Defining a PivotTable Range

1. To begin, you need to specify the range of data to use in the PivotTable. Open the perception_PivotTableData.xlsx file. If it is not already active, click the Perception Data worksheet tab at the bottom left of the worksheet, and you see the survey data.
2. In this example, you will use all the columns from *ID* through School Affiliation. Click in cell A2, which contains the column header *ID*. With the mouse button pressed, drag down to row 101 and right to column A so that all the data from cell A2 through S101 are selected (see Figure 5.64)

These are the data you will use in the PivotTable report. If you plan to add additional rows of information later, you can do so. However, after entering the data, you need to click the Refresh button, which can be found in the Data group on the Options tab under PivotTable Tools. The PivotTable Tools tab becomes active when you click in the PivotTable. You can also right-click in the PivotTable and select Refresh.

3. On the Ribbon, click the Insert tab. Click PivotTable and select the PivotTable Drop-Down option (see Figure 5.65). The Create PivotTable box appears (see Figure 5.66).
4. Select a Table or Range is currently active. If your data existed in an external file, you would choose the Use an External Data Source option. The two options under Choose Where You Want the PivotTable Report to Be Placed allow you to specify the location for the PivotTable. Choose the default, New Worksheet, and Excel creates a new worksheet and places the PivotTable within it. Click OK. The worksheet presents a new PivotTable (see Figure 5.67).

Excel refers to columns in your source data as *fields*. Notice in this example that the column headers of your source data are listed under PivotTable Field List. In addition, notice the Drop Report Filters Fields Here, Drop Row Fields Here, Drop Column Fields Here, and Data Value Items Here regions of the PivotTable.

5. If the PivotTable does not display regions and looks like Figure 5.68, right-click inside the PivotTable area and select PivotTable Options. Click the Display tab and check the Classic PivotTable Layout (Enables Dragging of Fields in the Grid) item. Click OK.

PDToolkit for *Microsoft® Office 2010 for Teachers*

Go to PDToolkit for **Microsoft® Office 2010 for Teachers** to locate a completed version of the letter in the Examples folder. Open the perception_PivotTableData.xlsx file.

	A	B	C	D	E	F	G	H	I	J	K	L	M	N	O	P	Q	R	S
71	70	Alumnus	0	5	0	0	9	5	0	4	4	5	4	9	7	6	9	HSD	HHS
72	71	Parent	0	2	9	8	3	1	0	3	2	7	1	7	4	4	4	HSD	KD8
73	72	Parent	1	2	1	1	7	8	7	1	7	3	0	9	9	2	3	MAD	MID
74	73	Community citizen	8	6	0	6	6	6	6	2	3	8	4	2	0	6	5	MAD	ALL
75	74	Alumnus	7	1	7	7	4	4	0	4	4	9	7	0	5	6	4	COL	HHS
76	75	Community Citizen	1	6	5	6	9	5	0	4	1	1	8	3	8	7	7	HSD	HHS
77	76	Parent	4	6	9	5	6	5	0	1	9	6	6	4	6	9	5	HSD	PRE
78	77	Alumnus	5	9	0	8	2	3	6	7	6	9	1	4	4	6	1	COL	HHS
79	78	Alumnus	0	2	3	5	2	2	4	7	2	0	3	0	9	7	8	HSD	HHS
80	79	Administrator	1	9	0	6	0	2	9	7	0	6	4	0	6	0	1	MA+	MID
81	80	Community business	8	6	3	3	1	8	3	0	9	5	6	7	3	4	4	COL	MID
82	81	Teacher	6	9	2	6	8	6	2	4	5	7	9	1	1	9	4	MA+	MID
83	82	Parent	7	4	5	2	7	0	8	4	3	3	4	3	0	5	0	COL	MID
84	83	Teacher	4	8	8	4	0	1	0	6	7	4	5	2	0	7	8	COL	MID
85	84	Community business	8	5	0	2	3	7	3	5	3	0	7	7	1	2	9	COL	ALL
86	85	Teacher	1	2	0	0	6	0	9	9	7	6	4	7	7	6	7	MAD	HHS
87	86	Alumnus	7	2	6	0	3	7	1	5	8	7	2	7	7	9	9	COL	HHS
88	87	Community business	3	9	6	0	3	1	4	1	4	4	5	5	1	6	1	COL	ALL
89	88	Teacher	5	7	8	0	6	7	0	2	9	0	2	0	9	9	8	COL	PRE
90	89	Administrator	7	7	6	3	2	7	4	2	0	0	7	3	6	0	3	MA+	PRE
91	90	Teacher	2	3	4	7	3	4	0	6	0	5	8	5	8	8	5	COL	KD8
92	91	Parent	7	4	7	3	2	4	3	1	4	5	7	2	5	5	6	COL	HHS
93	92	Teacher	4	9	2	4	4	9	8	8	6	4	1	3	6	7	8	COL	PRE
94	93	Community citizen	5	1	2	1	9	6	4	7	1	9	2	4	7	8	8	HSD	HHS
95	94	Teacher	8	2	2	6	3	4	5	4	7	9	3	9	7	8	8	MA+	HHS
96	95	Administrator	4	9	2	4	1	6	6	7	1	2	2	8	0	0	4	MA+	PRE
97	96	Parent	5	6	8	5	7	5	8	2	4	5	5	8	0	1	6	HSD	ALL
98	97	Alumnus	7	1	5	7	9	9	0	4	4	6	5	3	8	9	4	HSD	HHS
99	98	Community business	6	9	4	1	5	7	0	1	3	0	3	4	9	4	3	HSD	KD8
100	99	Alumnus	5	2	6	6	5	1	2	4	6	8	9	4	5	7	8	COL	HHS
101	100	Teacher	0	8	4	3	0	6	6	4	9	5	9	6	9	3	3	COL	PRE

FIGURE 5.64 A Data Range

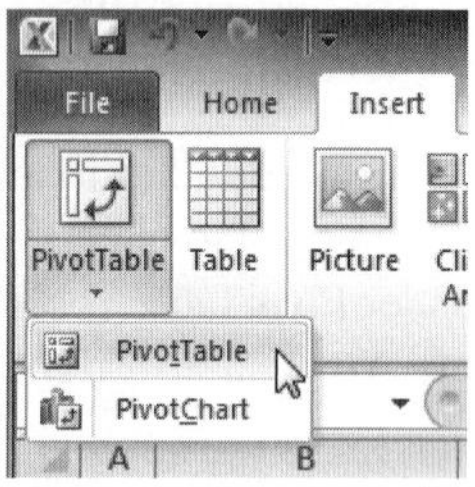

FIGURE 5.65 A PivotTable

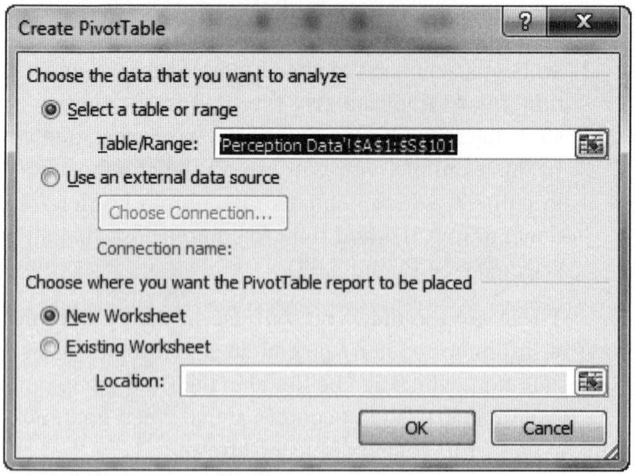

FIGURE 5.66 The Create PivotTable Box

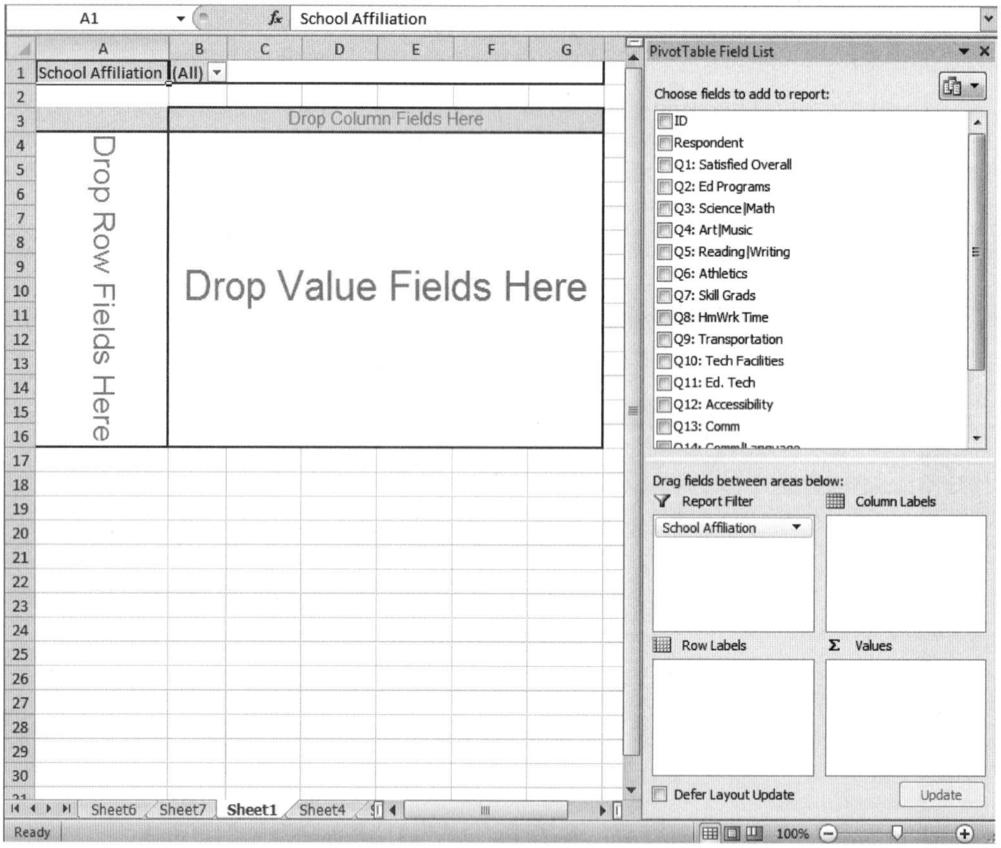

FIGURE 5.67 PivotTable Regions

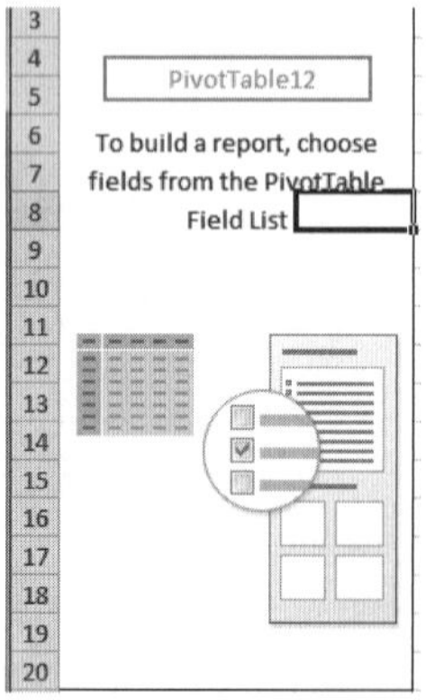

FIGURE 5.68 A PivotTable Display

To examine the data, you can drag fields listed under PivotTable Field List and drop them on any one of the regions. You may also drag fields into any of the four areas (Report Filter, Column Labels, Row Labels, and Values) at the bottom of the PivotTable Field List box. To remove a field, click inside any cell corresponding to the region, right-click, and select Remove. Alternatively, click the down arrow on the field item at the bottom of the PivotTable Field List box and select Remove (and the Corresponding Field Name).

If the PivotTable Field List box gets hidden, click inside the PivotTable to make the PivotTable Tools tab active. Click the Options tab under PivotTable Tools and then click the Field List button in the Show group. Following is a short description of each region:

- *Drop Row Fields Here*—By placing a field in this region, the data in the field are displayed as rows.
- *Drop Column Fields Here*—By placing a field in this region, the data in the field are displayed as columns at the top of the report.
- *Drop Value Field Items Here*—In this region, you place the fields for which you want to obtain subtotals or averages. For example, suppose you are interested in the education level of respondents.
- *Drop Report Filters Fields Here*—You can filter an entire report based on the item placed in this region.

Suppose you are interested in examining how respondents rated question 1, *I am satisfied with the school*. More specifically, you want to know if ratings differ by the type of school/grade level, such as preschool, K–8, and high school. To do this, the PivotTable might look like the one shown in Figure 5.69.

6. To create the table, drag the School Affiliation field to the Drop Report Filters Fields Here region; the Respondent field to the Drop Row Fields Here region; and the Q1: Satisfied Overall field to the Drop Value Data Items Here region. Notice that these fields are also present at the bottom of the PivotTable Field List box (at the bottom right of Figure 5.69).
7. Figure 5.69 displays the averages. To get averages, click the down arrow on the Sum of Q1: Satisfied Overall field located at the bottom of the PivotTable Field List box and then select Value Field Settings (see Figure 5.70).
8. On the Value Field Settings box, select Average and click OK (see Figure 5.71).

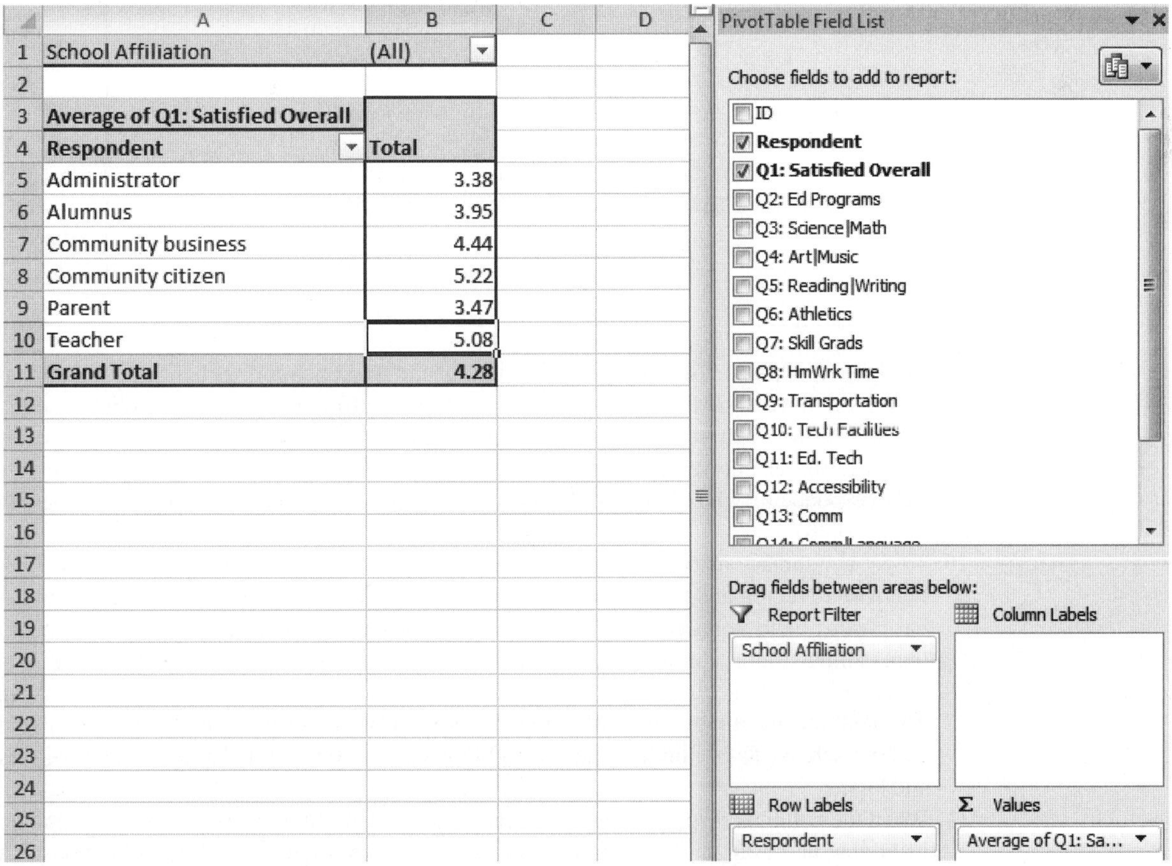

FIGURE 5.69 A Filtered PivotTable

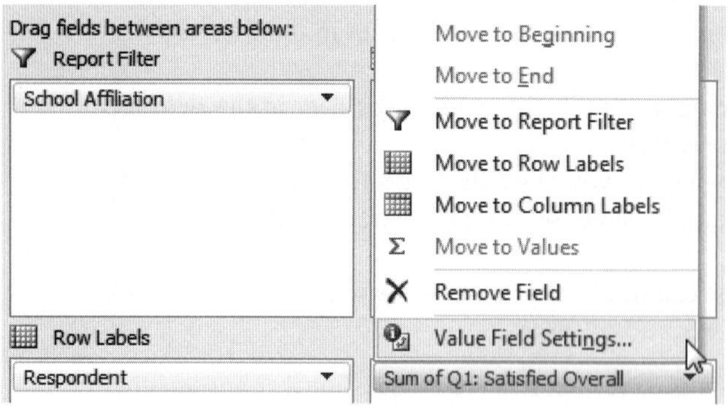

FIGURE 5.70 Value Field Settings

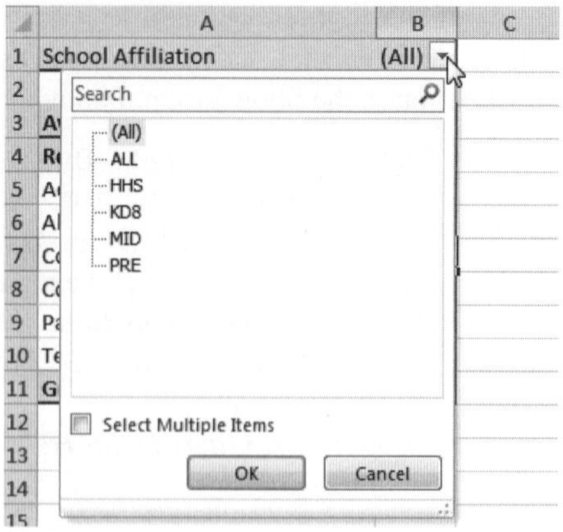

FIGURE 5.72 Filtering by Affiliation or Grade Level

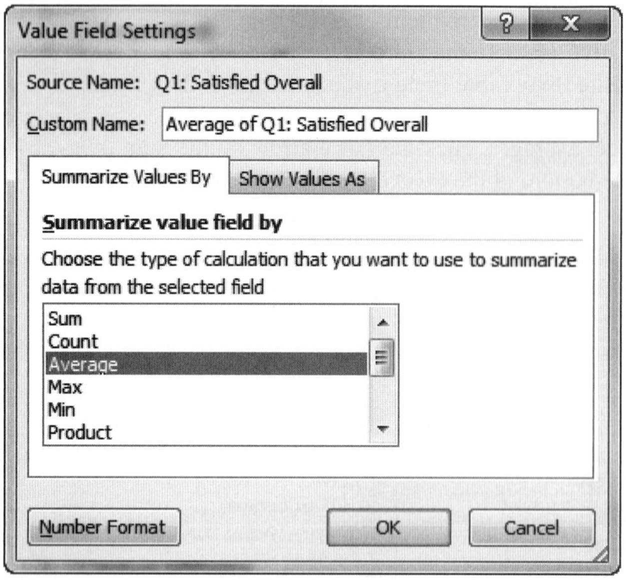

FIGURE 5.71 The Value Field Settings Box

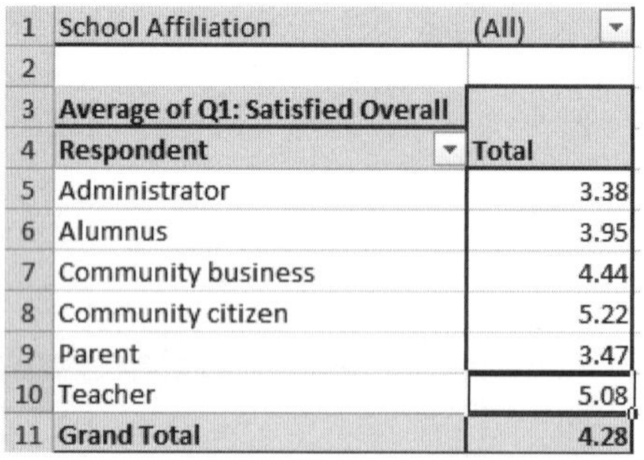

FIGURE 5.73 Filtering by School Affiliation

9. In Figure 5.72, an arrow appears to the right of the word School Affiliation (cell B1) that allows the data to be filtered based on school/grade affiliation. When you click it, a list appears from which you can select the school/grade affiliation; data about those respondents' rating are presented. For instance, Figure 5.73 shows the ratings for question 1 from respondents who identified themselves as being affiliated with the high school grade levels (HHS).
10. To get a summary of these data, you could place the Respondent field in the Drop Row Fields Here region and then place the Ed. Level in the Drop Column Fields Here and in the Drop Value Field Items Here regions. The result is a count of degrees by type of respondent (e.g., administrator, alumnus). Additionally, if you drag the School Affiliation to the Drop Report Filter Fields Here region, you can filter the data based on the type of affiliation. This could be useful, to determine how many school administrators and teachers affiliated with preschool, K–8, middle school, and high school grade levels have graduate degrees and higher.
11. When the columns display, you can rearrange them by highlighting a column, clicking on its border, and dragging it to the appropriate location. In Figure 5.74, the MAD (master's degree) column is selected. Clicking the border and dragging moves it.

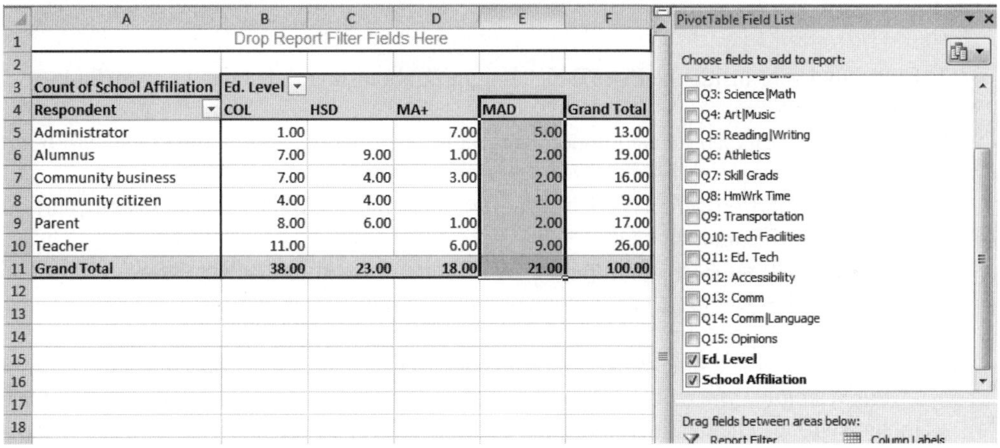

FIGURE 5.74 School Affiliation and Education Level

Examining Communications Data

Now that the data range is defined, let's examine the data. For the next example, assume that you are interested in how respondents rated communications, survey items 13, Communications with school staff are useful and 14, Written communications about students (e.g., report cards, newsletters) are available in a language I understand. You want to see these ratings by school/grade affiliation. Follow these steps:

1. Drag the School Affiliation field to the Drop Row Fields Here region or into the Row Labels box at the bottom of the PivotTable Field List box.
2. Drag the Q13: Comm and Q14: Comm | Language fields into the Drop Value Field Items Here region or into the Values box at the bottom of the PivotTable Field List box.
3. If the averages are not already shown, click the down arrow on the SumofQ13: Comm field located at the bottom of the PivotTable Field List box and then select Value Field Settings.
4. On the Value Field Settings box, select Average and click OK. Repeat this step for the Sum of Q14: Comm | Language field.
5. Your PivotTable should look similar to Figure 5.75, which shows that the communications ratings for the high school (HHS) were higher than all other ratings, which overall were low.

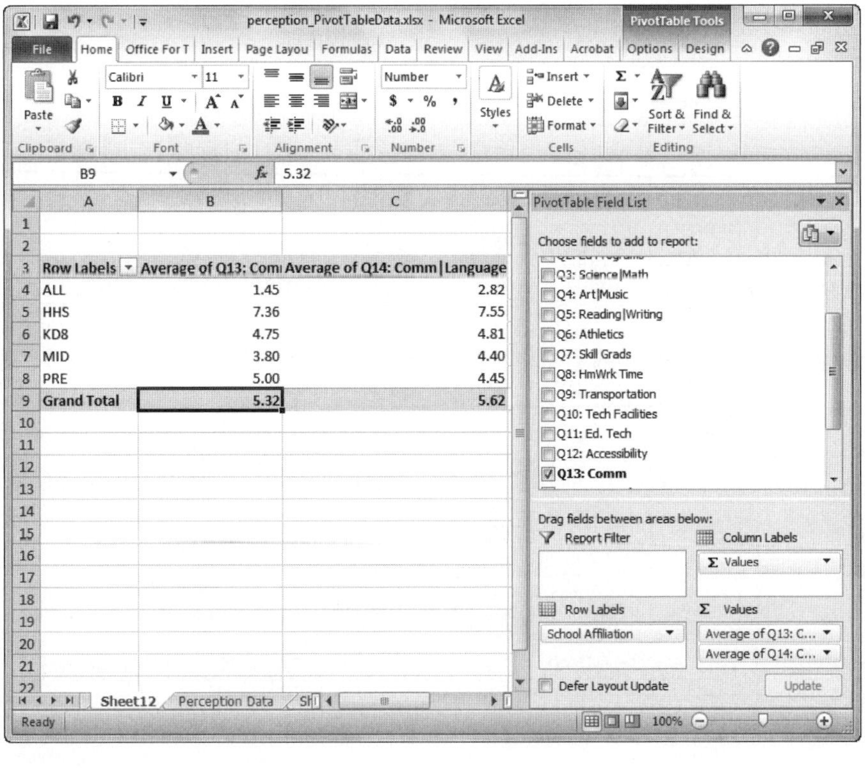

FIGURE 5.75 Ratings on Communications

Making a PivotChart

1. Click anywhere inside the PivotTable, and the Ribbon should display the PivotTable Tools tab.
2. Click the Options tab located under PivotTable Tools and then click the PivotChart button in the Tools group (see Figure 5.76).
3. The Insert Chart box displays. Click the first item under Column on the Insert Chart box (see Figure 5.77) and click OK.
4. A column chart appears (see Figure 5.78). To alter the settings, select the chart. If you inadvertently deselect the chart, Ribbon options change. To return to the chart options, click in the chart area, and on the Ribbon, under PivotChart Tools, click the Design tab.
5. Change the color and style of the chart with options in the Chart Styles group (see Figure 5.79). In this example, you will change the chart layout. Click the More option in the Chart Layouts group. The Chart Layouts box appears; select Layout 5.
6. The new layout presents a data table in the lower half of the chart. Click the title and change it from Communications and Language to a title of your choice. Simply click the title, type a new title, and press Enter. Click the Axis Title and change it to Ratings. Your complete chart should look as shown in Figure 5.80. You can now select the chart, copy it, and then open Word or PowerPoint and paste it.
7. Notice the button in the lower-left portion of the chart. Click it to filter the chart by school affiliation. For instance, you can easily change the chart so that it displays the communication ratings of only persons affiliated with the preschool or high school. This could be especially useful during a presentation.
8. You could present your data with Excel and use the Filter button on the chart to adjust how the data are represented. In addition, you could copy the chart to PowerPoint and use the copy in Excel to filter the data. The chart in PowerPoint will change accordingly.

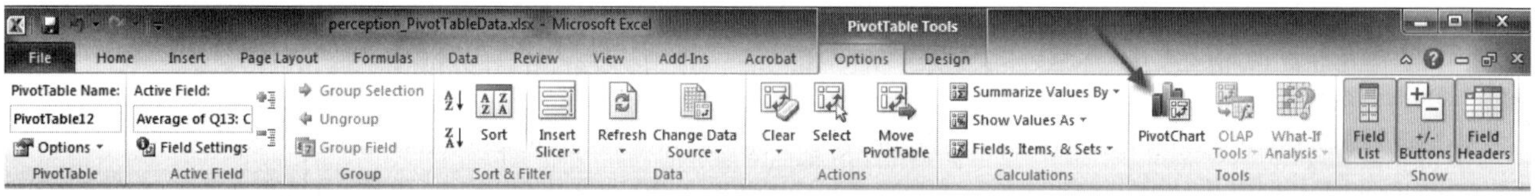

FIGURE 5.76 A PivotChart

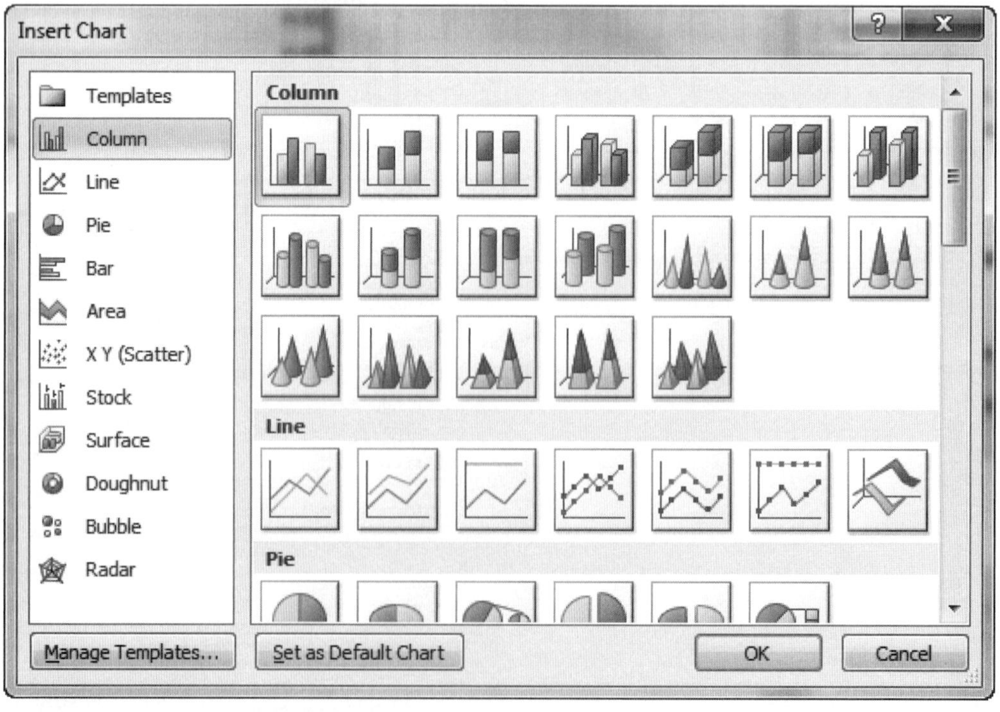

FIGURE 5.77 Inserting Chart Options

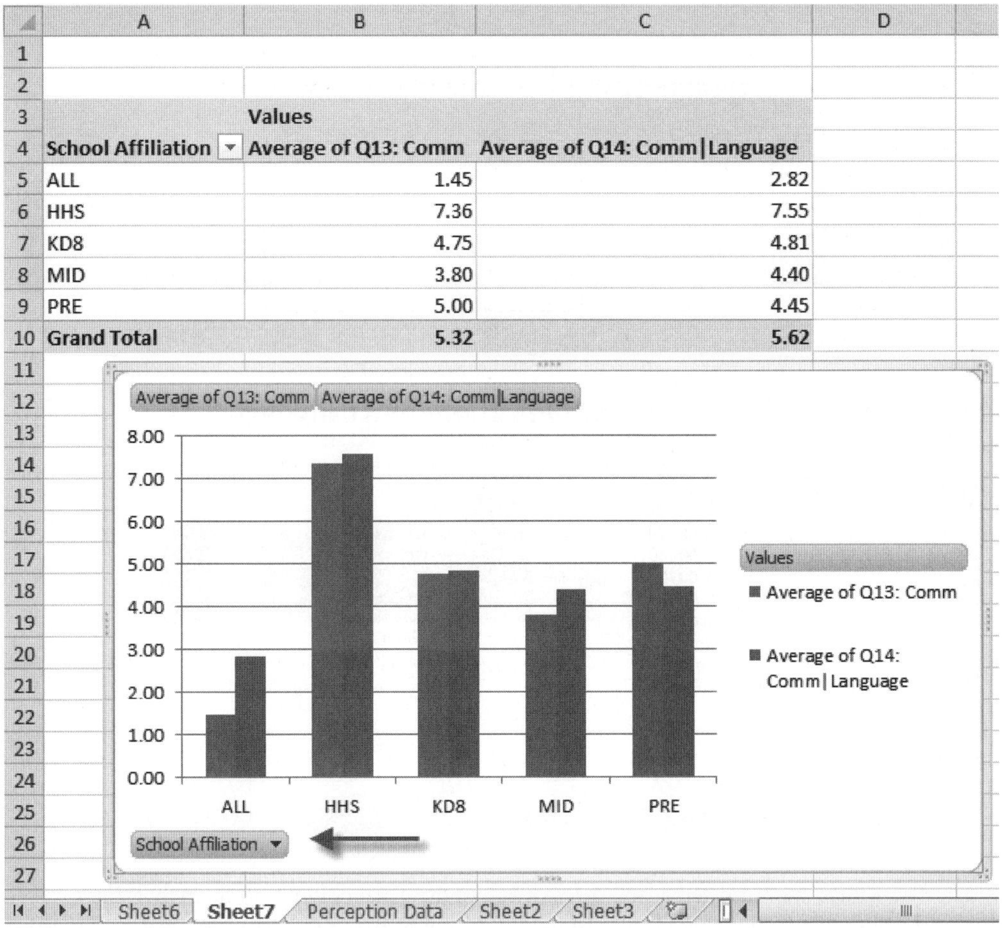

FIGURE 5.78 The Chart and Filter Options

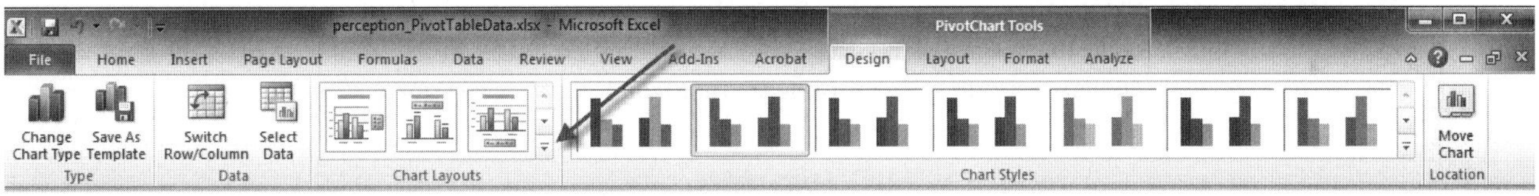

FIGURE 5.79 Chart Layouts

Examining All Survey Results

1. To get the survey results for all 15 questions, create a new PivotTable. Click in cell A2 that contains the column header ID. With the mouse button pressed, drag down to row 101 and right so that all data from cell A2 through S101 are selected.
2. On the Ribbon, click the Insert tab.
3. Click PivotTable and select the PivotTable drop-down option.
4. On the Create PivotTable box, the table or range is active. Choose New Worksheet, and Excel creates a new worksheet and places the PivotTable within it. Click OK.
5. Drag School Affiliation to the Drop Report Field Filters Here region. You will have a list of all the questions, with the average rating.
6. Drag the first question field, Q1: Satisfied Overall, to the Drop Value Fields Here region.
7. After you drop the Q1 field, you can simply check the remaining survey items under Choose Fields to add to report in the PivotTable Field List box. As you add the fields, you may notice that the data are placed in columns. For this example, you want all the survey items listed in one column, rather than each item listed in its own column.
8. Notice in Figure 5.81 that Values is listed under Column Labels on the lower-right side of the PivotTable Field List box. Drag the Values item under Row Labels. All the survey items should then be listed under one column in the PivotTable (see Figure 5.82).

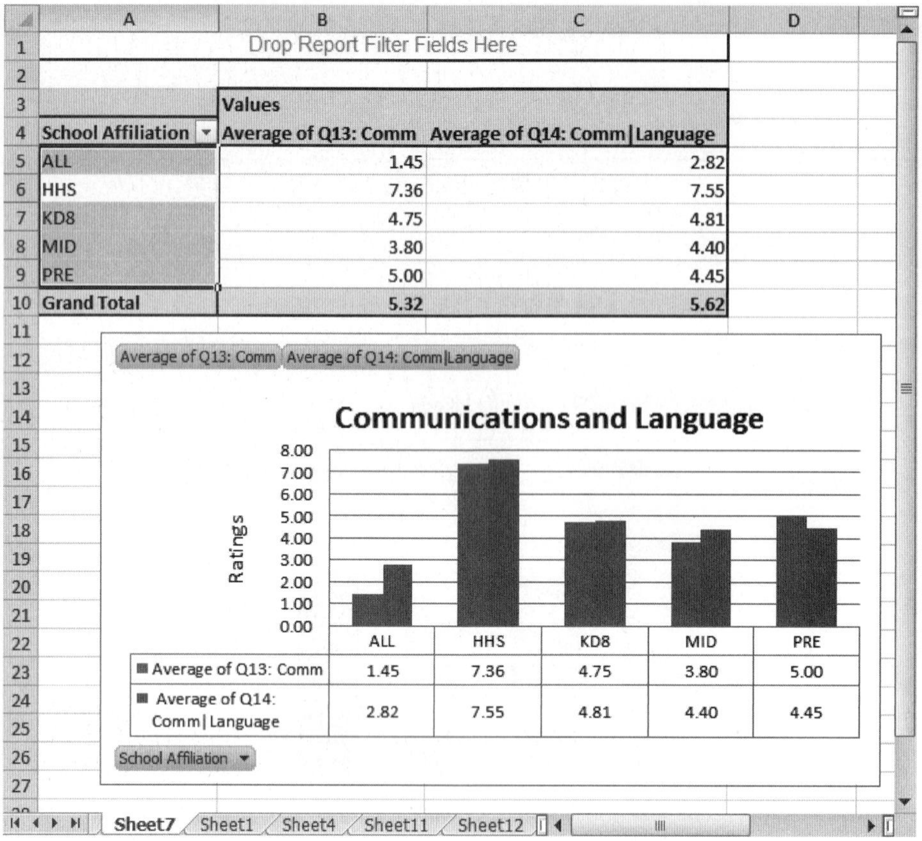

FIGURE 5.80 A Completed Chart

9. The values are not listed as averages. Click in the Total column of the PivotTable to select a value. Go to the PivotTable Tools Options tab in the Calculations group and select Summarize Values By Average. You can also right-click on the value and select Summarize Values By Average.
10. Drag the Respondents field to Column Labels in the PivotTable Field List box to see how the various types of respondents rated each item (see Figure 5.83).

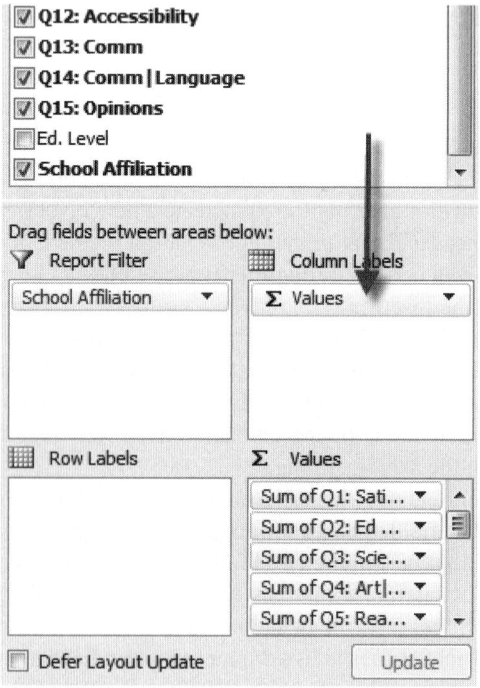

FIGURE 5.81 Column Labels

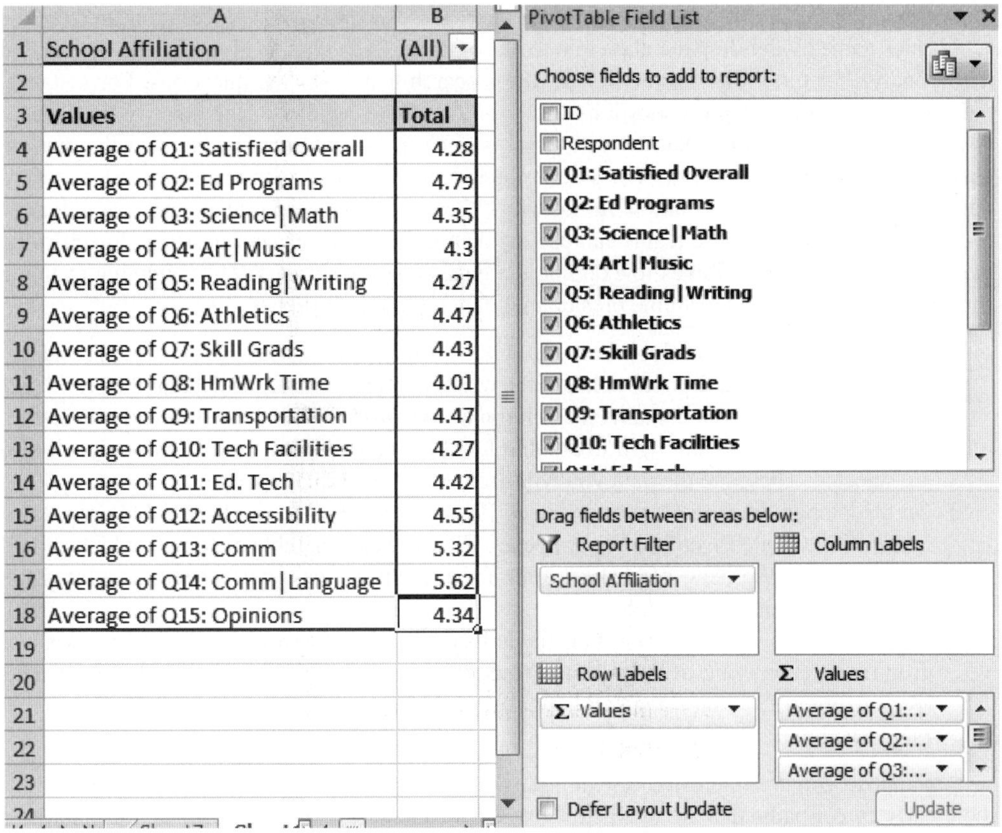

FIGURE 5.82 Row Labels

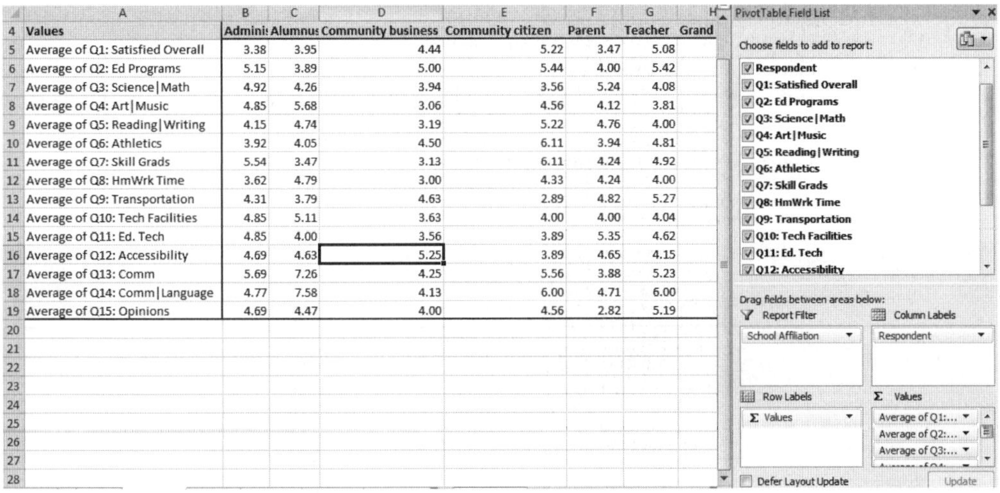

FIGURE 5.83 Respondent Ratings

PROJECT FOR STUDENTS: USING A PIVOTTABLE TO EXAMINE DATA ABOUT THE PRESIDENTS

Defining a PivotTable Range to Study the Presidents

Suppose you ask a few students to research information about all of the presidents of the United States. They collect facts and figures related to each president. After the data are collected, you and the research team glean the most important items and then generate questions. You have this research team compile the relevant data in an Excel workbook. You create a presidential scholastics game by dividing the class into teams of three. Each team is given the Excel data that it can analyze as questions are presented. The research team asks the questions. For instance, the research team might pose questions such as, "Are there regions of the country that appear to produce more presidents than others? If so, why?" or "Are there early career paths that are characteristics of presidents? or "Does being president affect one's life span?" or "Does where one lives influence party affiliation? If so, why?" You and the research team serve as judges to evaluate team responses. The teams can use the data in Excel to answer questions. Specifically, the teams could use PivotTables to examine the data to derive answers. The following example shows how students could examine presidential data to derive answers:

1. Open the President_PivotTableData.xlsx file. If it is not already active, click the President_ Data worksheet tab at the bottom left of the worksheet, and you see the data for the presidents.
2. Click in cell A2, which contains the column header Name. With the mouse button pressed, drag down to row 46 and right to column L so that all data from cell A2 through cell L46 are selected. These are the data you will use in the PivotTable report.
3. On the Ribbon, click the Insert tab. Click PivotTable and select the PivotTable drop-down option. The Create PivotTable box appears. Choose Select a Table or Range, which should be active. Choose New Worksheet, and Excel creates a new worksheet and places the PivotTable within it. Click OK.
4. To examine the data, you can drag fields listed under the PivotTable Field List box and drop them on any one of the regions. You may also drag fields into any of the four areas (Report Filter, Column Labels, Row Labels, and Values) at the bottom of the PivotTable Field List box.

Suppose you are interested in examining the presidents based on their occupation ("Are there early career paths that are characteristics of presidents?"). When you view your data, you want to know the president's name, state of birth, party affiliation, and age in first term of office. The PivotTable might look as shown in Figure 5.84. However, say that you want to examine this information based on occupation. In other words, when you ask to identify the presidents who were soldiers, the table should display all corresponding information for those who served as soldiers before the presidency.

5. To create the table, drag the Occupation field to the Drop Report Filters Fields Here region The Name, State, Party, and Age in First Term fields would be placed in the Drop Row Fields Here region. In addition, notice that these fields are also present at the bottom of the PivotTable Field List box (at the bottom right of Figure 5.84).

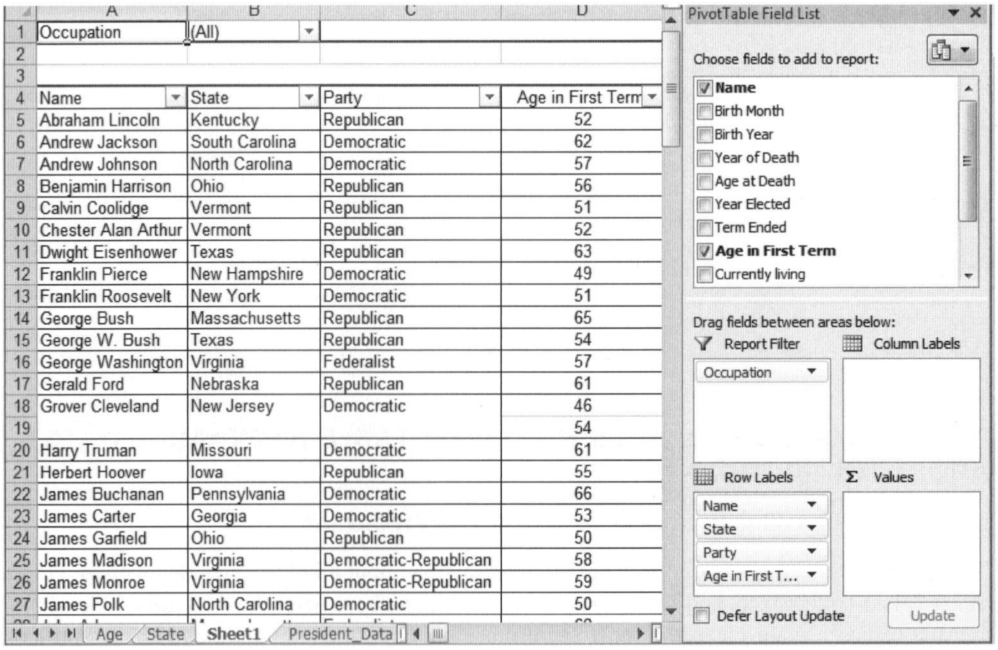

FIGURE 5.84 Career Paths That Are Characteristics of Presidents

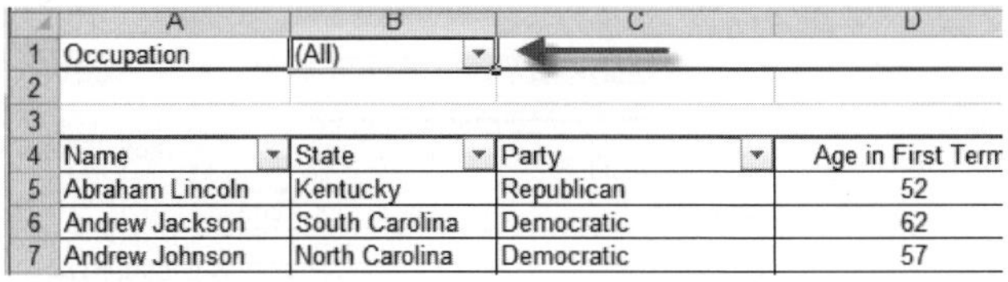

	A	B	C	D
1	Occupation	(All)		
2				
3				
4	Name	State	Party	Age in First Term
5	Abraham Lincoln	Kentucky	Republican	52
6	Andrew Jackson	South Carolina	Democratic	62
7	Andrew Johnson	North Carolina	Democratic	57

FIGURE 5.85 Filter Data

FIGURE 5.86 The Soldier Filter

6. In Figure 5.85, a down arrow appears to the right of the word ALL (cell B1); it allows the data to be filtered based on occupation. When it is clicked, a list appears, from which you can select the occupation of interest, and then information about those presidents who served in that occupation is presented (see Figure 5.86). In this example, select Soldier and click OK. The PivotTable presents a list of presidents who were soldiers prior to their presidency (see Figure 5.87).

CALCULATING THE NUMBER OF YEARS EACH PRESIDENT LIVED AFTER HIS TERM IN OFFICE ENDED

7. Open the President_PivotTableData.xlsx file if it is not already open. Define a data range as you did in the "PivotTable Report: Defining a PivotTable Range" section. Click in cell A2, which contains the column header Name. With the mouse button pressed, drag down to row 46 and right to column L so that all data from cell A2 through cell L46 are selected.
8. Click the Insert tab and then click the PivotTable button and select PivotTable to create a new PivotTable report. Place the report in a new worksheet. After Excel creates the PivotTable report, ensure that the Classic PivotTable layout is turned on.
9. Drag the Name field from the PivotTable Field List box to the Drop Row Fields Here region.
10. Drag the Year of Death and the Term Ended fields to the Drop Row Fields Here region also. You can accomplish this by dragging Year of Death to the top of the Row Fields region, where the Name header is located. Alternatively, you can drag Year of Death to the Row Labels box at the bottom right of the PivotTable Field List box.
11. Place the Year of Death field first and then the Term Ended field so that the row fields appear in the same order (Name, Term Ended, and then Year of Death) (see Figure 5.88). If needed, you can rearrange a field by clicking on it and dragging it to another location.

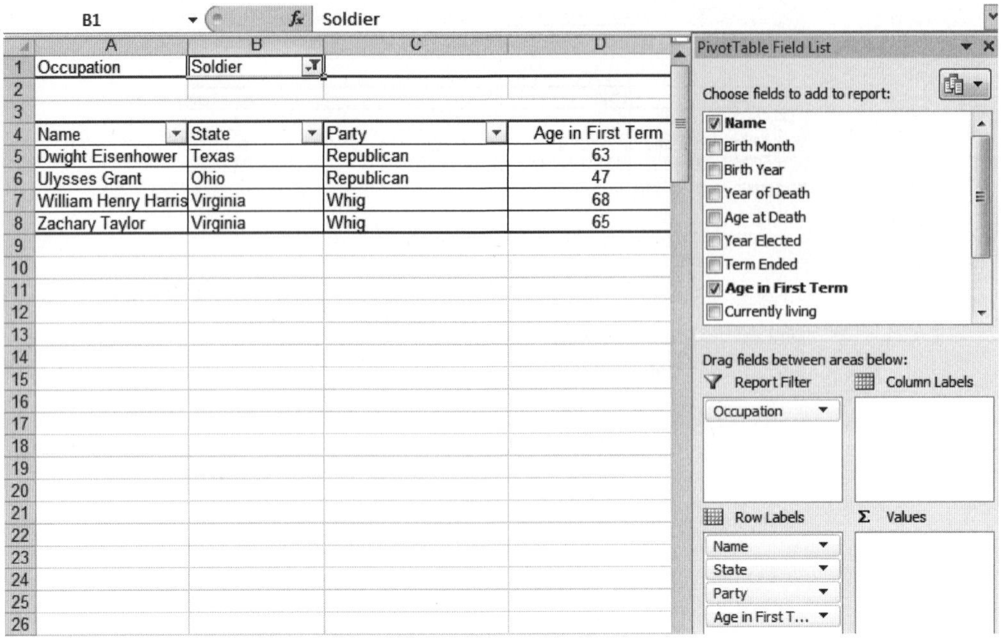

FIGURE 5.87 Presidents Who Were Soldiers

12. Notice in Figure 5.88 that an additional row (Total) appears after each name and date. You don't need the additional rows for this example, so remove them by clicking the down arrow on each field item in the Row Labels box (see Figure 5.89) and select Field Settings. You can also access the Field Settings option by right-clicking inside the table and selecting Field Setting. The Field Settings box appears.

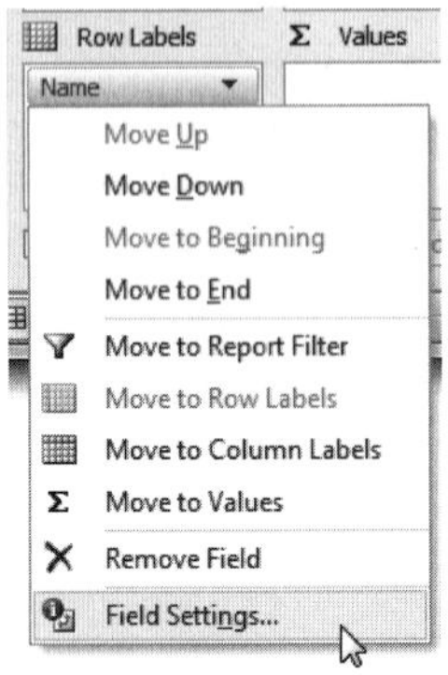

FIGURE 5.88 Row Filters

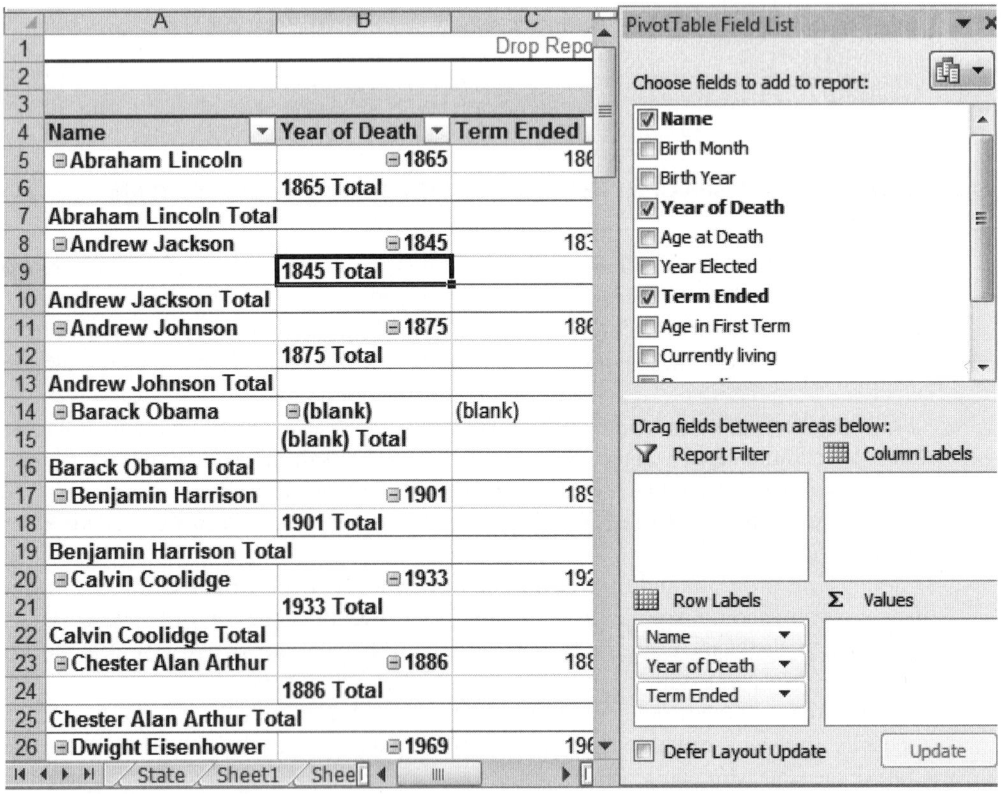

FIGURE 5.89 Field Settings

13. In the Field Settings box, select the None option and click OK (see Figure 5.90). Repeat this step for the Name, Term Ended, and Year of Death fields. In addition, notice that the table items have small (show/hide) buttons that you do not need. Turn them off by clicking in the PivotTable area, which activates the PivotTable Tools and Options. Click the Button+/- button in the Show group (see Figure 5.91). Your PivotTable should look as shown in Figure 5.92.

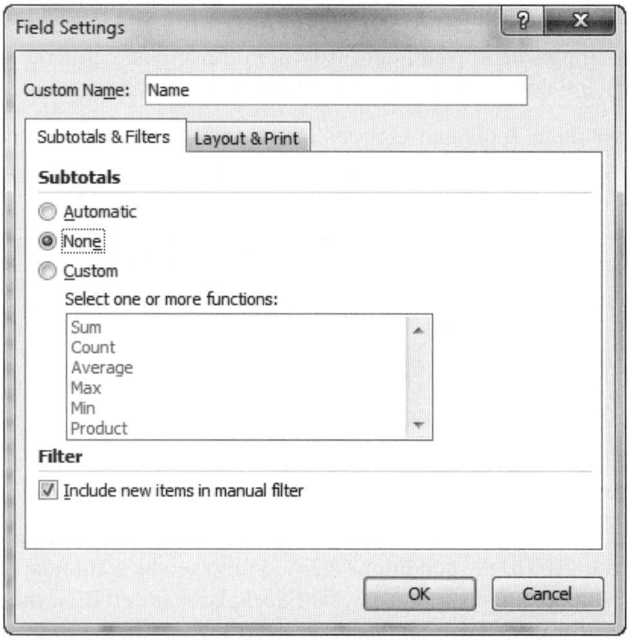

FIGURE 5.90 The Field Settings Box

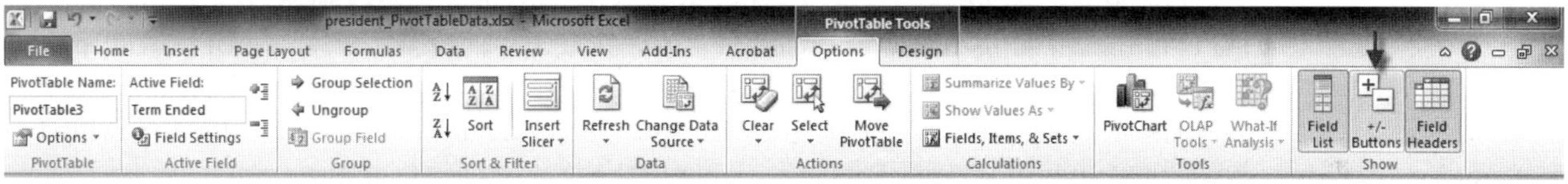

FIGURE 5.91 The Show Buttons

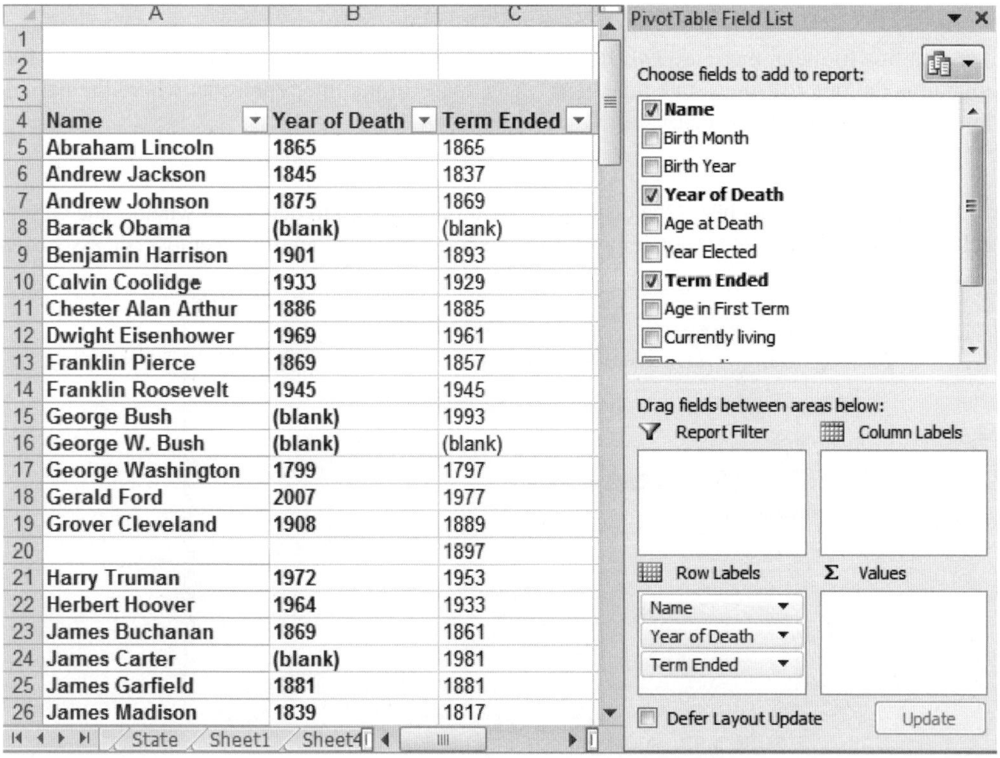

FIGURE 5.92 A PivotTable Without a Total and Buttons

14. In Figure 5.92, notice that an empty cell appears below Grover Cleveland because his two terms in office were separated by several years. It would be preferable to replace the empty cell with Cleveland's name. To do this, make the PivotTable Tools and Options tabs active by clicking in the table. On the left side of the Ribbon, click Options in the PivotTable group, and the PivotTable Options box appears. Check the item Merge and Center with Labels and click OK.

CALCULATING THE YEARS A PRESIDENT LIVED AFTER HIS TERM ENDED To calculate the number of years each president lived after his term in office, you can write a formula that subtracts the Term Ended field from the Year of Death field. Follow these steps:

15. With the PivotTable Tools and Options tabs active, click Fields, Items, and Sets in the Calculations group and select Calculated Field. The Insert Calculated Field box appears (see Figure 5.93).
16. In the Name box, type a name for the calculated field: Years Presidents Lived After Presidency. In the Formula box, type the following formula and then click OK:

```
=IF('Term Ended'<>0,IF('Year of Death'<>0,'Year of Death'- 'Term
Ended', NA()),NA())
```

The formula contains a nested IF-then conditional statement or one IF-then statement within another. To better understand it, let's review an example. Suppose you typed the following IF-then statement into Excel's formula bar for cell B2:

```
=IF(A2=95, "Good Job", "Keep Trying")
```

This statement has several parts: (a) the IF statement preceded by an equals sign to denote that it's an Excel formula; (b) the condition (A2=95) followed by a comma; (c) the result-if-true (in this case, Good Job), or, in other words, what Excel places in cell B2 if the condition turns out to be true; and (d) the result-if-false (in this case, Keep Trying). In the formula, the result-if-true precedes the result-if-false. The statement first checks the condition, if the contents of cell A2 equal 95. If the condition is true (A2=95), then the result-if-true (Good Job) is placed in cell B2, the cell for which the formula was written. If cell A2 does not equal 95, then the result-if-false (Keep Trying) is placed in cell B2.

Now let's go back to the presidential spreadsheet example and examine the following formula more closely:

```
=IF('Term Ended'<>0,IF('Year of Death'<>0,'Year of Death'-'Term Ended',
NA()),NA())
```

In this formula, there are two IF-then statements; one is nested within the other. The following is the outer IF-then statement. The blank space in the line represents where the nested/inner IF-then should be placed:

```
=IF ('Term Ended'<>0 ,,NA())
```

The outer IF-then checks the condition (Term Ended < >0) to determine whether the current cell in the Term Ended field is not empty. Using this form, you can identify the empty cell associated

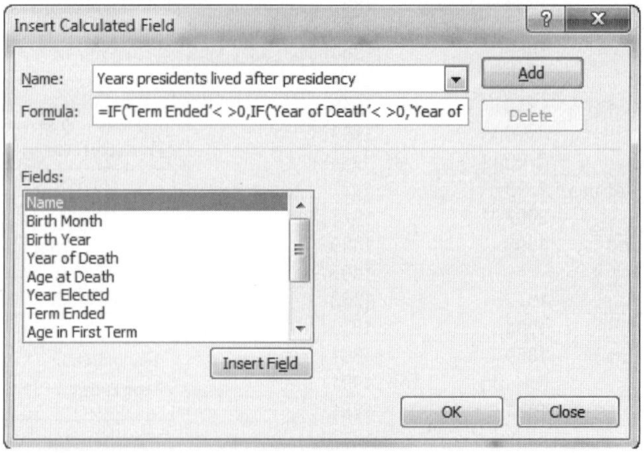

FIGURE 5.93 A Calculated Field

with the current president because his term has not yet ended and the spreadsheet contains no term ending date. You need to identify the empty cell so that it is not used in the calculation. When Term Ended < > 0 is true, or, in other words, when Term Ended is not empty and there is a date for when the term ended, the result-if-true occurs. In the earlier example, the result-if-true was Good Job, but in this case the inner/nested IF-then statement is executed. When Term Ended < > 0 is false or Term Ended is empty and there is no date, the result-if-false occurs, and Excel places #N/A in the corresponding cell (see Table 5.1). The NA() function places #N/A in PivotTable to mark empty cells.

The following is the nested/inner IF-then statement:

```
=IF('Year of Death'<>0,'Year of Death'-'Term Ended', NA())
```

The inner IF-then statement is executed only if Term Ended < >0 is true or the cell is not empty. It checks the Year of Death field for empty cells because the spreadsheet contains no year of death date for presidents who are not yet deceased. When Excel locates empty cells, it places #N/A in them. You do this to exclude empty fields from calculations. The format of this IF-then statement is similar to the outer IF-then (see Table 5.2). When Year of Death < > 0 is false or, in other words, Year of Death is empty, Excel places #N/A in the corresponding cell. When Year of Death < > 0 is true or is not empty, Excel subtracts the value in the Term Ended field from the value in the Year of Death field, which gives the number of years lived after the term in office ended.

The Years Presidents Lived After Presidency field appears in the PivotTable Field List box. If it is not already checked, drag it to the Drop Data Items Here region or under Values in the PivotTable Field List box (see Figure 5.94). The totals column appears; it calculates the years the

TABLE 5.1 Outer IF-Then Statement

Condition	When Condition Is TRUE, Do This	When Condition Is FALSE, Do This
IF('Term Ended' < >0,	IF('Year of Death'< >0,'Year of Death'-'Term Ended', NA()),	NA())

TABLE 5.2 Inner/Nested IF-Then Statement

Condition	When Condition Is TRUE, Do This	When Condition Is FALSE, Do This
IF('Year of Death'< >0,	'Year of Death'-'Term Ended',	NA())

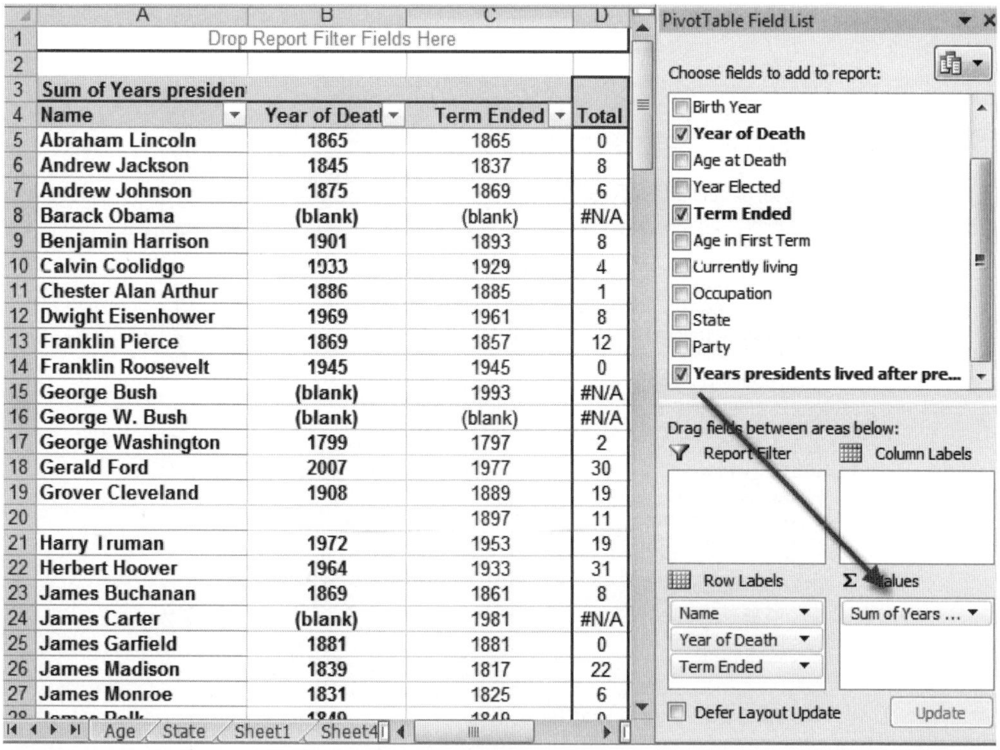

FIGURE 5.94 Years Presidents Lived After Presidency

president lived after his presidency. #NA is placed in the cell for presidents who are still living. You may notice a Grand Total of 5570 at the bottom of your table. To remove this figure from the table, click in the cell containing the words Grand Total and then right-click and select Remove Grand Total.

To edit or delete the Calculated field, click inside the PivotTable to make the PivotTable Tools and Options tabs active. In the Calculation group on the Ribbon, click Fields, Items, & Sets and then select Calculated Field. The Insert Calculated Field box displays. Click the selection list arrow in the Name box to display a list of formulas. Select the formula you want to edit and then type changes in the Formula box. Delete the formula by clicking the Delete button.

CALCULATING THE AVERAGE AGES OF PRESIDENTS IN THEIR FIRST TERMS For this example, suppose you are interested in knowing the average age of the presidents in their first term in office and the presidents who were under age 50 when elected to the presidency. Follow these steps:

1. Open the President_PivotTableData.xlsx file if it is not already open. Define a data range as you did in the "PivotTable Report: Defining a PivotTable Range" section. Click in cell A2, which contains the column header Name. With the left mouse button pressed, drag down to row 46 and right to column L so that all data from cell A2 through cell L46 are selected.
2. Click the Insert tab and then click the PivotTable button and select PivotTable to create a new PivotTable report. Place the report in a new worksheet. After Excel creates the PivotTable report, ensure that the Classic PivotTable layout is turned on.
3. Drag Age in First Term to the Drop Report Filters Fields Here region or to Report Filter on the PivotTable Field List box.
4. Drag the Name field to the Drop Row Fields Here region or to Row Labels on the PivotTable Field List box.
5. Drag the Age in First Term field to the Data Value Items Here region or to Values on the PivotTable Field List box. Your PivotTable should look similar to Figure 5.95. Notice in the figure that the values are set to Sum of Age, and as a result, Grover Cleveland's age is listed as 100 because he had two first terms in office. You will get the average age.
6. Click the down arrow on the Sum of Age field located under Values. In Value Field Settings, click the Summarize By tab and then select Average and click OK. Alternatively, you can right-click in any cell that contains a president's age and select Summarize Value by Average. You should see that the grand total is 55.4651128 years of age.

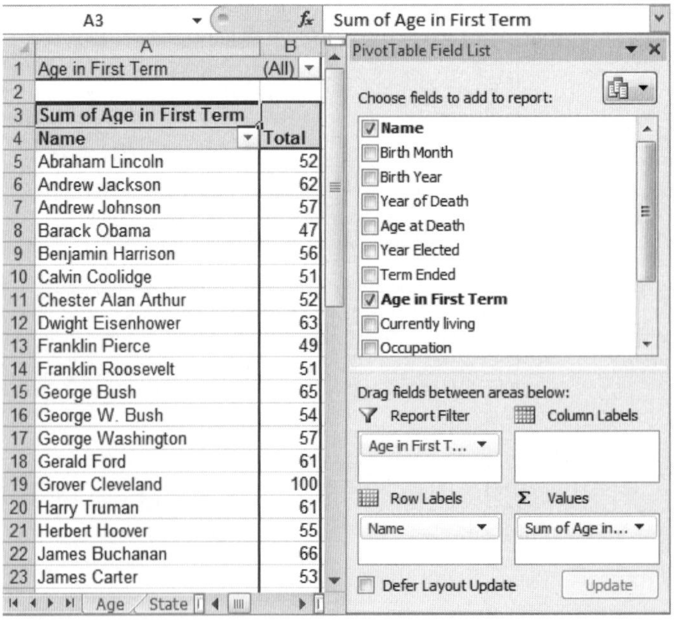

FIGURE 5.95 Age in First Term

7. To reduce the number of decimal places, right-click in the Grand Total cell and select Number Format. In the Format Cell box, click Number under Category and then click the down arrow to the right of the Decimal Places box to reduce the decimal places to 0. The grand total should change to 55, indicating that the average age of all presidents in their first term in office is 55 years.
8. To determine what presidents who were under the age of 50 in their first term of office, click the down arrow at the top of the PivotTable in the Page fields region, and the list of ages displays (see Figure 5.96).
9. Click Select Multiple Items and then click All to deselect all the ages. Next, click all the ages below age 50, and a check appears next to the selected items. Click OK. Your PivotTable should look similar to the one in Figure 5.97.

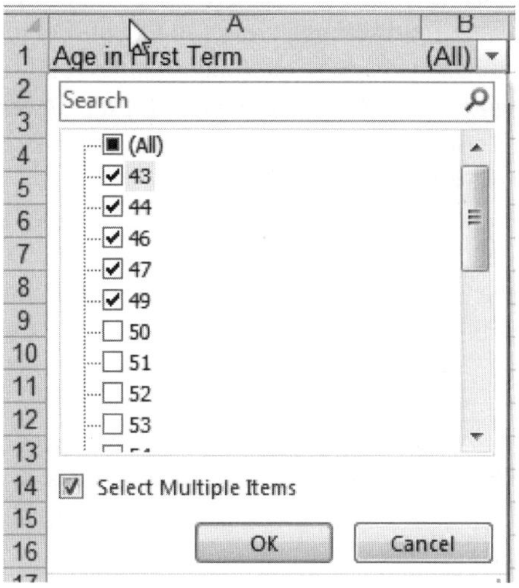

FIGURE 5.96 Filter for Presidents Under Age 50

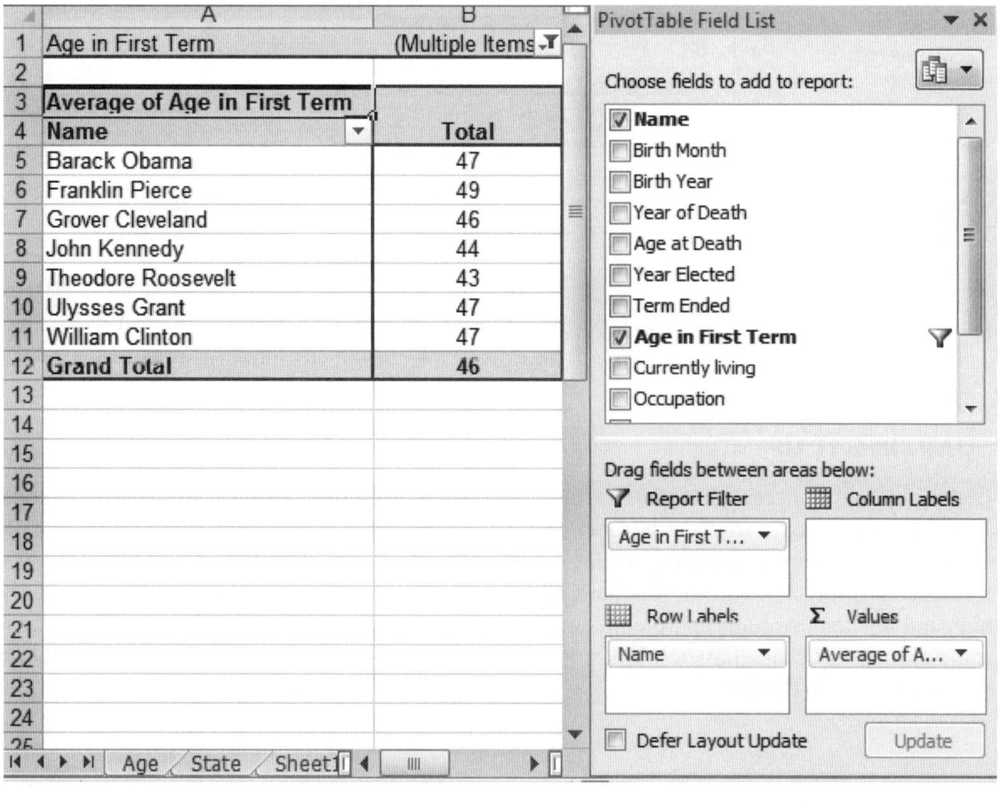

FIGURE 5.97 Presidents Under Age 50

USING A PIVOTTABLE AND PIVOTCHART TO ANALYZE THE STATES IN WHICH PRESIDENTS WERE BORN

10. Open the President_PivotTableData.xlsx file if it is not already opened. Define a data range as you did in the "PivotTable Report: Defining a PivotTable Range" section. Click in cell A2, which contains the column header Name. With the mouse button pressed, drag down to row 46 and right to column L so that all data from cell A2 through cell L46 are selected.
11. Click the Insert tab and then click the selection arrow under the PivotTable button and select PivotChart to create a PivotTable with a PivotChart in a new worksheet. After Excel creates the PivotTable with the PivotChart, ensure that the Classic PivotTable layout is turned on.
12. Drag State to the Drop Row Fields Here region or to Row Labels on the PivotTable Field List box.
13. Drag the Name field to the Data Value Items Here region or to Values on the PivotTable Field List box. Ensure the value field settings are set to Count. On the PivotTable Field List box, click the selection arrow on the Name field (under Values) and select Value Field Settings. In the Value Field Settings box, click the Summarize By tab and then select Count. Click OK. You should now have a count of the presidents born in each state (see Figure 5.98) as well as a chart depicting these results.
14. Click in the chart title and type a new title, President Birth States.
15. Remove the chart legend by clicking the chart to select it. The PivotChart Tools tab becomes active. Click the Layout tab. In the Labels group, click the selection arrow under Legend and select None.

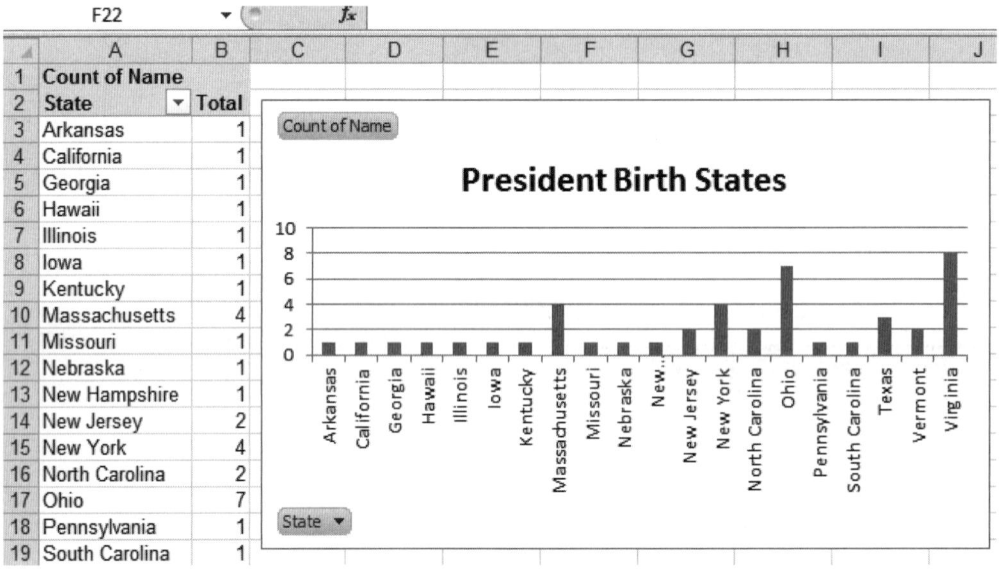

FIGURE 5.98 Presidents' Birth States

SUMMING IT UP

In this chapter, you created an Excel workbook containing several worksheets. Your workbook served as an electronic weather data recorder. You organized data according to Excel's row-and-column format and formatted the worksheet layout, including font type, size, and style. Excel's formula capability and built-in functions allowed you to calculate the differences between daily high and low temperatures and precipitation averages. You explored PivotTables and charts and some of their key characteristics. You walked through the steps of saving the file in a workbook (.xlsx) and in Web format.

Additional Activities Using Excel

- *Let's get counting*—Create a change-counting worksheet. In one column, list the amount of money that was spent. In a second column, list the amount of money that was given to the cashier. The students can enter a value in a third column for how much change should be given. A fourth column could provide feedback about whether the change amount is correct.
- *What we eat*—Create a worksheet that tracks the amount of food students eat in the following food groups: fruits, meats, milk, grains, and junk foods. The rows of column A should list the days of the week. Label column A *Days of Week*. Make column headers for each food group starting at column B. Create a *Total* column. You should have a total of seven columns, including *Days of the Week* and *Total*. Decide how you want to record the amounts (e.g., serving size) and enter those values for each food group for each day. Use the SUM function or write a formula that calculates the totals. Chart the data.
- *Temperature*—Using Excel, record the daily high and low temperatures and precipitation for a month. For each day, ask students to calculate the temperature change and to record the average change in temperature for the month. Ask students to calculate the average high and low temperatures and the total precipitation.
- *What we like to read*—Have students create reading lists. In one column (column A) list all student names, and in column B list the book titles. Create columns for descriptors, such as fiction/nonfiction, mystery, science, animals, book length, time taken to read, and so on. Write a description for each book. Compile the data for the class and ask students to identify, among other things, the most common types of books, the number of books read, and the average length of pages. Discuss the kind of books that were read and the kind of books that students have not yet explored.
- *The presidents*—Create an Excel worksheet that lists all the presidents of the United States. Include the presidents' dates of birth, dates of death, states of birth, election years to office, years terms ended, and occupations. With this information, ask students to calculate the states with the most presidents, the age of each deceased president when he died, the most popular occupation other than president, and the number of presidents from each state. Finally, ask students to create a column chart that represents all states in which a president was born and the number of presidents from those states.
- *The solar system*—Create a worksheet of data pertaining to the planets in the solar system, including their distance from the sun. Calculate the distance each planet is from one another.
- *Study habits*—Create a study habits worksheet. For a month, ask students to record the number of hours they study, read, and watch television each day. Record this information by day of the week and date. At the end of the month, chart the data to observe trends in studying, reading, and television viewing.
- *Showing respect*—Discuss with students what it means to show respect to others, such as treating people the way you want to be treated. Ask students to watch three of their favorite television programs during a weekend. Each student should record the number of times someone in each of the programs shows respect as well as the number of times someone shows disrespect. If possible, students should record how the respect or disrespect is shown, such as someone saying thank you or someone laughing at another person. Students should rate how much they like the program (e.g., on a 10-point scale). Create an Excel worksheet and enter all student data by program and by indicators of respect and disrespect. Ask students to identify the programs that have the highest indicators of respect and those with the lowest. Conduct comparisons by program and by how much students like the program. Discuss the implications of these data with students.

References and Resources

Grolier Incorporated. (1994). *The American presidents*. Danbury, CT: Grolier.

Learning Points Associates and NCREL. (2004). *Guide to using data in school improvement efforts*. Retrieved July 1, 2011, from www.learningpt.org/pdfs/datause/guidebook.pdf.

Microsoft Corporation. (2010). *XML paper specification: Overview*. Retrieved July 18, 2011, from http://msdn.microsoft.com/en-us/windows/hardware/gg463373.

Microsoft Corporation. (2011a). *Mortgage acceleration calculator*. Retrieved June 1, 2011, from http://office.microsoft.com/en-us/templates/results.aspx?qu=amortization&CTT=1#ai:TC030001668l.

Microsoft Corporation. (2011b). *Mortgage refinance calculator*. Retrieved July 1, 2011, from http://office.microsoft.com/en-us/templates/mortgage-refinance-calculator-TC001056621.aspx?CTT=5&origin=HA001034640.

Microsoft Corporation. (2011c). *Using the loan amortization and loan analysis templates*. Retrieved June 1, 2011, from http://office.microsoft.com/en-us/excel-help/using-the-loan-amortization-and-loan-analysis-templates-HA001034640.aspx.

Microsoft Corporation. (2011d). *What is SharePoint?* Retrieved July 15, 2011, from http://sharepoint.microsoft.com/en-us/product/capabilities/Pages/default.aspx.

6 ACCESS 2010

Chapter Outline

WHAT YOU ARE GOING TO LEARN

At the completion of this chapter you will be able to:

- Start a new database
- Create tables for data display
- Create forms for input of data
- Create reports of the database
- Edit the data and fields that display data
- Print reports
- Save the database

CHAPTER OVERVIEW

This chapter provides an introduction to Access 2010. The content focuses on Access fundamentals and how to apply them to a variety of learning activities. You will create four different databases throughout this chapter, and using the databases, you will create reports that provide specific information about the reports. Again, using databases that are created, forms and queries will be formulated. Studying the chapter contents and working through the projects will enable you to create databases suitable for many school-based activities.

HOW YOU CAN USE ACCESS

Microsoft Access can be used in a variety of activities by students, teachers, and administrators. You can use Access to support learning in relationship to Bloom's taxonomy of cognitive levels in conjunction with the National Educational Technology Standards for Teachers. Teachers can utilize Access to accomplish instruction, and, it is hoped, learning at a variety of levels and address multiple standards. Some examples of student use of Access could include the following:

- ***Knowledge***—Students can create their own database to list information about the planets in the solar system and create reports of the data they have compiled.
- ***Comprehension***—Students can compare data collected about the states in their region and summarize the information collected.
- ***Application***—After reading *Sarah, Plain and Tall*, students can research and create a database collecting data about the two states where Sarah lived.
- ***Analysis***—After collecting data about the planets in the solar system, students can compare and contrast the attributes of the planets.
- ***Synthesis***—Students can collect Census Bureau data on three large cities in their area and hypothesize why populations of persons 65 or older increased or decreased in those cities.
- ***Evaluation***—After reading *Vacation Under the Volcano*, students can collect data related to the Pompeii volcano eruption and evaluate whether the novel is plausible.

NETS FOR TEACHERS*

Access can be utilized in the classroom to address the following standards:

- ***Facilitate and Inspire Student Learning and Creativity***—Teachers use their knowledge of subject matter, teaching and learning, and technology to facilitate experiences that advance student learning, creativity, and innovation in both face-to-face and virtual environments.
- ***Design and Develop Digital-Age Learning Experiences and Assessments***—Teachers design, develop, and evaluate authentic learning experiences and assessment, incorporating contemporary tools and resources to maximize content learning in context and to develop the knowledge, skills, and attitudes identified in *NETS Teachers*.
- ***Model Digital-Age Work and Learning***—Teachers exhibit knowledge, skills, and work processes representative of an innovative professional and digital society.

WHAT'S NEW IN ACCESS 2010

Access 2010 uses a Ribbon similar to that of Access 2007, but the arrangement of the Ribbon differs somewhat from that of 2007. Access 2010 includes a suite of designed database templates for tracking contacts, tasks, events, students, and assets, among other types of data. You can create a database by clicking Blank database, naming that database, and on the Create icon below the File Name, you can start entering data. Access automatically determines the best type of data for each field. The Navigation pane is the pane on the left side of the Access program window that allows you to work with database objects and replaces the Database window in Access 2007.

If you have access to the SharePoint site with Access Services configured, you can create a Web database using Access 2010. You can publish an existing application to the Web. Not all desktop database features are supported on the Web, so you may have to adjust some features of your application. (Microsoft SharePoint is designed as a centralized replacement for multiple Web applications and supports various combinations of enterprise website requirements. It is typically associated with Web content management and document management systems.)

The File tab replaces the Microsoft Office Button found in earlier versions of the Office suite. The File tab is where you can see the Microsoft Office Backstage view. The Office Backstage view is where you manage your files and save, create, and find setting options.

---

*Reprinted with permission from *NETS for Teachers*, © 2008, International Society for Technology in Education, www.iste.org. All rights reserved.

WORKING WITH ACCESS

Access is a database program that allows you to store and manage information. You can think of a database program as an electronic stack of index cards that can be sorted and reported electronically. Common databases include telephone directories and television program schedules. A database consists of objects such as tables, forms, reports, and queries. Access allows you and your students to collect information, organize it, and report the information.

It is important to plan a database prior to creating the file. You need to think about what sort of data you want to collect and manage. What do you want to do with data? What kind of reports do you want to generate with the data? Taking time in advance to plan the database will save you time when you try to create reports or queries later.

In Access, a table is a list of information organized into rows and columns. Every entry you make in a table in Access is a record, and every record appears in a row in your database. Each column in a record is a field. An example of a record would be student contact information. The fields in that record might include address, phone number, and e-mail address. The field name appears at the top of the table. A form in Access presents your table fields in a fill-in-the-blank format, allowing you or others to enter data into the database without seeing all data in the database at one time. After creating a database and entering data, you can use reports to summarize your data and generate printouts. You can use queries to sort and filter your data. For example, you can choose to view only part of your fields in a table and have them match certain criteria.

The primary purpose of this chapter is to introduce fundamental components and features of Access so you can use Access in productive ways. To accomplish this objective, this chapter presents several examples. Although the examples are specific, the steps and procedures they present for developing databases, tables, forms, reports, and queries are generic and are applicable to a variety of school-based activities and learning activities. As you work through the chapter, you can substitute your own examples for the ones shown here.

Opening Access 2010

Access requires that a database be created and saved prior to data entry. When you open the database program, you will find a Ribbon common to those in other Microsoft products; however, similarly to Publisher, in Access you get options related to what type of database you would like to create rather than a blank document, as in Word or Excel (see Figure 6.1).

There are several ways of starting a database. You can create a new blank database, create a blank Web database, open a recent database, open sample templates, or create a database based on a template that comes with the program or one that is found on Office.com, if you have Web access.

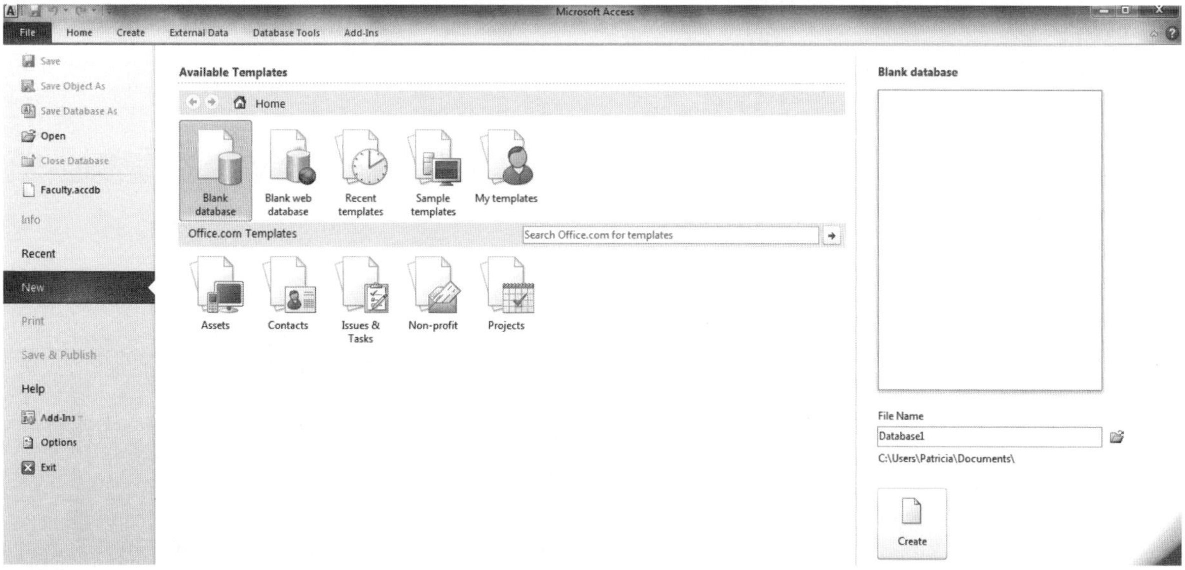

FIGURE 6.1 The Access Opening Screen

PROJECT FOR TEACHERS: CREATING A CLASSROOM LIBRARY DATABASE

PDToolkit for ***Microsoft® Office 2010 for Teachers***

Go to PDToolkit for **Microsoft® Office 2010 for Teachers** to locate a completed example in the Examples folder (Classroom Library.accdb).

To start creating a classroom library database:

1. Click Start on the Windows taskbar, move the mouse pointer over All Programs, and the Programs submenu appears. Move the mouse pointer over Microsoft Office and click; the Office submenu appears. Click on Microsoft Access 2010 to open the software program. The Access opening screen appears (see Figure 6.1).
2. For this project you will want to create a new blank database. Select Blank Database by clicking on the Blank database icon, typing Classroom Library in the Space for File Name, and then clicking on the Create button on the left side of the screen. A new table appears, ready for you to input data (see Figure 6.2).
3. By clicking on Field Name and Caption in the Fields tab, you can name the fields (see Figure 6.3).
4. Add the following field names to the database:
   - Author
   - Title
   - Publisher
   - Copyright
   - Date of publication
   - Series
   - Reading level
5. To increase the width of the columns, place the mouse cursor between the columns at the field label; hold down the left mouse button and drag the column until it is the appropriate width (see Figure 6.4).

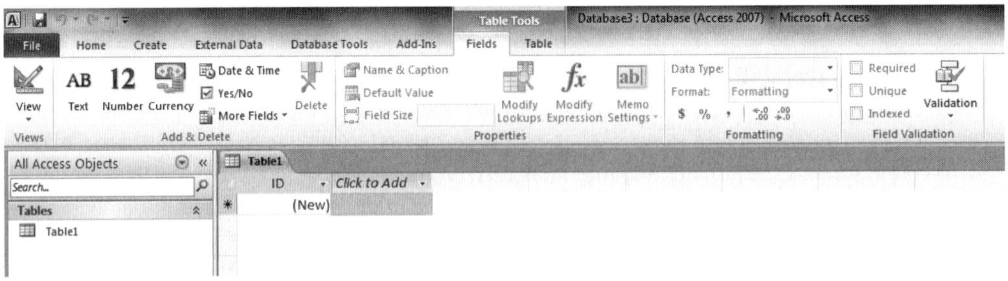

FIGURE 6.2 The Opening Screen of a Blank Database

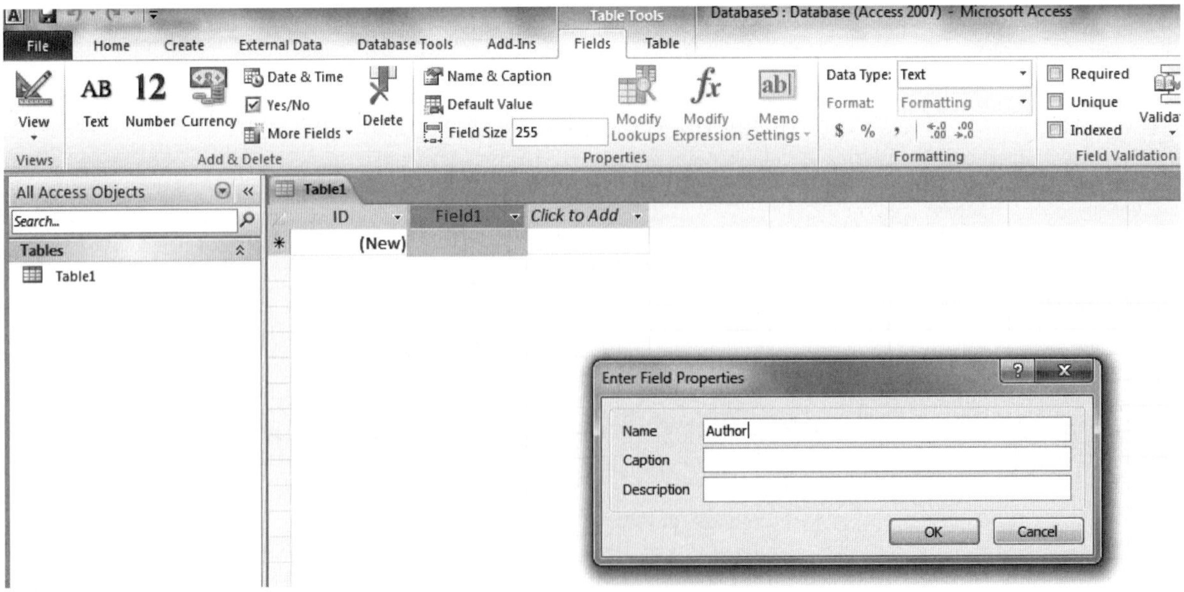

FIGURE 6.3 Field Names

FIGURE 6.4 Adjusting the Column Width

Author	Title	Publisher	Copyright	Date of Publ	Series	Reading Lev
Gailman, Neil	The Graveyard Book	HarperCollins	2008			5-8
Lowry, Louis	The Giver	Random House Press	1993			5-8
Patron, Susan	The Higher Power of Lucky	Simon & Schuster	2006			4-6
Stead, Rebecca	When You Reach Me	Wendy Lamb Books	2009			4-9
Vanderpool, Clare	Moon over Manifest	Delacorte Press	2010			4-7

FIGURE 6.5 Data to Enter

6. After the fields have been identified, you can start to enter data in the respective fields. The data for this database should include the data in Figure 6.5.
7. Now that you have entered data, you can examine the Ribbon in Access. The components on the Home tab of the Ribbon include:
   - *Views*—Allows you to see different view of the database
   - *Clipboard*—Allows you to cut, copy, and paste to and from the Clipboard
   - *Sort & Filter*—Allows you to arrange and sort information within the database
   - *Records*—Allows you to work with the data in the database, such as spell-checking
   - *Find*—Allows you to find data, replace data, and go to particular parts of the database
   - *Text Formatting*—Allows you to change the font, size, and style of text in the database (see Figure 6.6).
8. The next tab on the Ribbon is the Create tab. The options in this tab include the following:
   - *Templates*—Allows you to insert or create portions of a database
   - *Tables*—Allows you to create a new table, use a template, or show the Table Design view
   - *Queries*—Allows you to answer very specific questions about your data
   - *Forms*—Enables you to create a user interface that allows individuals to enter and edit your data
   - *Reports*—Allows the presentation of information that is pulled from tables or queries as well as information stored with report design, such as graphics, headings, and labels
   - *Macros & Code*—Allows a program to execute a series of instructions (see Figure 6.7)

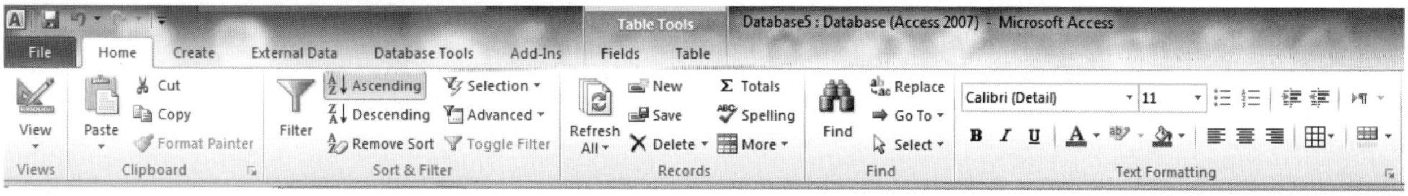

FIGURE 6.6 The Access Ribbon Home Tab

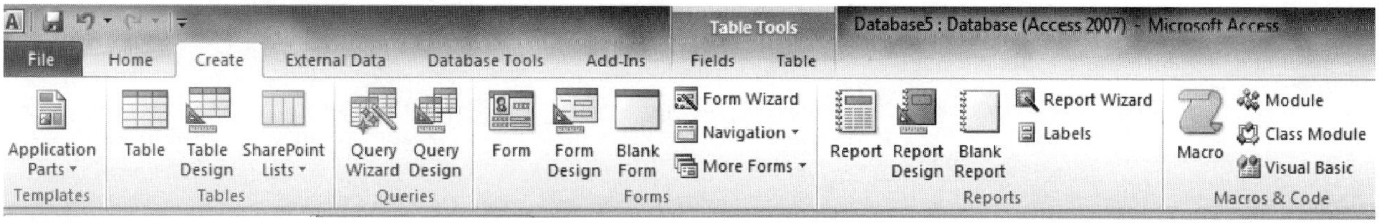

FIGURE 6.7 The Create Tab

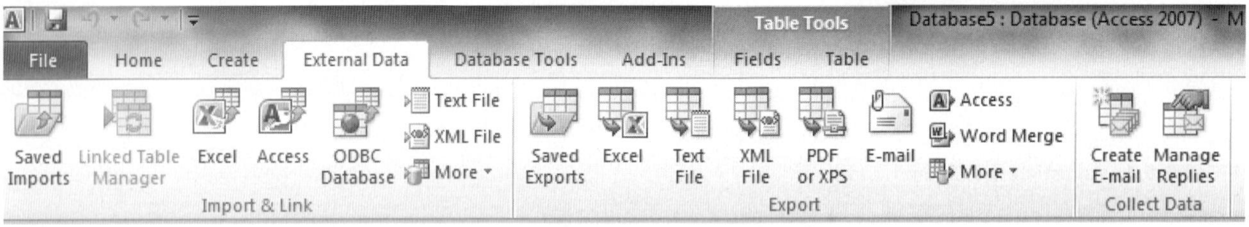

FIGURE 6.8 The External Data Tab

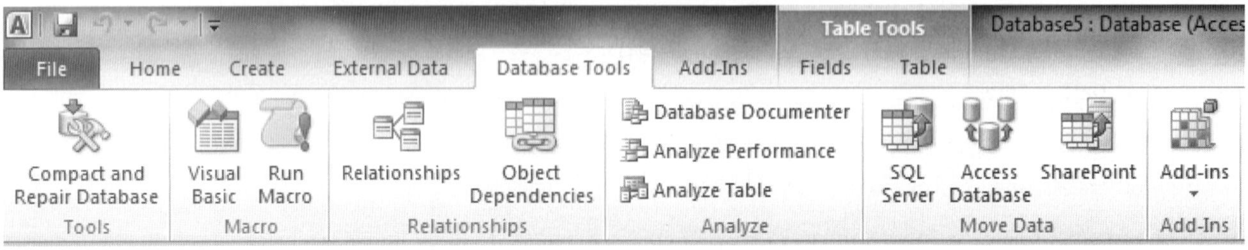

FIGURE 6.9 The Database Tools Tab

9. The External Data tab on the Ribbon allows you to import information from other sources, export databases, and collect data (see Figure 6.8).
10. The Database Tools tab allows you to compact and repair databases, run macros, determine relationships in databases, analyze tables and databases, move all or parts of a database to other storage places, and use an add-in manager (see Figure 6.9).
11. The Add-Ins tab is for commands that were available as add-ins in Office 2007 and earlier. Bluetooth is the one add-in that is automatically in the tab (see Figure 6.10).
12. The Table Tools tab has two tabs within this tab: Field and Table. The Fields tab section of Table Tools allows you to modify the way fields are presented, the properties of the fields, and the formatting of the data in the fields (see Figure 6.11).
13. Having gone through the Ribbon tabs in Access, turn back to your library database that you created earlier. Periodically save what you are working on.
14. The database you created can generate a report of the information in the database for others to review. To start this process, click on the Create tab and select Report Wizard (see Figure 6.12).

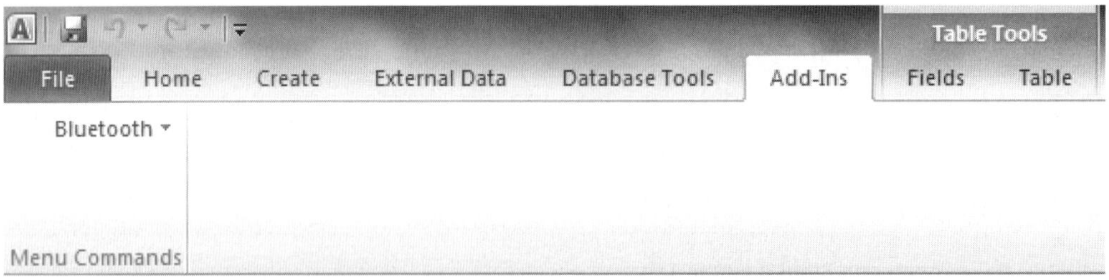

FIGURE 6.10 The Add-Ins Tab

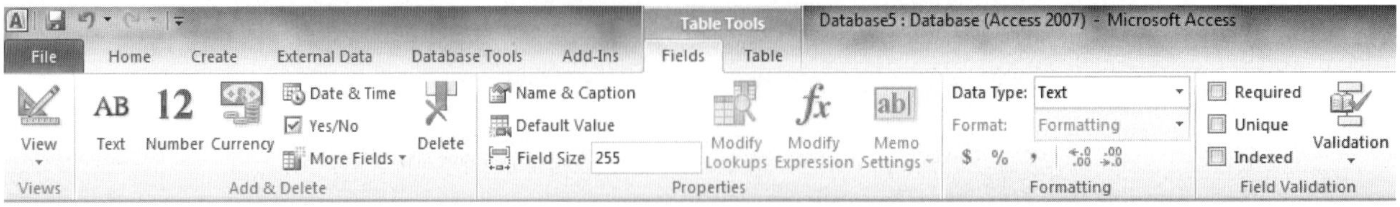

FIGURE 6.11 The Table Tools—Fields Tab

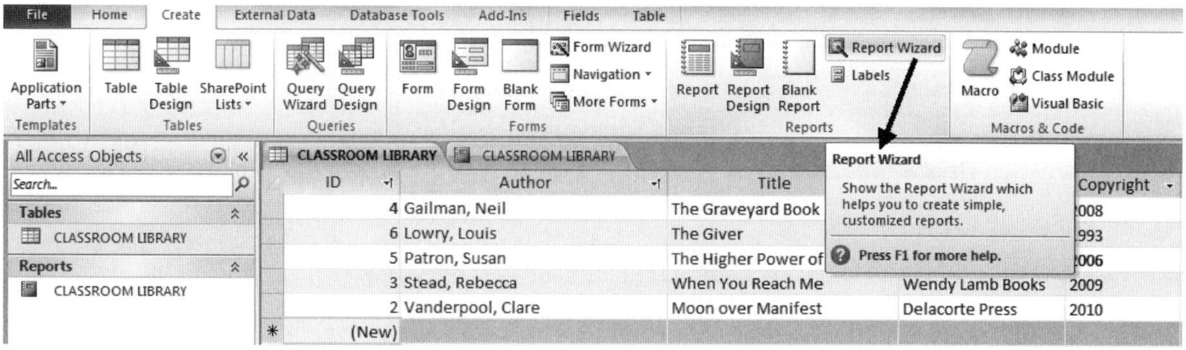

FIGURE 6.12 The Report Wizard

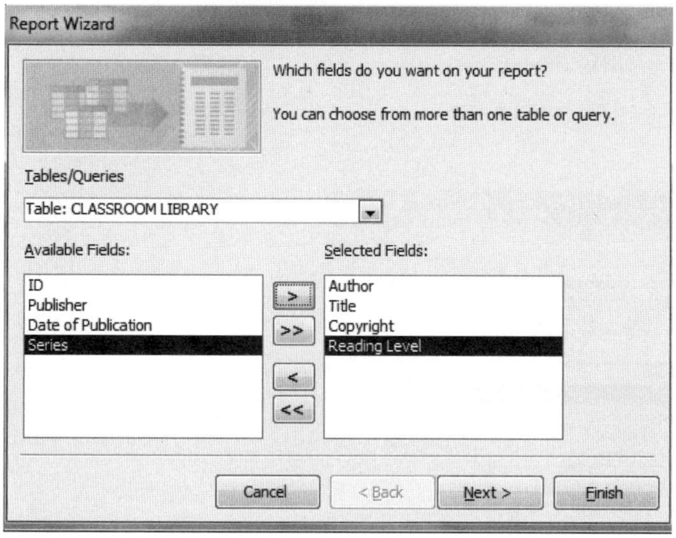

FIGURE 6.13 Selecting Fields

15. As you create a report, you can select the table or query on which to base your report. Because you have created only one database, there will be no other options except to create a report on the classroom library database you have created. In the Report Wizard, select the fields Author, Title, Copyright, and Reading level by using the arrow over from Available Fields to Selected Fields (see Figure 6.13). After doing so, click the Next button to continue with the wizard to create the report.
16. The Report Wizard asks if you would like to have grouping levels and what field you would like to use. This allows you to have a particular field stand out above the rest of the information in that record. In this case, you do not want to group any of the fields, so click the Next button (see Figure 6.14).
17. The next screen in the Report Wizard asks what sort order you would like for your records. Select Author from the list and then select ascending order. Click Next (see Figure 6.15).
18. Select the layout of your report. In this case, select Tabular as the layout for the report and Landscape for the orientation, making sure that there is a check in the box that adjusts the field width so all fields fit on a page. Then click Next (see Figure 6.16).
19. The next screen asks you to create a title for your report. In this case, call it Classroom Library, making sure the Preview the Report radio button is clicked. Next, click Finish (see Figure 6.17). The finished report should look similar to the example shown in Figure 6.18 in the Print Preview tab.
20. Print your report from the Preview tab using the Print icon. You will notice that the Landscape icon and One Page icon are highlighted because these are the layout styles chosen for this report. If you choose not to print this report, click on the Close Print Preview icon (see Figure 6.19).

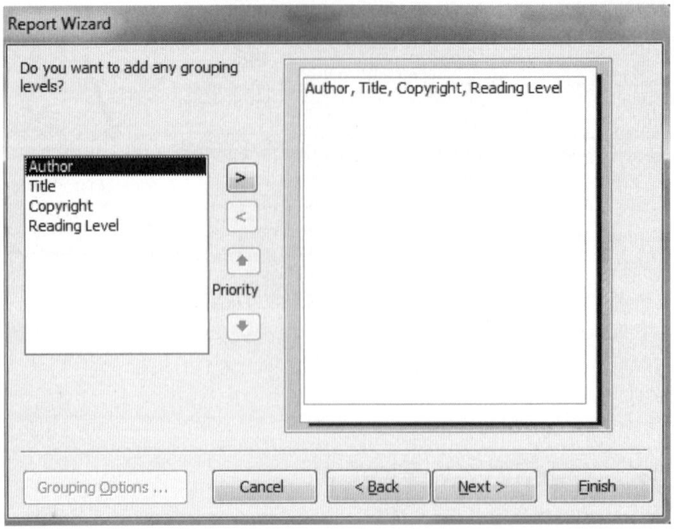

FIGURE 6.14 Grouping Levels

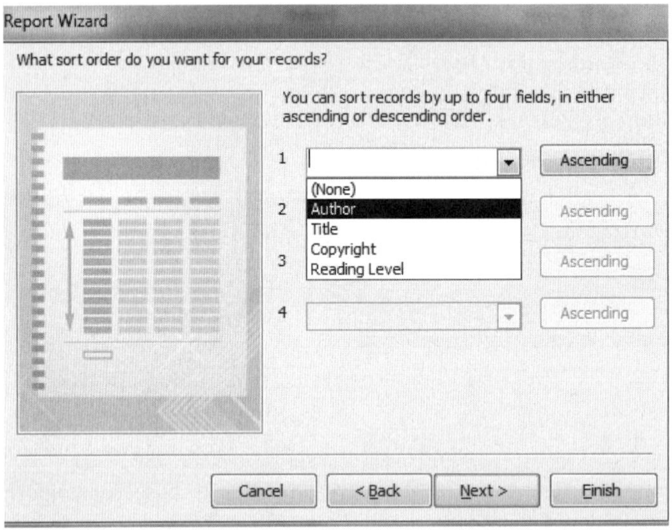

FIGURE 6.15 The Order of Records

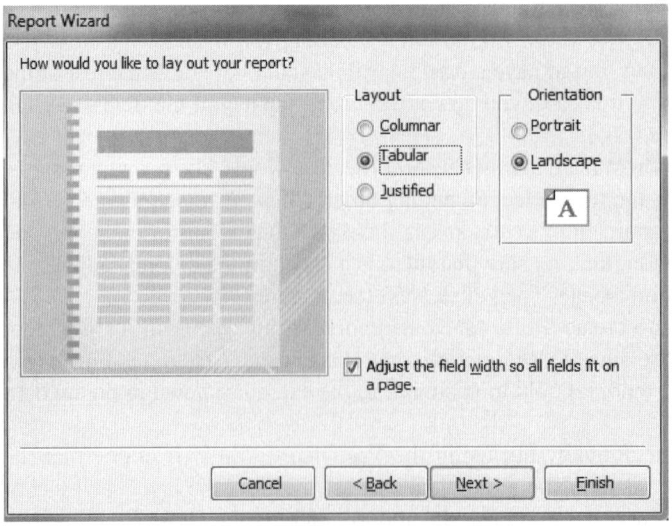

FIGURE 6.16 The Layout of a Report

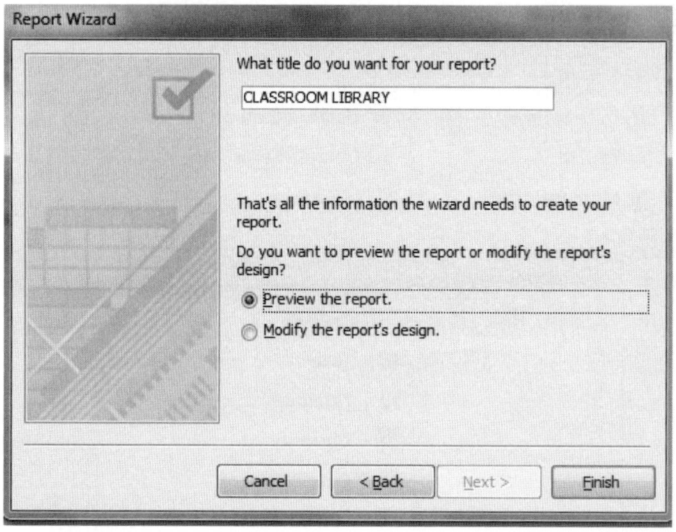

FIGURE 6.17 The Title of the Report

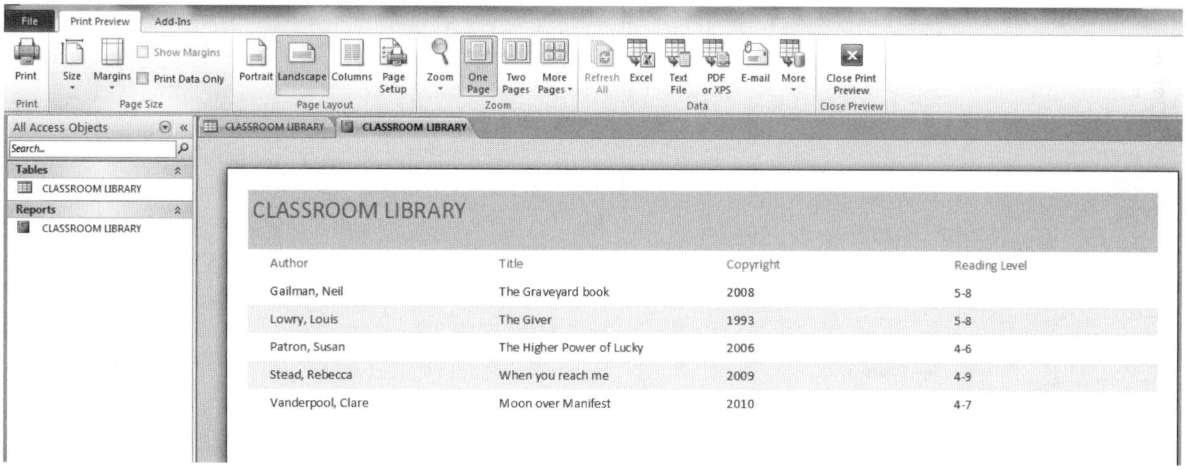

FIGURE 6.18 The Finished Report

FIGURE 6.19 The Print Preview Tab

PROJECT FOR STUDENTS: CREATING A PLANET DATABASE

Students are asked to know the planets in the solar system and information about them. Scientists have sent missions to many of the planets for exploration. Students can be assigned to find information about a particular planet and place that information in a database, where the information can be compared. In this section, you will create a form for students to add information about planets. In order to create a form, the fields need to be established in the table format. Follow these steps:

1. Open Access and create a new database.
2. Click on the field, which is next to the ID, labeled Click to Add; click on the arrow for the pull-down menu, highlight text. You will then be able to type in the text to name each field of the database (see Figure 6.20).

PDToolkit for *Microsoft® Office 2010 for Teachers*

Go to PDToolkit for **Microsoft® Office 2010 for Teachers** to locate a completed example in the Examples folder (Planet Database.accdb).

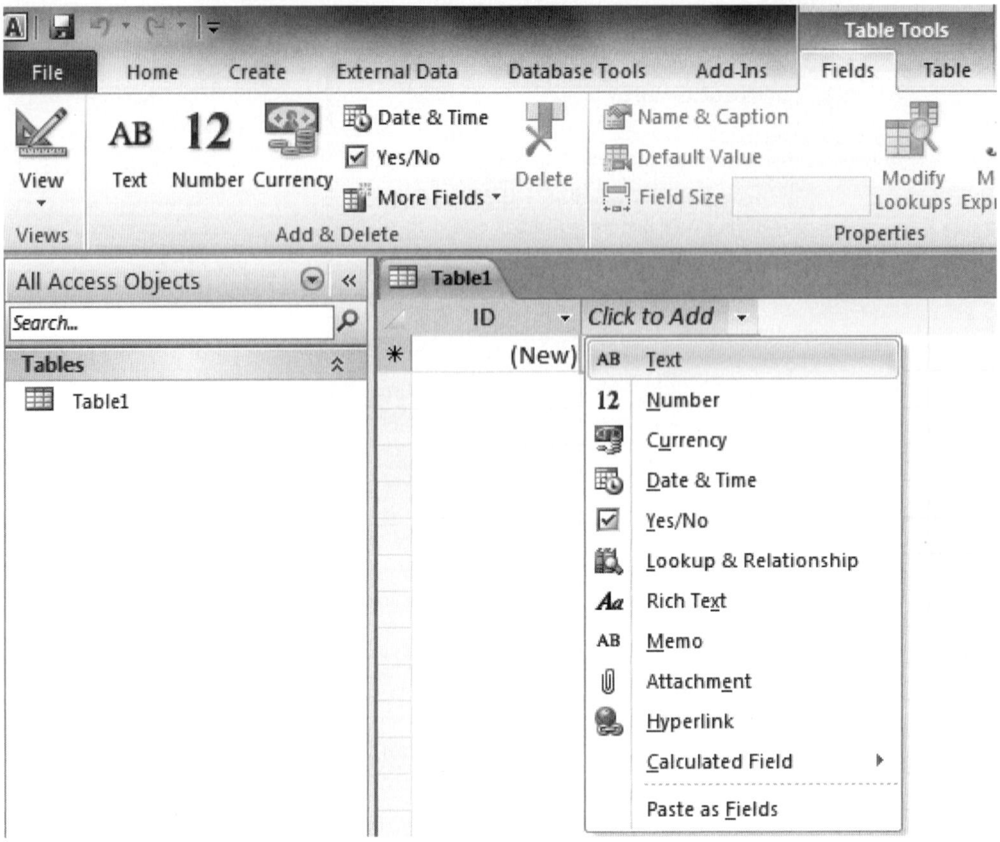

FIGURE 6.20 Naming Fields

3. Type in the following fields for this database:
   - Planet
   - Size
   - Diameter
   - Rotation on axis
   - Satellites
   - Your weight
   - Missions
4. Save the table as Planet Data.
5. Click on the Create tab on the Ribbon. Select Form Wizard from the Form section on the Ribbon, and a pop-up menu appears (see Figure 6.21).
6. Select all the available fields by using the double arrow to move all fields. You will use the back arrow to remove ID from the selected fields and then click on the Next button (see Figure 6.22).
7. Select Columnar as the layout for the form and click Next (see Figure 6.23).
8. Provide a title for your form on the next screen. Use the title Planet Data. Open the form to view or enter information and then click Finish (see Figure 6.24). The finished form appears on the screen.
9. Enter information in the form as shown in Figure 6.25.
10. To add the next set of information, click on the right arrow at the bottom of the work area and create a new blank record to enter the data for the next planet (see Figure 6.26).
11. Add records until you have all the information needed. In the File tab, click Save As and name and save your database.
12. After all the information is in the database, print the database by using the Report Wizard as described in the previous example. You can also go to the Form layout section along the left side of the screen (below Tables), and print the information in the form (see Figure 6.27).

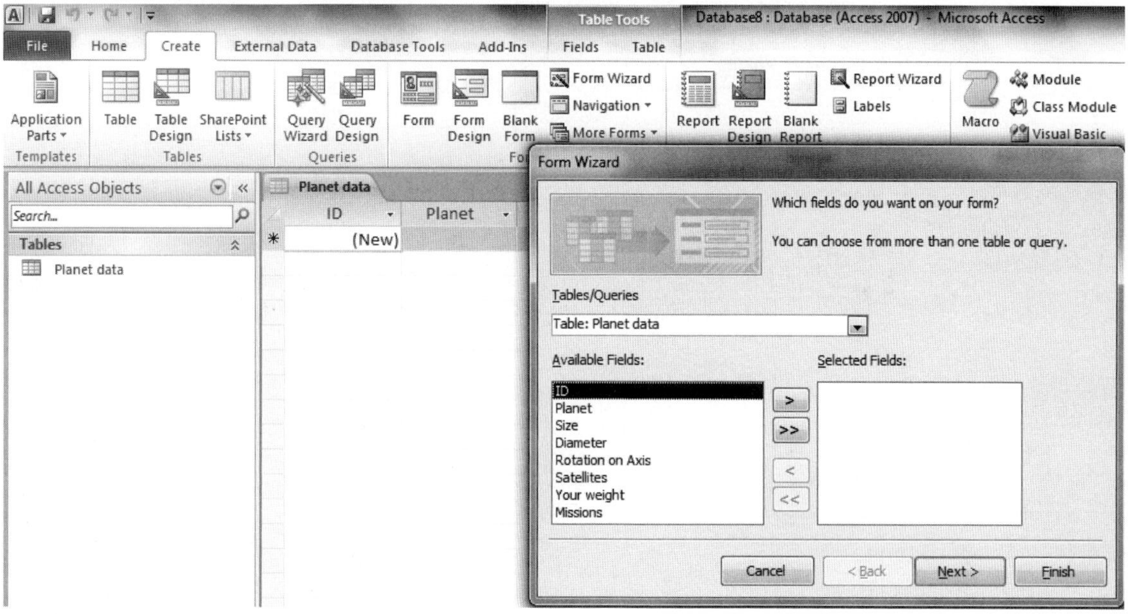

FIGURE 6.21 The Form Wizard

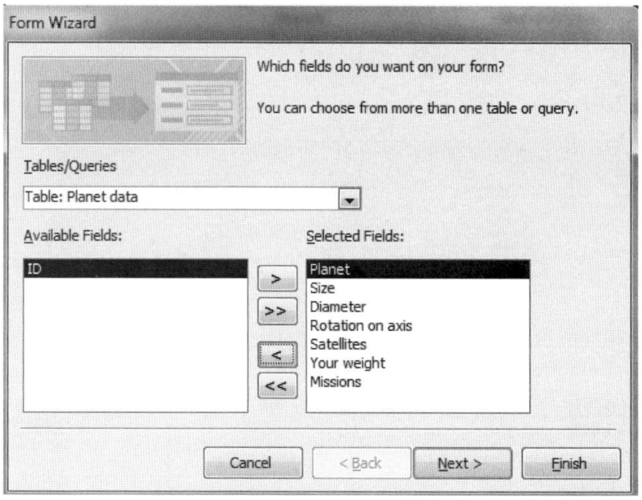

FIGURE 6.22 Selected Fields on a Form

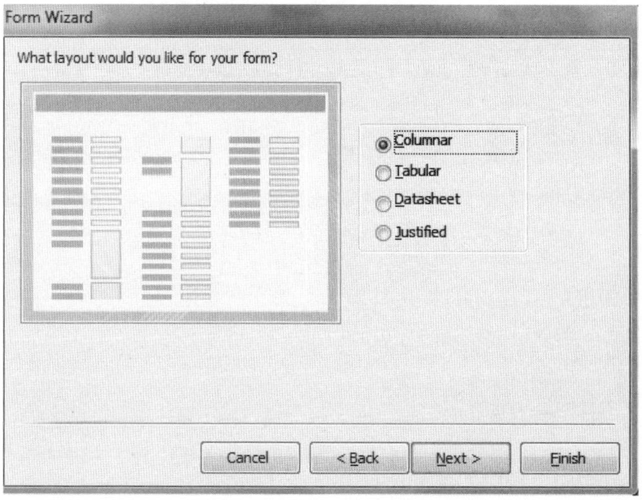

FIGURE 6.23 Selecting a Layout for a Form

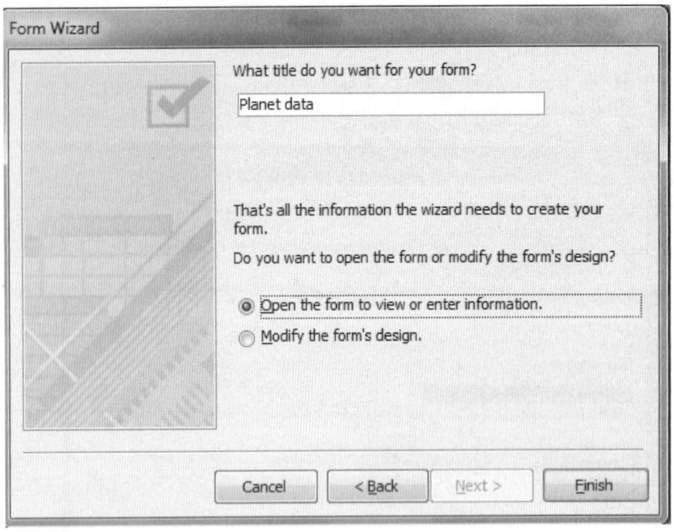

FIGURE 6.24 A Title for a Form

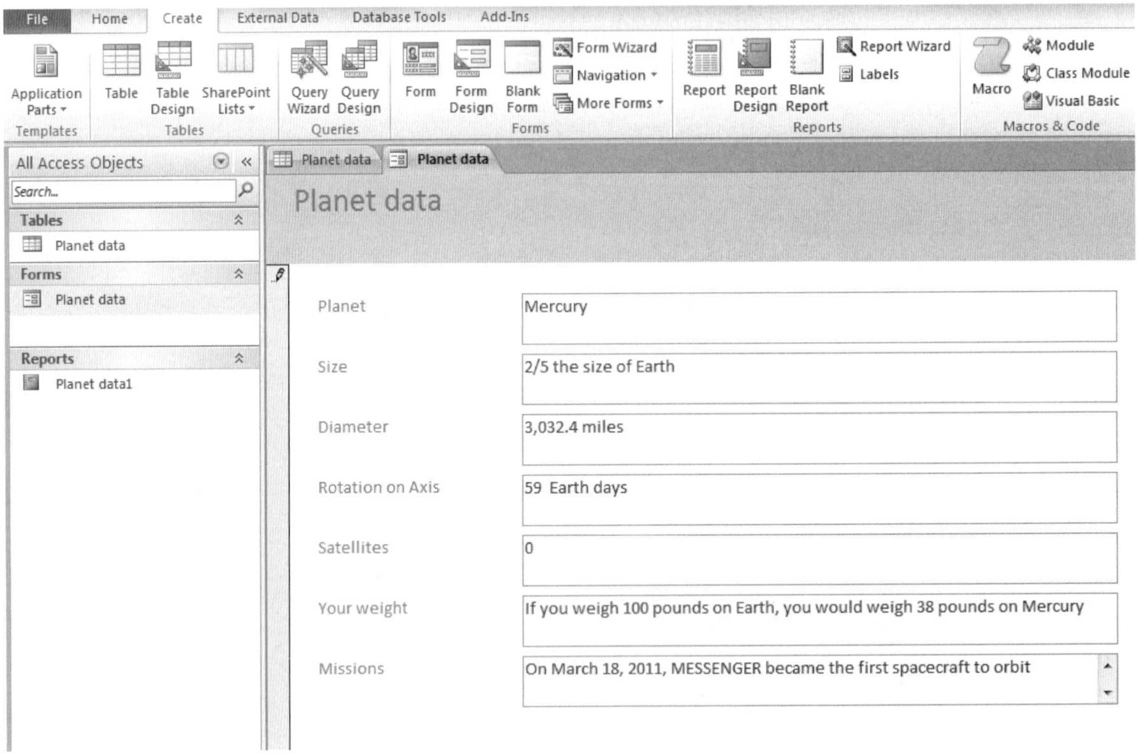

FIGURE 6.25 Entering Data in a Form

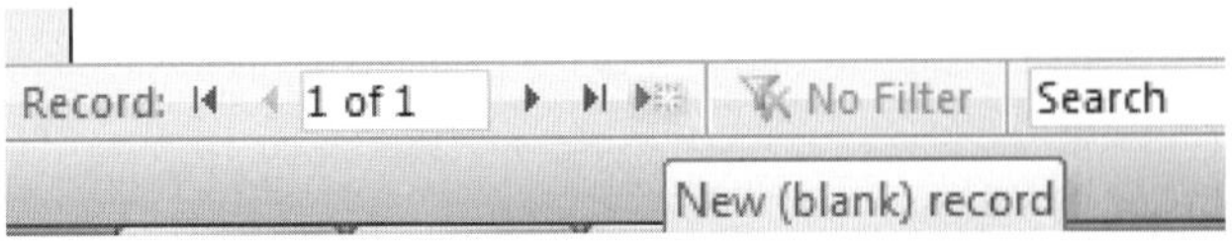

FIGURE 6.26 A New Blank Record

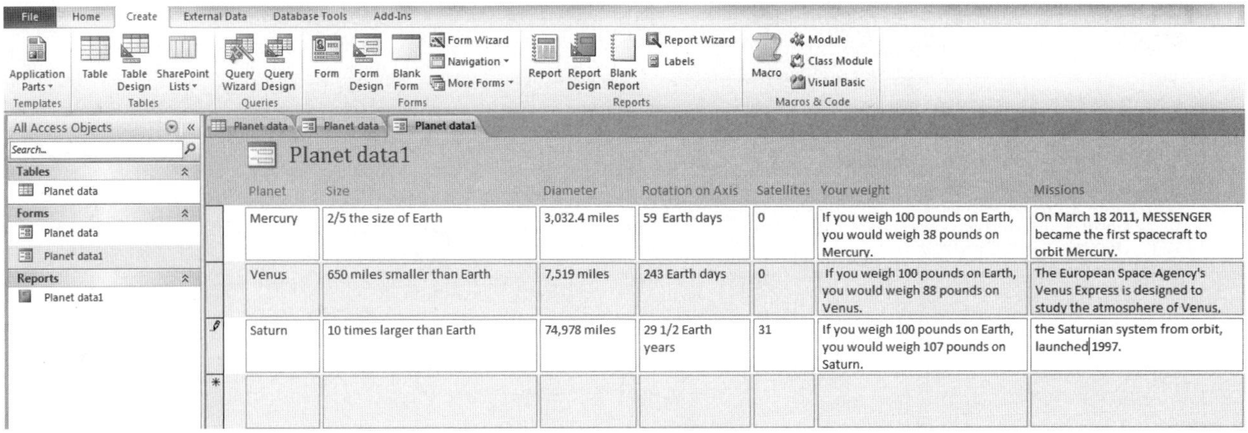

FIGURE 6.27 Form Layout

PROJECT FOR ADMINISTRATORS: CREATING A FACULTY DATABASE

As an administrator, you need to keep information related to the faculty you work with. Access provides templates that have fields already established that allow you to input information in a created database. Follow these steps to create a faculty database:

1. Open Access and select a template from the Samples section for the new database that you are creating (see Figure 6.28).
2. From the Sample templates, select the Faculty template (see Figure 6.29).

PDToolkit for *Microsoft® Office 2010 for Teachers*

Go to PDToolkit for **Microsoft® Office 2010 for Teachers** to locate a completed example in the Examples folder (Faculty Listing.accdb).

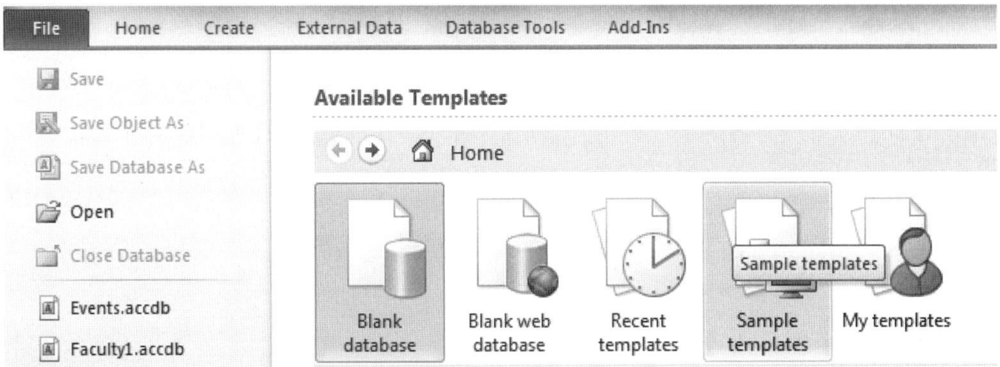

FIGURE 6.28 The Samples Section Template

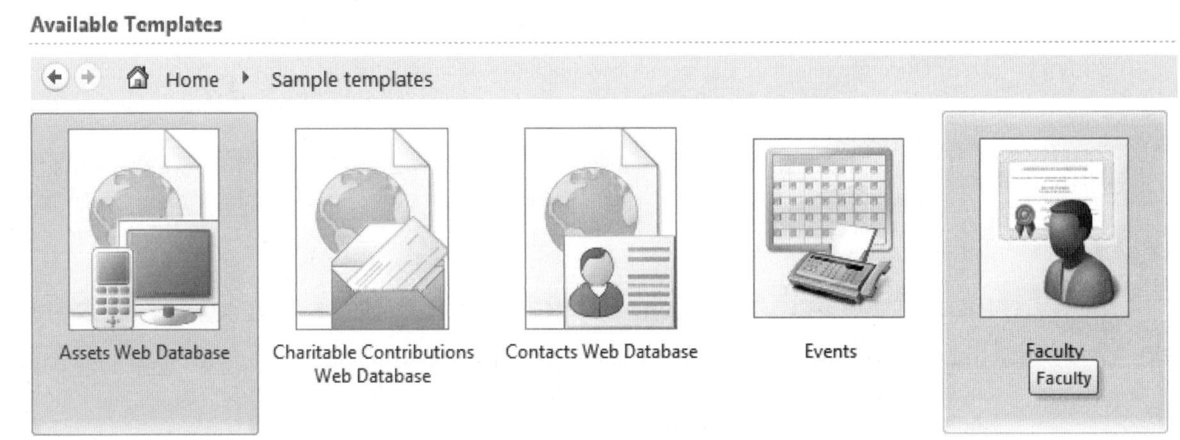

FIGURE 6.29 The Faculty Template

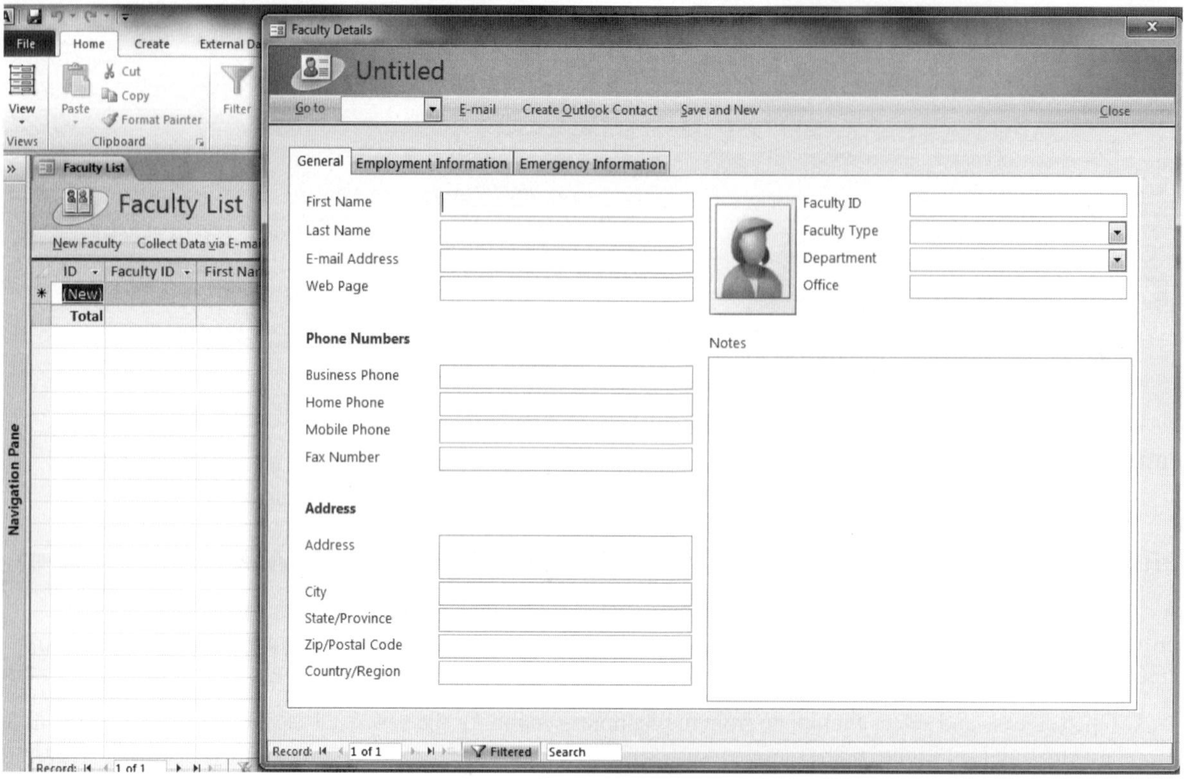

FIGURE 6.30 A New Faculty Form

Faculty — Tuesday, August 09, 2011 2:30:30 AM

Last Name	First Name	E-mail Address	Department	Faculty Type
Aster	Helen	Aster@ourschool.com	English	Teacher
Beckett	LeRoy	Beckett@ school.com	Mathematics	Teacher
Montalto	Juan	Jmontalto@mycohool.com	Science	Teacher
Lawyer	Livingston	llawyer@myschool.com	Physics	Teacher
Campbell	Kelly	kcampbell@myschool.com	Physical Education	Teacher's Assistar
Lando	Joy	jlando@myschool.com	English	Teacher
Bonzi	Rebecca	rbonzi@myschool.com	Mathematics	Teacher
Gong	Lori	lgong@myschool.com	English	Teacher
Key	Monica	mkey@myschool.com	Science	Teacher

FIGURE 6.31 A Faculty Report

3. Once the template has been downloaded, you can enter data directly into the table. Or by clicking on (New) in the ID column, a form appears, titled Faculty Details, and on it you can input data (see Figure 6.30).
4. When the database is populated with your information, explore the forms, reports, and materials you have already created. Figure 6.31 shows an example of one of the reports you can create.

PDToolkit for *Microsoft® Office 2010 for Teachers*

Go to PDToolkit for **Microsoft® Office 2010 for Teachers** to locate a completed example in the Examples folder (Mailing List.accdb).

PROJECT FOR EVERYONE: USING MAILING LISTS AND MAIL MERGE

From time to time, you will have a mailing that needs to go out to a group of people. It may be an announcement for a meeting, a letter, or an announcement for a celebration. To use mailing lists and mail merge, follow these steps:

1. Open Access and click on a blank database to create a mailing list.

2. In the new database, include the following field names:
   - First Name
   - Last Name
   - Address
   - City
   - State
   - Zip
3. Enter the data shown in Figure 6.32.
4. Open Microsoft Word and a new blank document.
5. Select the Mailings tab, select Start Mail Merge, and highlight Step by Step Mail Merge Wizard (see Figure 6.33). The Mail Merge Wizard pane appears along the right side of the Word document.
6. Select Letters from the list of documents you want to work on. At the very bottom of the pane are directions about the next step in the mail merge. Click Next: Starting Document (see Figure 6.34).
7. Use the current document, as indicated on the screen, and click on Select recipients (see Figure 6.35).
8. Select Browse from the list on the Mail Merge pane. Then select your mailing list from the location where it is stored (see Figure 6.36).

First name	Last Name	Address	City	State	Zip
Marshall	Ioeger	R.R. 1	Toluca	IL	62739
Lowell	Black	301 Oak	Minonk	IL	61760
Marie	Wool	212 State	El Paso	IL	61738
JoAnn	Long	543 Edgewood	Keller	TX	54911
Mitch	Rogers	320 First	Normal	OK	74707
Elaine	Small	543 Michigan	St. Louis	MO	81291
Bob	Hill	443 Lincoln	Washington	DC	31329
Mattew	Bonzi	760 Court	Mattoon	IL	61920

FIGURE 6.32 A Mailing List

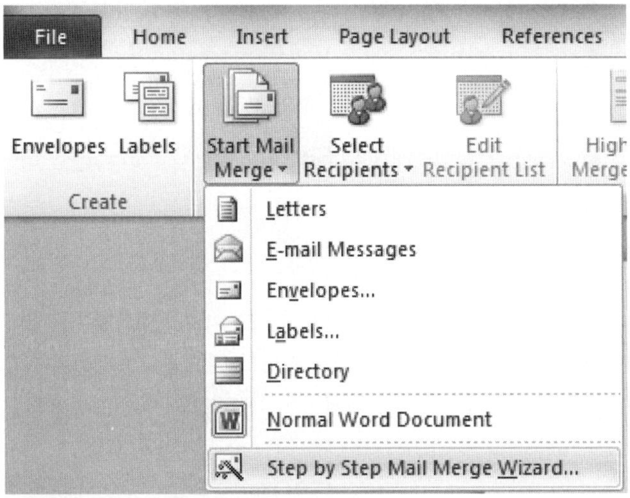

FIGURE 6.33 The Mail Merge Wizard

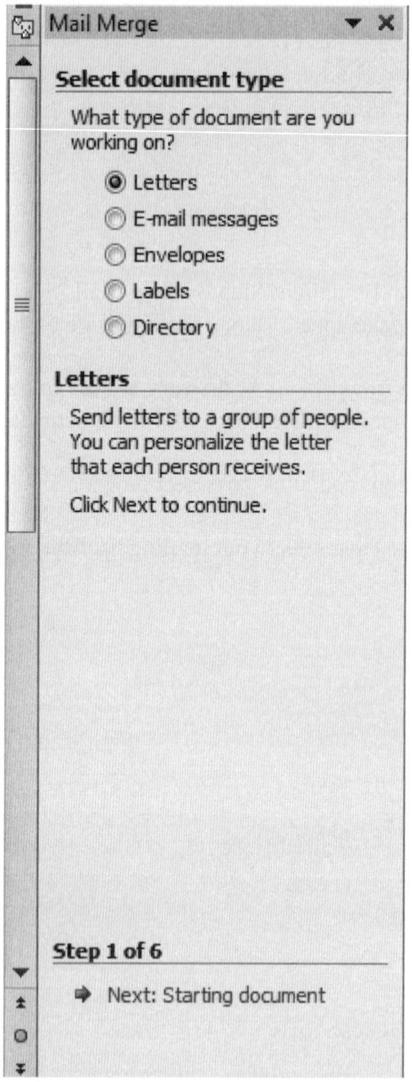

FIGURE 6.34 Starting a Document

FIGURE 6.35 Selecting Recipients

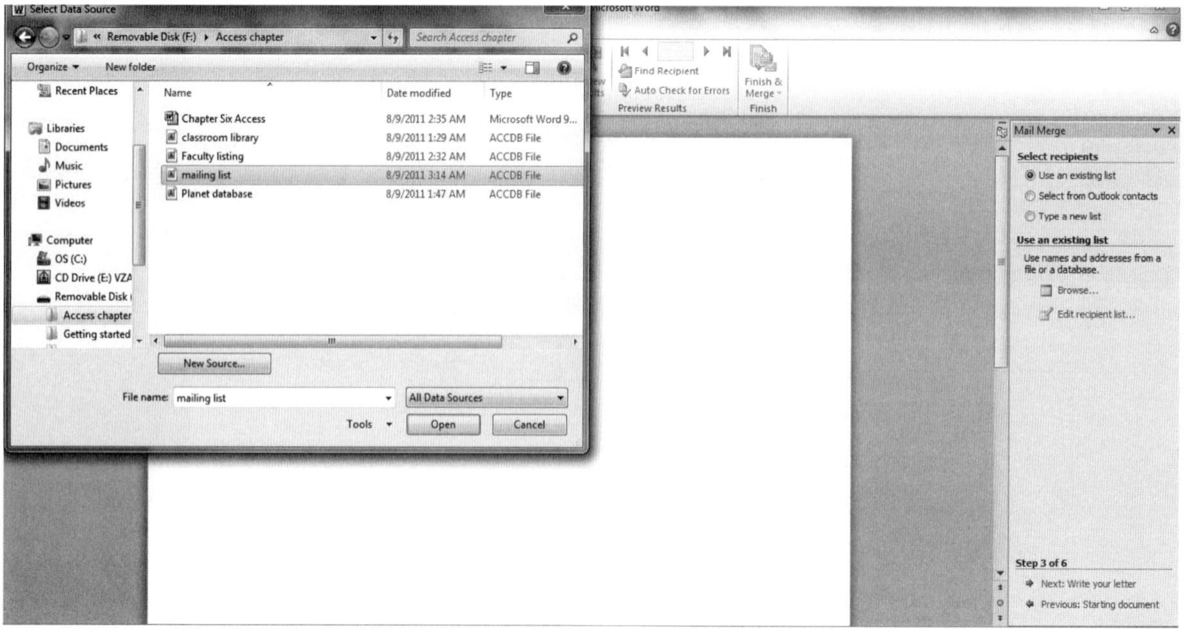

FIGURE 6.36 Selecting a Data File

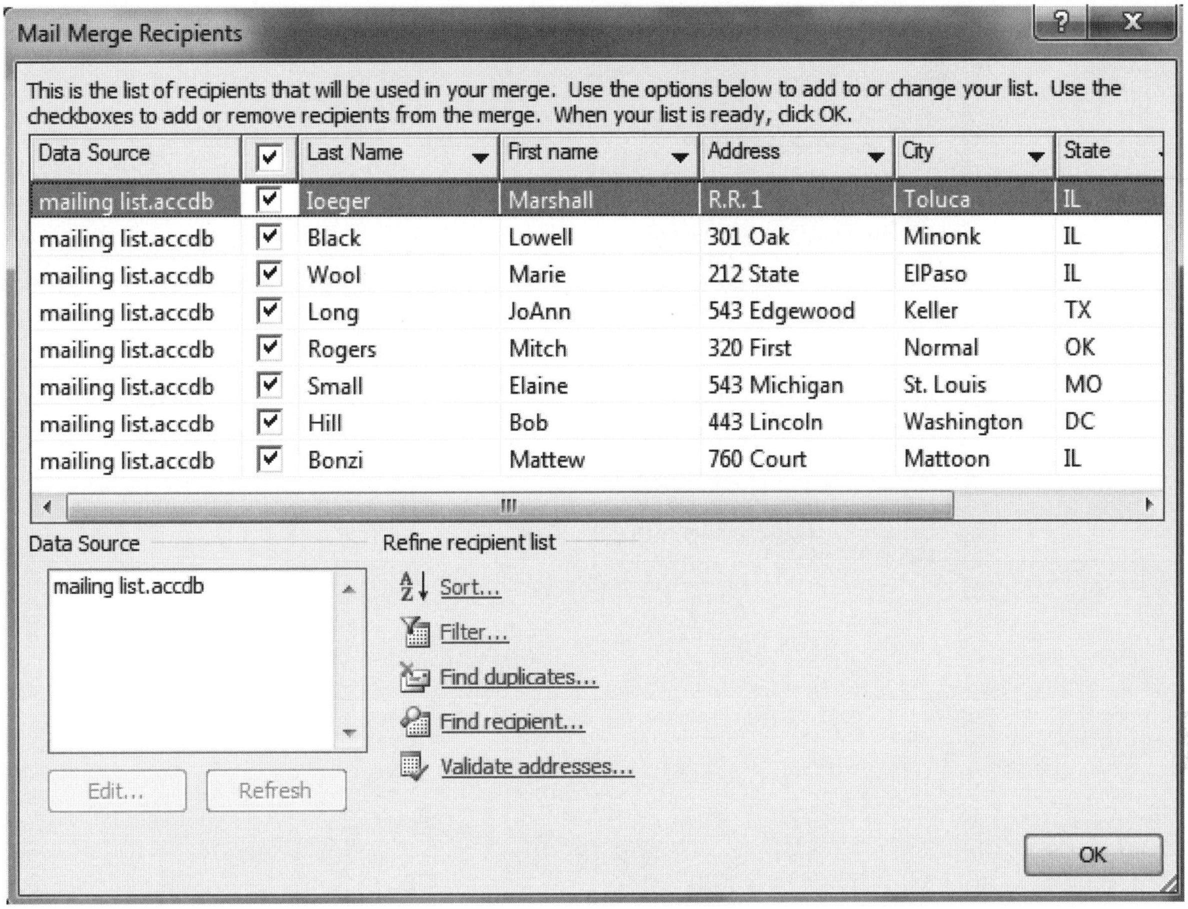

FIGURE 6.37 Mail Merge Recipients

9. Open the database. Each individual you want to include in the mail merge will have a check mark next to his or her name. In this case, just click OK, which will include all individuals in the database (see Figure 6.37).
10. The next step in the wizard is to write the letter and insert an address block. To do so, click on Address block in the Mail Merge pane (see Figure 6.38).
11. When the address pane appears in the work area, use the address block that appears by default in the pane and click OK (see Figure 6.39).
12. The address block appears in the work pane in Word. Press the Enter key twice and click on the greeting line. When the Insert Greeting Line window appears, accept the default greeting line by clicking OK (see Figure 6.40).
13. Continue writing the letter until it is complete and then click on Next: Preview Your Letters (see Figure 6.41). Then click on Completed Merge to create letters for each of the recipients in the database.
14. To print your letters, click Print in the Wizard pane and select the printer associated with your computer. Then select how many of the mail merge letters to print.

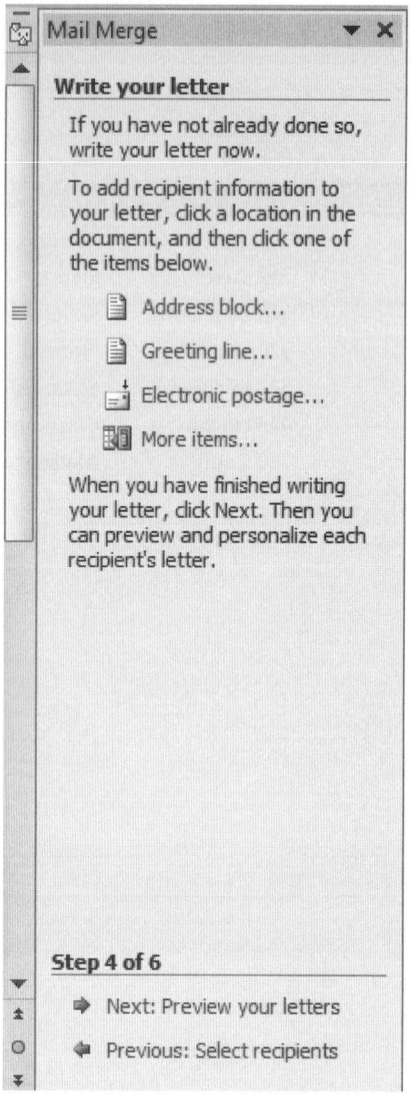

FIGURE 6.38 Inserting an Address Block

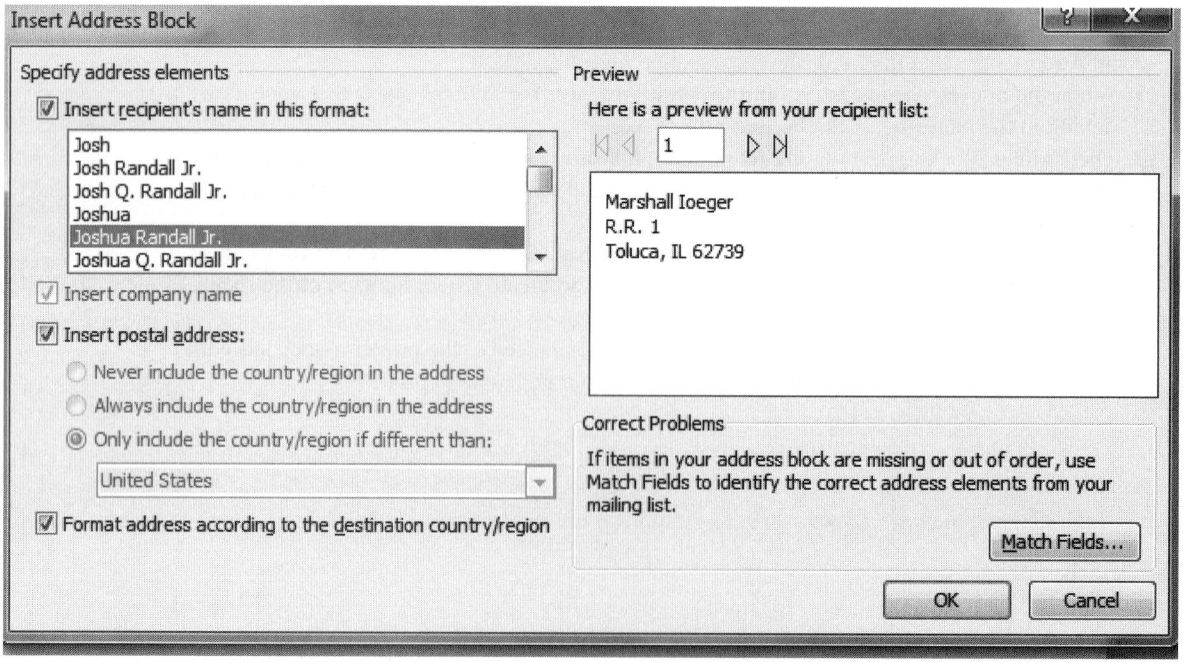

FIGURE 6.39 An Address Block Pane

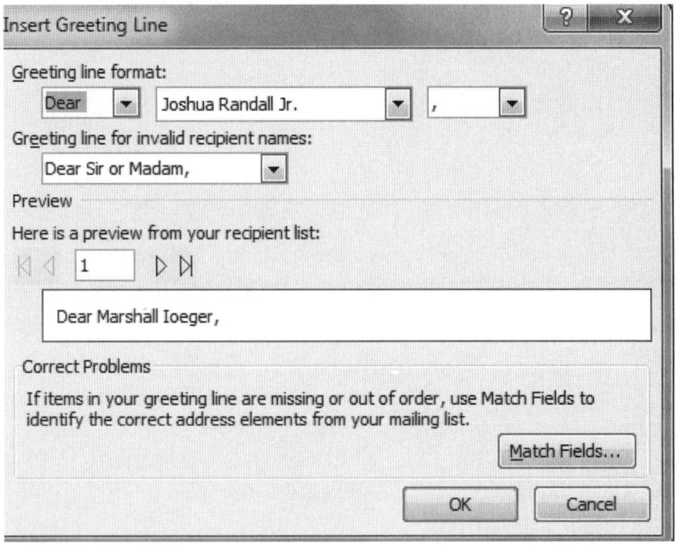

FIGURE 6.40 Inserting a Greeting Line

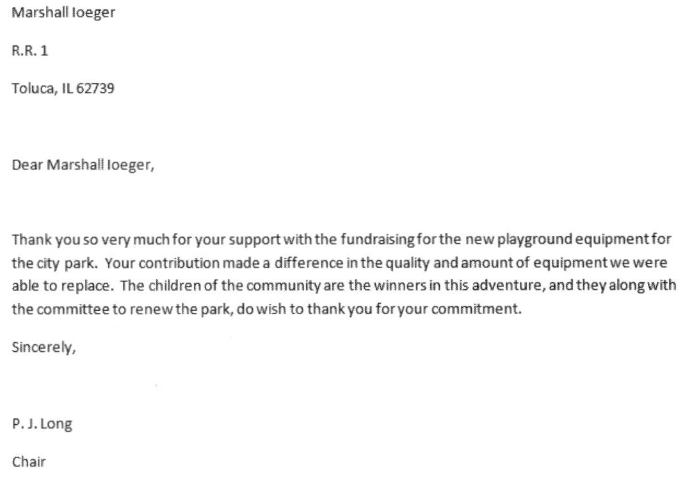

Marshall Ioeger

R.R. 1

Toluca, IL 62739

Dear Marshall Ioeger,

Thank you so very much for your support with the fundraising for the new playground equipment for the city park. Your contribution made a difference in the quality and amount of equipment we were able to replace. The children of the community are the winners in this adventure, and they along with the committee to renew the park, do wish to thank you for your commitment.

Sincerely,

P. J. Long

Chair

FIGURE 6.41 A Completed Letter

SUMMING IT UP

In this chapter, you created a class library database, a planetary database for students, a faculty contact database, and a mail merge letter. You can produce all these items yourself or teach your students how to do so. These and other activities allow you to fulfill some of the ISTE standards for teachers, making you and your classroom look more professional and providing technology that enhances student learning.

References and Resources

Bloom, B. (Ed.). (1956). *Taxonomy of educational objectives*. New York: David McKay.

International Society for Technology in Education. (2008). *NETS for teachers*. Retrieved March 4, 2011, from www.iste.org/standards/nets-for-teachers.aspx.

SELECTED WEBSITES

NASA: Website About the Solar System
http://solarsystem.nasa.gov/planets/profile.cfm?Object=SolarSys

Fact Monster About Planets
www.factmonster.com/ipka/A0769141.html

7 PUBLISHER 2010

Chapter Outline

WHAT YOU ARE GOING TO LEARN

At the completion of this chapter you will be able to:

- Create a new Publisher document
- Navigate the Publisher workspace
- Use a Publisher template
- Resize a text box in a publication
- Add a frame or artwork to a document
- Modify a picture in a document
- Cut, copy, and paste in a document
- Preview a document for printing
- Create a new blank Publisher document
- Work with bullets and numbering

CHAPTER OVERVIEW

This chapter provides an introduction to Publisher 2010. It focuses on Publisher fundamentals and how to apply them to a variety of learning activities. This chapter provides instruction on how to use many of Publisher's tools for creating, editing, and manipulating information in a document. The exercises provide real-life examples of activities you do on a daily basis that may make your classroom or school more productive and provide a richer educational experience for students. The following section provides ideas on how you can use Publisher at a variety of cognitive levels.

HOW YOU CAN USE PUBLISHER

Both you and your students can use Microsoft Publisher for a variety of activities. You can use Access to support learning in relationship to Bloom's taxonomy of cognitive levels, in conjunction with the National Educational Technology Standards for Teachers. You can use Publisher to accomplish instruction and learning at a variety of levels and address multiple standards. Examples of Bloom's taxonomy of cognitive levels that Publisher can apply are as follows:

- ***Knowledge***—Students can create their own "dictionary," using the catalog template or newsletter template to create their own lists of words found in their reading that they do not know and define them. Students can select a brochure template and list the 50 states and capitals, adding appropriate clip art.
- ***Comprehension***—Students can use the postcard template to create a postcard of one of their favorite plant species they have studied. After reading a book such as *A Year Down Yonder* by Richard Peck, students can create a book report using the newsletter template.
- ***Application***—Students can create a brochure describing a location described in a book or a region of the world they learned about in class by doing further research. Students can prepare a flier to illustrate the concepts behind the life cycle of a butterfly.
- ***Analysis***—Students can create a brochure that relates a biography of a famous scientist whom they have studied. Students can use a newsletter format to compare and contrast the main characters in two books, such as Brian in *Hatchet* by Gary Paulsen and Sam in *My Side of the Mountain* by Jean Craighead George.
- ***Synthesis***—Students can design and create advertisements for their inventions. Students can also use the menu template to create a "healthy" menu for a restaurant they are hypothetically establishing.
- ***Evaluation***—Students can use a brochure template to create a brochure comparing and contrasting videos they have seen in class, and they can use their comparison to recommend a video to see, and why. Students can also use a flier template to create a rubric for evaluating newsletters that have been created by companies and organizations; the students can use the information they learn from this rubric to improve their own creations and to provide criticism for newsletters in written form.

NETS FOR TEACHERS*

Publisher can be utilized in the classroom to address the following standards:

- ***Facilitate and Inspire Student Learning and Creativity***—Teachers use their knowledge of subject matter, teaching and learning, and technology to facilitate experiences that advance student learning, creativity, and innovation in both face-to-face and virtual environments.
- ***Design and Develop Digital-Age Learning Experiences and Assessments***—Teachers design, develop, and evaluate authentic learning experiences and assessment, incorporating contemporary tools and resources to maximize content learning in context and to develop the knowledge, skills, and attitudes identified in *NETS Teachers*.
- ***Model Digital-Age Work and Learning***—Teachers exhibit knowledge, skills, and work processes representative of an innovative professional and digital society.

WHAT'S NEW IN PUBLISHER 2010

Publisher allows you to design, create, and publish publications that range from very simple to sophisticated, both on paper and on the Web. Publisher 2010 utilizes the Ribbon that is found in the other Microsoft Office products, such as Word 2010. There are new image tools in Publisher that allow you to crop pictures and provide a picture-style gallery. The print preview and printing settings are now found in the File tab with this version.

*Reprinted with permission from *NETS for Teachers*, © 2008, International Society for Technology in Education, www.iste.org. All rights reserved.

WORKING WITH PUBLISHER

The primary purpose of this chapter is to introduce you to the fundamental components and features of Publisher so you can use it in productive ways. To accomplish this objective, you will work through examples. Publisher is desktop publishing software. Unlike Word, Publisher allows you to add text and pictures to pages, and Publisher places these items as individual objects on the page. This allows you to move text boxes, reposition headings, and layer objects on the page. When you open Publisher, the opening screen shows blank templates as well as examples of templates, including those for the following types of publications:

- Brochures
- Business cards
- Calendars
- Greeting cards
- Labels
- Newsletters
- Postcards
- Advertisements
- Award certificates
- E-mail
- Flyers
- Resumes
- Gift certificates

As you work through the chapter, you can substitute your own examples for the ones shown here to make your finished products unique.

OPENING PUBLISHER 2010

To create a Publisher document, you need to open Publisher 2010. Click Start on the Windows taskbar; move the mouse pointer over All Programs, and the Programs submenu appears. Move the mouse pointer over Microsoft Office and click, and the Office submenu appears. Click Microsoft Publisher, and Publisher 2010 opens (see Figure 7.1). The Publisher workspace is delineated by tabs at the top of the Ribbon that are activated when selected, allowing the user to utilize the tools that are located on each tab.

Click Microsoft Publisher 2010, and Publisher 2010 opens (see Figure 7.2). For this illustration, in the Most Popular section, click on the Newsletters icon. (The other templates work the same way as the newsletter template.)

FIGURE 7.1 Opening Publisher

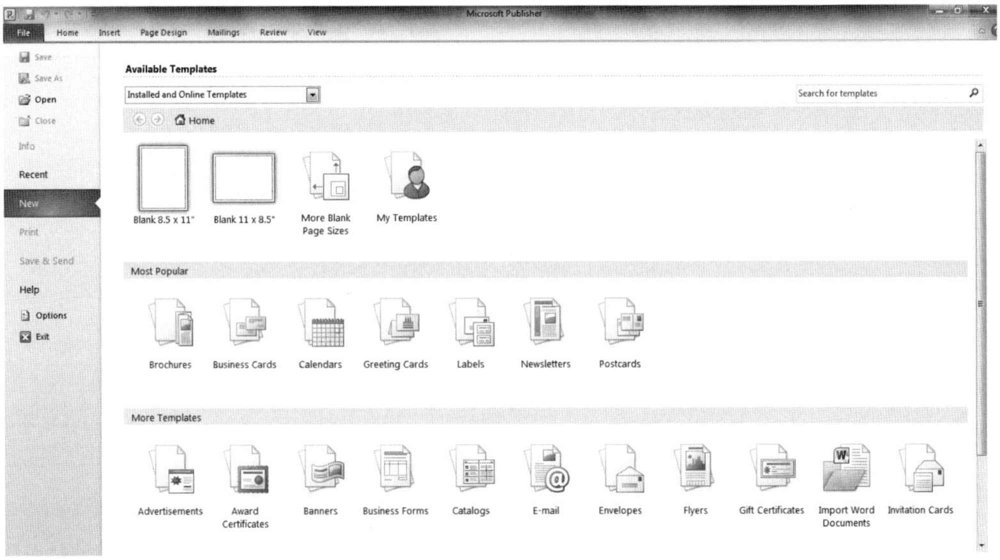

FIGURE 7.2 The Opening Screen of Publisher

Once you have clicked the icon, a screen of newsletter options appears. If your computer is attached to the Internet, newsletter options from Office.com appear. For this example, you will use installed newsletters. You need to scroll down to see all the newsletter templates installed on your computer (see Figure 7.3). In this case, Kid Stuff is the selected template. Notice that on the right of the screen is a larger image of the template, along with color scheme options, font scheme options, business information, and page size. All these options have pull-down menus that you can modify to meet your design requirements.

In this case, you want to create a one-page newsletter by pulling down the drop-down menu and selecting one page (see Figure 7.4). To start the document once all customizing has been done, you click on the Create icon, and the template appears in the workspace for you to further design.

The workspace for Publisher 2010 is different than in the previous editions of Publisher. The software now uses the Ribbon that the rest of the Microsoft Office products utilize. The Ribbon is divided into tabs, and each tab is divided into sections of operations (see Figure 7.5).

FIGURE 7.3 The Newsletter Template Screen

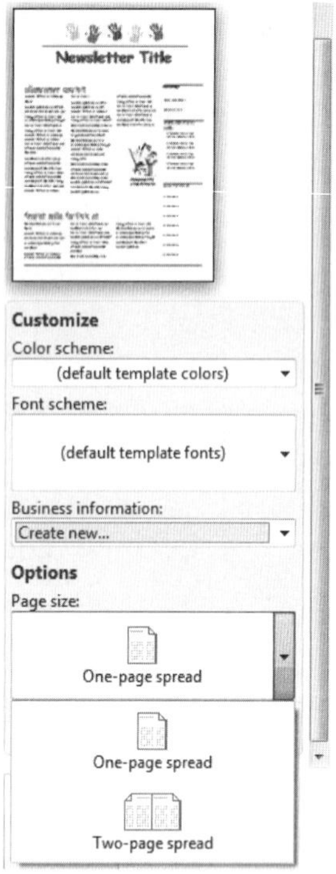

FIGURE 7.4 Page Size Options

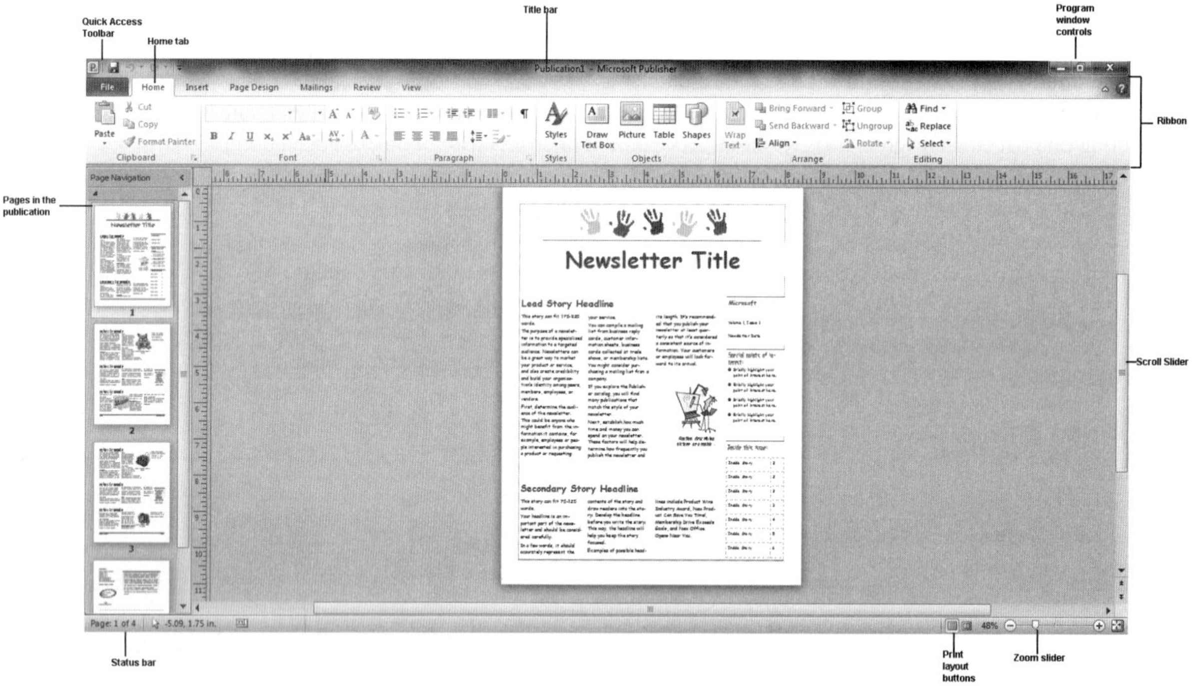

FIGURE 7.5 The Publisher Workspace

PDToolkit for *Microsoft® Office 2010 for Teachers*

Go to PDToolkit for **Microsoft® Office 2010 for Teachers** to locate a completed example in the Examples folder (Hands on Science Newsletter.pub).

PROJECT FOR TEACHERS: CREATING A NEWSLETTER

As an example of a project that a teacher could develop, in this section you will create a newsletter for the beginning of the school year for your classroom. You need to start with a plan of what to include in this newsletter and decide what information you need to collect prior to writing the newsletter. Taking this planning step now will save you time later on. To create a newsletter for your classroom, follow these steps:

FIGURE 7.6 The Newsletter Title

1. Unlike Word, Publisher has templates that come with the software package, and you don't need access to the Web to access them. Using the Kid Stuff template selected earlier, you can basically fill in the blanks of the template with information that relates to your classroom. You can create documents in Word and copy and paste them into the Publisher template, or you can type directly into the template itself. In order to work in the template, move the zoom slider to 100% so you can see what your document looks like more clearly and so you can manipulate the information on the template with greater ease (see Figure 7.6).
2. The template is divided into individual boxes that you can click on and change by typing or pasting in information to replace the template placeholders. In this case, click on the Newsletter Title box. The text box turns dark, and you are able to type directly in the box. In this case, type a new title for the newsletter: Hands-On Science (see Figure 7.7).
3. Moving down the template, the next text box is Lead Story Headline. Place your main story title here by clicking on the text box and typing the title: Creating a Recycling Plan for Our School (see Figure 7.8).
4. Click on the text box below the lead story headline to highlight this text box, which will contain the story. You can type directly into this text box as you did with the title boxes. Or you can open a Word document, copy the information it contains, and paste that information in this text box. In this case, type directly in the text box. As you type, you will notice that your words automatically flow into the next column of the article (see Figure 7.9).
5. To change the illustration next to the lead story, click on the illustration and then click on the Insert tab on the Ribbon. In this example, the clip art and the caption are grouped together as one box, but if you click on the illustration again, you will see that there is a box within the box that relates to the clip art only (see Figure 7.10). You can group and ungroup items by clicking on the Group and Ungroup icons in the Arrange section of the Home tab of the Ribbon (see Figure 7.11).

FIGURE 7.7 Changing the Title

FIGURE 7.8 The Lead Story Headline

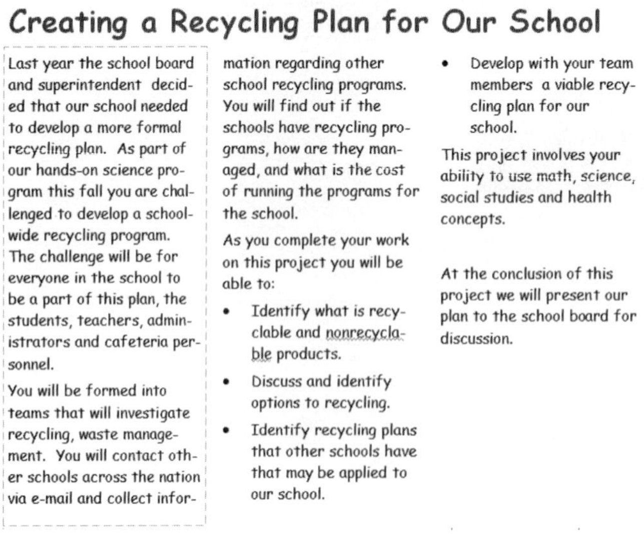

Creating a Recycling Plan for Our School

Last year the school board and superintendent decided that our school needed to develop a more formal recycling plan. As part of our hands-on science program this fall you are challenged to develop a schoolwide recycling program. The challenge will be for everyone in the school to be a part of this plan, the students, teachers, administrators and cafeteria personnel.

You will be formed into teams that will investigate recycling, waste management. You will contact other schools across the nation via e-mail and collect information regarding other school recycling programs. You will find out if the schools have recycling programs, how are they managed, and what is the cost of running the programs for the school.

As you complete your work on this project you will be able to:

- Identify what is recyclable and nonrecyclable products.
- Discuss and identify options to recycling.
- Identify recycling plans that other schools have that may be applied to our school.
- Develop with your team members a viable recycling plan for our school.

This project involves your ability to use math, science, social studies and health concepts.

At the conclusion of this project we will present our plan to the school board for discussion.

FIGURE 7.9 Lead Story Copy

FIGURE 7.10 Inserting Clip Art

6. Select Clip Art on the Insert tab (see Figure 7.12). A window appears on the right of the workspace. In the box labeled Search For, type in the clip art you are looking for. If you are connected to the Web, you will be able to find additional clip art on Office.com. In this case, type in the word recycle, and a piece of clip art appears, as shown in Figure 7.13.
7. Place the mouse pointer over the clip art image, and a pull-down menu appears. Make sure the image on the newsletter you want to replace is still selected; you can tell that it is if you can see the box around the image on the page. In this case, the image is in a box grouped with a text box. Select Insert from the pull-down menu (see Figure 7.14).

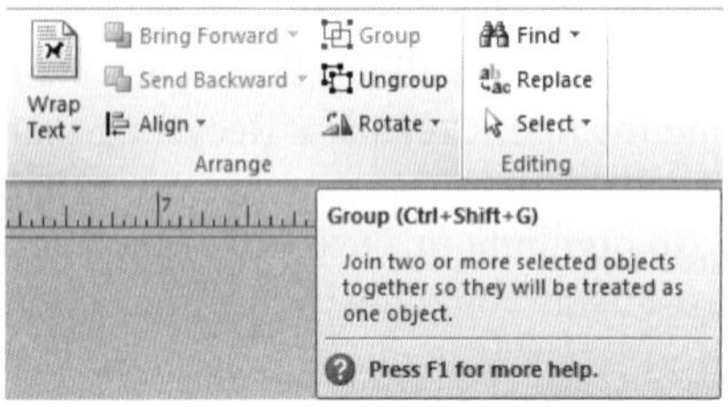

FIGURE 7.11 Grouping and Ungrouping Items

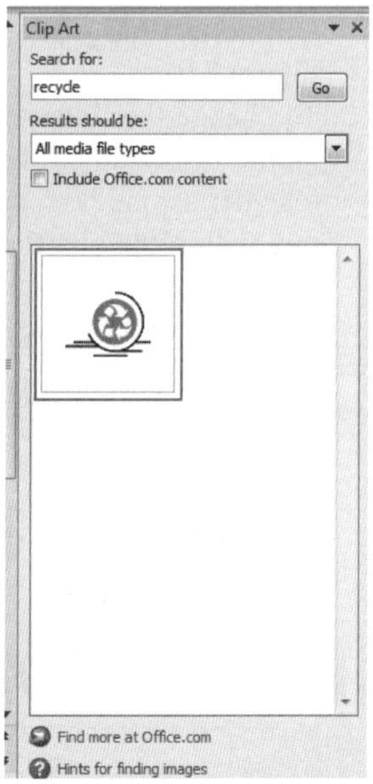

FIGURE 7.13 Recycle Clip Art

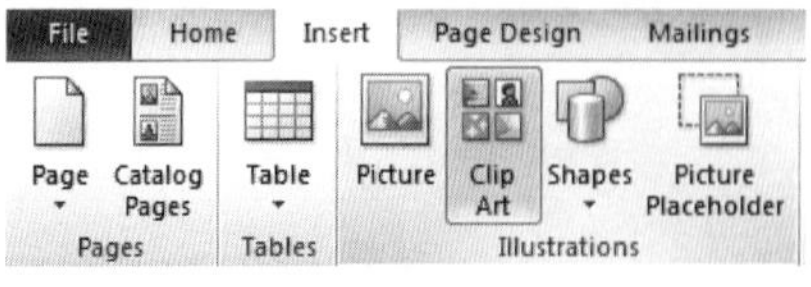

FIGURE 7.12 The Clip Art Insert Tab

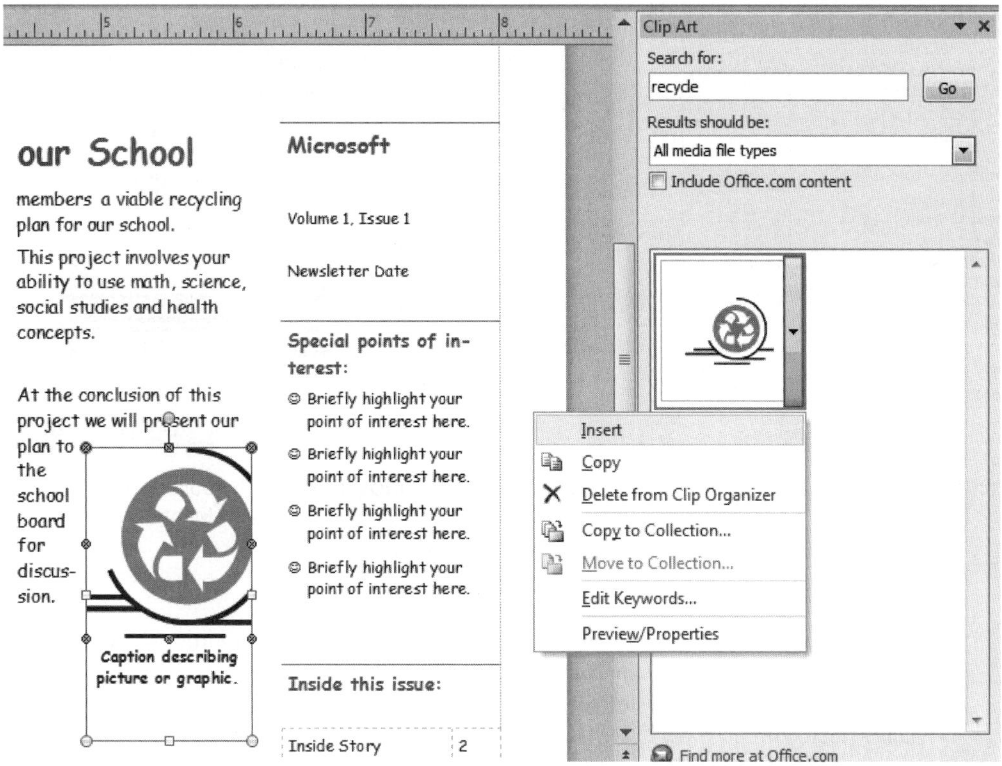

FIGURE 7.14 Inserting Clip Art

FIGURE 7.15 Adding a Caption for Clip Art

8. Resize the clip art by using the sizing handles that appear at the corners and sides of the clip art by moving your mouse over the box until the pointer turns to a double-sided arrow. Hold down the right mouse button and drag the circles or boxes to make the image the size you want. To size the clip art proportionally, use the circles on the corners of the image. The green circle at the top of the image allows you to rotate the image to get an angular effect. (You can do this trick with any text box in Publisher.)
9. Change the caption description for the clip art: by clicking on the lower half of the box where you just inserted the clip art. This activates the text box and allows you to replace the type. Provide a title that is appropriate for the clip art: Reduce, Reuse, Recycle (see Figure 7.15).
10. Identify your newsletter. In the last column on the right, replace Microsoft with the text Mrs. Longman's Science Class and change the date by clicking on the box and modifying the information to August 2011 (see Figure 7.16).
11. Replace the special points of interest with interesting points about your main article. To do so, click on the text box and type the information you want to appear. In this case, provide information about recycling and be sure to cite the source of the information (see Figure 7.17). This is a bulleted list using smiley faces. To find different types of bulleted and number lists, on the Home tab select the Paragraph section of the Ribbon and click on the bulleted list. Selections of more popular bullets are presented. In this case, select Bullets and Numbering at the bottom of the list. A screen appears, allowing you to select a bullet and modify its size, if you wish (see Figure 7.18).

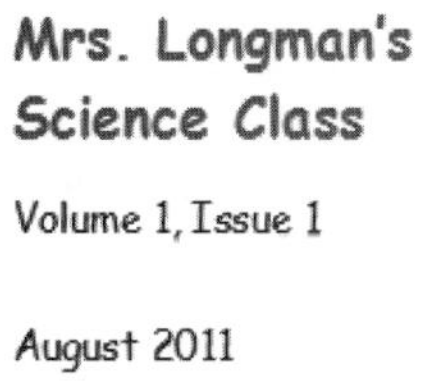

FIGURE 7.16 Indicating the Newsletter Volume

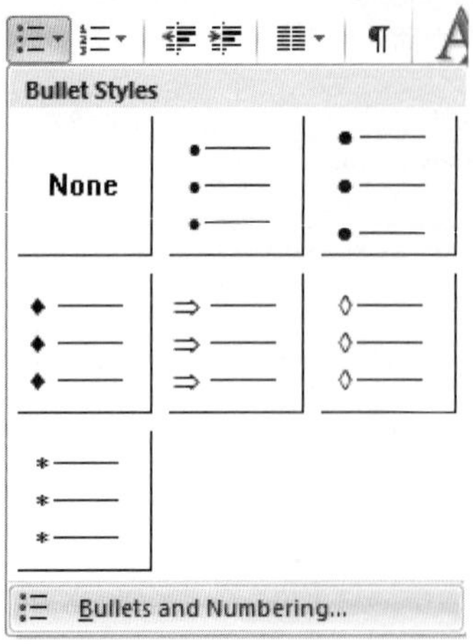

FIGURE 7.17 Bullets and Numbering

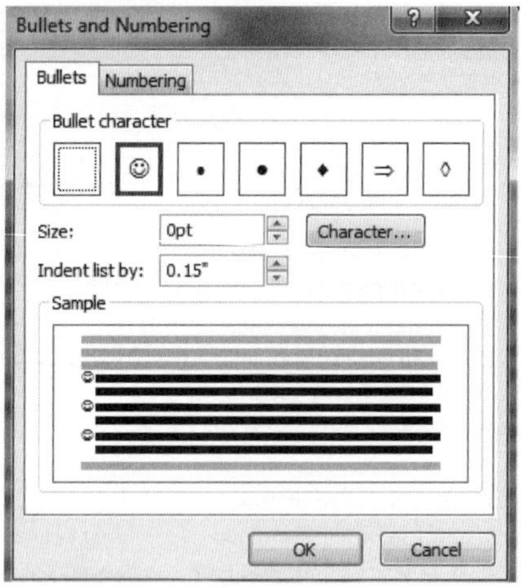

FIGURE 7.18 The Bullets and Numbering Pop-up Menu

12. In the newsletter section Inside This Issue, change the title to read Additional units we will cover this year, followed by the following units:
    - Natural disasters; Science and technology of toys; Kitchen science; Insect chemical warfare; What's in the water?

Delete the page numbers and the additional Inside Story slots in the table by selecting the appropriate number and/or words and pressing either the Delete key or the Backspace key. The table will not print because the lines are dotted, indicating that there is no solid line in the table format (see Figure 7.19).

13. Highlight the secondary story headline and replace it with information that goes with the topic of your newsletter—a definition and explanation of recycling (see Figure 7.20). The first page of the newsletter is now complete.
14. To work on the second page of the newsletter, click on the second page in the page navigation section on the workspace. In this example, though, you want only a one-page newsletter. To delete an additional page, select the page, right-click, and select Delete (see Figure 7.21).
15. To print the newsletter page, select the File tab on the Ribbon. A preview of the newsletter appears, along with printers that may be attached to your computer (see Figure 7.22).
16. Save the document and, if desired, send it as an e-mail attachment, a webpage, or a PDF. On the File tab, select Save and Send; you see options for saving your document and publishing it electronically (see Figure 7.23).

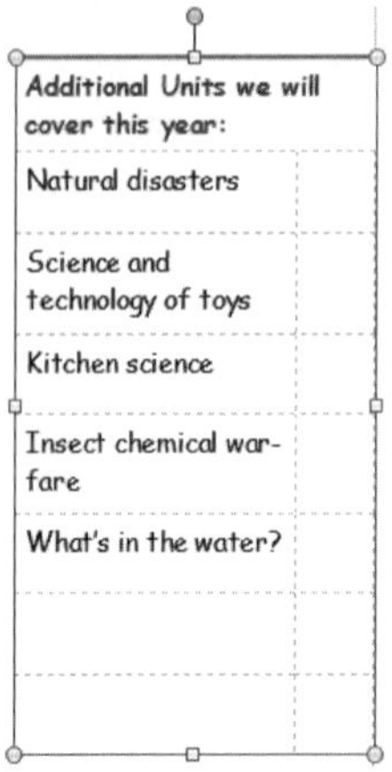

FIGURE 7.19 Additional Units

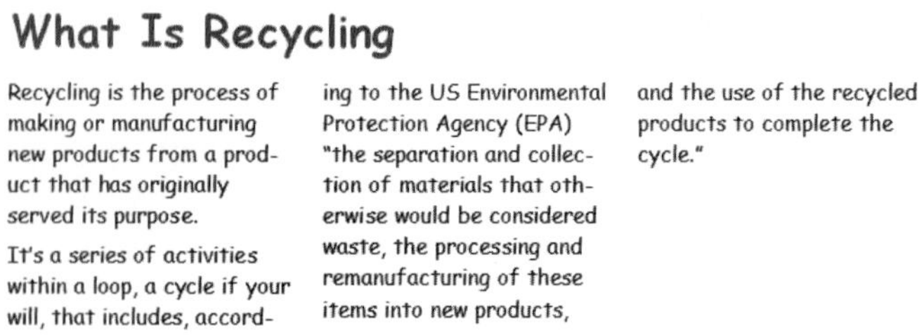

FIGURE 7.20 The Second Story

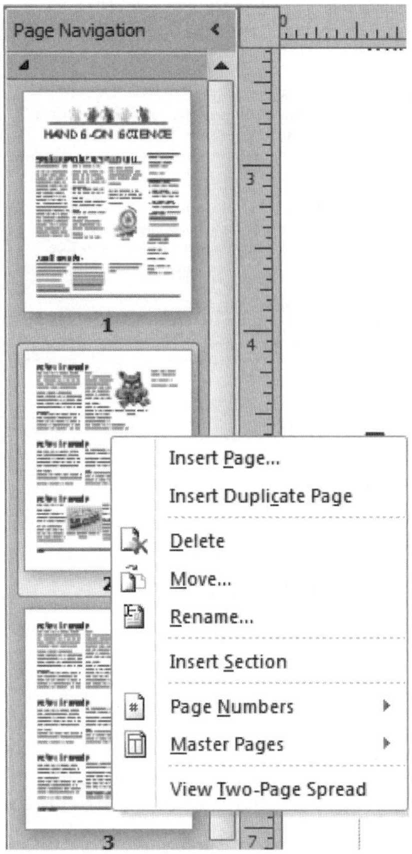

FIGURE 7.21 Deleting Additional Pages

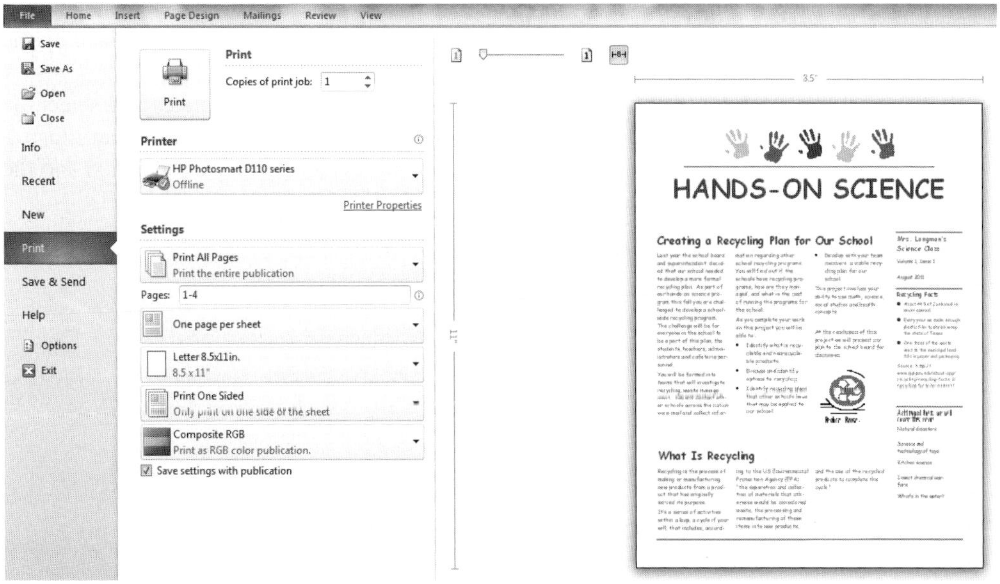

FIGURE 7.22 Printing the Document

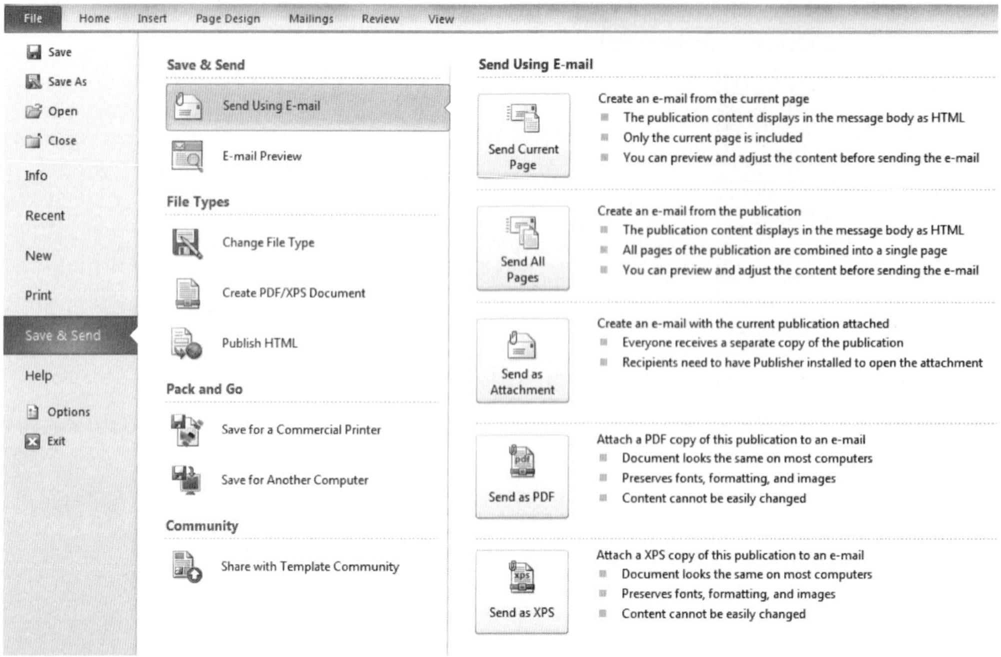

FIGURE 7.23 Saving and Sending a Document

PROJECT FOR STUDENTS: CREATING A BROCHURE

Students are often asked to write book reports or reports about topics such as people. Creating a brochure allows a student to illustrate the information presented and gives the student an opportunity for creativity in sharing the information with others. Say that as part of a mathematics unit, students are asked to prepare a brochure that relates the biography of a prominent mathematician. Creating such a brochure involves the following steps:

1. Open a new document in Publisher by clicking on the Start button and opening the software as in the previous project. If you kept the program open from the previous document, you can select New from the File tab on the Ribbon. Available templates are listed on the screen. Select Brochures from the Most Popular section (see Figure 7.24).
2. To select the brochure template for this project, use the installed templates and select the template named Simple Divider. As with the newsletter you created earlier, an illustration of the template appears along the right side of the screen, giving information and the "look" of the brochure template (see Figure 7.25).

PDToolkit for *Microsoft® Office 2010 for Teachers*

Go to PDToolkit for **Microsoft® Office 2010 for Teachers** to locate a completed example in the Examples folder (Maria Agnesi Brochure.pub).

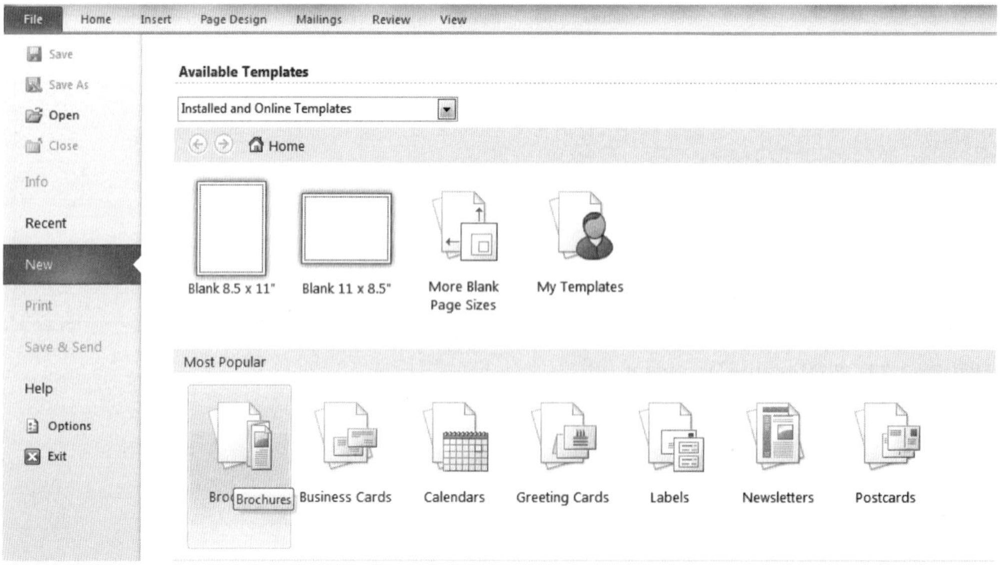

FIGURE 7.24 New Brochures

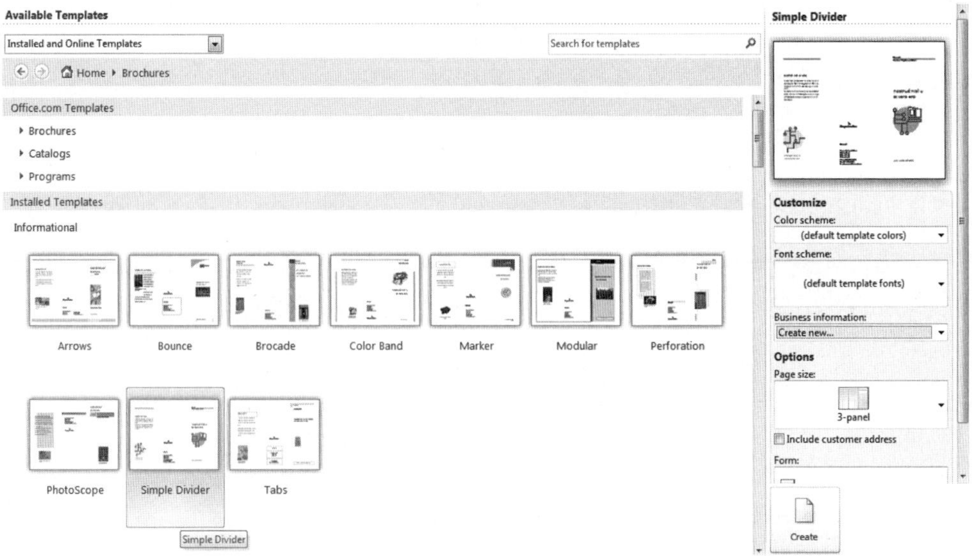

FIGURE 7.25 Installed Templates

3. For this brochure, you want to include business information: individual name, job position, organization name, address and phone number among other information. You have to do this only once if you use the same computer with the same software and save a document with this information on the computer (i.e., your home computer or the computer you use consistently in your classroom). To input this information, use the drop-down menu in the Customize section of the screen, where you see Business Information and Create New (see Figure 7.26). Include as little or as much information as you would like to include on your publications.
4. Click Create at the bottom of the Customizing panel to start creating your brochure using the template selected. Notice on the template that the business information you typed now appears in the brochure. Working on the brochure is easiest if you increase the viewing size, so use the zoom slider at the bottom of the workspace to increase the size to 100% (see Figure 7.27).
5. Notice that the workspace for the brochure is the same as that used for the newsletter, with the two sides of the three-fold brochure shown in the Page Navigation area. The front of the brochure is the page that automatically appears in the workspace (see Figure 7.28).

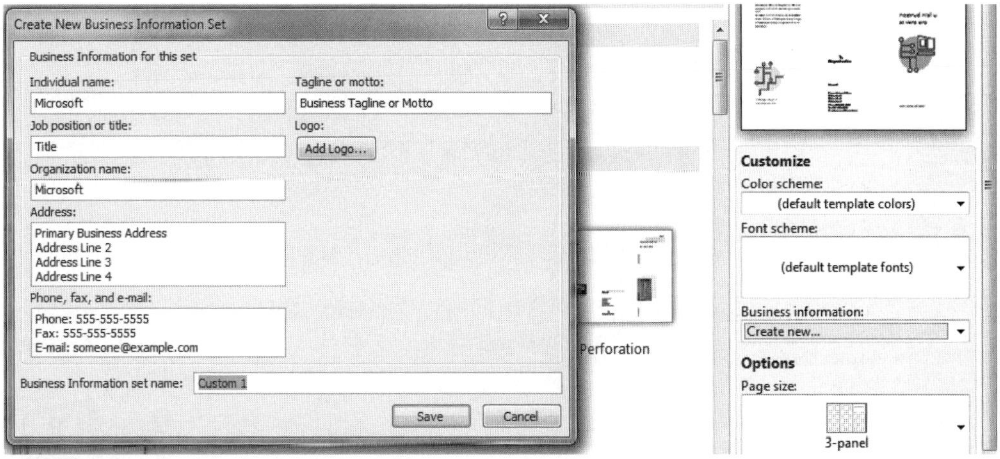

FIGURE 7.26 New Business Information

FIGURE 7.27 The Zoom Slider

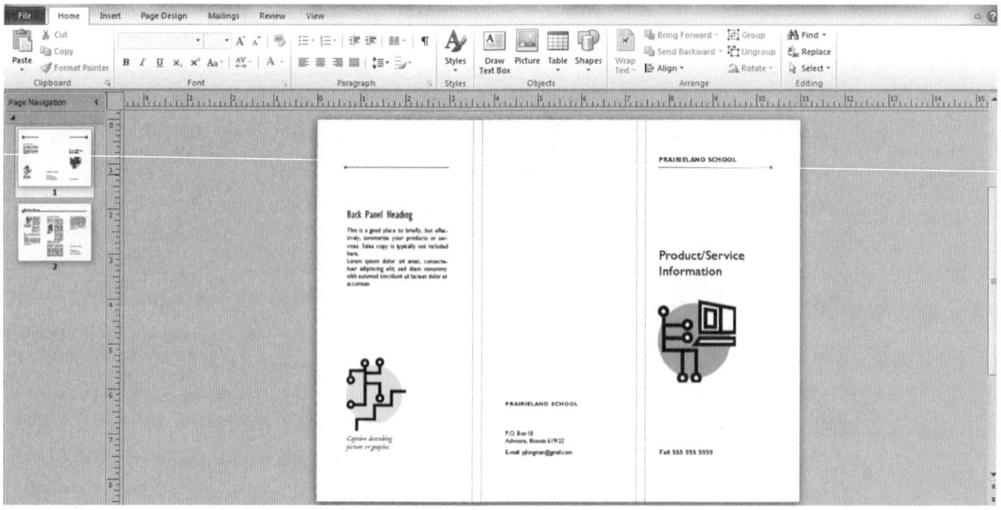

FIGURE 7.28 A Brochure Template

6. To change the title of the brochure, click on the Product/Service Information text box. Then type the name of the mathematician you have chosen to write about, Maria Agnesi, and select a font from the Font section of the Ribbon. The font will automatically change to reflect the style you have selected, so you can get a good idea of what your text will look like (see Figure 7.29).

Next, replace the picture on the front of the brochure. If you have access to the Web, you might want to do a search for an image of Agnesi. If you use an image from the Internet, make sure to visit the site where you found the image and receive permission to use the image. In this case, though, use an example of Agnesi's work, the Witch of Agnesi diagram, which is available on a public domain website: http://en.wikipedia.org/wiki/File:WitchOfAgnesi03a.png#file. Once the image has been located on the website, copy the image to the computer for use.

1. Select the graphic on the brochure by right-clicking it and selecting Change Picture (see Figure 7.30).
2. An Insert Picture screen appears. Select the file Witch of Agnesi from the location where you have saved it, highlight the title of the image, and click the Insert button (see Figure 7.31).

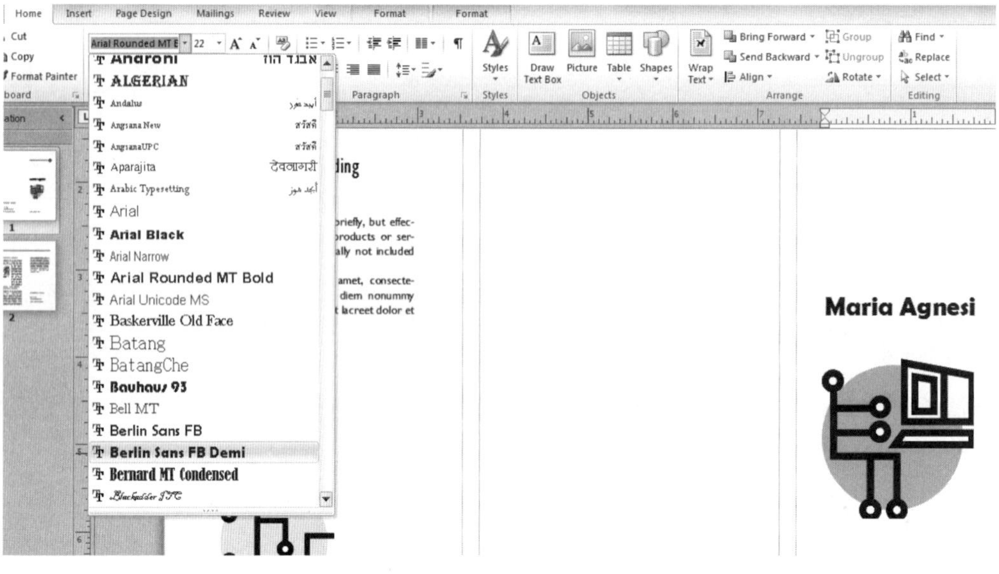

FIGURE 7.29 Changing Font Style

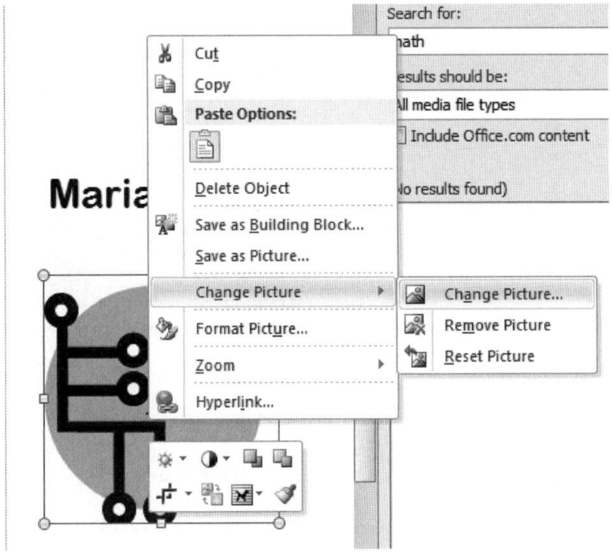

FIGURE 7.30 Changing a Picture

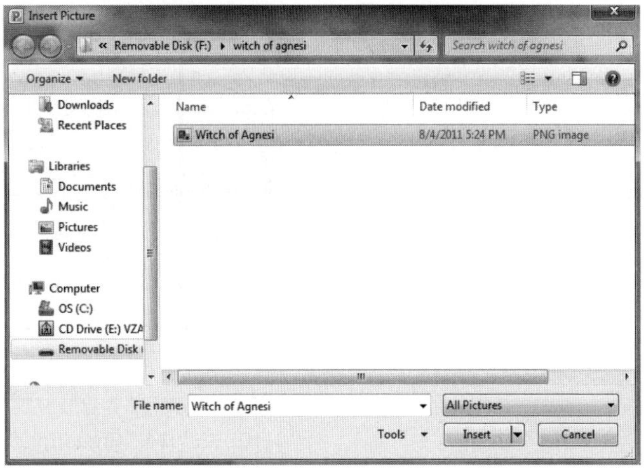

FIGURE 7.31 Inserting a Picture

3. The picture appears in place of the original image. You may need to adjust the image by using the sizing handles at the edges of the picture to make it the appropriate size for the brochure. To keep the picture in proportion, use the circles at the corners and hold down the mouse button while dragging to make the image smaller or larger (see Figure 7.32).
4. To give the reader of the brochure an idea of what this image is, create a text box and place the title Witch of Agnesi in it. Select the Insert tab from the Ribbon and select Draw Text Box (see Figure 7.33).
5. As you move the mouse to the brochure page, it will turn into a crosshair. Hold down the left mouse button and drag to create a text box. Once the text box is created, a cursor appears in the text box, and you can type in it (see Figure 7.34).

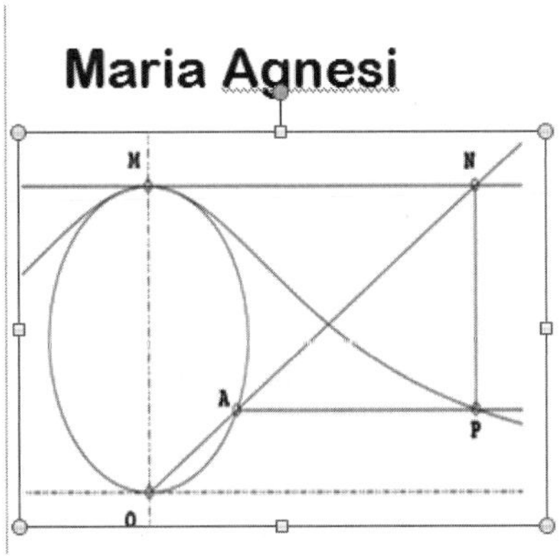

FIGURE 7.32 Sizing a Picture

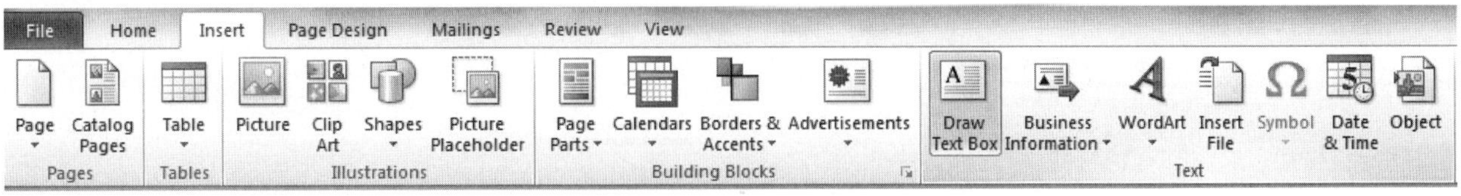

FIGURE 7.33 Drawing a Text Box

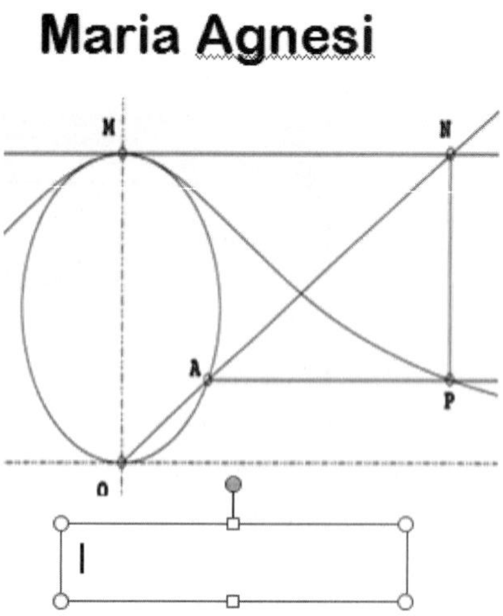

FIGURE 7.34 Creating a Text Box

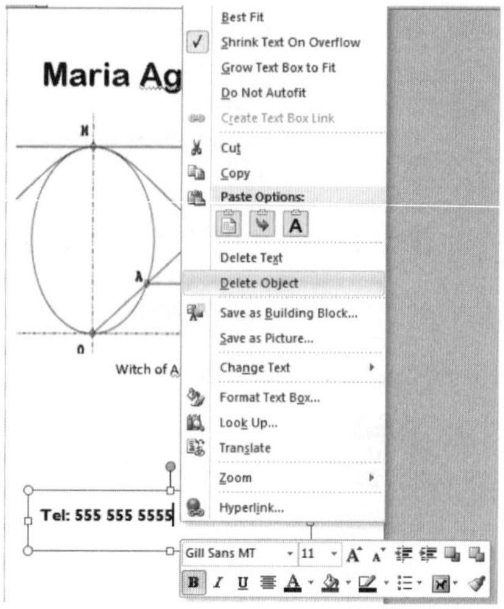

FIGURE 7.35 Deleting a Text Box

6. After you have typed in the title of the picture or graphic, remove the telephone number that appears on the front of the brochure. This is part of the information that is automatically created when contact information is entered in the program. To delete the text box, simply highlight it, right-click, and select Delete Object (see Figure 7.35).
7. Highlight the back panel heading and type Maria Agnesi Contributions.
8. In the text box below the heading, type in the following information:
   - Wrote and published the first comprehensive calculus textbook
   - First woman to be appointed as a professor at a university
   - Wrote the first mathematics book by a woman that still survives
   - Italian mathematician and philosopher
   - Lived from 1718 to 1799
9. Delete the graphic object at the bottom of the page in the same way you deleted the telephone number on the front panel. The completed front of the brochure should look as shown in Figure 7.36.

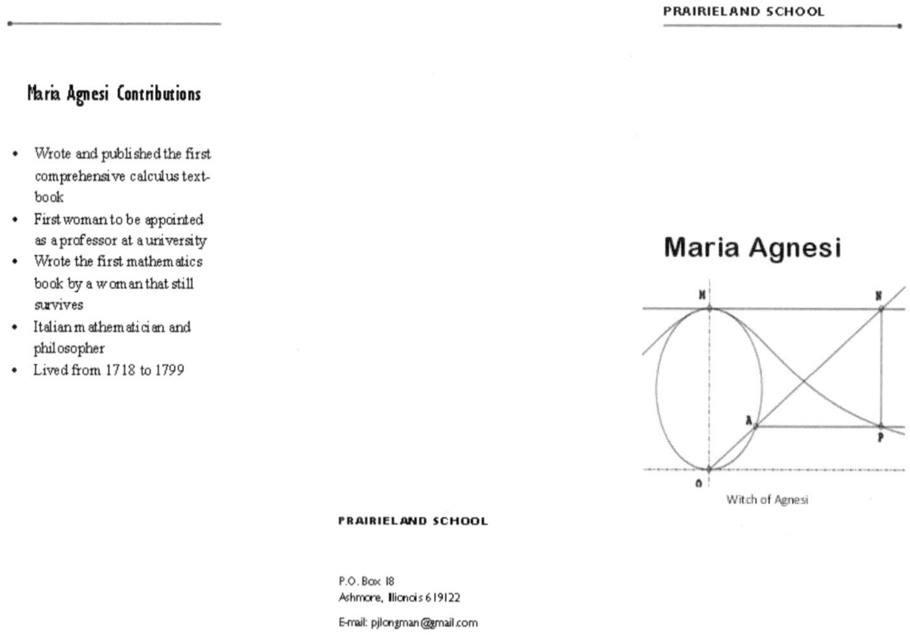

FIGURE 7.36 The Completed Front Cover

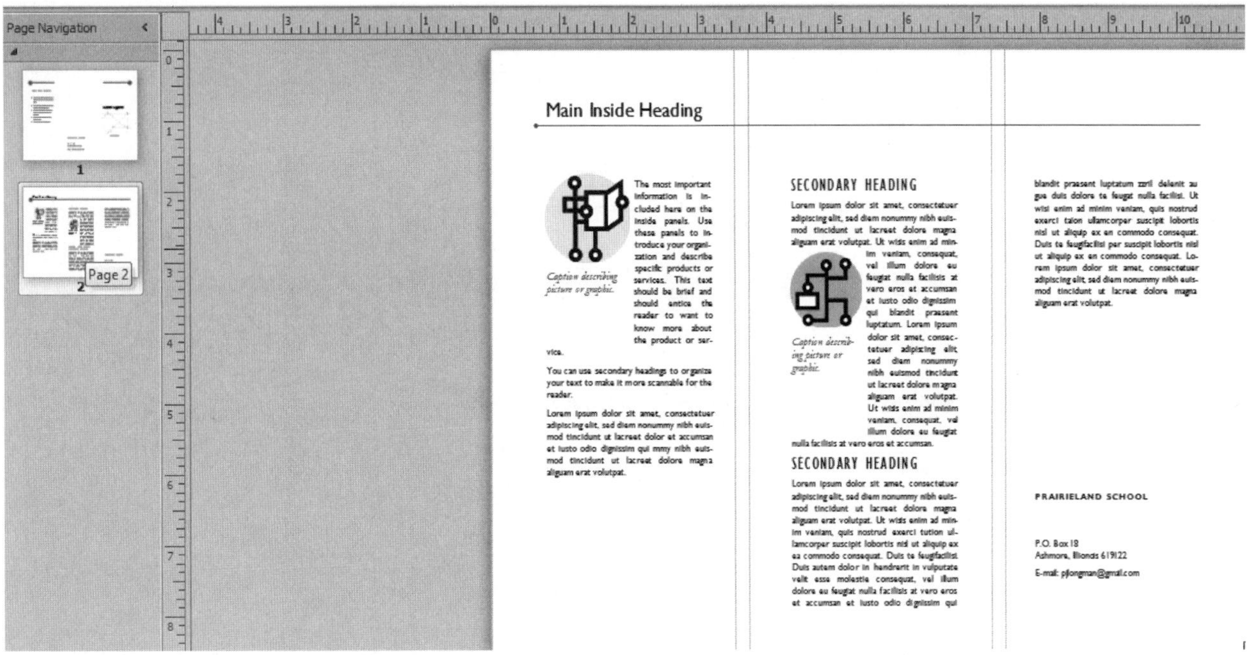

FIGURE 7.37 Page Two of the Brochure

10. To start the second page or the inside of the brochure, click on Page Two in the navigation panel on the left of the workspace (see Figure 7.37).
11. To place information in the brochure, start in the left-hand column. Replace Main Inside Heading with Maria Agnesi: Italian Algebraist, Geometer, and Logician. Then, in the first and second columns, insert information about Agnesi's life.
12. Replace Secondary Heading with Her Mathematical Contributions. Then provide information regarding Agnesi's work in mathematics and an explanation of the Witch of Agnesi.
13. Insert a clip art picture at the bottom of the first column. As you add a picture, you may want to format the text around the picture. To do this, right-click on the picture and select Format Picture (see Figure 7.38).
14. Select the Layout tab on the Format Picture window that pops up after you make your selection. Select the tight wrapping style, allowing text and pictures to wrap around the format (see Figure 7.39). The finished second page of the brochure might look like the illustration in Figure 7.40.

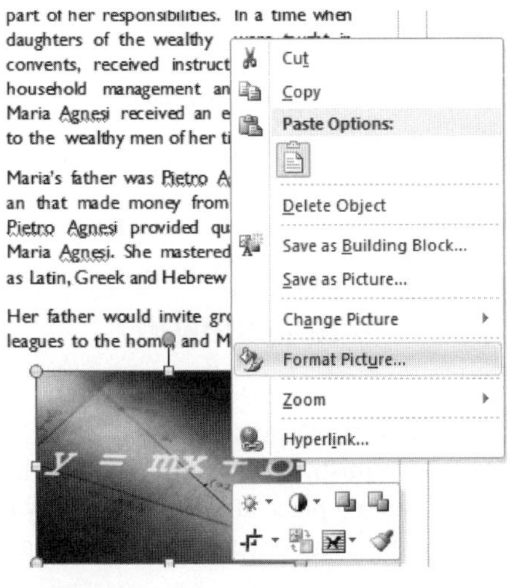

FIGURE 7.38 Formatting a Picture

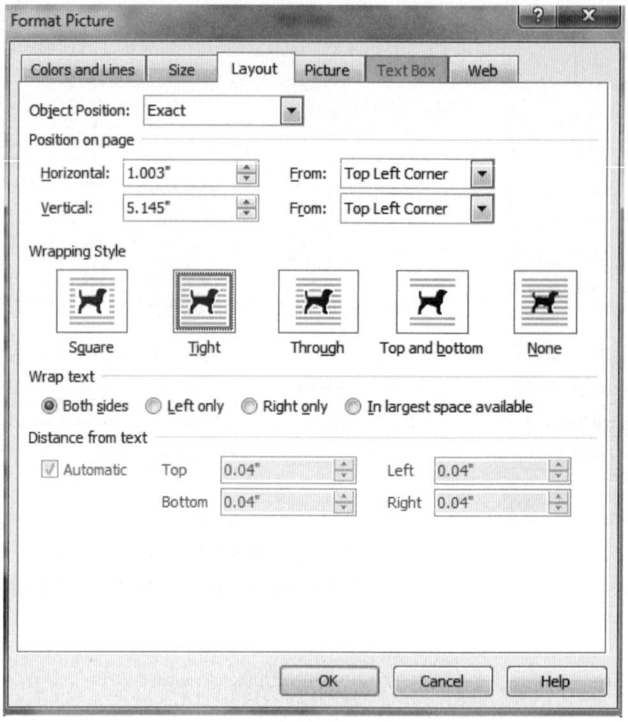

FIGURE 7.39 The Tight Text Wrap

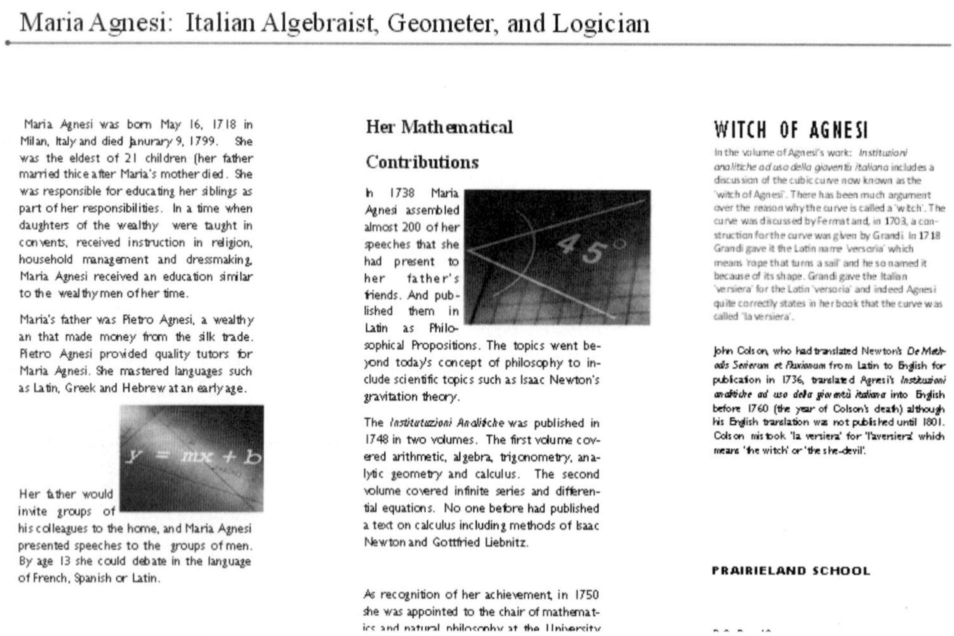

Maria Agnesi: Italian Algebraist, Geometer, and Logician

Maria Agnesi was born May 16, 1718 in Milan, Italy and died Janurary 9, 1799. She was the eldest of 21 children (her father married thice after Maria's mother died. She was responsible for educating her siblings as part of her responsibilities. In a time when daughters of the wealthy were taught in convents, received instruction in religion, household management and dressmaking, Maria Agnesi received an education similar to the wealthy men of her time.

Maria's father was Pietro Agnesi, a wealthy an that made money from the silk trade. Pietro Agnesi provided quality tutors for Maria Agnesi. She mastered languages such as Latin, Greek and Hebrew at an early age.

$y = mx + b$

Her father would invite groups of his colleagues to the home, and Maria Agnesi presented speeches to the groups of men. By age 13 she could debate in the language of French, Spanish or Latin.

Her Mathematical Contributions

In 1738 Maria Agnesi assembled almost 200 of her speeches that she had present to her father's friends. And published them in Latin as Philosophical Propositions. The topics went beyond today's concept of philosophy to include scientific topics such as Isaac Newton's gravitation theory.

45°

The *Institutazioni Analitiche* was published in 1748 in two volumes. The first volume covered arithmetic, algebra, trigonometry, analytic geometry and calculus. The second volume covered infinite series and differential equations. No one before had published a text on calculus including methods of Isaac Newton and Gottfried Liebnitz.

As recognition of her achievement, in 1750 she was appointed to the chair of mathematics and natural philosophy at the University

WITCH OF AGNESI

In the volume of Agnesi's work: *Instituzioni analitiche ad uso della gioventù italiana* includes a discussion of the cubic curve now known as the 'witch of Agnesi'. There has been much argument over the reason why the curve is called a 'witch'. The curve was discussed by Fermat and, in 1703, a construction for the curve was given by Grandi. In 1718 Grandi gave it the Latin name 'versoria' which means 'rope that turns a sail' and he so named it because of its shape. Grandi gave the Italian 'versiera' for the Latin 'versoria' and indeed Agnesi quite correctly states in her book that the curve was called 'la versiera'.

John Colson, who had translated Newton's *De Methodis Serierum et Fluxionum* from Latin to English for publication in 1736, translated Agnesi's *Instituzioni analitiche ad uso della gioventù italiana* into English before 1760 (the year of Colson's death) although his English translation was not published until 1801. Colson mistook 'la versiera' for 'l'aversiera' which means 'the witch' or 'the she-devil'.

PRAIRIELAND SCHOOL

FIGURE 7.40 The Second Page of the Brochure

PDToolkit for Microsoft® Office 2010 for Teachers

Go to PDToolkit for **Microsoft® Office 2010 for Teachers** to locate completed examples in the Examples folder (Cyberbullying email.pdf and Cyberbullying email.pub).

PROJECT FOR ADMINISTRATORS: CREATING A PROFESSIONAL E-MAIL TEMPLATE

An administrator may want a teacher or a student to send out an e-mail to a group but want the document to be something other than a standard e-mail. An administrator may also need to distribute information to others regarding an activity that will be taking place at school. One way to save paper, postage, and time is to e-mail the information to groups and/or parents and guardians who have provided their e-mail addresses to the school.

Before you create a template such as the one in the following exercise, you should check with the technology coordinator in your school to see if there are any restrictions regarding what may be sent through your school's e-mail accounts.

To create an e-mail using a Publisher template follow these steps:

1. Open Publisher, select E-mail in the More Templates section, and click on the icon to see what templates are available (see Figure 7.41).
2. Select the template labeled Bounce. As with other templates in Publisher, the thumbnail of the e-mail appears on the right side of the screen. Keep in mind that you have already input business information from the project you created for students. To create a new business information profile, use the pull-down menu to create one. Click the Create button (see Figure 7.42).
3. Replace the information on the template with information regarding a public speaker who will be presenting at the school on cyberbullying. The public is invited. Replace Event or Activity Title with Cyberbullying : What is it? How does it work? How do we prevent it? What is the law? To do so, click on the text box, highlight the text, and type in the new title (see Figure 7.43).
4. In the event heading, you identify the speaker and perhaps the credentials of the speaker. To do so, highlight the text box and insert the following information: E. J. Long, M.S.,

FIGURE 7.41 The E-mail Template Icon

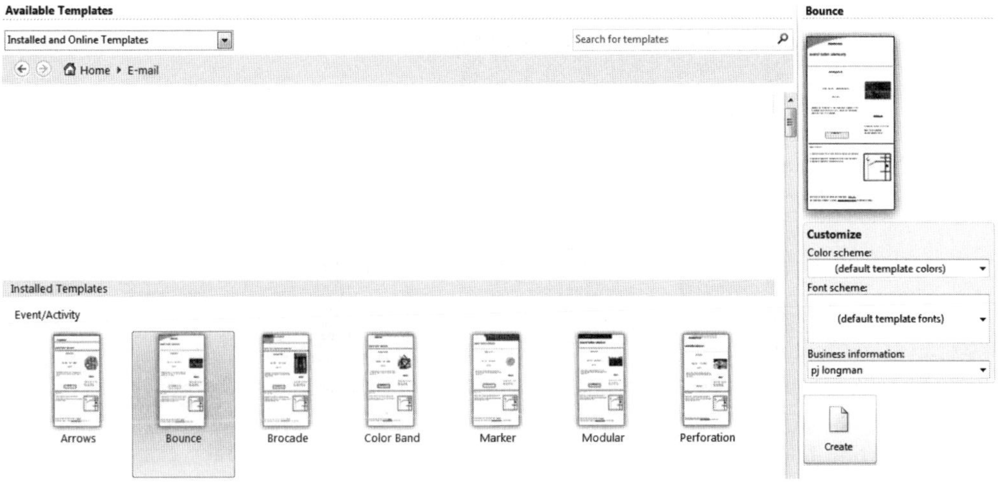

FIGURE 7.42 The Bounce Template

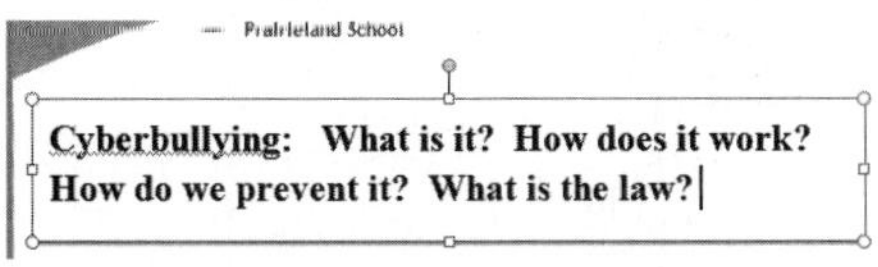

FIGURE 7.43 Replacing the Event Title

J.D., Director of Safe Space, a national speaker on cyberbullying, will present and answer questions.

5. Highlight the numbers next to Time and insert 7:00 p.m.
6. Highlight the numbers next to Date and insert 09/15/2012 (see Figure 7.44).
7. Leave the location in the text box but add a specific location—Prairieland School Auditorium, Room 112—by placing the cursor after the word Location in the text box and then typing the location information.
8. To replace the artwork on the e-mail with clip art, click on the clip art currently in the e-mail document. Select the Insert tab on the Ribbon and click on Clip Art in the Illustrations section of the Ribbon. The clip art workspace appears on the right side of the workspace. In Search For, type computer. Select a piece of clip art by clicking on it. In the pull-down menu that appears, highlight Insert. The clip art automatically replaces the clip art highlighted in the e-mail document (see Figure 7.45).
9. To write a description of the event, highlight the text box and type the following:
   - Topics that will be addressed include: What is cyberbullying? What can parents do about cyberbullying? What is the law about cyberbullying? How does the school get involved in prevention? Tip sheets and handouts will be provided. A question and answer period will follow the presentation.
10. Highlight the contact information person and telephone number and replace that information with S. Schertz, 309-549-8737.
11. Highlight the contact person's e-mail address and type S. Schertz, e-mail: s.schertz@prairielandschool.net.
12. Because this event is open to the public, highlight the text Sign Up Now and replace it with Open to the Public (see Figure 7.46).
13. Replace the location details with the address 1300 East Raab Road, Normal, IL 61761.

E. J. Long, M.S., J.D., Director of Safe Space, a national speaker on cyberbullying, will present and answer questions.

Time: 7:00 p.m. Date: 09/15/2012

FIGURE 7.44 Inserted Text

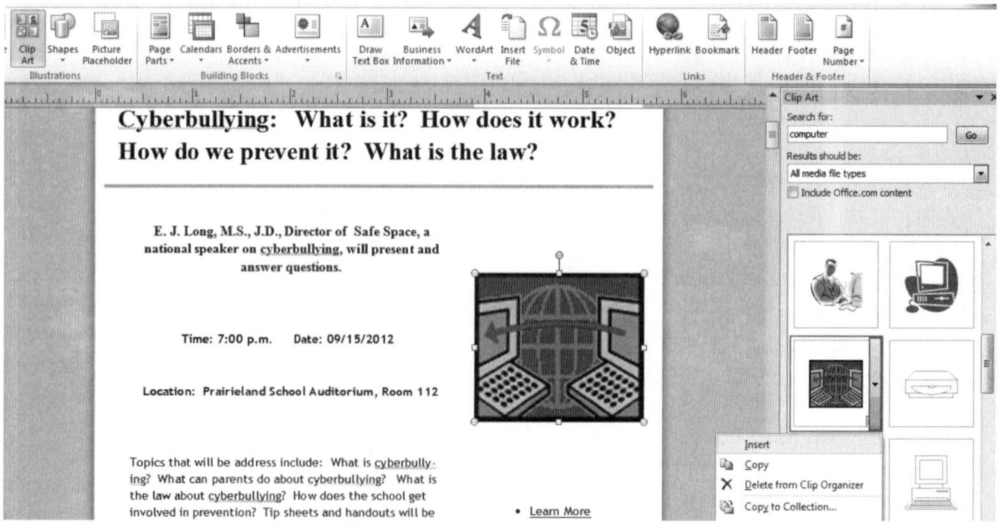

FIGURE 7.45 Inserting Clip Art

14. Replace the map with a map scanned in from a document provided by the school. For this example, you do not have to replace the map, but to do this, you would use the same techniques as for replacing clip art or a picture.
15. Remove the following information: To remove your name from our mailing list, please click here. Questions or comments? E-mail us at someone@example.com or call 555-555-5555. To do so, click on the text box and press the Delete key. The complete e-mail might now look as shown in Figure 7.47.
16. Select the File tab on the Ribbon and select Save and Send from the menu bar. The sending options appear. If you are using Microsoft Outlook as your e-mail software, you may use the Send Using E-mail option. If you are not using the software or would like to send this document as an attachment, you can select Save As on the menu bar and save the document as a PDF that can be attached to any e-mail message (see Figure 7.48).

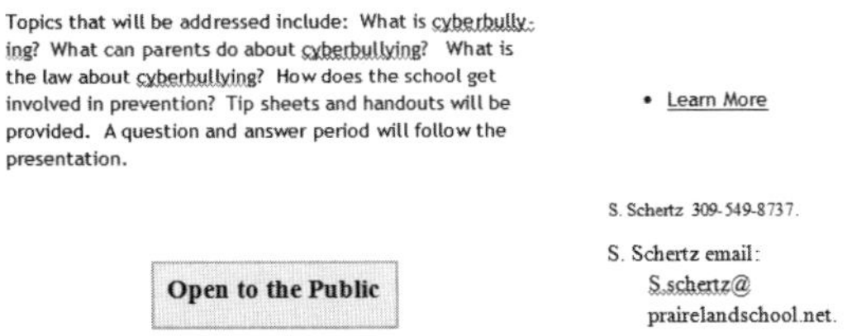

FIGURE 7.46 Text Replacement Segments

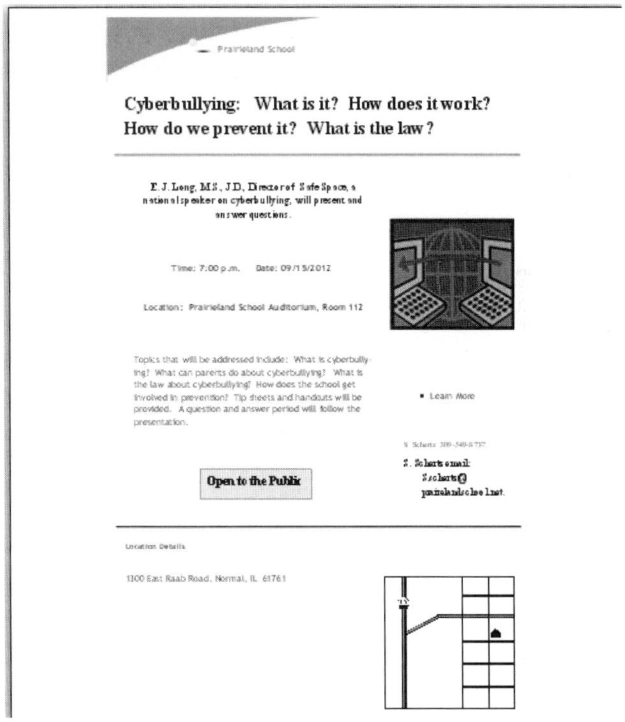

FIGURE 7.47 A Completed E-mail Document

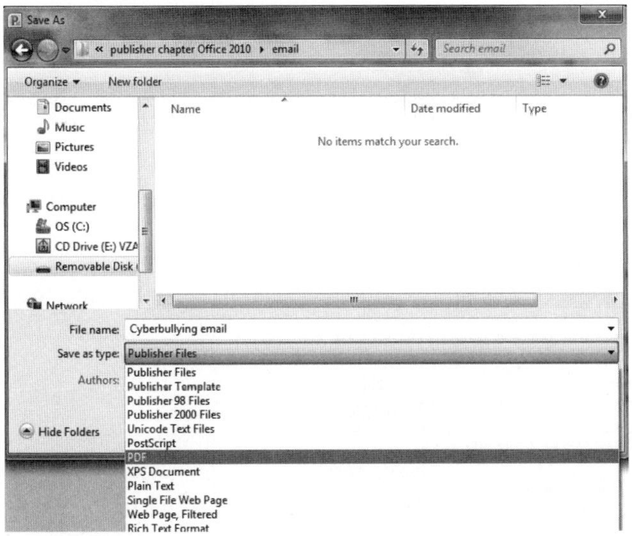

FIGURE 7.48 Saving as a PDF

PDToolkit for *Microsoft® Office 2010 for Teachers*

Go to PDToolkit for **Microsoft® Office 2010 for Teachers** to locate a completed example in the Examples folder (Catman Postcard.pub).

PROJECT FOR EVERYONE: CREATING A POSTCARD

Educators often want to send information through the postal service to share important events with others. For example, they might want to send a postcard to parents and guardians, indicating that their students have done well in school. Or they might want to send a card to celebrate a season, such as fall and the beginning of the school year. To create a postcard announcing that a school has a new friend in the barn, follow these steps:

1. Select the Arrows postcard template and click Create (see Figure 7.49).
2. On the front of the postcard (there are two sides in this template) or page one, highlight Product/Service Information and replace it with Welcome "Catman" to the Barn!
3. Highlight the text box below the title and press Delete to erase the text box.
4. To create a shape for a picture that you want to place in the postcard, select the Insert tab from the Ribbon and then select Picture Placeholder from the Illustrations section (see Figure 7.50).
5. The box for the picture placeholder appears on the postcard. Mouse over the square sizing handles at the corners of the placeholder until the double-sided arrow appears, hold down the left mouse button, and drag until the space is the appropriate size (see Figure 7.51).
6. You can use pictures from clip art, or in this case, a file that has been sent electronically as a picture and then saved as a file on the computer. To place the picture in the placeholder space, select Insert from the Ribbon and 10 select Picture. In this example, the picture is in the picture library on the hard drive of the computer that was taken with a digital camera and loaded on the hard drive of the computer. Select the picture you want to use and click Insert (see Figure 7.52)

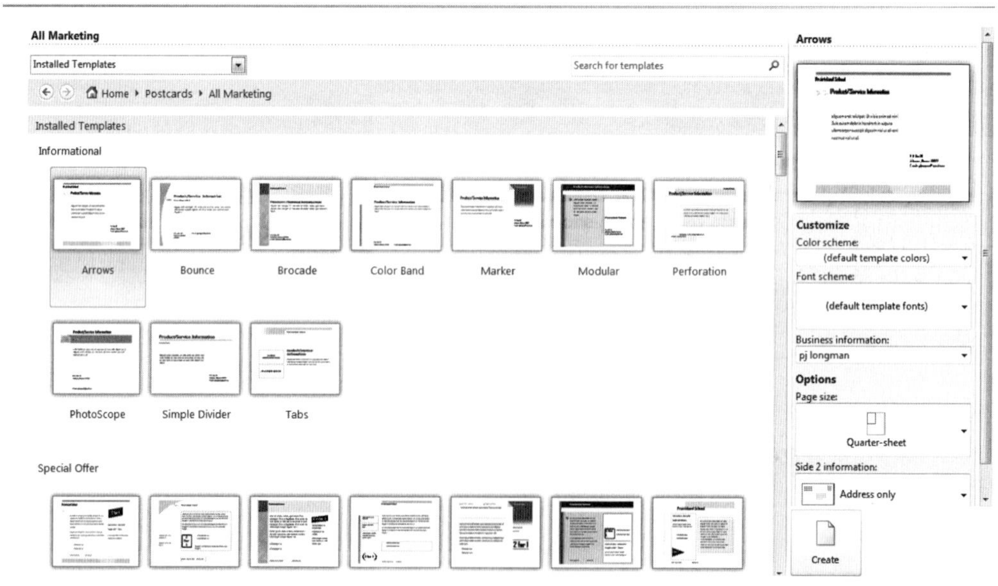

FIGURE 7.49 Creating a Postcard

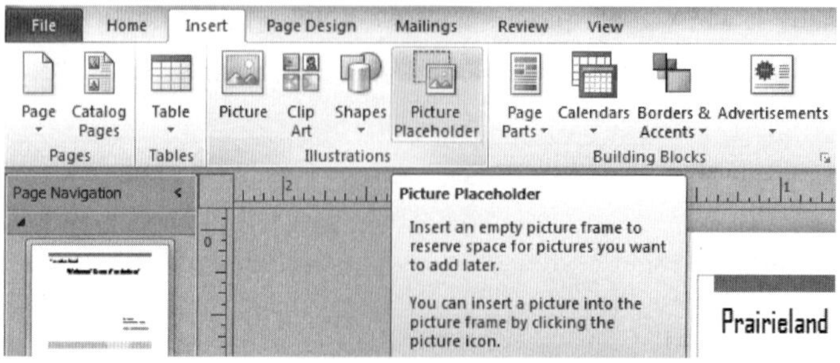

FIGURE 7.50 A Picture Placeholder

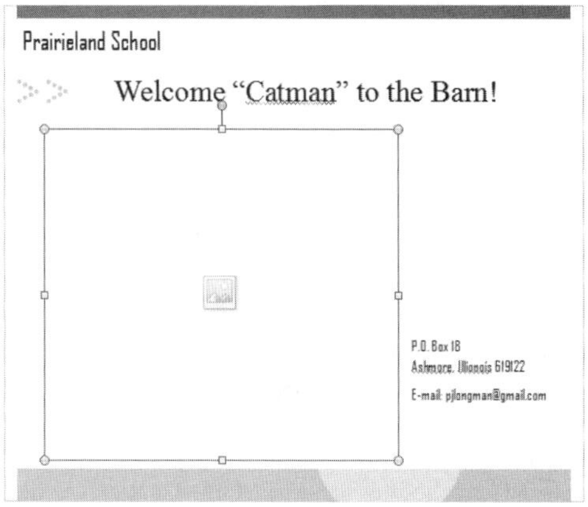

FIGURE 7.51 A Picture Placeholder

FIGURE 7.52 Inserting a Picture

FIGURE 7.53 A Finished Postcard

7. Once the picture appears, click outside the placeholder space, and the picture is cropped to size of the placeholder. The front of the postcard is now finished and should look something like Figure 7.53.

SUMMING IT UP

In this chapter, you created a newsletter, a brochure, an e-mail message, and a postcard. You can now produce all these communications on your own and teach your students to use the techniques. These and other activities allow you to fulfill some of the ISTE standards for teachers, making you and your classroom look more professional and providing technology that enhances student learning.

References and Resources

Bloom, B. (Ed.). (1956). *Taxonomy of educational objectives.* New York: David McKay.

George, J.C. (1988). *My side of the mountain.* New York: Puffin Books.

Paulsen, G. (1999). *Hatchet.* New York: Simon Pulse.

International Society for Technology in Education. (2008). *NETS for teachers.* Retrieved March 4, 2011, from www.iste.org/standards/nets-for-teachers.aspx.

SELECTED WEBSITES

National Recycling Facts, Penn State
www.opp.psu.edu/about-opp/recycling/recycling-facts-1/recycling-facts-by-material

Source of Student Work About Agnesi
http://mrsvesseymathematicians.wikispaces.com/Agnesi

The Witch of Agnesi
http://en.wikipedia.org/wiki/File:WitchOfAgnesi03a.png#file

Maria Gaetana Agnesi
www.britannica.com/EBchecked/topic/9316/Maria-Gaetana-Agnesi

Website Addressing Issues Related to Cyberbullying
www.stopcyberbullying.org/index2.html

National Crime Prevention Center Website Section on Cyberbullying
www.ncpc.org/topics/cyberbullying

8 INTEGRATING OFFICE 2010

Chapter Outline

- What You Are Going to Learn
- Chapter Overview
- About Integrating the Office Products
- Project for Students: Creating a Multimedia Project
- Project for Teachers: Creating a Question and Answer Game
- Project for Administrators: Posting School Board Files on SkyDrive
- Additional Activities
- Summing It Up
- Reference

WHAT YOU ARE GOING TO LEARN

At the completion of this chapter you will be able to:

- Copy and paste text from a Word document to a PowerPoint slide
- Place an Excel worksheet into a Word document and a PowerPoint slide show
- Edit an Excel chart in a Word document and a PowerPoint slide show
- Embed an Excel worksheet in a Word document
- Link an Excel worksheet to a Word document and a PowerPoint slide show
- Embed a PowerPoint slide in a Word document
- Run a PowerPoint slide show from a Word document
- Create contacts in Outlook and export them to Access
- Place Access data in a PowerPoint slide

CHAPTER OVERVIEW

PDToolkit for *Microsoft® Office 2010 for Teachers*

You can find files that correspond to the chapter activities at http://pdtoolkit.pearson.com.

Each Office application has a unique purpose and function. The ability to integrate their functionality expands your capacity to efficiently design and produce materials and to incorporate diverse informational sources and media. Given this capability, it is fitting that an entire chapter of this text is devoted to approaches to integrating these products. In this chapter, you will find instruction on how to develop materials that incorporate PowerPoint slides, Word documents, Excel worksheets, Outlook data, and Access data. The examples presented are only a few of the many options for developing materials. The activities give step-by-step instructions for quickly accomplishing tasks.

ABOUT INTEGRATING THE OFFICE PRODUCTS

As you work with Office, you will undoubtedly encounter situations in which you need files or portions of a file created with one application in a file created with another application. You may even need to work with one file and from it update, open, or run another file in a different application. For instance, suppose you use Word to create a class newsletter in which you highlight a student project, such as a PowerPoint slide show illustrating a student's artwork. In Word, you provide a text description of the project as well as illustrations of the slide show. Because PowerPoint and Word integrate so easily, you can select slides from PowerPoint and place them in the newsletter. In addition, if you show colleagues the newsletter you created in Word, and they want to view the student project in more depth, you can click on the slide illustration and run the PowerPoint slide show.

Integrating files across the Office products is extremely useful. It broadens the possibilities for the types of materials you can make and the efficiency with which you can produce them.

Say that you create a chart and place it in a document that you plan to distribute to an audience. Just before you click the Print button, you notice an error in the chart. Depending on how you made the chart, you may need to open an application, alter chart text and numeric values, prepare the chart for a word processing program, and then place and format it. These tasks can be time-consuming. Alternatively, by creating the document with Word and the chart with Excel and then linking them, you could quickly modify numeric values in Excel, which would automatically update the Word document and make it ready for printing. This is a good illustration of the power of integrating Office programs.

This chapter presents a few more approaches to integrating Office programs. As your familiarity with Office deepens, you will no doubt discover inventive ways to use its integrative capabilities to create interesting and engaging classroom materials and activities.

PROJECT FOR STUDENTS: CREATING A MULTIMEDIA PROJECT

Suppose students must create a multimedia project to present their research. The teacher designates teams composed of three or four individuals each. Each team must write a proposal that provides an overview of the topic, a rationale for why it is important to develop the project, project objectives, ideas about how the project will look when it is finished, a projected timeline, and a budget. Since it is important for students to document their work, they keep a project journal in which they write details about the development process. At a minimum, each time the team works on the project, a team member records the date, time, how much time was spent working, the tasks or what was accomplished, and any thoughts about how the project is progressing.

Over a 4-month period, teams must deliver two 15-minute class presentations. The first, a project proposal presentation, provides an overview of the topic proposal, the development plan, and work already accomplished. During the presentation, teams seek feedback from the class about how to improve the project. After this presentation, teams spend time collecting additional information and materials and developing the project. At the second presentation, teams present the finished multimedia project. When the assignment is complete, students complete a self-evaluation consisting of a written summary of what they learned, an overall evaluation of the finished project, and an assessment of how well members worked together. The classroom is equipped with a computer and projector so that teams can project their projects onto a screen for the entire class to see.

This activity is divided into five segments. The first segment presents the following:

- Making a project journal-log in Excel
- Copying and pasting text from Word to PowerPoint
- Inserting PowerPoint slides into Word using Copy and Paste
- Dragging and dropping a slide
- Inserting objects

PDToolkit for *Microsoft® Office 2010 for Teachers*

Go to PDToolkit for **Microsoft® Office 2010 for Teachers** to locate a completed example in the Examples folder (Project Log_Complete_2011.xlsx).

Suppose that team 1 chooses to create a PowerPoint slide show that informs the class about how to create webpages and transfer them to a webserver. The project will also present information about Hypertext Markup Language (HTML). Using an Excel worksheet, team 1 begins by creating a project journal-log (see Figure 8.1).

Team members set up columns for date, time, hours worked, tasks, and thoughts. Corresponding to the tasks column, they create a column named Identifier, in which they place codes to help them identify task types. The identifiers are RSH for research, DEV for

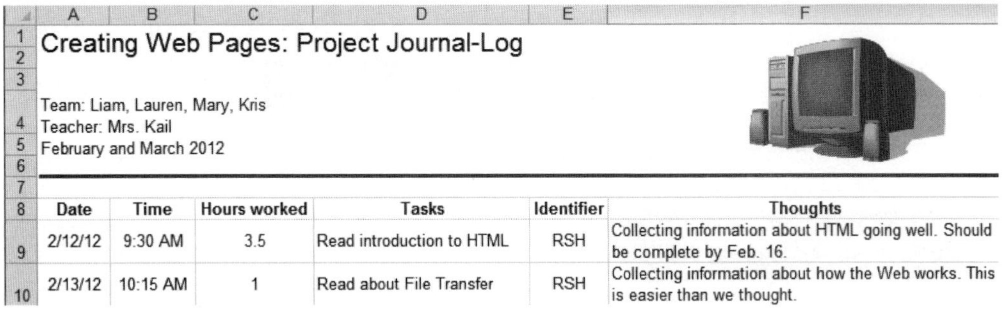

Creating Web Pages: Project Journal-Log

Team: Liam, Lauren, Mary, Kris
Teacher: Mrs. Kail
February and March 2012

Date	Time	Hours worked	Tasks	Identifier	Thoughts
2/12/12	9:30 AM	3.5	Read introduction to HTML	RSH	Collecting information about HTML going well. Should be complete by Feb. 16.
2/13/12	10:15 AM	1	Read about File Transfer	RSH	Collecting information about how the Web works. This is easier than we thought.

FIGURE 8.1 Journal-Log Sample

development, ADM for administrative, and OTH for other. When they enter task descriptions, they identify them by one of the four identifiers to help members determine the amount of time spent on different types of tasks.

After making the project journal-log, team 1 creates several PowerPoint slides that represent the finished project. The members also begin developing a project proposal that contains the following sections: title page, table of contents, project summary, project rationale, project objectives, creative strategy (what the project will be like when finished), project timeline, and budget. They will use the proposal to guide their development of the PowerPoint slide show to be delivered at the first (proposal) presentation. That slide show will include a title slide, project objectives, sample screens (creative strategy), and a timeline. In addition, the team intends to place slides from the PowerPoint slide show into the Creative Strategy section of the proposal to illustrate to the teacher (and other readers of the proposal) what the finished slide show will look like.

PDToolkit for *Microsoft® Office 2010 for Teachers*

Go to PDToolkit for **Microsoft® Office 2010 for Teachers** to locate the corresponding file in the Examples folder. For the completed file see ProposalSlideShow_Complete_2011.pptx.

Copying and Pasting Text from Word to PowerPoint

The members of team 1 developed several sections of the project proposal in Word. They also created several sample screens in PowerPoint. In this example, you will use text from the Objectives section of the proposal to add to a PowerPoint slide. Follow these steps:

1. Open the ProposalSlideShow_2011.pptx and click on the first slide.
2. Click the New Slide button or select New Slide from the Home tab.
3. Set the slide layout to Title and Content.
4. Open the Proposal_2011.docx Word file.
5. Locate the Objectives section of the proposal and select the word Objectives.
6. Click the Copy button on the Home tab or press Ctrl+C.
7. Go to PowerPoint and click in the Title box (Click to Add Title) of the slide you just inserted. Click the Paste button, and the title text appears (see Figure 8.2). If you copied the Return character after the word Objectives, delete it by pressing the Backspace key.
8. Return to Word. Below the Objectives section heading are three objectives. Select them and then go back to PowerPoint.
9. Click in the Click to Add Text text box and click the Paste button. The bulleted items appear (see Figure 8.3).

PDToolkit for *Microsoft® Office 2010 for Teachers*

Go to PDToolkit for **Microsoft® Office 2010 for Teachers** to locate the corresponding file in the Examples folder. See Proposal_Complete_2011.docx to view a completed proposal.

FIGURE 8.2 Objectives Text

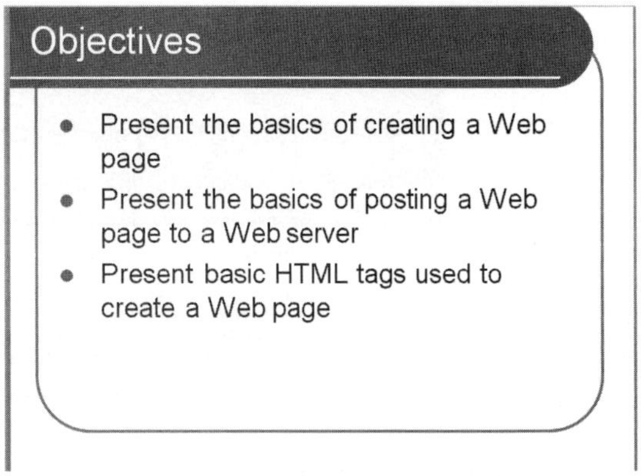

FIGURE 8.3 A Completed Slide

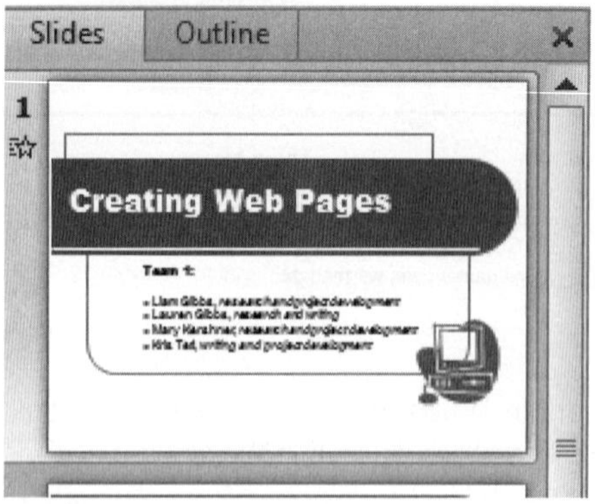

FIGURE 8.4 The Slide Pane

FIGURE 8.5 Paste Special

PDToolkit for *Microsoft® Office 2010 for Teachers*

Go to PDToolkit for **Microsoft® Office 2010 for Teachers** to locate the corresponding file in the Examples folder.

Inserting PowerPoint Slides into Word Using Copy and Paste

In this section, you will place two slides from PowerPoint into the Creative Strategy section of the proposal. There are several ways to place PowerPoint slides into Word. The easiest method is to copy a slide from PowerPoint and paste it into Word. A slide placed in Word is referred to as a *slide object.* Follow these steps:

1. Open the PowerPoint slide show. In this example, you will open a file named ProposalSlideShow_2011.pptx. In the PowerPoint workspace, select the Normal view by selecting Normal from the View tab to see the slide pane (Figure 8.4).
2. Copy the first slide and insert it into Word. In PowerPoint, click slide 1 and then click the Copy button (or select Copy on the Home tab or press Ctrl+C).
3. Open Word and place the cursor where you would like to insert the PowerPoint slide. You will position both slides in the Creative Strategy section of the proposal. Place the first slide after the sentence "After the title slide, it will present the objectives of the presentation and information about where the class can view the presentation online." Position the second slide at the end of the section. To do this, with the cursor positioned after the words ". . . presentation online," click the Paste Special button (see Figure 8.5), and the slide (slide object) appears (see Figure 8.6).
4. Format the slide object by right-clicking it in Word and selecting Format Object (see Figure 8.7). The Format Object box appears (see Figure 8.8). In this case, resize the slide object to 70% of its original size.

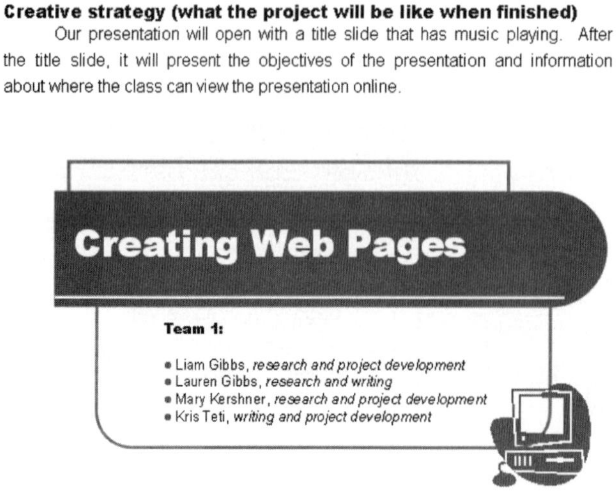

FIGURE 8.6 A Pasted Slide

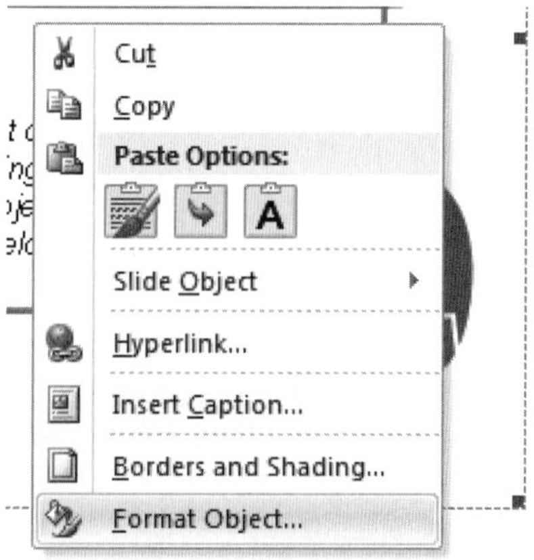

FIGURE 8.7 The Format Object Menu Item

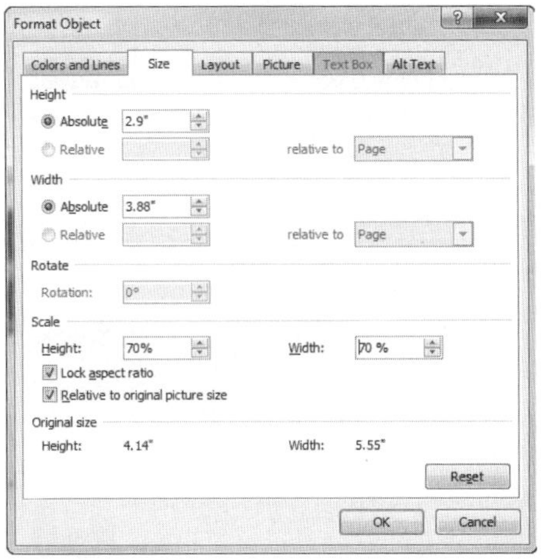

FIGURE 8.8 The Format Object Box

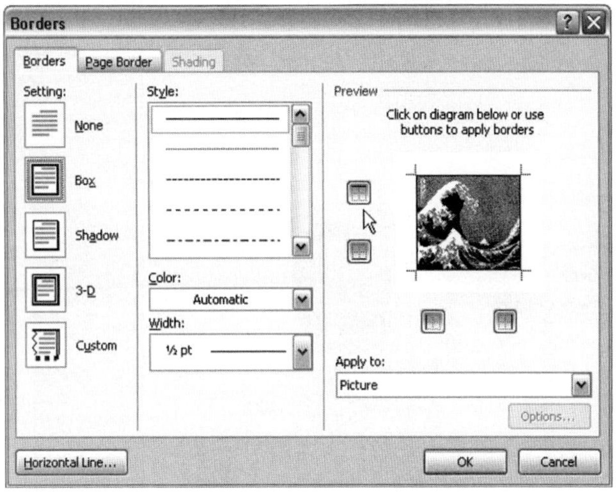

FIGURE 8.9 The Borders Box

5. Click the Size tab and type *70* in the Height box. (If the Lock Aspect Ratio box is checked, the width automatically adjusts.) Click OK.
6. Place a border around the slide to set it apart from the text. Right-click on the slide and select Border and Shading. The Borders box appears (see Figure 8.9). Click the Borders tab. In the Preview section of the Borders box, click the sides of the small image that displays or click the buttons at the left and bottom of the image. Click OK.
7. With the slide object selected, click the Align Center icon (see Figure 8.10) on the Home tab (in the Paragraph group) to center the slide on the page. The slide should look as shown in Figure 8.11.
8. Place the second slide object into Word. Go back to PowerPoint and click on slide 3 in the slide pane or select one of the slides titled Storage: Online.
9. Select Copy from the Home tab or press Ctrl+C.
10. Go back to Word and position the cursor where you would like to place the slide. For this example, place it at the end of the Creative Strategy section of the project proposal, on the empty line after the sentence "The presentation will end with a black slide."
11. Select Paste Special on the Home tab or press Ctrl+V, and the slide object appears.
12. Resize the slide to 70% of its original size.
13. Place a border around the slide to separate it from the text. Center-align it.
14. Edit the slide object by right-clicking on it and selecting Edit from the Slide Object menu item (see Figure 8.12). In the Edit mode, some of the functions on Word's Ribbon change to correspond to functions available on PowerPoint's Ribbon so that you can modify the slide layout, design, and color schemes (see Figure 8.13).

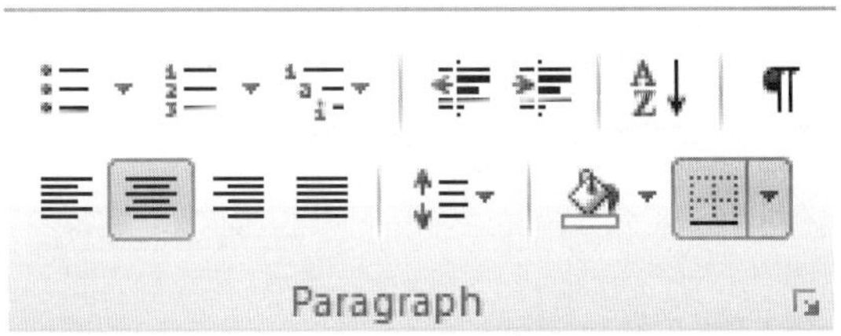

FIGURE 8.10 The Align Center Icon

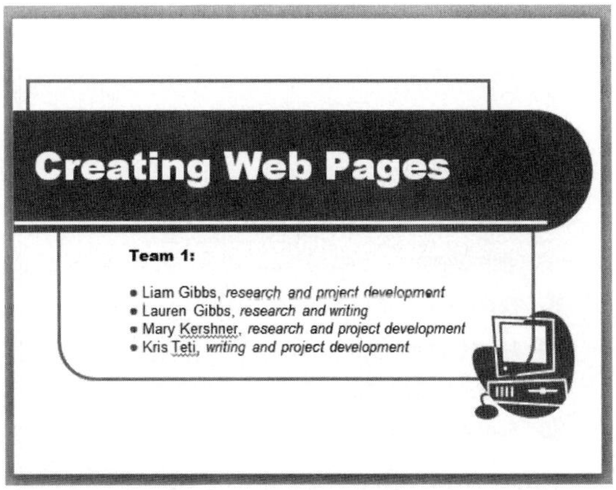

FIGURE 8.11 The Completed Title Slide

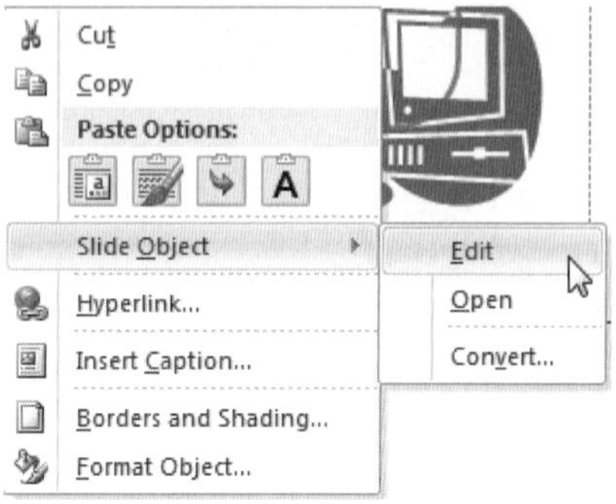

FIGURE 8.12 The Slide Object Menu Item

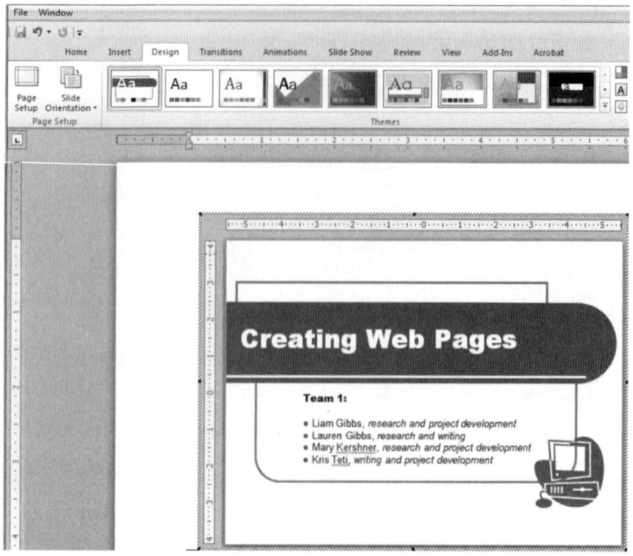

FIGURE 8.13 Themes

15. Click anywhere outside the slide area to exit the Edit mode. You can also edit the slide in PowerPoint. Right-click on the slide object in the Word document and then select Open from the Slide Object menu. Diagonal lines appear through the slide, and PowerPoint opens with the single slide in it. As you edit the slide in PowerPoint, the changes display in the slide object that you placed in Word. To save the slide as a PowerPoint file, select Save *As* from the File tab. As you modify the slide, you do not affect the original PowerPoint file. Notice that when you choose to edit a slide in PowerPoint, PowerPoint's New Slide button on the Home tab is inactive. This is because you are working with a single slide object, and additional slides cannot be added. To add slides to the PowerPoint file, you need to convert it from a slide object to a presentation object.
16. To convert the slide object, go to the slide in your Word document, right-click on it, and select Convert from the Slide Object menu (see Figure 8.14). The Convert box appears (see Figure 8.15).
17. Click the Convert To button and then select Microsoft PowerPoint Presentation. Click OK. The object is now a presentation into which you can add slides. For example, if you are in Word and right-click on the Presentation object and select Open from the Presentation Object menu, the file opens in PowerPoint. When in PowerPoint, you can add slides by clicking the New Slide button or selecting Insert New Slide from the Insert menu.
18. Once a slide object is converted to a presentation, you can run the PowerPoint slide show from Word by double-clicking the object or by right-clicking on it and selecting Show from the Presentation Object menu (Figure 8.16).

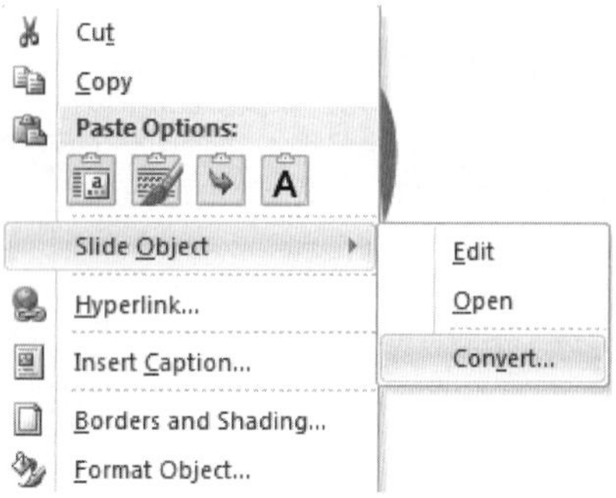

FIGURE 8.14 Converting a Slide Object

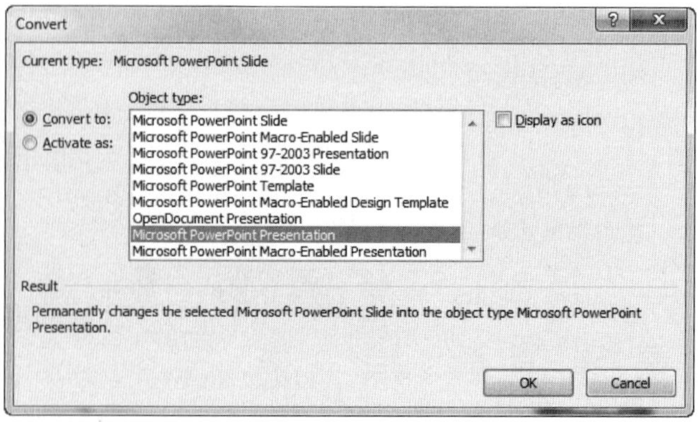

FIGURE 8.15 The Convert Box

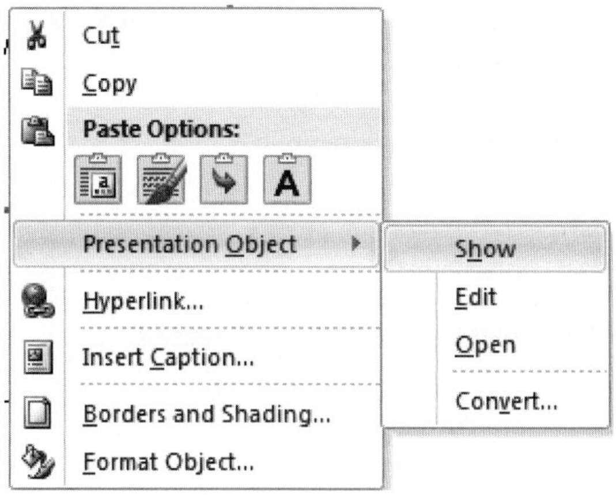

FIGURE 8.16 Showing a Presentation Object

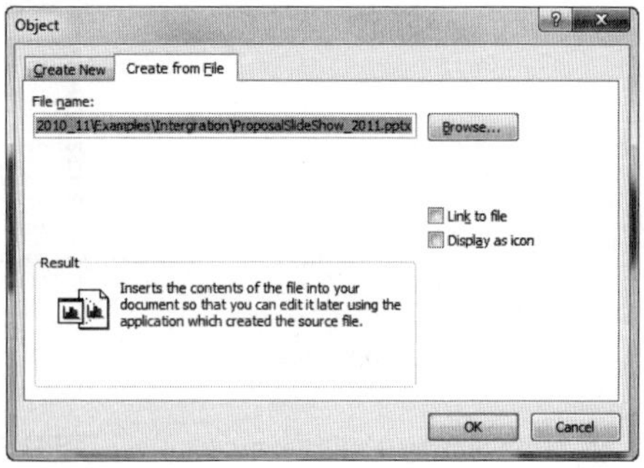

FIGURE 8.17 The Object Box

Inserting a Presentation Object and Converting It to a Slide Object

Another method of placing a slide into Word is to use Object on the Insert tab. Follow these steps:

1. Position the cursor at the location in Word where you want the slide to appear. Select Object from the Insert tab (Text group), and the Object box appears (see Figure 8.17).
2. Click the Create from File tab. Select the Link to File option from the Object box (Figure 8.17). When you insert a presentation object (or any other inserted object) without selecting Link to File, a copy of the object embeds into the file. For example, if you insert a PowerPoint presentation titled Presentation 1 into Word, Word embeds a copy of that file. Any changes that you make to the file embedded in Word will not affect the original file, Presentation 1. Likewise, when you edit the original file (e.g., Presentation 1), you do not affect the copy embedded in Word. Since an object becomes part of the document, it is available as you move the document from computer to computer. For instance, if you move a Word document containing an embedded presentation object to another computer, you can run the slide show and edit the object if the other computer has PowerPoint. Keep in mind that a document's file size increases when you insert or embed an object.

   The Link to File option links to the presentation object (or any other inserted object). The object is not embedded—it does not become part of the Word document. After you insert a linked object, you can work in the source application (e.g., PowerPoint), and the changes will be reflected in Word when you run the slide show or when you right-click on the presentation object and select Update Link. Since Word links to the object, you must remember to move the linked file with the Word file when you move the Word document from one computer to another. If you move only the Word document, the linked object (e.g., the PowerPoint slide show) will not run from Word.
3. Click the Browse button, and the Browse window appears. Locate the PowerPoint file that contains the slide you want to insert.
4. Single-click on the file ProposalSlideShow_2011.pptx to select it and then click the Insert button on the Browse window.
5. Click OK. The first slide of the PowerPoint file appears.
6. At this point, the presentation object is actually a PowerPoint file that, when double-clicked, displays the slides in the slide show. If you do not need to run the PowerPoint slide show and want to place only one slide into Word, you must convert the presentation object to a slide.
7. Right-click on the presentation object and select Convert from the Presentation Object menu (see Figure 8.18).
8. When the Convert box appears, click the Convert To option and then click Microsoft PowerPoint Slide under Object Type (see Figure 8.19). Click OK. The presentation object is now a single slide rather than a PowerPoint presentation file.

PDToolkit for *Microsoft® Office 2010 for Teachers*

Go to PDToolkit for **Microsoft® Office 2010 for Teachers** to locate the corresponding file in the Examples folder.

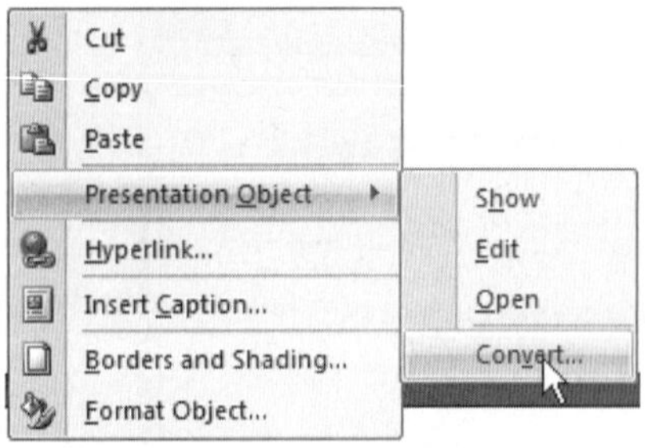

FIGURE 8.18 Converting an Object

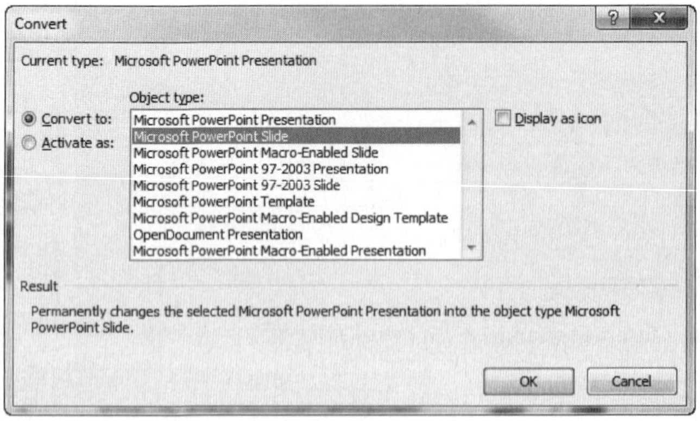

FIGURE 8.19 Converting a Box

Pasting an Excel Worksheet into a Word Document and a PowerPoint Slide Show

PDToolkit for *Microsoft® Office 2010 for Teachers*

Go to PDToolkit for **Microsoft® Office 2010 for Teachers** to locate the corresponding file in the Examples folder.

In developing the projected timeline section of the project proposal, team 1 plans to include a sample of the project log. The sample will illustrate the work that the team has completed, and it will help justify the budget and projected completion date the team has set. In addition, the team will create a chart that illustrates the time that the members have spent on specific project tasks. You will place these materials in the PowerPoint slide show. To create the slide show, follow these steps:

1. To paste a section of the project log into Word, open the Excel file. In this example, open the file named Project Log_2011.xlsx. Team 1 would like to show the work that has been completed so far on the project, which is represented in columns A through F and in rows 8 through 19.
2. Click in column A at row 8 and, while holding down the left mouse button, drag downward and to the right to column F at row 19. The contents of the worksheet are now selected (see Figure 8.20).
3. Click the Copy button on the Home tab or press Ctrl+C.
4. Position the cursor at the location in Word where you want to place the worksheet—in this case, after the first paragraph in the Project Timeline section of the proposal.
5. Click the Paste button or press Ctrl+V. The worksheet appears in the Word document as a table. In this example, the worksheet table extends beyond the border of the Word document (see Figure 8.21).
6. To adjust the table, click inside it, and under the Table Tools tab click the Layout tab. In the Cell Size group of the Layout tab, select AutoFit and then AutoFit Window (see Figure 8.22).

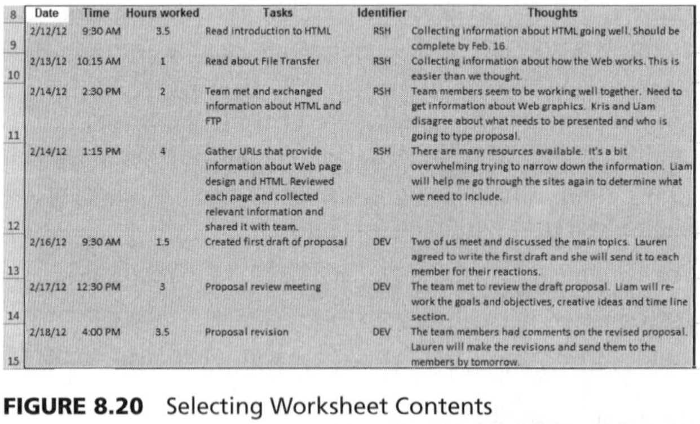

8	Date	Time	Hours worked	Tasks	Identifier	Thoughts
9	2/12/12	9:30 AM	3.5	Read introduction to HTML	RSH	Collecting information about HTML going well. Should be complete by Feb. 16.
10	2/13/12	10:15 AM	1	Read about File Transfer	RSH	Collecting information about how the Web works. This is easier than we thought.
11	2/14/12	2:30 PM	2	Team met and exchanged information about HTML and FTP	RSH	Team members seem to be working well together. Need to get information about Web graphics. Kris and Liam disagree about what needs to be presented and who is going to type proposal.
12	2/14/12	1:15 PM	4	Gather URLs that provide information about Web page design and HTML. Reviewed each page and collected relevant information and shared it with team.	RSH	There are many resources available. It's a bit overwhelming trying to narrow down the information. Liam will help me go through the sites again to determine what we need to include.
13	2/16/12	9:30 AM	1.5	Created first draft of proposal	DEV	Two of us meet and discussed the main topics. Lauren agreed to write the first draft and she will send it to each member for their reactions.
14	2/17/12	12:30 PM	3	Proposal review meeting	DEV	The team met to review the draft proposal. Liam will re-work the goals and objectives, creative ideas and time line section.
15	2/18/12	4:00 PM	3.5	Proposal revision	DEV	The team members had comments on the revised proposal. Lauren will make the revisions and send them to the members by tomorrow.

FIGURE 8.20 Selecting Worksheet Contents

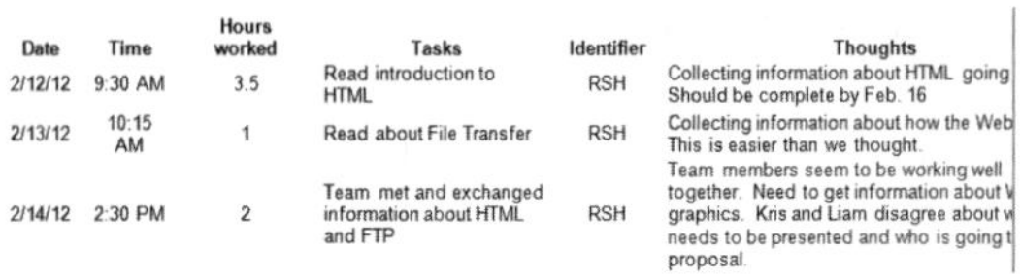

Date	Time	Hours worked	Tasks	Identifier	Thoughts
2/12/12	9:30 AM	3.5	Read introduction to HTML	RSH	Collecting information about HTML going Should be complete by Feb. 16
2/13/12	10:15 AM	1	Read about File Transfer	RSH	Collecting information about how the Web This is easier than we thought.
2/14/12	2:30 PM	2	Team met and exchanged information about HTML and FTP	RSH	Team members seem to be working well together. Need to get information about V graphics. Kris and Liam disagree about w needs to be presented and who is going t proposal.

FIGURE 8.21 A Pasted Worksheet

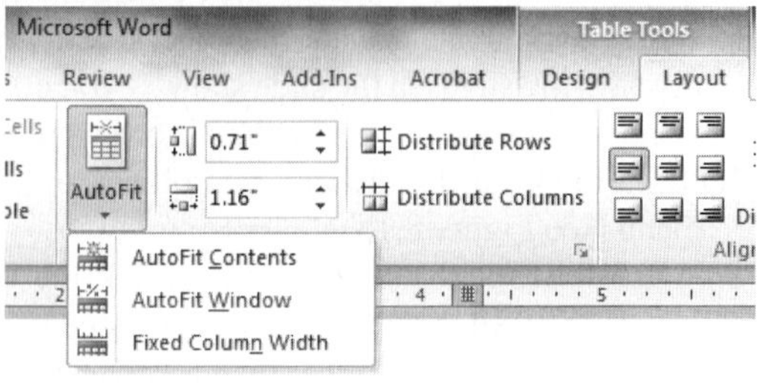

FIGURE 8.22 AutoFit

Date	Time	Hours worked	Tasks	Identifier	Thoughts
2/12/12	9:30 AM	3.5	Read introduction to HTML	RSH	Collecting information about HTML going well. Should be complete by Feb. 16.
2/13/12	10:15 AM	1	Read about File Transfer	RSH	Collecting information about how the Web works. This is easier than we thought.
2/14/12	2:30 PM	2	Team met and exchanged information about HTML and FTP	RSH	Team members seem to be working well together. Need to get information about Web graphics. Kris and Liam disagree about what needs to be presented and who is going to type proposal.
2/14/12	1:15 PM	4	Gather URLs that provide information about Web page design and HTML. Reviewed each page and collected relevant information and shared it with team.	RSH	There are many resources available. It's a bit overwhelming trying to narrow down the information. Liam will help me go through the sites again to determine what we need to include.

FIGURE 8.23 Table Styles

7. Click the Design tab under Table Tools, and in the Table Styles group select a style for the table. In Figure 8.23, Medium Grid 3-Accent 1 is used.
8. Set the font style and font size by clicking in the table, clicking the Layout tab (under Table Tools), and then choosing Select Table from the Select option in the Table group. The table text is selected. Make the Home tab active and set the font to Arial and the size to 8 points.

PDToolkit for *Microsoft® Office 2010 for Teachers*

Go to PDToolkit for **Microsoft® Office 2010 for Teachers** to locate the corresponding file in the Examples folder.

Copying and Pasting a Worksheet into PowerPoint

You will now add the journal-log sample to PowerPoint and make a new slide to present information about the project timeline. Follow these steps:

1. Open the PowerPoint presentation file ProposalSlideshow_2011.pptx. In this file, click on the Project Timeline slide.
2. Click the New Slide button. Make this slide a Title Only slide.
3. Type Project Timeline in the title box. Click outside the title to deselect it.
4. Go to Excel, to the file ProjectLog_2011.xlsx. Since this slide is only a sample of the journal-log, select the contents of the worksheet from cell A8 down to F12. Click the Copy button.
5. Go to the Project Timeline slide in PowerPoint. Click in the open area of the slide and click the Paste button. The table appears (see Figure 8.24).
6. Extend the width of the table. Click the sizing handles and drag left or right.
7. Place borders around the cells to separate them. Select the table by right-clicking inside it and choosing Select Table or clicking in the table and pressing Ctrl+A. With the table selected, click the Design tab (under Table Tools), click the Borders button in the Table Styles group, and select Inside Borders (see Figure 8.25). Alternatively, you can apply a table style by selecting a style from the Table Styles group on the Design tab.

PDToolkit for *Microsoft® Office 2010 for Teachers*

Go to PDToolkit for **Microsoft® Office 2010 for Teachers** to locate the corresponding file in the Examples folder.

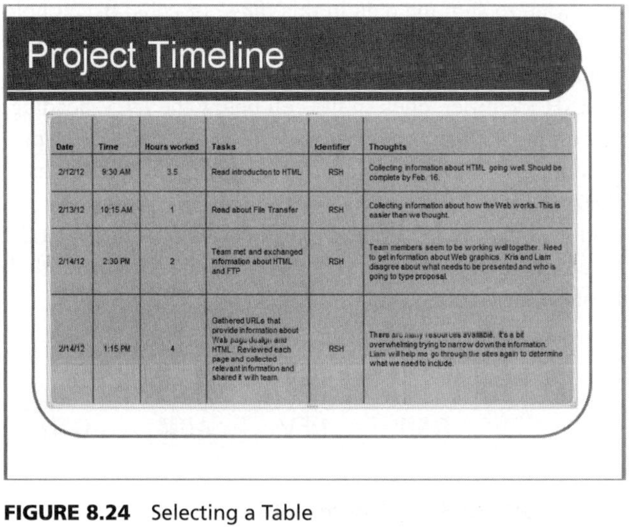

FIGURE 8.24 Selecting a Table

FIGURE 8.25 Borders

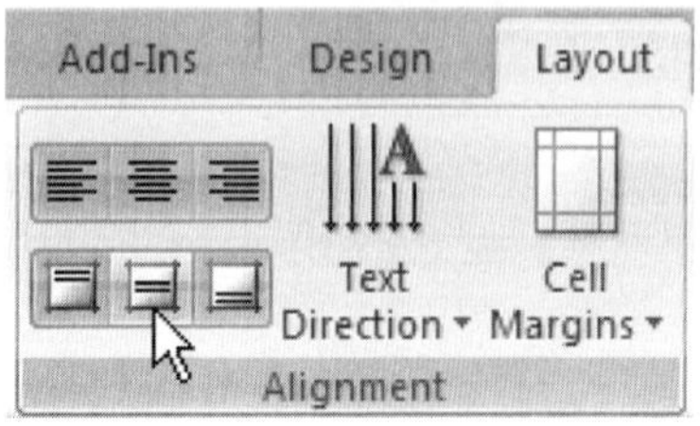

FIGURE 8.26 Alignment

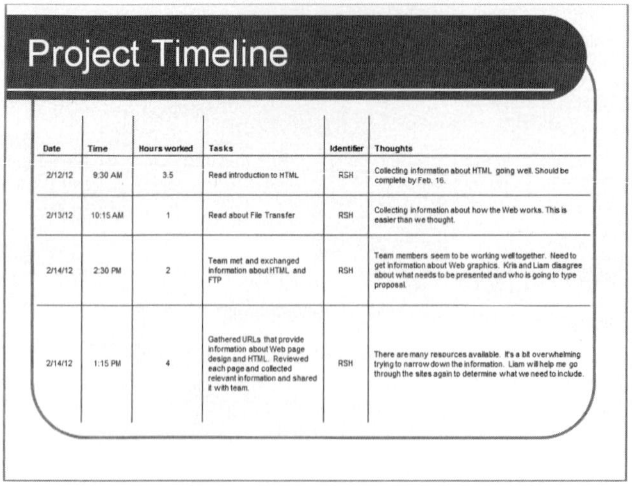

FIGURE 8.27 The Completed Slide

8. With the table still selected, click the Layout tab and in the Alignment group click the Centered Vertically button (see Figure 8.26). Click the Cell Margins button and select Normal. If portions of text wrap around the cells, enlarge a column by clicking on the column border and drag it left or right.

   The finished slide should look as shown in Figure 8.27.

PDToolkit for *Microsoft® Office 2010 for Teachers*

Go to PDToolkit for **Microsoft® Office 2010 for Teachers** to locate the corresponding file in the Examples folder.

Creating a Chart That Shows the Time Members Have Spent on Project Tasks

In the proposal as well as in the presentation, the members of team 1 think it is important to illustrate how they have spent their time on the project. You will create a chart that shows how they allocated their time to various tasks and place it in Word and in PowerPoint.

ADDING AN EXCEL CHART TO WORD In column C of the project journal-log (ProjectLog_2011.xlsx), the members recorded time on task (Hours Worked), and in column E they categorized specific tasks (Identifier). For instance, in Figure 8.28, cell C9 contains *3.5*, and cell E9 contains *RSH*. This indicates that members spent 3.5 hours on a research (RSH) task.

1. The members would like to chart the time they have spent on all tasks so far. In Excel, create four column headings: RSH, DEV, ADM, and OTH (see Figure 8.29).
2. Click in the cell below the RSH heading and click the Sum button in the Editing group of the Home tab (see Figure 8.30). After you click Sum, Excel waits for you to select the cells. Since you have labeled this column RSH, you want to select only the cells that correspond to the RSH (research) label. Click in cell C9 and drag down to cell C12 (see Figure 8.31). Doing this informs Excel that you want to sum the data in this range of cells. If you hold down the Ctrl key while clicking, you can select cells that are not adjacent to one another.
3. Press the Enter key, and the value appears.
4. After you add the values for the RSH identifier, click in the cell below the DEV heading. Click Sum and select the cells in column C that correspond to DEV (development) tasks.
5. Repeat this procedure for the ADM and OTH identifiers (see Figure 8.32) so that you have summed the hours spent on all tasks.
6. To chart the data, click the left mouse button and drag across the data headings and the values. The headings and values are in cells G8 through J9. With the data selected, click the pie chart in the Charts group of the Insert tab.

9	2/12/12	9:30 AM	3.5	Read introduction to HTML	RSH
10	2/13/12	10:15 AM	1	Read about File Transfer	RSH

FIGURE 8.28 A Project Journal-Log

	G	H	I	J
8	RSH	DEV	ADM	OTH
9				

FIGURE 8.29 Task Identifiers

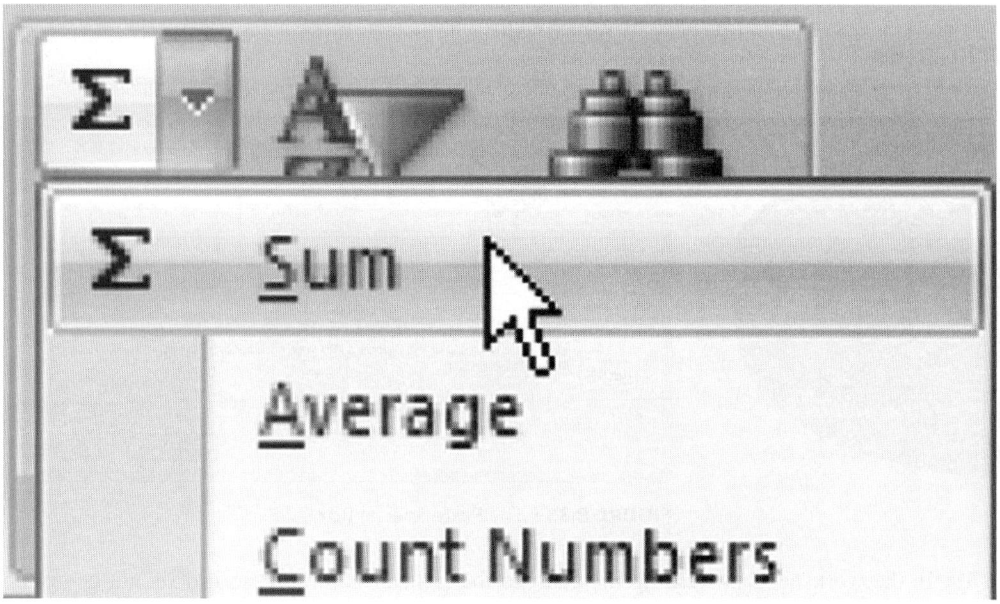

FIGURE 8.30 AutoSum

8	Hours worked	Tasks	Identifier	Thoughts
9	3.5	Read introduction to HTML	RSH	Collecting information about HTML going well. Shoulc be complete by Feb. 16.
10	1	Read about File Transfer	RSH	Collecting information about how the Web works. Thi is easier than we thought.
11	2	Team met and exchanged information about HTML and FTP	RSH	Team members seem to be working well together. Need to get information about Web graphics. Kris and Liam disagree about what needs to be presentec and who is going to type proposal.
12	4	Gathered URLs that provide information about Web page design and HTML. Reviewed each page and collected relevant information and shared it with team.	RSH	There are many resources available. It's a bit overwhelming trying to narrow down the information. Liam will help me go through the sites again to determine what we need to include.

FIGURE 8.31 Selected Cells

RSH	DEV	ADM	OTH
10.5	13	2	1

FIGURE 8.32 Summed Values

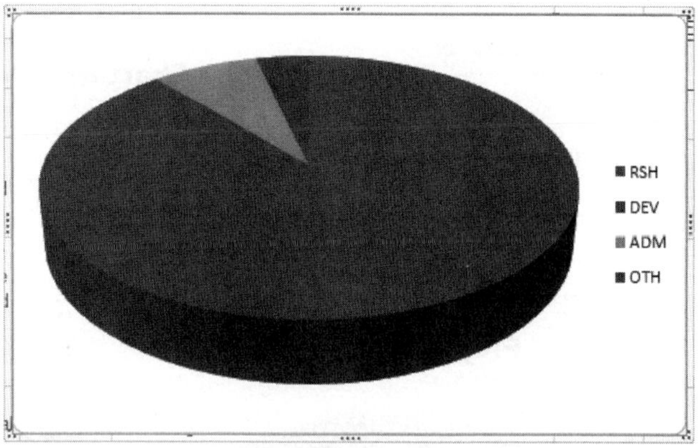

FIGURE 8.33 A Pie Chart

7. Select 3-D Pie, and a pie chart appears (see Figure 8.33).
8. Click on the border of the chart. Under the Chart Tools tab, click Design. In the Chart Layouts group, choose Layout 1. Click on the chart title and type Project Work Tasks.
9. Click on any of the series labels (ADM, OTH, DEV, or RSH) to select it. Make the Home tab active, choose Arial as the font, set the text to bold, and set the size to 10 points. You may have to reposition the series labels so they are readable. To move a label, click it and drag it to a new location. The completed chart should look similar to Figure 8.34.

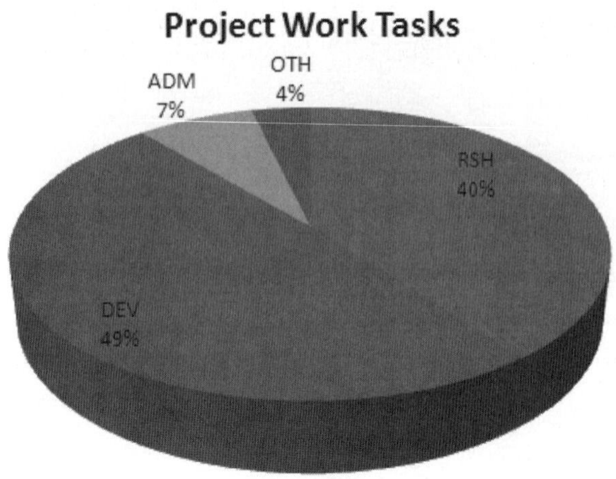

FIGURE 8.34 A Completed Chart

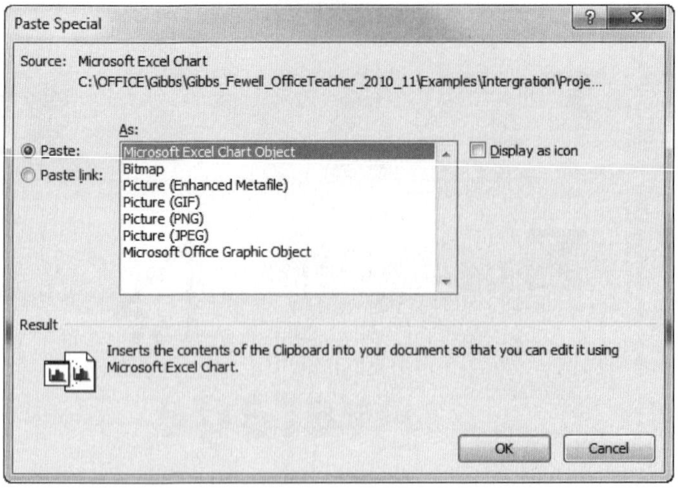

FIGURE 8.35 The Paste Special Box

10. In the worksheet, move/drag the chart to the right of column F so it does not cover the worksheet contents.
11. Click on the chart to select it and then click the Copy button (on the Home tab) or press Ctrl+C.
12. Go to Word and position the cursor where you would like to place the chart. In this example, you will place it in the Project Timeline section.
13. Since team members may need to add more data to the chart, paste it as an Excel chart object. Click the Paste button and then select Paste Special. The Paste Special box appears (see Figure 8.35).
14. Click the Microsoft Office Excel Chart Object option and click Paste.
15. Click OK, and the chart appears as a chart object in Word.
16. Suppose you need to increase the hours on the OTH tasks. Right-click on the chart and select Edit from the Worksheet Object menu. In the Edit mode, you have access to worksheets as well as the chart (see Figure 8.36).
17. Click the Sheet1 tab to view the data sheet.
18. Click in the cell that contains the value for the OTH category and type the number 5 (see Figure 8.37). Click the Chart1 tab and then click outside the Object area to exit Edit mode. If you exit Edit mode without clicking the Chart1 tab, the worksheet and not the chart displays in Word.

    The finished chart should look as shown in Figure 8.38.

PDToolkit for *Microsoft® Office 2010 for Teachers*

Go to PDToolkit for **Microsoft® Office 2010 for Teachers** to locate the corresponding file in the Examples folder.

Inserting a Chart into PowerPoint from Excel

Placing a chart created in Excel in a PowerPoint slide:

1. Since you made the chart in Excel, you do not need to re-create it in PowerPoint. Open the PowerPoint file ProposalSlideShow_2011.pptx and insert a new slide after the

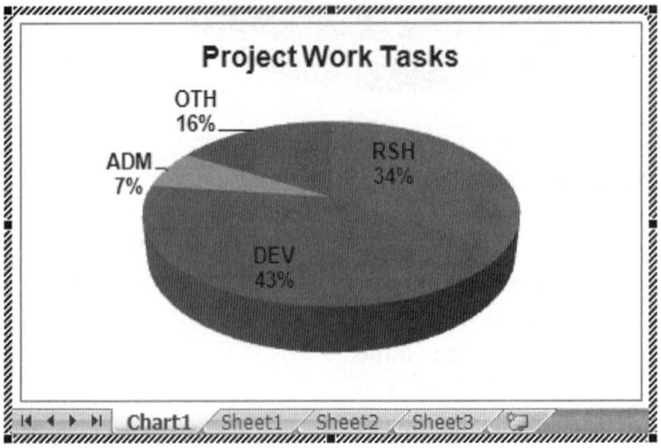

FIGURE 8.36 Edit Mode

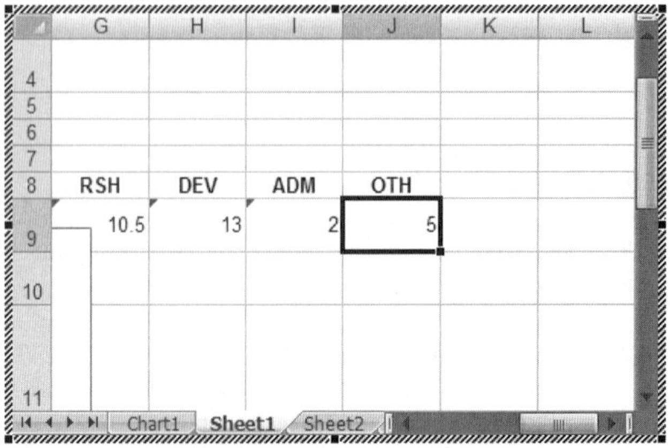

FIGURE 8.37 Edit Mode, Sheet1

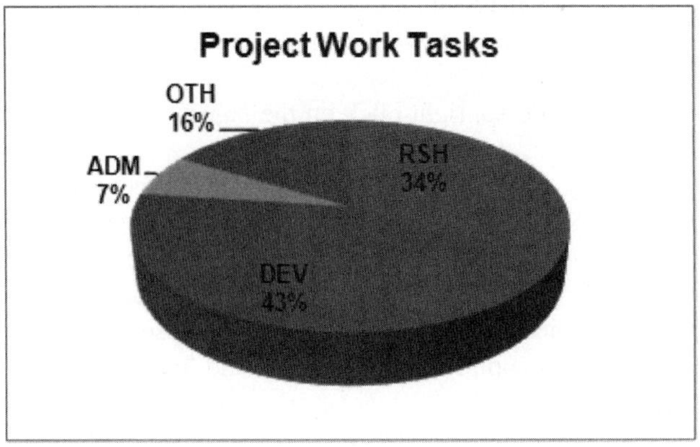

FIGURE 8.38 The Completed Chart

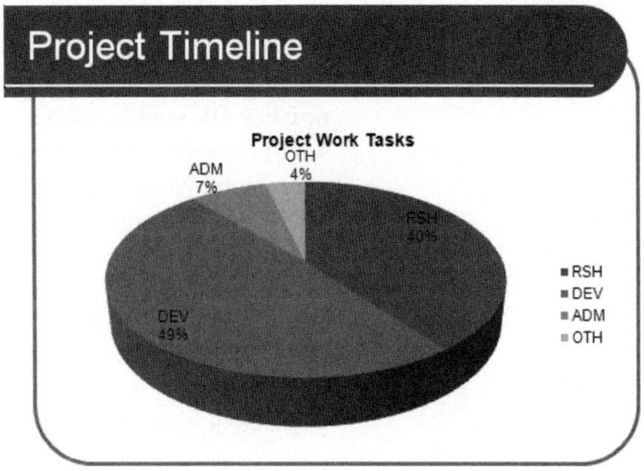

FIGURE 8.39 A Chart in PowerPoint

last Project Timeline slide. Make this slide Title Only and type Project Timeline in the title box.

2. Open the project journal-log in Excel.
3. Previously, you created a pie chart, which should be in Sheet1 of Excel. Click on the pie chart and then click the Copy button.
4. Return to PowerPoint and click in the Project Timeline slide you created and then click the Paste button. The chart appears.
5. Resize the chart by selecting it and dragging a sizing handle outward. Resize so that it is large enough to read but does not overlap the slide borders.
6. Click the chart to select it and then click the Design tab under the Chart Tools tab. Select a style from the Chart Styles group. For this example, choose Style 4.

   The chart should now look as shown in Figure 8.39.

Embedding an Excel Worksheet into a Word Document

Team 1 has taken time to develop the project journal-log, and the members intend to place a copy of the entire project journal-log at the end of the proposal (as an appendix) for the teacher to review. In this case, you will embed the worksheet object. Follow these steps:

1. With the proposal open in Word, position the cursor at the bottom of the last page. Click the Page Layout tab and then click Breaks. A list of options appears. Under Section Breaks, select Next Page (see Figure 8.40).
2. Click on the new blank page. On the Page Layout tab, click Orientation and select Landscape.
3. With the cursor positioned at the top of the new page, select Object from the Insert tab. The Object box appears.
4. Click the Create from File tab. Click the Browse button, and the Browse window appears. Locate the Excel worksheet that you want to insert—in this case, Project_Log_Word_2011.xlsx. Click on the Project Log_Word_2011.xlsx file to select it and then click the Insert button on the Browse window. Click *OK*.

PDToolkit for *Microsoft® Office 2010 for Teachers*

Go to PDToolkit for **Microsoft® Office 2010 for Teachers** to locate the corresponding file in the Examples folder.

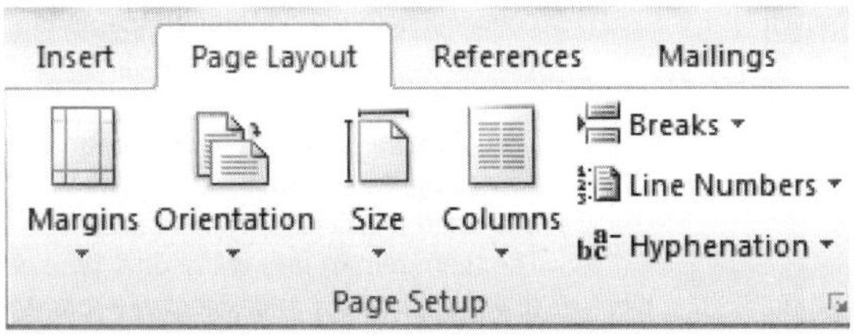

FIGURE 8.40 Layout

5. Make the object smaller. To do so, right-click on the worksheet and select Format Object. When the Format Object box displays, click the Size tab (see Figure 8.41). Enter *6* for the height. Select the Lock Aspect Ratio option, and the width changes automatically.
6. Click OK, and the object appears smaller.
7. If necessary, resize the object window. To do so, right-click on the object and select Edit from the Worksheet Object menu.
8. In Edit mode, resize the object window. Go to the bottom-right side of the object and position the cursor over the corner. The cursor changes to a double arrow (see Figure 8.42). While holding down the left mouse button, drag upward and to the left so that the empty rows and columns do not appear.
9. Exit Edit mode by clicking outside the object area. You may need to increase the object's size by using the Format Object box. When complete, the object should look as shown in Figure 8.43.

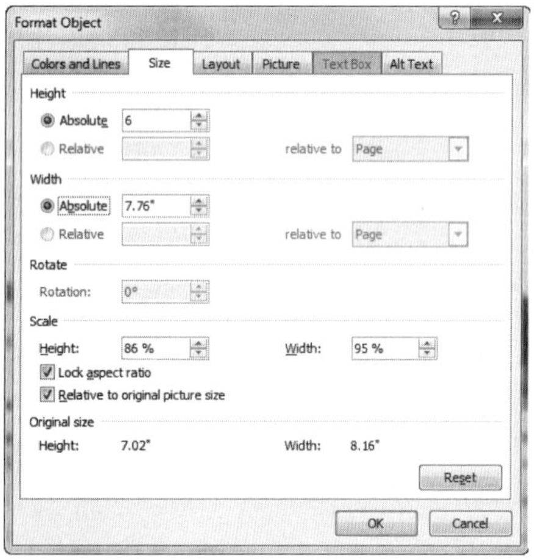

FIGURE 8.41 The Format Object Box

FIGURE 8.42 The Double Arrow Cursor

Creating Web Pages: Project Journal-Log

Team: Liam, Lauren, Mary, Kris
Teacher: Mrs. Kail
February and March 2012

Date	Time	Hours worked	Tasks	Identifier	Thoughts
2/12/12	9:30 AM	3.5	Read introduction to HTML	RSH	Collecting information about HTML going well. Should be complete by Feb. 16.
2/13/12	10:15 AM	1	Read about File Transfer	RSH	Collecting information about how the Web works. This is easier than we thought.
2/14/12	2:30 PM	2	Team met and exchanged information about HTML and FTP	RSH	Team members seem to be working well together. Need to get information about Web graphics. Kris and Liam disagree about what needs to be presented and who is going to type proposal.
2/14/12	1:15 PM	4	Gathered URLs that provide information about Web page design and HTML. Reviewed each page and collected relevant information and shared it with team.	RSH	There are many resources available. It's a bit overwhelming trying to narrow down the information. Liam will help me go through the sites again to determine what we need to include.
2/16/12	9:30 AM	1.5	Created first draft of proposal	DEV	Two of us met and discussed the main topics. Lauren agreed to write the first draft and she will send it to each member for their reactions.
2/17/12	12:30 PM	3	Proposal review meeting	DEV	The team met to review the draft proposal. Liam will re-work the goals and objectives, creative ideas and time line section.

FIGURE 8.43 A Completed Table

Creating a Credit Slide: Outlook and Access

Suppose that for the duration of the project, the members of team 1 maintained an e-mail contact list in Microsoft Outlook of individuals who assisted with the project proposal and presentation. As the list developed, team members added information in addition to e-mail addresses, such as phone numbers, fax numbers, and addresses. They would now like to export the list to Access to create a database of experts that will be a valuable resource for them and their classmates. From the database, they will make a Credits slide to give those individuals credit for their assistance.

CREATING A CONTACT IN OUTLOOK Outlook contacts can be created by following these steps:

1. Select New Items in the New group on the Home tab and then select Contact from the submenu (see Figure 8.44). An untitled contact box appears.
2. Enter the contact information, as shown in Figure 8.45.
3. Select Save & Close in the Actions group of the Contact tab. To add more contacts, select New Items and then Contacts from the Home tab.

EXPORTING CONTACTS TO ACCESS To export contacts to Access:

4. Click the File tab. Select Options and then click Advanced (see Figure 8.46).
5. Click the Export button under Export within the Advanced category.
6. The Import and Export Wizard appears. Choose the Export to a File option and click Next (see Figure 8.47).
7. In the Export to a File box that appears, click the Microsoft Access option and then click Next.
8. On the next Export to a File screen, click Contacts under Select Folder to Export From (see Figure 8.48). Click Next.
9. On the next Export to a File screen, give the file a name and specify a location in which to save it. For this example, name the file Team1Contacts and save it in the My Documents folder. Click Next. The next screen informs you of the action to be taken. Ensure that Export "Contacts" from Folder; "Contacts" is checked. Click Finish.
10. The contacts export to Access, and an .accdb file is created, with the name you assigned. Because you named the file Team1Contacts, you should find a file in the My Documents folder named Team1Contacts.accdb.
11. Open Access. Click the File tab, select Open, and locate the Team1Contacts.accdb file.
12. The Team1Contacts database window appears. On the left side of the window, double-click Contacts Table (see Figure 8.49).
13. From the Access View menu, select Datasheet View. The data records appear (see Figure 8.50).

PDToolkit for *Microsoft® Office 2010 for Teachers*

Go to PDToolkit for **Microsoft® Office 2010 for Teachers** to locate the corresponding file in the Examples folder.

PDToolkit for *Microsoft® Office 2010 for Teachers*

Go to PDToolkit for **Microsoft® Office 2010 for Teachers** to locate the corresponding file in the Examples folder.

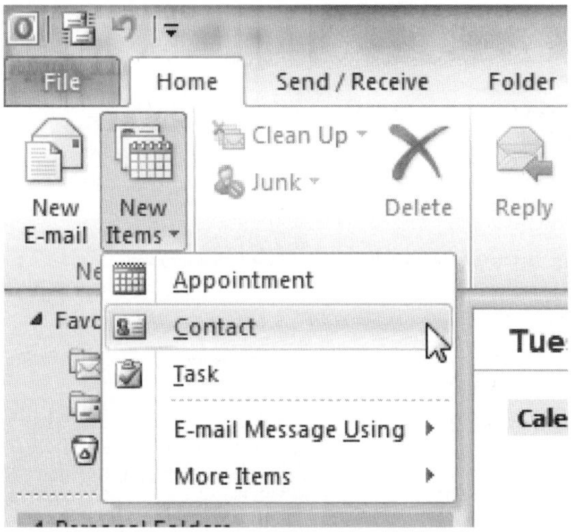

FIGURE 8.44 Outlook Contacts

FIGURE 8.45 Contact Information

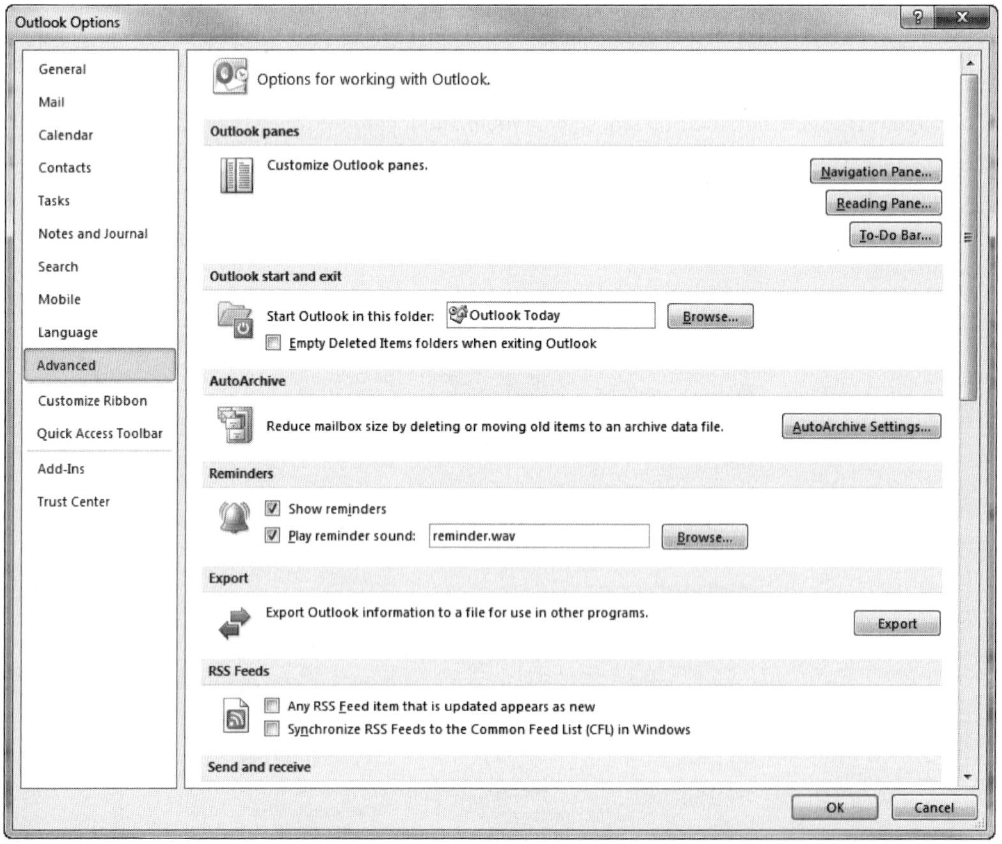

FIGURE 8.46 Contact Information

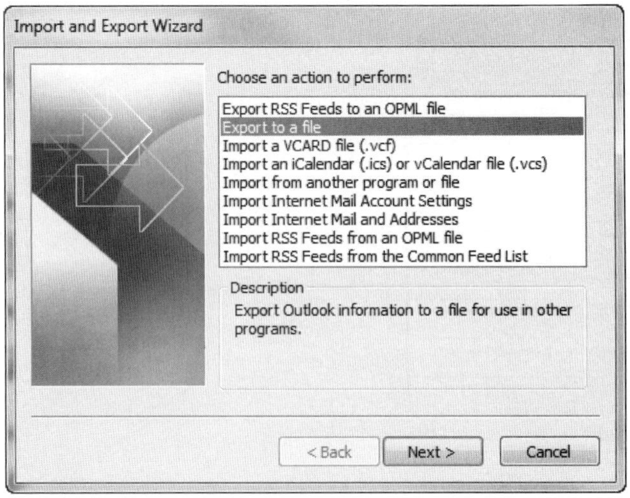

FIGURE 8.47 The Import and Export Wizard

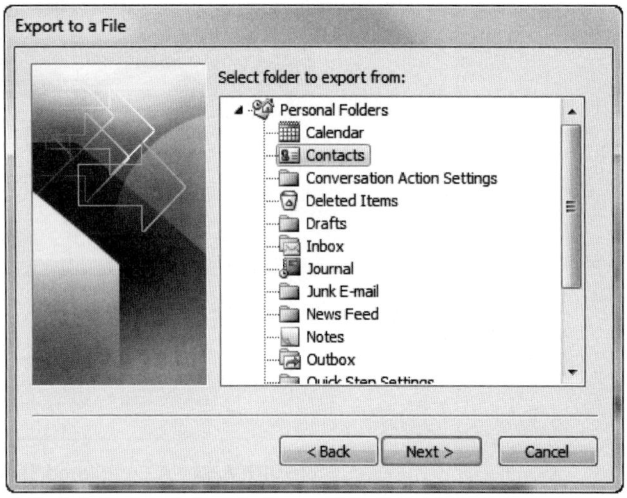

FIGURE 8.48 Exporting to a File

COPYING AND PASTING DATA RECORDS FROM ACCESS TO POWERPOINT Now that you have created a database, you can copy some of the data records and paste them into PowerPoint to create the credits slide. For the credits slide, you need only the person's name and company. However, the columns with this information are not adjacent, so you will move them. Follow these steps:

14. In the Datasheet view, position the cursor over the field selector for the Company column, and the cursor changes to an inverted arrow (see Figure 8.51). Click anywhere in the gray title area to select the column.
15. Move the Company column so that it is next to (to the right of) the LastName column. Select the Company column and, while holding down the left mouse button, drag it so it is positioned to right of the LastName column. The Contacts: Table should look as shown in Figure 8.52.

FIGURE 8.49 Team1 Contacts

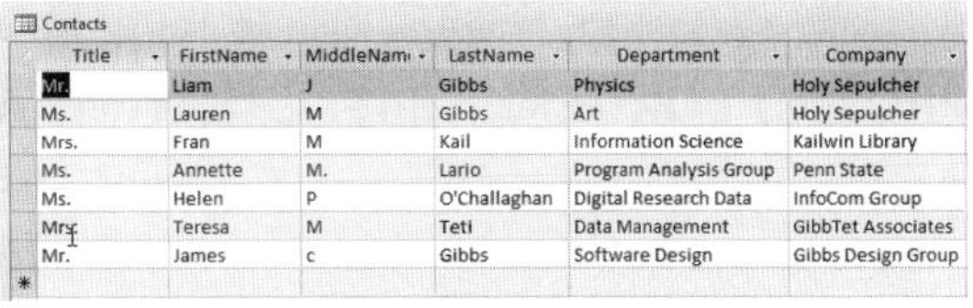

FIGURE 8.50 The Access Datasheet View

FIGURE 8.51 A Field Selector

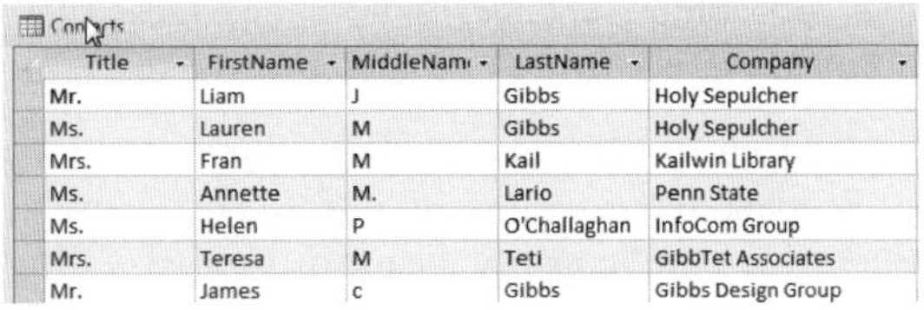

FIGURE 8.52 The Contacts Table

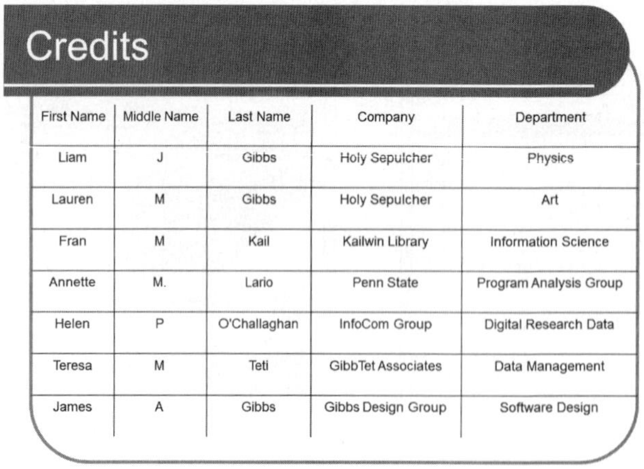
Credits

First Name	Middle Name	Last Name	Company	Department
Liam	J	Gibbs	Holy Sepulcher	Physics
Lauren	M	Gibbs	Holy Sepulcher	Art
Fran	M	Kail	Kailwin Library	Information Science
Annette	M.	Lario	Penn State	Program Analysis Group
Helen	P	O'Challaghan	InfoCom Group	Digital Research Data
Teresa	M	Teti	GibbTet Associates	Data Management
James	A	Gibbs	Gibbs Design Group	Software Design

FIGURE 8.53 A Completed Slide

16. Select the Title, FirstName, MiddleName, LastName, and Company columns by dragging the mouse over the field selector (the gray area with a column name) of each column.
17. Click the Copy button in the Clipboard group on the Home tab.
18. Go to PowerPoint. Click the last side and then click the New Slide button.
19. Set the slide layout to Title Only. Type Credits in the Title box.
20. Click outside the Title box to deselect it.
21. Click the Paste button, and the Access data displays in the slide. Notice that the title (Contacts) of the data table also appears on the slide. You can delete it for this example by right-clicking in the row and selecting Delete Rows.
22. Resize the table so that it fits below the title and within the slide frame.
23. When you first click on an object, its border changes to a dashed line, indicating that it can be modified. Clicking on the border a second time changes it from a dashed line to a solid line. The line indicates that the contents of the object are selected and that changes (e.g., font size or style) will affect the entire contents of the object.
24. Click inside the table and press Ctrl+A to select it. With the table selected, click the Layout tab under Table Tools. Set the text alignment to Center and Center Vertically.
25. Click the Design tab and select Inside Borders in the Table Styles group.
26. Click the Home tab and set the font to Arial, the size to 14 points, and the style to bold.

When you are done, the slide should look similar to the slide in Figure 8.53.

PDToolkit for *Microsoft® Office 2010 for Teachers*

Go to PDToolkit for **Microsoft® Office 2010 for Teachers** to locate the corresponding file in the Examples folder.

PDToolkit for *Microsoft® Office 2010 for Teachers*

Go to PDToolkit for **Microsoft® Office 2010 for Teachers** to locate the corresponding file in the Examples folder.

PROJECT FOR TEACHERS: CREATING A QUESTION AND ANSWER GAME

Teachers can quickly and easily create a PowerPoint game to use in classes. However, if you want to change questions, you have to modify them on each slide, which is time-consuming. In this example, you will use Excel to store questions. When you want to change a question, you can make the change in Excel rather than PowerPoint, which will allow for more rapid updates. You can review a sample file (Jeopardy.pptx) on the website that corresponds to this book. The Jeopardy.pptx file is linked to an Excel file (JeopardyData.xlsx) and simply serves as a menu that connects to other PowerPoint files. Inside Jeopardy.pptx is one slide that has five buttons on it. Only the Multiplication button is active, and when clicked, it opens another PowerPoint file titled Multiplication.pptx. The button labels and questions in Jeopardy.pptx and Multiplication.pptx have been entered into the Excel file JeopardyData.xlsx. The PowerPoint files are set up to display these labels and questions. As you change the labels or questions in Excel, the PowerPoint files reflect those changes. You can use these files to expand on the game. To expand the game, follow these steps:

PDToolkit for *Microsoft® Office 2010 for Teachers*

Go to PDToolkit for **Microsoft® Office 2010 for Teachers** to locate the corresponding file in the Examples folder.

PDToolkit for *Microsoft® Office 2010 for Teachers*

Go to PDToolkit for **Microsoft® Office 2010 for Teachers** to locate the corresponding file in the Examples folder.

1. Open Jeopardy_Game_Linked.pptx and Jeopardy_Game_Linked.xlsx.
2. Make Jeopardy_Game_Linked.pptx active and click on slide 2.
3. Go to the Jeopardy_Game_Linked.xlsx file. Click in cell A2 and click the Copy button or press Ctrl+C.

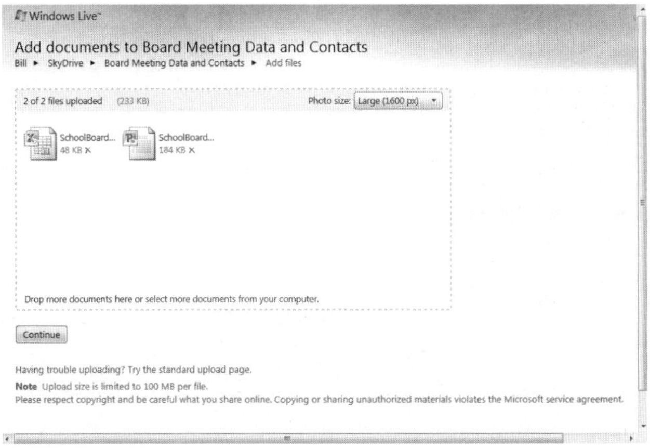

FIGURE 8.54 Adding Documents

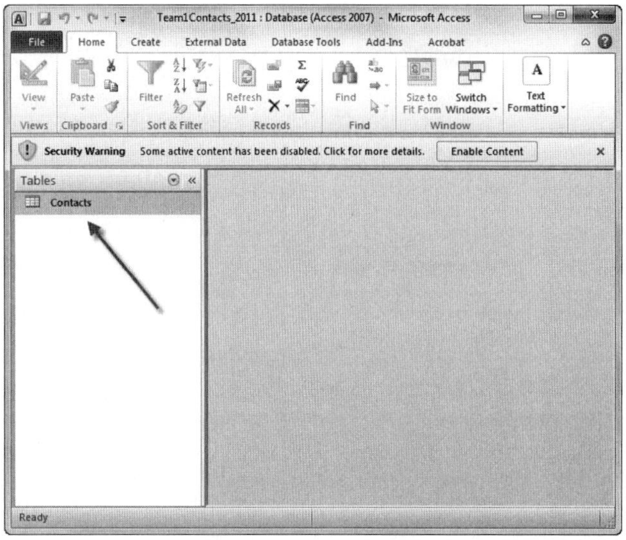

FIGURE 8.55 Accessing Contacts

4. Go to the Jeopardy_Game_Linked.pptx (PowerPoint) file. Click slide 2 and click the Paste button and select Paste Special.
5. Select Paste Link and Microsoft Office Excel Worksheet Object in the Paste Special box and click OK. The text 3 Times 4 appears.
6. Click on slide 3.
7. Go to the Jeopardy_Game_Linked.xlsx file. Click in cell B2 and click the Copy button or press Ctrl+C.
8. Go to the Jeopardy_Game_Linked.pptx (PowerPoint) file. Click slide 3 and from the Paste button and select Paste Special.
9. Select Paste Link and Microsoft Office Excel Worksheet Object in the Paste Special box and click OK. The text What Is 12? appears.
10. Go back to the Jeopardy_Game_Linked.xlsx file and change the statement in cell A2 from 3 Times 4 to 4 Times 7 and change the question in cell B2 from What Is 12? to What Is 28? Save the Excel file. Go back to PowerPoint, and you should see the changes you made in Excel.

Using this approach, you can add more questions and change the formatting (fonts, color, etc.) from Excel, leaving the PowerPoint slide to look the same, with only the content changing.

PDToolkit for *Microsoft® Office 2010 for Teachers*

Go to PDToolkit for **Microsoft® Office 2010 for Teachers** to locate the corresponding file in the Examples folder.

PDToolkit for *Microsoft® Office 2010 for Teachers*

Go to PDToolkit for **Microsoft® Office 2010 for Teachers** to locate the corresponding file in the Examples folder.

PROJECT FOR ADMINISTRATORS: POSTING SCHOOL BOARD FILES ON SKYDRIVE

Suppose you make a presentation to the school board, and after it, you want to give the school board members access to your materials. In this example, you will upload the materials to the Windows Live SkyDrive so people can access them. In addition, you will create a list of contacts that the board members may want to review. You will copy the contact list from Access to an Excel workbook in the SkyDrive. Follow these steps:

1. Log in to Windows Live (https://login.live.com) and go to the SkyDrive.
2. Click Add Files.
3. Double-click on New Folder to make a new folder and title the folder Board Meeting Data and Contacts.
4. Drag the SchoolBoard_2011.pptx and SchoolBoard_2011_perceptionData.xlsx files onto the drop area (see Figure 8.54). Click Continue.
5. Copy the list of contacts from Access to an Excel file in the SkyDrive.
6. Open the file Team1Contacts_2011.accdb.
7. In the Tables column, double-click Contacts. The data in table Contacts appear (see Figure 8.55).

PDToolkit for *Microsoft® Office 2010 for Teachers*

Go to PDToolkit for **Microsoft® Office 2010 for Teachers** to locate the corresponding file in the Examples folder.

PDToolkit for *Microsoft® Office 2010 for Teachers*

Go to PDToolkit for **Microsoft® Office 2010 for Teachers** to locate the corresponding file in the Examples folder.

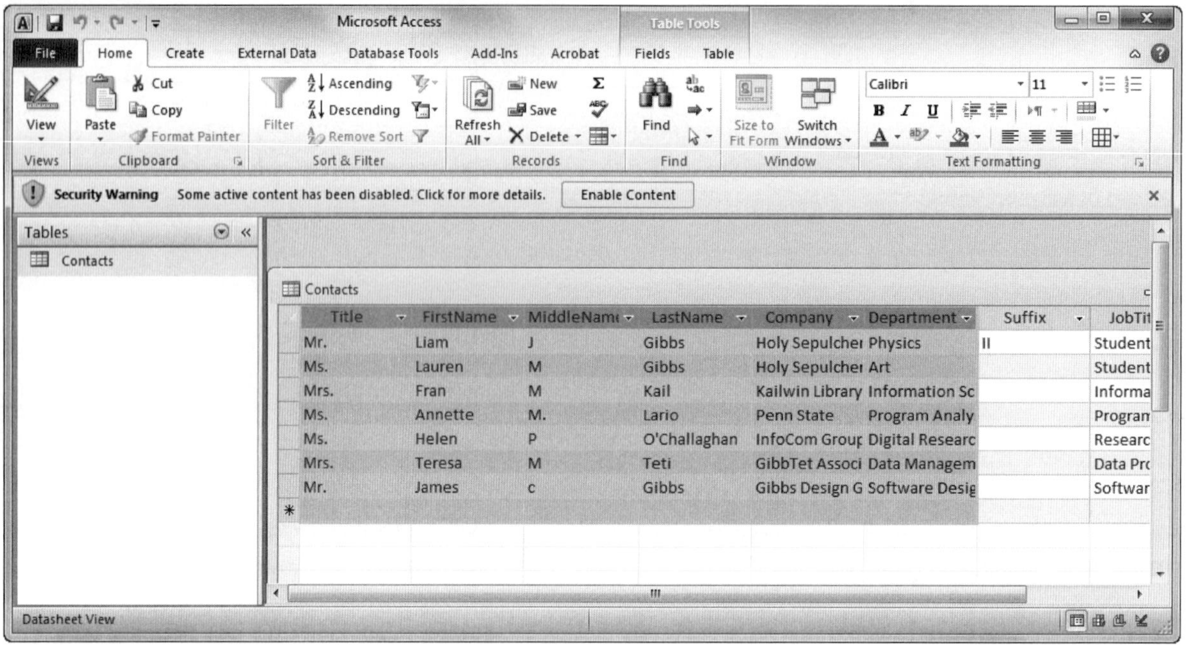

FIGURE 8.56 Accessing Data

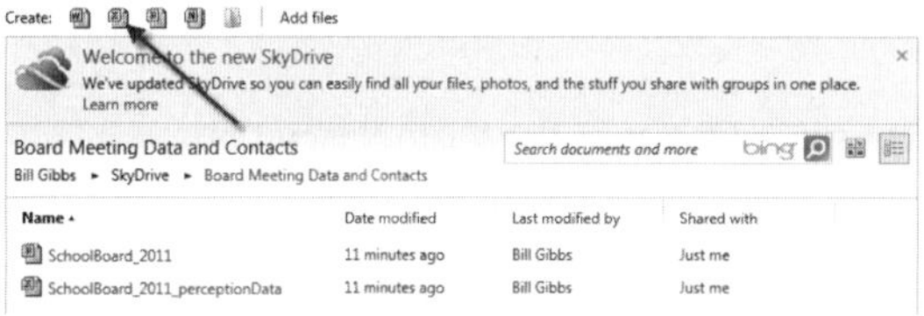

FIGURE 8.57 SkyDrive

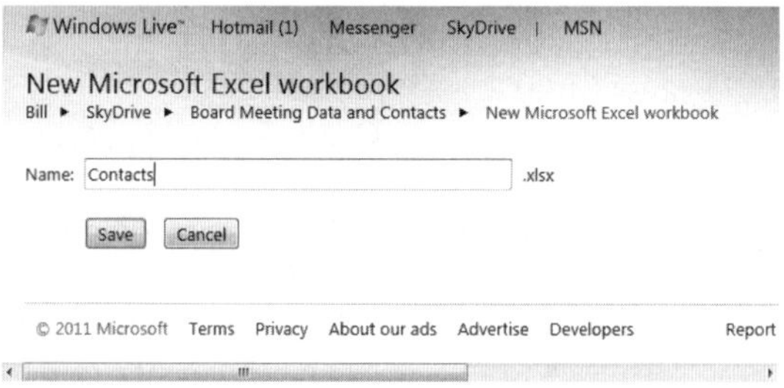

FIGURE 8.58 Naming an Excel File

8. Click the column headings Title, FirstName, MiddleName, LastName, Company, and Department (see Figure 8.56) to select the data in those columns.
9. On the Home tab, click Copy.
10. Go to Windows Live. In the Board Meeting and Contacts folder in SkyDrive, click the Excel icon (see Figure 8.57).
11. The next screen presents a box for you to name the file. Name it Contacts (see Figure 8.58) and click the Save button.
12. A new blank worksheet appears in the browser. With cell A1 active, click the Paste button. A prompt appears, asking you to allow access. Click the Allow Access button.
13. Your Contact data should now appear in Excel. Adjust the column widths so you can see all the data (see Figure 8.59).
14. Click the File tab and select Close. You should now have three files in the Board Meeting Data and Contacts folder: Contacts.xlsx, SchoolBoard_2011.pptx, and SchoolBoard_2011_perceptionData.xlsx (see Figure 8.60).
15. You must now set the permissions on the Board Meeting Data and Contacts folder so others can look at or download the files it contains. In Figure 8.61, the path information starts with the User's Name > SkyDrive > Board Meeting Data and Contacts folder. Click on SkyDrive to go back up a level or folder. You now see the contents of the SkyDrive folder. The Board Meeting Data and Contacts folder is inside the SkyDrive folder.

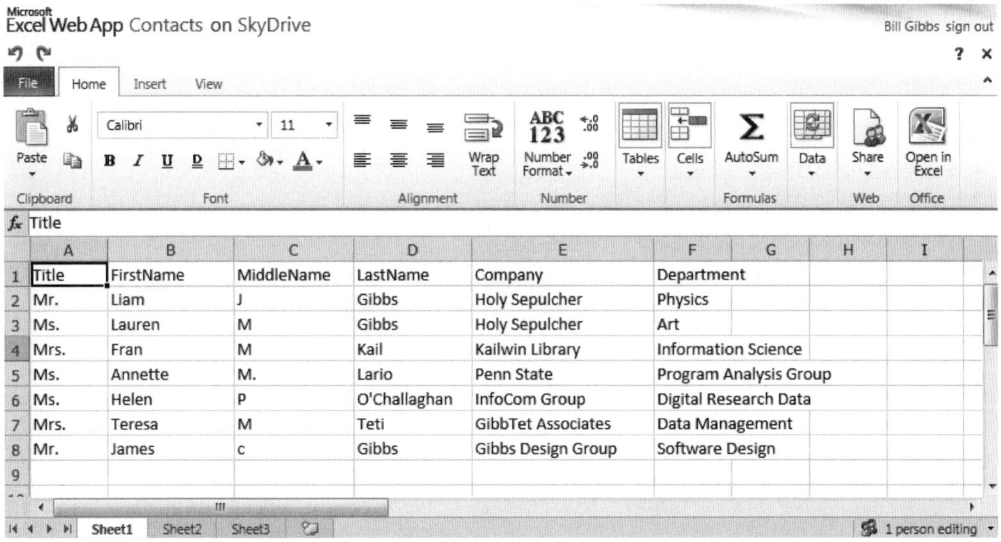

FIGURE 8.59 An Excel App

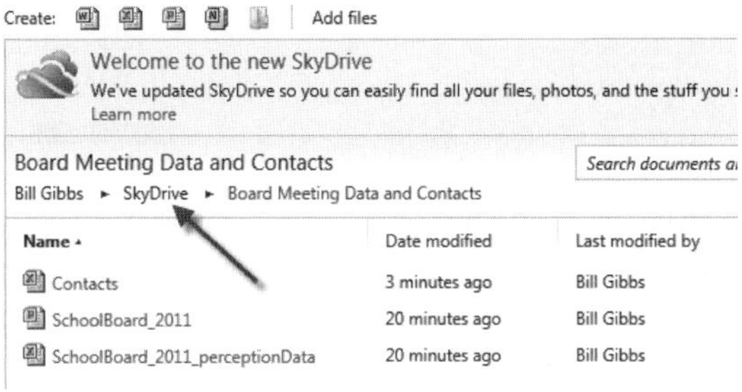

FIGURE 8.60 SkyDrive

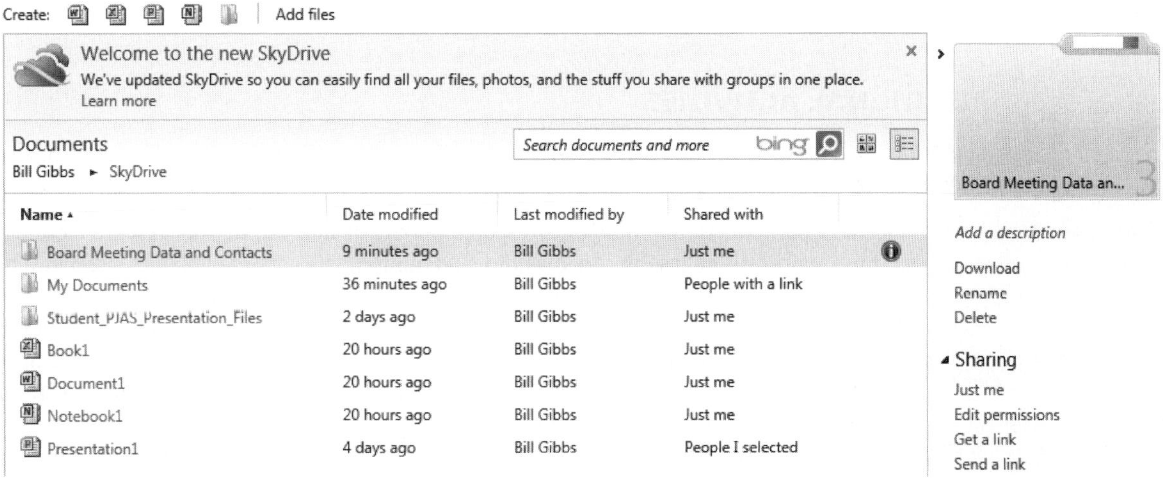

FIGURE 8.61 File/Folder Listing

16. Click on the Board Meeting Data and Contacts folder to select it (see Figure 8.61).
17. Click Get a Link. The Get a Link screen appears. For this example, allow access to anyone who receives the link.
18. Click in the Copy This Link to Share box and copy the address (see Figure 8.62). If the box is empty, click the Create Link button.

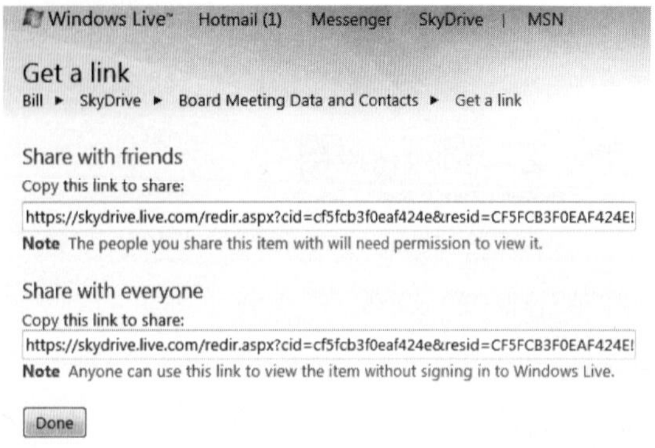

FIGURE 8.62 Getting a Link

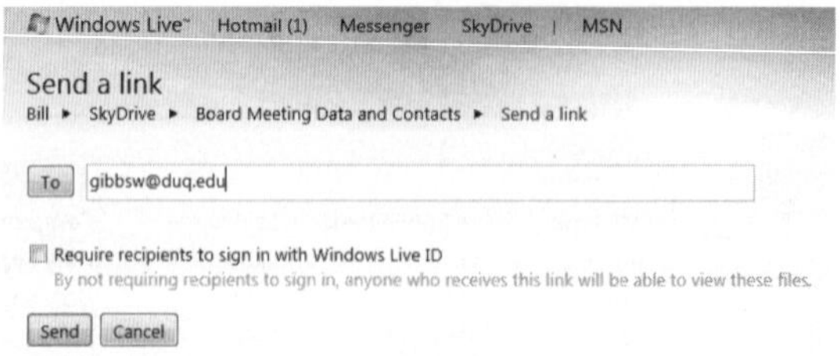

FIGURE 8.63 E-mailing a Link

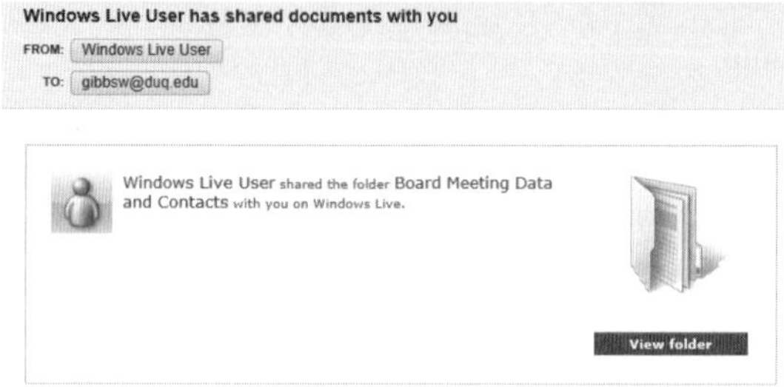

FIGURE 8.64 E-mailing a Recipient

19. Click Send a Link. Type the e-mail address of the person to whom you are sending the link (see Figure 8.63). Click the Send button.
20. The e-mail recipient gets a message (see Figure 8.64). He or she can click the View Folder button to view the contents of the Board Meeting Data and Contacts folder. The recipient can open the files to view them or click Download to download the files to a local computer.

ADDITIONAL ACTIVITIES

The following are additional activities that can be created integrating the products in the Microsoft Office suite of products:

- Create a multimedia research report. Research a topic of interest. In your research, collect text information, photographs, video, audio, and numeric data about the topic. Use Word to compile the text information; PowerPoint to assemble the photographs, video, and audio; and Excel to organize the numeric data. After you compile your research findings with the respective program, integrate your data and provide access to the data through one program (e.g., Word). Assume that the reader of your research report will be able to view it on a computer. As the reader reads, he or she should be able to click on illustrations (figures and tables) to view more in-depth information in either a PowerPoint slide show or Excel.
- Create a short PowerPoint presentation. Insert it into a Word document as an embedded object. Insert the same object as a linked object and compare the two.
- Insert an Excel worksheet object into a PowerPoint slide. Enter data and view them on the slide. Try saving the worksheet as a separate file.
- Create a PowerPoint slide show that links to two or more presentation objects. Assume that multiple students will each develop PowerPoint slide shows and present them to the class on the instructor's workstation, connected to a projector. Early in the development process, create a folder to store all the slide shows. Have students create drafts of their slide shows

and name them descriptively. Place them in the folder. Create a master slide show and link all draft files to it. Prior to the students' presentations, collect all the completed slide shows and place them in the folder. If the names of the files are identical, you will overwrite the draft versions of the files as you do this.

SUMMING IT UP

In this chapter, you modified materials in ways that required you to integrate the Office products. You used several integration approaches, including copy and paste, drag and drop, and insertion of objects involving embedding them in files and linking to them. In addition, you made a contact list in Outlook and exported it to Access. You then took data records from Access and placed them in PowerPoint. The examples presented in this chapter serve as an introduction to some of the many ways you can use and incorporate the Office programs to work more effectively and efficiently.

Reference

Microsoft Corporation. (2011). *Copy Excel data or charts to Word.* Retrieved June 10, 2011, from http://office.microsoft.com/en-us/excel-help/copy-excel-data-or-charts-to-word-HP010198874.aspx?CTT=1.

9 MULTIMEDIA AND WEB TECHNOLOGIES

Chapter Outline

WHAT YOU ARE GOING TO LEARN

At the completion of this chapter you will be able to:

- Create contacts in Windows Live
- Share pictures and video
- Upload content to Windows Live
- Collaboratively work in Excel

CHAPTER OVERVIEW

Current iterations of Web technologies are often referred to as Web 2.0 because they support social relations. Anderson (2007), citing Tim Berners-Lee (2006), the creator of the Web, points out that this characterization or delineation between Web 1.0 and 2.0 may be imprecise. Berners-Lee contends that the intent of Web 1.0 was interactivity and connectivity, or connecting people to one another. Web 2.0 is really about using the Web standards developed by those who worked on Web 1.0. "'Web 2.0' should not therefore be held up in opposition to 'Web 1.0,' but should be seen as a consequence of a more fully implemented Web" (Anderson, 2007, p. 6). O'Reilly (2007) identified a number of features now seen as conceptualizing Web 2.0 but that were actually based on Web 1.0 standards, such as user-generated content, the harnessing of the power of the crowd, participation, and rich user experiences. Correspondingly, a number of Web-based services are generally seen to embody Web 2.0, including blogs, wikis, multimedia sharing services, and podcasting.

Much content on the Web is multimedia. It is pervasive. Multimedia is the integration of two or more media in digital form, controlled by a computer (Chapman & Chapman, 2004). Mayer (2009) refers to multimedia learning as learning from words and pictures, either static or dynamic images. The prevalence of multimedia may benefit teachers who try to engage learners with diverse learning styles and preferences and who are accustomed to digital content. Some learners learn best from text information, while others prefer visualization and tactile experiences in which they see, hear, and interact with content.

Multimedia content can be shared across networks. Using what are now referred to as Web 2.0 services, teachers, students, and administrators can share and manipulate pictures, text, video, audio, and animation. They can create multimedia content collaboratively as well as connect with others not just with text but with audio, video, and pictures. In terms of Office, these experiences can take place in a suite of free programs called Windows Live, with which you can create and share multimedia content, organize files, and communicate with others, among other things (Microsoft, 2011). This chapter examines the foundations of multimedia Web services and Office applications.

PROJECT FOR TEACHER AND STUDENTS: SHARING MULTIMEDIA

In this activity, the teacher assigns students teams to work on a multimedia report about plants. The teacher creates groups in Windows Live. Student team members log in to their assigned groups to get Office files, work collaboratively on documents, discuss projects, and share media. The instructor and all students need Windows Live accounts. You create an account by going to https://login.live.com.

Creating Contacts

The teacher creates a contact list. He or she then creates a group to which contacts (students) are invited to join. Once a group is created and students join, group members can interact and share media with each other. Only persons in a group can interact; nonmembers do not have access.

In this activity, you create a contact and a group, and you invite people to join the group. Group members work on a multimedia project collaboratively, discuss it, and share photos and video. Follow these steps:

1. To work with a group in Windows Live, you make a contact, so select Contacts from the Messenger menu (see Figure 9.1).
2. On the Contacts screen, click New (see Figure 9.2).
3. The New Contact screen appears. Fill in the new contact information (see Figure 9.3).
4. Instead of typing the contact information, you can import contacts. To do so, click Manage and then select Import (see Figure 9.4).
5. On the Add People screen, type the e-mail address of the person you want to add as a contact (see Figure 9.5). Click Next.
6. Windows Live sends the person an e-mail/notification indicating that you want him or her to be a friend/contact. The person has to accept by clicking the Accept button (see Figure 9.6).
7. Select Contacts from the Messenger menu, and you see your newly added contacts (see Figure 9.7).

FIGURE 9.1 Making a New Contact

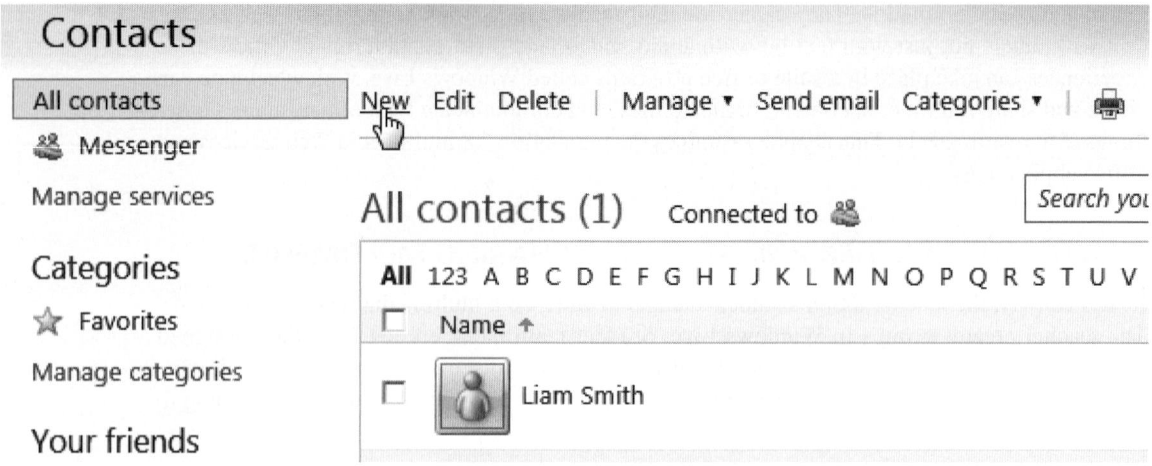

FIGURE 9.2 A New Contact

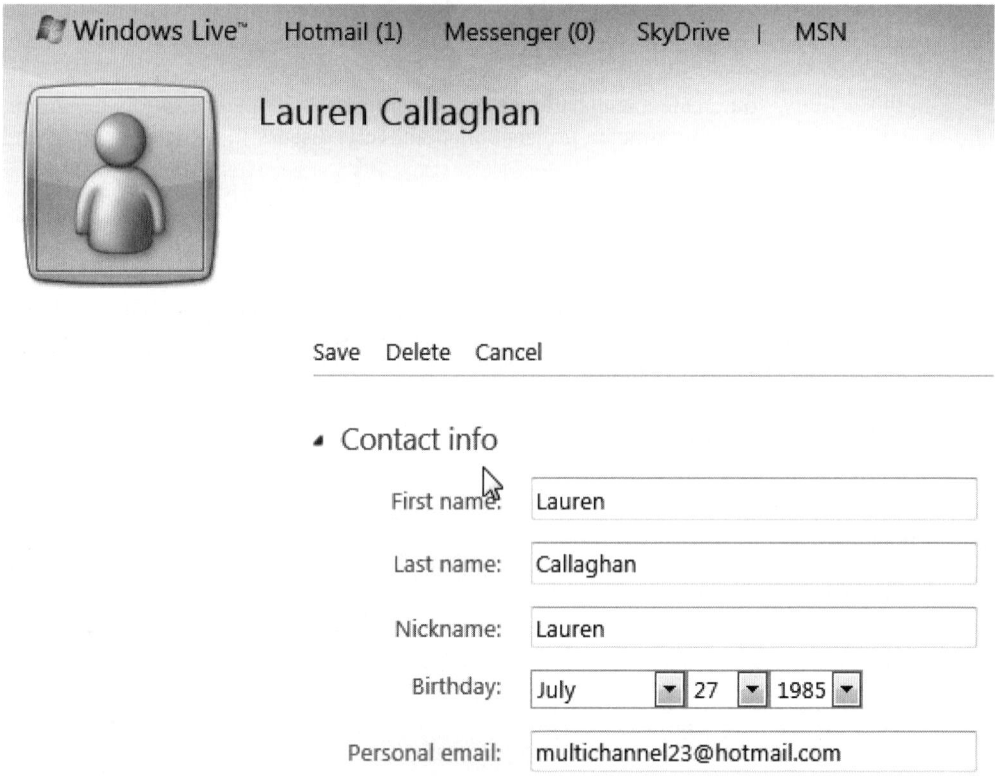

FIGURE 9.3 Entering New Contact Information

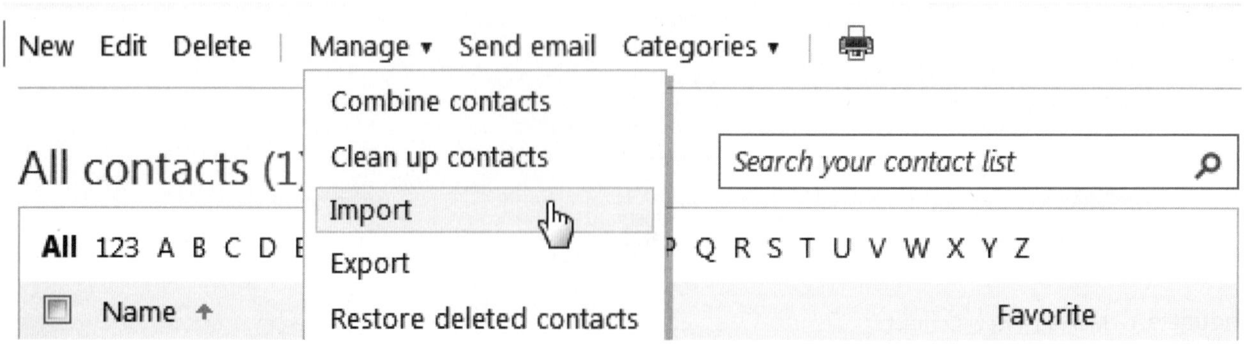

FIGURE 9.4 Importing Contacts

FIGURE 9.5 Importing Contacts by E-mail Address

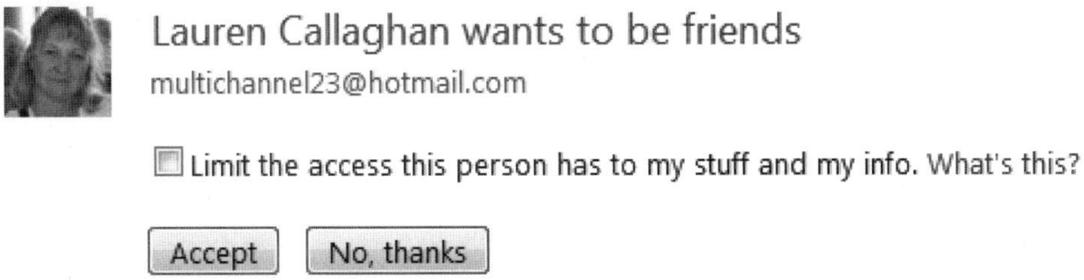

FIGURE 9.6 Accepting an Invitation

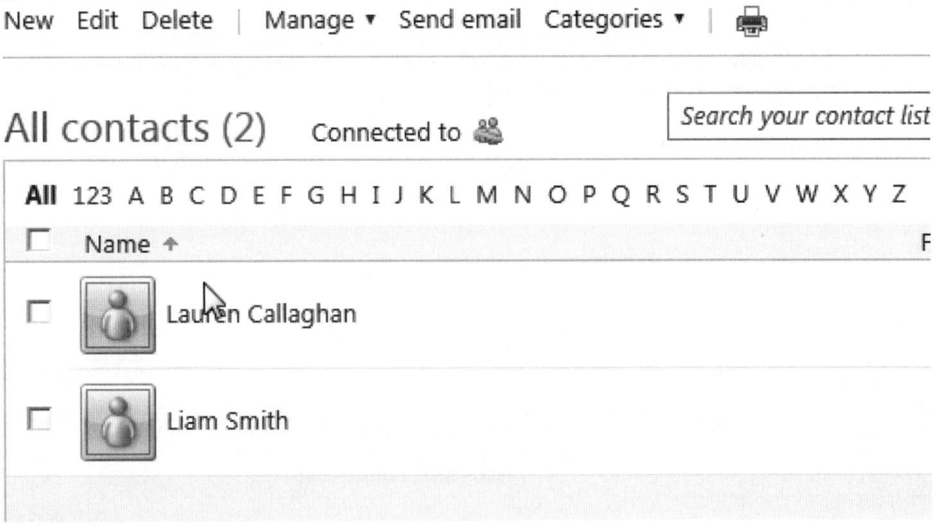

FIGURE 9.7 A Contacts List

Making a Group

Now that you've made some contacts, you can create a group and ask those individuals (new contacts) to join. Follow these steps:

1. Select the SkyDrive menu item and click Groups (see Figure 9.8). The Groups screen appears.
2. On the Groups screen, click Create a Group (see Figure 9.9).
3. Enter a group name. Notice in Figure 9.10 that the name Plants and Things is used as the e-mail (PlantsandThings@groupslive.com).
4. If you added contacts previously, click Select from Contact List. A list of contacts appears. Choose the individuals you want to add/invite to the group. Click the Create button.
5. After you click Create, an e-mail/invitation is sent to the person you want to add in the group (see Figure 9.11). The invitation notice also appears under the Messenger menu

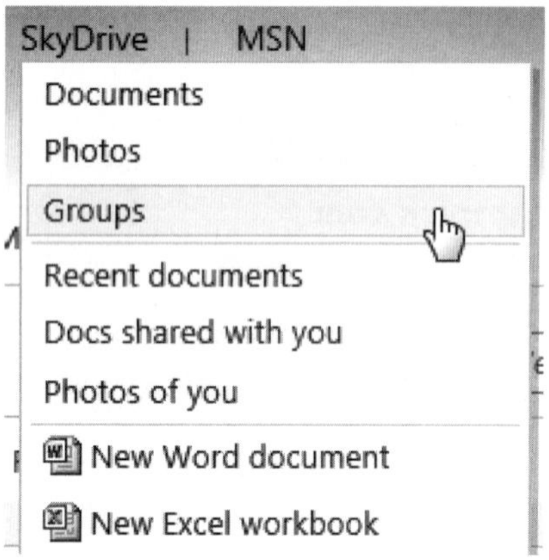

FIGURE 9.8 Groups

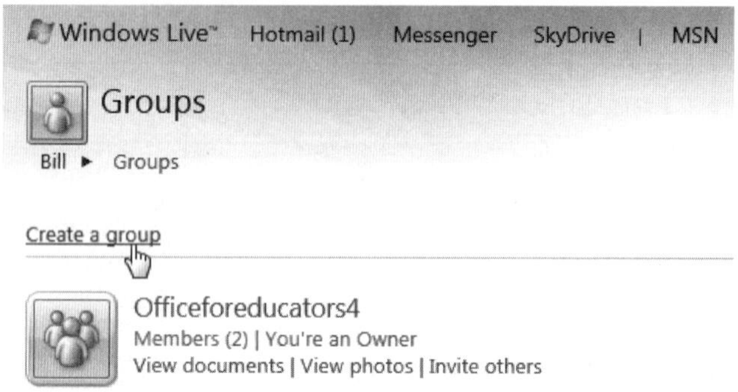

FIGURE 9.9 Creating a Group

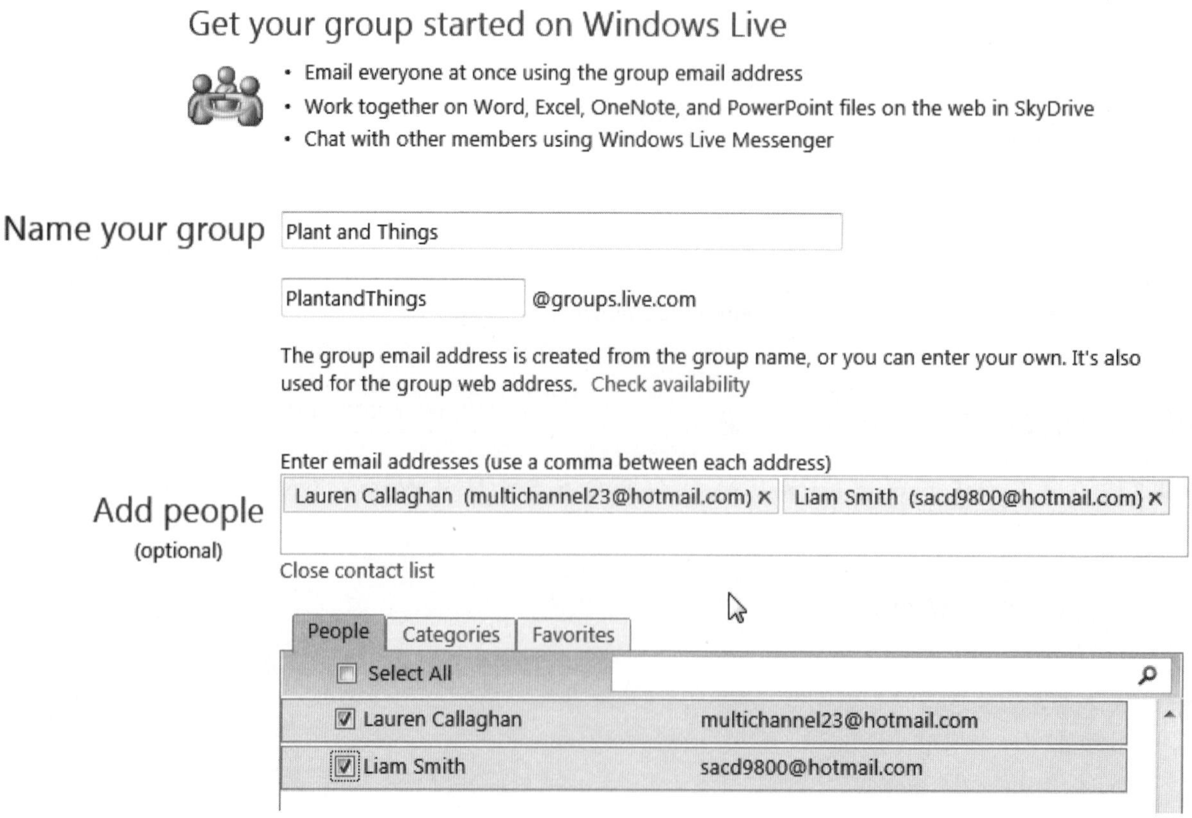

FIGURE 9.10 Creating a Group and Inviting Members

(see Figure 9.12). Additionally, you can see the invitation by selecting Profile from the Messenger menu. When you see the invitation, click the Accept button.

6. Before someone can receive invitations from you, he or she must have the proper privacy settings. To set the appropriate privacy setting, click Profile in the upper-right portion of the Windows Live screen (see Figure 9.13). The Profile screen appears. Click Privacy Settings (see Figure 9.14).
7. On the Privacy Settings screen, choose the Limited option (see Figure 9.15). With the Limited setting, students to whom you send invitations will be able to receive them. Notice that if students set their privacy settings to Limited, everyone can send invitations to them. This may not be appropriate for your students. You can limit the persons from whom your students get invitations. To do so, click the Advanced option at the bottom of the Privacy Settings screen. Go to the *Who Can Contact Me* section. In this example, the setting is My Friends and Their Friends (see Figure 9.16). This means that unless a student invited you (or anyone else) to be a friend/contact, he or she will be unable to get invitations from you. In this example, all team members must make each other and the teacher friends/contacts. This prevents students from getting unwanted invitations.

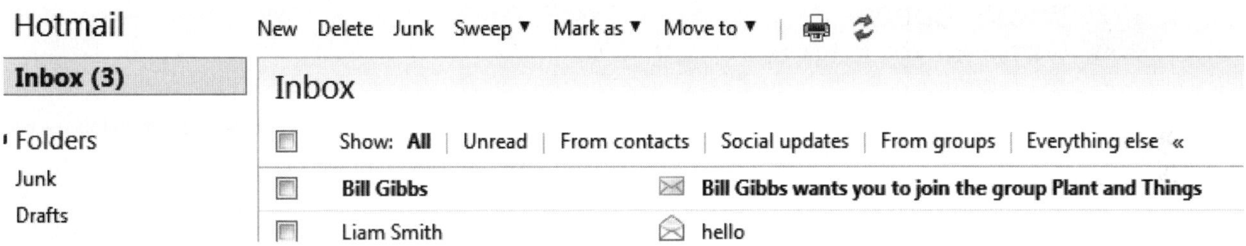

FIGURE 9.11 An Invitation Sent to a Member

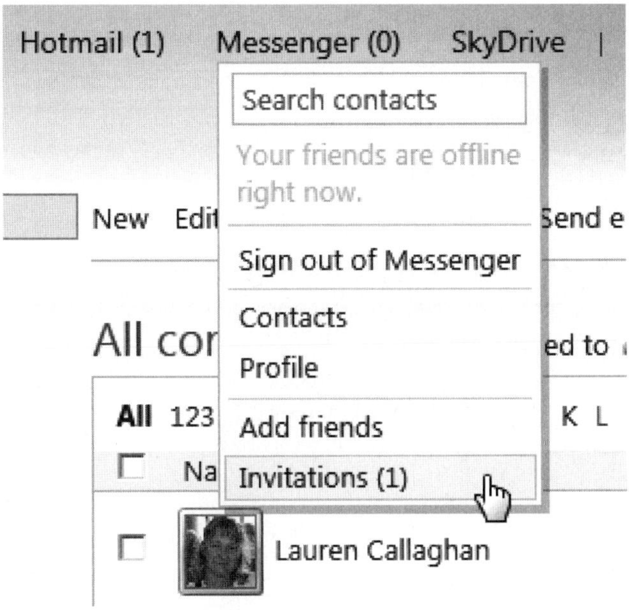

FIGURE 9.12 An Invitation Sent to a Member

FIGURE 9.13 Profile Settings

FIGURE 9.14 Privacy Settings

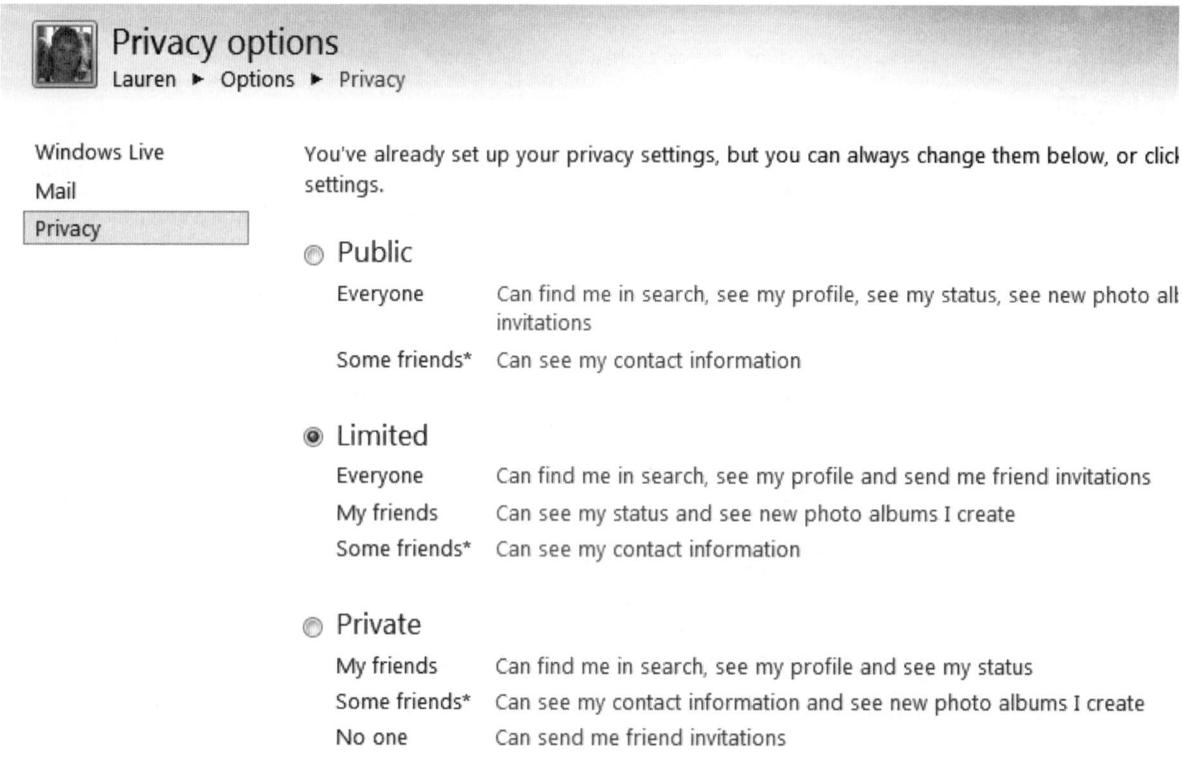

FIGURE 9.15 Limited Privacy Settings

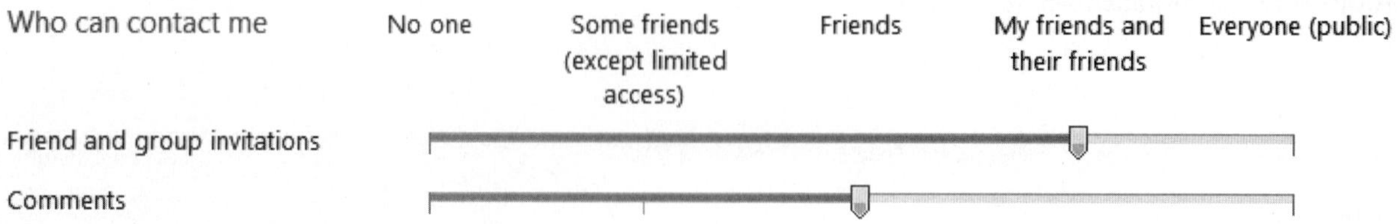

FIGURE 9.16 Modifying Privacy Settings

Uploading Content

Now that the groups are set up, invitations have been sent, and recipients (students) have accepted invitations, it's time to upload the project guide. This guide helps your students create the project step-by-step. Because you created the group, you are the group owner. You can upload the guide so that students can work on it. In this example, the guide is uploaded to just one group. If there were multiple groups, the teacher would upload the guide to a common space where all students could access it. Each team would then copy the project guide into its respective group space.

To upload content, follow these steps:

1. Go to group SkyDrive menu item and select Groups.
2. Click on Plants and Things or click whatever group name you chose.
3. Click Upload or Create Documents (see Figure 9.17). Alternatively, you can click Documents. The SkyDrive space shows any files that have been uploaded to the group.
4. Click Add Files (see Figure 9.18).
5. Click New Folder and give the folder the name Plants Report Team 1. Then select Members Can Add, Edit, Details, and Delete Files and click Next (see Figure 9.19)
6. Drag and drop files in the drop area to upload them (see Figure 9.20). Click Continue, and you see the file that has been uploaded (see Figure 9.21).

Now that the project guide has been uploaded by you (the teacher), the team members can work on it.

Say that you are Lauren Callaghan, on the team to work on the project. Here are the steps you follow:

7. Log in to Windows Live at https://login.live.com.
8. To open and edit the project guide document, go to the SkyDrive menu item and select Groups.
9. The Plants and Things group appears. Click on the title of the group to enter it (see Figure 9.22).

PDToolkit for ***Microsoft® Office 2010 for Teachers***

Go to PDToolkit for **Microsoft® Office 2010 for Teachers** to locate the corresponding file in the Examples folder (PlantAndThings_ReportGuide.docx).

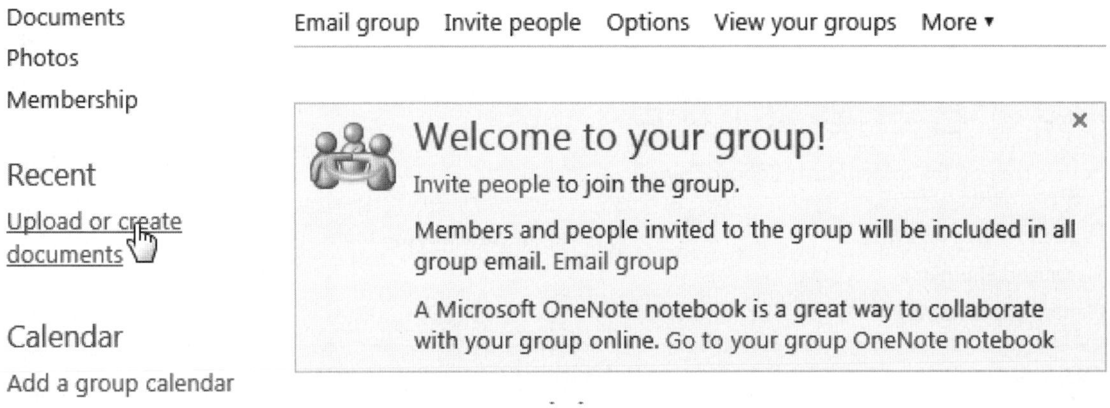

FIGURE 9.17 Upload or Create Documents

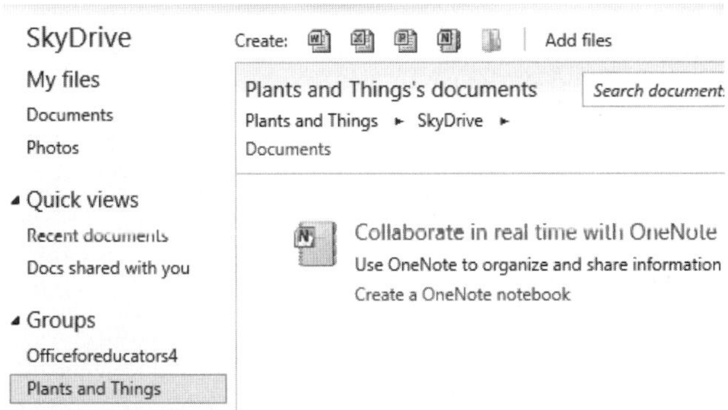

FIGURE 9.18 Add Files

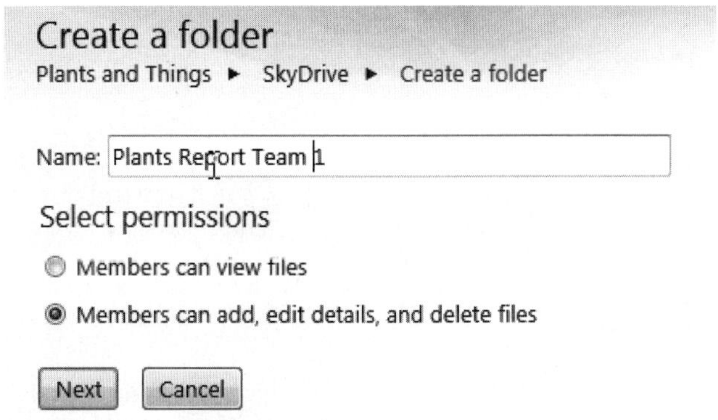

FIGURE 9.19 Create a Folder

PDToolkit for Microsoft® Office 2010 for Teachers

Go to PDToolkit for **Microsoft® Office 2010 for Teachers** to locate the corresponding file in the Examples folder.

10. Look at the group members under Messenger Social (see Figure 9.23). Click Documents on the upper left of the screen to see the shared documents in the Plants and Things group (see Figure 9.24).
11. Click on the folder Plants Report Team 1, which contains the document PlantAndThings_ReportGuide (see Figure 9.24).

FIGURE 9.20 Add Documents

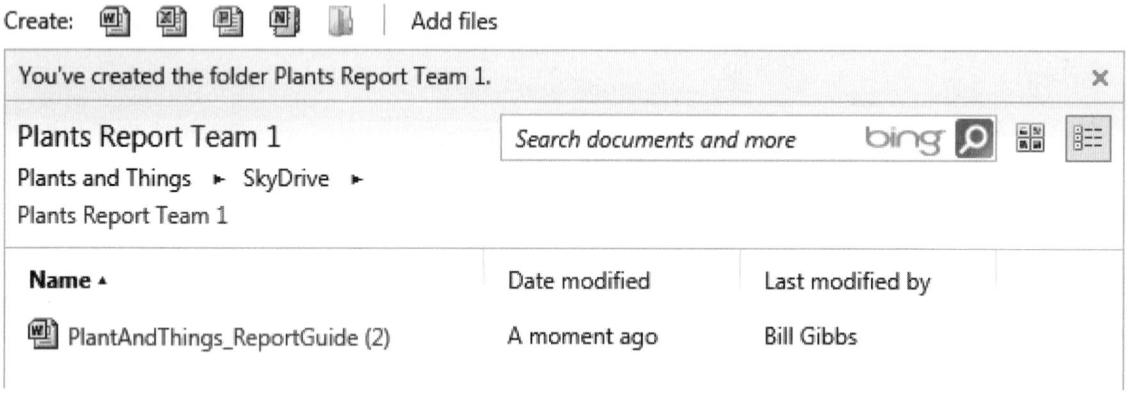

FIGURE 9.21 Document Listing

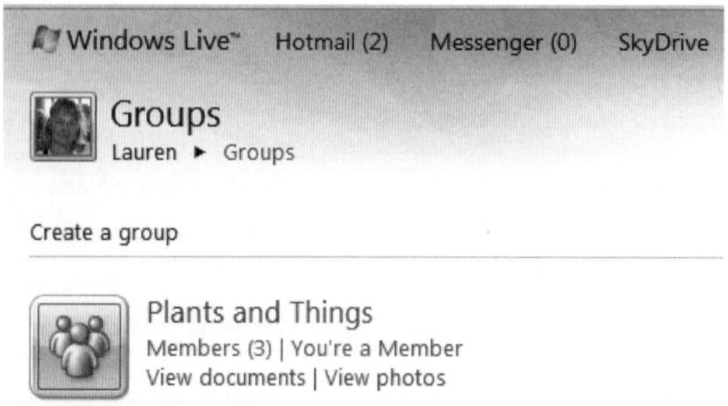

FIGURE 9.22 Clicking the Group Title to Enter

12. Click on the PlantAndThings_ReportGuide document to select it. If you click the document name it opens in the browser. However, if you click to the right of the document name, it becomes selected. You will see options appear on the right side of the screen. Click Edit in Browser (see Figure 9.25).
13. Add the initial portion of the report (see Figure 9.26). Save it by clicking the *File* tab and selecting *Save* and then select the *Close* option to return Plants and Things group space.
14. To let the group members know that you have completed the initial portion of the report, add a comment. To do so, click on the document to select it. In the lower-right portion of the screen, add a comment (see Figure 9.27).

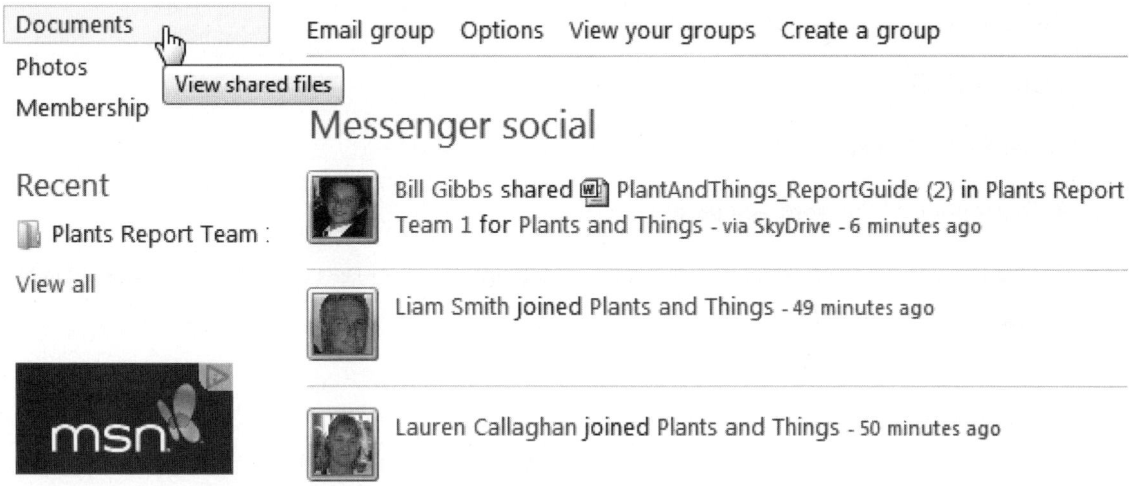

FIGURE 9.23 Shared Documents

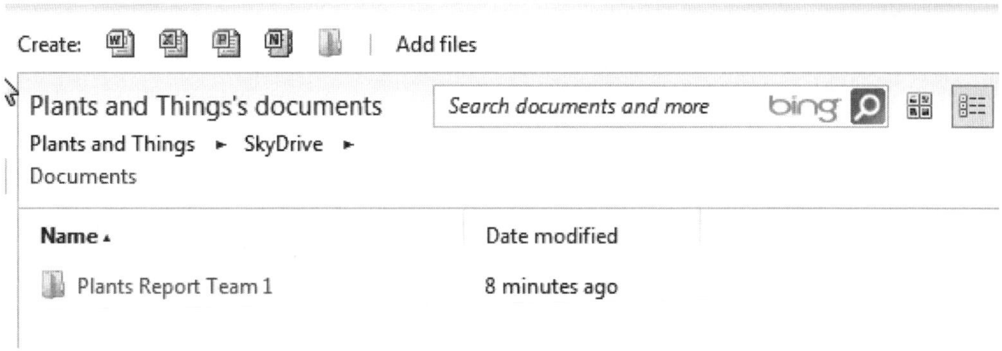

FIGURE 9.24 Plants Report Team 1

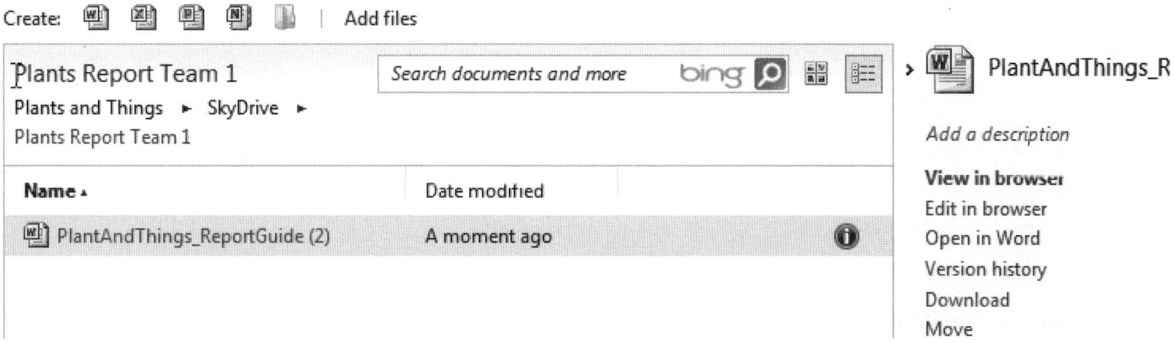

FIGURE 9.25 A Selected Document and Options

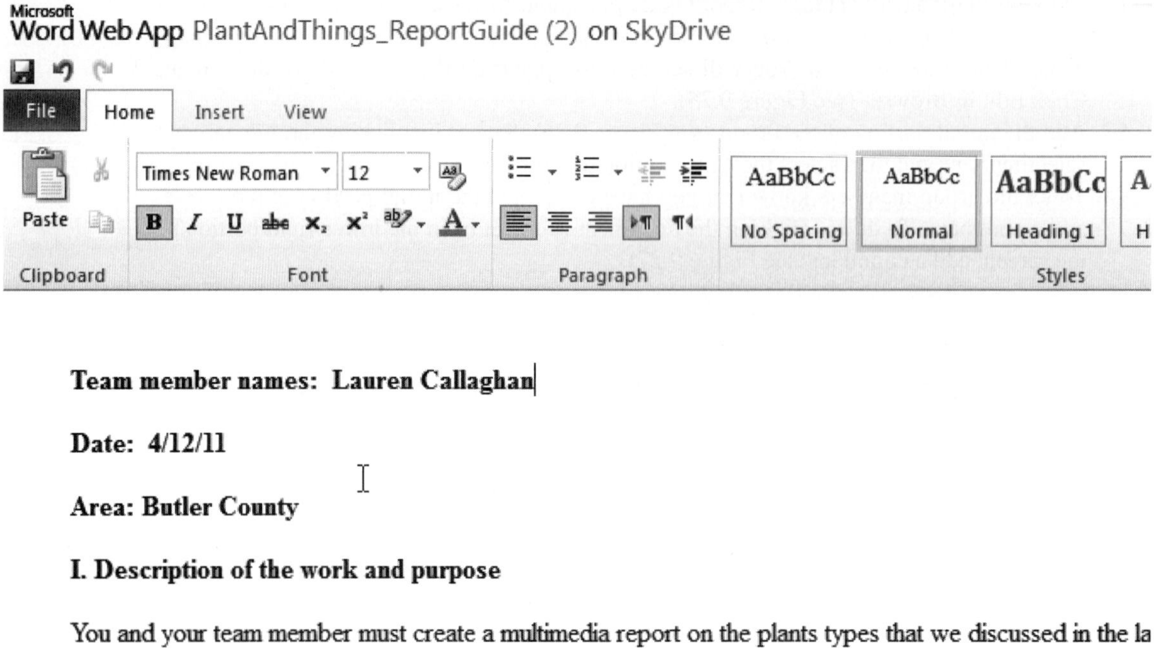

FIGURE 9.26 Opened Document

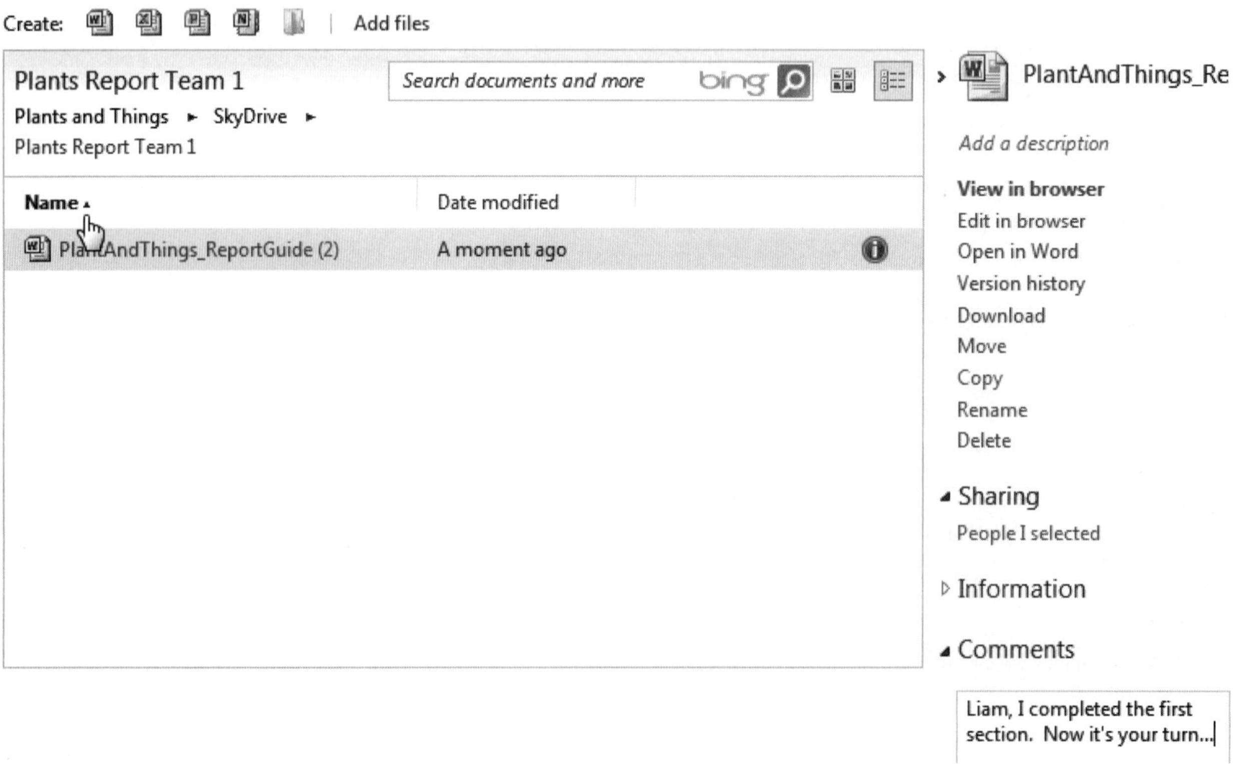

FIGURE 9.27 Adding a Comment

Now say that you're another team member, Liam. You follow these steps:

15. Log in to Windows Live and into the Plants and Things group. After logging in, go to the Plants and Things group by selecting SkyDrive and then Group and then clicking on the group name to enter it. In the group space, you see Lauren's comment (see Figure 9.28) as well as all the activity that took place in the group.
16. To access the report from the group space, click Documents in the upper left of the screen.
17. Click on the Plants Report Team 1 folder and then select the PlantAndThings_ReportGuide document.
18. Click Edit in Browser. The document with the content that Lauren added appears. Add more text, as well as two photographs. To align the photographs, make a table. To make the table, click the Insert tab and select the number of cells (see Figure 9.29).
19. Click in a cell of the table to specify a location to insert the image (see Figure 9.30).

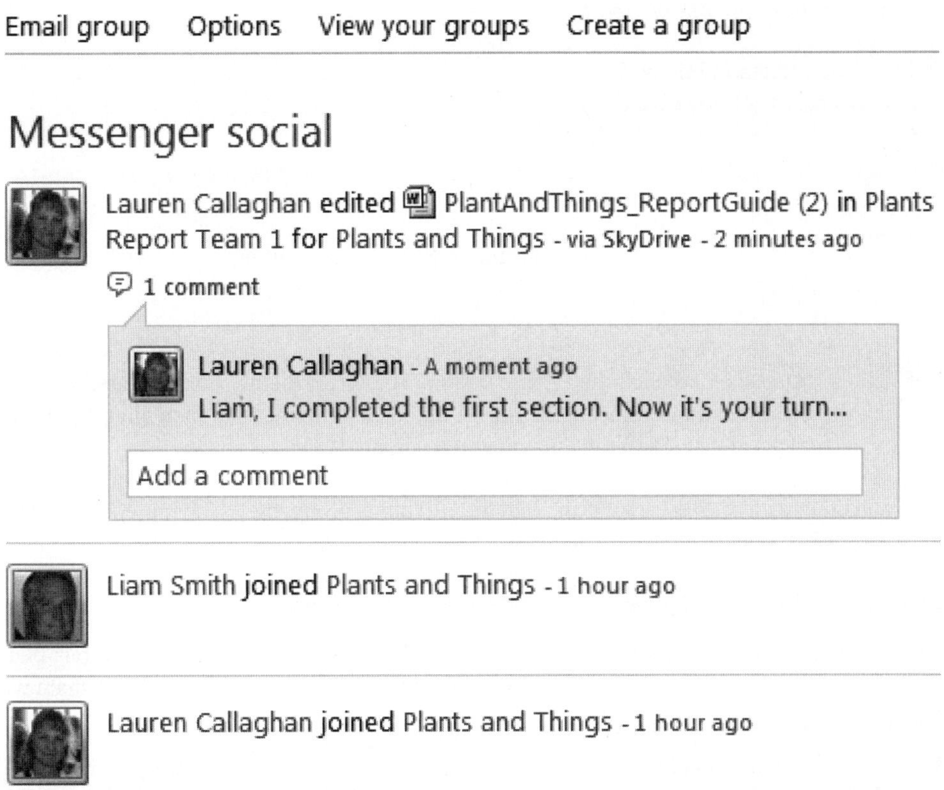

FIGURE 9.28 Reading Group Comments

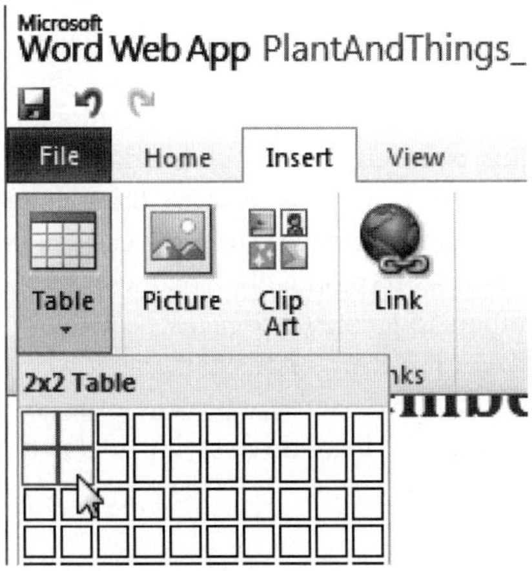

FIGURE 9.29 Inserting a Table

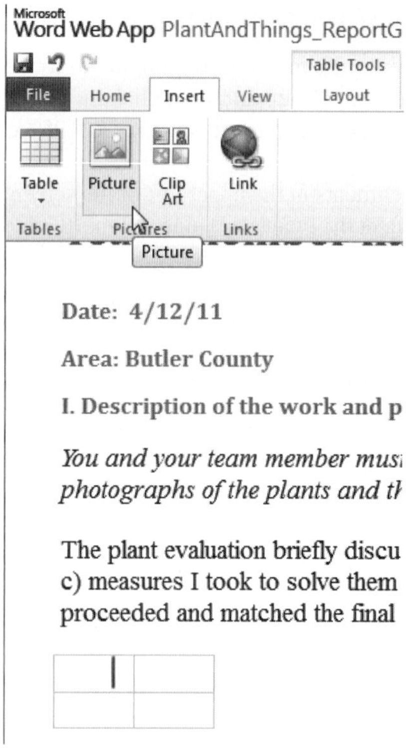

FIGURE 9.30 Inserting a Picture

20. Click the Insert tab and click the Picture button. The Insert Picture box appears.
21. Click the Browse button to locate the file on the local computer and then click Insert. The text and images are added to the document (see Figure 9.31).
22. To inform the group members you have added content, add a comment to the document. When other team members view the Plants and Things group, they see your comments (see Figure 9.32).

Copying Media from Cameras and Portable Devices

The team used a digital camera and an iPod to take pictures and record video of various plants and the surrounding environment. One of the team members will upload the content to share with the group and the teacher.

1. After taking photographs with a digital camera, the camera's universal serial bus (USB) cable is plugged into the camera and the computer so the images can be copied to the local computer and/or uploaded to the Plants and Things group. When the camera is connected to the USB port, the computer should recognize that a device is connected and display the AutoPlay box (see Figure 9.33).
2. Click Import Pictures and Videos under Device Options (see Figure 9.33). The Import Pictures and Videos box appears, and you can use it to give the images optional tag names. Click *Import*.
3. The images are imported into the Pictures folder within Libraries on the local computer. The imported images will be contained in a folder that is usually named with a date, such as 2011-7-30 Plants (see Figure 9.34). From this folder, you can copy or move the files to any folder on the local computer. An alternative way to get the images from the camera is to connect the camera to the local computer. Open Windows Explorer, click on the icon for the camera (see Figure 9.35), and then browse the folders to locate the images.
4. Whether you copied the images to the local hard drive or left them on the camera, you can upload them to the Plants and Things group at Windows Live. Before uploading the images to Windows Live, transfer the video from the iPod to the local drive so it can also be uploaded to the Plants and Things group.

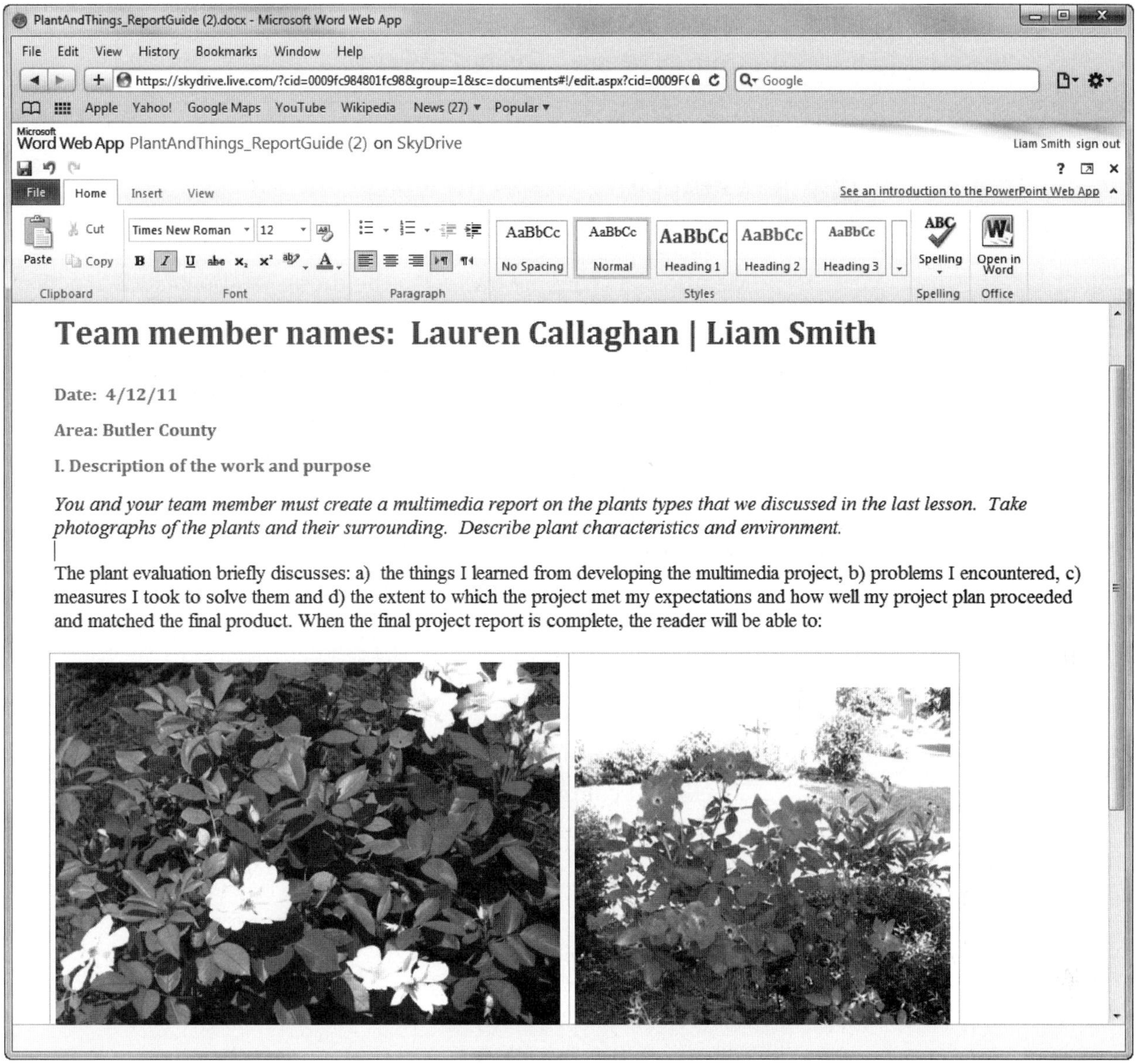

FIGURE 9.31 Adding a Comment

5. To transfer the video, connect the iPod's USB cord to the computer's USB port. The computer should recognize the device. Use Windows Explore to browse the iPod to locate the video files. The movie files are located in a folder named 800AAAAA that is inside the folder DCIM (see Figure 9.36). Once you find the files, you can drag them to a folder on the local drive.

PDToolkit for *Microsoft® Office 2010 for Teachers*

Go to PDToolkit for **Microsoft® Office 2010** for Teachers to locate the corresponding file in the Examples folder (PlantEnvironment1.MOV, PlantEnvironment2.MOV, and PlantEnvironment3.MOV).

Uploading Media to the Group Space

In this example, assume that you are once again Lauren. You have taken several photographs and recorded video that you want the other members to review. After the group members review the media, they'll decide which images and video to use in their project and the media to share with others. Follow these steps:

1. Click the SkyDrive menu item and select Groups. Under the Plants and Things title, click View Photos (see Figure 9.37).
2. In the Photos space, click Create Album (see Figure 9.38). The Create a Photo Album screen appears. Enter a name for your album: Team 1 Plant Media (see Figure 9.39). Click Next.

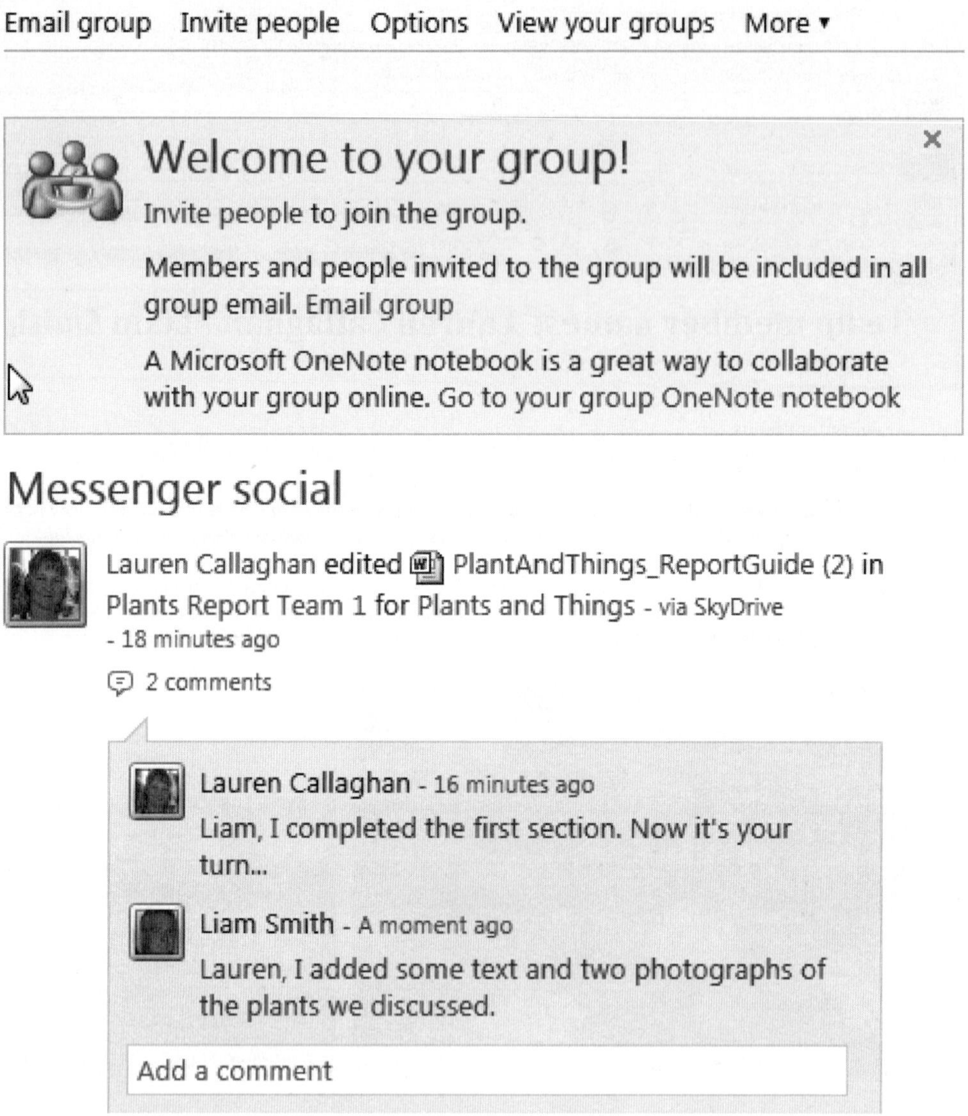

FIGURE 9.32 Reading Group Comments

FIGURE 9.33 AutoPlaying a USB Device

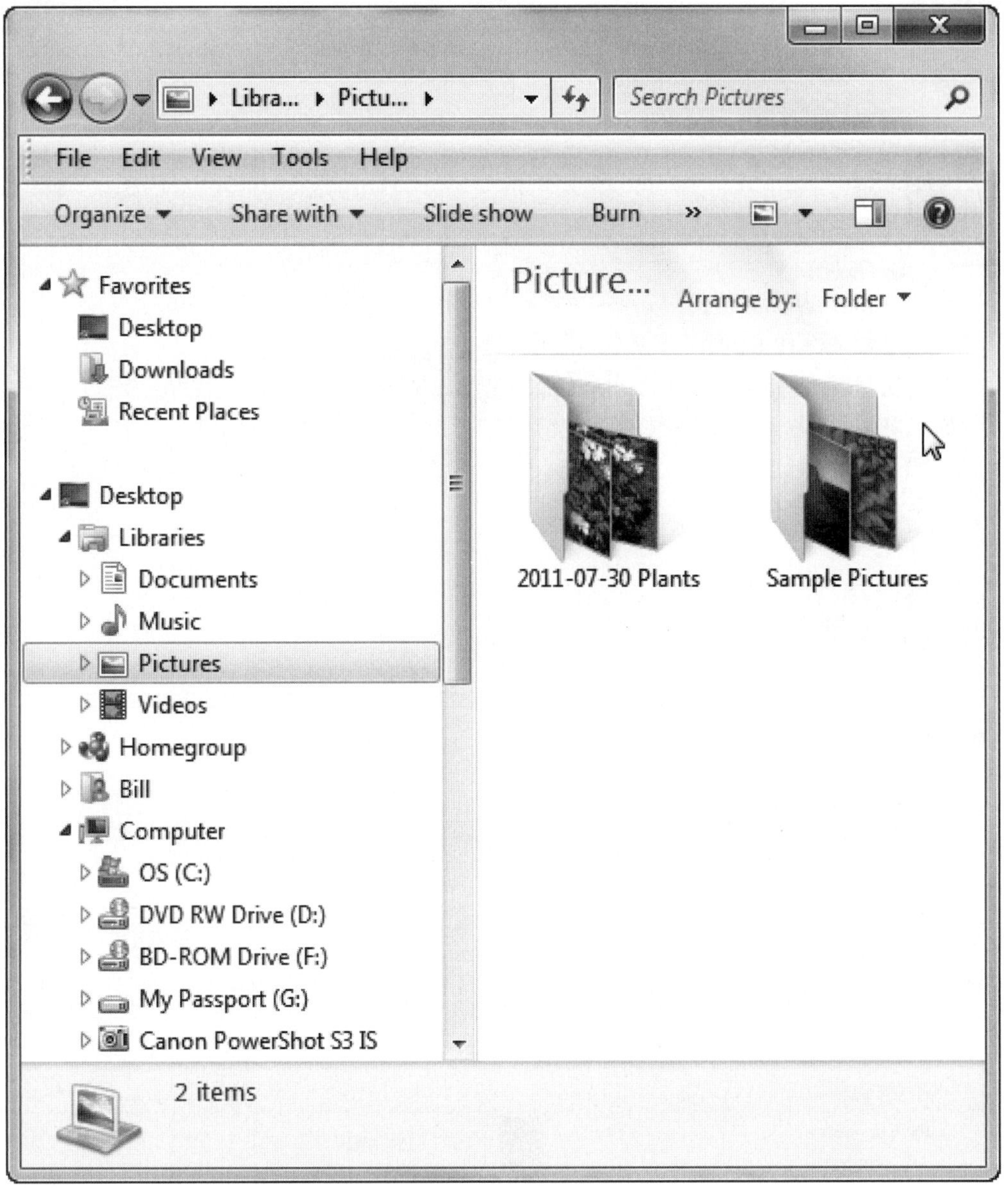

FIGURE 9.34 Images Folder in My Pictures

3. When the area where you can upload photos appears, click Select Photos from Your Computer (see Figure 9.40). The Open box appears. Browse your computer for the images you want to upload. You can upload multiple images at one time by holding down the Ctrl key while clicking on an image (see Figure 9.41). The images upload, and thumbnails of them appear (see Figure 9.42). Click the Continue button.
4. The uploaded images appear in the Team 1 Plant Media album. You want the other team members to review these images, so add a note, instructing them to do so (see Figure 9.43). When the group members go to the Plants and Things group space, they see the activity that took place, as well as your comment to review the images (see Figure 9.44).
5. To upload additional files to the album, click the SkyDrive menu item and select Groups. On the Group screen, click View Photos. In this example, you want to add a video file to the Team 1 Plant Media album, so click on the folder to open it and then click Add Files (see Figure 9.45).
6. On the Add Photos screen, you can click Choose File and browse to the video file. Alternatively, you can use Windows Explore to locate the file and then drag it on top of the

PDToolkit for ***Microsoft® Office 2010 for Teachers***

Go to PDToolkit for **Microsoft® Office 2010 for Teachers** to locate the corresponding files in the Plants folder within the Examples folder (Plants 001.JPG, Plants 002.JPG, Plants 003.JPG, Plants 004.JPG, Plants 005.JPG, and Plants 005.JPG).

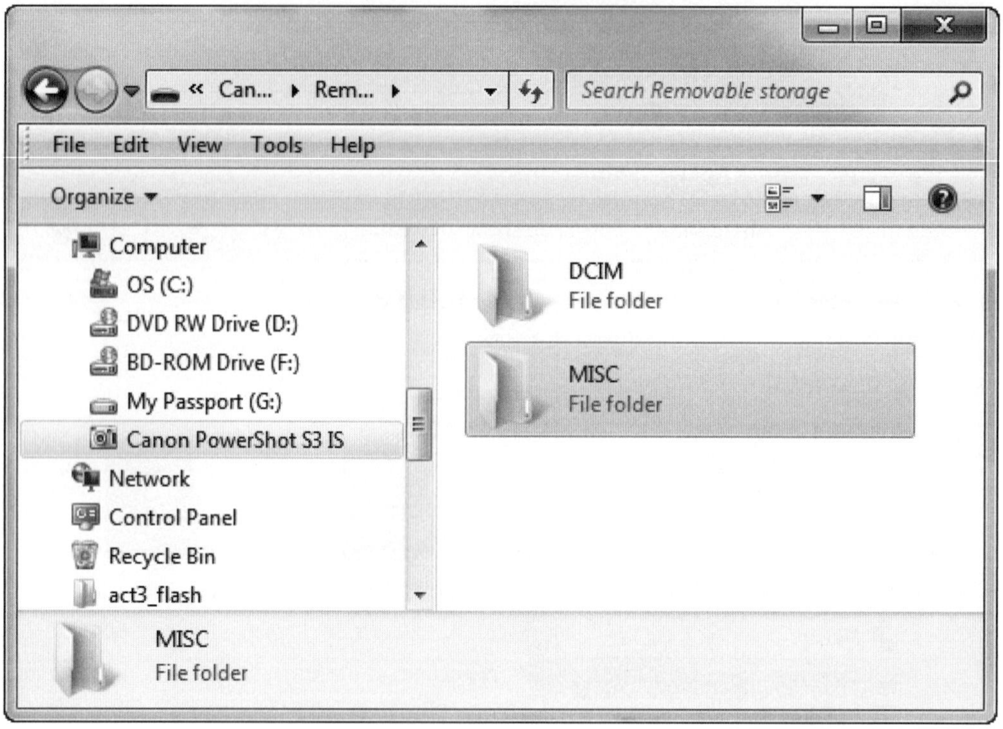

FIGURE 9.35 Browsing a Camera

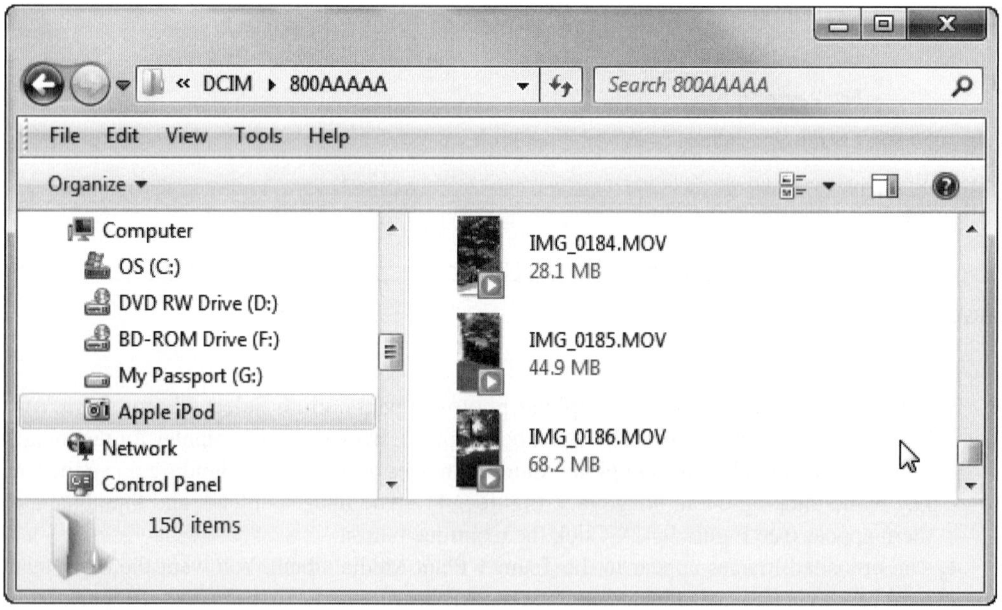

FIGURE 9.36 iPod Files

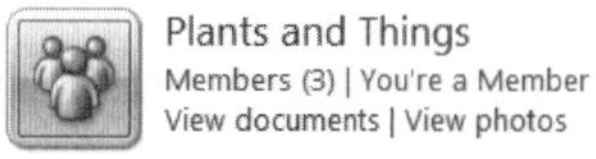

FIGURE 9.37 Viewing Photos

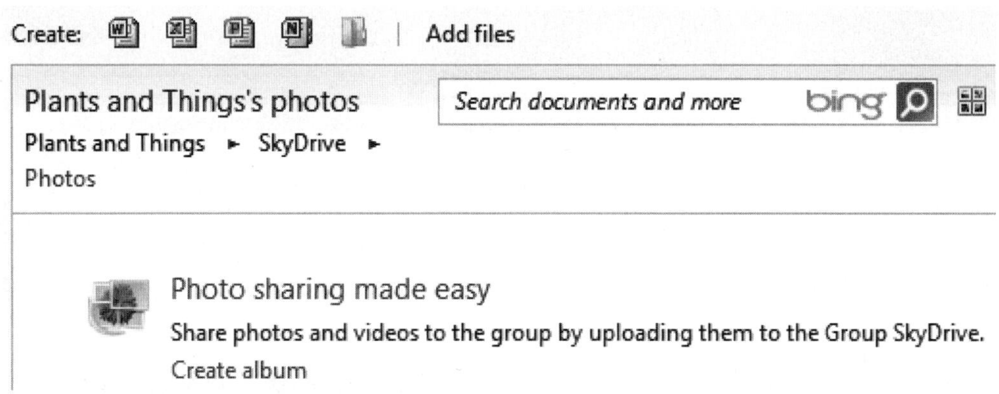

FIGURE 9.38 Creating a Photo Album

FIGURE 9.39 The Create a Photo Album Screen

FIGURE 9.40 Uploading Photos

FIGURE 9.41 Selecting Multiple Photos

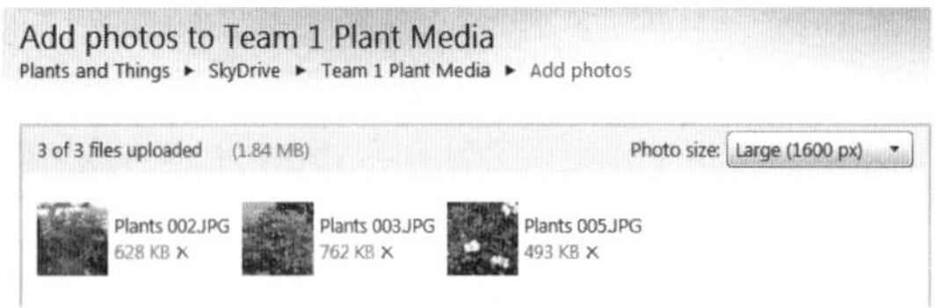

FIGURE 9.42 Uploaded Photos

Choose File button. No File Selected is replaced by the file name to indicate that it is ready to be uploaded (see Figure 9.46). Click Upload.

7. The uploaded video files appear in the Team 1 Plant Media album (see Figure 9.47).
8. Once the video and images are uploaded, members can view or download them. In fact, all group members can upload their own media content to the group.
9. When members go to the group space, they see a list of all group activity, with thumbnail images of the uploaded media (see Figure 9.48). To view the media, click on the thumbnail image. The photo album opens, and you can preview or download media files (see Figure 9.49). In addition to viewing these media files, group members can download, move, copy, rename, and delete them to include them in PowerPoint or in the other Office applications.

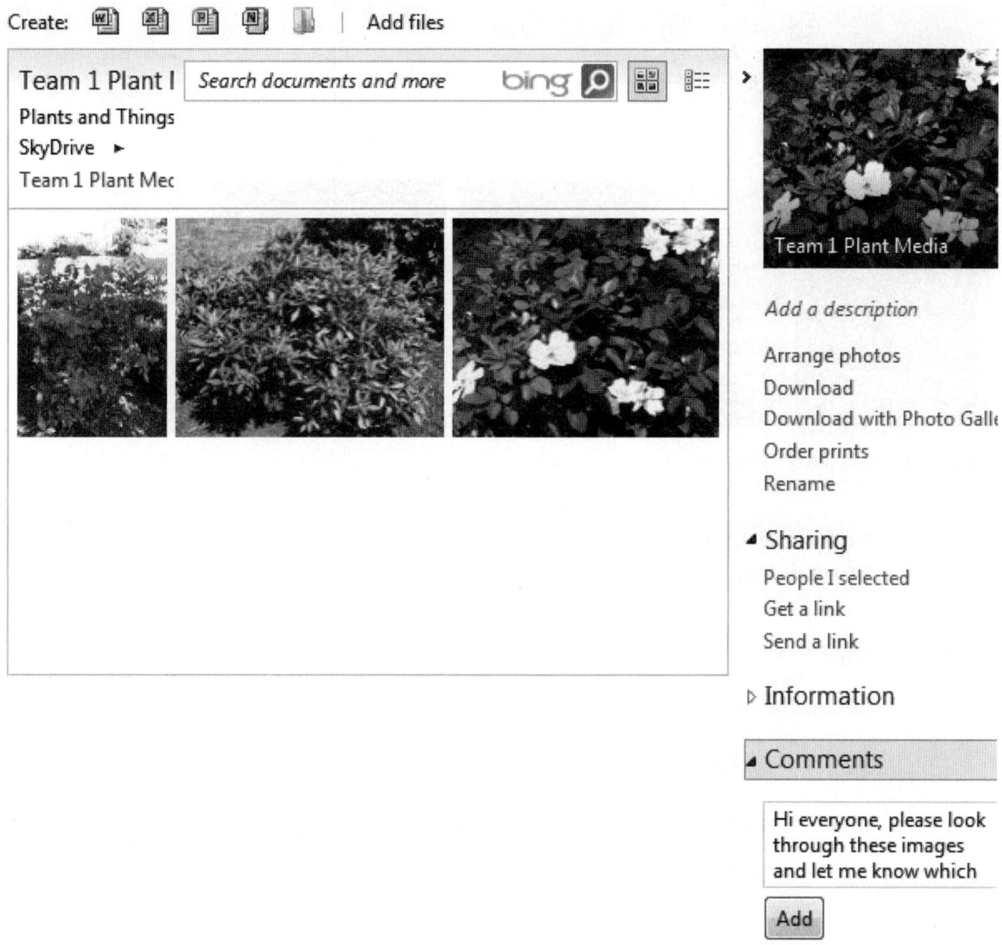

FIGURE 9.43 A Photo Album and Comments

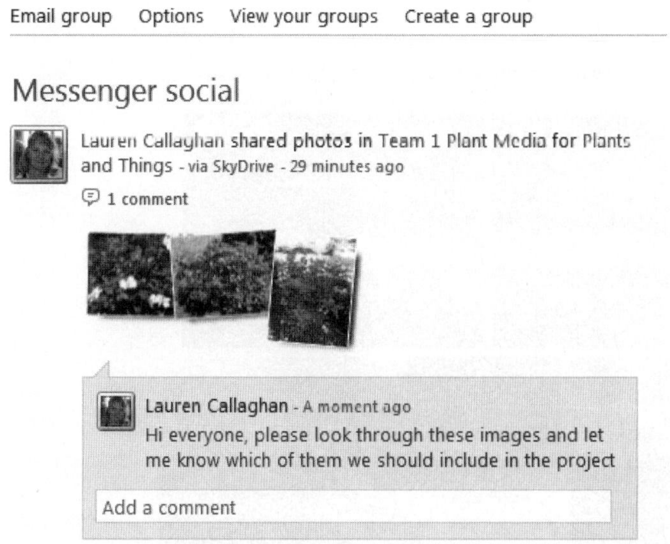

FIGURE 9.44 Comments

FIGURE 9.45 Folder Contents

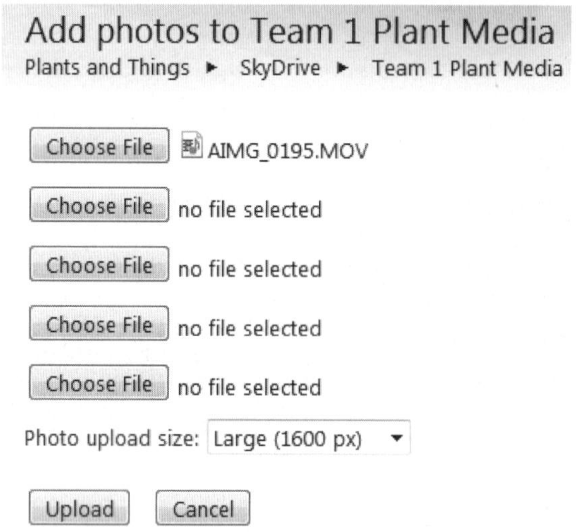

FIGURE 9.46 Adding Video

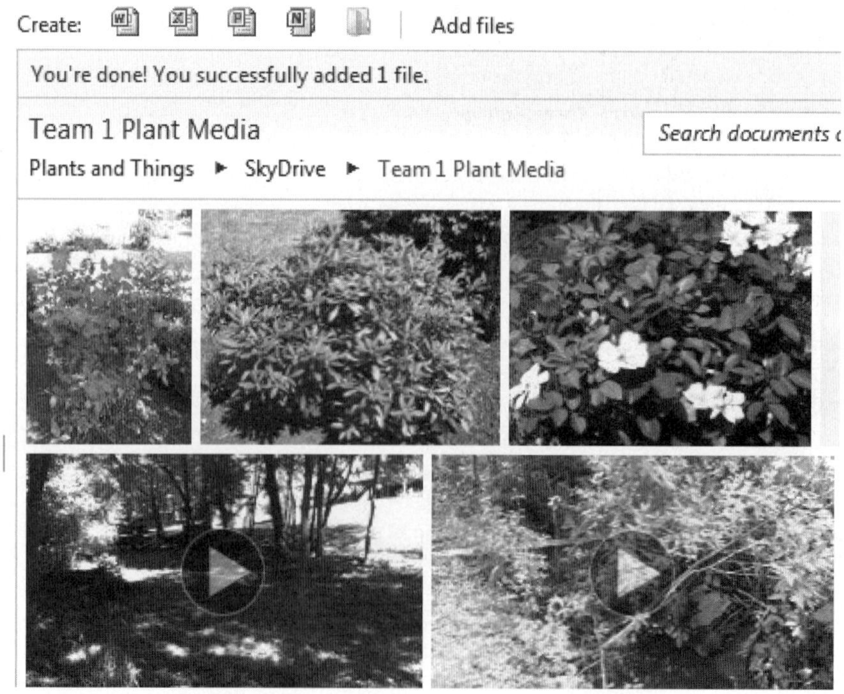

FIGURE 9.47 Uploaded Video

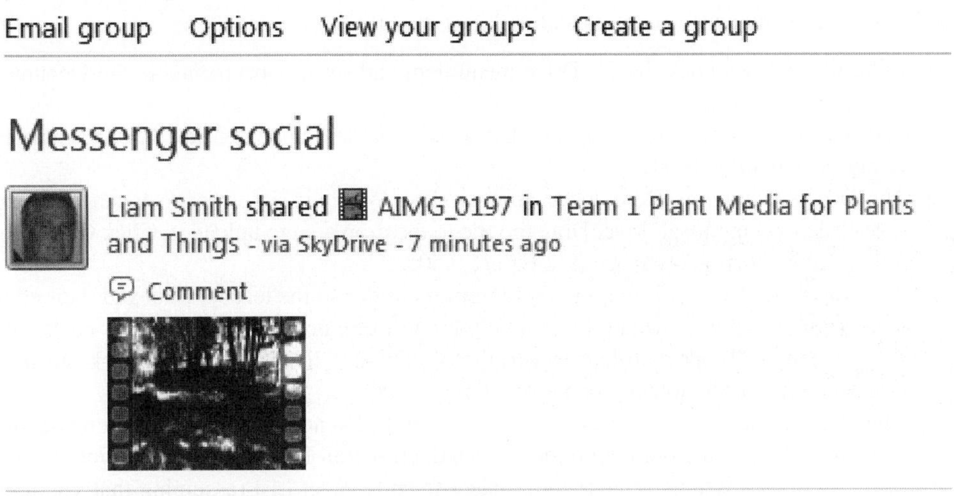

FIGURE 9.48 Group Activity

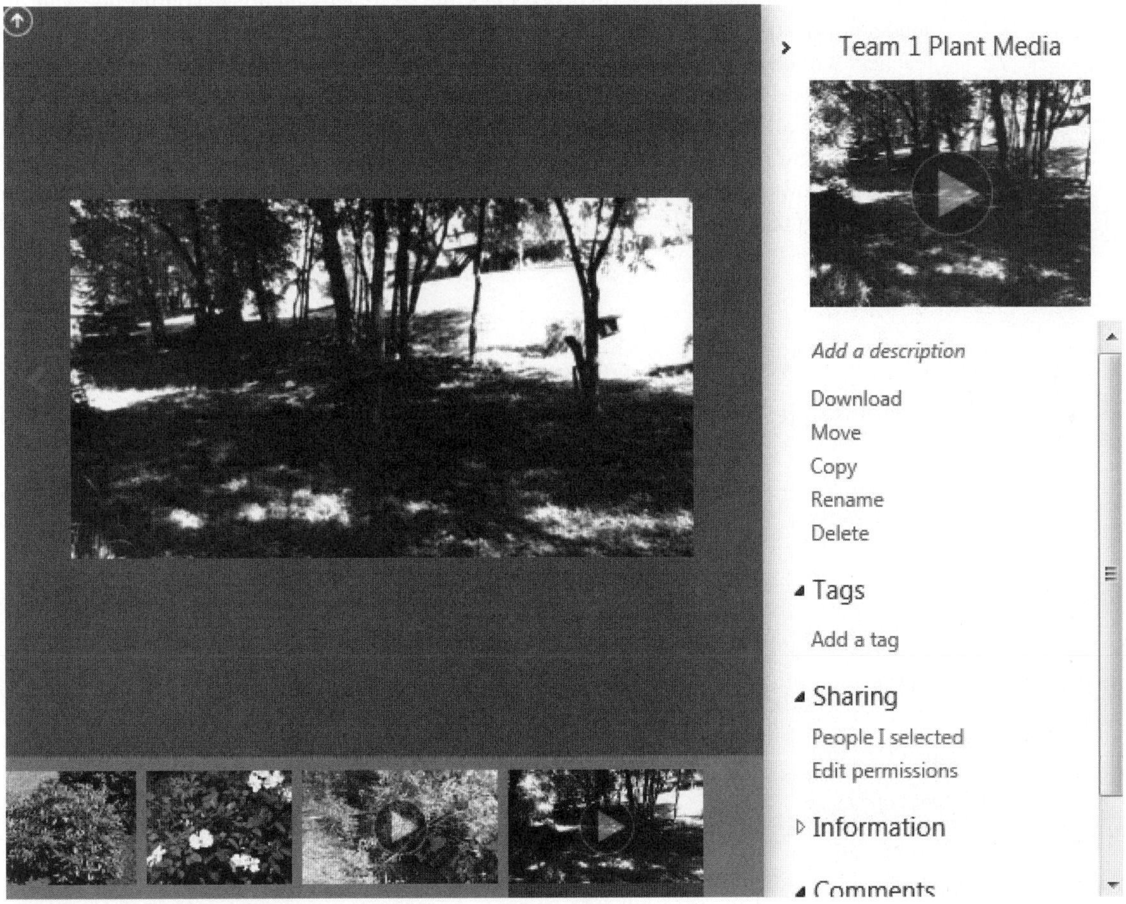

FIGURE 9.49 A Photo/Media Album

PROJECT FOR ADMINISTRATORS: MAKING AN EQUIPMENT INVENTORY

Each year you ask teachers to list their equipment requests. You created an Excel worksheet that requests the following information: quantity, equipment item (e.g., computer, camera), description, unit price, and total price. In addition, you ask teachers to give each item a priority ranking on a scale of 1 to 5, with 1 being high priority and 5 low priority. After you compile the equipment list, you pass it around to the department heads for them to rank items from a departmental perspective. You use the information you collect to justify your equipment purchases. You upload

PDToolkit for *Microsoft® Office 2010 for Teachers*

Go to PDToolkit for **Microsoft® Office 2010 for Teachers** to locate the corresponding file in the Examples folder (YearEquipmentRequest.xlsx).

the Excel worksheet to Windows Live and make it available to all the teachers and department heads so they can enter their requests and rankings directly.

1. In Windows Live, click the SkyDrive menu item and select Documents. In the Documents space, click Add File.
2. The Select a Folder Screen appears. Click New Folder, name the new folder Equipment Requests, and click Next.
3. The Drop Documents Here space appears. Use Windows Explorer to locate the Excel spreadsheet on the local drive. Drag the file to the drop area to upload it. Click Continue to return to the Documents space (see Figure 9.50).
4. Set the permissions on the Equipment Requests folder so the teachers can add their equipment requests. If your screen looks like the one in Figure 9.51, you need to back out of the Equipment Requests folder and to the SkyDrive. Click SkyDrive to back out of the Equipment Requests folder (see Figure 9.51).
5. Click on the Equipment Requests folder to select it. (Do not click on the folder name, or its contents will appear.) With the folder selected, click Edit Permissions (see Figure 9.52).
6. In the Edit Permissions screen, click Select from Contact List (assuming that you added the teachers to your contact list). For each teacher, choose Can Add, Edit Details (see Figure 9.53). Click Save.
7. When the notification screen displays, click the Skip This button if you do not want to send a notification (assuming that the teachers are notified in a faculty meeting). Now the teachers will be able to add their requests. They will need to make the administrator (you) a contact/friend by clicking the Messenger menu item and selecting Add Friends.
8. Type the e-mail address of the administrator. The administrator and all teachers need to have a Windows Live account to participate.
9. Go to Windows Live, click the SkyDrive menu item, and select Documents Shared with You (see Figure 9.54).

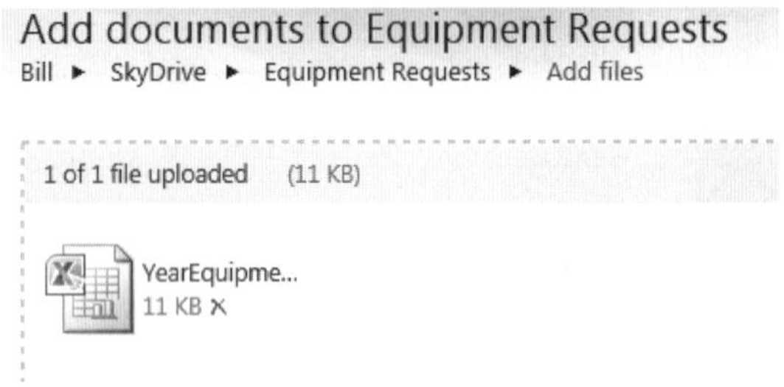

FIGURE 9.50 An Uploaded Excel File

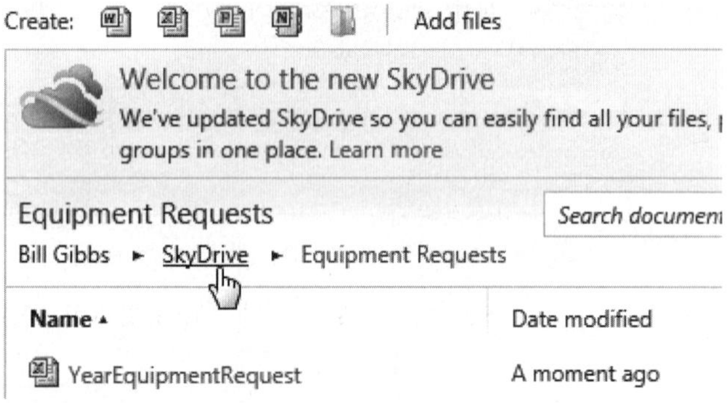

FIGURE 9.51 Equipment Requests

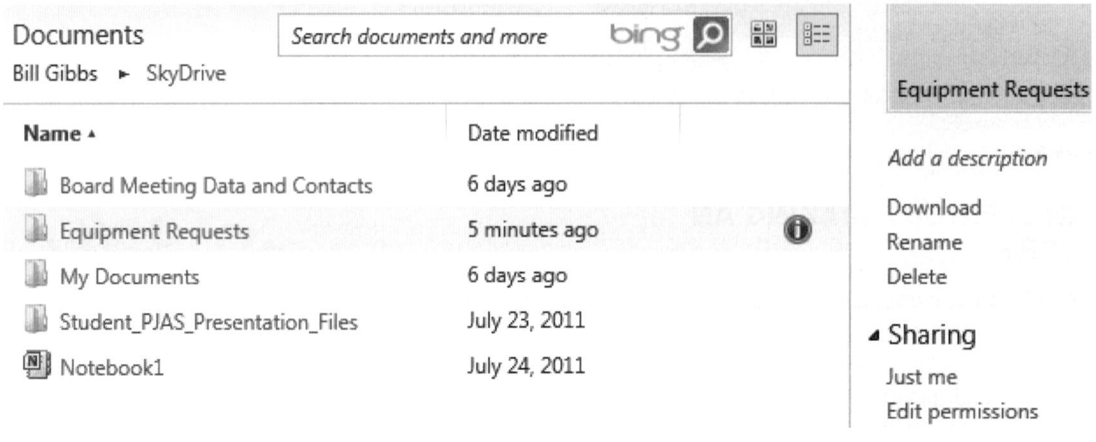

FIGURE 9.52 Selecting Edit Permissions

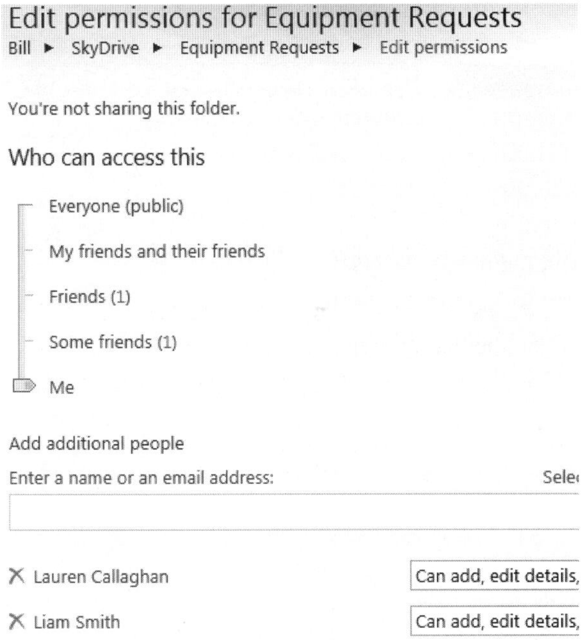

FIGURE 9.53 Editing Permissions

FIGURE 9.54 Opening Shared Files

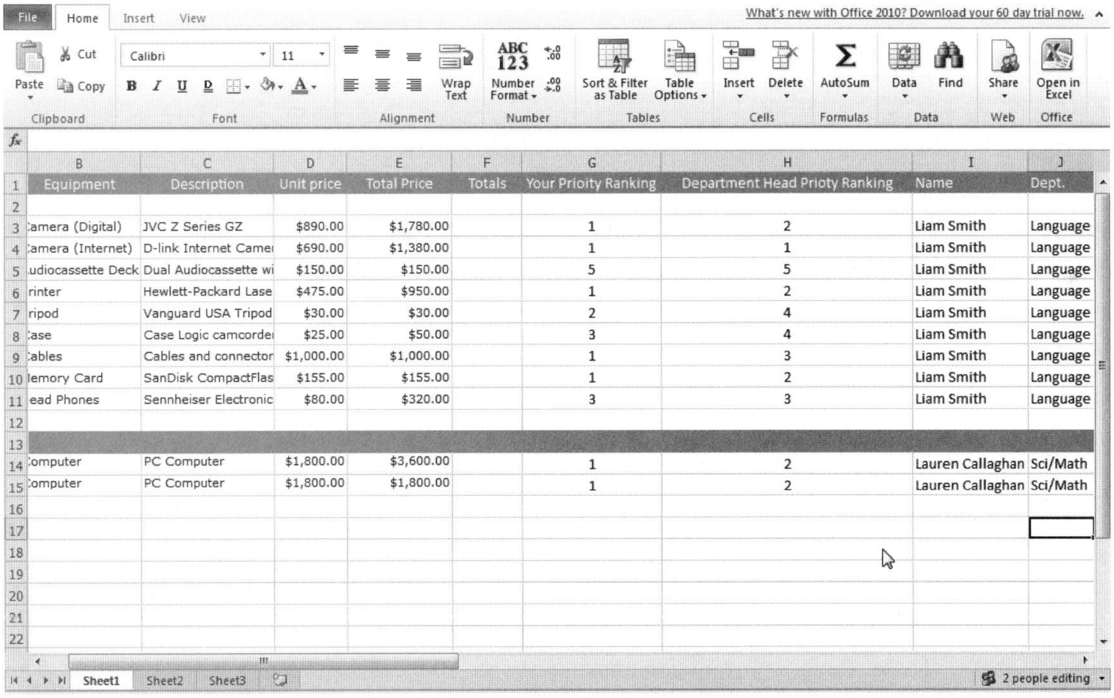

FIGURE 9.55 Opening Shared Files

10. The Equipment Requests Folder appears. Click on it to access the Excel worksheet.
11. Click on the spreadsheet item to select it and then click Edit in Browser.
12. The worksheet opens. Type your equipment requests (see Figure 9.55). The number of people working on the document appears in the lower-right corner of the document (see Figure 9.56). As one person makes changes in the document, the document is immediately updated. People can access the worksheet (or PowerPoint or Word file) from anywhere.
13. After teachers have entered their requests, you, as the administrator, may create another column to get an average priority ranking for each request. For simplicity in this example, we calculated an average based on rankings of the teacher and the department head. Once an average ranking column is created, select all data and on the Home tab, in the Tables

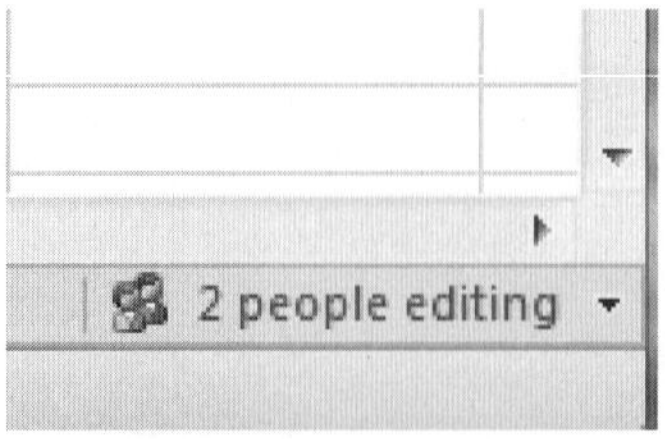

FIGURE 9.56 Indicator of the Number of People Working on the Document

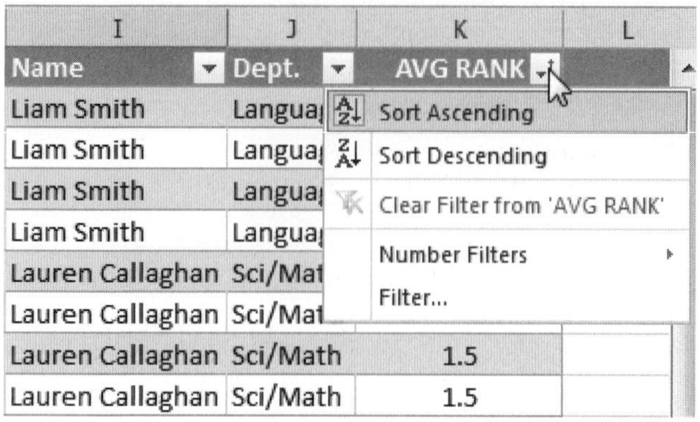

FIGURE 9.57 Sorting Requests by Average Ranking

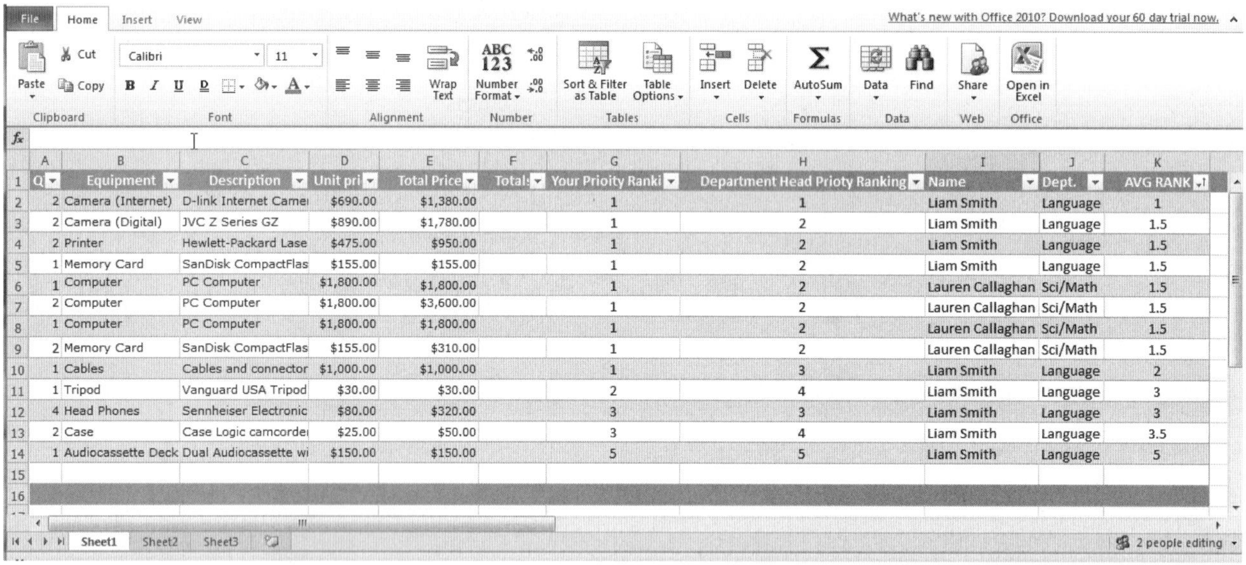

FIGURE 9.58 Items with Highest-Priority Ranking

group, click the Sort & Filter button. A drop-down arrow appears in the column headings. In this example, the average ranking is in column K. Click the drop arrow at the top of column K and select Sort Ascending (see Figure 9.57). The items with the highest-priority ranking are now easily identified (see Figure 9.58).

Those who have permission immediately see all the changes made in the worksheet. This feature could be especially useful if you were working on budgets collaboratively with others who are at distant locations. You can create charts, and you can modify and analyze data; all those changes are immediately accessible to everyone who has appropriate permission.

SUMMING IT UP

This chapter introduced multimedia and Web technologies. It presented fundamentals to help you get started with capturing multimedia files with digital cameras and portable devices and copying them to your computer. In the chapter, you used Windows Live and the Office applications to work with and share multimedia content. Windows Live opens up many possibilities for working with Office. You can work collaboratively with colleagues and students, regardless of where they are located. You can co-develop multimedia content by using the Office applications, share it, discuss it, and revised it—all through Windows Live.

References and Resources

Anderson, P. (2007). What is Web 2.0? Ideas, technologies and implications for education. *JISC Technology and Standards Watch.* Retrieved July 27, 2011, from www.jisc.ac.uk/media/documents/techwatch/tsw0701b.pdf.

Chapman, N., & Chapman, J. (2004). *Digital multimedia* (2nd ed.). Chichester, UK: John Wiley & Sons Ltd.

Laningham, S., & Berners-Lee, T. (2006). *DeveloperWorks Interviews: Tim Berners-Lee. Originator of the Web and director of the World Wide Web Consortium talks about where we've come, and about the challenges and opportunities ahead.* Retrieved July 27, 2011, from www.ibm.com/developerworks/podcast/dwi/cm-int082206txt.html.

Mayer, R.E. (2009). *Multimedia learning* (2nd ed.). New York: Cambridge University Press.

Microsoft. (2011). *Windows Live essentials.* Retrieved July 1, 2011, from http://windows.microsoft.com/en-US/windows7/products/features/windows-live-essentials.

O'Reilly, T. (2007). What is Web 2.0: Design patterns and business models for the next generation of software. *Communications & Strategies, 65*(1), 17–37. Retrieved July 27, 2011, from http://mpra.ub.uni-muenchen.de/4580/1/MPRA_paper_4580.pdf.

APPENDIX A

Windows 7

This appendix provides a basic overview of the Windows 7 operating system and fundamental features of Windows 7 that can help you use Office 2010.

Before you open and work with any of the Microsoft Office products, it is important to have a basic understanding of Windows 7. As the name *Windows* implies, interaction with programs is facilitated through adjustable rectangular areas, or windows, that appear on your computer screen. Windows 7, like earlier versions of the operating system, has a graphical user interface that contains objects (e.g., buttons and icons) through which you access and work with files, folders, and programs. The interface helps you access, store, and organize information or data on your computer as well as to easily find and navigate documents, programs, and menus. It makes working with the computer easy and efficient.

Windows 7 offers many notable features, including a visually rich interface named Windows Aero that provides transparent windows, built-in search, libraries to manage files, sidebar gadgets, and a refined taskbar to launch and manage programs and files (Manjoo, 2009). In addition, it features Aero Peek, which enables you to hover the mouse pointer over an icon on the taskbar to see a preview of the associated program or file; Shake, which allows you to click on a window and drag it back and forth to minimize all other windows; and Snap, with which you can drag a window to the top of the desktop to cause the desktop to snap in place and fill the screen (maximize it) or drag a window to the left or right side of the desktop to cause it to fill the respective half of the screen. These are a few of the features included in the Windows 7 operating system that aim to make your experience interacting with your computer easy, efficient, and fun.

THE DESKTOP

When you turn your computer on, the desktop displays (see Figure A.1). The desktop is the work area where you place files and folders. The folders, programs, or files that you open display in rectangular windows on the desktop. Icons such the Recycle Bin icon represent applications, files, or system resources (e.g., scanner). To activate these objects, you click them with the left mouse button.

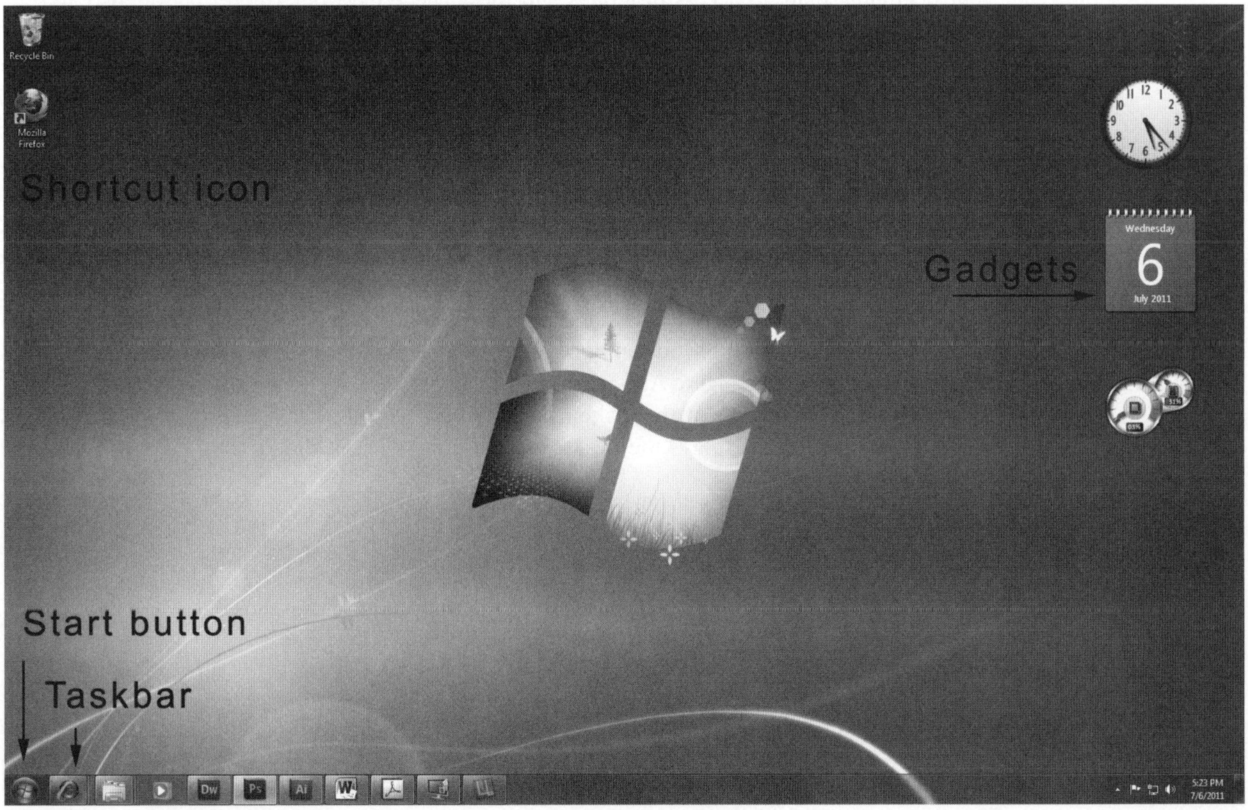

FIGURE A.1 The Windows Desktop

Your desktop may contain the following features, although the configuration of your system may differ.

Desktop Gadgets

Gadgets include calendars, news and weather feeds, and clocks, as shown in Figure A.1.

The Computer Object

The Computer object allows you to see the contents of your disk drives and to access your computer's configuration settings. It contains the C: drive icon, the E: drive icon, icons for any other disk drives you have connected to your computer, and the Control Panel. When you double-click a drive icon, the contents of that drive appear on the screen. For instance, double-clicking the C: drive icon displays a list of all the folders, directories, and files contained on the C: drive. You may not see the Computer icon. To display it, you right-click on the desktop, select Personalize, and then select Desktop icons. Then you check the Computer item and click OK.

The Recycle Bin

The Recycle Bin temporarily stores deleted files. All files deleted from the C: drive first go to the Recycle Bin. Only when the Recycle Bin is emptied are the files removed from your computer. You can retrieve files from the Recycle Bin if you deleted them erroneously. If you do not empty the Recycle Bin, your deleted files still occupy disk space. Files deleted from external disk drives do not go to the Recycle Bin. They are removed from your computer as soon as you delete them. If you want to delete a file from the C: drive without sending it to the Recycle Bin, hold down the Shift key while you delete it. If you do not see the Recycle Bin icon on the Desktop, right-click on the desktop, select Personalize, and then select Desktop Icons. Check the Recycle Bin item and click OK.

The Taskbar

The taskbar provides access to opened folders and files and makes switching between them convenient (see Figure A.2). It contains the Start button, on the left side of the taskbar, which is your beginning point to access programs and files. The Windows Explorer button also appears on the taskbar. The icon looks like a folder. Clicking it provides you quick access to your disk drives, folders, and files. As you open items, a button representing each program displays on the taskbar. You can switch between programs by clicking the appropriate button icon. In Figure A.2, Microsoft Word is open, along with several other programs and resources. Clicking on the Word icon makes it active by bringing the application window to the forefront on the desktop. Depending on the computer's configuration, icons appear in the Notification area on the right side of the taskbar, providing information and access to programs and resources. For instance, the icons on the right of the taskbar in Figure A.2 provide access to and information about audio and network resources.

You can pin icons of frequently used programs to the taskbar to access them quickly. When a pinned program is running, you can right-click its button on the taskbar and then select Pin This Program to Taskbar (see Figure A.2).

On the far right side of the taskbar is the Show Desktop button. Clicking it minimizes all open windows and displays the desktop. In Figure A.2 it is shown to the right of the time and date.

FIGURE A.2 The Taskbar

Shortcuts

Instead of searching your computer each time you want to open a frequently used file or program, you can create a shortcut to it on the desktop. When you double-click the shortcut, the file or program opens. Each shortcut icon has a small arrow at the bottom-left corner (see Figure A.3) to distinguish it from other icons. As mentioned, you can also pin items to the taskbar for quick access.

FIGURE A.3 A Shortcut Icon

THE MOUSE AND WINDOWS

The computer's mouse is integral to working with Windows. You use the mouse to scroll documents, select icons, make choices from dialog boxes and pull-down menus, and move and resize windows.

A typical computer mouse has at least two buttons (left and right) and a scroll wheel. You use the left mouse button to select and open objects and to resize and position windows. The right mouse button helps open shortcut menus that display commands for a particular object. The scroll wheel allows for efficient scrolling, especially for long documents.

Selecting an object with the mouse informs Windows that you are going to work with the object in some way, such as opening or moving it. Objects become highlighted when selected. Figure A.4 illustrates the Computer object as not selected and selected (when a border appears around the icon). The selected Computer object is on the right side of Figure A.4.

Double-clicking the left mouse button on an object opens it in a window on the desktop. For example, you can double-click the left mouse button on the Computer object to open its contents (see Figure A.5).

FIGURE A.4 Icons Not Selected and Selected

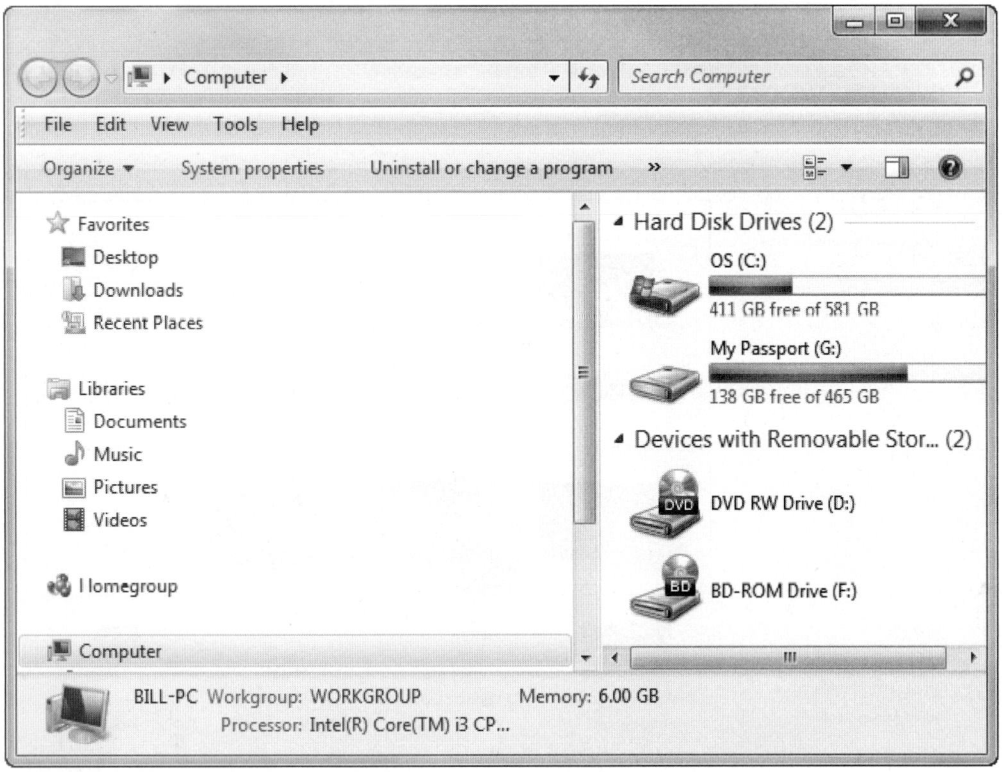

FIGURE A.5 The Computer Object

PERSONALIZING WINDOWS 7

You can personalize many features of Windows 7 so that the operating system is tailored to your preferences and needs. To access the personalization options, you right-click on the desktop to display the shortcut menu and click Personalize (see Figure A.6). The Personalize box appears (see Figure A.7); you can use this box to access options to alter Windows 7 features. For instance, clicking the Window Color option displays the Window Color and Appearance box, where you can set the color and styles of windows. In Figure A.8, the default is selected, and it will be applied to all windows. With the Desktop Background option, you can choose a background color or image for your desktop. When this option is selected, the Choose a Desktop Background box appears (see Figure A.9); you can use this box to select or browse for a desktop image. The remaining items on the Personalize box afford similar access to options for customizing Windows 7 features.

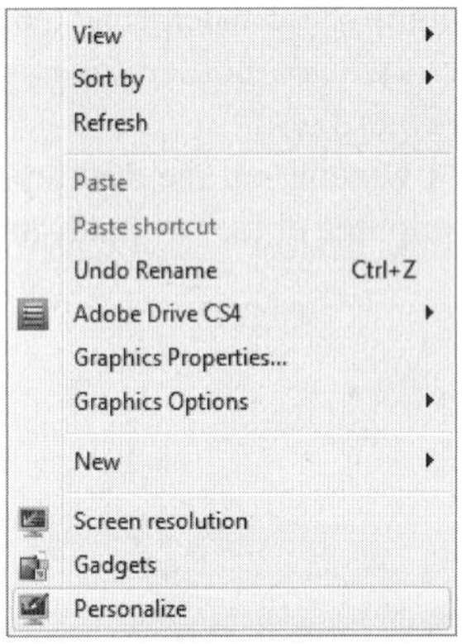

FIGURE A.6 A Desktop Shortcut Menu

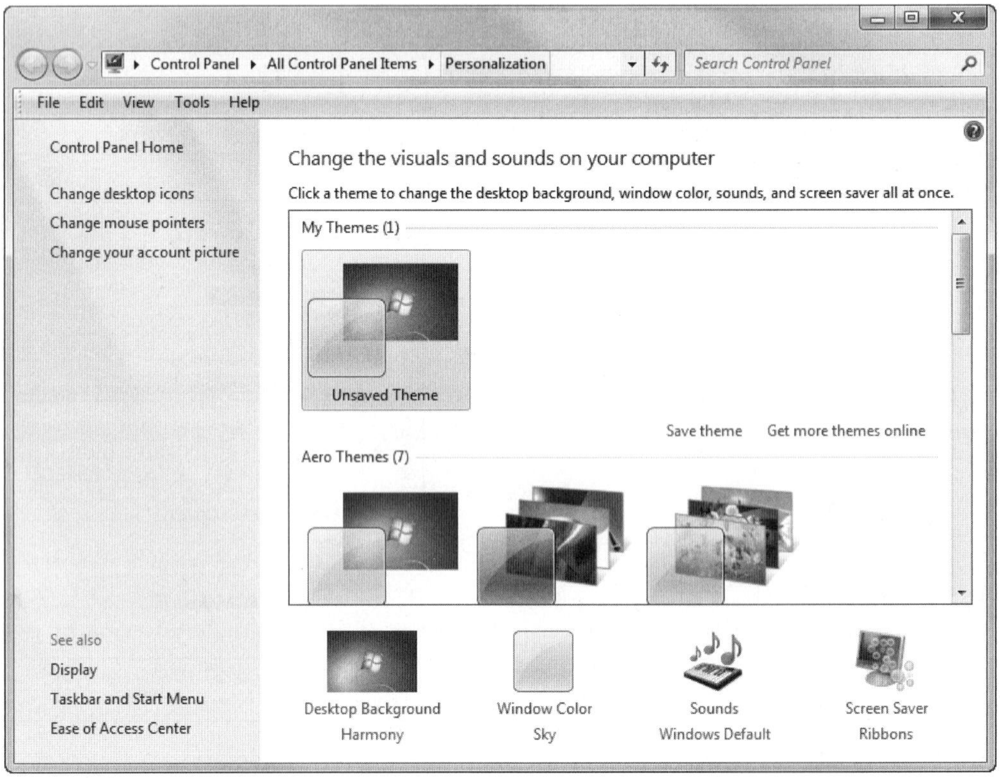

FIGURE A.7 The Personalize Box for Personalizing Windows

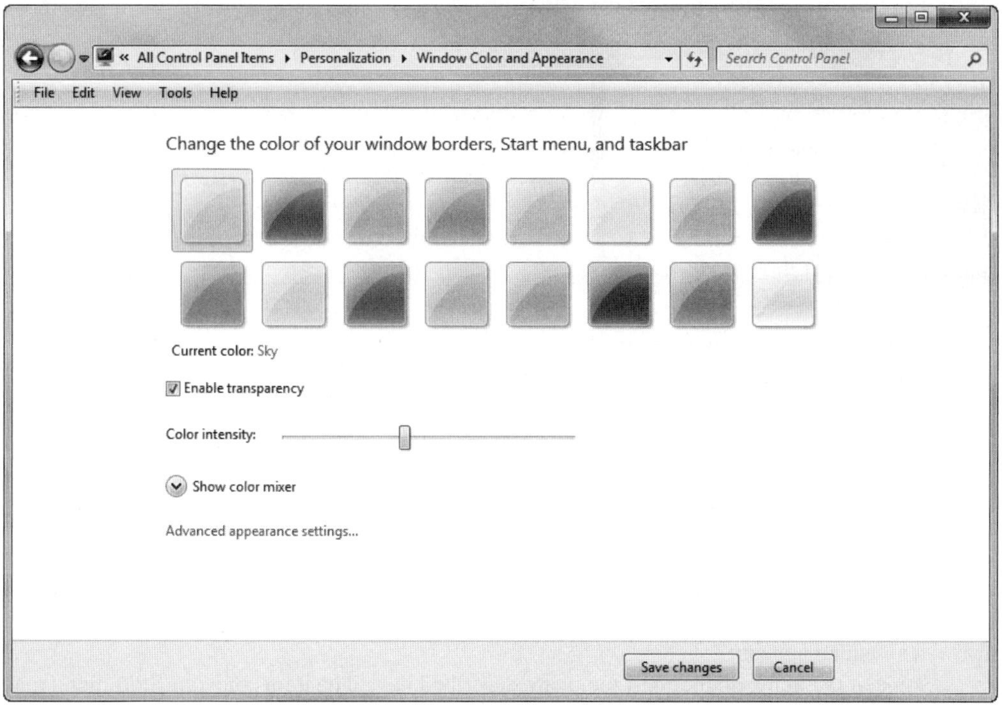

FIGURE A.8 Changing Window Color and Appearance

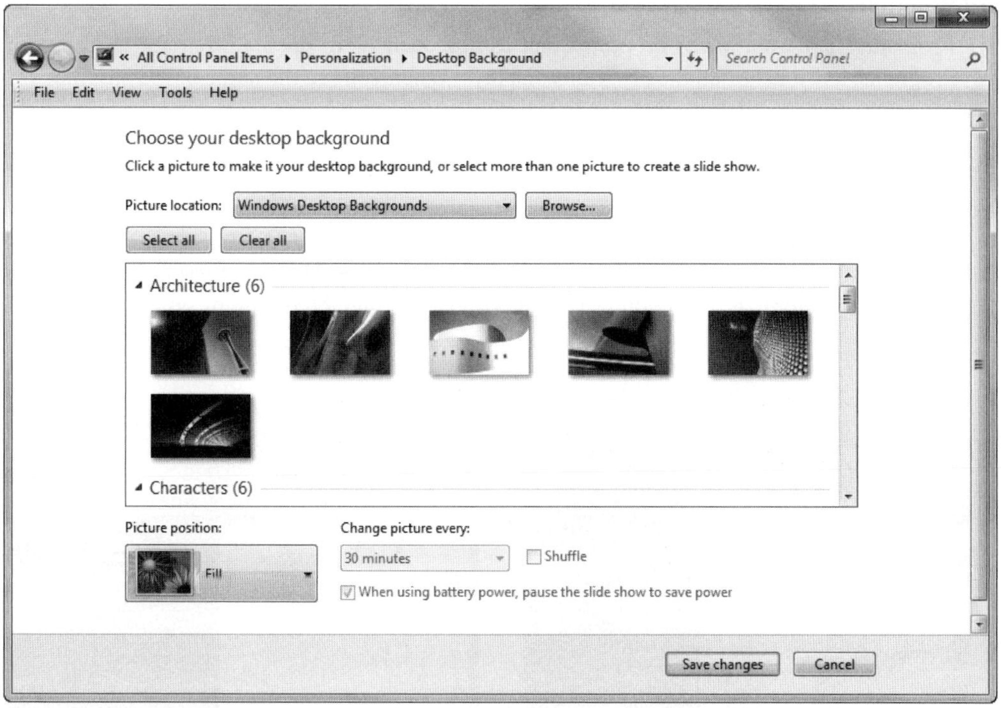

FIGURE A.9 Changing the Desktop Background

SHORTCUT MENUS

Using shortcut menus can be an efficient way to access files, programs, and system resources, among other things. If you position your mouse on a folder, an object, the desktop, or the taskbar and then right-click, a shortcut menu appears, displaying the commands for that object. Right-clicking on Computer, for example, displays its shortcut menu (see Figure A.10). Holding the Shift key while right-clicking displays an extended shortcut menu. As mentioned earlier, if you position the mouse on the desktop and right-click, the desktop shortcut menu appears (see Figure A.6).

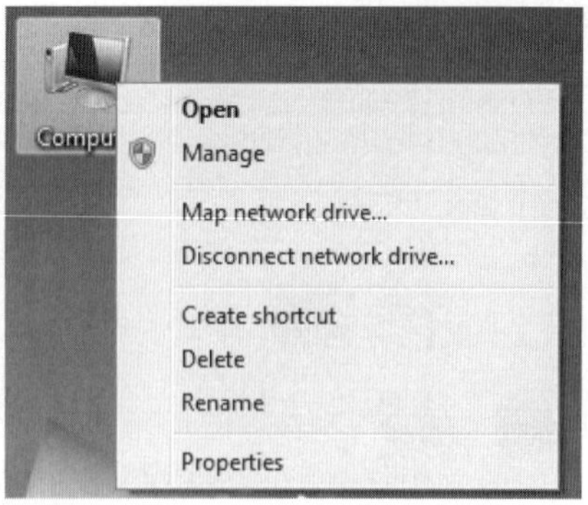

FIGURE A.10 A Shortcut Menu

THE START MENU

If you click the Start button on the taskbar, the Start menu displays (see Figure A.11). The items on this menu contain most of the things you need to begin using Windows 7. An arrow next to a menu item indicates that more items or submenus are present. When you pass the mouse over the arrow, a submenu appears.

Some of the items on the Start menu are described next. The items on your Start menu may vary from those presented here because your computer is likely configured differently from the one used in this example.

All Programs

All Programs displays a list of programs that can be opened. To open a program, you click on All Programs, and a list of all the programs displays. When you see the name of the program you want to open, you can click it.

Recent Items

Recent Items presents a list of recently opened documents. This item is useful for quickly opening a document without searching for it on your computer. If you do not see Recent Items, you can right-click on the Start button and select Properties. In the Taskbar and Start Menu Properties box, you click Customize. Then you scroll down and check the Recent Items box and click OK.

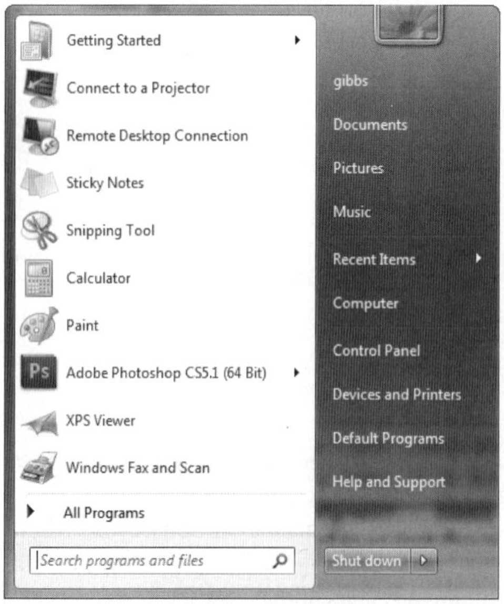

FIGURE A.11 The Start Menu

FIGURE A.12 Start Menu: Shut Down

Search

Search allows you to find files and folders located on your computer. You can also search the Internet by using this option.

Help and Support

Help and Support opens the Help and Support module, which provides information about Windows and many of its features and functions.

Shut Down/Turn Off Computer

This option shuts down Windows and turns off the computer. It can also be used to restart the computer or to put it in Sleep mode. Shutdown options are located at the bottom right of the Start menu (see Figure A.12).

REPOSITIONING AND RESIZING WINDOWS

As you work in Windows 7, you will likely open several files or programs at the same time and may need to reposition windows to work efficiently. Every window has an address bar (see Figure A.13) that displays breadcrumbs, or the current location of the file or folder. For instance, Figure A.13 displays the Public folder in the address bar. You can reposition a window by clicking on the title bar (the area above the address bar) and, while holding down the left mouse button, dragging the window to a new location. You can also activate a window simply by clicking on the title bar.

A title bar contains three buttons on the upper-right side. The button on the left reduces, or minimizes, the window. The button in the center enlarges, or maximizes, a window to the full size of the desktop. When the window is enlarged to full screen, the Maximize button changes to the Restore Down button. Restore Down returns the window to its original size prior to the window being maximized. The button on the right closes the window or program. When you have a program open (e.g., Word), clicking the Close/Quit Program button exits the program. Right-clicking on the title bar displays a pop-up menu with Minimize, Maximize, and Close/Quit options. As mentioned earlier, you can use Shake and Snap to work with windows. You use Shake by clicking on a window and dragging it back and forth to minimize all other windows. When windows are minimized and you use Shake, the windows are maximized. You use Snap by dragging a window to the top of the desktop so it snaps in place and fills the screen (i.e., maximizes it). You can drag a window to the left or right side of the desktop, and it fills the respective half of the screen.

To make a window larger or smaller, you move the mouse pointer to any of the four sides of the window. The pointer will change to a double arrow. You drag the border to enlarge or reduce the window size. A box appears around the window as you resize it. Resizing from the bottom-right corner sizes the window proportionally. If you just want to adjust the width, you can place the cursor over the left or right side of the window and drag. You change the length by placing the cursor at the top or bottom of the window and drag.

You may also alter how windows present information. Clicking the Organize button provides options for adjusting the layout of windows (see Figure A.14). For example, clicking Menu Bar displays the File, Edit, View, Tools, and Help menu options. Clicking Views (see Figure A.15) provides options for how the contents of the window get displayed. For instance, clicking Details presents detailed information about files.

FIGURE A.13 A Window

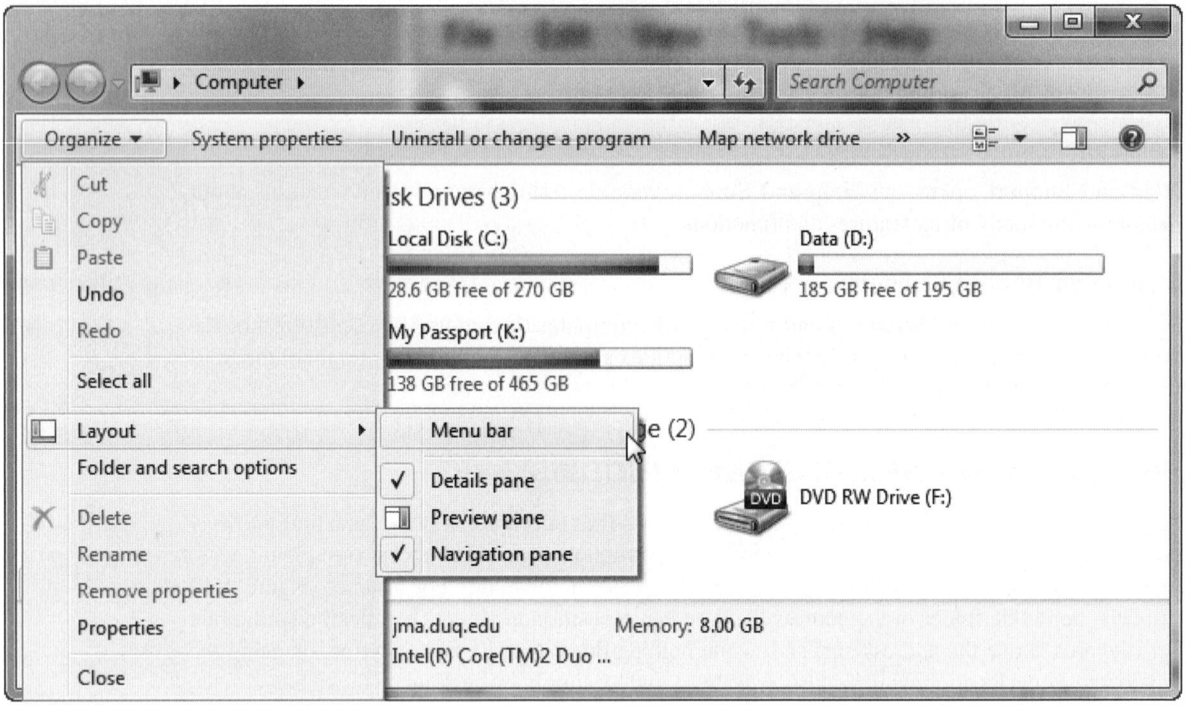

FIGURE A.14 Window Layout Options

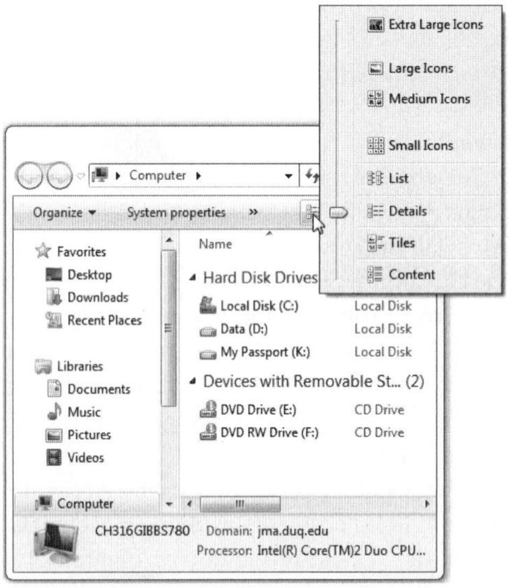

FIGURE A.15 Window View Options

FIGURE A.16 A Program List

WORKING WITH PROGRAMS AND FILES

Opening Programs

To open a program such as Microsoft Word, you click the Start button on the taskbar. On the Start menu, you click All Programs to display the Program list. You click Microsoft Office to display the Microsoft Office group (see Figure A.16).

You click Microsoft Office Word 2010 to open it. Word opens, with a blank untitled document. A button representing Word appears on the taskbar. Depending on how you installed Office 2010, the menu item for it may be located in various locations on the Start menu. In most cases, it can be found under All Programs and within the Microsoft Office folder.

Opening Files

There are multiple ways to open a file. In this section, we discuss three methods: (a) opening a file using the application that created it, (b) accessing and opening a file using the Computer object, and (c) opening a file using Recent Items on the Start menu.

OPENING A FILE USING THE APPLICATION THAT CREATED IT Using the Start menu, you can open the application with which you created the file. For example, to open a file created with Microsoft Word, you ensure that Word is open and the click the File tab and select Open (see Figure A.17). The Open dialog box appears (see Figure A.18).

Use the Open dialog box to locate the file you want to open. If you need to open a file in a different folder, click the down arrow in the address bar and then select the disk drive that contains the folder. Once you locate the file, select it by clicking on it one time and then click Open. In this example, the file to be opened is Lecture_week1.docx, and it is in the A_week1 folder.

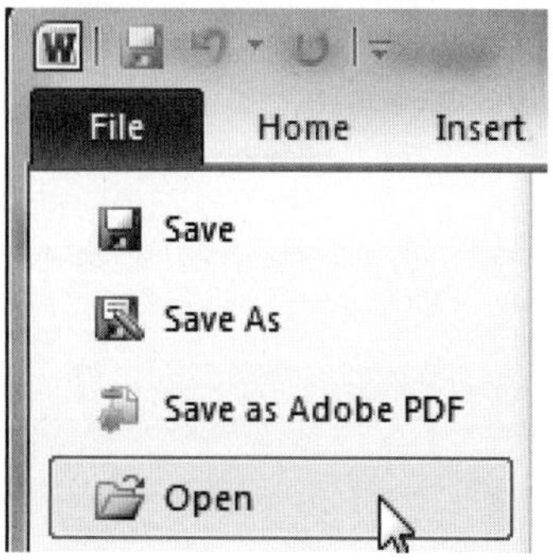

FIGURE A.17 Opening a File

ACCESSING AND OPENING A FILE USING THE COMPUTER OBJECT For this example, you want to access and open a file named Lecture_week1.doc located on the local disk, or C: drive, in a folder named A_week1. Double-click Computer on the desktop or select Computer from the Start menu (see Figure A.19), and the Computer window appears (see Figure A.20). Double-click the drive where the file is located. In this case, the drive is the C: drive.

In the local disk (C:) window, locate and double-click the A_week1 folder (see Figure A.20) to open it and then double-click the file Lecture_week1.docx. Notice the breadcrumbs, or path (Computer>Local Disk(C:) > A_week1), in the address bar.

OPENING A FILE USING RECENT ITEMS The Recent Items option on the Start menu presents a list of recently opened files. As mentioned earlier, if you do not see Recent Items, right-click on the Start button and select Properties. In the Taskbar and Start Menu Properties box, click Customize. Scroll down and check the Recent Items box. Click OK. Keep in mind that the list changes as you open and close files. Using Recent Items, you can quickly open a file that you have been working on without searching for it on your computer or opening the application that created it. Both the file and its application open when you open a file with Recent Items.

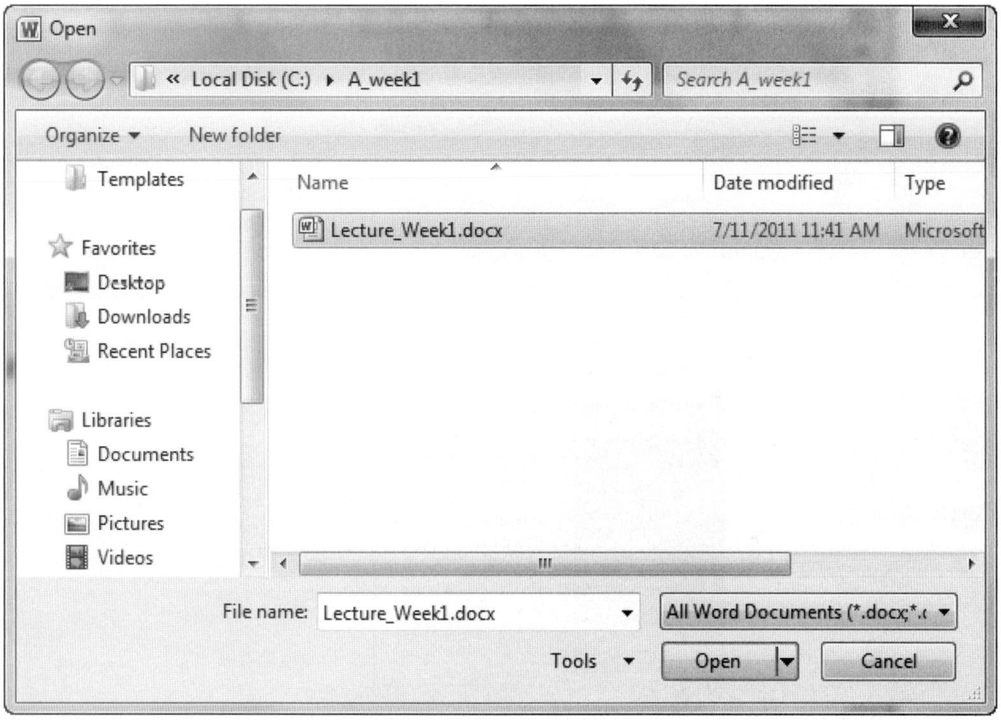

FIGURE A.18 The Open Dialog Box

Click the Start button and then select Recent Items, and a submenu appears. Click the name of the file that you want to open (see Figure A.21). This step assumes that you already have a file created and that you recently opened it. In this example, the Microsoft Word file Lecture_week1.docx opens.

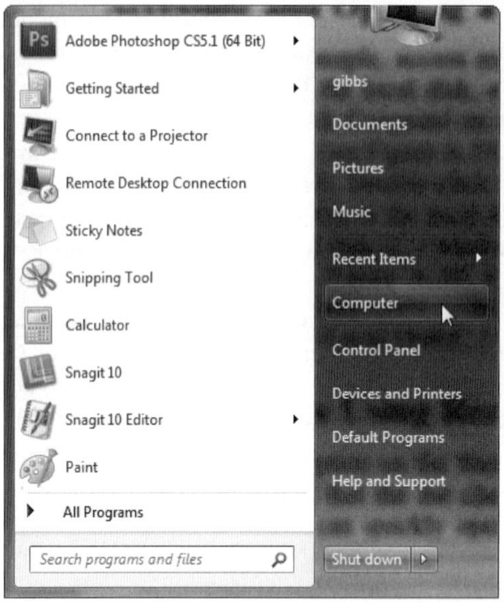

FIGURE A.19 The Computer Object

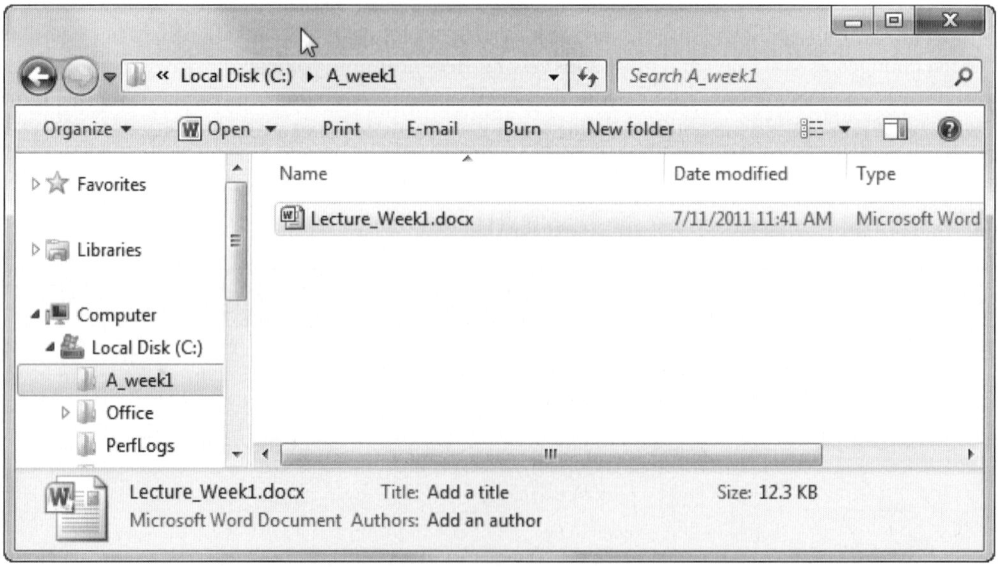

FIGURE A.20 The Computer Window

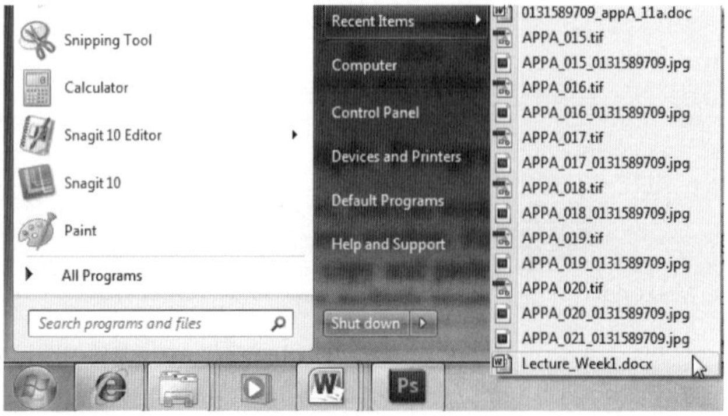

FIGURE A.21 Recent Items

OPENING MULTIPLE PROGRAMS

When using Windows, you can work with several files simultaneously, each of which opens in its own window. For example, you can open Microsoft Word and Excel files and copy and paste data between them. The following sections illustrate how to open multiple programs, switch between programs, reposition and resize program windows, and exchange data between programs.

Opening Programs

Click the Start button on the Windows taskbar. On the Start menu, click All Programs, and the Programs list appears. Click Microsoft Office to display the Microsoft Office group. Click Microsoft Word to open it. Word opens, with one blank untitled document. Notice that a button representing Word appears on the taskbar.

Open Microsoft Excel, and Excel opens with one blank workbook. You now have two programs open, Word and Excel, and each of these programs has one blank file.

Switching Between Programs

Word and Excel documents appear on the taskbar. If you are viewing an Excel document, switch to Word by clicking the Word button on the taskbar. Alternatively, you can switch between programs by pressing the Alt and Tab keys simultaneously (see Figure A.22). Pressing the Tab key repeatedly (while holding down the Alt key) changes the selection. Release the keys, and the selected program becomes active.

In addition to using the Alt and Tab keys, you can switch between programs by clicking the appropriate button on the taskbar (see Figure A.2). Clicking on a button makes the program active by bringing the application window to the forefront on the desktop.

Repositioning and Resizing Program Windows

In this example, you can resize the Word and Excel windows and then copy data from Excel into Word. If Word and Excel are open to full screen, restore them to adjust the window size. Click the Restore Down button at the top right of the window on the Word file. Remember that when a window is full screen, the Restore Down button replaces the Maximize button.

Switch to Excel by clicking the button that corresponds to it on the taskbar. Click the Restore Down button at the top right of the Excel window. *Note:* If, when you restore a Word file, you see Excel in the background, click on Excel's window. This makes Excel active, and it is an alternative to switching between programs using the taskbar. Clicking on windows in the background brings them to the foreground and makes them active.

Make either the Word or Excel window active. Resize the window by positioning the mouse pointer at the bottom-right corner of the window. The pointer changes to a double arrow (see Figure A.23). While holding down the left mouse button, drag upward and to the left. The length and width of the window should change.

Resize the Word and Excel windows so that they are both visible (see Figure A.24). For this example, assume that you have data in an Excel worksheet and you will copy the data to Word. Make the Excel window active by clicking its title bar or by selecting the Excel button on the taskbar. With the Excel window active, select the data in the spreadsheet and copy it.

FIGURE A.22 Program Switching (Using Alt+Tab)

Make the Word window active by clicking its title bar or by clicking the Word button on the taskbar. Now paste the data from Excel into the Word file. Notice in Figure A.24 that the Word window title bar (on the left) is darker and that the Excel window title bar is a lighter shade. The darker title bar indicates that the Word window is active.

To reposition either window, click on the title bar and, while pressing the left mouse button, drag the window to the desired location. You can also use Snap by clicking on a window's title bar and dragging the window to the right or left side of the desktop. When the cursor pointer intersects with the edge of the desktop, the window snaps or fills the respective half of the screen.

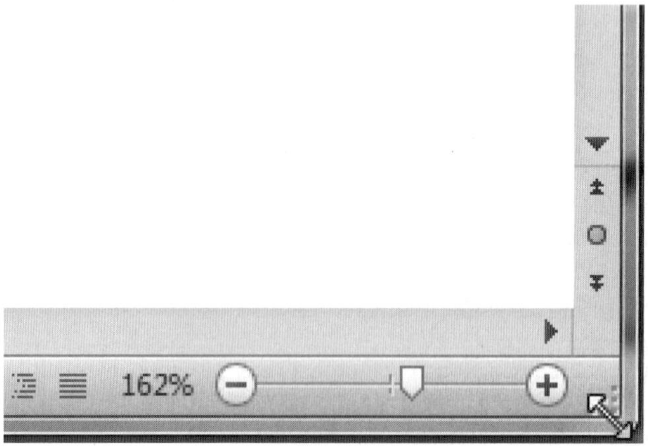

FIGURE A.23 Resizing a Window

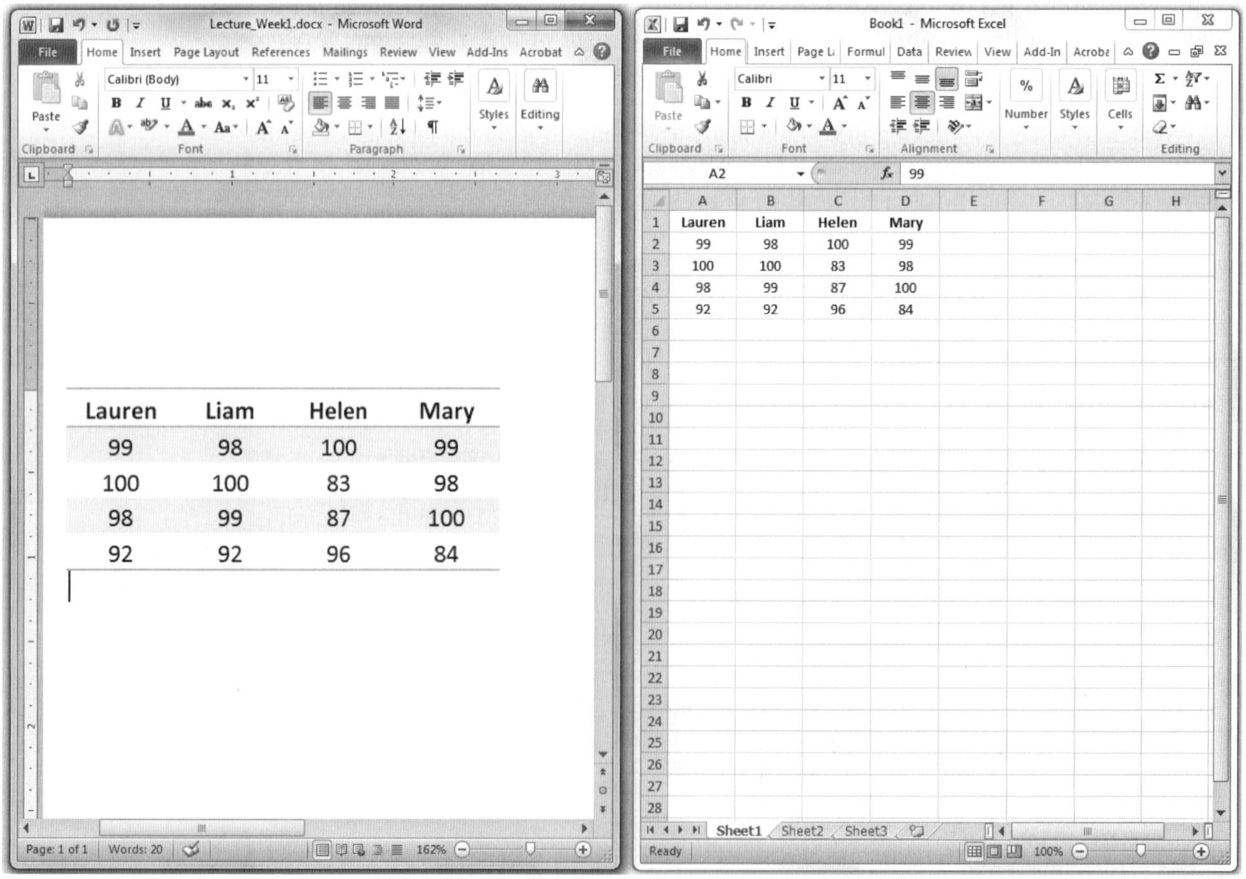

FIGURE A.24 Resizing Word and Excel Windows

QUITTING A PROGRAM

You can quit, or close, a program by clicking the Close/Quit button at the top-right corner of a window (see Figure A.25). The Close button also closes windows associated with folder. In addition, right-clicking on the title bar and selecting Close from the shortcut menu closes or quits the program. Also, right-clicking on the button icon on the taskbar displays a list of open files for that program. You can close them all by selecting Close All Windows (see Figure A.26).

When working in a program, you may have multiple documents open. In such cases, there is a main program window and within it are individual document windows. Each window has a Close button, and each window may appear as a button on the taskbar. For example, in Figure A.27, the Excel program window has Minimize, Maximize, and Close buttons, as do the individual document (Book1 and Book2) windows. The Book2 buttons will not display until the book is active. Clicking the Close button on Excel's program window closes Excel and all open documents. Clicking the Close button on a document window closes that document only. Excel and all other documents remain open.

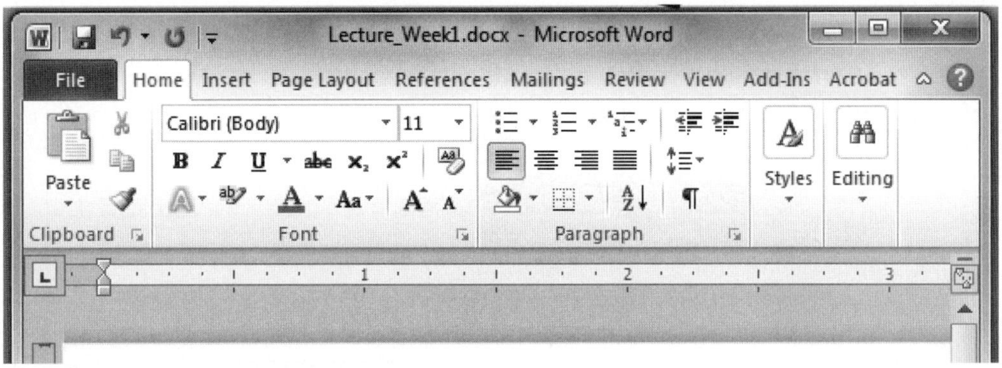

FIGURE A.25 A Close Button

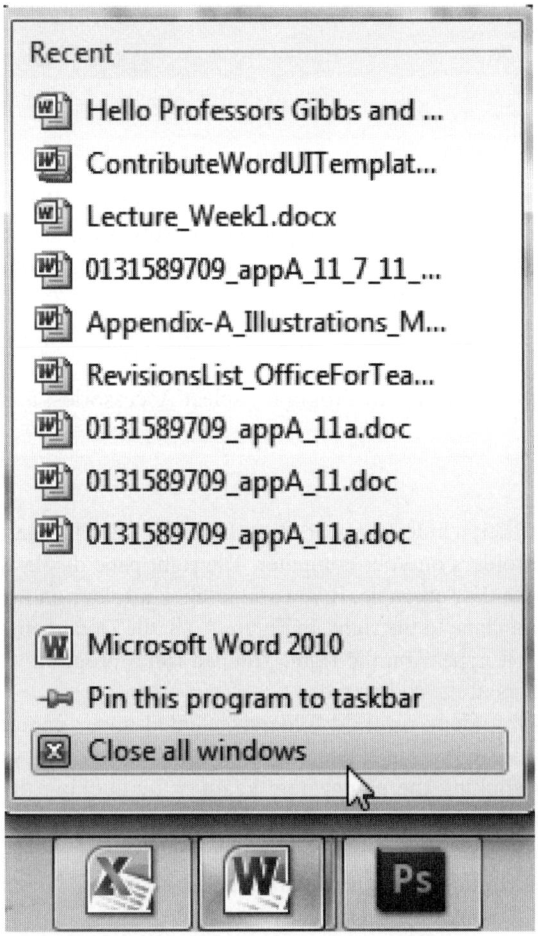

FIGURE A.26 Closing a Program

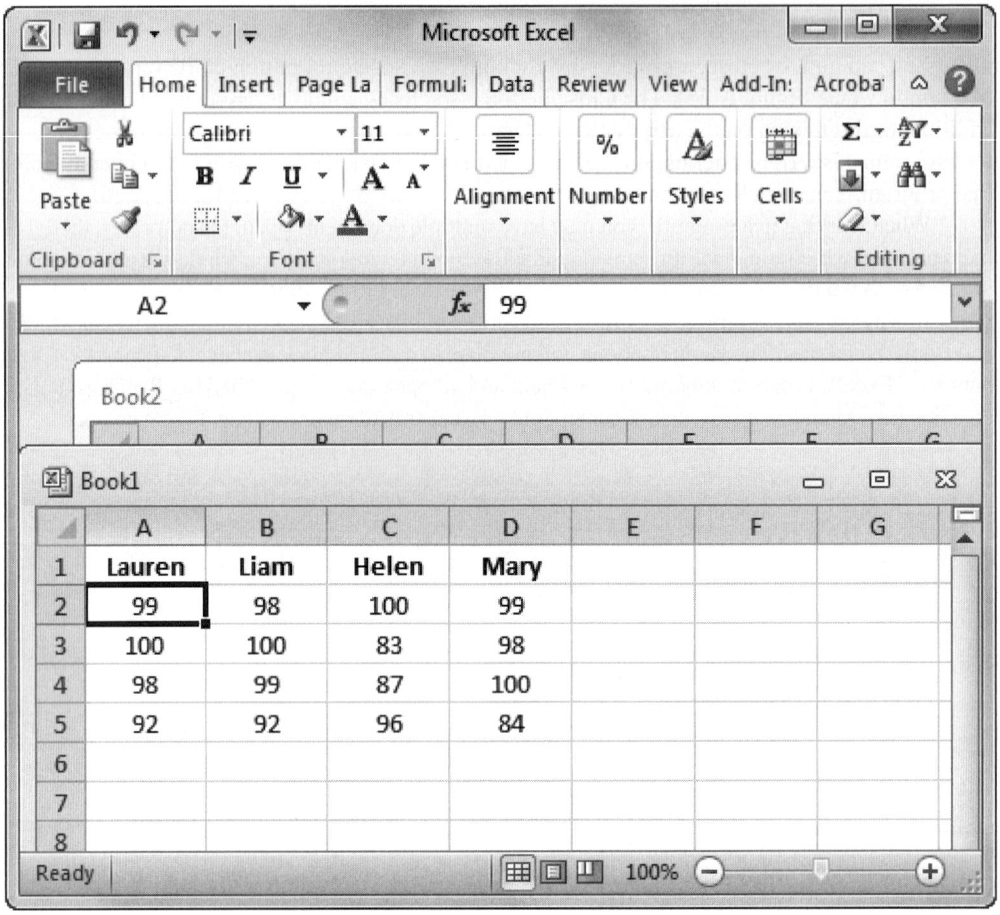

FIGURE A.27 Multiple Document Windows

WINDOWS EXPLORER

Windows Explorer allows you to view and manage files and folders on your computer. When you open Windows Explorer, you get a detailed view of your computer's contents, such as the contents of disk drives, folders, and any connected network drives. You can also manage your files and folders by using the Copy, Delete, and Move functions.

Opening Windows Explorer

To open Windows Explorer, click the Start menu, select All Programs, select Accessories, and then click Windows Explorer.

The Explorer Window

Once you open Windows Explorer, the Explorer window appears (see Figure A.28). The left pane of the window displays disk drives and folders on your computer. The right pane displays the contents of the item selected in the left pane. For example, if you single-click a folder on the left side of the screen, its contents display in the pane to the right. In Figure A.28, the Documents folder is selected, and the items contained in it appear on the right. You can run a program or open a file by double-clicking it when it appears in the right pane.

The panels present a hierarchy with subfolders, or child folders, indented under parent objects, such as disks and folders. Clicking disks or parent folders expands the list and displays the subfolders. You can collapse the list by clicking the parent item again or by clicking the small arrow that appears to the left of the item. In Figure A.29, the arrow to the left of the parent Computer object is selected, and items such as Local Disk (C:) appear. Clicking the arrow or parent object (Computer) again collapses the list. In this example, Local Disk (C:), Data (D:), and the other items are child objects of the parent Computer object.

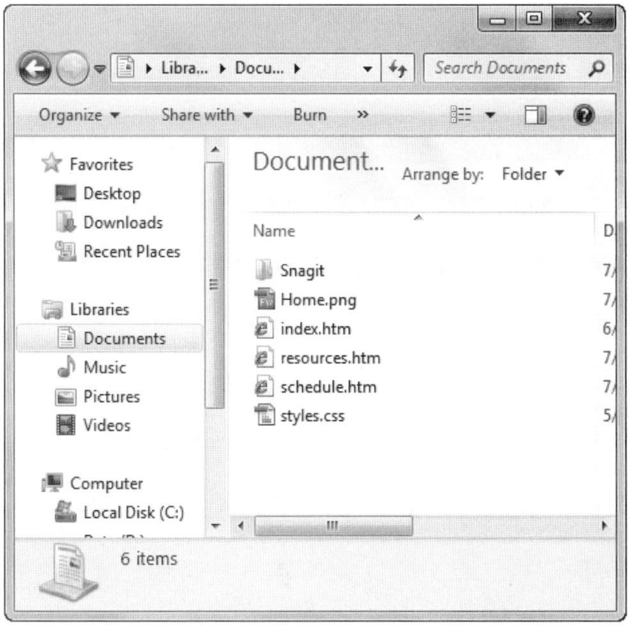

FIGURE A.28 Windows Explorer

FIGURE A.29 A Window Explorer Folder List

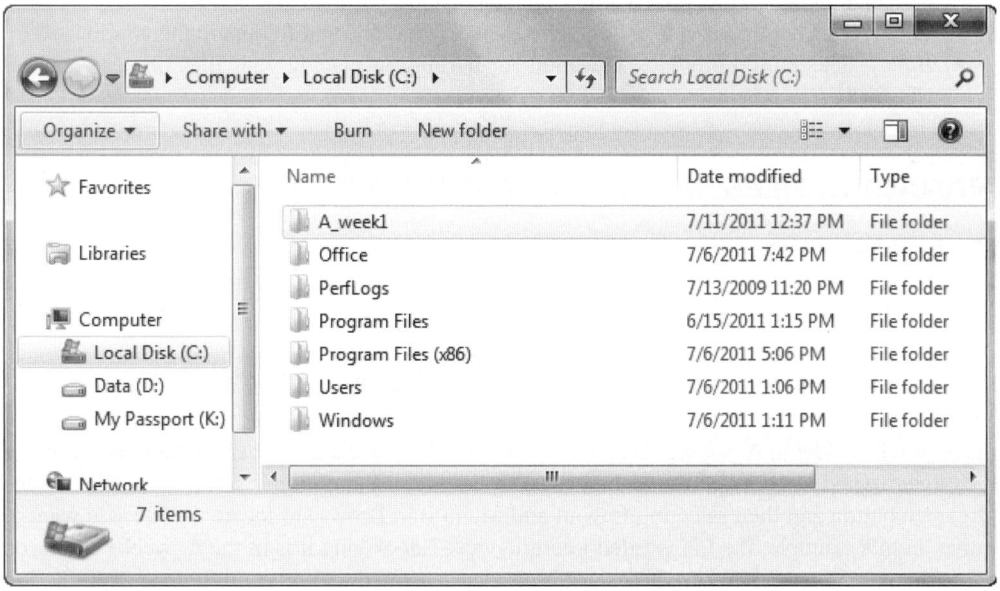

FIGURE A.30 The Explorer Toolbar

The Explorer Toolbar

The Windows Explorer toolbar makes working with files and folders easy. The Explorer toolbar (see Figure A.30) contains buttons to view and organize folders and to copy, move, and delete files, among other things:

- ***Back and Forward buttons***—The back arrow at the top left of the window takes you back through the most recently visited folders. After going back through recently visited folders using the Back button, Forward takes you forward though these same folders. You may also navigate across folders by using the drop-down list, as show in Figure A.31.
- ***Address bar***—The address bar provides the path (breadcrumbs) of the current folder. Click the down arrow to navigate to other locations on your computer. In Figure A.30, Computer. Local Disk (C:) is in the address bar.
- ***Search Local Disk (C:)***—This button allows you to type a search query in the search box to search the contents of your computer and all disks connected to it.

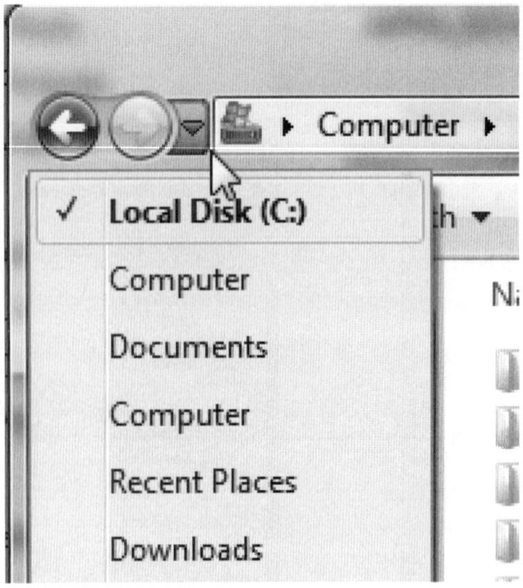

FIGURE A.31 A Drop-Down List

- ***Organize***—This button provides options for how the information in the window displays. The Layout option under Organize provides an option for adding a menu bar on the window that includes File, Edit, View, Tools, and Help.
- ***View***—This button provides alternative ways to view file and folders in the window.
- ***Burn***—This button provides an option for burning or placing your files on disk, such as CDs or DVDs.

MANAGING FILES: MOVING AND COPYING FILES

Moving a File

When moving a file or folder, the object you want to move is removed from one location (e.g., folder or disk) and placed in another location. Note that the Move command differs from Copy. Copy places a duplicate file in the location of your choice and leaves the original file unaltered. To move a file or folder, open Windows Explorer. Find the file or folder that you want to move and click on it one time to select it. For this example, move the file Lecture_week1.docx from the A_week1 folder to A_week2. One way to do this is to place a menu bar on the window, using the Organize and Layout options. In Figure A.32, the Menu Bar option is selected by clicking the Organize button and then selecting Layout and Menu Bar. Browse to locate the file you want to move. In this example, the file is titled Lecture_week1.docx, and it is in the A_week1 folder on the local disk drive (C:). When the A_week1 folder is located and selected, it appears in the left panel, and the file appears in the right panel. Select the file by clicking on it one time.

Select Move to Folder from the Edit menu (see Figure A.33), and the Move Items box appears (see Figure A.34). Select the folder where you want to move the file, which in this example is A_week2. Click Move, and Windows Explorer moves Lecture_week1.docx from A_week1 to A_week2.

Alternatively, you can move files by dragging and dropping them. Using the same example as previously, move Lecture_week1.docx from the A_week1 folder to A_week2 by dragging and dropping it.

Locate and select the Lecture_week1.docx file. Click on it and, while holding down the left mouse button, drag it to the A_week2 folder. The A_week2 folder is highlighted as the mouse pointer approaches it. With the folder highlighted, release the mouse button, and the file moves to A_week2.

A third method you can use to move a file or folder is to select the object you want to move by clicking it one time. From the Edit menu, select Cut or press Ctrl+X. Determine the new location where you want to place the file or folder. Select Paste from the Edit menu or press Ctrl+V. This cuts the object from its present location and places it in the new location.

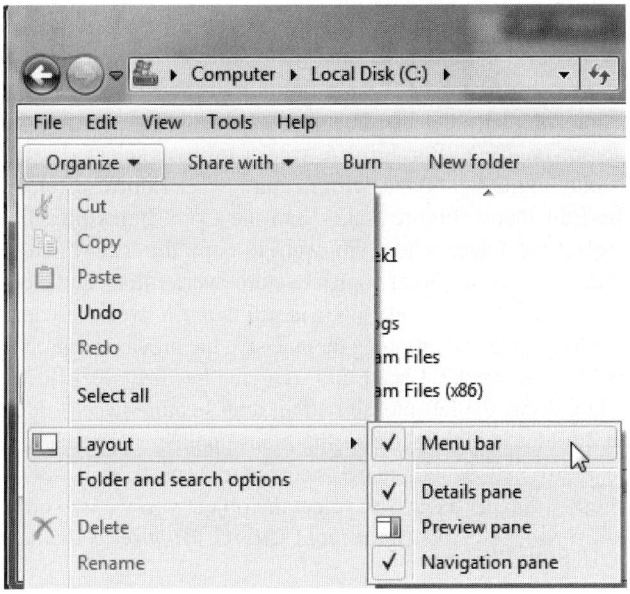

FIGURE A.32 Organize Layout Options

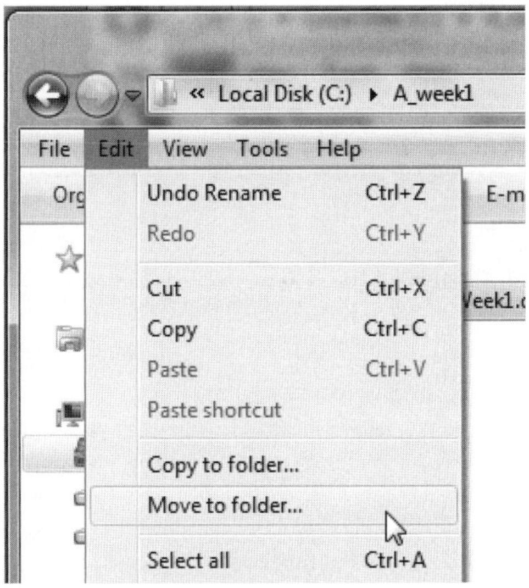

FIGURE A.33 Moving a File

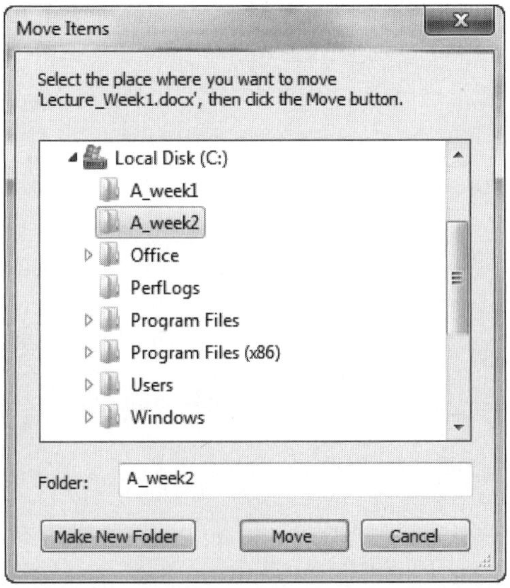

FIGURE A.34 The Move Items Box

Copying a File

The Copy function duplicates a file or folder. Find and select the file or folder that you want to copy. For this example, make a copy of the Lecture_week1.docx file in the A_week1 folder and place the copy in A_week2. Ensure that the menu bar displays in the window by clicking the Organize button and then selecting Layout and Menu Bar. If the A_week1 folder is selected in the left pane, the contents of A_week1 display in the right pane, with Lecture_week1.docx selected.

Select Copy to Folder from the Edit menu (Figure A.35), and the Copy Items box displays (see Figure A.36). Locate and select the folder where you want to copy the file, which in this example is A_week2. Click OK, and Windows Explorer copies Lecture_week1.docx and places the copy in A_week2. The original copy of Lecture_week1.docx is still in the A_week1 folder.

Alternatively, you can copy files by dragging and dropping them. Using the previous example, you will copy the Lecture_week1.docx file to A_week2. Locate and select the Lecture_week1.docx file. Press the Ctrl key and, while holding down the left mouse button, drag Lecture_week1.docx onto the A_week2 folder. The A_week2 folder is highlighted as the mouse pointer approaches it. With the folder highlighted, release the mouse button, and the file is copied to A_week2.

A third method you can use to copy a file or folder is to select the object you want to copy by clicking it one time. From the Edit menu, select Copy or press Ctrl+C. Browse to the new

FIGURE A.35 The Copy to Folder Option

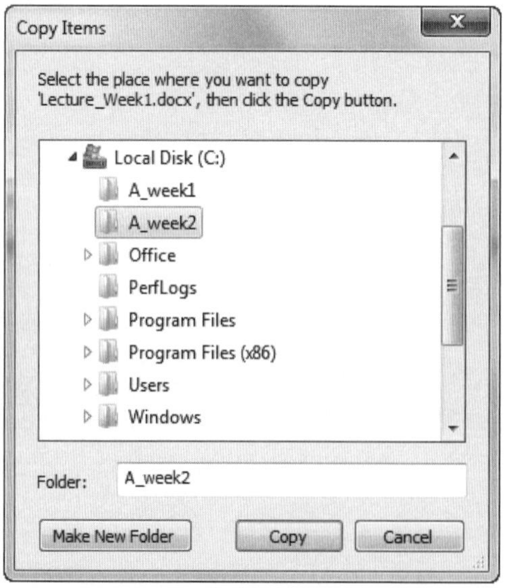

FIGURE A.36 The Copy Items Box

location where you want to place the copied file or folder. Select Paste from the Edit menu or press Ctrl+V. This copies the object and places a copy of it in the new location.

DELETING FILES AND FOLDERS

There are several ways to delete files and folders, two of which are presented next: (a) using a shortcut menu and (b) using the Delete key.

Using a Shortcut Menu to Delete Files

Suppose you want to delete a file named Lecture_week1.docx located in the A_week1 folder. Find and select Lecture_week1.docx and right-click it. Right-clicking on a file or folder displays a shortcut menu (see Figure A.37).

Select Delete, and the Confirm File Delete box appears (see Figure A.38). Click Yes to send the file or folder to the Recycle Bin.

To remove a file or folder from your computer without sending it to the Recycle Bin, press the Shift key while selecting Delete.

Using the Delete Key to Delete Files or Folders

Another way to delete files or folders is to select the item to be deleted and press the Delete key. The Delete File box appears, asking whether you want to send the file to the Recycle Bin. Click Yes if you want to remove the file from its current location and place it in the Recycle Bin. Remember that files or folders in the Recycle Bin can be recovered. In addition, they take up disk storage space and remain on the computer until you empty the Recycle Bin.

Emptying the Recycle Bin

Windows sends all deleted files and folders to the Recycle Bin before removing them from your computer. You must empty the Recycle Bin to remove deleted files or folders.

Windows does not send items on removable disks to the Recycle Bin. Instead, Windows removes files or folders on removable disks from your computer as soon as you issue the delete command. They are not sent to the Recycle Bin.

To empty the Recycle Bin, right-click Recycle Bin on the desktop and then select Empty Recycle Bin from the shortcut menu (see Figure A.39). The Delete File box appears. Click Yes to remove the files or folders. When you empty the Recycle Bin, deleted files are permanently removed from your computer.

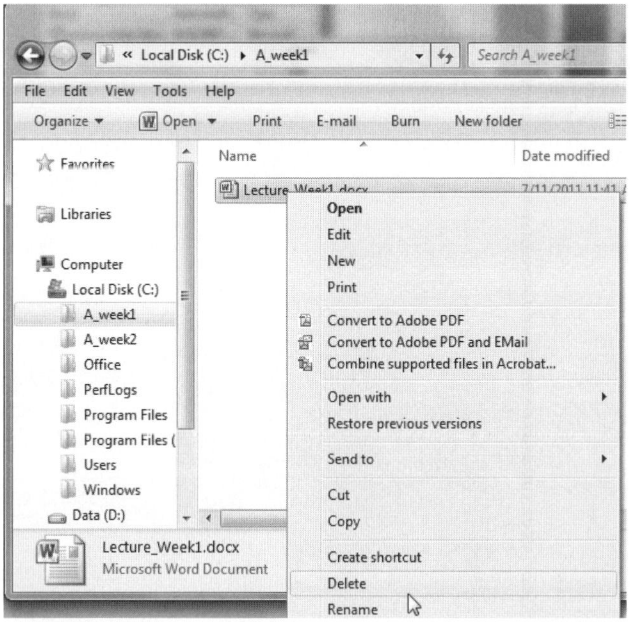

FIGURE A.37 Deleting Files

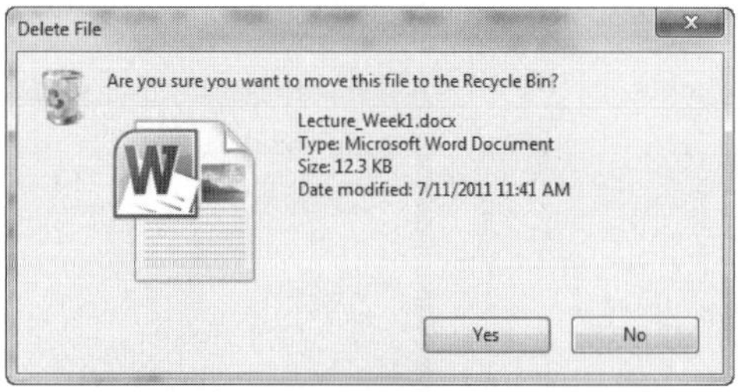

FIGURE A.38 Deleting a File

FIGURE A.39 Emptying the Recycle Bin

SELECTING MULTIPLE FILES

In the preceding discussion, the examples illustrate moving, copying, and deleting one file at a time. You can also select multiple items at one time to be moved, copied, or deleted.

To select multiple items that are adjacent, press the Shift key and click the first and last items. If, for example, you have 14 files that you want to select, press the Shift key and click items 1 and 14. This action selects all items between and including 1 and 14. When items to be selected are not adjacent, press the Ctrl key and click the files, folders, or programs that you want to select.

You can select numerous files and folders by clicking the left mouse button and, while holding it down, dragging across the items that you want selected.

RENAMING A FILE

Right-click the file or folder that you want to rename and select Rename from the shortcut menu that appears. The file name becomes selected, and a blinking cursor appears in the name box. Type a new name and press Enter or click outside the name box.

Another way to change a file or folder name is to click on the item two times, pausing briefly between clicks. The first click selects the item, and the second click makes the name available for editing.

SEARCHING FOR FILES OR FOLDERS

Search is a useful tool for locating files or folders on your computer and information on the Internet. To locate a file or folder on your computer, click the Start button and type directly into the Search Programs and Files box. Press Enter to begin the search. A list of results appears (see Figure A.40).

You can search from Windows Explorer. In the Search box at the top right, type the name of the file or folder you want to locate. Press Enter to begin the search. For example, typing Lecture_week1.docx will locate files with this name in all locations on your computer (see Figure A.41).

Specify where to search for files or folders by clicking the down arrow on the right side of the Address box.

In Figure A.42, notice the word Lecture1 under the Tags column on the right side of the window. Suppose you have several files, each of which relates to the first lecture of the term, Lecture1. You can right-click each one of the four files and on the shortcut menu select Properties. When the Properties box appears, click the Details tab (see Figure A.43) and next to the Tags item type a word or phrase (i.e., Lecture 1) that will help you identify the file. You can type multiple items as long as you separate them with semicolons. Then when you search, you can type the tag identifier in the search box, and Windows 7 will locate all the files with that tag, such as those shown in Figure A.42.

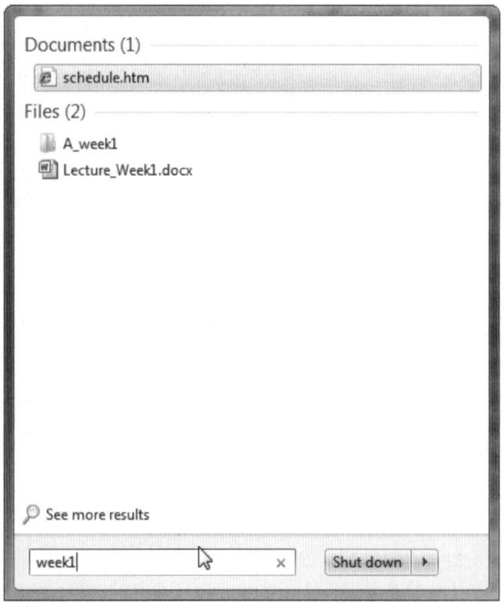

FIGURE A.40 Searching

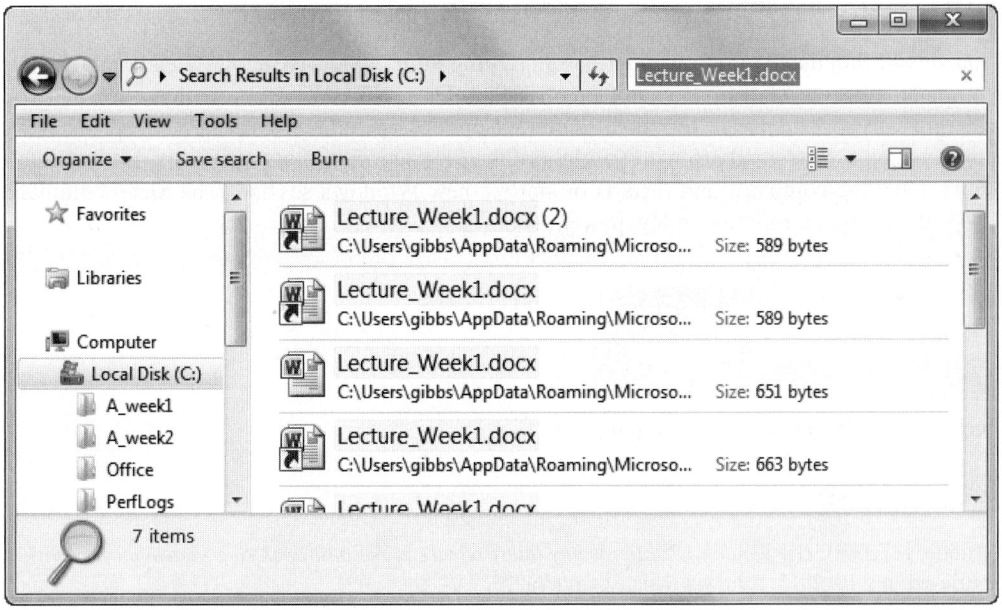

FIGURE A.41 Searching from Windows Explorer

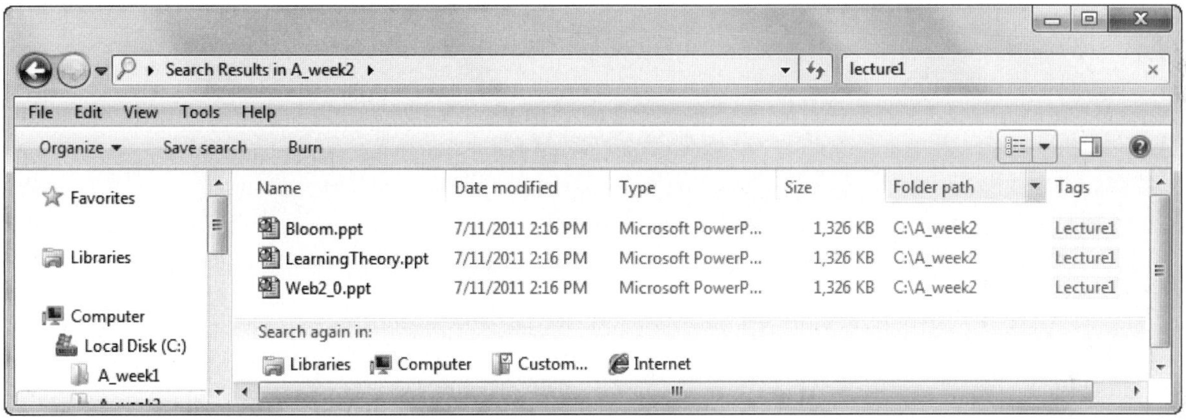

FIGURE A.42 Searching by Tags

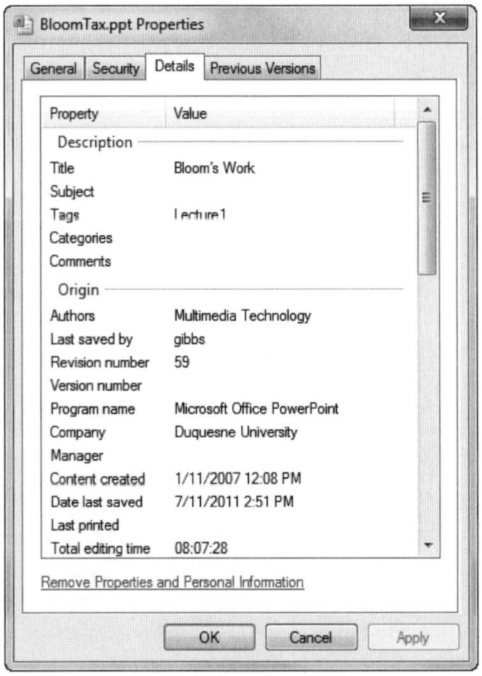

FIGURE A.43 Tagging Files

SHUTTING DOWN YOUR COMPUTER

You should shut down your computer before turning it off. To exit Windows 7 and turn off your computer, click the Start button and then click Shut Down. The Windows session ends, and you can turn off your computer. Additional shutdown options, including Restart and Sleep, are available by clicking the small arrow to the right of the Shut Down option (see Figure A.44). Restart shuts down the computer and restarts or starts a new Windows session. The Sleep command keeps the computer running on low power.

FIGURE A.44 Shutting Down a Computer

REFERENCE

Manjoo, F. (2009). *Get Windows 7. Microsoft's latest release is the best operating system on the market.* Retrieved July 10, 2011, from www.slate.com/id/2233294/.

APPENDIX B

Macintosh

This appendix provides a basic overview of the Macintosh operating system. It presents fundamental features of the operating system (OS) and explains how to use them when working with Office.

The Macintosh OS helps you access Office applications and organize information or data on your computer. You interact with the applications and associated files through adjustable rectangular areas, or windows, that appear on your computer screen. The OS has a graphical user interface. It contains objects (e.g., buttons and icons) through which you access and work with files, folders, and programs. The interface makes working with a computer easy and efficient, and it eliminates the need to type commands, which are often confusing.

THE DESKTOP

Typically, the desktop displays when the computer is turned on. The desktop is the work area where you place files and folders. The folders, programs, and files that you open display in rectangular windows on the desktop. Several objects appear on the desktop and represent disks, folders, applications, files, or system resources. To activate these items, double-click on them. For example, the hard drive (HD) icon when double-clicked provides access to the contents of your computer or to the contents of a folder.

ALIASES

A useful item for obtaining quick access to your computer contents is the alias. Aliases on the desktop provide easy access to files and programs. Instead of searching your computer each time you want to open a frequently used file or program, you can place an alias to it on the desktop. When you double-click the alias, the file, program, or disk opens.

Aliases look different from other desktop icons. The icon of each alias has a small arrow at the bottom-left corner, and the icon's text is italicized.

You can place an alias on the desktop to access Office applications. For example, to make an alias, locate the Office applications icons. Click on the icon (e.g., Word) and press the Command key and the letter L at the same time. Once the alias is created, drag it to the desktop or to the Dock.

ITEMS ON THE DESKTOP

A desktop may contain the following features:

- ***Macintosh HD icon***—This icon allows you to see the contents of your computer's hard drive. For instance, double-clicking the Macintosh HD icon opens the Macintosh HD window that displays all the folders or directories and files contained on your computer. You can change the name of the Macintosh HD icon by clicking the icon's name and typing.
- ***Trash***—The Trash temporarily stores files that you want to delete. A Trash icon can be found on the Dock. All files that you intend to delete get sent first to the Trash, and only when the Trash is emptied are the files removed from your computer permanently. You can retrieve files from the Trash as long as you have not emptied it.
- ***The Dock***—The Dock gives access to frequently used items. The Dock is located at the bottom of the screen (desktop) but can be moved or resized. The Trash icon is found on the Dock. Click an item in the Dock, and it opens. Minimized documents contract to the Dock. You can add to it by dragging an item over the Dock and dropping it.
- ***Desktop menu***—The desktop menu contains several items that help you work with your computer and its files. The items include Apple, Finder, File, Edit, View, Go, Window, and Help. The desktop menu is located at the top of the screen.

DESKTOP MENU ITEMS

When working with the Microsoft Office applications, you use the desktop menu often. The desktop menu contains the following items:

- *Apple*—Allows quick access to system preferences. You can shut down, restart, or put your computer to sleep. Clicking the Apple on the desktop menu bar displays the Apple menu. An arrow to the right of a menu item indicates that more items, or submenus, are available. When you pass the mouse over the arrow, a submenu appears.
- *File*—This item allows you to perform operations with disks, files, folders, windows, and applications. You can also use the File menu to search the contents of the hard drive and other disks.
- *Edit*—You use the Edit menu to copy and paste when working on the desktop, to select items, and to set desktop preferences.
- *View*—You use the View menu to change the way files, programs, folders, and information about them display on your computer screen.
- *Go*—You use Go to access folders, drives, files, and applications on your computer.
- *Window*—You use the Window menu to close or activate windows opened on the desktop.
- *Help*—You use Help to get information about your computer and how to use it. This menu option opens the Help module, which provides information about the Macintosh OS and many of its features and functions.
- *The Dock*—Located on the bottom of the desktop, the Dock allows you to alternate among all open applications. As you open applications, their icons appear in the Dock. You switch among them by clicking the Applications menu and selecting the item you need.

SELECTING ICONS

The mouse is an integral component of your computer, and it enables you to work with applications such as Office. You can use the mouse to select icons, make choices from dialog boxes and pull-down menus, and move and resize windows.

You select items by clicking on them one time with the mouse, and you open items by double-clicking on them. Selecting an item signals to the computer that you are going to work with the selected object in some way, such as opening or moving it. Icons are highlighted when they are selected.

Double-clicking an object or icon opens it in a window on the desktop. For example, double-clicking a hard drive icon on the desktop opens its contents.

Icons appear in different states. By default, icons are unselected. When you click an icon one time, it becomes selected, a border appears around the icon, and it becomes highlighted. If you want to change the file name, click on the icon name and then type the new name. To select the icon's name, click on the file name rather than the document's icon.

CONTEXTUAL MENUS

Using contextual menus can be an efficient way to access and work with files, folders, and windows, among other things. By clicking the mouse pointer on a folder, a file, a window's title, or the desktop and holding down the Ctrl key, a menu appears, displaying the commands for that item.

REPOSITIONING AND RESIZING WINDOWS

Often you will have several files or programs open at the same time. To work efficiently, you may want to reposition the document windows. Every window has a title bar that displays the window name. You can reposition a window by clicking on the title bar and, while holding down the mouse button, dragging the window to a new location. You can also activate a window by clicking on the title bar or any location within the window.

Title bars contain three buttons. Close closes the active window. Minimize makes the window larger or reduces the window to its previous size after it has been enlarged. Collapse collapses the window so that only the title bar is visible.

You scroll horizontally in a window by clicking the scroll arrows at the bottom of the window. You scroll vertically by clicking the arrows to the right of the window. You may also move quickly across or up and down a window by dragging the scroll bar.

To make a window larger or smaller, move the mouse pointer over the resize box at the window's bottom-right corner. Drag the border to enlarge or reduce the size of the window. A box appears around the window as you resize it. When resizing a window, dragging diagonally resizes the window proportionally.

WORKING WITH PROGRAMS AND FILES

Opening Programs

There are several ways to open an application such as Microsoft Word. If you see the application's icon (e.g., Word) on the Dock, click it, and the application opens.

Another way to open an application (e.g., Word) is to double-click the Macintosh HD icon on the desktop, locate the Applications folder, and double-click it. Within Applications, double-click the Microsoft Office folder and then double-click the application's icon.

Opening Files

There are multiple ways to open a file. In this section, we discuss three methods of opening a file: (a) opening a file using the application that created it, (b) accessing and opening a file by using the Macintosh HD icon, and (c) opening a file by using Recent Documents from the Apple menu.

Opening a File Using the Application That Created It

To begin using this method, open the application with which you created the file. For this example, open a file created with Microsoft Word.

Once Word is open, click File and select Open. The Open dialog box appears. Use the Open dialog box to locate the folder or file you want to open. If you need to open a file in a different folder, click the double arrows on the location box and then select the disk drive or folder that contains the item. Once you locate the file, select it by clicking on it one time and then click Open.

Accessing and Opening a File by Using the Macintosh HD Icon

You can use the Macintosh HD icon to access and open a file located on the computer's hard drive in a folder named Classes. Double-click the Macintosh HD icon on the desktop, and its window appears. Double-click the folder that contains the file you want to open. Suppose the file Lecture_week4.doc is in a folder titled Classes. Locate and double-click the Classes folder to open the Classes window. In the Classes window, locate the file Lecture_week4.doc and double-click it to open the file.

Opening a File by Using Recent Items

Recent Items on the Apple menu presents a list of recently opened files and applications. Using Recent Items, you can quickly open a file that you have been working on without searching for it on your computer or opening the application that created it. The Recent Items option opens both the file and its application. Keep in mind that the Recent Items list changes as you open and close files.

Click Apple and then select Recent Items. The Recent Items submenu appears. Click the name of the file you want to open. This method assumes that you already have a file created and that you recently opened it.

OPENING MULTIPLE PROGRAMS

You can work with several files simultaneously, with each file open in its own window. For instance, you might open Microsoft Word and Excel files and copy and paste data between them. The following sections illustrate how to open multiple programs, switch between programs, and reposition and resize program windows.

Opening Programs

Open Word by clicking its icon on the Dock or by accessing it through the computer hard drive. Word opens, with one blank untitled document. Repeat the process for Excel. You now have two programs open, Word and Excel, and each program displays one blank document. Both program icons appear on the Dock.

Switching Between Programs

Use the Dock to switch between Word and Excel. If you are viewing an Excel document, switch to Word by clicking the Word icon on the Dock. Alternatively, you can switch between applications by pressing the Command and Tab keys simultaneously. When you press Command+Tab, program icons display onscreen, indicating the active program. Repeatedly pressing the Tab key changes the selection. Release the key, and the selected program becomes active.

Repositioning and Resizing Program Windows

You can resize Word and Excel windows and then copy data from Excel into Word. If Word and Excel are open to full screen, restore them to adjust the window size. Click the Zoom (expand/contract) button at the top-left corner of the window on the Word file. Switch to Excel by selecting it on the Dock and, if it is full screen, reduce it. *Note:* If you are in Word and see Excel in the background, click on Excel's window. This makes Excel active; it is an alternative to switching between programs using the Dock. When programs are visible, clicking on them in the background brings them to the foreground and makes them active.

Resize document windows. Make either the Word or Excel window active. Position the mouse cursor at the bottom-right corner of the window. The cursor changes to an arrow. While holding down the mouse button, drag upward and to the left. A shadowed box displays around the window as it resizes.

Resize the Word and Excel windows so that are both visible. If you need to reposition either window, click on the title bar and, while pressing the mouse button, drag the window to the desired location. For this example, suppose you have a data set entered into Excel. Make the Excel window active by clicking its title bar or by selecting the Excel icon on the Dock. With the Excel window active, select the data in the spreadsheet and copy it. Make the Word window active by clicking its title bar or by selecting the Word icon on the Dock. Now paste the data from Excel into the Word file. The data appear in a table within Word. You may notice that the Word window is darker than Excel's window. The darker shaded window indicates the active program.

CLOSING A FILE

Clicking the Close button at the top-left corner of a window closes the file. In addition, the Close button closes windows associated with folders. You can also close a file by selecting Close from the application's File menu. When you close a file, only the active file is closed. The program and any other files remain open. When working in a program, you may have multiple documents open. In such cases, each document has a window, and each window has a Close button. For example, suppose you have two Word documents open (Document 4 and Document 5). Clicking the Close button on Document 5 closes only the Document 5 file. The Document 4 file remains open.

QUITTING AN APPLICATION

To quit a program, select Quit from the program's menu or press the Command+Q. Quitting a program closes the application (e.g., Word or Excel) and all open files created in that program.

VIEWING THE CONTENTS OF YOUR COMPUTER

There are several ways to view the contents of your computer. Double-clicking the hard drive icon on the desktop is an easy way to access the contents of your computer. You can also select Computer from the Go menu. This allows you to view and manage files and folders. You get a detailed view of your computer's contents, such as the folder contents, files, and programs.

THE COMPUTER WINDOW

When you open the Computer window, you will see the programs, files, and folders contained on your computer's hard drive, as well as devices (disk drives) connected to your computer. You can view these items in a variety of ways, including as lists, icons, or columns.

You can alter the view (e.g., icon, list, and columns) of window contents by selecting As Icons, As List, or As Columns from the View menu on the desktop. Double-click a folder to view its contents or, when in the List view, click the arrow to the left of the folder to expand or collapse it. When a folder is expanded (by clicking the arrow to its left), the arrow turns downward. The contents of the folder appear indented under it. From the Computer window, you can also open files and programs by double-clicking their icons.

MANAGING FILES: MOVING, COPYING, DELETING, AND RENAMING FILES

This section explains how to manage files with the Macintosh operating system.

Moving a File

When moving a file or folder, you move it from one location (e.g., folder or disk) to another. If, for example, you have a file titled MyLesson.doc in a folder titled Week1, when you move MyLesson.doc from the Week1 folder to another folder, MyLesson.doc is no longer in the Week1 folder. The Move command differs from Copy. Copy places a duplicate file in the location of your choice. It leaves the original file in place and unaltered.

You can move files by dragging and dropping them. To move a file or folder, open the Computer window by selecting Computer from the Go menu or double-clicking the hard drives icon on the desktop. Find the file or folder you want to move and click it one time to select it. While holding down the left mouse button, drag the file or folder onto the destination folder. The folder highlights as the mouse pointer approaches it. With the folder highlighted, release the mouse button, and the file or folder moves to the destination folder.

Copying a File

The Copy function duplicates a file or folder. Find and select the file or folder you want to copy. For this example, make a copy of a file and place the copy in a folder. Click on a file to select it. From the desktop File menu, select Duplicate (or press Command+D), and a copy of the file appears. Notice that the duplicated file appears next to the original, with the word Copy in the name. Now move the duplicate file to a folder by dragging it on top of the destination folder and dropping it.

Alternatively, to copy a file, you can drag and drop it onto the destination folder while holding down the Option key. This duplicates the file and places the copy inside the folder. With this method, Copy is not appended to the file name.

Deleting Files and Folders

There are several ways to delete files and folders, two of which are presented here: using the Move to Trash option and dragging and dropping files to the Trash.

Suppose you want to delete a file named Lecture_week4.doc located in a folder named Data. Find and select Lecture_week4.doc and then select Move to Trash on the desktop File menu. This command removes the file from its current location and places it in the Trash. Alternatively, once you select the file, you can send it to the Trash by pressing Command+Delete.

Remember that files or folders in the Trash can be recovered or retrieved. In addition, files or folders in the Trash take up disk storage space, and only after emptying the Trash are they removed from your computer permanently.

Another way to delete files is to drag and drop them in the Trash. Locate the file that you want to delete. Click it once to select it and, while holding down the mouse button, drag the file to the Trash on the Dock. As the mouse pointer approaches the Trash icon on the Dock, the icon becomes highlighted. With the Trash icon highlighted, release the mouse, and the file is moved to the Trash.

Emptying the Trash

All deleted files and folders are sent to the Trash before they are removed from your computer. You must empty the Trash to permanently remove deleted files or folders. Empty the Trash by selecting Empty Trash from the Finder menu. You can also empty the Trash by pressing Command+Shift+Delete. Another way to empty the Trash is by pressing the Control key while clicking the Trash icon on the Dock.

An alert box appears, asking if you want to remove the items from the Trash. Click Empty Trash to remove the items.

Selecting Multiple Files

In the preceding discussion, the examples illustrate moving, copying, and deleting one file at a time. You can also select multiple items at one time to be moved, copied, or deleted.

To select multiple items that are adjacent, click the mouse button and, while holding it down, drag across the items you want to select. After highlighting all the items that you want selected, release the mouse button.

When items to be selected are not adjacent, press the Command key and click the files, folders, or programs that you want to select.

Renaming a File

Click the file or folder that you want to rename. Click on the item's name rather than on the icon. Clicking the name selects the text. With the text selected, you can edit it or type a new name.

SEARCHING FOR FILES OR FOLDERS

Search is a useful tool for locating files, folders, or applications on your computer and information on the Internet. To locate a file or folder on your computer, click the File menu on the desktop and select Find. The Find box appears. In the Search in box, type the name of the file or folder you want to locate. You can search for items by file name or by content. Specify where to search for files or folders by selecting the location with the Search In box option. Begin the search by clicking the Search button, and the Search Results screen appears. You can stop the search at any time by closing the Search Results screen.

SHUTTING DOWN YOUR COMPUTER

You should shut down your computer before turning it off. To exit the Mac OS and turn off your computer, click the Apple menu on the desktop and select Shut Down.

On the Apple menu, you will notice several options, including Restart and Sleep. Restart shuts down and restarts the computer or starts a new session. Sleep keeps the computer running on low power, but it maintains the contents of memory. While the computer is in the Sleep mode, touching a key wakes the computer.

THE MICROSOFT OFFICE WORKSPACES: MACINTOSH AND WINDOWS

Overall, the menu items, toolbars, and workspaces between the Macintosh and Windows versions of Office are similar. Both versions offer many of the same options and features. The Macintosh and Windows versions of Microsoft Office offer a variety of methods for accomplishing similar tasks. An understanding of the Macintosh operating system components, such as the desktop, and knowledge of the varied approaches that it offers for opening and managing files and programs will be beneficial to you when using Microsoft Office.

GLOSSARY

Acceptable Use Policies: A set of rules for students, teachers, staff, and administrators that govern the use of school or school district computers, networks, and the Internet.

Alias: A file that provides quick access to frequently used items, such as programs, folders, documents, or disks. An alias is equivalent to a shortcut on the Windows platform.

Application: A software program that performs a specific function or purpose. For example, Word is an application that helps you compose a letter or a report and Excel is an application that helps you analyze data. Word, Excel, and PowerPoint are all applications.

Attachment: A file sent along with an e-mail message. Documents, pictures, and multimedia objects may be sent; the receiving computer must have the software installed to read the attached file.

AutoCorrection: A Word feature that allows you to undo automatic corrections or select a different AutoCorrect option.

Cell: A unit in an Excel worksheet column that holds information such as text and numerical data.

Clip Art: Professionally prepared art stored as files that may be inserted in Office applications.

Commands: Tasks that are performed in an Office program, such as Open and Save, and that are found in the Office menu bars.

Contacts: An Outlook folder that maintains an address book.

Copyright: Laws that regulate and describe the manner in which materials may be used and copied.

Design Templates: Predefined colors, layout formats, and font styles that give PowerPoint presentations and Word documents a specific look.

Desktop: A work area on a computer where you place files and folders. The desktop is the screen that typically appears when you first turn on the computer.

Document Object: A Word document that has been inserted into a file.

Drag and Drop: A method of moving objects by dragging them with a mouse and dropping them in a desired location by releasing the mouse button.

Dragging: A method of moving objects by dragging them with a computer mouse.

Embedding: A method of inserting an object in an Office application file whereby the object embeds or becomes part of the file.

Expanded Menu: A menu format that displays all the commands in a pull-down list.

Field: In a database, a specific category or location to store information. For example, a field called *first name* could store students' first names.

File: A unit of information produced by a program (e.g., Microsoft Word). For example, Word documents, PowerPoint presentations, and Excel workbooks are files. To organize files, you put them in folders.

Folder: Often referred to as a directory, a place to store digital work files. Placing work files into folders keeps them organized.

Form: A database object that presents display boxes where information can be displayed or entered. A form usually displays one record at a time.

Formatting: Refers to characteristics (e.g., bold, italic, color, size, type, and so on) applied to text, tables, lists, and documents. In a document, it allows for paragraph formatting or changing columns.

Formula: An Excel expression in the form of a series of numbers or cell references that produces a new value. The formula = (A1 + B1) when placed in cell C1 adds the contents of cells A1 and B1 and places the results in C1. All formulas must start with an equals sign (=).

Frame: A space in Publisher that contains pictures. Pictures may be clip art, circles, arrows, lines, or AutoShapes, as well as a variety of graphic files, such as GIF (graphic interchange format), JPEG (joint photographic experts group), or scanned photographs taken with a digital camera.

Function: Formulas built into Excel. (*See* formula)

Homepage: The first Web document a user sees when entering a website.

HTML (Hypertext Markup Language): The computer language used to format Web documents. You can save Word documents, PowerPoint presentations, and Excel worksheets as HTML documents and put them on the Web.

Hyperlink: A link that creates a connection between a word or phrase in a document and another document on the computer or on the Internet.

Hypertext Links: Text and/or pictures that can be clicked to take the user to another screen, Web document, or media object (e.g., video, audio). These screens, documents, and objects may be within the same file, the same website, or at a website around the world. They are often referred to as hyperlinks. They are often associated with Web documents but may also be in other files such as PowerPoint presentations.

Independent Design Elements: In Publisher, text and picture portions of a publication that act as independent entities when designing publications.

Insert Object: A method of placing an object or a portion of an object into an Office application file. For example, when a PowerPoint slide is placed or inserted into Word, it is referred to as a *slide object*.

Internet: A large, worldwide network of computers (computing hardware and software) in which the computers communicate with one another.

ISTE (International Society for Technology in Education): An international organization of educators that has developed teaching standards for students and teachers.

Link to File: A method of inserting an object in an Office application file whereby the object is linked to the file. The object is not embedded and does not become part of the file.

Mac OS: The Macintosh operating system.

NCATE (National Council for Accreditation of Teacher Education): A council that developed a set of standards for the accreditation of teachers. NCATE also accredits teacher education organizations.

Objects: A Word document, PowerPoint slide or presentation, Excel worksheet, image, sound, video, or other file that can be embedded or linked to Office application files. When a file created by a separate application is placed into the Office file, it is referred to as an *object*.

Outline Tab: One of several view options available for viewing a PowerPoint presentation while it is being developed. The Outline tab presents slides in text outline form.

Presentation Object: A PowerPoint presentation that has been inserted into a file.

Queries: Searches in Access that allow users to find specific information in a database, such as who lives in a particular zip code.

Quick Access Toolbar: A toolbar that displays quick access buttons, such as buttons for undo and save commands. It is located at the top of the application window.

Record: A collection of information about a thing or person (e.g., name, address, phone number, e-mail address, and so on) in a table of an Access database.

Relative Cell Reference: In Excel, a reference to a cell (e.g., C1) that, when used in a formula, changes when the formula is copied to another cell. If cell E1 contains the formula = (C1 + D1) and E1 is copied to E2, then E2's formula changes to = (C2 + D2).

Report: A document that summarizes Access database information.

Ribbon: In the Office 2010 interface, a menu that displays groups of related commands in tabs across the top of the application window. Tabs on the Ribbon provide access to major program functions and features.

Right-click: On Windows computers, clicking the right mouse button. The computer mouse often has two buttons, a left mouse button and a right mouse button. In most instances, the left mouse button is used for selecting menu options, moving objects, and dragging and dropping. Clicking the right mouse button frequency brings up menu choices associated with the selected object.

Shortcut Menus: Menus that appear on the screen when you right-click an item and that display the most frequently used commands.

Shortcuts: Icons that provide quick access to frequently used files and programs. You can place shortcuts on the desktop or in folders. Instead of searching the computer for a file or program, you can create a shortcut to it that opens the file or program.

Slide: A screen that may contain text and content such as pictures, clip art, graphs, tables, diagrams, video, and audio. Several slides make up a presentation.

Slide Object: A single PowerPoint slide that has been inserted into a file.

Slide Show: A PowerPoint view that presents the finished slides of a presentation. In this mode, slides cannot be edited.

Slide Sorter: One of several PowerPoint view options that presents small images of each slide in the presentation. It is useful for seeing the order of all slides. You can copy, paste, delete, and rearrange slides in the Slide Sorter view.

Slides Tab: One of several options available for viewing a presentation while it is being developed. The Slides view presents miniature slides of the presentation.

Start Button: A button that appears to the left of the taskbar. Clicking Start displays the Start menu and provides access to programs, files, help, and search facilities, among other things.

Table: (1) A graphic that allows you to display information in a tabular format in a document. (2) A collection of information in an Access database about a specific topic (e.g., student information, class materials inventory). A table consists of fields and records. There may be more than one table in a database.

Task Pane: A window that allows users to work with common tasks, such as opening a new document and formatting text.

Taskbar: A bar that contains buttons that provide access to opened folders and files and that makes switching between them convenient. Although you can position the taskbar at the top of sides of the screen, it typically appears at the bottom.

Tasks: An Outlook folder that allows for the creation of lists of activities.

Text Box: A space that acts as a container for text and can be arranged, reshaped, and created within a publication.

URL (Uniform Resource Locator): Frequently referred to as an address or a Web address, such as www.duq.edu.

Web Browser: A software application used to view Web content. Some popular Web browsers include Internet Explorer, Netscape, and Mozilla Firefox.

Webpage: A singe Web document that may contain images, text, graphics, video, and audio.

Website: A collection of Web documents that may contain images, text, graphics, video, and audio.

Windows 7: The current Windows operating system. Windows Vista, XP, 98, NT, and 95 are earlier versions of the Windows operating system.

Workbook: An Excel spreadsheet file composed of one or more worksheets. Excel identifies worksheets as Sheet1, Sheet2, Sheet3, and so on. A single workbook may contain numerous worksheets.

Worksheet: A screen in an Excel workbook made up of columns, rows, and cells. Each worksheet may contain as many as 256 columns and 65,536 rows.

Worksheet Object: An Excel worksheet that has been inserted into a file.

World Wide Web: Often referred to as the Web, a collection of information viewed with a Web browser that is available through computing networks.

INDEX